RED MOON

RED MOON

STORY
CARLOS TRILLO

ART
EDUARDO RISSO

TRANSLATION
ZELJKO MEDIC

Dark Horse Books

COMICS

PRESIDENT & PUBLISHER MIKE RICHARDSON

U.S. EDITOR SIERRA HAHN

ASSISTANT EDITOR SPENCER CUSHING

DIGITAL PRODUCTION CHRISTINA McKENZIE

DESIGNER KAT LARSON

Special thanks to Josip Gudlin at SAF.

Published by Dark Horse Books
A division of Dark Horse Comics, Inc.
10956 SE Main Street
Milwaukie, OR 97222

First edition: September 2014
ISBN 978-1-61655-447-7

1 3 5 7 8 10 8 6 4 2
Printed in China

International Licensing: (503) 905-2377
Comic Shop Locator Service: (888) 266-4226

This volume collects *Red Moon* #1–#4, originally published by SAF COMICS.

TABLE OF CONTENTS

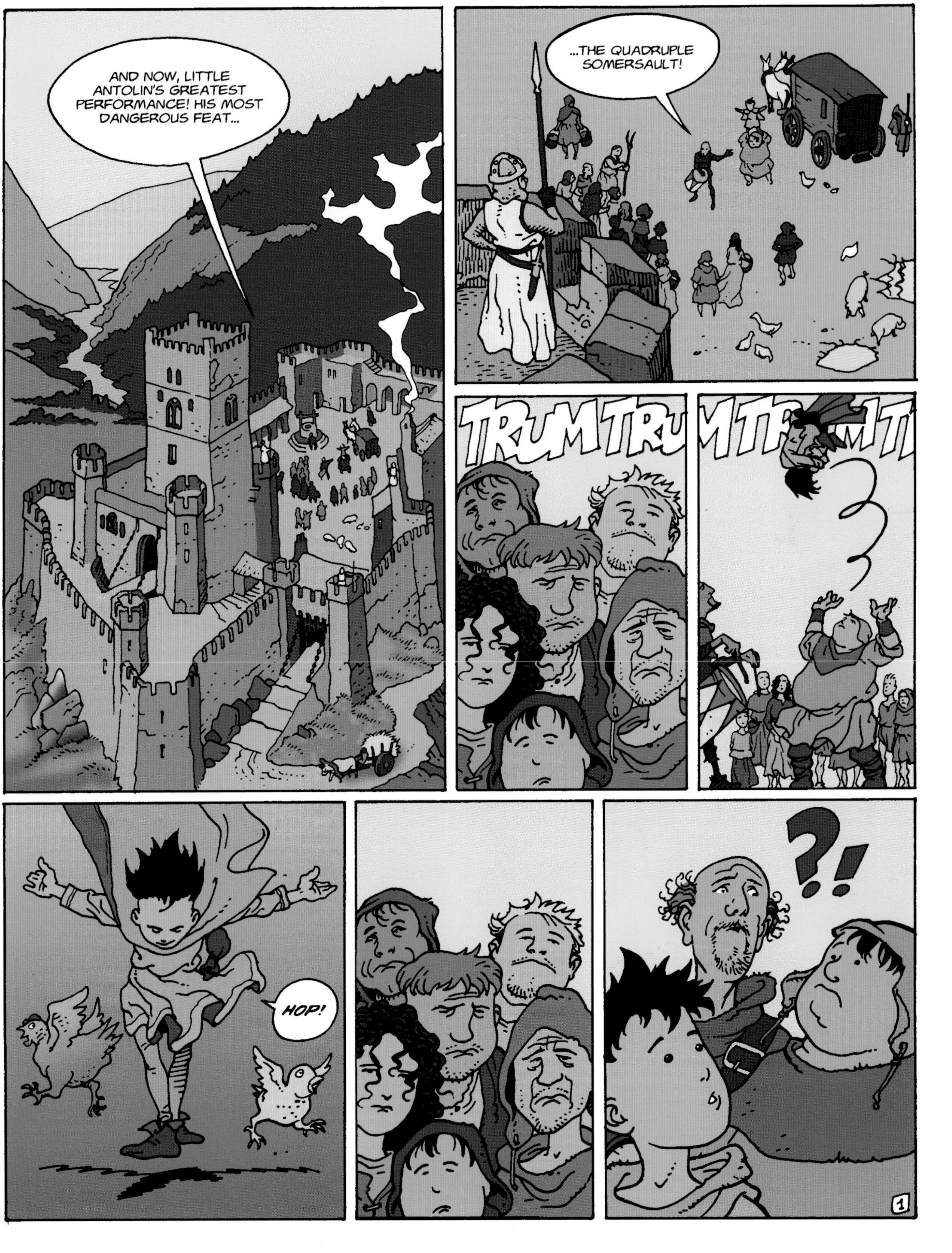
AND NOW, LITTLE ANTOLIN'S GREATEST PERFORMANCE! HIS MOST DANGEROUS FEAT...
...THE QUADRUPLE SOMERSAULT!
TRUM TRUM TRUM TR
HOP!
?!
1

WE'VE NEVER PERFORMED BEFORE AN AUDIENCE WITH SO LITTLE INTEREST IN OUR MAGIC AND ACROBATICS, THEO.

YES, CROCKER, IT WAS LIKE TRYING TO GET LAUGHS AT A FAMILY FUNERAL.

I'D REALLY LIKE TO KNOW WHY EVERYBODY IS SO SAD.

I'LL TELL YOU, BOY...

IN EXCHANGE FOR THOSE COOKIES.

CAREFUL, ANTOLIN. YOU'D BETTER NOT MAKE THAT DEAL.

WE HAVE FEW PROVISIONS LEFT; YOUR SHARE FOR THE NEXT COUPLE OF DAYS IS BARELY BIGGER THAN WHAT YOU'VE GOT IN YOUR HAND.

IT DOESN'T MATTER. HERE YOU GO, WOMAN.

I TOLD YOU, CROCKER; THE ONLY THING THIS KID CARES ABOUT SATISFYING IS HIS CURIOSITY.

NOW, TELL ME EVERYTHING.

OF COURSE.

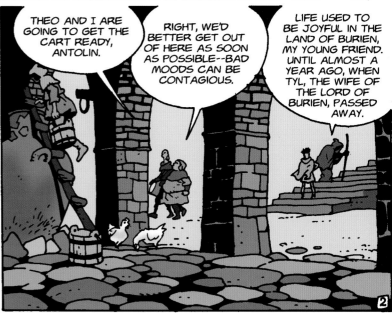

THEO AND I ARE GOING TO GET THE CART READY, ANTOLIN.

RIGHT, WE'D BETTER GET OUT OF HERE AS SOON AS POSSIBLE--BAD MOODS CAN BE CONTAGIOUS.

LIFE USED TO BE JOYFUL IN THE LAND OF BURIEN, MY YOUNG FRIEND. UNTIL ALMOST A YEAR AGO, WHEN TYL, THE WIFE OF THE LORD OF BURIEN, PASSED AWAY.

2

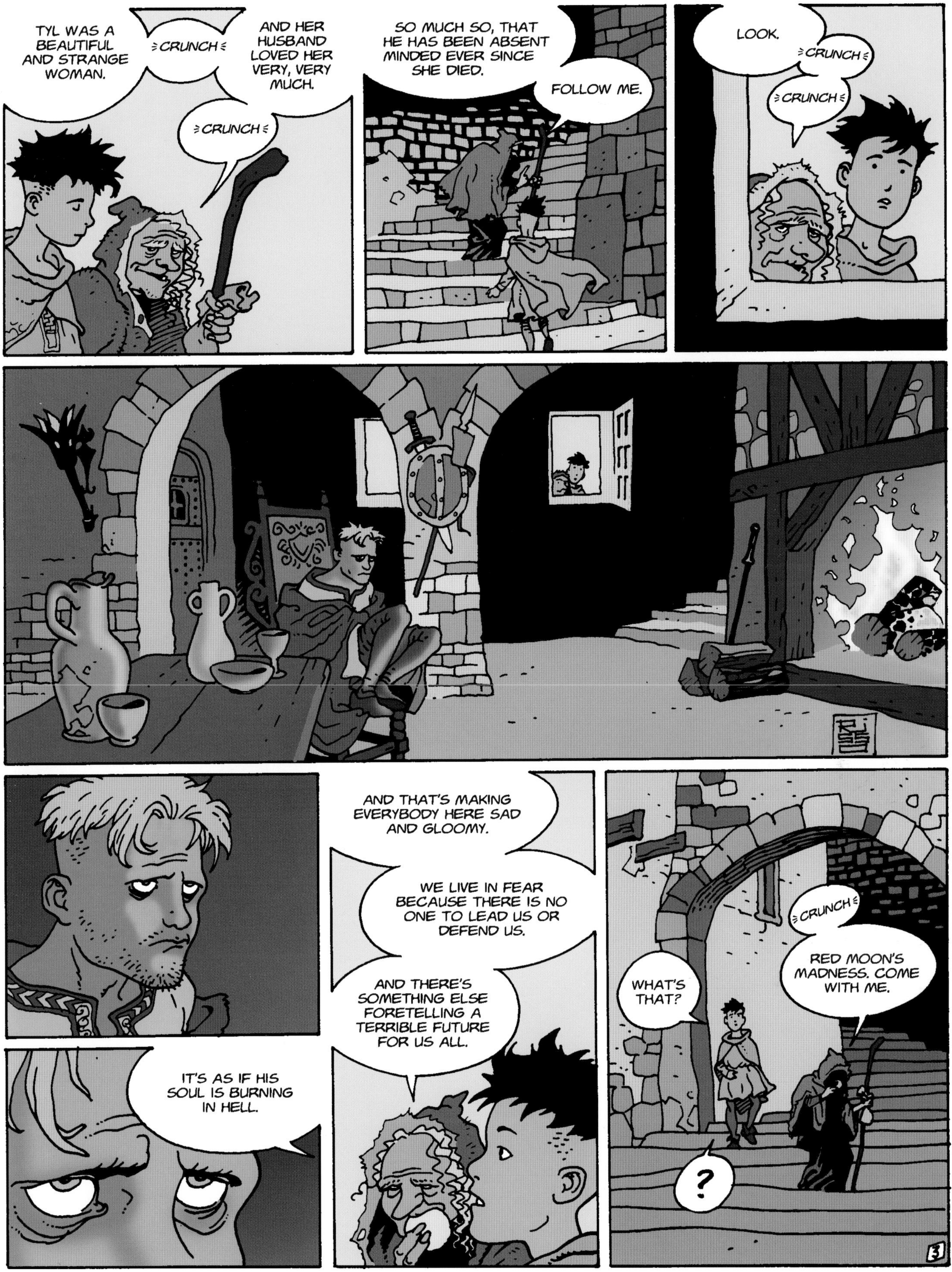
TYL WAS A BEAUTIFUL AND STRANGE WOMAN.
CRUNCH
AND HER HUSBAND LOVED HER VERY, VERY MUCH.
CRUNCH
SO MUCH SO, THAT HE HAS BEEN ABSENT MINDED EVER SINCE SHE DIED.
FOLLOW ME.
LOOK.
CRUNCH
CRUNCH
AND THAT'S MAKING EVERYBODY HERE SAD AND GLOOMY.
WE LIVE IN FEAR BECAUSE THERE IS NO ONE TO LEAD US OR DEFEND US.
AND THERE'S SOMETHING ELSE FORETELLING A TERRIBLE FUTURE FOR US ALL.
IT'S AS IF HIS SOUL IS BURNING IN HELL.
CRUNCH
WHAT'S THAT?
RED MOON'S MADNESS. COME WITH ME.
?
3

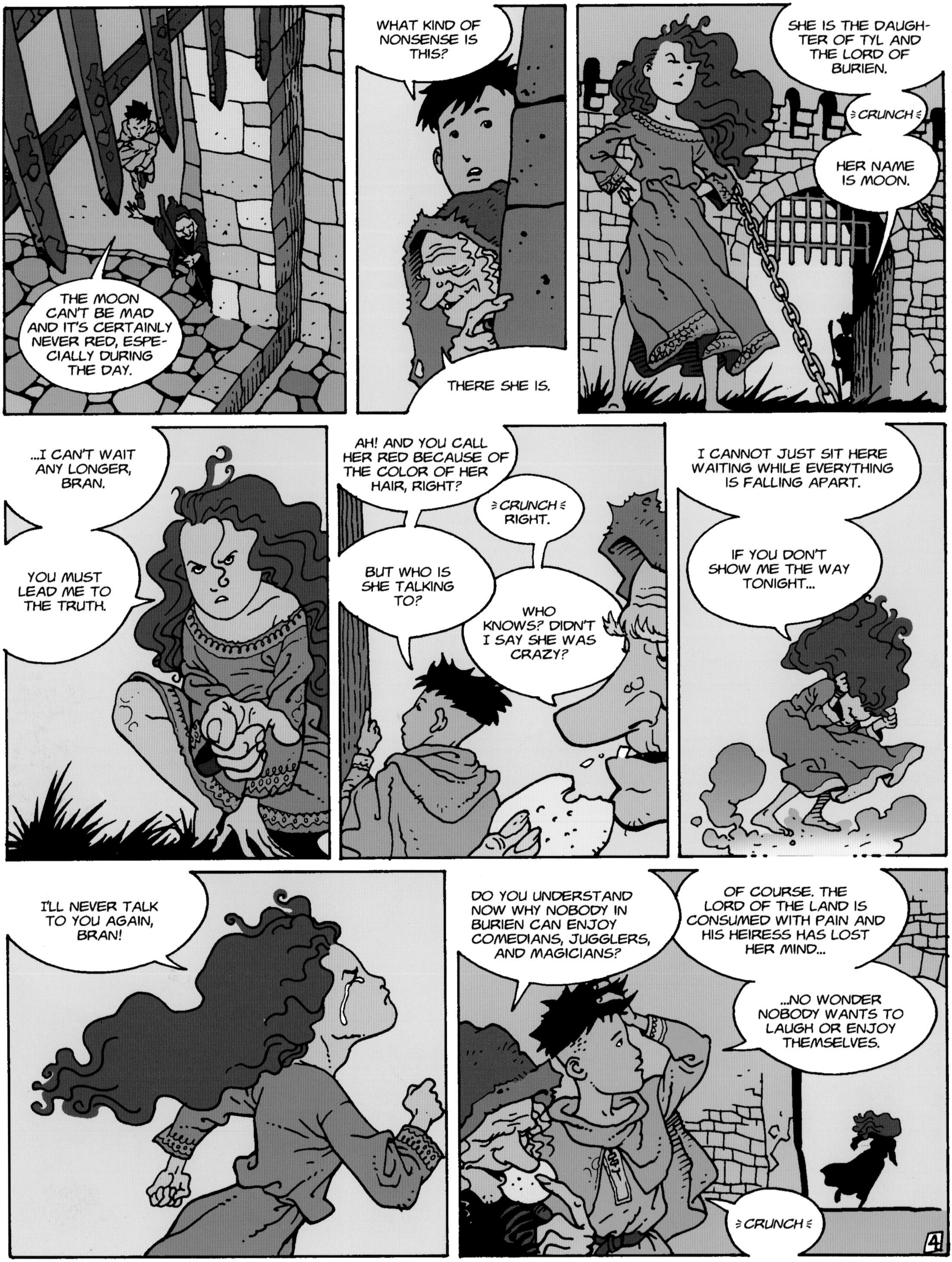
THE MOON CAN'T BE MAD AND IT'S CERTAINLY NEVER RED, ESPECIALLY DURING THE DAY.
WHAT KIND OF NONSENSE IS THIS?
THERE SHE IS.
SHE IS THE DAUGHTER OF TYL AND THE LORD OF BURIEN.
CRUNCH
HER NAME IS MOON.
...I CAN'T WAIT ANY LONGER, BRAN.
YOU MUST LEAD ME TO THE TRUTH.
AH! AND YOU CALL HER RED BECAUSE OF THE COLOR OF HER HAIR, RIGHT?
CRUNCH RIGHT.
BUT WHO IS SHE TALKING TO?
WHO KNOWS? DIDN'T I SAY SHE WAS CRAZY?
I CANNOT JUST SIT HERE WAITING WHILE EVERYTHING IS FALLING APART.
IF YOU DON'T SHOW ME THE WAY TONIGHT...
I'LL NEVER TALK TO YOU AGAIN, BRAN!
DO YOU UNDERSTAND NOW WHY NOBODY IN BURIEN CAN ENJOY COMEDIANS, JUGGLERS, AND MAGICIANS?
OF COURSE. THE LORD OF THE LAND IS CONSUMED WITH PAIN AND HIS HEIRESS HAS LOST HER MIND...
...NO WONDER NOBODY WANTS TO LAUGH OR ENJOY THEMSELVES.
CRUNCH
4

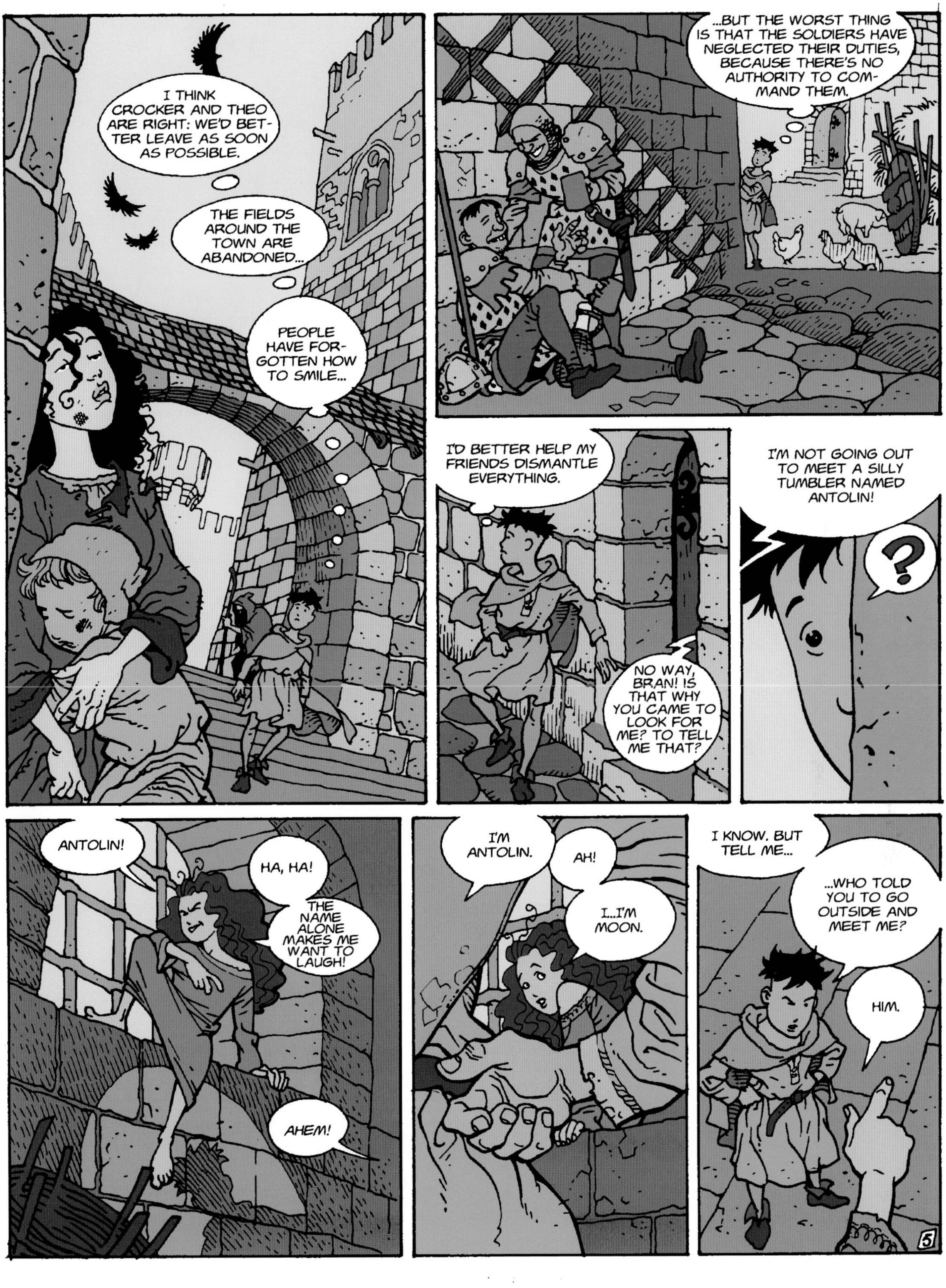
I THINK CROCKER AND THEO ARE RIGHT: WE'D BETTER LEAVE AS SOON AS POSSIBLE.
THE FIELDS AROUND THE TOWN ARE ABANDONED...
PEOPLE HAVE FORGOTTEN HOW TO SMILE...
...BUT THE WORST THING IS THAT THE SOLDIERS HAVE NEGLECTED THEIR DUTIES, BECAUSE THERE'S NO AUTHORITY TO COMMAND THEM.
I'D BETTER HELP MY FRIENDS DISMANTLE EVERYTHING.
NO WAY, BRAN! IS THAT WHY YOU CAME TO LOOK FOR ME? TO TELL ME THAT?
I'M NOT GOING OUT TO MEET A SILLY TUMBLER NAMED ANTOLIN!
?
ANTOLIN!
HA, HA!
THE NAME ALONE MAKES ME WANT TO LAUGH!
AHEM!
I'M ANTOLIN.
AH!
I...I'M MOON.
I KNOW. BUT TELL ME...
...WHO TOLD YOU TO GO OUTSIDE AND MEET ME?
HIM.
5

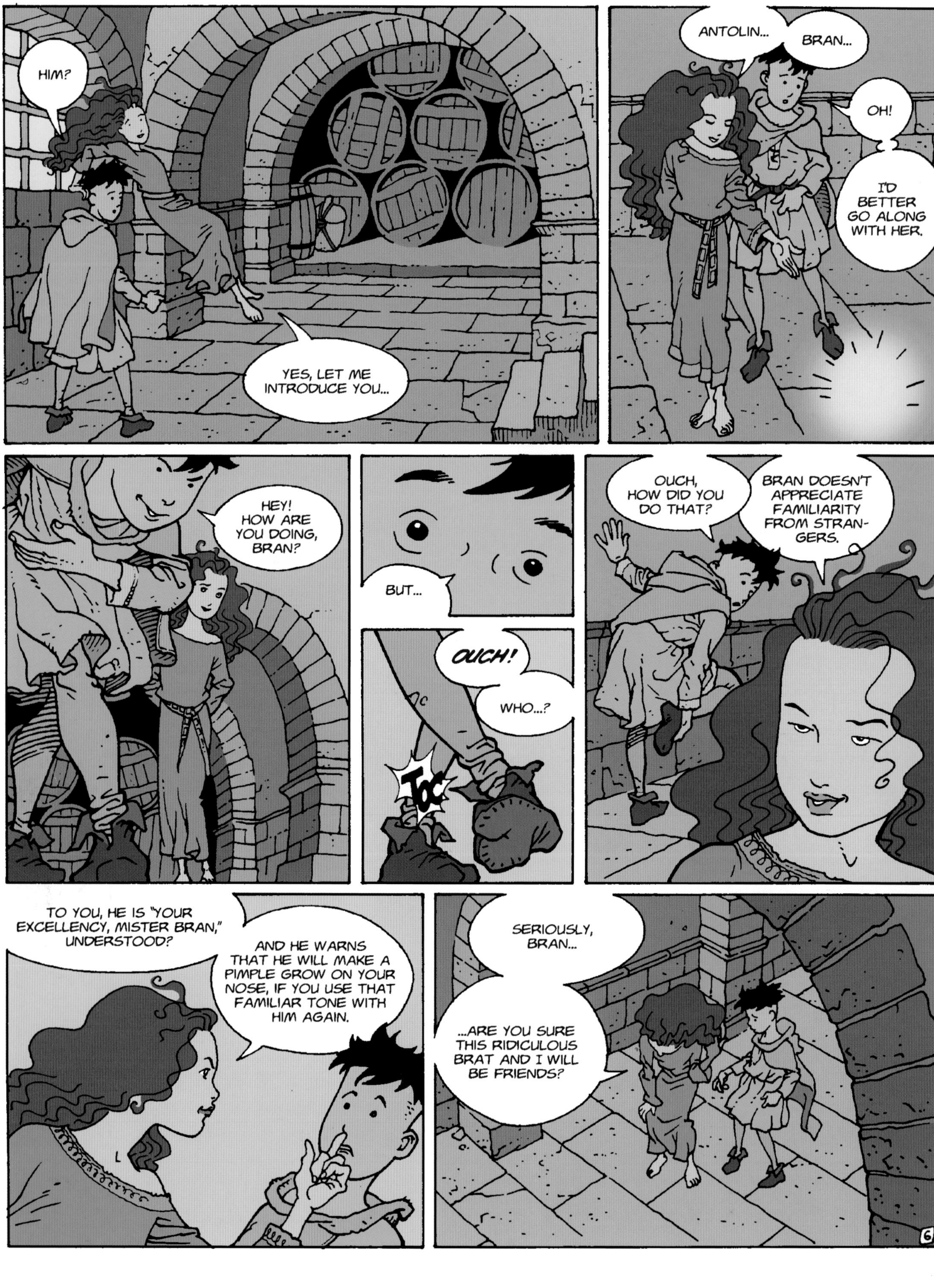

HIM?
YES, LET ME INTRODUCE YOU...
ANTOLIN...
BRAN...
OH!
I'D BETTER GO ALONG WITH HER.
HEY! HOW ARE YOU DOING, BRAN?
BUT...
OUCH!
WHO...?
TOC
OUCH, HOW DID YOU DO THAT?
BRAN DOESN'T APPRECIATE FAMILIARITY FROM STRANGERS.
TO YOU, HE IS "YOUR EXCELLENCY, MISTER BRAN," UNDERSTOOD?
AND HE WARNS THAT HE WILL MAKE A PIMPLE GROW ON YOUR NOSE, IF YOU USE THAT FAMILIAR TONE WITH HIM AGAIN.
SERIOUSLY, BRAN...
...ARE YOU SURE THIS RIDICULOUS BRAT AND I WILL BE FRIENDS?
6

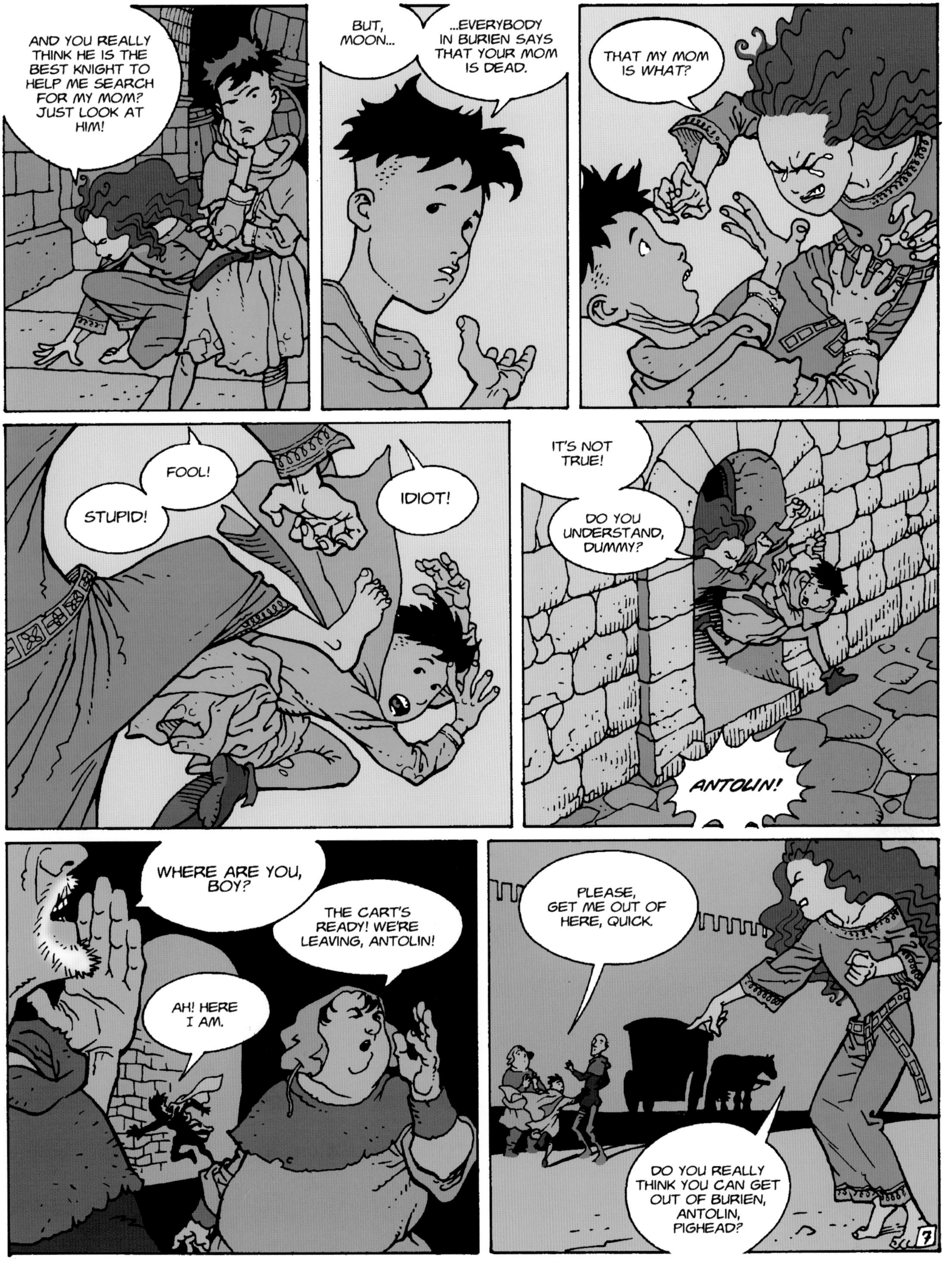
AND YOU REALLY THINK HE IS THE BEST KNIGHT TO HELP ME SEARCH FOR MY MOM? JUST LOOK AT HIM!
BUT, MOON...
...EVERYBODY IN BURIEN SAYS THAT YOUR MOM IS DEAD.
THAT MY MOM IS WHAT?
STUPID!
FOOL!
IDIOT!
IT'S NOT TRUE!
DO YOU UNDERSTAND, DUMMY?
ANTOLIN!
WHERE ARE YOU, BOY?
THE CART'S READY! WE'RE LEAVING, ANTOLIN!
AH! HERE I AM.
PLEASE, GET ME OUT OF HERE, QUICK.
DO YOU REALLY THINK YOU CAN GET OUT OF BURIEN, ANTOLIN, PIGHEAD?
7

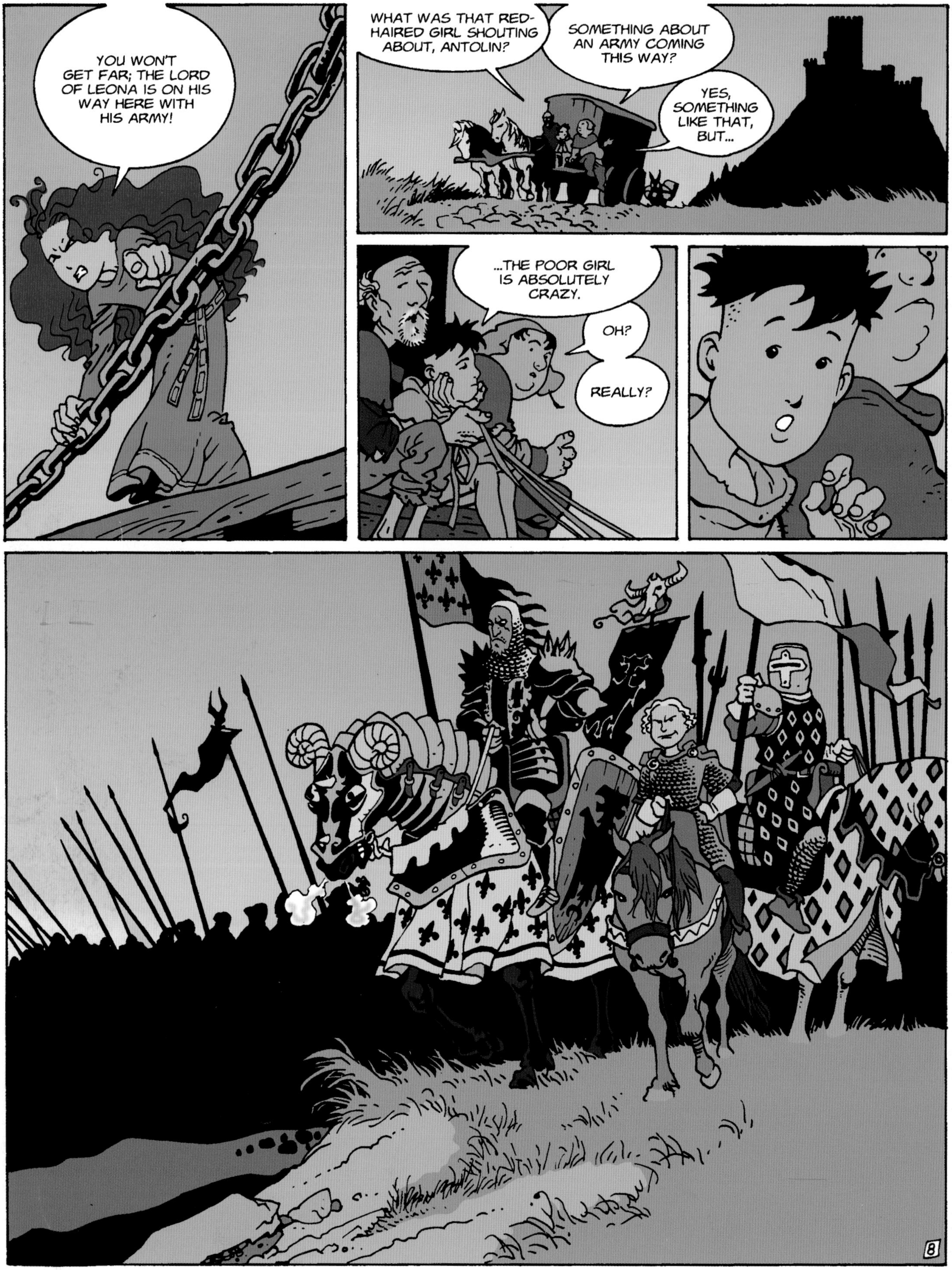

YOU WON'T GET FAR; THE LORD OF LEONA IS ON HIS WAY HERE WITH HIS ARMY!
WHAT WAS THAT RED-HAIRED GIRL SHOUTING ABOUT, ANTOLIN?
SOMETHING ABOUT AN ARMY COMING THIS WAY?
YES, SOMETHING LIKE THAT, BUT...
...THE POOR GIRL IS ABSOLUTELY CRAZY.
OH?
REALLY?
8

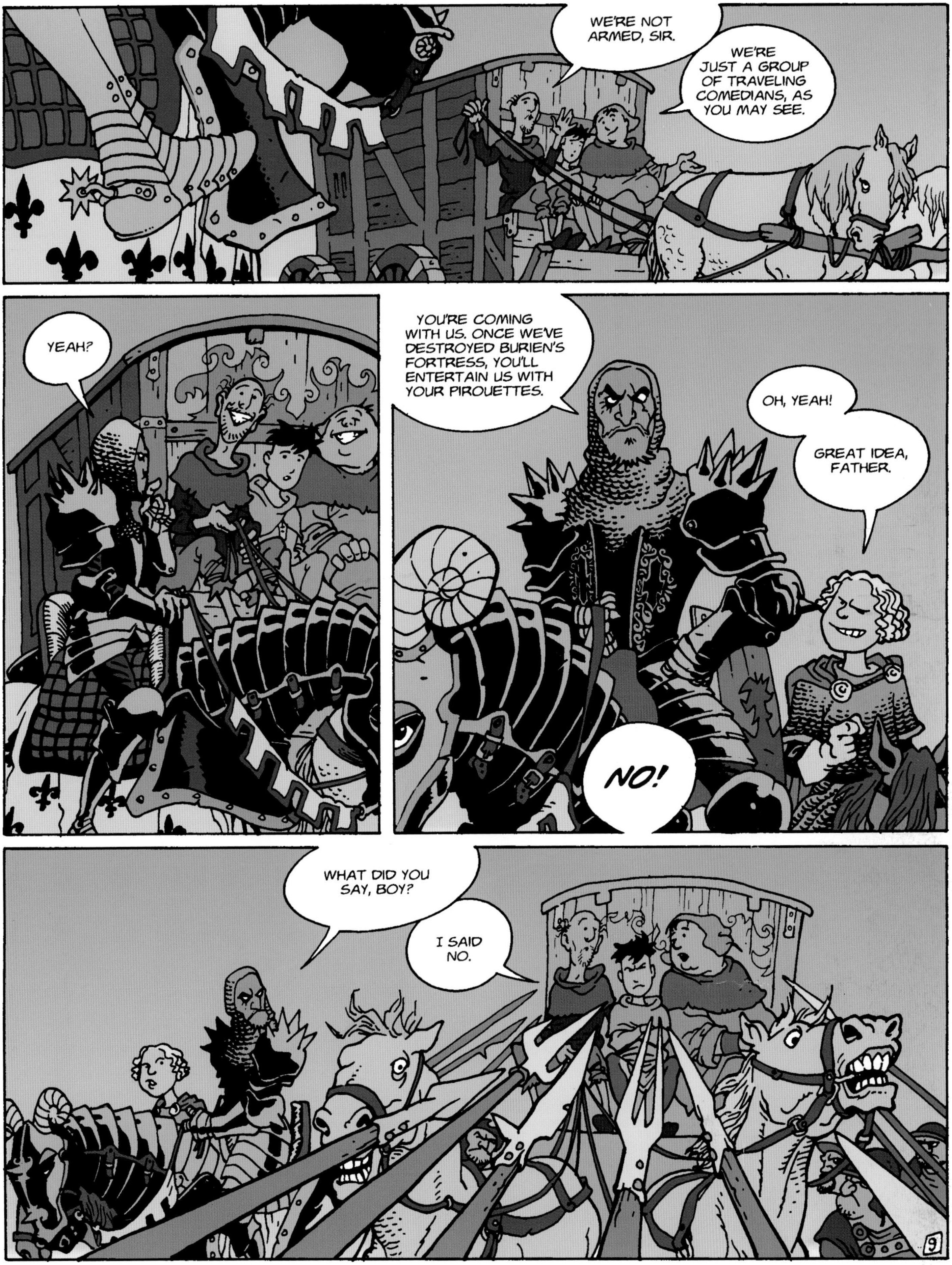
WE'RE NOT ARMED, SIR.
WE'RE JUST A GROUP OF TRAVELING COMEDIANS, AS YOU MAY SEE.
YEAH?
YOU'RE COMING WITH US. ONCE WE'VE DESTROYED BURIEN'S FORTRESS, YOU'LL ENTERTAIN US WITH YOUR PIROUETTES.
OH, YEAH!
GREAT IDEA, FATHER.
NO!
WHAT DID YOU SAY, BOY?
I SAID NO.
9

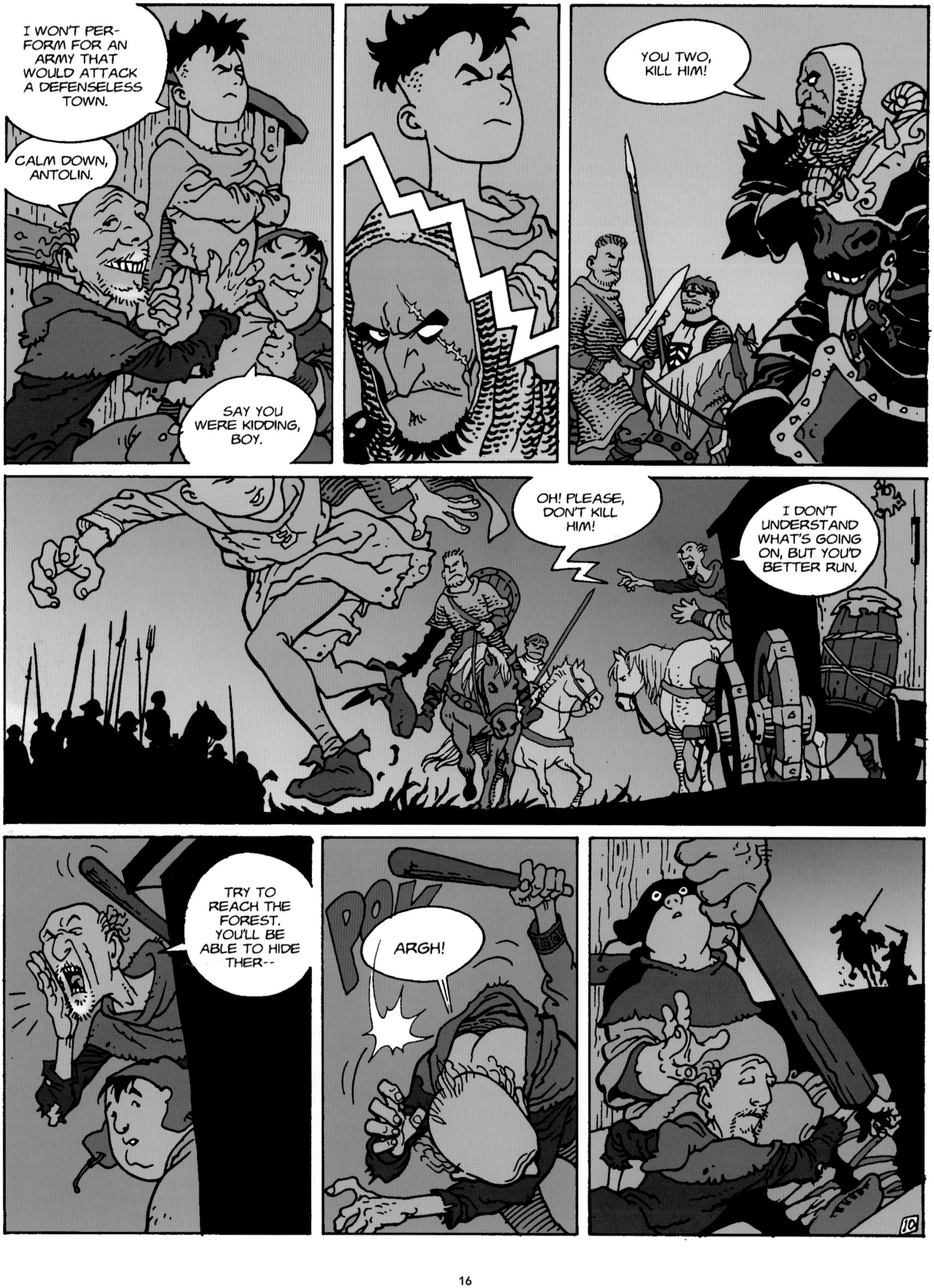
I WON'T PERFORM FOR AN ARMY THAT WOULD ATTACK A DEFENSELESS TOWN.
CALM DOWN, ANTOLIN.
SAY YOU WERE KIDDING, BOY.
YOU TWO, KILL HIM!
OH! PLEASE, DON'T KILL HIM!
I DON'T UNDERSTAND WHAT'S GOING ON, BUT YOU'D BETTER RUN.
TRY TO REACH THE FOREST. YOU'LL BE ABLE TO HIDE THER--
POK
ARGH!
10

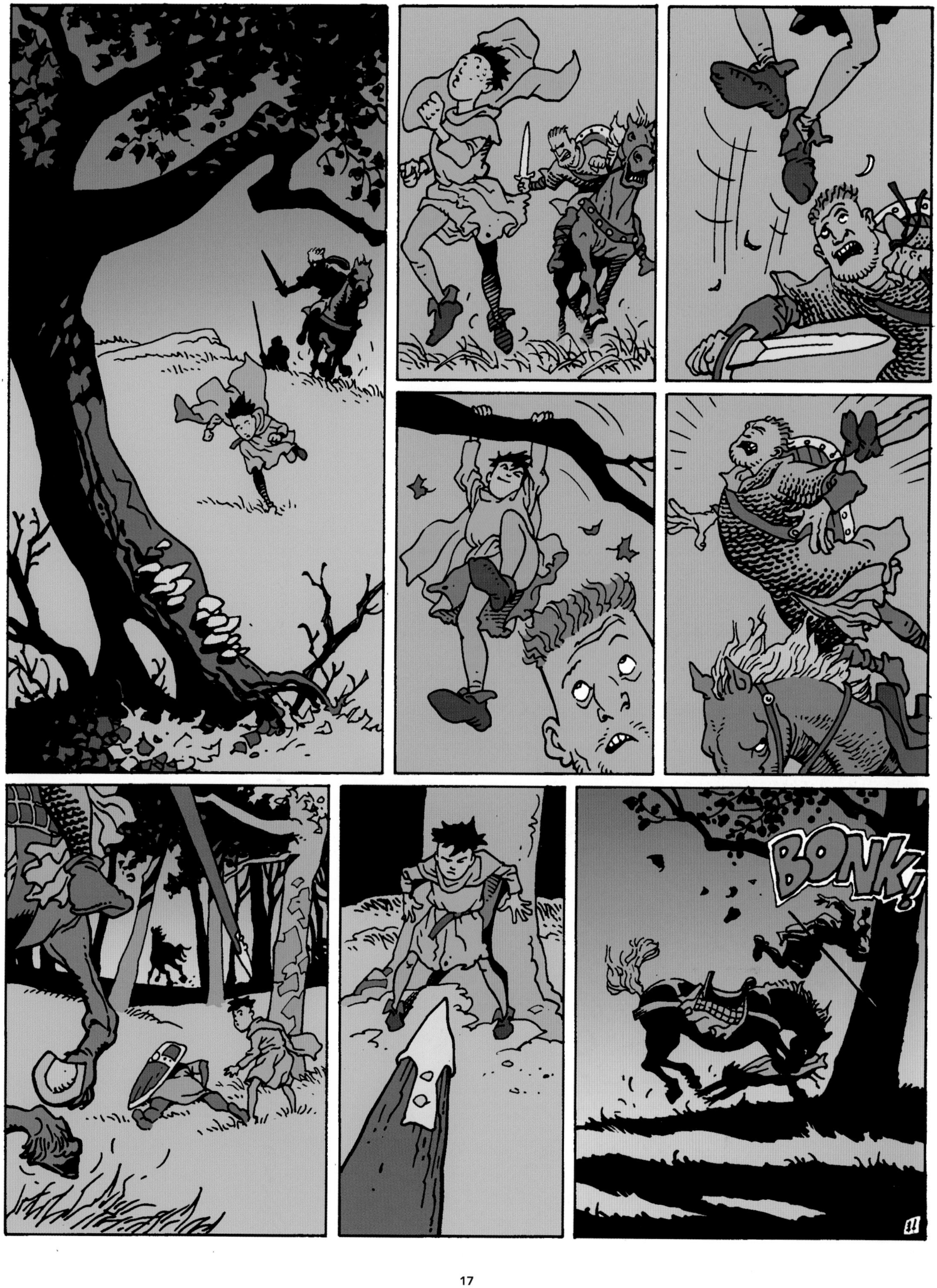
BONK!

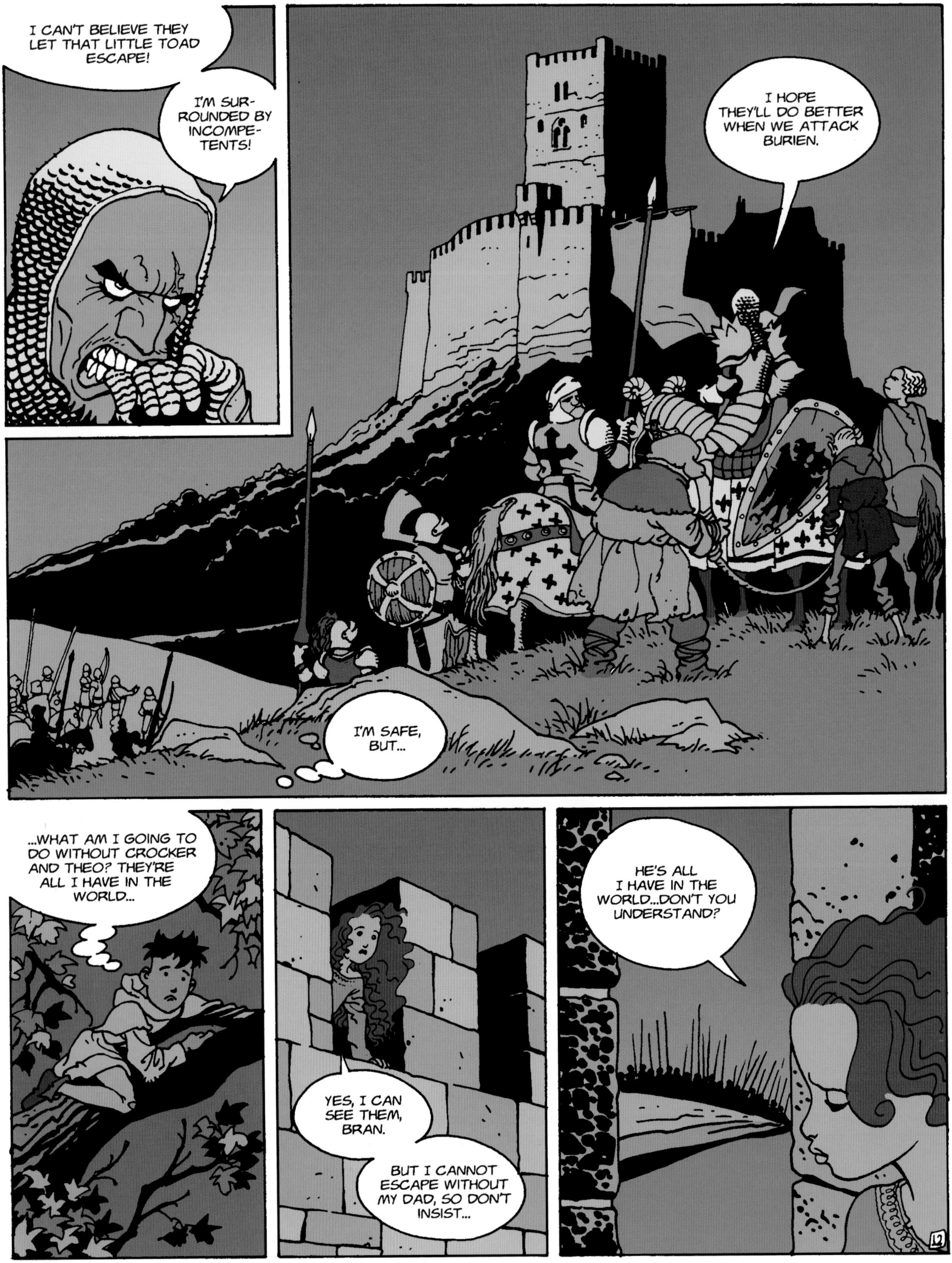
I CAN'T BELIEVE THEY LET THAT LITTLE TOAD ESCAPE!
I'M SUR-ROUNDED BY INCOMPE-TENTS!
I HOPE THEY'LL DO BETTER WHEN WE ATTACK BURIEN.
I'M SAFE, BUT...
...WHAT AM I GOING TO DO WITHOUT CROCKER AND THEO? THEY'RE ALL I HAVE IN THE WORLD...
YES, I CAN SEE THEM, BRAN.
BUT I CANNOT ESCAPE WITHOUT MY DAD, SO DON'T INSIST...
HE'S ALL I HAVE IN THE WORLD...DON'T YOU UNDERSTAND?
12

LEONA'S ARMY IS ATTACKING, SIR!

LEONA'S ARMY IS ATTACKING, SIR!

WHAT SHALL WE DO?

TELL US, PLEASE.

YOU ARE OUR LEADER.

YOU MUST LEAD US INTO COMBAT, SIR!

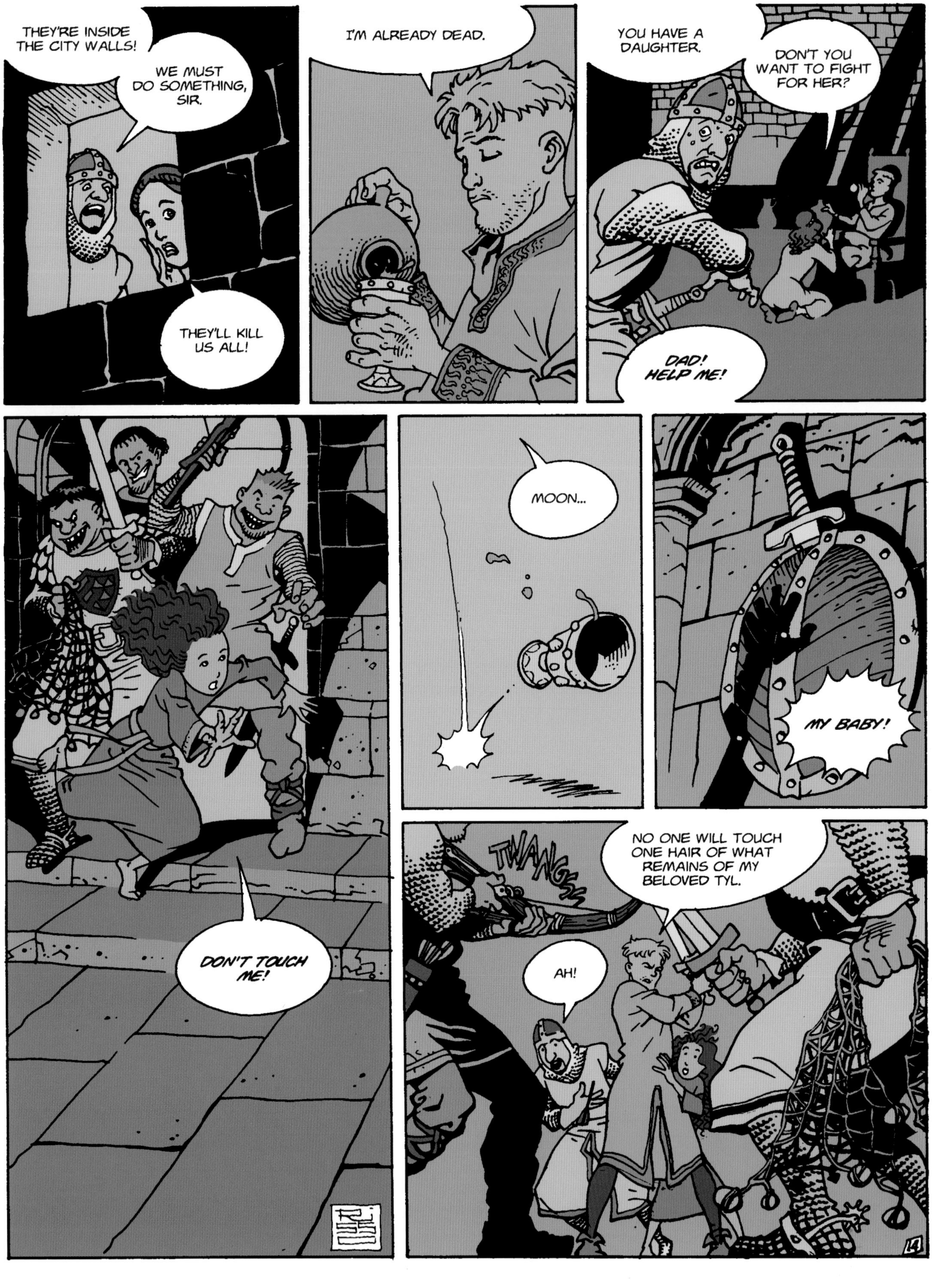
THEY'RE INSIDE THE CITY WALLS!
WE MUST DO SOMETHING, SIR.
THEY'LL KILL US ALL!
I'M ALREADY DEAD.
YOU HAVE A DAUGHTER.
DON'T YOU WANT TO FIGHT FOR HER?
DAD! HELP ME!
DON'T TOUCH ME!
MOON...
MY BABY!
TWANGSS
NO ONE WILL TOUCH ONE HAIR OF WHAT REMAINS OF MY BELOVED TYL.
AH!
14

BACK OFF!

AND YOU, LITTLE ONE, RUN!

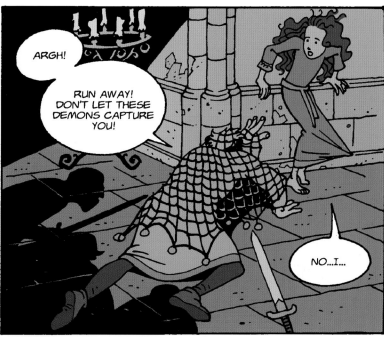

ARGH!

RUN AWAY! DON'T LET THESE DEMONS CAPTURE YOU!

NO...I...

...I WANT TO STAY WITH YOU, DAD.

LET GO OF ME, BRAN!

STOP PULLING AT MY CLOTHES.

I'M ORDERING YOU TO ES-CAPE BEFORE THEY GET YOU, SILLY GIRL!

ALL RIGHT THEN!

WHERE?

TO THE BASEMENT?

THERE'S NO PLACE TO HIDE THERE. THEY'D FIND ME RIGHT AWAY.

OKAY. STOP SHOUTING AND I WON'T ANSWER BACK ANYMORE!

EH? THAT'S THE LORD OF BURIEN'S DAUGHTER! WAIT UP, GIRL! COME HERE!

I'M FOLLOWING YOU.

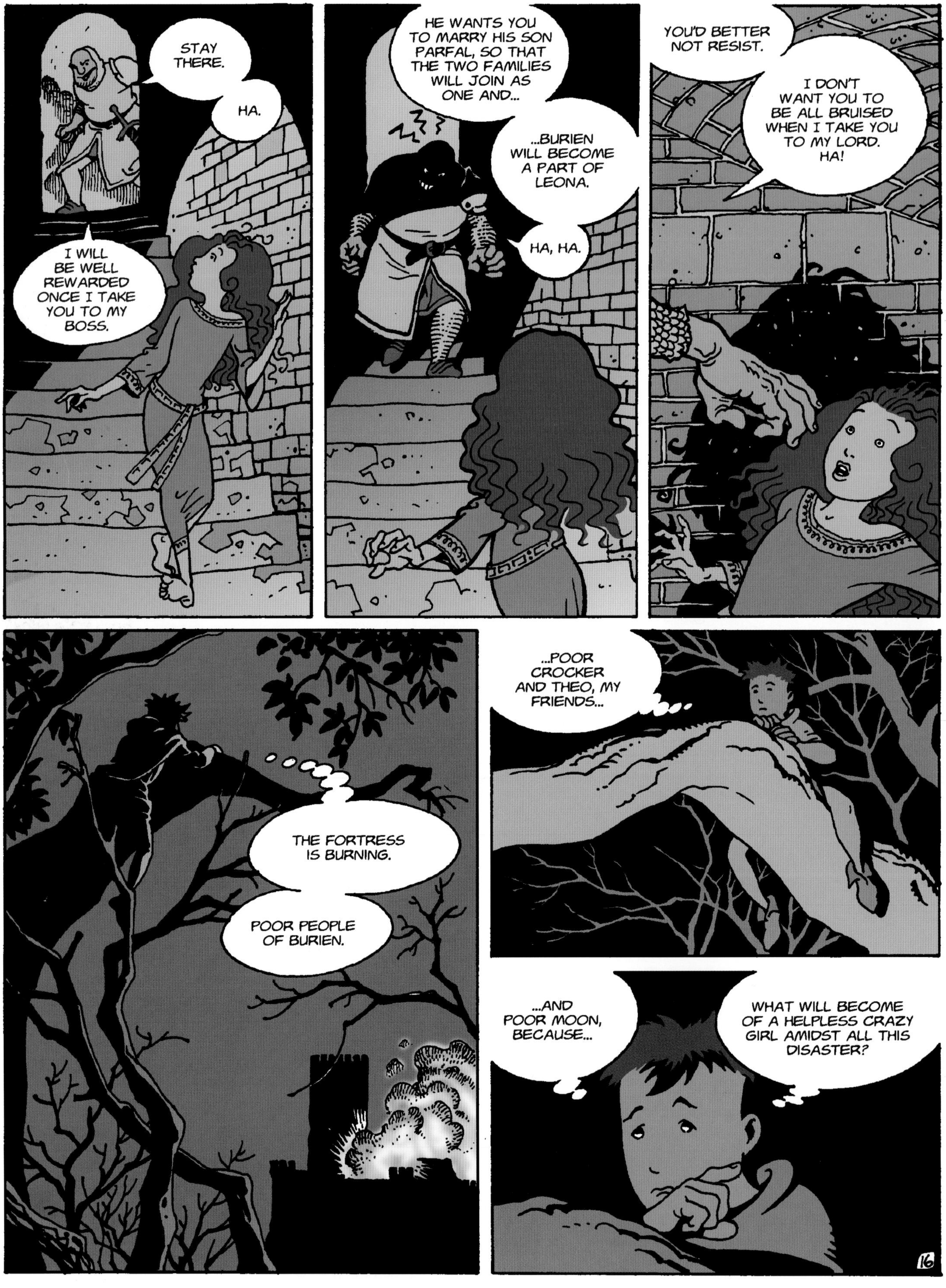
STAY THERE.
HA.
I WILL BE WELL REWARDED ONCE I TAKE YOU TO MY BOSS.
HE WANTS YOU TO MARRY HIS SON PARFAL, SO THAT THE TWO FAMILIES WILL JOIN AS ONE AND...
...BURIEN WILL BECOME A PART OF LEONA.
HA, HA.
YOU'D BETTER NOT RESIST.
I DON'T WANT YOU TO BE ALL BRUISED WHEN I TAKE YOU TO MY LORD. HA!
THE FORTRESS IS BURNING.
POOR PEOPLE OF BURIEN.
...POOR CROCKER AND THEO, MY FRIENDS...
...AND POOR MOON, BECAUSE...
WHAT WILL BECOME OF A HELPLESS CRAZY GIRL AMIDST ALL THIS DISASTER?
16

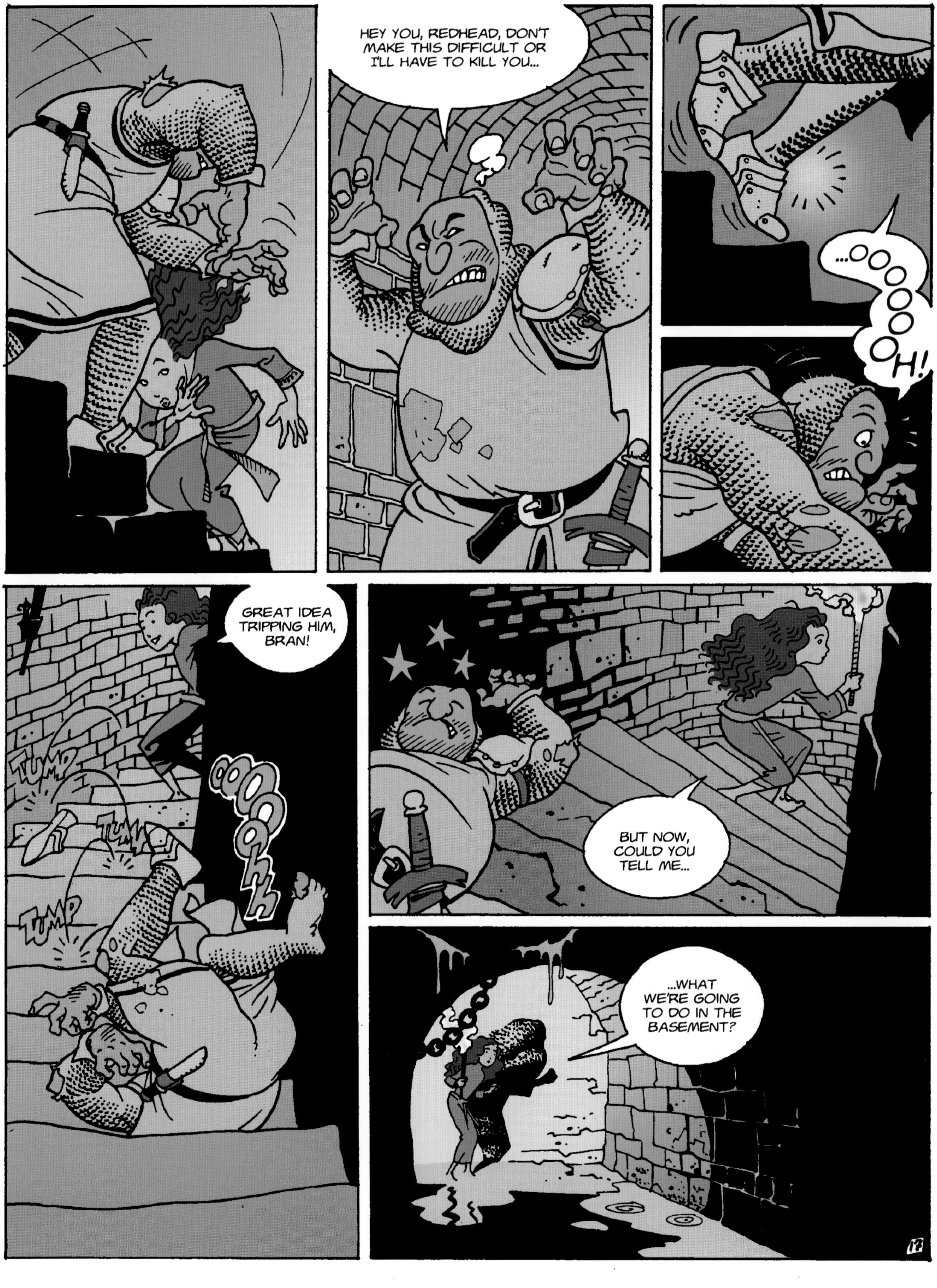
HEY YOU, REDHEAD, DON'T MAKE THIS DIFFICULT OR I'LL HAVE TO KILL YOU...
...OOOOOOOH!
GREAT IDEA TRIPPING HIM, BRAN!
TUMP
TUMP
TUMP
OOOOOOhh
BUT NOW, COULD YOU TELL ME...
...WHAT WE'RE GOING TO DO IN THE BASEMENT?

WHAT? THE THIRD STONE...

SHE MUST NOT ESCAPE! GET HER AND BRING HER TO ME!

WE'VE LOOKED EVERYWHERE, SIR!

...IN THE FOURTH ROW?

THIS ONE?

THE BASEMENT IS THE ONLY PLACE WE HAVEN'T SEARCHED YET.

THEN WHAT ARE YOU WAITING FOR? GO!

I HAVE TO PUSH IT?

BRAN, DO YOU THINK THIS IS THE TIME TO BE PLAYING GAMES?

CLIC

DOWN-STAIRS! LET'S GO!

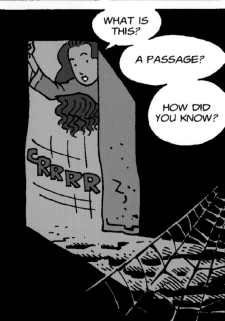

WHAT IS THIS?

A PASSAGE?

HOW DID YOU KNOW?

CRRRR

LOOK! THERE'S JACKOT LYING ON THE STAIRS, UNCONSCIOUS!

WHOEVER MADE HIM FALL COULDN'T GET BACK UPSTAIRS, SO THAT MEANS THEY MUST STILL BE...

OOF! ALL RIGHT! I'M COMING!

...DOWN HERE!

BUT...

NIK

THERE'S NO ONE HERE!

PLIC

18

24

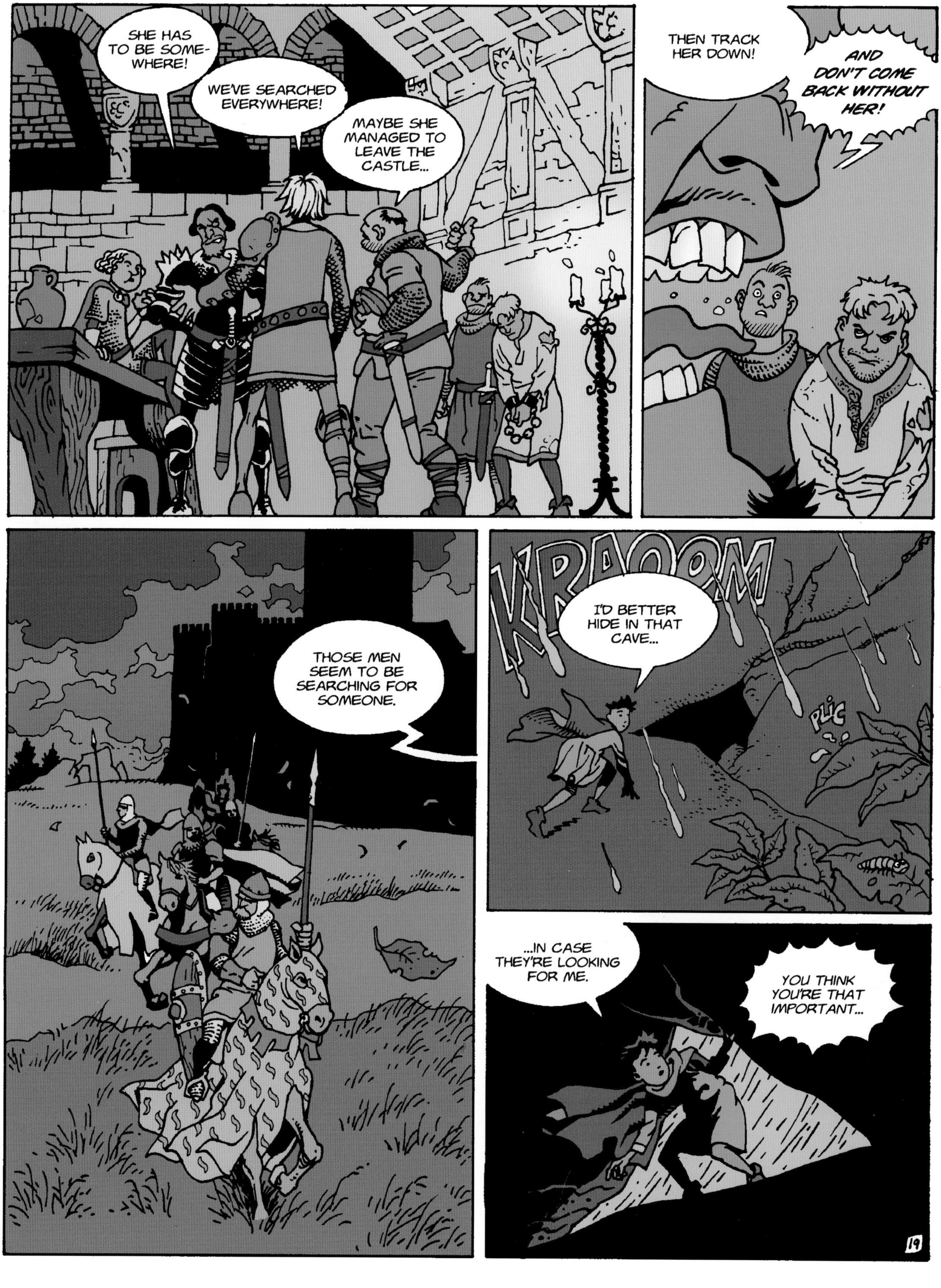
SHE HAS TO BE SOME-WHERE!
WE'VE SEARCHED EVERYWHERE!
MAYBE SHE MANAGED TO LEAVE THE CASTLE...
THEN TRACK HER DOWN!
AND DON'T COME BACK WITHOUT HER!
THOSE MEN SEEM TO BE SEARCHING FOR SOMEONE.
KRAOOM
I'D BETTER HIDE IN THAT CAVE...
PLIC
...IN CASE THEY'RE LOOKING FOR ME.
YOU THINK YOU'RE THAT IMPORTANT...
19

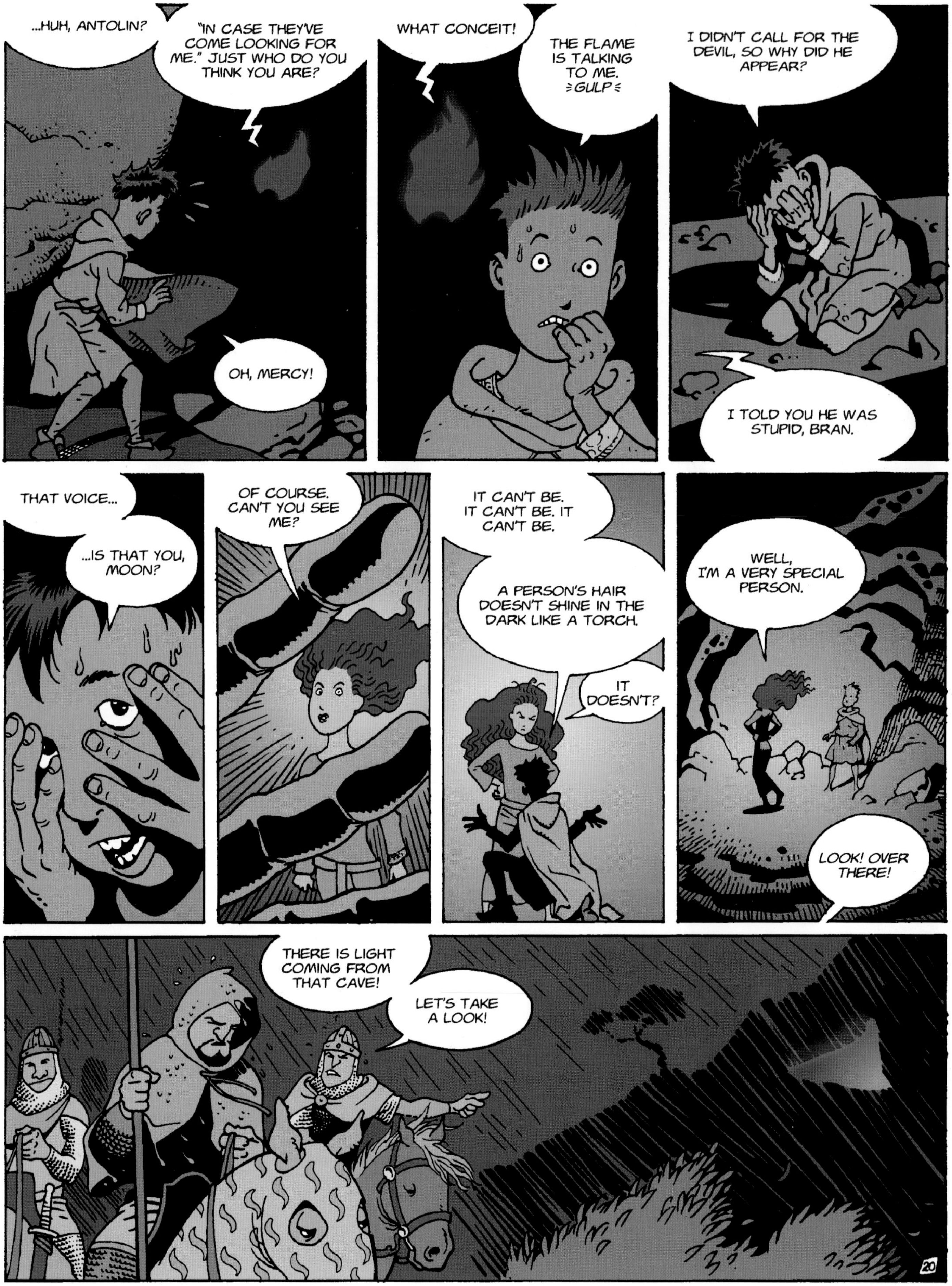
...HUH, ANTOLIN?
"IN CASE THEY'VE COME LOOKING FOR ME." JUST WHO DO YOU THINK YOU ARE?
OH, MERCY!
WHAT CONCEIT!
THE FLAME IS TALKING TO ME. GULP
I DIDN'T CALL FOR THE DEVIL, SO WHY DID HE APPEAR?
I TOLD YOU HE WAS STUPID, BRAN.
THAT VOICE...
...IS THAT YOU, MOON?
OF COURSE. CAN'T YOU SEE ME?
IT CAN'T BE. IT CAN'T BE. IT CAN'T BE.
A PERSON'S HAIR DOESN'T SHINE IN THE DARK LIKE A TORCH.
IT DOESN'T?
WELL, I'M A VERY SPECIAL PERSON.
LOOK! OVER THERE!
THERE IS LIGHT COMING FROM THAT CAVE!
LET'S TAKE A LOOK!
20

I CAN'T SEE ANYTHING.

LET'S GO. WE'RE WASTING OUR TIME.

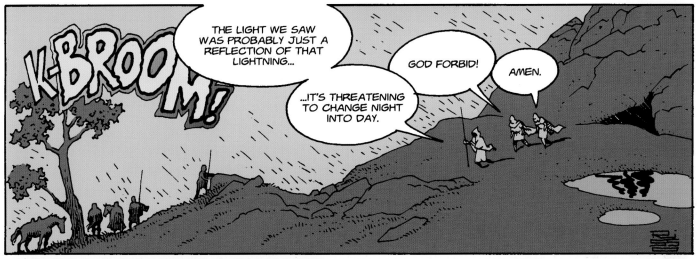

K-BROOM!

THE LIGHT WE SAW WAS PROBABLY JUST A REFLECTION OF THAT LIGHTNING...

...IT'S THREATENING TO CHANGE NIGHT INTO DAY.

GOD FORBID!

AMEN.

21

THEY'RE GONE.

CAN I TAKE THIS DIRTY RAG OFF MY HEAD NOW?

IT'S NOT A DIRTY RAG. IT'S MY JACKET.

PHEW! I KNOW WHAT IT IS, BUT YOU SHOULD WASH IT MORE OFTEN.

THANKS TO ME, THE SOLDIERS DIDN'T FIND YOU. MY IDEA OF COVERING YOUR STUPID HAIR WITH MY JACKET WORKED.

SO, YOU COULD THANK ME INSTEAD OF CRITICIZING...

COULD YOU REPEAT THAT, PLEASE?

I COULDN'T HEAR YOU SINCE THE TUMBLER HERE WAS SHOUTING.

THAT'S RIGHT. IT IS DANGEROUS.

WHAT IS THAT INVISIBLE FRIEND OF YOURS SAYING? IS HE GIVING YOU ANOTHER IDEA HOW TO BOTHER ME?

NO, HE'S JUST SAYING THAT SINCE WE ARRIVED HERE THROUGH A SECRET PASSAGE THAT HE KNEW ABOUT...

SOMEBODY WILL PROBABLY INFORM THE LORD OF LEONA ABOUT IT.

AND IF THE SOLDIERS FIND IT AND FOLLOW IT, THEY'LL ARRIVE HERE.

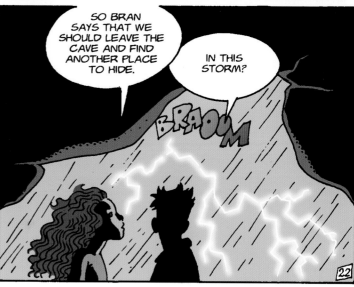

SO BRAN SAYS THAT WE SHOULD LEAVE THE CAVE AND FIND ANOTHER PLACE TO HIDE.

IN THIS STORM?

BRAOOM

22

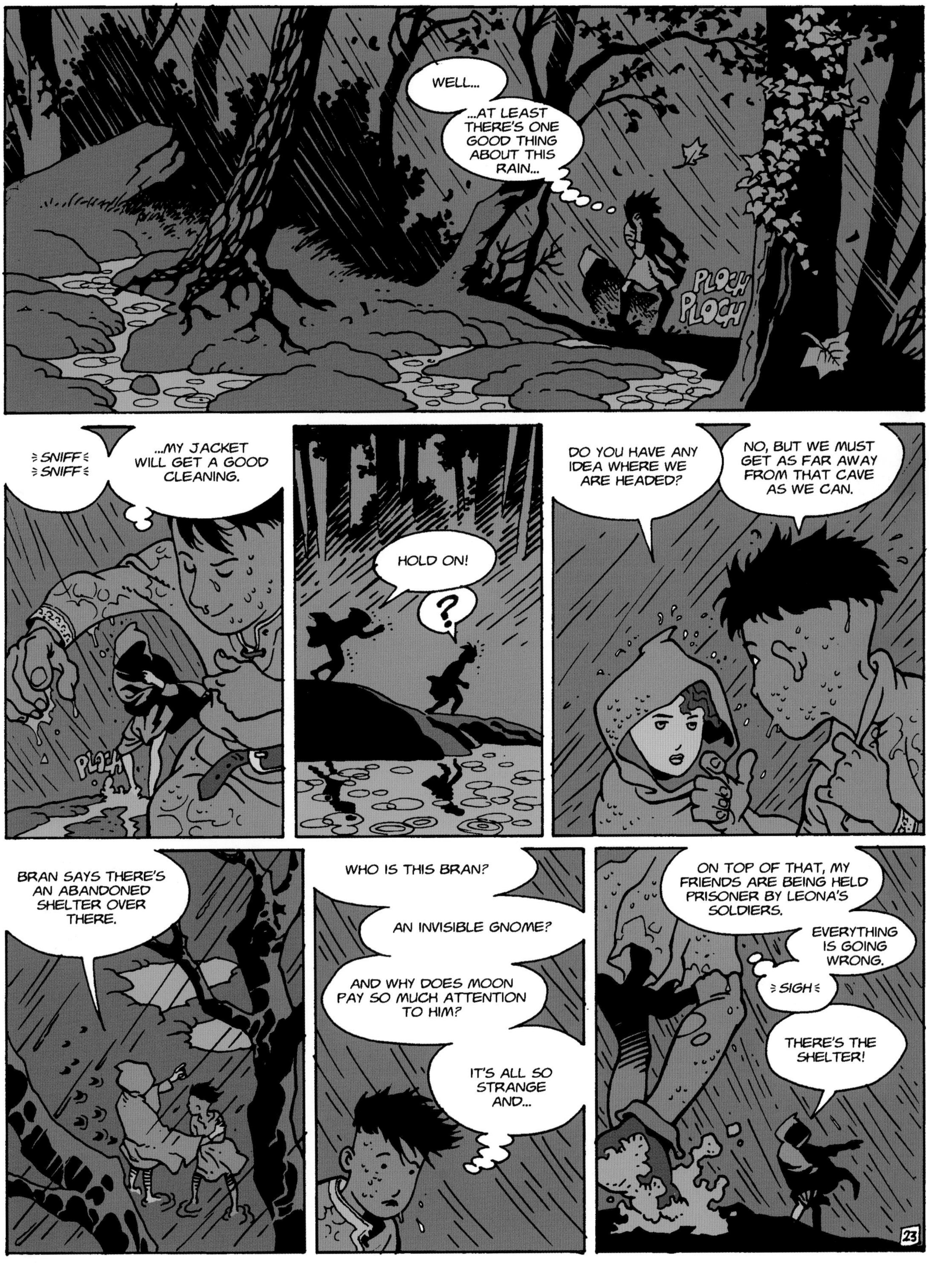
WELL...
...AT LEAST THERE'S ONE GOOD THING ABOUT THIS RAIN...
PLOCH PLOCH
SNIFF SNIFF
...MY JACKET WILL GET A GOOD CLEANING.
PLOCH
HOLD ON!
?
DO YOU HAVE ANY IDEA WHERE WE ARE HEADED?
NO, BUT WE MUST GET AS FAR AWAY FROM THAT CAVE AS WE CAN.
BRAN SAYS THERE'S AN ABANDONED SHELTER OVER THERE.
WHO IS THIS BRAN?
AN INVISIBLE GNOME?
AND WHY DOES MOON PAY SO MUCH ATTENTION TO HIM?
IT'S ALL SO STRANGE AND...
ON TOP OF THAT, MY FRIENDS ARE BEING HELD PRISONER BY LEONA'S SOLDIERS.
EVERYTHING IS GOING WRONG.
SIGH
THERE'S THE SHELTER!
23

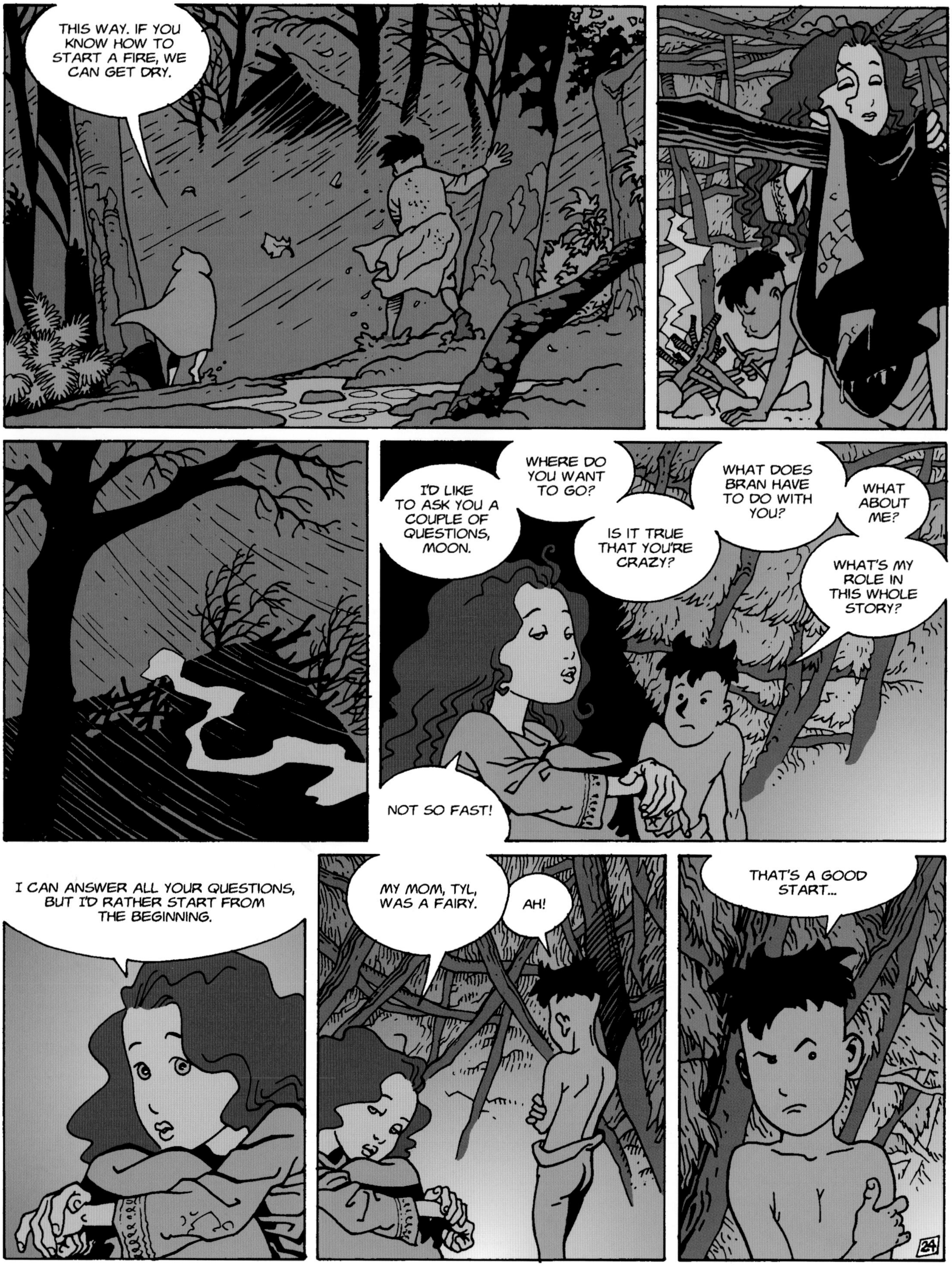
THIS WAY. IF YOU KNOW HOW TO START A FIRE, WE CAN GET DRY.
I'D LIKE TO ASK YOU A COUPLE OF QUESTIONS, MOON.
WHERE DO YOU WANT TO GO?
IS IT TRUE THAT YOU'RE CRAZY?
WHAT DOES BRAN HAVE TO DO WITH YOU?
WHAT ABOUT ME?
WHAT'S MY ROLE IN THIS WHOLE STORY?
NOT SO FAST!
I CAN ANSWER ALL YOUR QUESTIONS, BUT I'D RATHER START FROM THE BEGINNING.
MY MOM, TYL, WAS A FAIRY.
AH!
THAT'S A GOOD START...
24

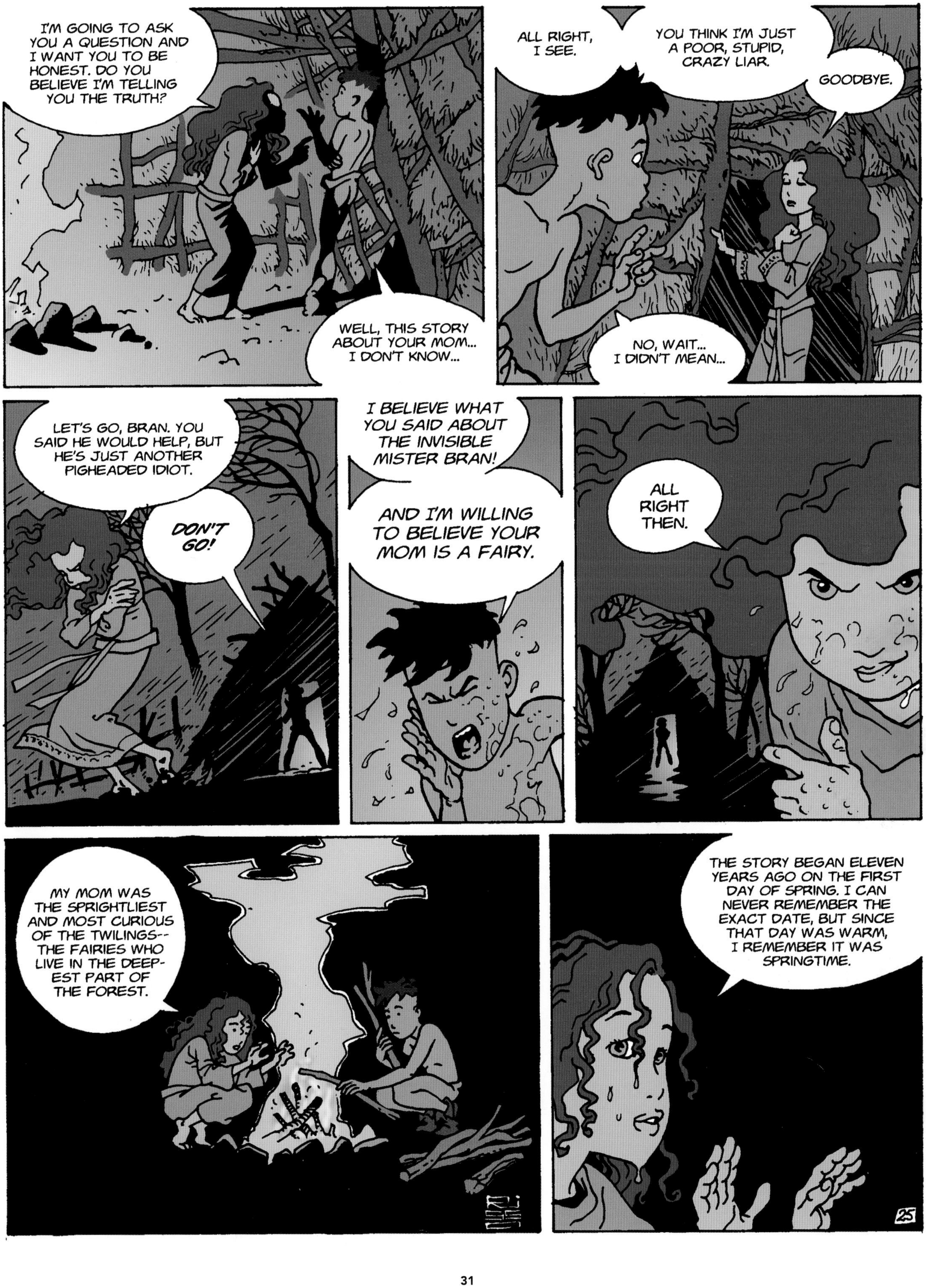
I'M GOING TO ASK YOU A QUESTION AND I WANT YOU TO BE HONEST. DO YOU BELIEVE I'M TELLING YOU THE TRUTH?
WELL, THIS STORY ABOUT YOUR MOM... I DON'T KNOW...
ALL RIGHT, I SEE.
YOU THINK I'M JUST A POOR, STUPID, CRAZY LIAR.
GOODBYE.
NO, WAIT... I DIDN'T MEAN...
LET'S GO, BRAN. YOU SAID HE WOULD HELP, BUT HE'S JUST ANOTHER PIGHEADED IDIOT.
DON'T GO!
I BELIEVE WHAT YOU SAID ABOUT THE INVISIBLE MISTER BRAN!
AND I'M WILLING TO BELIEVE YOUR MOM IS A FAIRY.
ALL RIGHT THEN.
MY MOM WAS THE SPRIGHTLIEST AND MOST CURIOUS OF THE TWILINGS-- THE FAIRIES WHO LIVE IN THE DEEP-EST PART OF THE FOREST.
THE STORY BEGAN ELEVEN YEARS AGO ON THE FIRST DAY OF SPRING. I CAN NEVER REMEMBER THE EXACT DATE, BUT SINCE THAT DAY WAS WARM, I REMEMBER IT WAS SPRINGTIME.
25

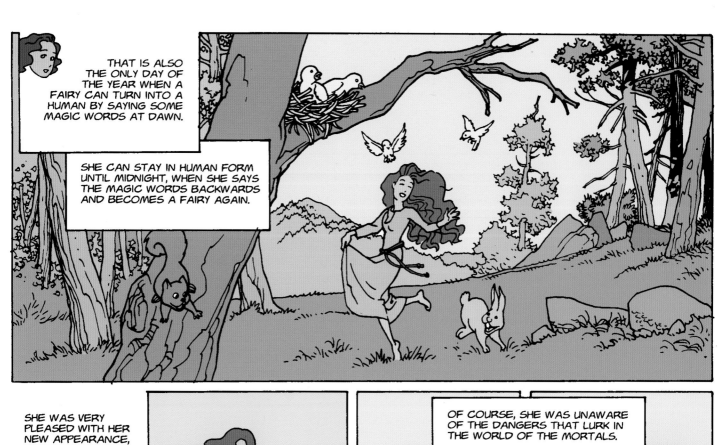

THAT IS ALSO THE ONLY DAY OF THE YEAR WHEN A FAIRY CAN TURN INTO A HUMAN BY SAYING SOME MAGIC WORDS AT DAWN.

SHE CAN STAY IN HUMAN FORM UNTIL MIDNIGHT, WHEN SHE SAYS THE MAGIC WORDS BACKWARDS AND BECOMES A FAIRY AGAIN.

SHE WAS VERY PLEASED WITH HER NEW APPEARANCE, ALTHOUGH IT SEEMED A LITTLE STRANGE TO HER. SHE WAS HAPPY AND CAREFREE.

OF COURSE, SHE WAS UNAWARE OF THE DANGERS THAT LURK IN THE WORLD OF THE MORTALS.

HM, BEAUTIFUL WOMAN.

IF YOU COME WITH ME, YOU'LL HAVE THE HONOR OF DANCING FOR ME, THE LORD OF LEONA, TEE-HEE.

NOT ON YOUR LIFE, TOADFACE!

I'D MUCH RATHER GO TO HELL.

THAT'S EXACTLY WHERE YOU'LL BE GOING FOR HAVING OFFENDED ME.

26

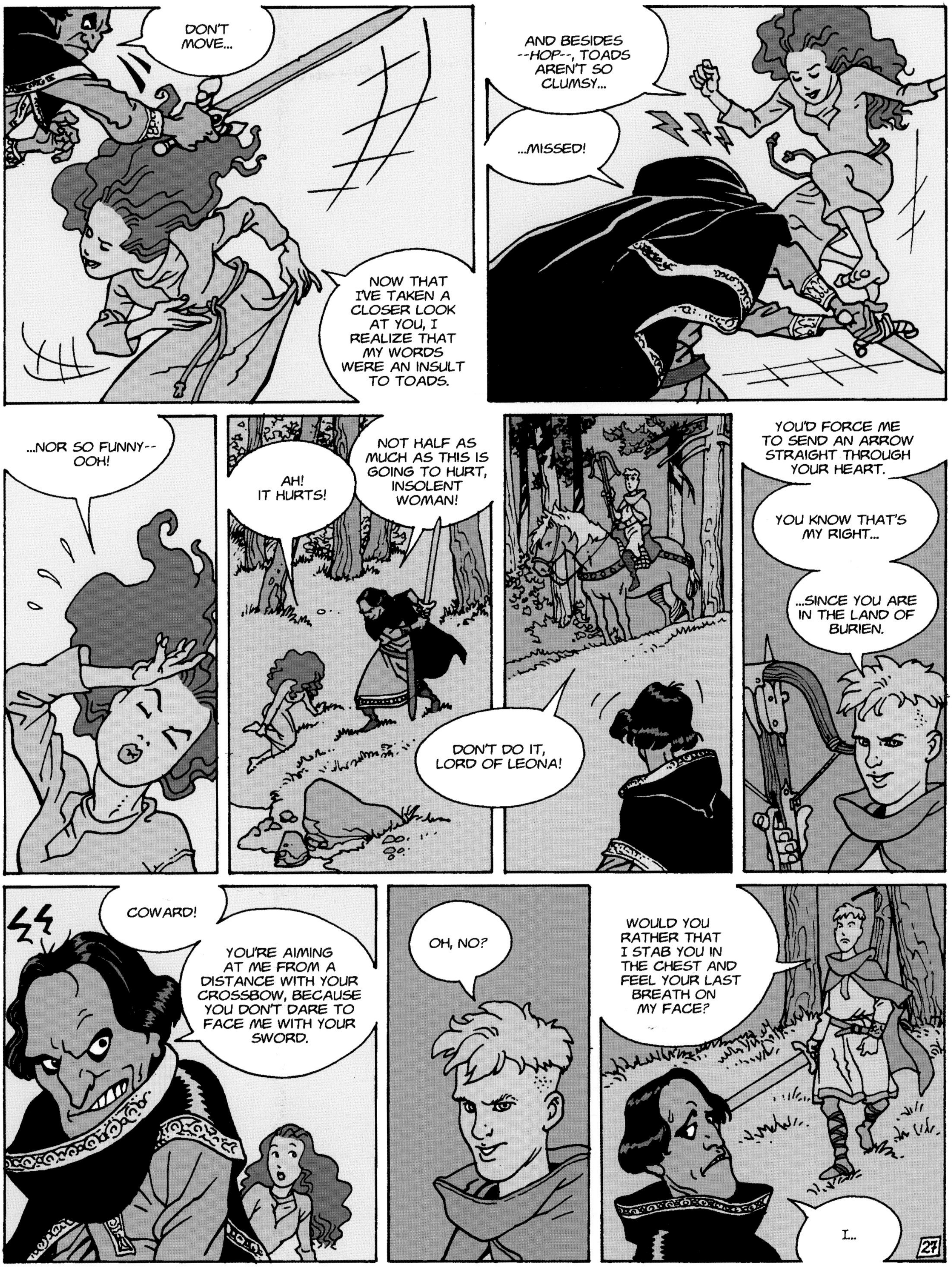
DON'T MOVE...
NOW THAT I'VE TAKEN A CLOSER LOOK AT YOU, I REALIZE THAT MY WORDS WERE AN INSULT TO TOADS.
AND BESIDES --HOP--, TOADS AREN'T SO CLUMSY...
...MISSED!
...NOR SO FUNNY-- OOH!
AH! IT HURTS!
NOT HALF AS MUCH AS THIS IS GOING TO HURT, INSOLENT WOMAN!
DON'T DO IT, LORD OF LEONA!
YOU'D FORCE ME TO SEND AN ARROW STRAIGHT THROUGH YOUR HEART.
YOU KNOW THAT'S MY RIGHT...
...SINCE YOU ARE IN THE LAND OF BURIEN.
COWARD!
YOU'RE AIMING AT ME FROM A DISTANCE WITH YOUR CROSSBOW, BECAUSE YOU DON'T DARE TO FACE ME WITH YOUR SWORD.
OH, NO?
WOULD YOU RATHER THAT I STAB YOU IN THE CHEST AND FEEL YOUR LAST BREATH ON MY FACE?
I...
27

...I'D BETTER LEAVE. I DON'T WANT TO START A WAR BETWEEN BURIEN AND LEONA OVER NOTHING.

GOOD-BYE!

ARE YOU ALL RIGHT, MISS?

ME?

I AM VERY, VERY WELL NOW.

YOUR COURAGE SURPRISES ME.

YOU FACED THAT BRUTE FOR ME...

...AND YOU DON'T EVEN KNOW ME.

I'D VERY MUCH LIKE TO GET TO KNOW YOU.

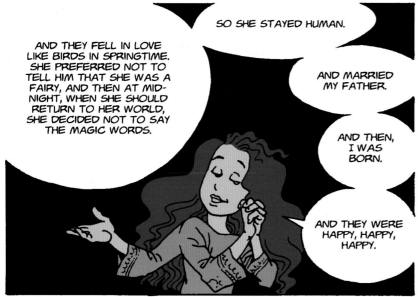

AND THEY FELL IN LOVE LIKE BIRDS IN SPRINGTIME. SHE PREFERRED NOT TO TELL HIM THAT SHE WAS A FAIRY, AND THEN AT MID-NIGHT, WHEN SHE SHOULD RETURN TO HER WORLD, SHE DECIDED NOT TO SAY THE MAGIC WORDS.

SO SHE STAYED HUMAN.

AND MARRIED MY FATHER.

AND THEN, I WAS BORN.

AND THEY WERE HAPPY, HAPPY, HAPPY.

UNTIL THE DAY WHEN EVERYTHING WENT WRONG.

≋SIGH≋

!

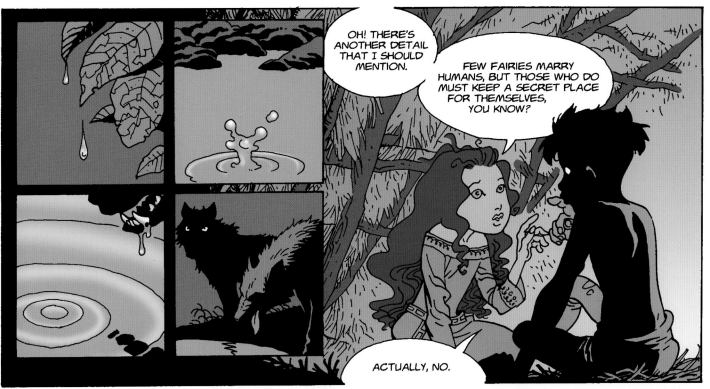

OH! THERE'S ANOTHER DETAIL THAT I SHOULD MENTION.

FEW FAIRIES MARRY HUMANS, BUT THOSE WHO DO MUST KEEP A SECRET PLACE FOR THEMSELVES, YOU KNOW?

ACTUALLY, NO.

YOU ARE A LITTLE DENSE, AREN'T YOU?

THE HUSBAND MUST NOT SUSPECT THAT HIS WIFE IS A FAIRY. BUT SHE NEEDS TO UNFOLD HER WINGS AND COLORS EVERY ONCE IN A WHILE TO KEEP THEM SHINY, SO...

MY MOM, BEFORE AGREEING TO MARRY MY FATHER, MADE A DEAL WITH HIM.

ALL RIGHT, I'M WILLING TO JOIN MY LIFE TO YOURS...

...BUT ONLY UNDER ONE VERY IMPORTANT CONDITION.

I'M LISTENING.

EVERY FRIDAY BETWEEN SIX IN THE AFTERNOON AND MIDNIGHT, I'LL BE GOING ALONE INTO THE WOODS. YOU HAVE TO PROMISE ME THAT YOU WILL NEVER, UNDER ANY CIRCUMSTANCES, FOLLOW ME. DO YOU AGREE?

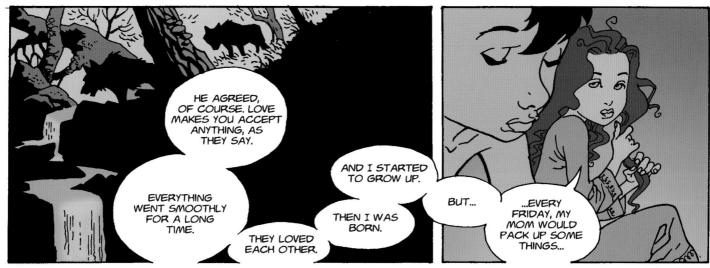

HE AGREED, OF COURSE. LOVE MAKES YOU ACCEPT ANYTHING, AS THEY SAY.

EVERYTHING WENT SMOOTHLY FOR A LONG TIME.

THEY LOVED EACH OTHER.

THEN I WAS BORN.

AND I STARTED TO GROW UP.

BUT...

...EVERY FRIDAY, MY MOM WOULD PACK UP SOME THINGS...

"...AND GO INTO THE WOODS. BUT NOBODY KNEW...

"...THAT THE SPIES OF LEONA WERE HIDING NEAR OUR CASTLE, WATCHING FOR SOMETHING WHICH COULD HURT MY FATHER...

"...AND WHICH WOULD ENABLE THEIR MASTER TO RETALIATE FOR THE HUMILIATION HE SUFFERED THE DAY MY FATHER CAME TO MY MOM'S RESCUE.

"SO, WHEN THE LORD OF LEONA LEARNED ABOUT MY MOM'S MOVE-MENTS, HE CAME UP WITH A CRUEL PLAN THAT WOULD STAB LIKE THE SHARPEST DAG-GER INTO THE HEART OF ANY MAN IN LOVE.

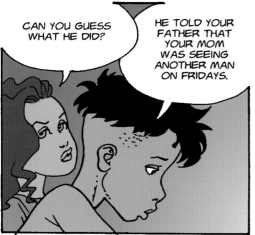

CAN YOU GUESS WHAT HE DID?

HE TOLD YOUR FATHER THAT YOUR MOM WAS SEEING ANOTHER MAN ON FRIDAYS.

THAT'S RIGHT! HOW DID YOU KNOW?

WELL...EVIL MEN ALWAYS INVENT THE WORST LIES.

AND I'VE HEARD OF SIMILAR THINGS HERE AND THERE.

BUT YOU DON'T KNOW HOW MY FATHER REACTED.

HMM...IT'S EASY TO GUESS.

"HE GOT SO ANGRY THAT HE TOOK HIS SWORD AND CHALLENGED THE LORD OF LEONA.

"AND I'LL TELL YOU MORE; IT WAS THAT DUEL...

KLANK

"THEY FOUGHT FEROCIOUSLY.

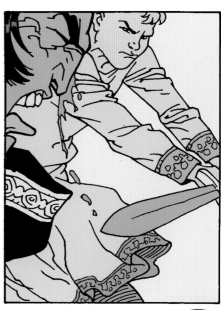

"...THAT LEFT THE LORD OF LEONA WITH THAT TERRIBLE SCAR AND THE WHITE EYE THAT APPEARS TO BE LOOKING INWARDS.

YOU SURPRISE ME, ANTOLIN. IT HAPPENED EXACTLY AS YOU SAID, BUT THERE IS MORE.

I KNOW.

THE LORD OF LEONA SUCCEEDED IN PLANTING A SEED OF DOUBT IN YOUR FATHER'S HEART.

"SO, THE NEXT FRIDAY, YOUR FATHER FOLLOWED TYL...

"...AND HE WITNESSED SOMETHING SPLENDID...

"...INDESCRIBABLE...

"...THE TRANSFORMATION OF A WOMAN INTO A FAIRY, WHICH IS SOMETHING NO MORTAL SHOULD EVER SEE.

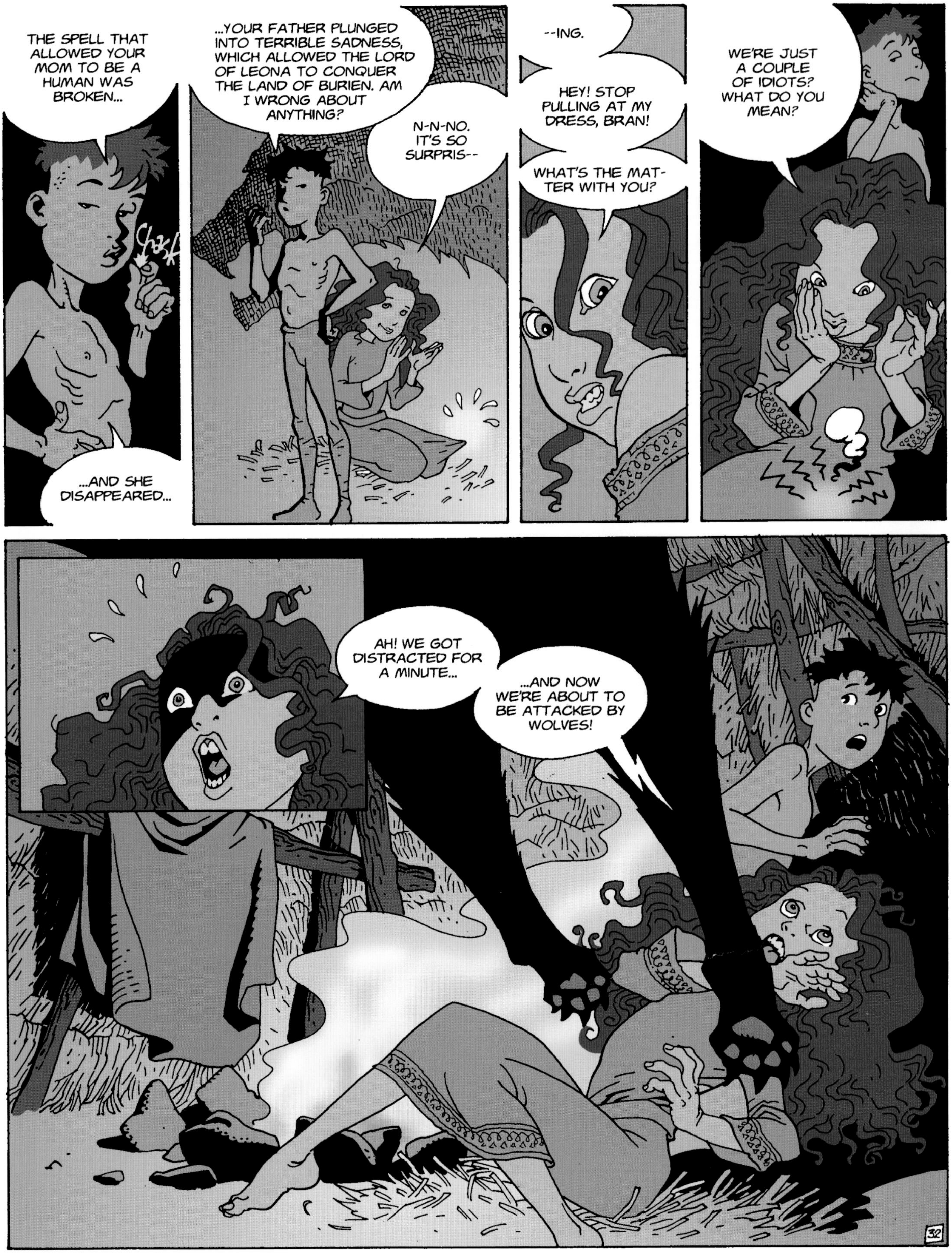
THE SPELL THAT ALLOWED YOUR MOM TO BE A HUMAN WAS BROKEN...
...AND SHE DISAPPEARED...
...YOUR FATHER PLUNGED INTO TERRIBLE SADNESS, WHICH ALLOWED THE LORD OF LEONA TO CONQUER THE LAND OF BURIEN. AM I WRONG ABOUT ANYTHING?
N-N-NO. IT'S SO SURPRIS--
--ING.
HEY! STOP PULLING AT MY DRESS, BRAN!
WHAT'S THE MAT-TER WITH YOU?
WE'RE JUST A COUPLE OF IDIOTS? WHAT DO YOU MEAN?
AH! WE GOT DISTRACTED FOR A MINUTE...
...AND NOW WE'RE ABOUT TO BE ATTACKED BY WOLVES!
32

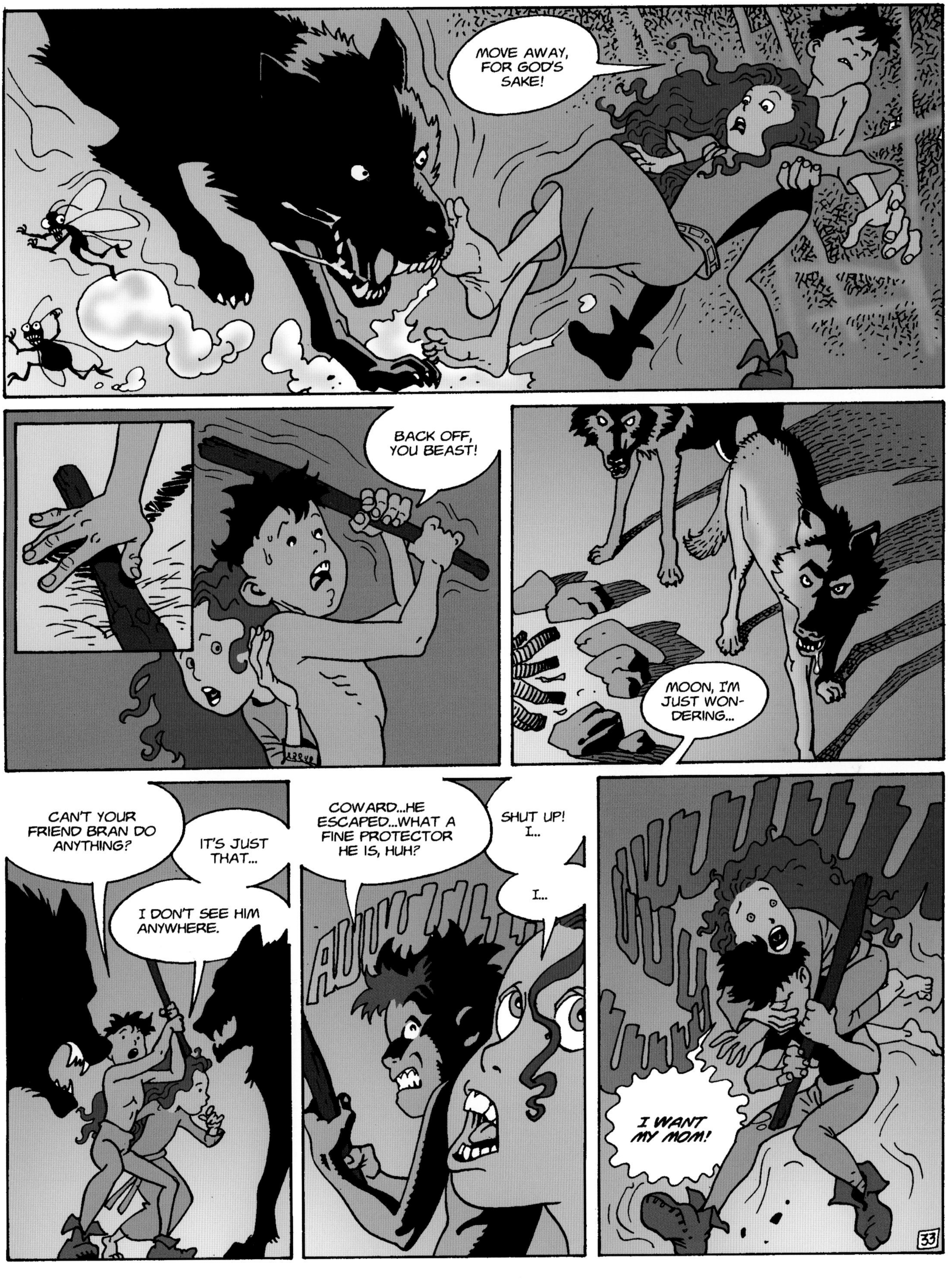

MOVE AWAY, FOR GOD'S SAKE!
BACK OFF, YOU BEAST!
MOON, I'M JUST WON- DERING...
CAN'T YOUR FRIEND BRAN DO ANYTHING?
IT'S JUST THAT...
I DON'T SEE HIM ANYWHERE.
COWARD...HE ESCAPED...WHAT A FINE PROTECTOR HE IS, HUH?
SHUT UP! I...
I...
I WANT MY MOM!
33

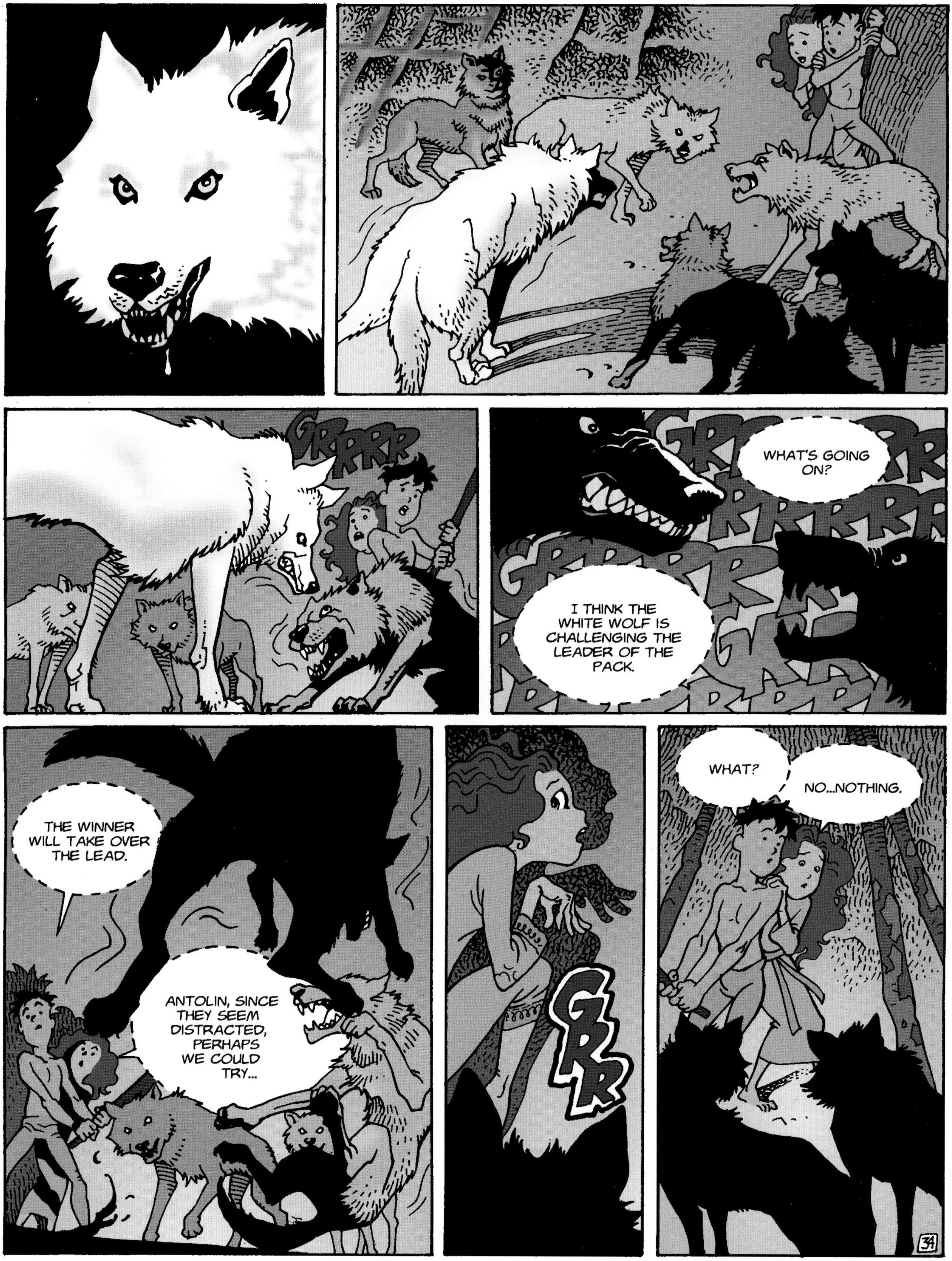
GRRRR
GRRRRRRRRR
WHAT'S GOING ON?
I THINK THE WHITE WOLF IS CHALLENGING THE LEADER OF THE PACK.
THE WINNER WILL TAKE OVER THE LEAD.
ANTOLIN, SINCE THEY SEEM DISTRACTED, PERHAPS WE COULD TRY...
GRR
WHAT?
NO...NOTHING.
34

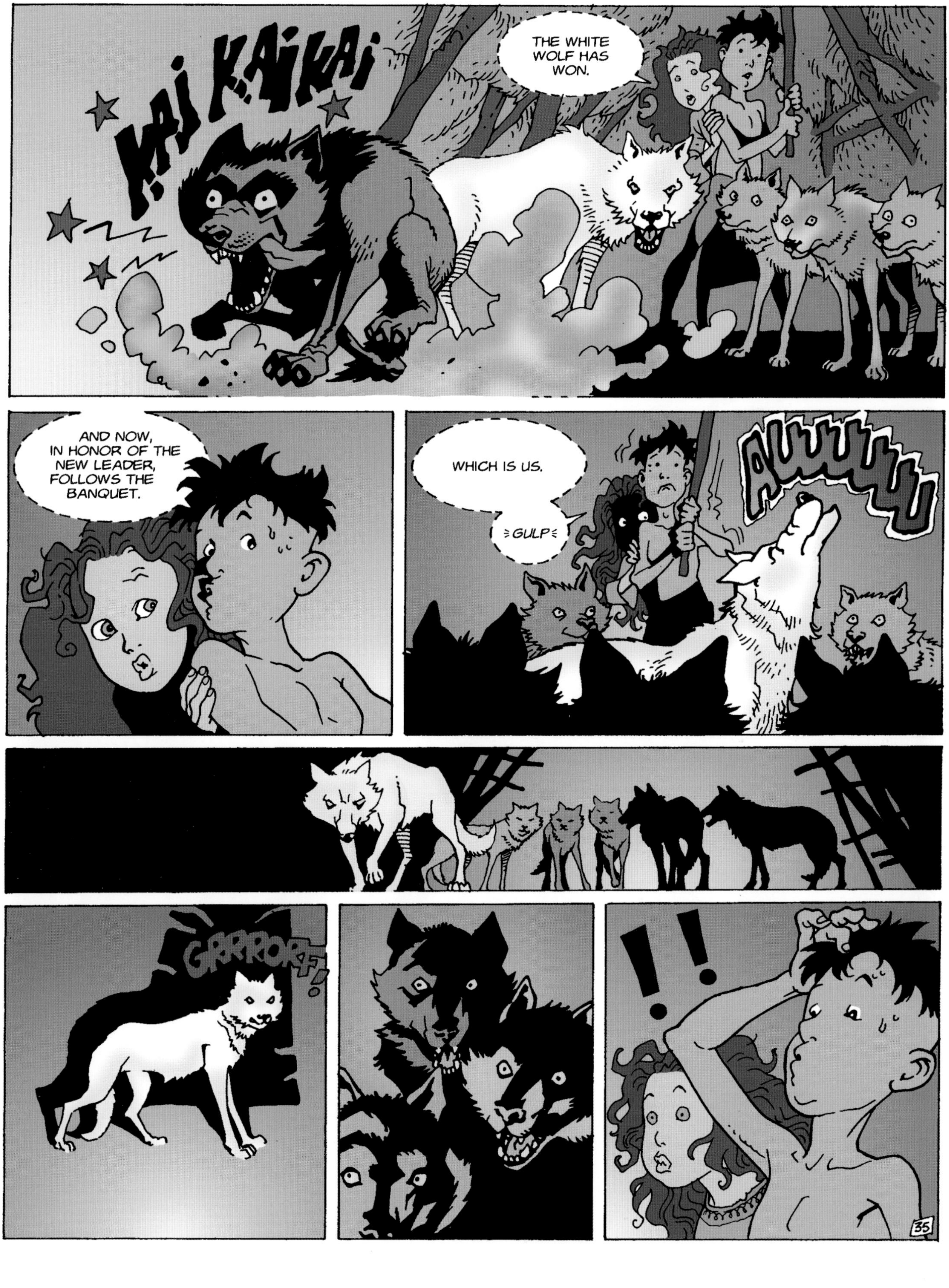
KAI KAI KAI
THE WHITE WOLF HAS WON.
AND NOW, IN HONOR OF THE NEW LEADER, FOLLOWS THE BANQUET.
WHICH IS US.
GULP
AUUUUUU
GRRRORF!
!!
35

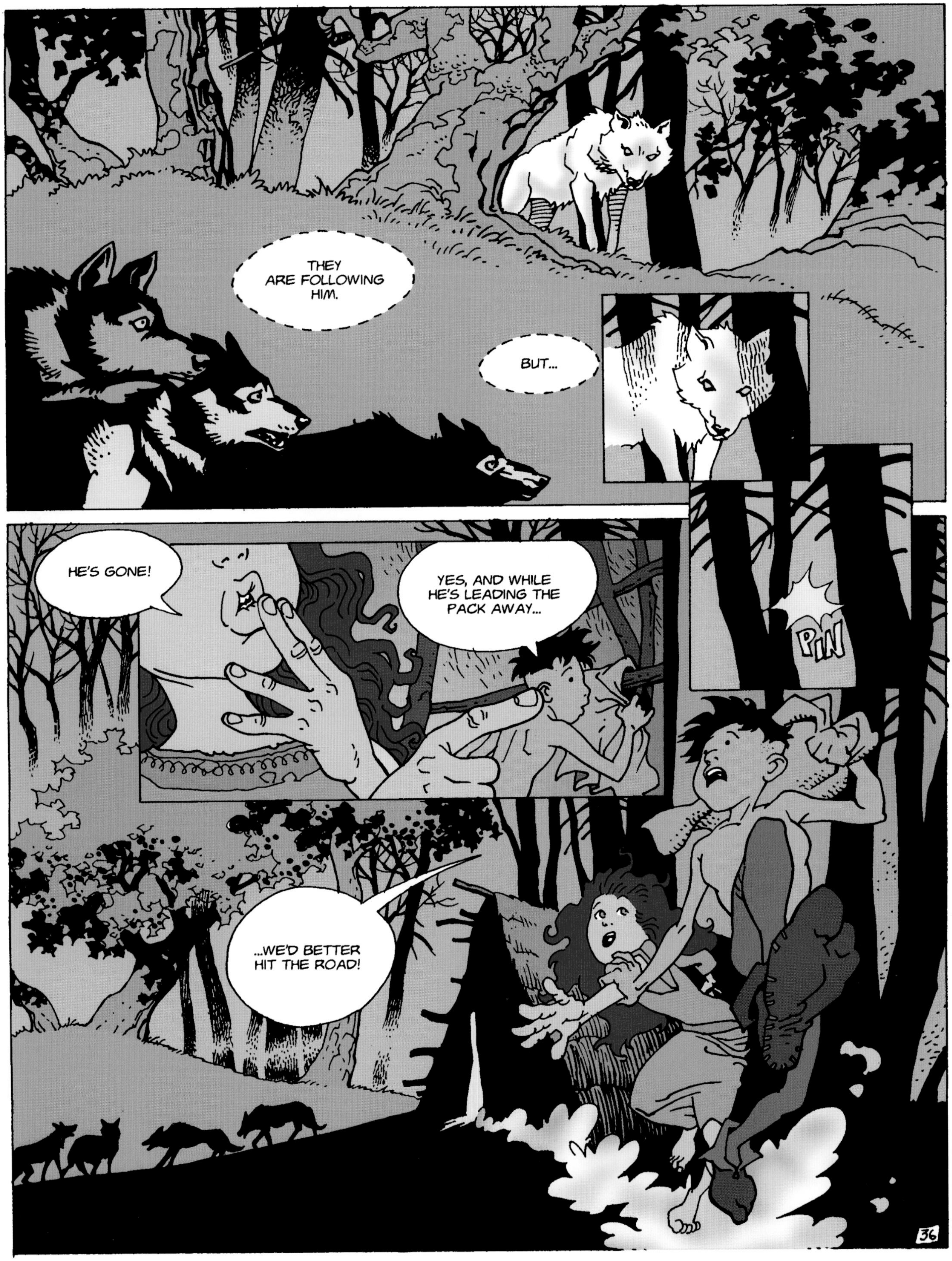
THEY ARE FOLLOWING HIM.
BUT...
HE'S GONE!
YES, AND WHILE HE'S LEADING THE PACK AWAY...
PIN
...WE'D BETTER HIT THE ROAD!
36

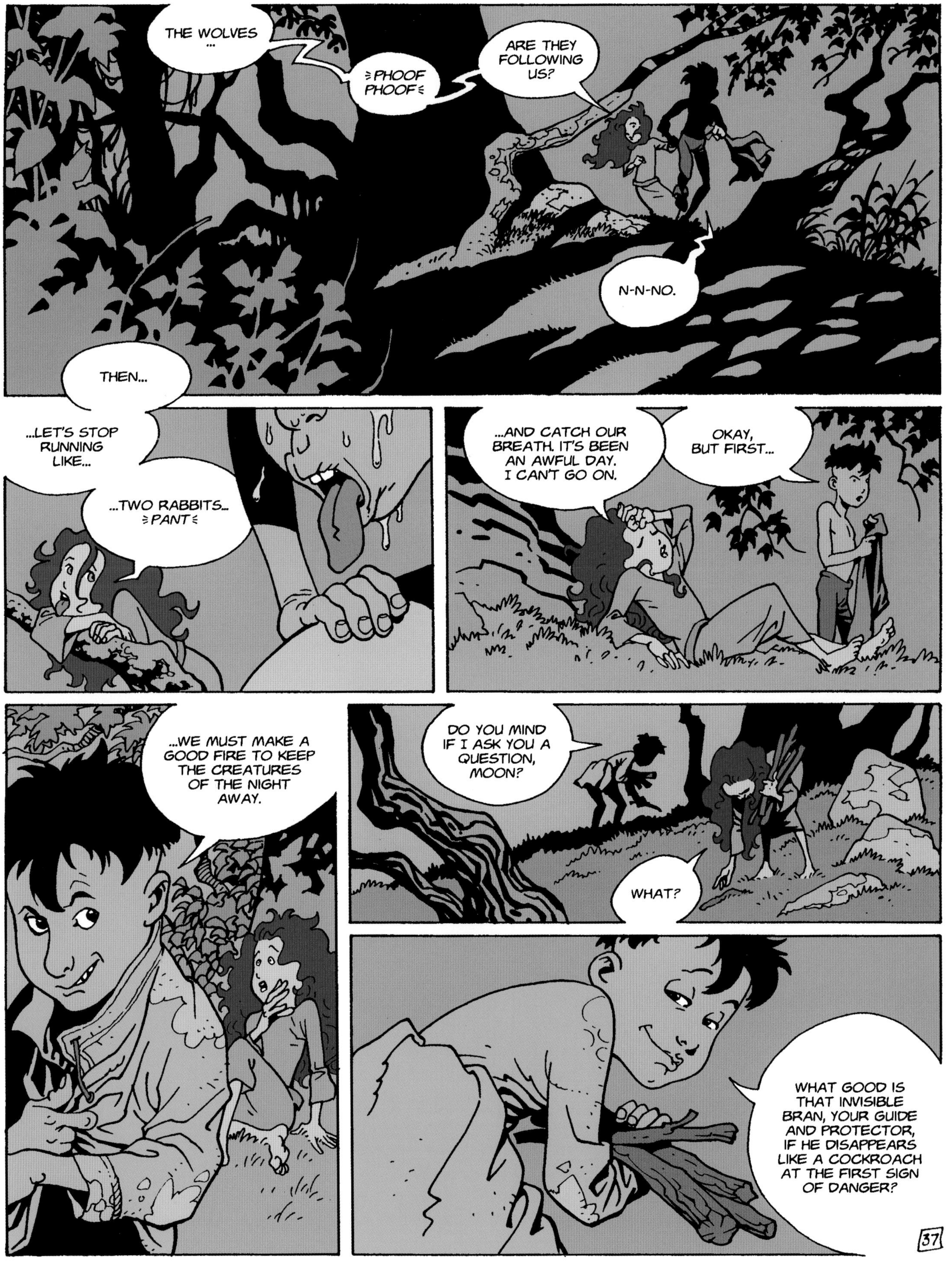
THE WOLVES ...
PHOOF PHOOF
ARE THEY FOLLOWING US?
N-N-NO.
THEN...
...LET'S STOP RUNNING LIKE...
...TWO RABBITS... PANT
...AND CATCH OUR BREATH. IT'S BEEN AN AWFUL DAY. I CAN'T GO ON.
OKAY, BUT FIRST...
...WE MUST MAKE A GOOD FIRE TO KEEP THE CREATURES OF THE NIGHT AWAY.
DO YOU MIND IF I ASK YOU A QUESTION, MOON?
WHAT?
WHAT GOOD IS THAT INVISIBLE BRAN, YOUR GUIDE AND PROTECTOR, IF HE DISAPPEARS LIKE A COCKROACH AT THE FIRST SIGN OF DANGER?
37

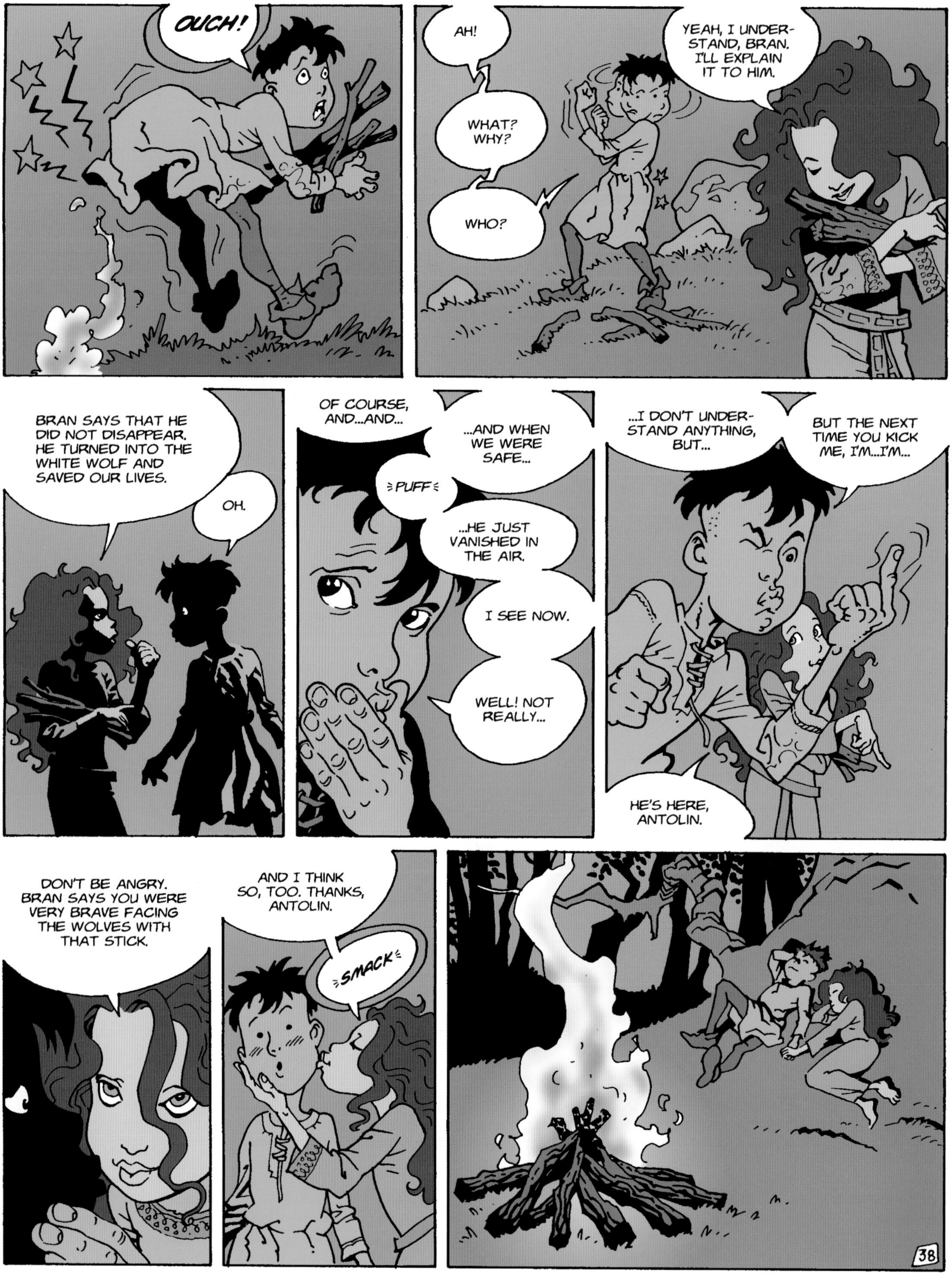
OUCH!
AH!
WHAT? WHY?
WHO?
YEAH, I UNDERSTAND, BRAN. I'LL EXPLAIN IT TO HIM.
BRAN SAYS THAT HE DID NOT DISAPPEAR. HE TURNED INTO THE WHITE WOLF AND SAVED OUR LIVES.
OH.
OF COURSE, AND...AND...
...AND WHEN WE WERE SAFE...
PUFF
...HE JUST VANISHED IN THE AIR.
I SEE NOW.
WELL! NOT REALLY...
...I DON'T UNDERSTAND ANYTHING, BUT...
BUT THE NEXT TIME YOU KICK ME, I'M...I'M...
HE'S HERE, ANTOLIN.
DON'T BE ANGRY. BRAN SAYS YOU WERE VERY BRAVE FACING THE WOLVES WITH THAT STICK.
AND I THINK SO, TOO. THANKS, ANTOLIN.
SMACK
38

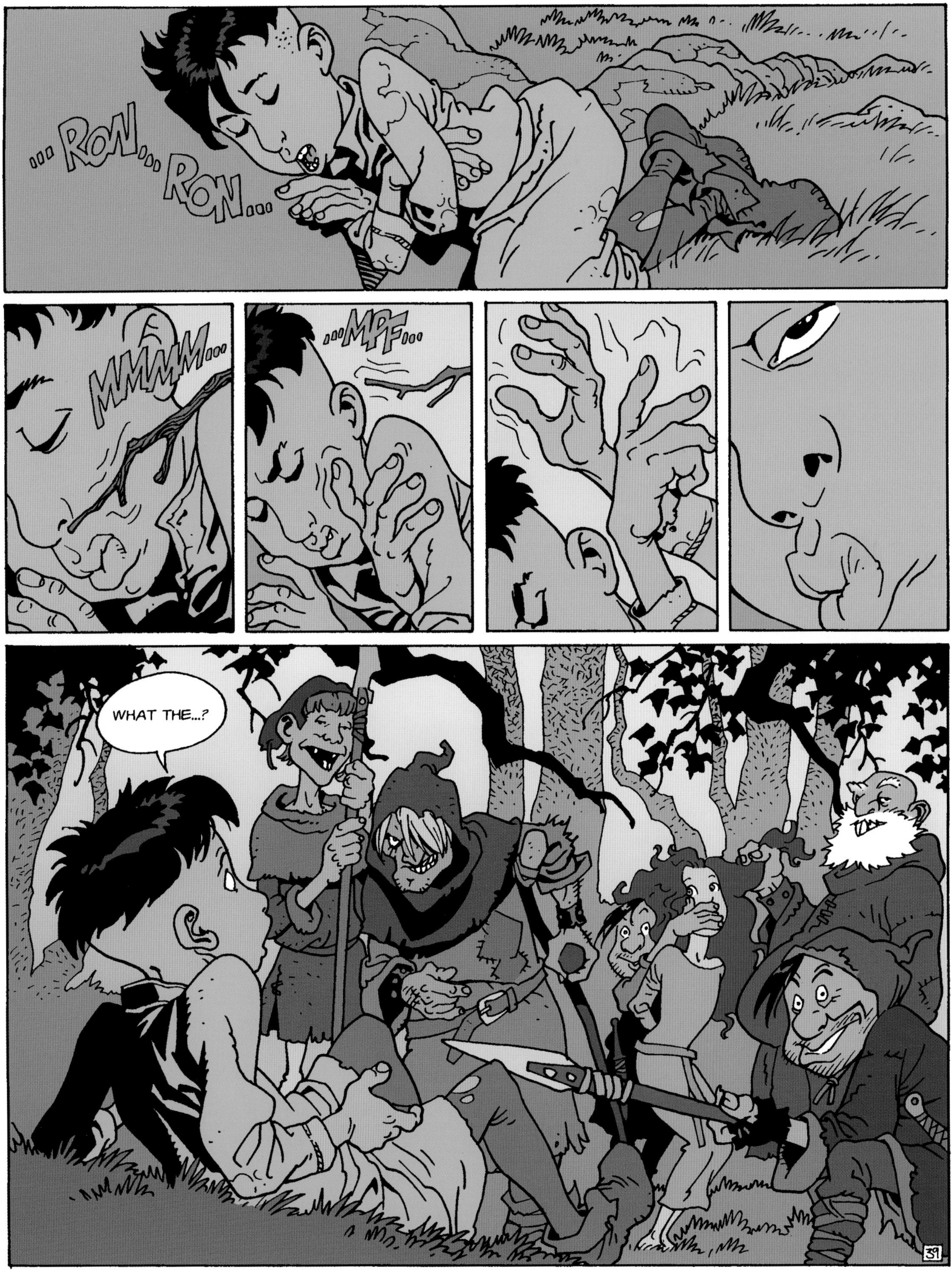
...RON...RON...
MMMM...
...MPF...
WHAT THE...?
39

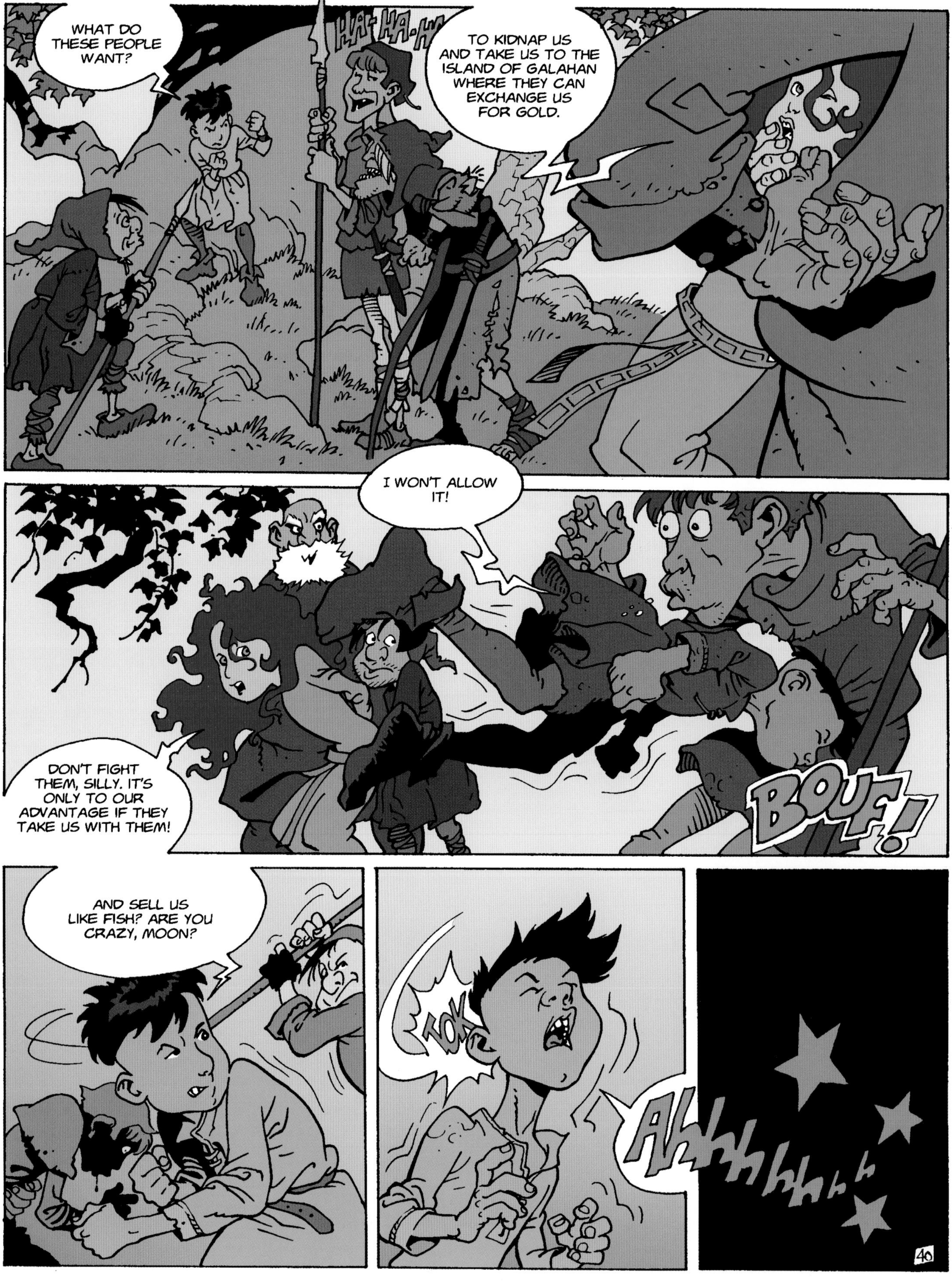
WHAT DO THESE PEOPLE WANT?
HA-HA-HA
TO KIDNAP US AND TAKE US TO THE ISLAND OF GALAHAN WHERE THEY CAN EXCHANGE US FOR GOLD.
I WON'T ALLOW IT!
DON'T FIGHT THEM, SILLY. IT'S ONLY TO OUR ADVANTAGE IF THEY TAKE US WITH THEM!
BOUF!
AND SELL US LIKE FISH? ARE YOU CRAZY, MOON?
KOK
Ahhhhhhhh
40

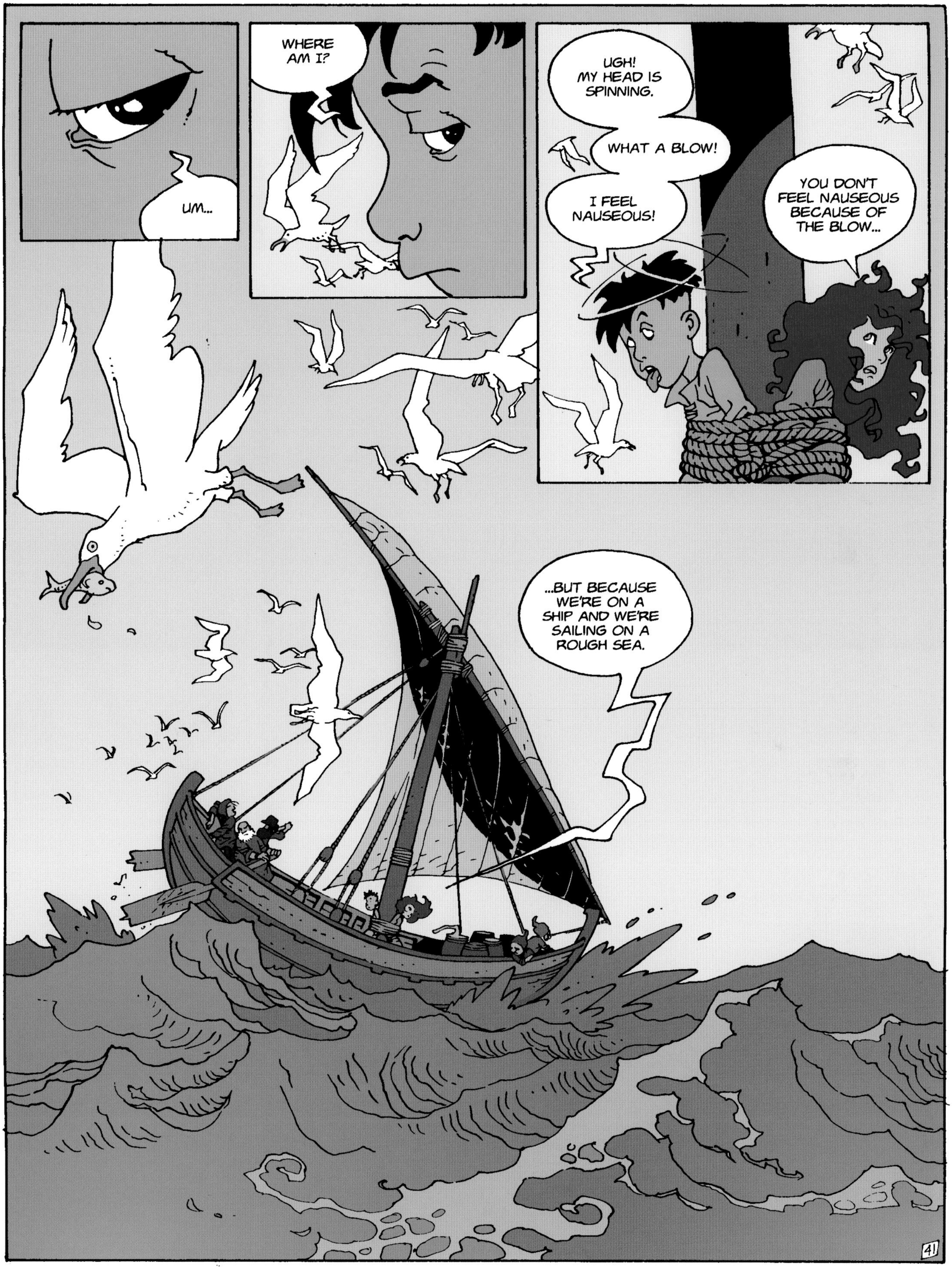
UM...
WHERE AM I?
UGH! MY HEAD IS SPINNING.
WHAT A BLOW!
I FEEL NAUSEOUS!
YOU DON'T FEEL NAUSEOUS BECAUSE OF THE BLOW...
...BUT BECAUSE WE'RE ON A SHIP AND WE'RE SAILING ON A ROUGH SEA.
41

I THINK YOUR IDEA WASN'T SO GOOD AFTER ALL.

THEY'RE KEEPING US TIED UP, AND I OVERHEARD THAT THERE WAS SOMEONE ON THE SHORE WAITING TO BUY ANTOLIN AND ME.

OKAY, I KNOW WE HAVE TO GET TO THE ISLAND BECAUSE MY MOM IS THERE, BUT...

...WHOEVER IS GOING TO BUY US IS LOOKING FOR A PAIR OF SLAVES.

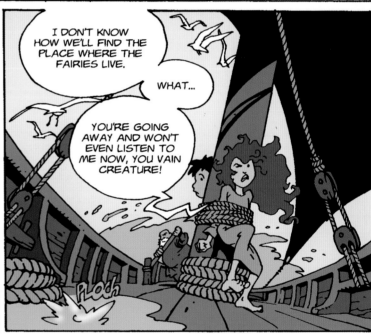

I DON'T KNOW HOW WE'LL FIND THE PLACE WHERE THE FAIRIES LIVE.

WHAT...

YOU'RE GOING AWAY AND WON'T EVEN LISTEN TO ME NOW, YOU VAIN CREATURE!

OH, IS THAT WHAT YOU'RE GOING TO DO?

MOON, WHAT ARE YOU AND BRAN TALKING ABOUT?

BRAN SAYS HE WON'T ALLOW ANYBODY TO SELL US.

OH...SO WHAT, IS HE GOING TO KILL US TO SAVE US FROM THAT SAD FATE?

NO, SILLY, HE'S ONLY GOING TO...

42

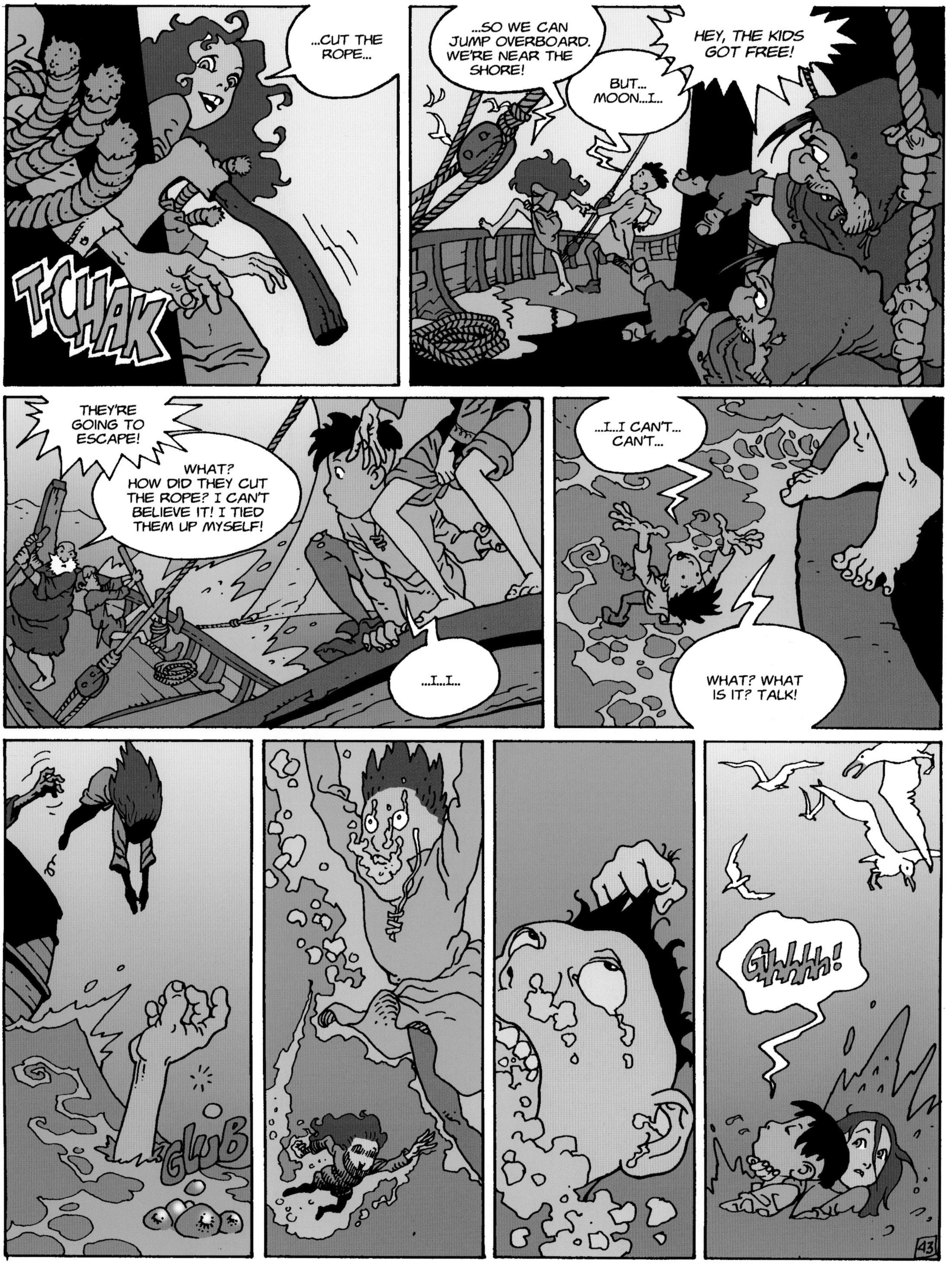
...CUT THE ROPE...
T-CHAK
...SO WE CAN JUMP OVERBOARD. WE'RE NEAR THE SHORE!
BUT... MOON...I...
HEY, THE KIDS GOT FREE!
THEY'RE GOING TO ESCAPE!
WHAT? HOW DID THEY CUT THE ROPE? I CAN'T BELIEVE IT! I TIED THEM UP MYSELF!
...I...I...
...I...I CAN'T... CAN'T...
WHAT? WHAT IS IT? TALK!
GLUB
Ghhhh!
43

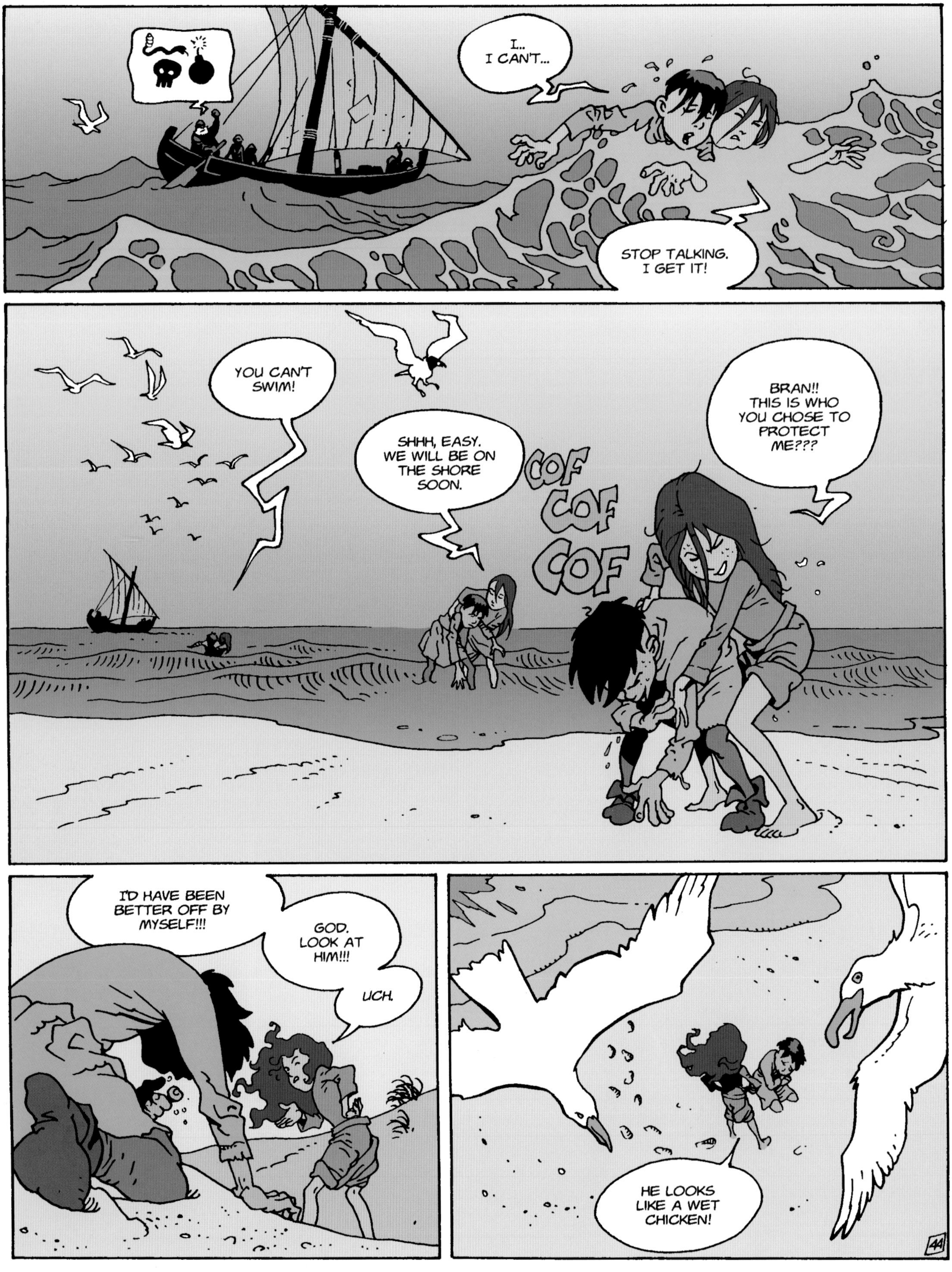
I..
I CAN'T...
STOP TALKING.
I GET IT!
YOU CAN'T SWIM!
SHHH, EASY. WE WILL BE ON THE SHORE SOON.
COF COF COF
BRAN!! THIS IS WHO YOU CHOSE TO PROTECT ME???
I'D HAVE BEEN BETTER OFF BY MYSELF!!!
GOD. LOOK AT HIM!!!
UCH.
HE LOOKS LIKE A WET CHICKEN!
44

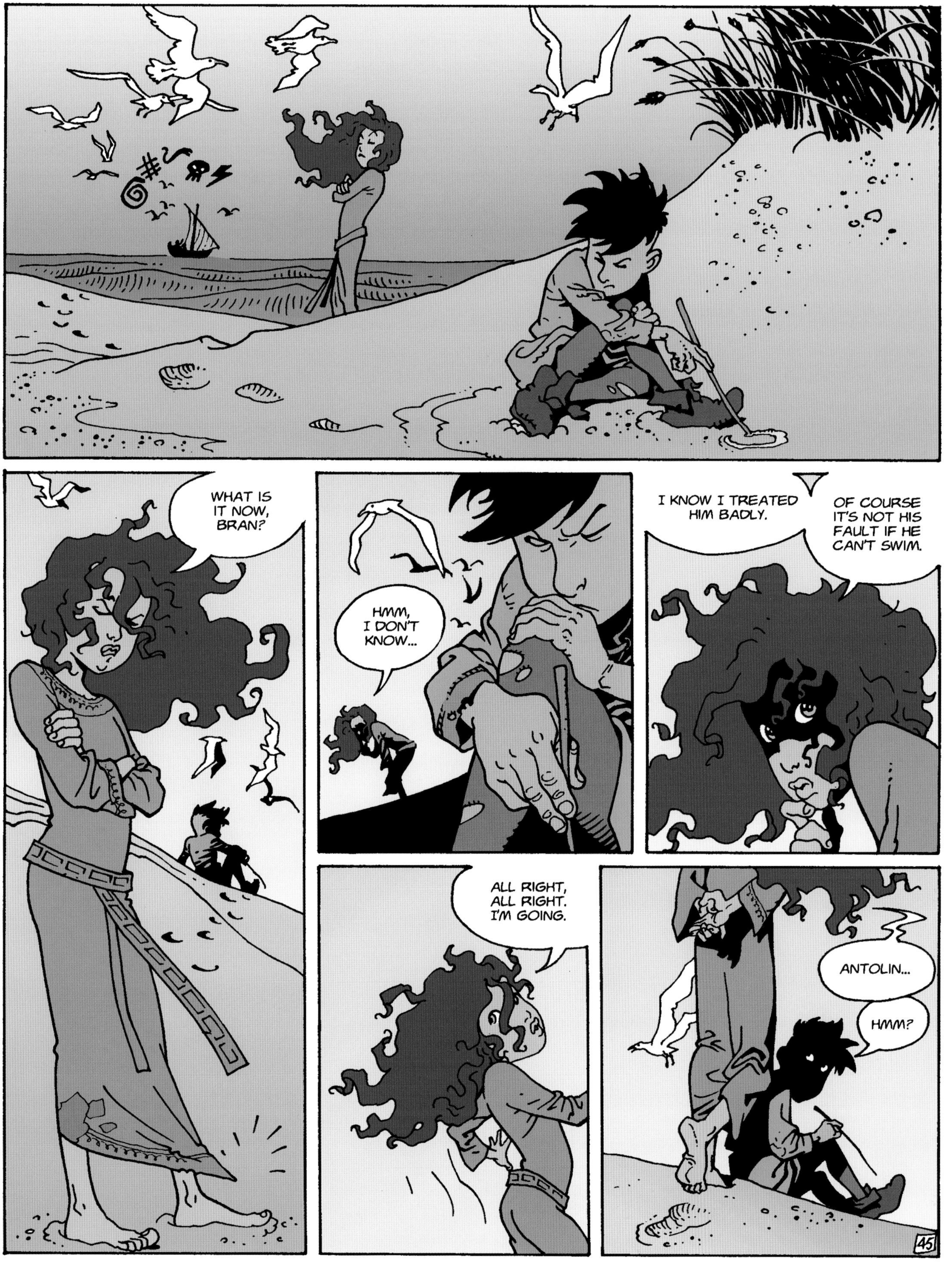
WHAT IS IT NOW, BRAN?
HMM, I DON'T KNOW...
I KNOW I TREATED HIM BADLY.
OF COURSE IT'S NOT HIS FAULT IF HE CAN'T SWIM.
ALL RIGHT, ALL RIGHT. I'M GOING.
ANTOLIN...
HMM?
45

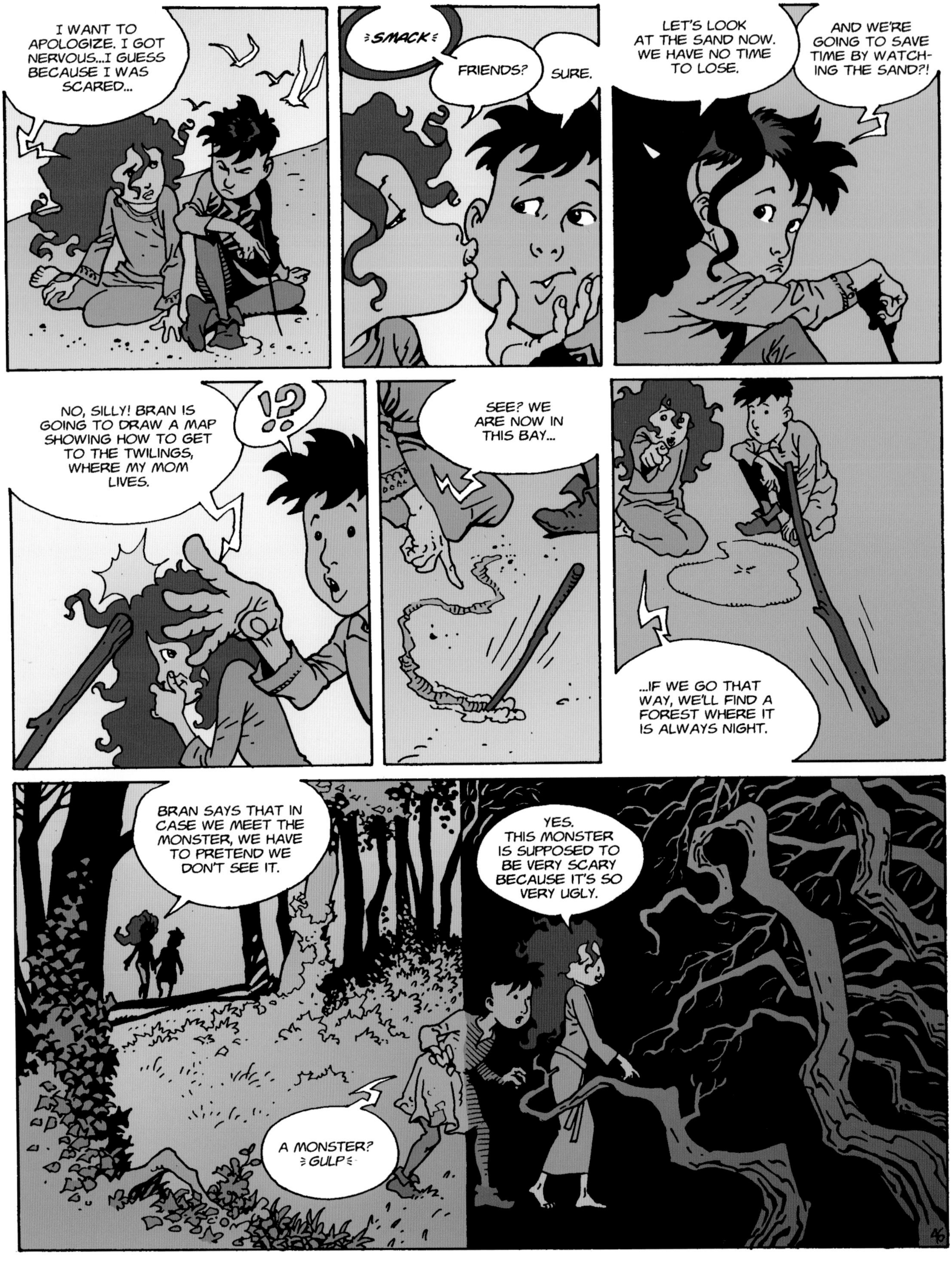
I WANT TO APOLOGIZE. I GOT NERVOUS...I GUESS BECAUSE I WAS SCARED...
SMACK
FRIENDS?
SURE.
LET'S LOOK AT THE SAND NOW. WE HAVE NO TIME TO LOSE.
AND WE'RE GOING TO SAVE TIME BY WATCHING THE SAND?!
NO, SILLY! BRAN IS GOING TO DRAW A MAP SHOWING HOW TO GET TO THE TWILINGS, WHERE MY MOM LIVES.
!?
SEE? WE ARE NOW IN THIS BAY...
...IF WE GO THAT WAY, WE'LL FIND A FOREST WHERE IT IS ALWAYS NIGHT.
BRAN SAYS THAT IN CASE WE MEET THE MONSTER, WE HAVE TO PRETEND WE DON'T SEE IT.
A MONSTER? GULP
YES. THIS MONSTER IS SUPPOSED TO BE VERY SCARY BECAUSE IT'S SO VERY UGLY.

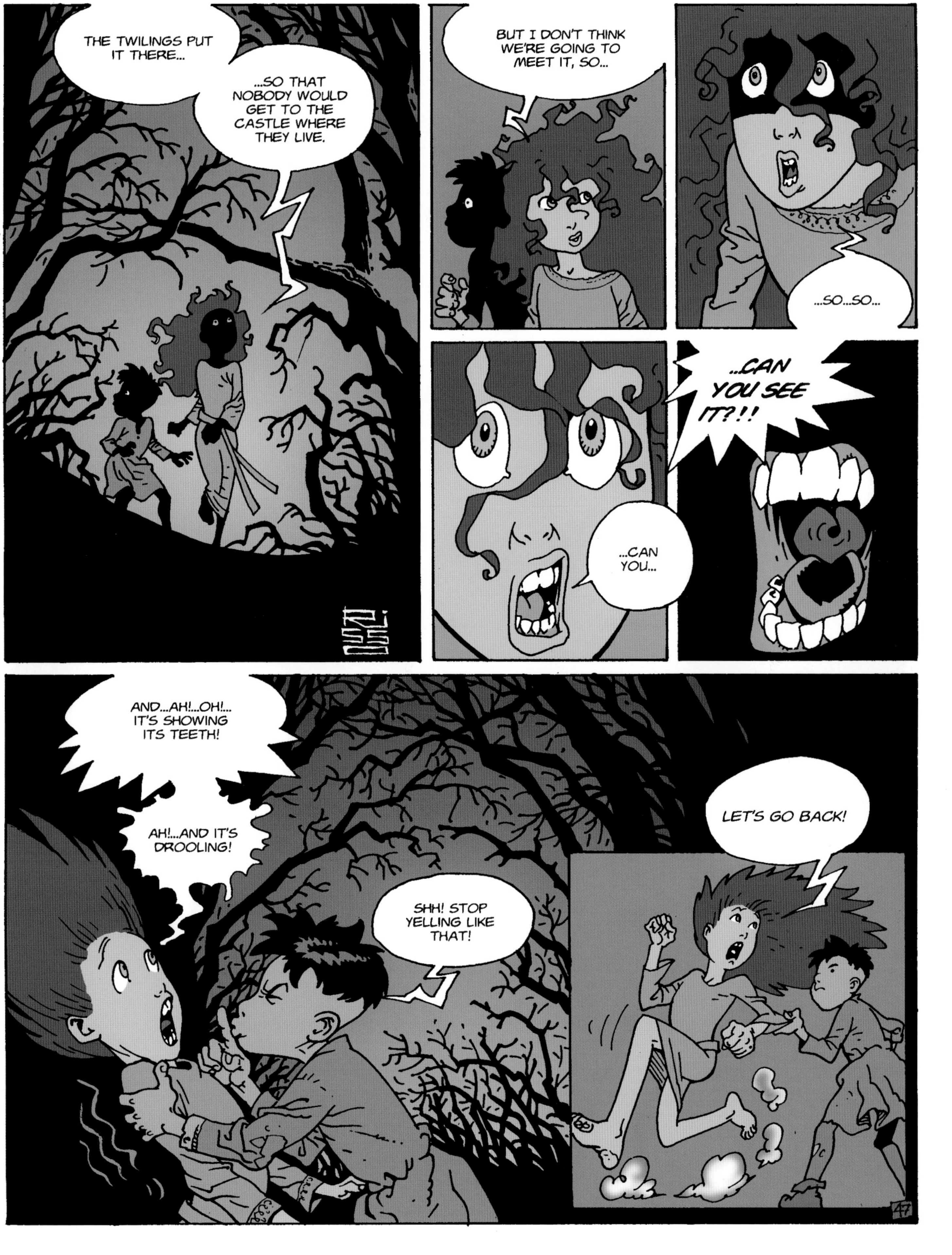
THE TWILINGS PUT IT THERE...
...SO THAT NOBODY WOULD GET TO THE CASTLE WHERE THEY LIVE.
BUT I DON'T THINK WE'RE GOING TO MEET IT, SO...
...SO...SO...
...CAN YOU...
...CAN YOU SEE IT?!!
AND...AH!...OH!... IT'S SHOWING ITS TEETH!
AH!...AND IT'S DROOLING!
SHH! STOP YELLING LIKE THAT!
LET'S GO BACK!
47

CALM DOWN, YOU BABY! I'M HERE TO TAKE CARE OF YOU.

LET GO OF MY DRESS! I WANT TO GO BACK!

DON'T BE SILLY! FOLLOW ME.

THERE IT IS. YOU SEE?

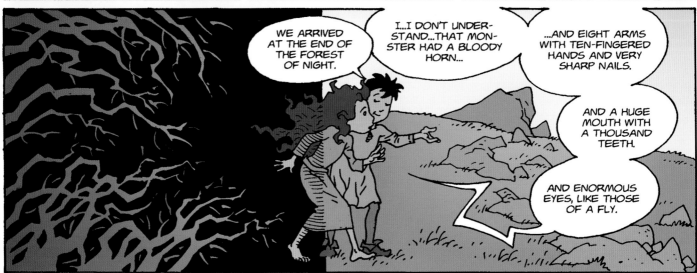

WE ARRIVED AT THE END OF THE FOREST OF NIGHT.

I...I DON'T UNDER-STAND...THAT MON-STER HAD A BLOODY HORN...

...AND EIGHT ARMS WITH TEN-FINGERED HANDS AND VERY SHARP NAILS.

AND A HUGE MOUTH WITH A THOUSAND TEETH.

AND ENORMOUS EYES, LIKE THOSE OF A FLY.

HOW COME YOU WEREN'T SCARED TO DEATH?

BECAUSE THERE WAS NO MONSTER. THAT WAS ONLY YOUR IMAGINATION.

YOU THINK SO?

54

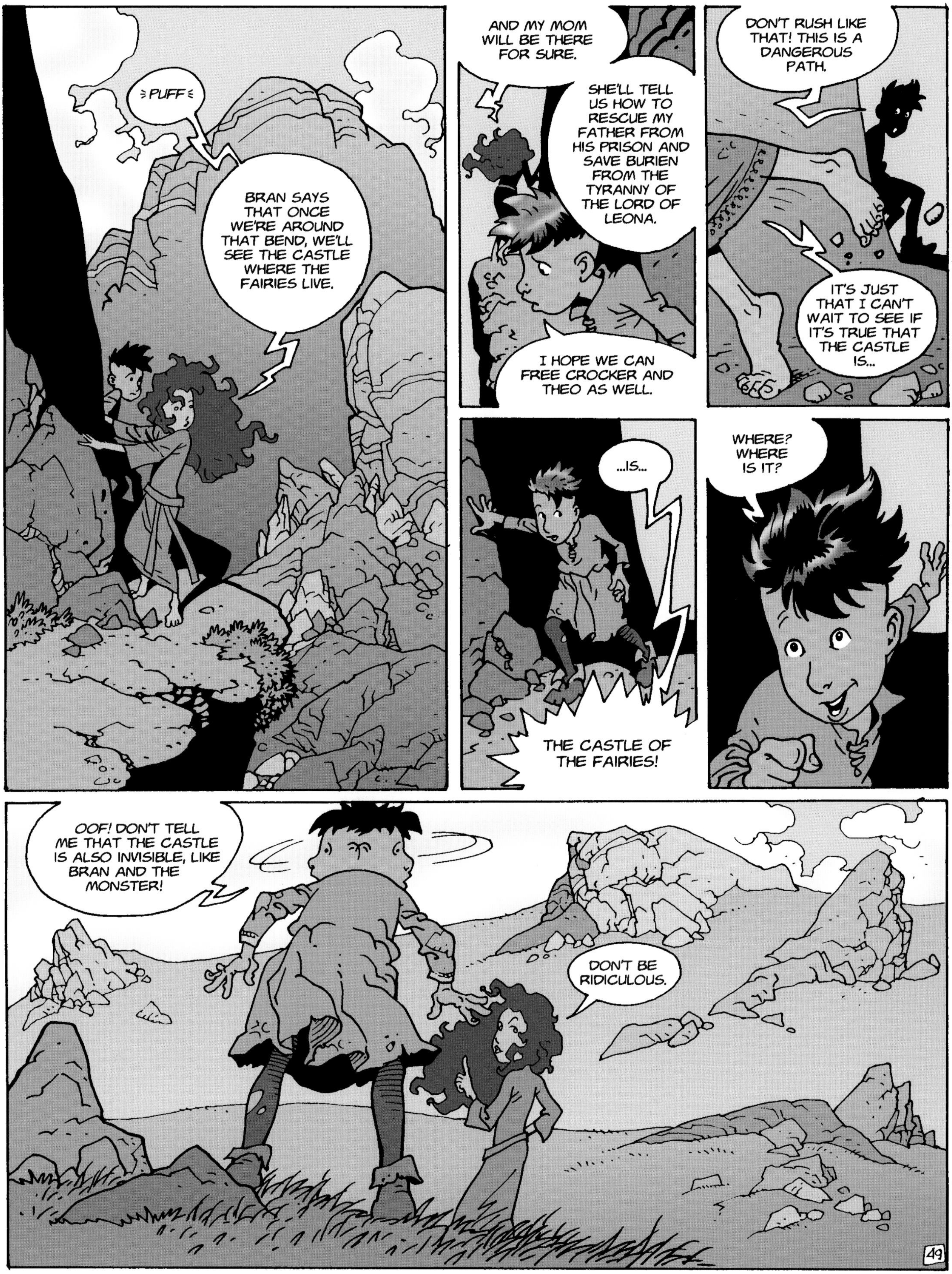
PUFF
BRAN SAYS THAT ONCE WE'RE AROUND THAT BEND, WE'LL SEE THE CASTLE WHERE THE FAIRIES LIVE.
AND MY MOM WILL BE THERE FOR SURE.
SHE'LL TELL US HOW TO RESCUE MY FATHER FROM HIS PRISON AND SAVE BURIEN FROM THE TYRANNY OF THE LORD OF LEONA.
I HOPE WE CAN FREE CROCKER AND THEO AS WELL.
DON'T RUSH LIKE THAT! THIS IS A DANGEROUS PATH.
IT'S JUST THAT I CAN'T WAIT TO SEE IF IT'S TRUE THAT THE CASTLE IS...
...IS...
THE CASTLE OF THE FAIRIES!
WHERE? WHERE IS IT?
OOF! DON'T TELL ME THAT THE CASTLE IS ALSO INVISIBLE, LIKE BRAN AND THE MONSTER!
DON'T BE RIDICULOUS.
49

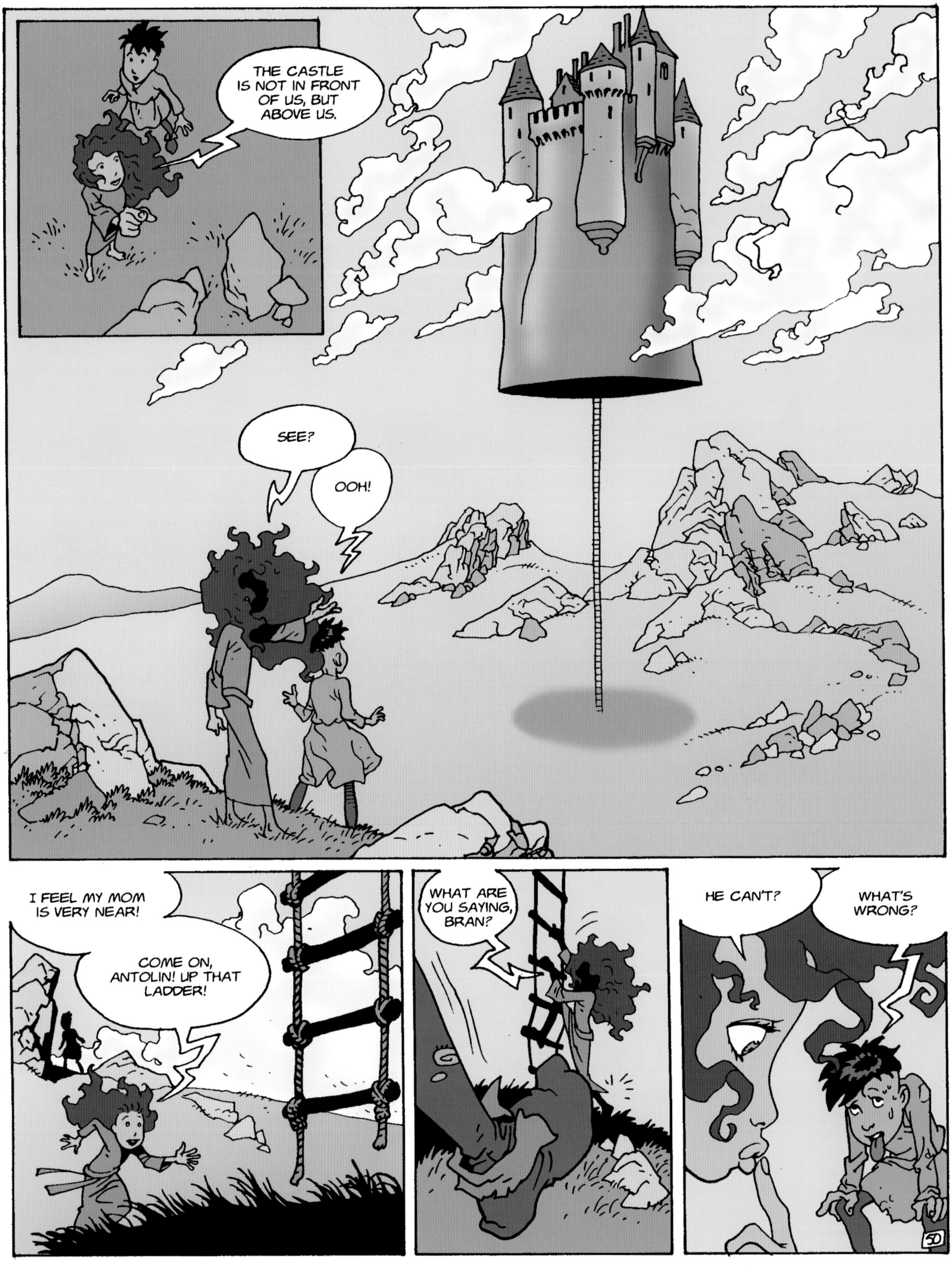
THE CASTLE IS NOT IN FRONT OF US, BUT ABOVE US.
SEE?
OOH!
I FEEL MY MOM IS VERY NEAR!
COME ON, ANTOLIN! UP THAT LADDER!
WHAT ARE YOU SAYING, BRAN?
HE CAN'T?
WHAT'S WRONG?
50

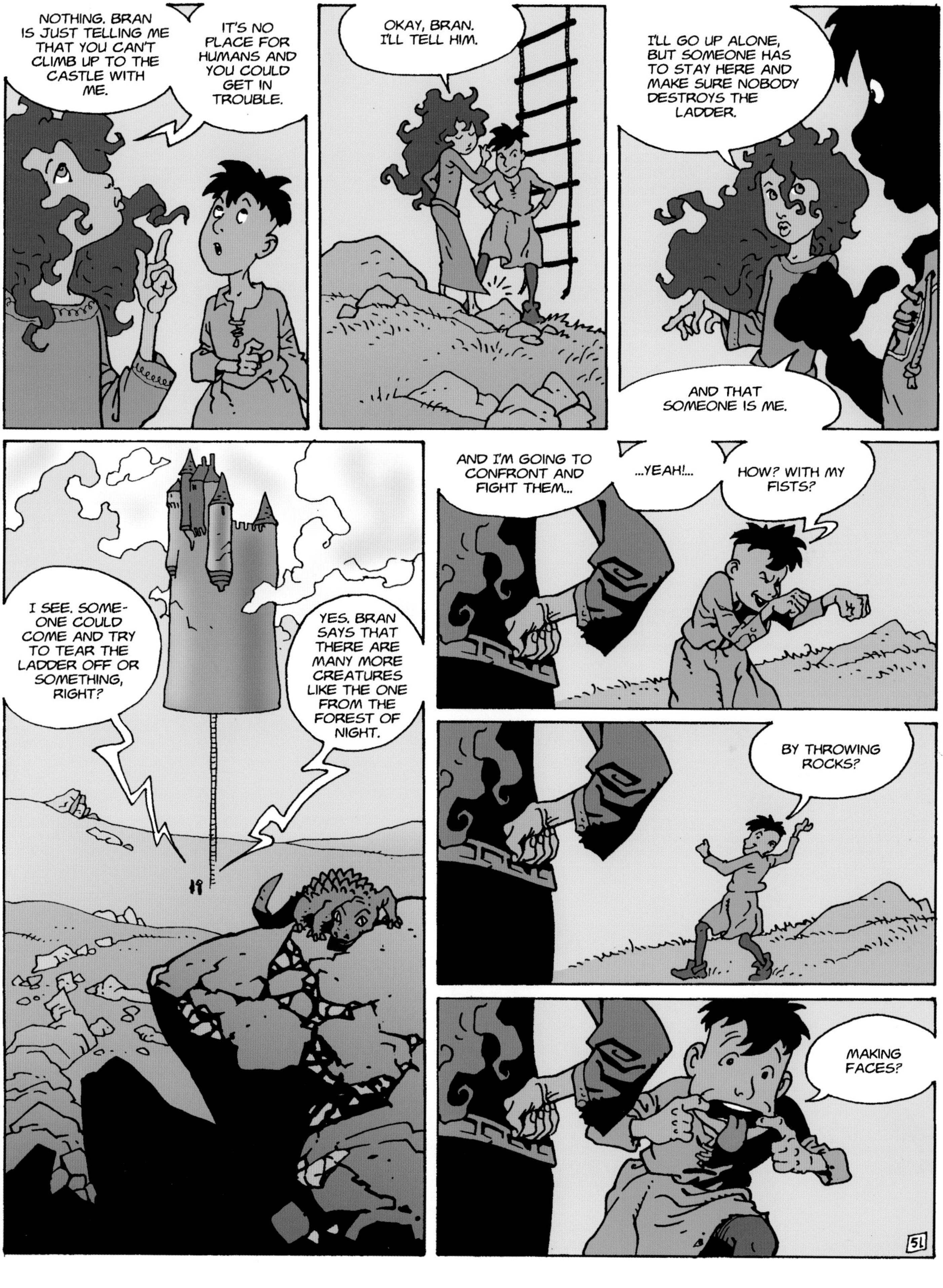
NOTHING. BRAN IS JUST TELLING ME THAT YOU CAN'T CLIMB UP TO THE CASTLE WITH ME.
IT'S NO PLACE FOR HUMANS AND YOU COULD GET IN TROUBLE.
OKAY, BRAN. I'LL TELL HIM.
I'LL GO UP ALONE, BUT SOMEONE HAS TO STAY HERE AND MAKE SURE NOBODY DESTROYS THE LADDER.
AND THAT SOMEONE IS ME.
I SEE. SOME-ONE COULD COME AND TRY TO TEAR THE LADDER OFF OR SOMETHING, RIGHT?
YES. BRAN SAYS THAT THERE ARE MANY MORE CREATURES LIKE THE ONE FROM THE FOREST OF NIGHT.
AND I'M GOING TO CONFRONT AND FIGHT THEM...
...YEAH!...
HOW? WITH MY FISTS?
BY THROWING ROCKS?
MAKING FACES?
51

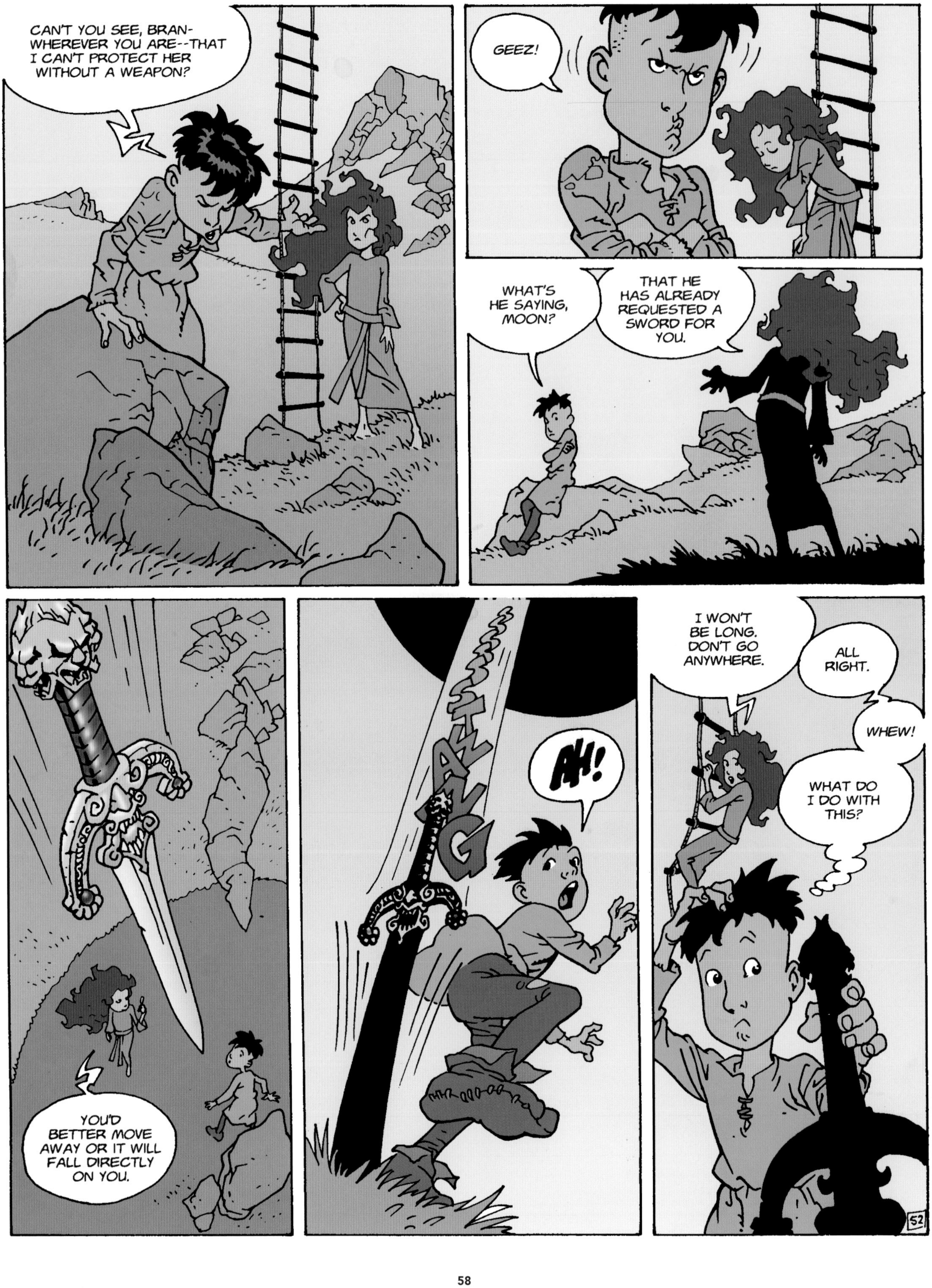
CAN'T YOU SEE, BRAN-WHEREVER YOU ARE--THAT I CAN'T PROTECT HER WITHOUT A WEAPON?
GEEZ!
WHAT'S HE SAYING, MOON?
THAT HE HAS ALREADY REQUESTED A SWORD FOR YOU.
YOU'D BETTER MOVE AWAY OR IT WILL FALL DIRECTLY ON YOU.
SSSSWANG
AH!
I WON'T BE LONG. DON'T GO ANYWHERE.
ALL RIGHT.
WHEW!
WHAT DO I DO WITH THIS?
52

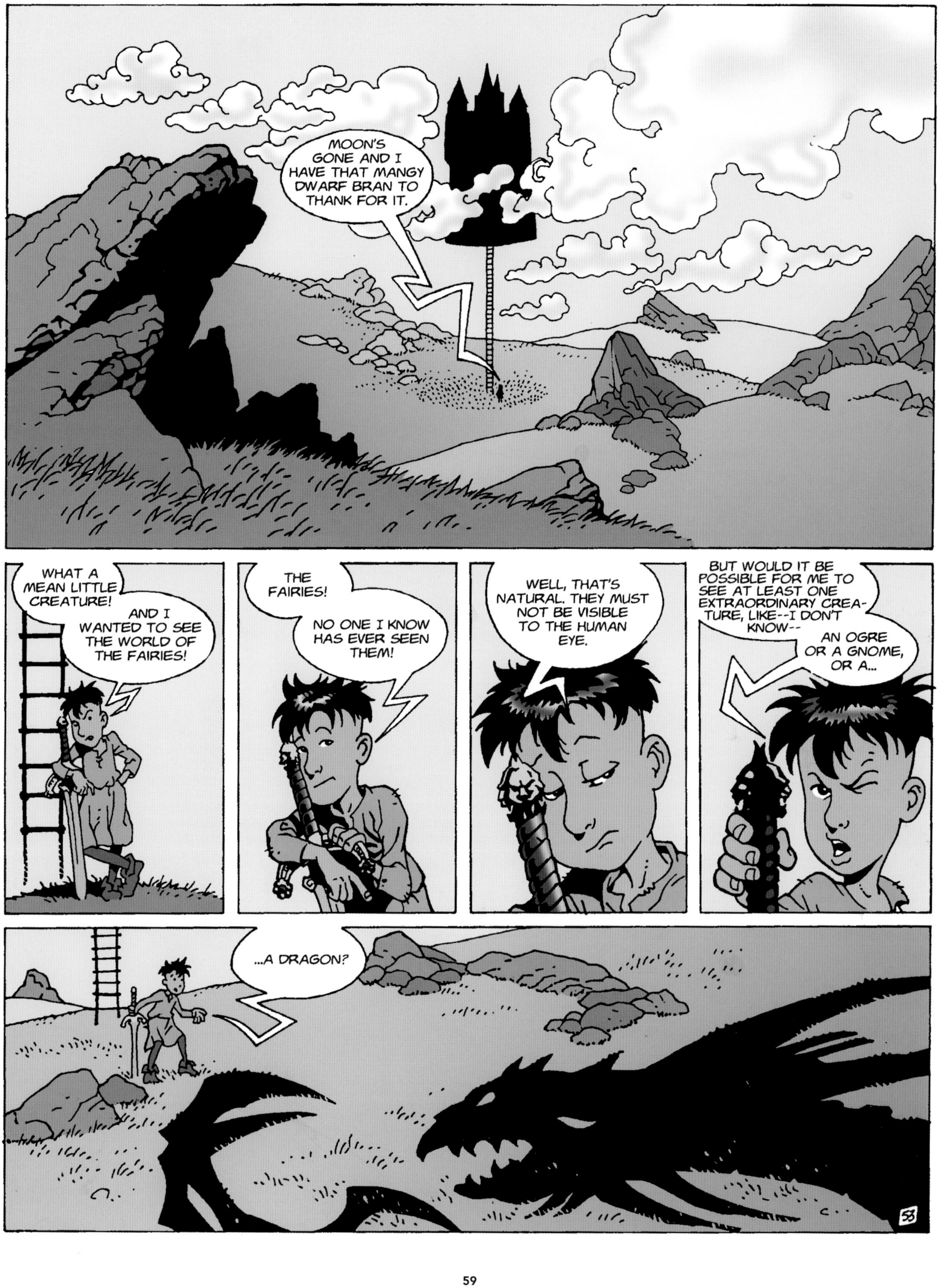
MOON'S GONE AND I HAVE THAT MANGY DWARF BRAN TO THANK FOR IT.
WHAT A MEAN LITTLE CREATURE!
AND I WANTED TO SEE THE WORLD OF THE FAIRIES!
THE FAIRIES!
NO ONE I KNOW HAS EVER SEEN THEM!
WELL, THAT'S NATURAL. THEY MUST NOT BE VISIBLE TO THE HUMAN EYE.
BUT WOULD IT BE POSSIBLE FOR ME TO SEE AT LEAST ONE EXTRAORDINARY CREA-TURE, LIKE--I DON'T KNOW--
AN OGRE OR A GNOME, OR A...
...A DRAGON?
53

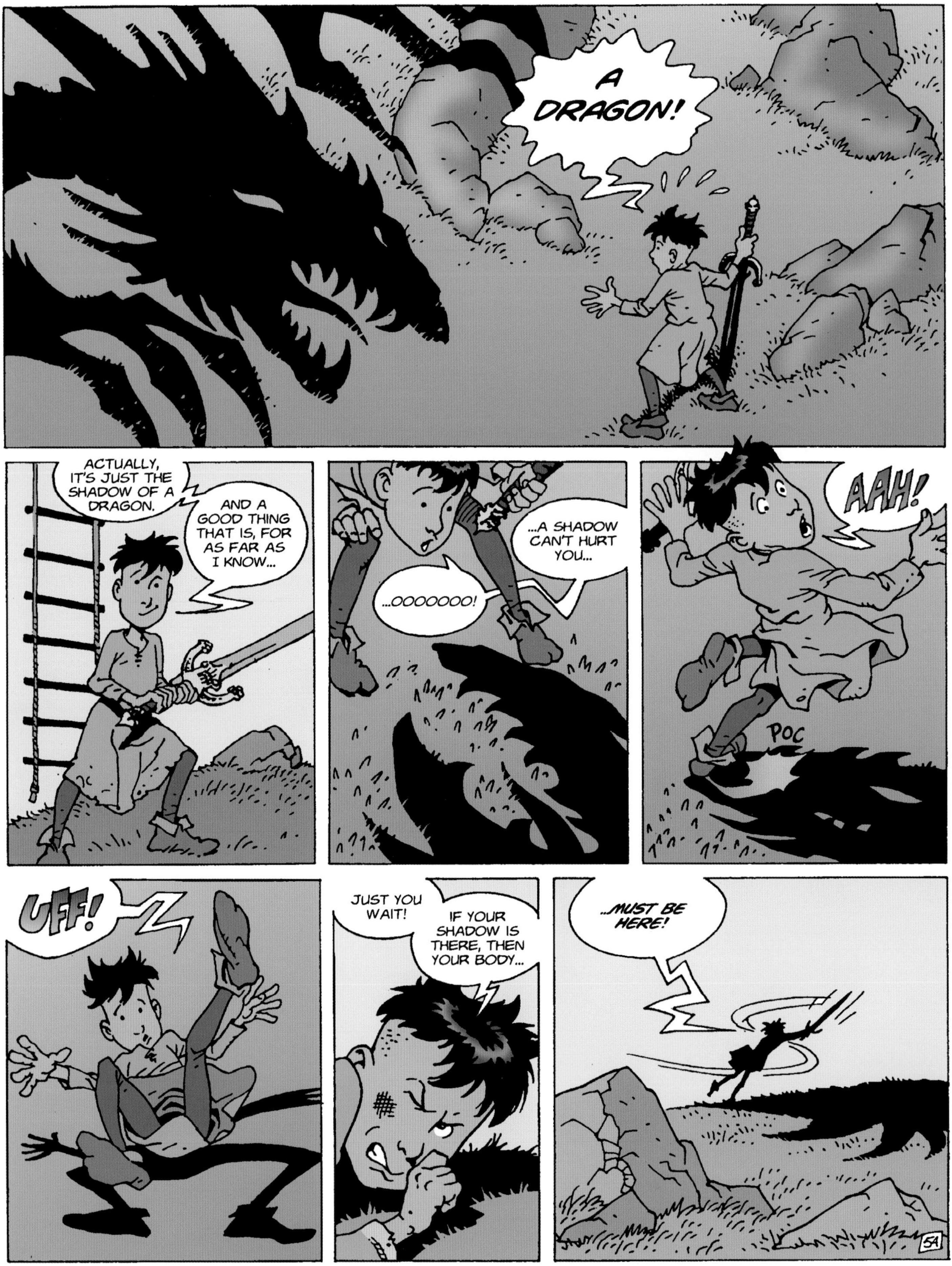
A DRAGON!
ACTUALLY, IT'S JUST THE SHADOW OF A DRAGON.
AND A GOOD THING THAT IS, FOR AS FAR AS I KNOW...
...A SHADOW CAN'T HURT YOU...
...OOOOOOO!
AAH!
POC
UFF!
JUST YOU WAIT!
IF YOUR SHADOW IS THERE, THEN YOUR BODY...
...MUST BE HERE!
54

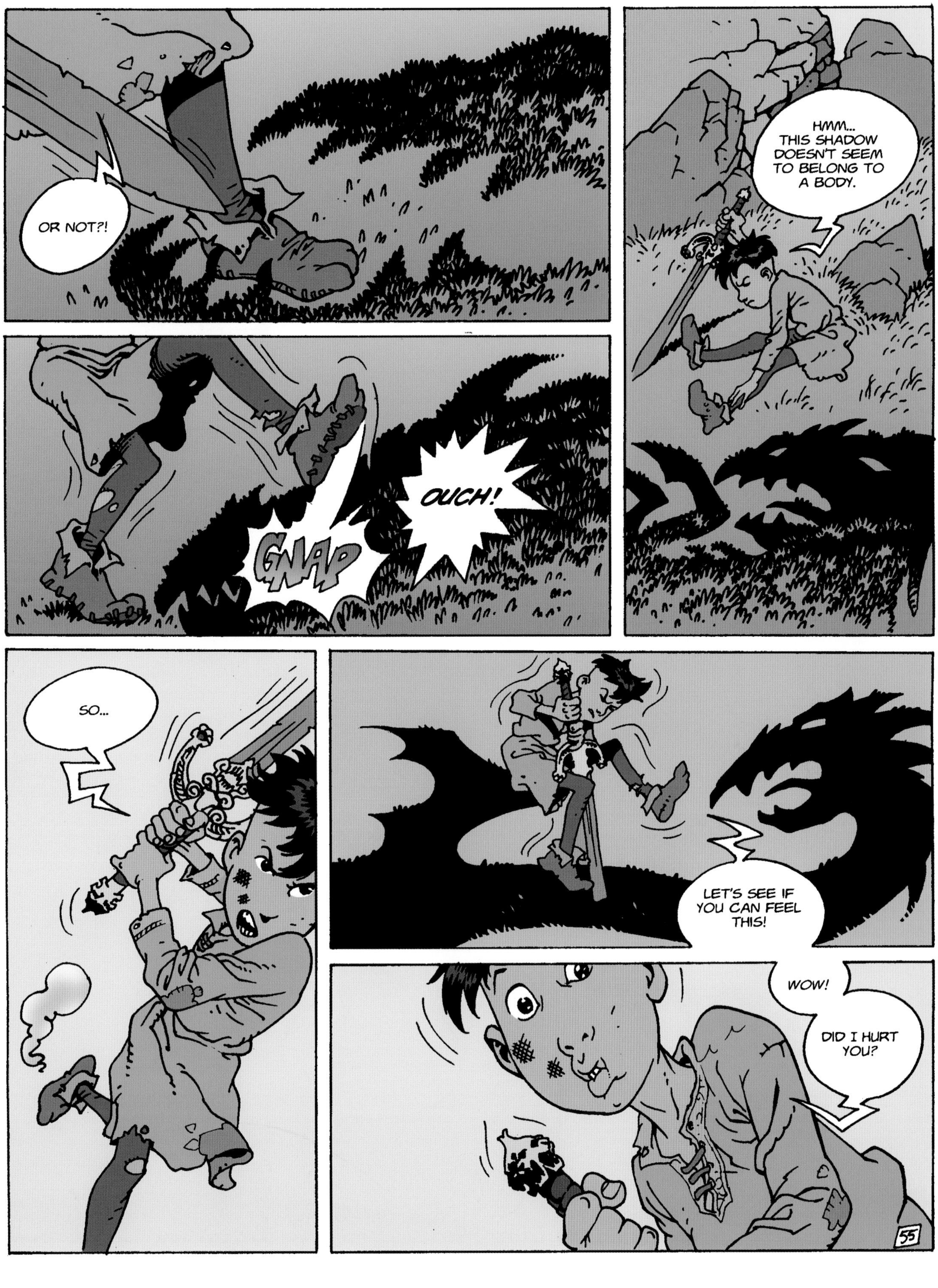
OR NOT?!
HMM... THIS SHADOW DOESN'T SEEM TO BELONG TO A BODY.
GNAP
OUCH!
SO...
LET'S SEE IF YOU CAN FEEL THIS!
WOW!
DID I HURT YOU?
55

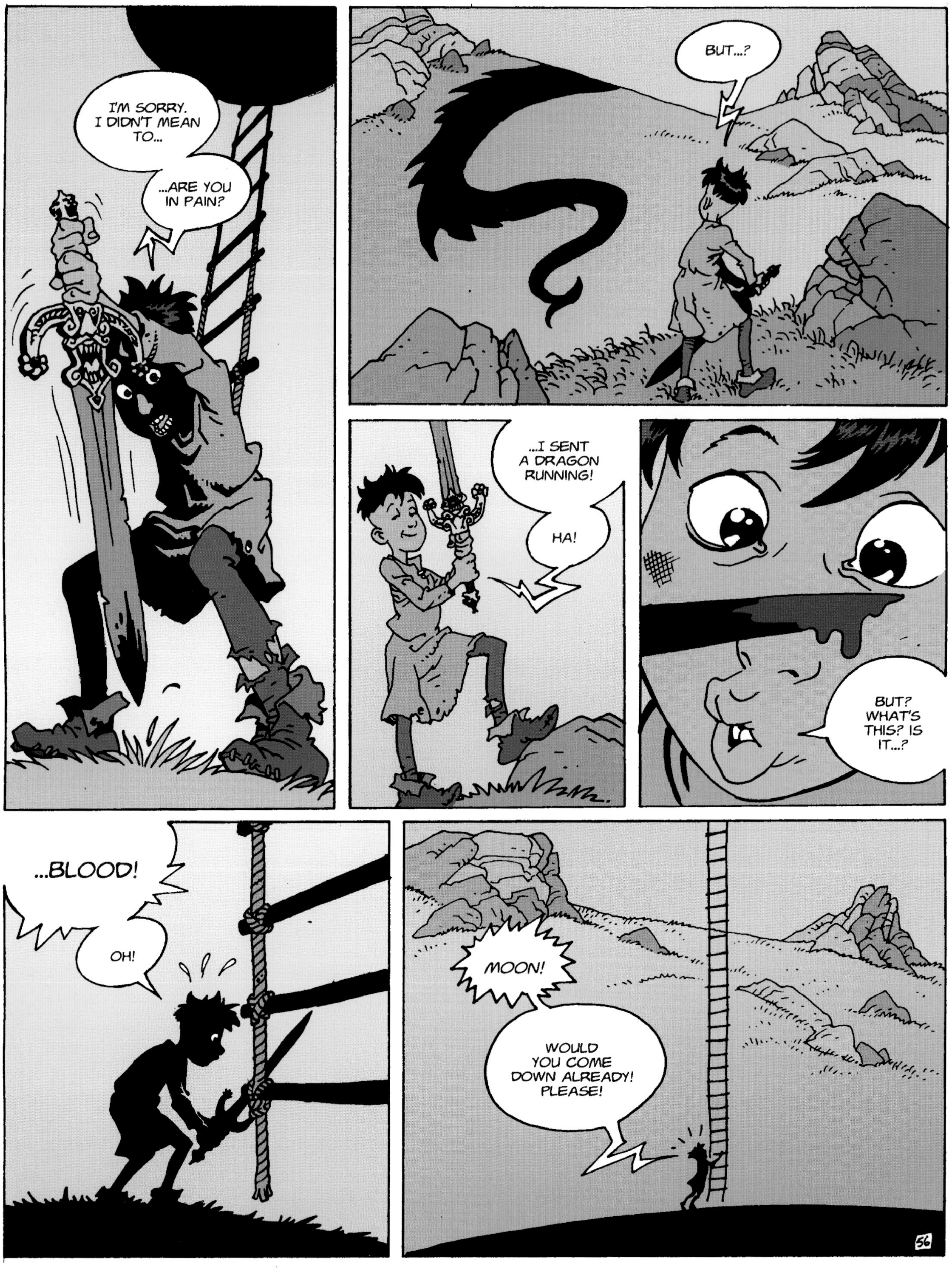
I'M SORRY. I DIDN'T MEAN TO...
...ARE YOU IN PAIN?
BUT...?
...I SENT A DRAGON RUNNING!
HA!
BUT? WHAT'S THIS? IS IT...?
...BLOOD!
OH!
MOON!
WOULD YOU COME DOWN ALREADY! PLEASE!
56

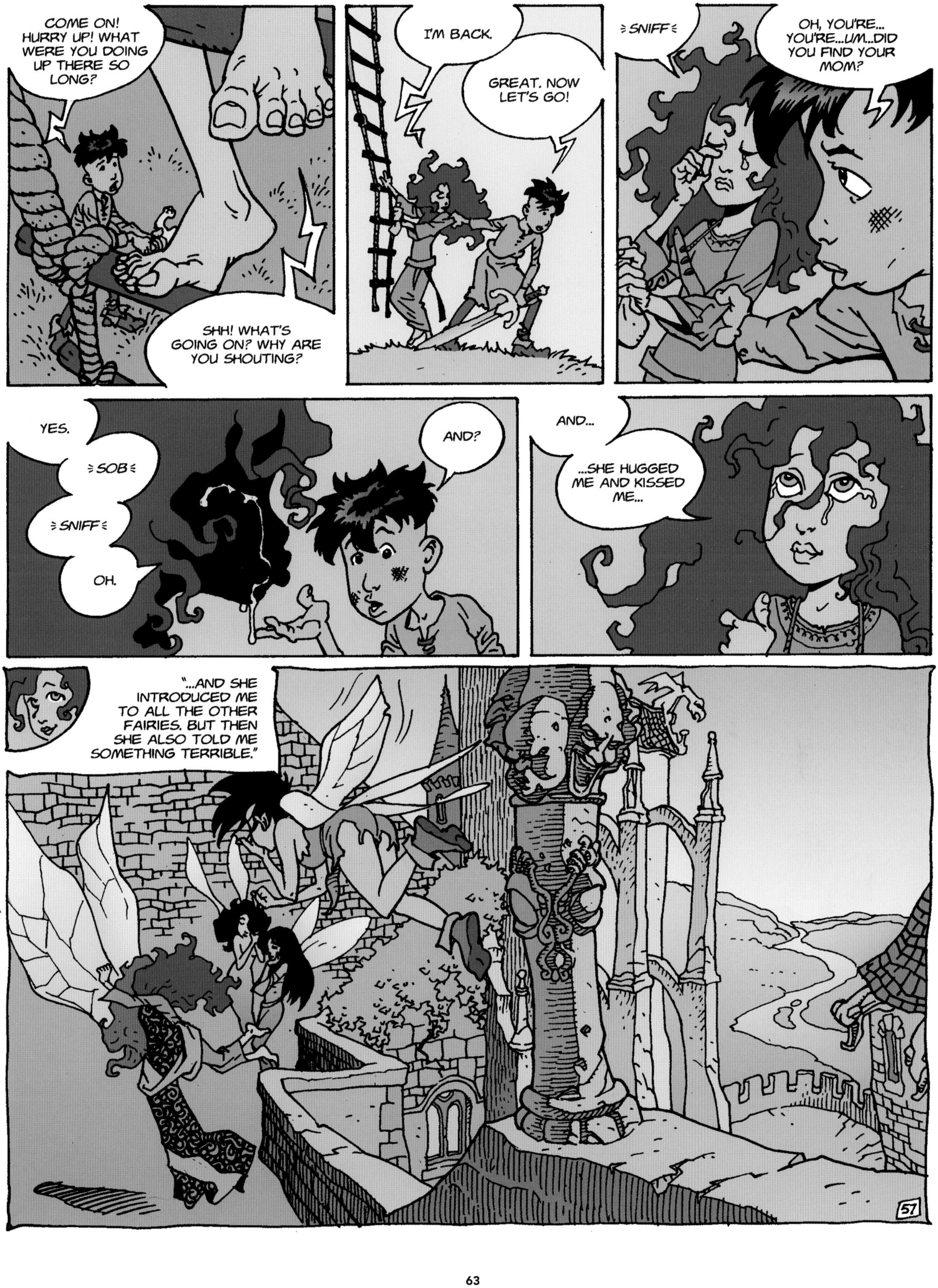
COME ON! HURRY UP! WHAT WERE YOU DOING UP THERE SO LONG?
SHH! WHAT'S GOING ON? WHY ARE YOU SHOUTING?
I'M BACK.
GREAT. NOW LET'S GO!
SNIFF
OH, YOU'RE... YOU'RE...UM...DID YOU FIND YOUR MOM?
YES.
SOB
SNIFF
OH.
AND?
AND...
...SHE HUGGED ME AND KISSED ME...
"...AND SHE INTRODUCED ME TO ALL THE OTHER FAIRIES. BUT THEN SHE ALSO TOLD ME SOMETHING TERRIBLE."
57

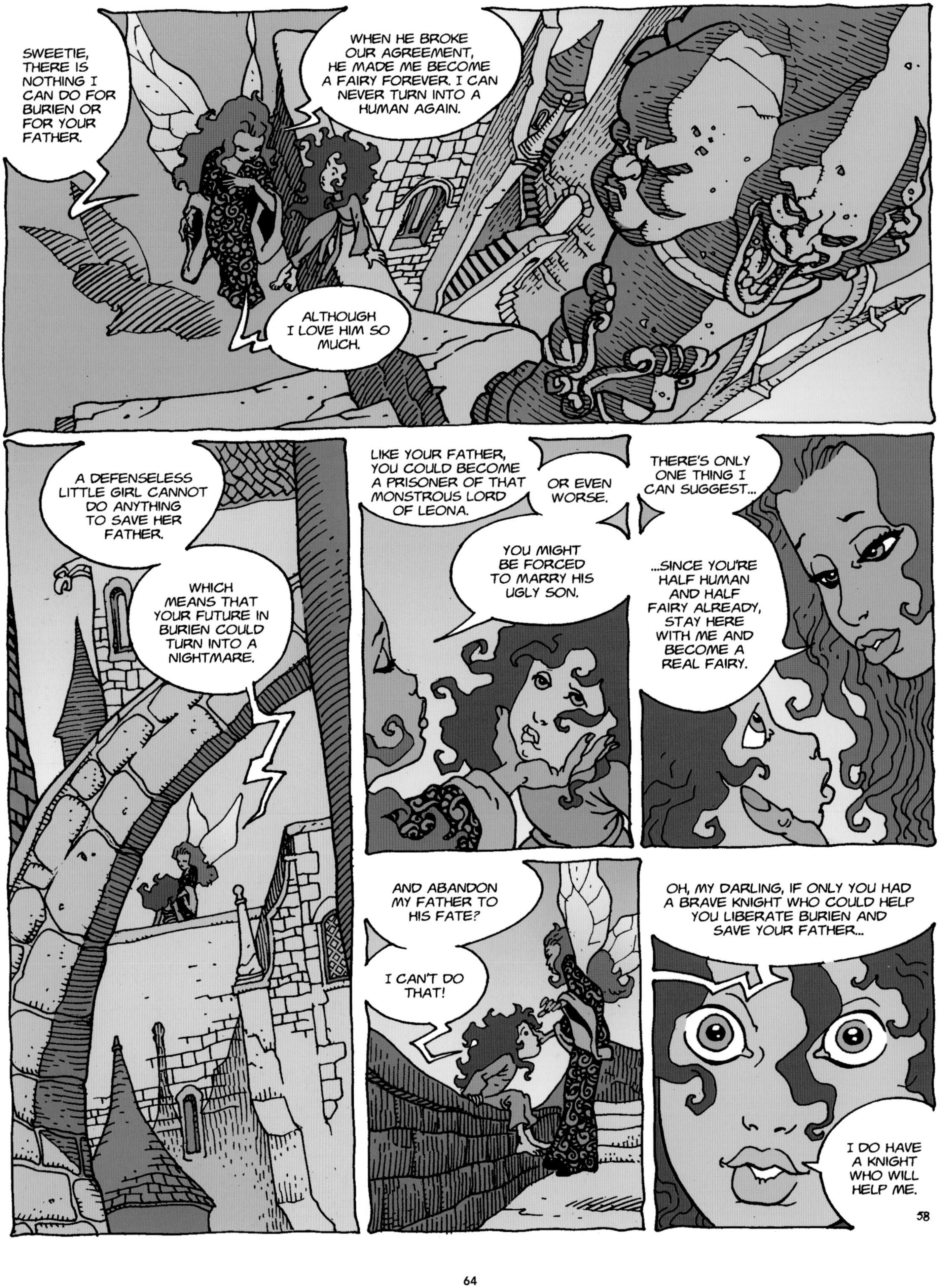
SWEETIE, THERE IS NOTHING I CAN DO FOR BURIEN OR FOR YOUR FATHER.
WHEN HE BROKE OUR AGREEMENT, HE MADE ME BECOME A FAIRY FOREVER. I CAN NEVER TURN INTO A HUMAN AGAIN.
ALTHOUGH I LOVE HIM SO MUCH.
A DEFENSELESS LITTLE GIRL CANNOT DO ANYTHING TO SAVE HER FATHER.
WHICH MEANS THAT YOUR FUTURE IN BURIEN COULD TURN INTO A NIGHTMARE.
LIKE YOUR FATHER, YOU COULD BECOME A PRISONER OF THAT MONSTROUS LORD OF LEONA.
OR EVEN WORSE.
YOU MIGHT BE FORCED TO MARRY HIS UGLY SON.
THERE'S ONLY ONE THING I CAN SUGGEST...
...SINCE YOU'RE HALF HUMAN AND HALF FAIRY ALREADY, STAY HERE WITH ME AND BECOME A REAL FAIRY.
AND ABANDON MY FATHER TO HIS FATE?
I CAN'T DO THAT!
OH, MY DARLING, IF ONLY YOU HAD A BRAVE KNIGHT WHO COULD HELP YOU LIBERATE BURIEN AND SAVE YOUR FATHER...
I DO HAVE A KNIGHT WHO WILL HELP ME.
58

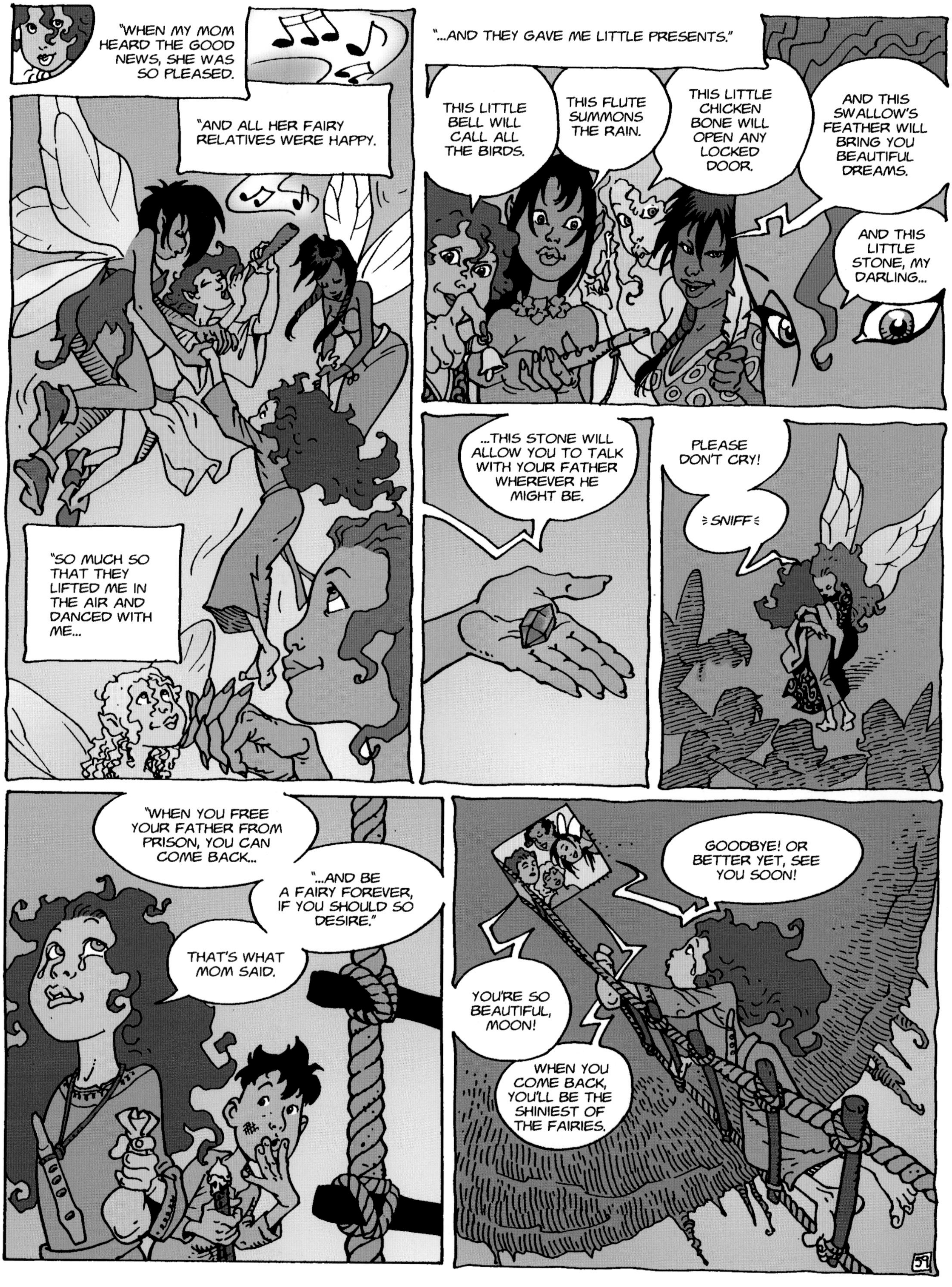

"WHEN MY MOM HEARD THE GOOD NEWS, SHE WAS SO PLEASED.
"AND ALL HER FAIRY RELATIVES WERE HAPPY.
"SO MUCH SO THAT THEY LIFTED ME IN THE AIR AND DANCED WITH ME...
"...AND THEY GAVE ME LITTLE PRESENTS."
THIS LITTLE BELL WILL CALL ALL THE BIRDS.
THIS FLUTE SUMMONS THE RAIN.
THIS LITTLE CHICKEN BONE WILL OPEN ANY LOCKED DOOR.
AND THIS SWALLOW'S FEATHER WILL BRING YOU BEAUTIFUL DREAMS.
AND THIS LITTLE STONE, MY DARLING...
...THIS STONE WILL ALLOW YOU TO TALK WITH YOUR FATHER WHEREVER HE MIGHT BE.
PLEASE DON'T CRY!
SNIFF
"WHEN YOU FREE YOUR FATHER FROM PRISON, YOU CAN COME BACK...
"...AND BE A FAIRY FOREVER, IF YOU SHOULD SO DESIRE."
THAT'S WHAT MOM SAID.
GOODBYE! OR BETTER YET, SEE YOU SOON!
YOU'RE SO BEAUTIFUL, MOON!
WHEN YOU COME BACK, YOU'LL BE THE SHINIEST OF THE FAIRIES.
59

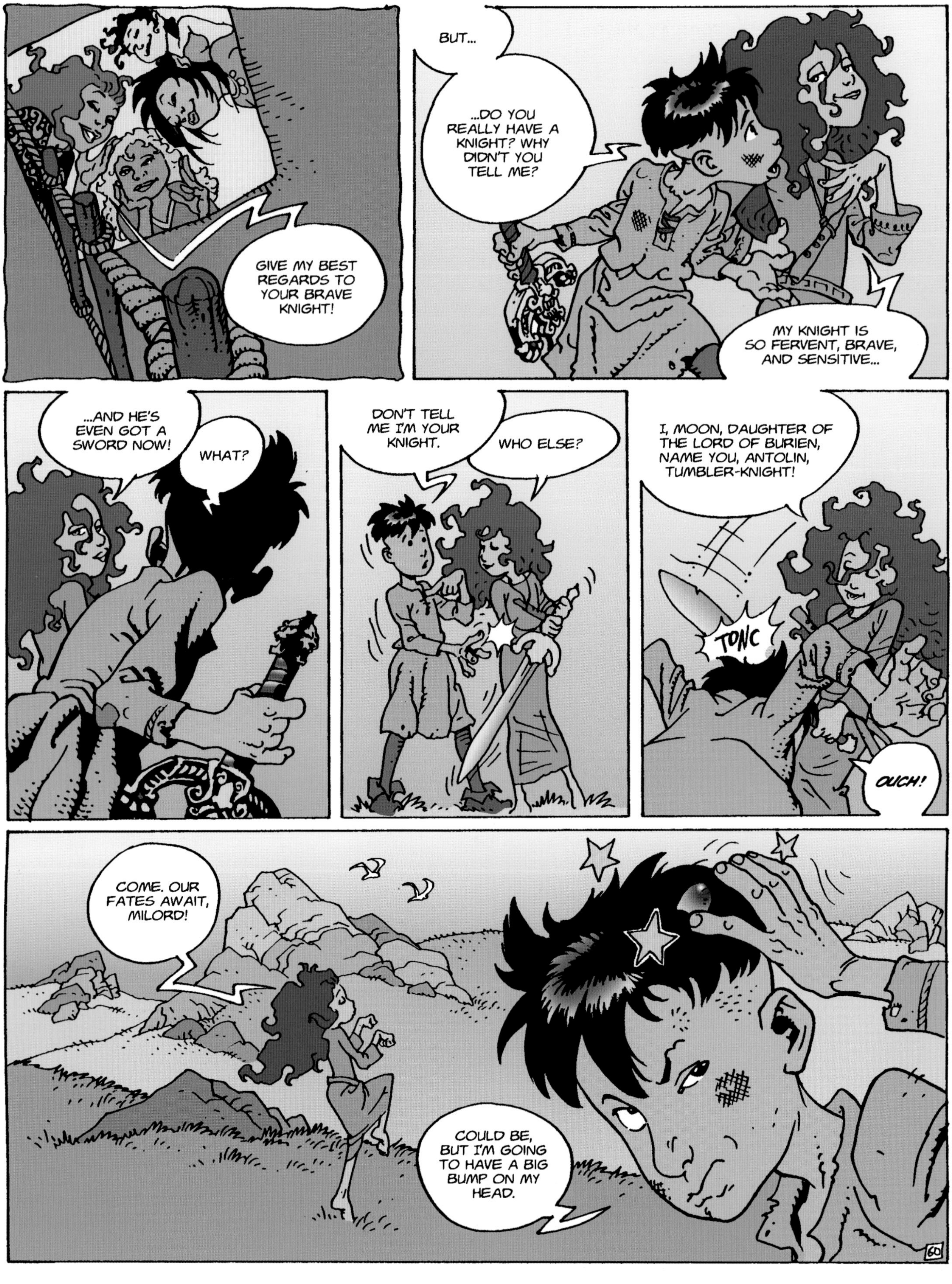
GIVE MY BEST REGARDS TO YOUR BRAVE KNIGHT!
BUT...
...DO YOU REALLY HAVE A KNIGHT? WHY DIDN'T YOU TELL ME?
MY KNIGHT IS SO FERVENT, BRAVE, AND SENSITIVE...
...AND HE'S EVEN GOT A SWORD NOW!
WHAT?
DON'T TELL ME I'M YOUR KNIGHT.
WHO ELSE?
I, MOON, DAUGHTER OF THE LORD OF BURIEN, NAME YOU, ANTOLIN, TUMBLER-KNIGHT!
TONC
OUCH!
COME. OUR FATES AWAIT, MILORD!
COULD BE, BUT I'M GOING TO HAVE A BIG BUMP ON MY HEAD.
60

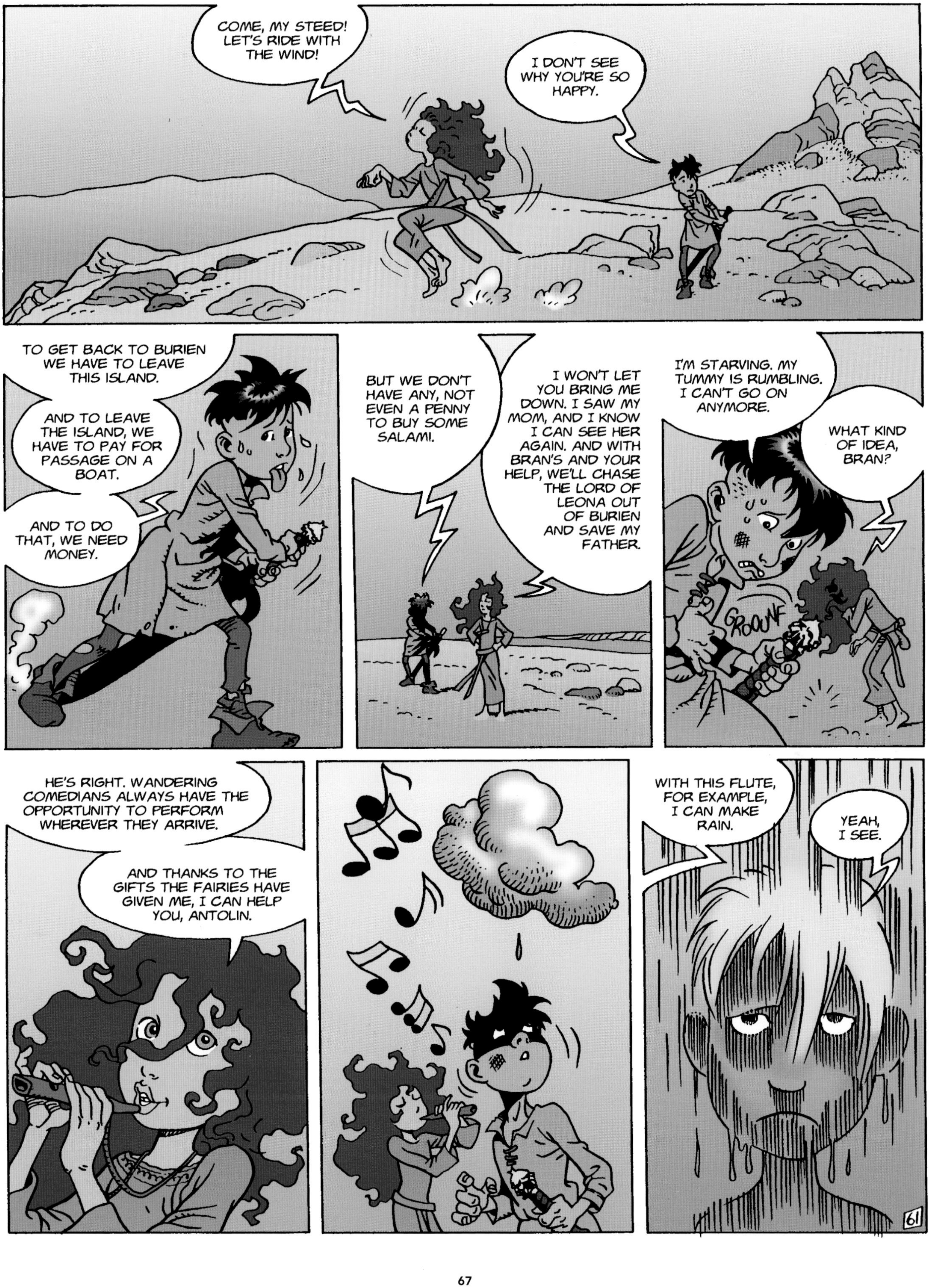
COME, MY STEED! LET'S RIDE WITH THE WIND!
I DON'T SEE WHY YOU'RE SO HAPPY.
TO GET BACK TO BURIEN WE HAVE TO LEAVE THIS ISLAND.
AND TO LEAVE THE ISLAND, WE HAVE TO PAY FOR PASSAGE ON A BOAT.
AND TO DO THAT, WE NEED MONEY.
BUT WE DON'T HAVE ANY, NOT EVEN A PENNY TO BUY SOME SALAMI.
I WON'T LET YOU BRING ME DOWN. I SAW MY MOM, AND I KNOW I CAN SEE HER AGAIN. AND WITH BRAN'S AND YOUR HELP, WE'LL CHASE THE LORD OF LEONA OUT OF BURIEN AND SAVE MY FATHER.
I'M STARVING. MY TUMMY IS RUMBLING. I CAN'T GO ON ANYMORE.
GROOUNF
WHAT KIND OF IDEA, BRAN?
HE'S RIGHT. WANDERING COMEDIANS ALWAYS HAVE THE OPPORTUNITY TO PERFORM WHEREVER THEY ARRIVE.
AND THANKS TO THE GIFTS THE FAIRIES HAVE GIVEN ME, I CAN HELP YOU, ANTOLIN.
WITH THIS FLUTE, FOR EXAMPLE, I CAN MAKE RAIN.
YEAH, I SEE.
61

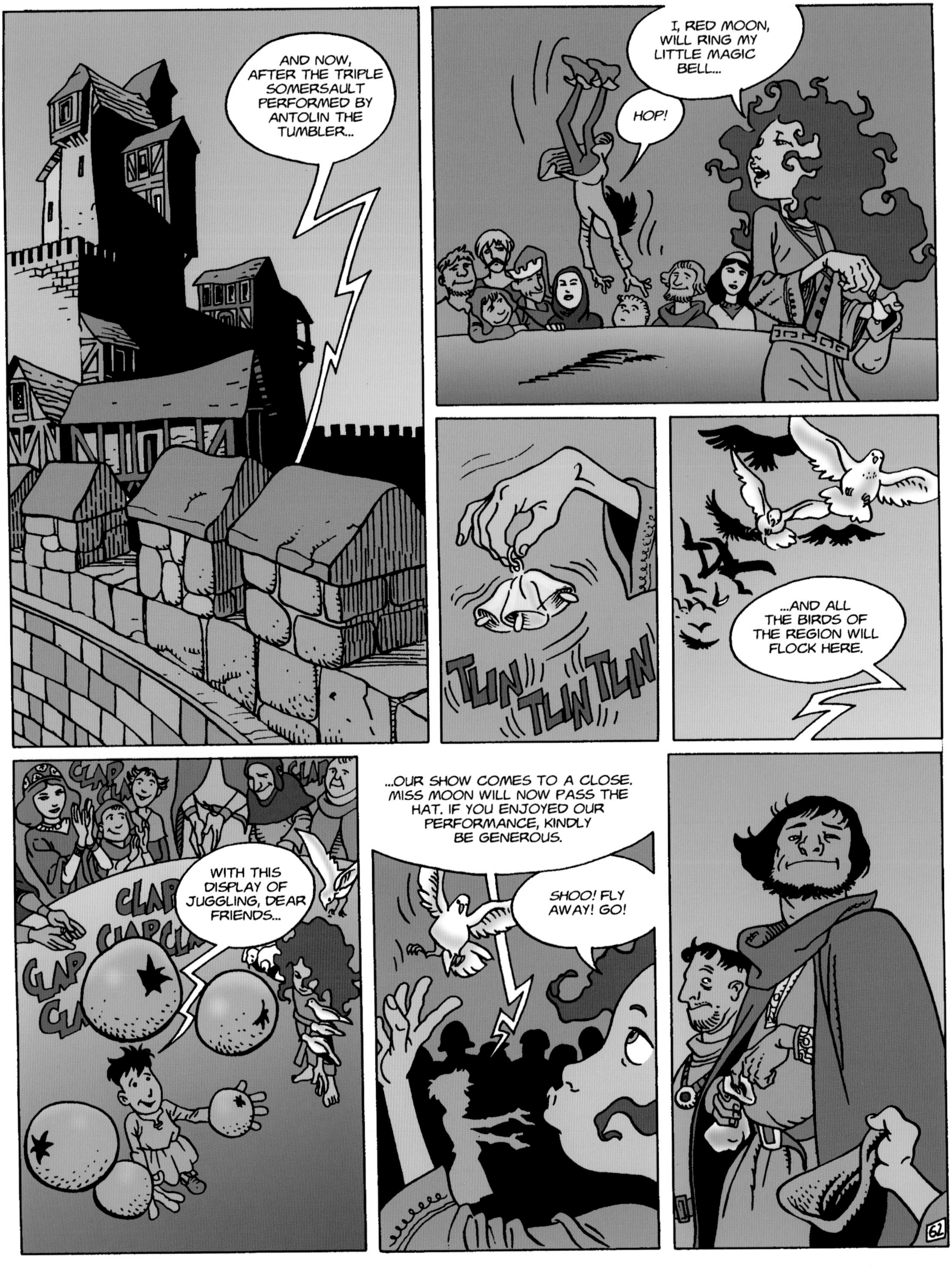
AND NOW, AFTER THE TRIPLE SOMERSAULT PERFORMED BY ANTOLIN THE TUMBLER...
I, RED MOON, WILL RING MY LITTLE MAGIC BELL...
HOP!
TLIN TLIN TLIN
...AND ALL THE BIRDS OF THE REGION WILL FLOCK HERE.
CLAP CLAP CLAP
WITH THIS DISPLAY OF JUGGLING, DEAR FRIENDS...
...OUR SHOW COMES TO A CLOSE. MISS MOON WILL NOW PASS THE HAT. IF YOU ENJOYED OUR PERFORMANCE, KINDLY BE GENEROUS.
SHOO! FLY AWAY! GO!
62

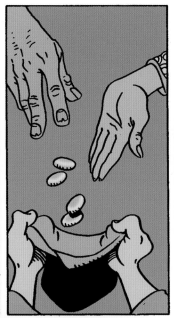

WE'RE A HIT, YUM. WE HAVE ENOUGH MONEY FOR THE TRIP BACK TO BURIEN, YUM, YUM.

≳MUNCH MUNCH≳ MMDON'T TALK WITH YOUR MOUTH FULLMM. ≳MUNCH MUNCH≳ WHERE'RE YOUR MANNERSMM?!

WHEW! THIS HAS BEEN QUITE AN ADVENTURE, SIR ANTOLIN.

DON'T MAKE FUN OF ME, MOON.

WE CROSSED THE SEA, WE'VE BEEN TO THE FLOATING CASTLE OF THE FAIRIES, I FOUND MY MOM...

I BECAME A WANDERING MAGICIAN (WHICH, BY THE WAY, I LIKE A LOT)...

AND NOW WE'RE GOING BACK HOME TO CHASE AWAY THE USURPER, THE LORD OF LEONA.

I BELIEVE THE HARD PART IS YET TO COME.

EVERYTHING WILL BE ALL RIGHT.

63

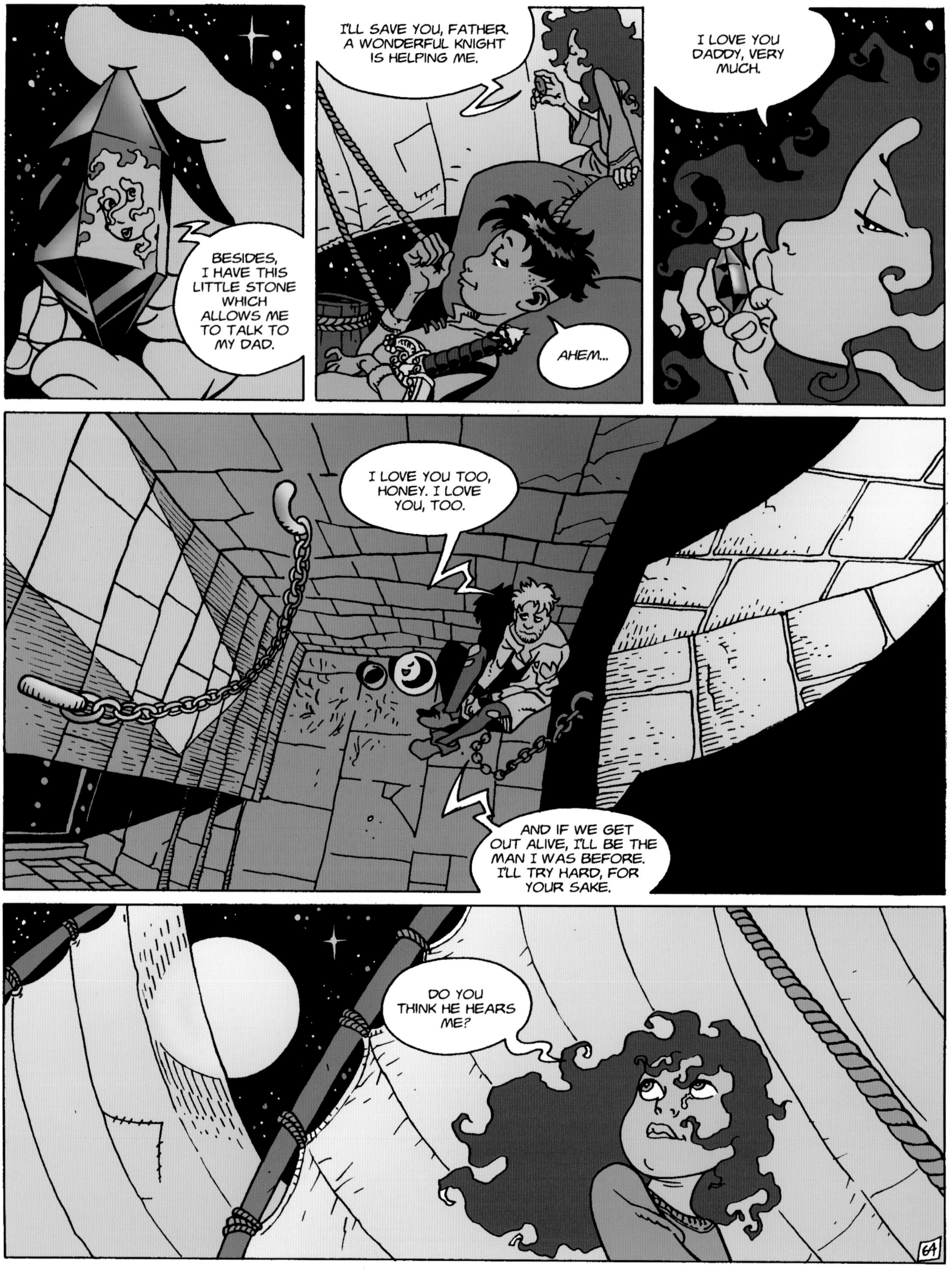
BESIDES, I HAVE THIS LITTLE STONE WHICH ALLOWS ME TO TALK TO MY DAD.
I'LL SAVE YOU, FATHER. A WONDERFUL KNIGHT IS HELPING ME.
AHEM...
I LOVE YOU DADDY, VERY MUCH.
I LOVE YOU TOO, HONEY. I LOVE YOU, TOO.
AND IF WE GET OUT ALIVE, I'LL BE THE MAN I WAS BEFORE. I'LL TRY HARD, FOR YOUR SAKE.
DO YOU THINK HE HEARS ME?
64

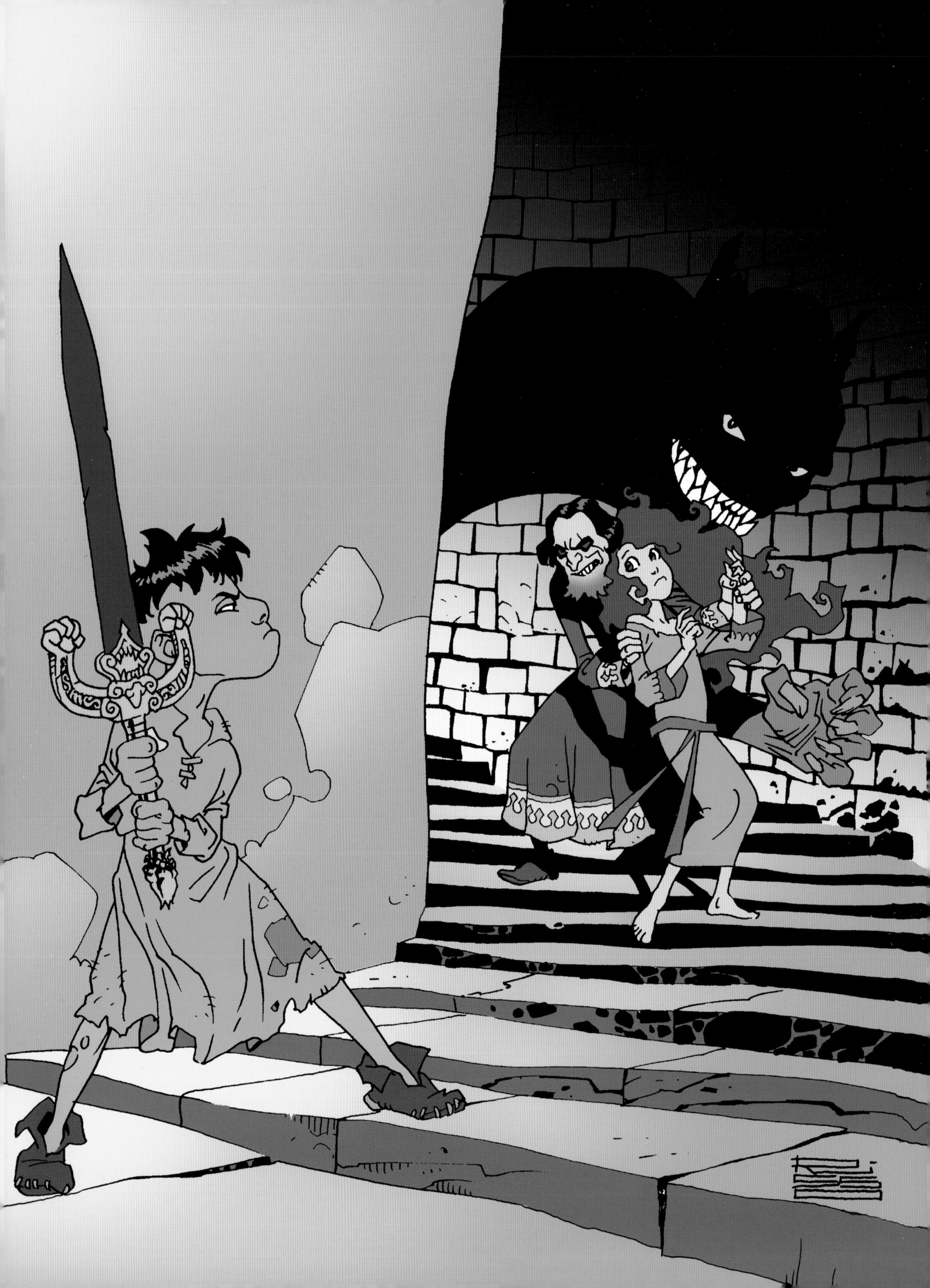

WILL WE ARRIVE SOON, CAPTAIN?

YES.

I DON'T THINK WE CAN DISEMBARK IN BURIEN, LITTLE ONE.

WHAT? WHY NOT? YOU PROMISED TO TAKE US THERE.

THAT'S WHAT WE PAID YOU FOR.

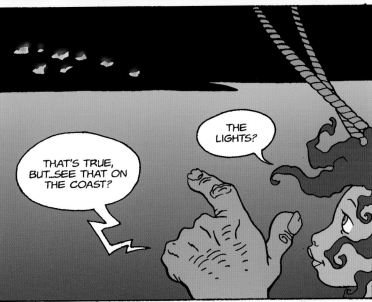

THAT'S TRUE, BUT...SEE THAT ON THE COAST?

THE LIGHTS?

THAT'S FIRE.

I'M AFRAID SOMETHING TERRIBLE IS GOING ON IN BURIEN. THE FIELDS AND HOUSES ARE BURNING.

GOD, NO! EVERY-THING I CHERISH IS THERE.

I DEMAND THAT YOU TAKE US THERE, LIKE WE AGREED!

ONLY IN YOUR DREAMS.

1

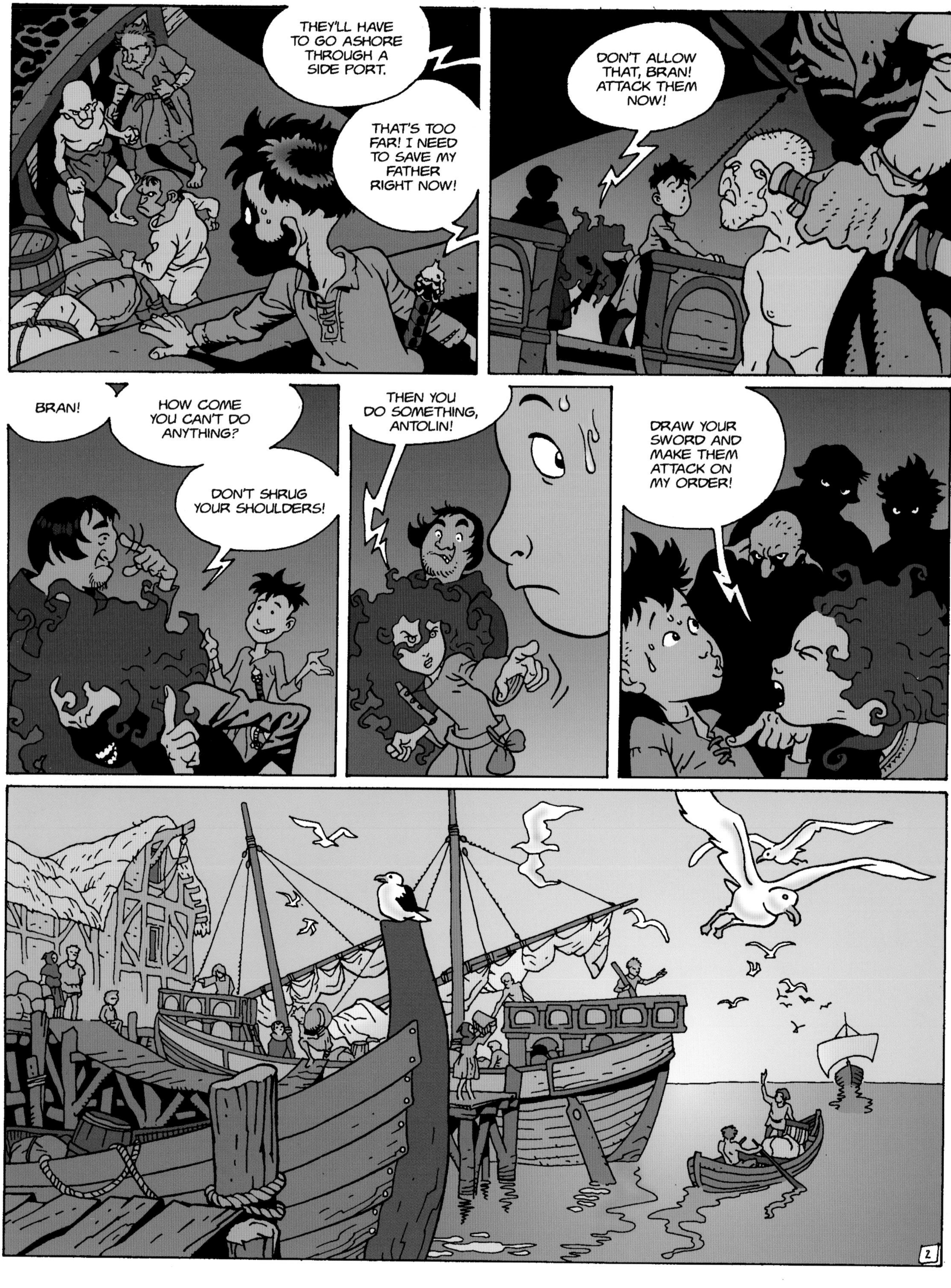
THEY'LL HAVE TO GO ASHORE THROUGH A SIDE PORT.
THAT'S TOO FAR! I NEED TO SAVE MY FATHER RIGHT NOW!
DON'T ALLOW THAT, BRAN! ATTACK THEM NOW!
BRAN!
HOW COME YOU CAN'T DO ANYTHING?
DON'T SHRUG YOUR SHOULDERS!
THEN YOU DO SOMETHING, ANTOLIN!
DRAW YOUR SWORD AND MAKE THEM ATTACK ON MY ORDER!
2

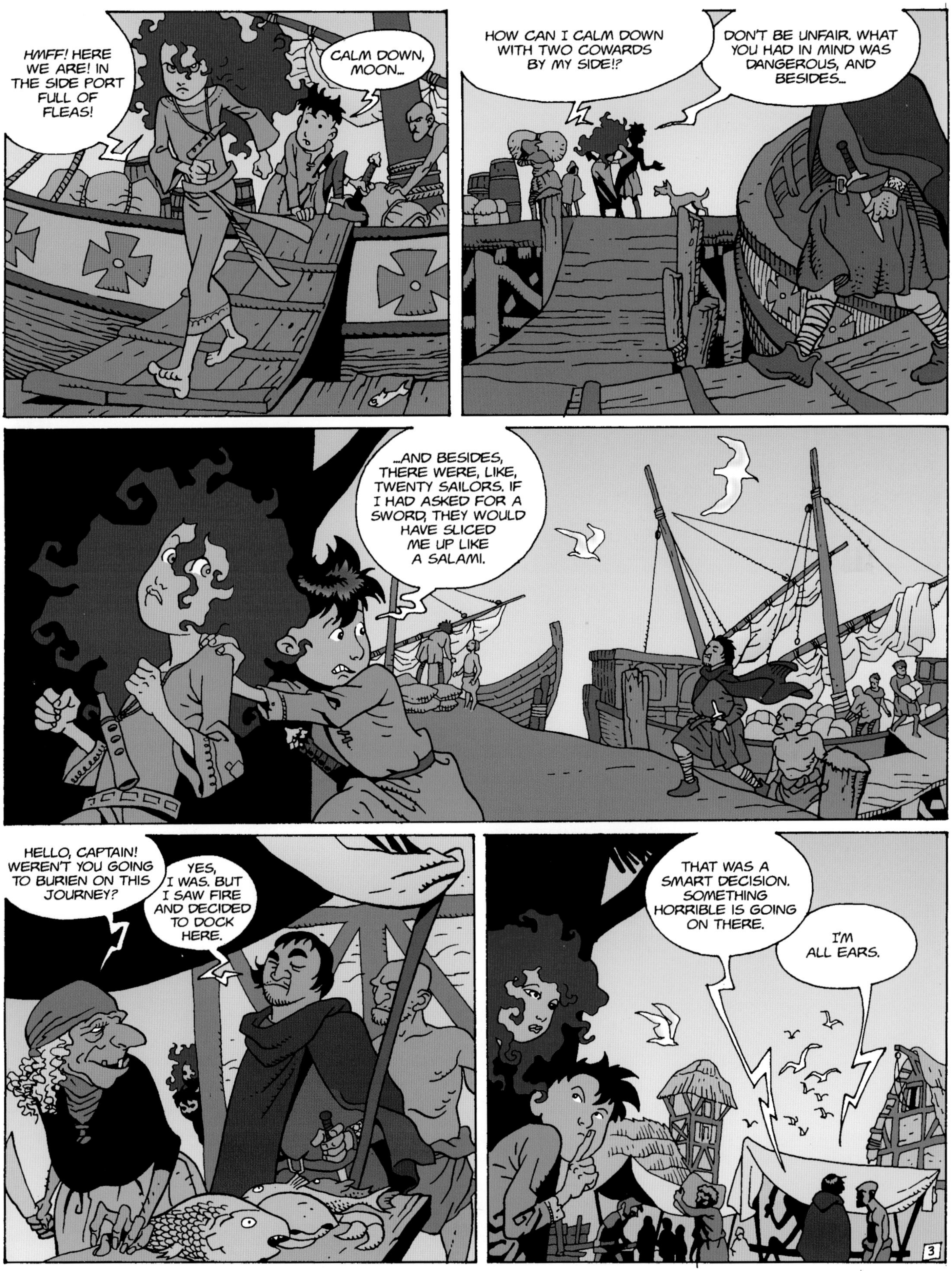
HMFF! HERE WE ARE! IN THE SIDE PORT FULL OF FLEAS!
CALM DOWN, MOON...
HOW CAN I CALM DOWN WITH TWO COWARDS BY MY SIDE!?
DON'T BE UNFAIR. WHAT YOU HAD IN MIND WAS DANGEROUS, AND BESIDES...
...AND BESIDES, THERE WERE, LIKE, TWENTY SAILORS. IF I HAD ASKED FOR A SWORD, THEY WOULD HAVE SLICED ME UP LIKE A SALAMI.
HELLO, CAPTAIN! WEREN'T YOU GOING TO BURIEN ON THIS JOURNEY?
YES, I WAS. BUT I SAW FIRE AND DECIDED TO DOCK HERE.
THAT WAS A SMART DECISION. SOMETHING HORRIBLE IS GOING ON THERE.
I'M ALL EARS.
3

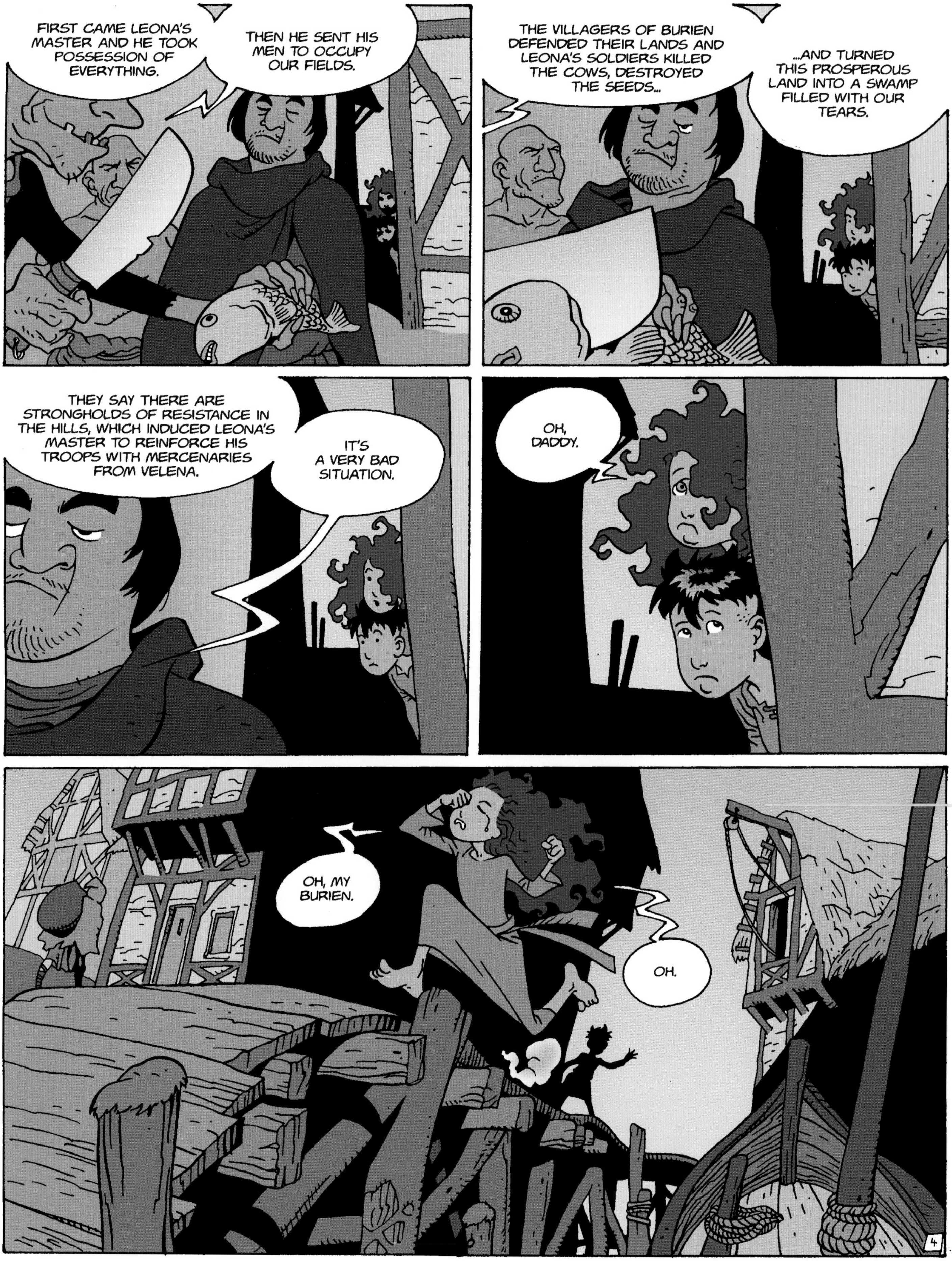
FIRST CAME LEONA'S MASTER AND HE TOOK POSSESSION OF EVERYTHING.
THEN HE SENT HIS MEN TO OCCUPY OUR FIELDS.
THE VILLAGERS OF BURIEN DEFENDED THEIR LANDS AND LEONA'S SOLDIERS KILLED THE COWS, DESTROYED THE SEEDS...
...AND TURNED THIS PROSPEROUS LAND INTO A SWAMP FILLED WITH OUR TEARS.
THEY SAY THERE ARE STRONGHOLDS OF RESISTANCE IN THE HILLS, WHICH INDUCED LEONA'S MASTER TO REINFORCE HIS TROOPS WITH MERCENARIES FROM VELENA.
IT'S A VERY BAD SITUATION.
OH, DADDY.
OH, MY BURIEN.
OH.
4

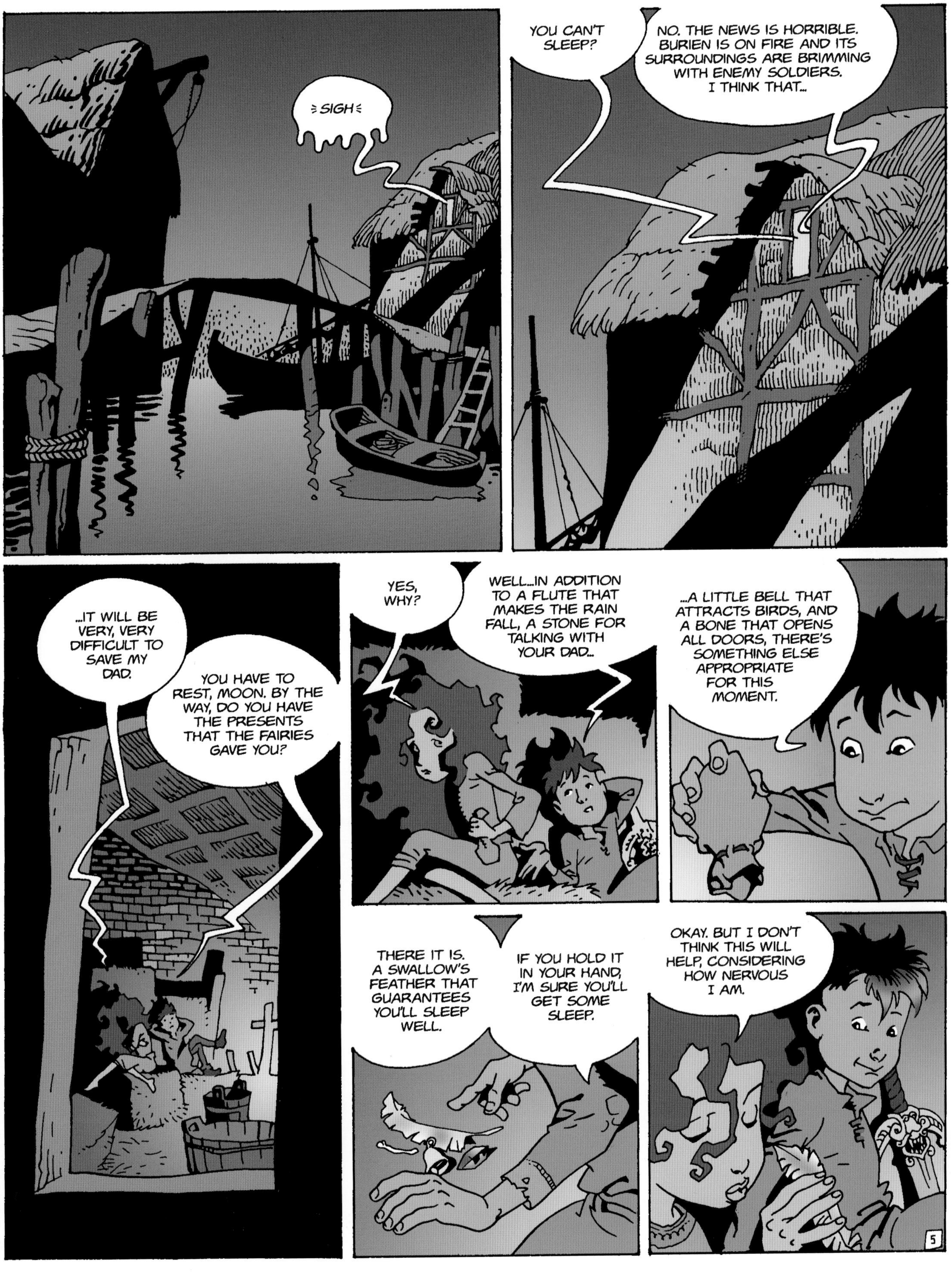

SIGH
YOU CAN'T SLEEP?
NO. THE NEWS IS HORRIBLE. BURIEN IS ON FIRE AND ITS SURROUNDINGS ARE BRIMMING WITH ENEMY SOLDIERS. I THINK THAT...
...IT WILL BE VERY, VERY DIFFICULT TO SAVE MY DAD.
YOU HAVE TO REST, MOON. BY THE WAY, DO YOU HAVE THE PRESENTS THAT THE FAIRIES GAVE YOU?
YES, WHY?
WELL...IN ADDITION TO A FLUTE THAT MAKES THE RAIN FALL, A STONE FOR TALKING WITH YOUR DAD...
...A LITTLE BELL THAT ATTRACTS BIRDS, AND A BONE THAT OPENS ALL DOORS, THERE'S SOMETHING ELSE APPROPRIATE FOR THIS MOMENT.
THERE IT IS. A SWALLOW'S FEATHER THAT GUARANTEES YOU'LL SLEEP WELL.
IF YOU HOLD IT IN YOUR HAND, I'M SURE YOU'LL GET SOME SLEEP.
OKAY. BUT I DON'T THINK THIS WILL HELP, CONSIDERING HOW NERVOUS I AM.
5

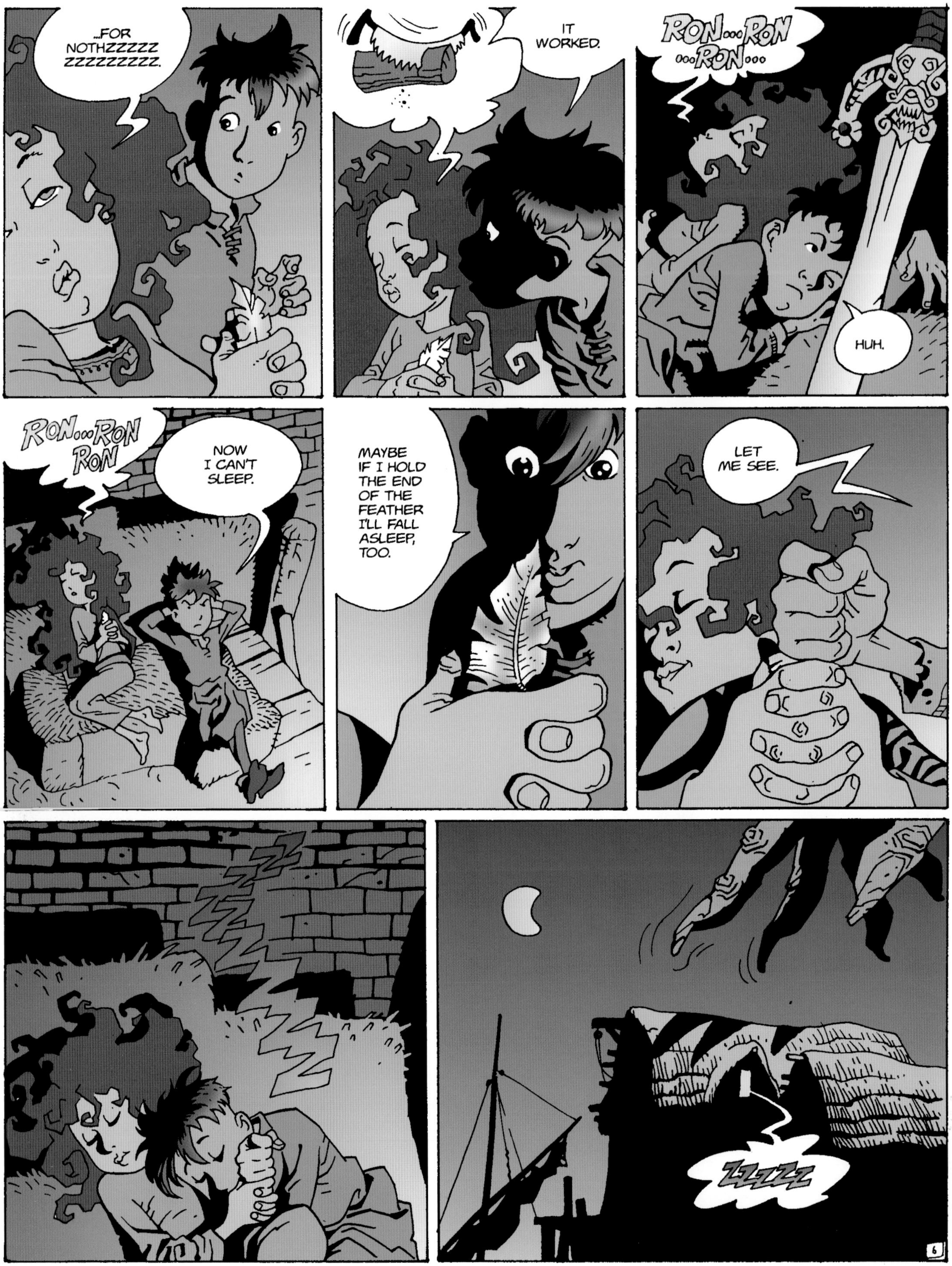

...FOR NOTHZZZZZ ZZZZZZZZZ.
IT WORKED.
RON...RON ...RON...
HUH.
RON...RON RON
NOW I CAN'T SLEEP.
MAYBE IF I HOLD THE END OF THE FEATHER I'LL FALL ASLEEP, TOO.
LET ME SEE.
ZZZZZ
6

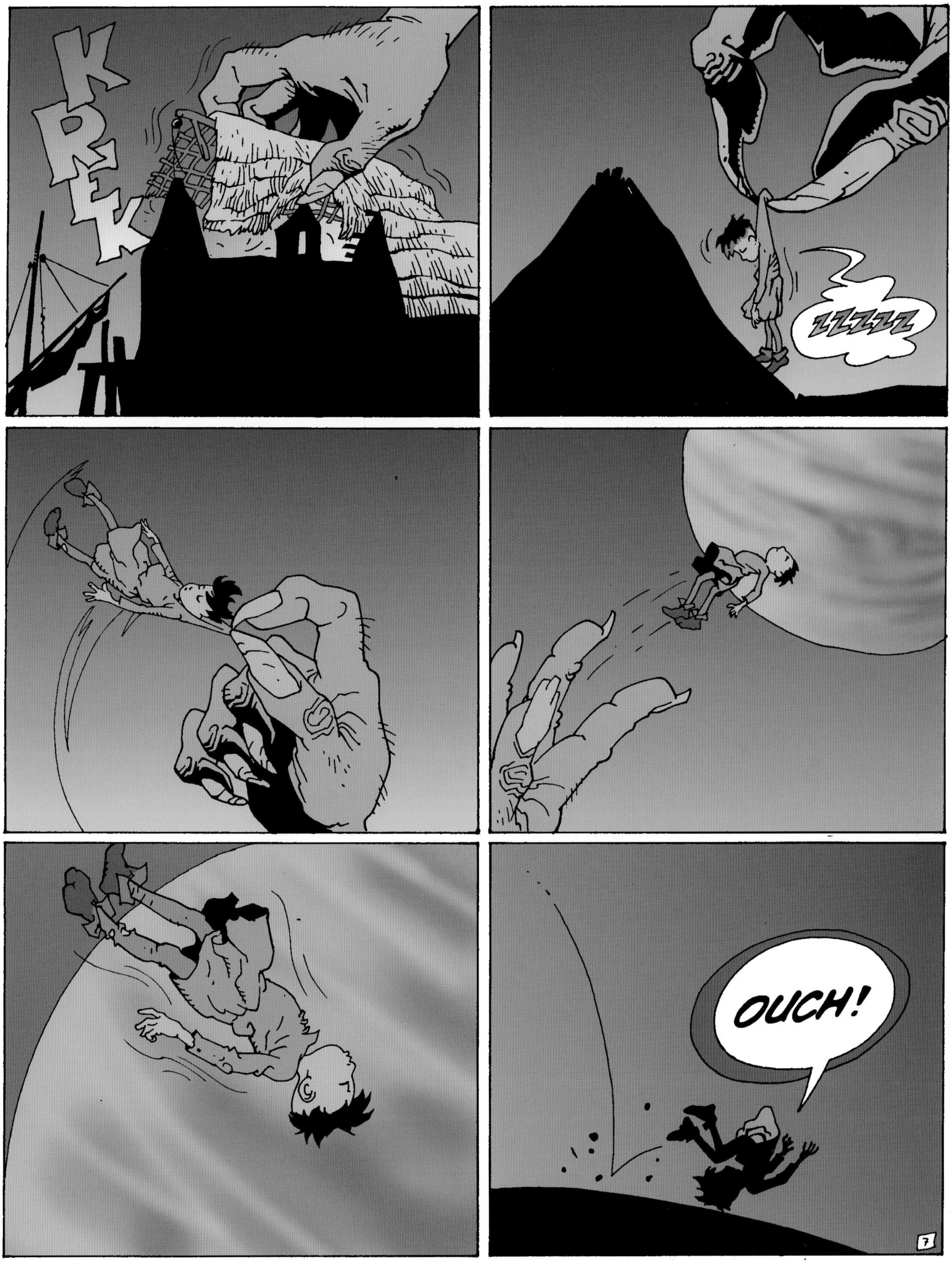
KREK
ZZZZZ
OUCH!
7

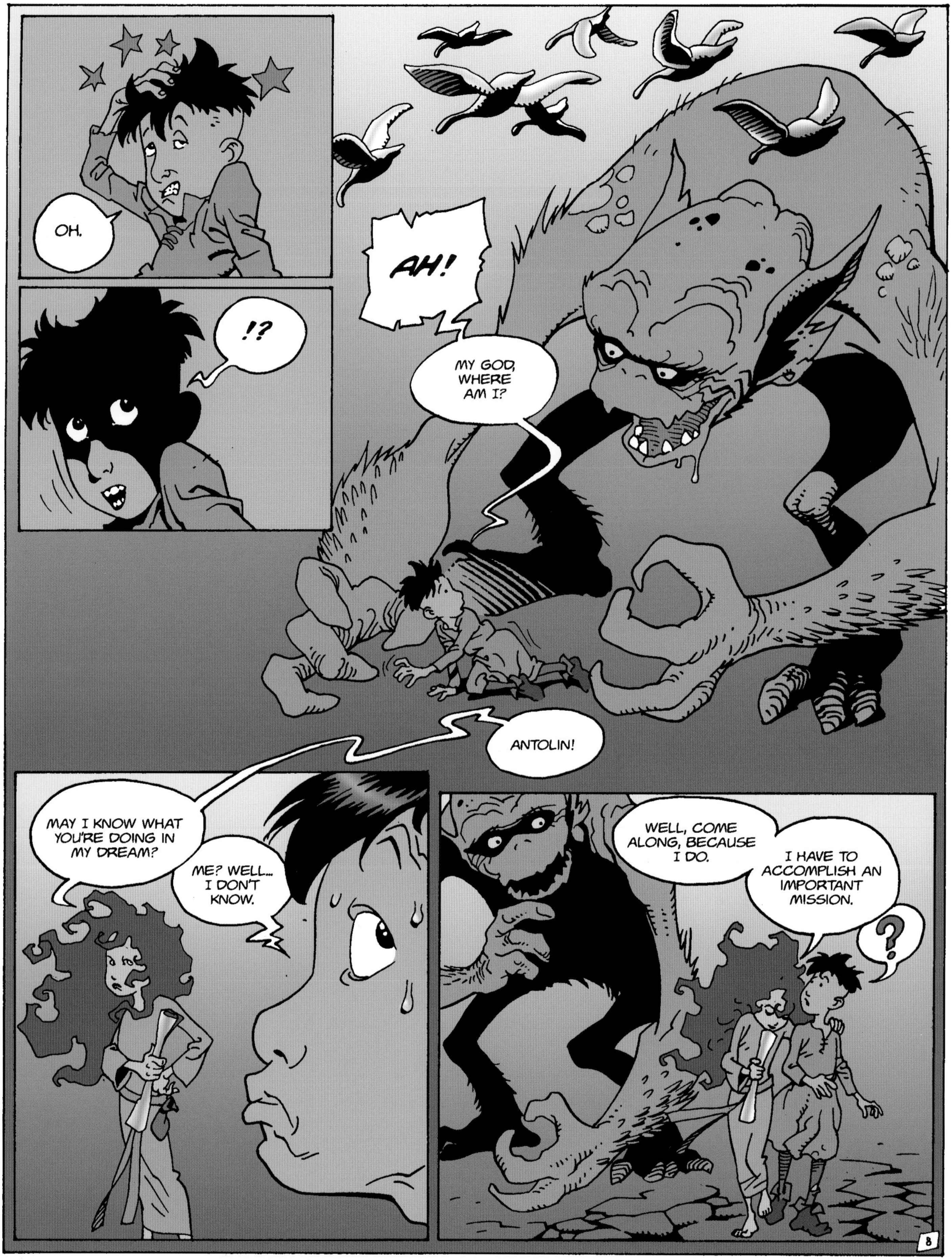

OH.
!?
AH!
MY GOD, WHERE AM I?
ANTOLIN!
MAY I KNOW WHAT YOU'RE DOING IN MY DREAM?
ME? WELL... I DON'T KNOW.
WELL, COME ALONG, BECAUSE I DO.
I HAVE TO ACCOMPLISH AN IMPORTANT MISSION.
?
8

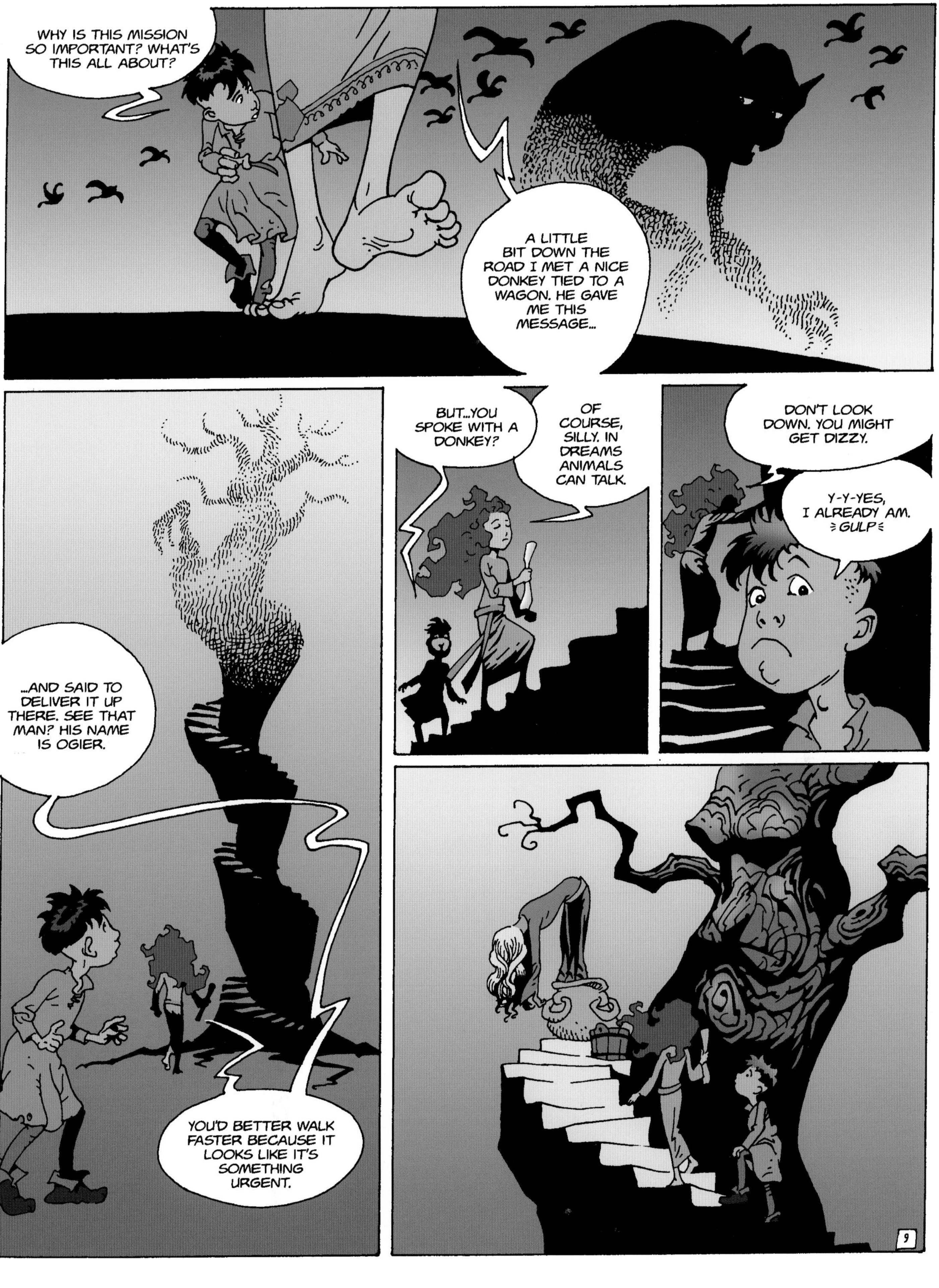
WHY IS THIS MISSION SO IMPORTANT? WHAT'S THIS ALL ABOUT?
A LITTLE BIT DOWN THE ROAD I MET A NICE DONKEY TIED TO A WAGON. HE GAVE ME THIS MESSAGE...
...AND SAID TO DELIVER IT UP THERE. SEE THAT MAN? HIS NAME IS OGIER.
YOU'D BETTER WALK FASTER BECAUSE IT LOOKS LIKE IT'S SOMETHING URGENT.
BUT...YOU SPOKE WITH A DONKEY?
OF COURSE, SILLY. IN DREAMS ANIMALS CAN TALK.
DON'T LOOK DOWN. YOU MIGHT GET DIZZY.
Y-Y-YES, I ALREADY AM. GULP
9

I DON'T SEE ANYONE.

WE SHOULD ASK THAT WOMAN IN THE FLOWERPOT.

HELLO, MA'AM. COULD YOU TELL ME WHERE I CAN FIND MR. OGIER?

SHE DOESN'T EVEN BOTHER TO ANSWER ME, ANTOLIN.

BECAUSE SHE FAINTED, POOR CUNEGUNDA. BUT DON'T YOU WORRY...

OGIER, I AM.

WOW! IN THIS DREAM TREES TALK AS WELL.

WE'VE BROUGHT YOU THIS MESSAGE FROM A DONKEY DOWN THERE.

AND WE HAVE TO LEAVE RIGHT AWAY BECAUSE...

...THE SOUP IS GETTING COLD.

WAIT A MINUTE! THAT'S AN ORDER!

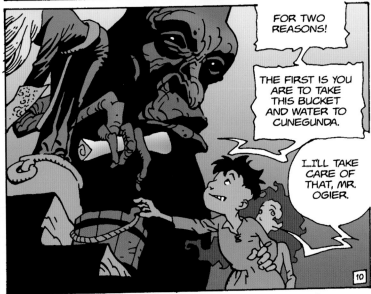

FOR TWO REASONS!

THE FIRST IS YOU ARE TO TAKE THIS BUCKET AND WATER TO CUNEGUNDA.

I...I'LL TAKE CARE OF THAT, MR. OGIER.

10

82

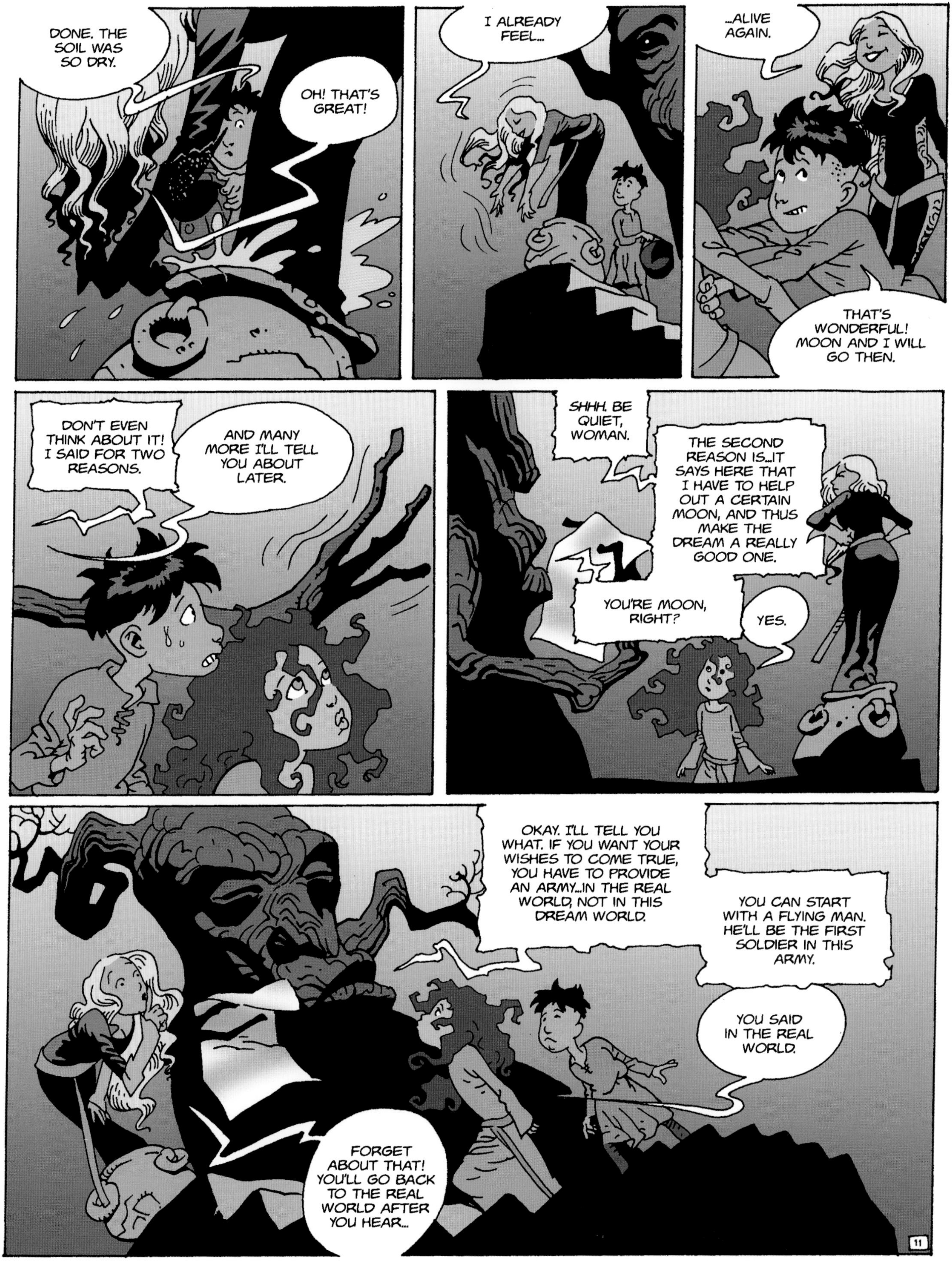
DONE. THE SOIL WAS SO DRY.
OH! THAT'S GREAT!
I ALREADY FEEL...
...ALIVE AGAIN.
THAT'S WONDERFUL! MOON AND I WILL GO THEN.
DON'T EVEN THINK ABOUT IT! I SAID FOR TWO REASONS.
AND MANY MORE I'LL TELL YOU ABOUT LATER.
SHHH. BE QUIET, WOMAN.
THE SECOND REASON IS...IT SAYS HERE THAT I HAVE TO HELP OUT A CERTAIN MOON, AND THUS MAKE THE DREAM A REALLY GOOD ONE.
YOU'RE MOON, RIGHT?
YES.
OKAY. I'LL TELL YOU WHAT. IF YOU WANT YOUR WISHES TO COME TRUE, YOU HAVE TO PROVIDE AN ARMY...IN THE REAL WORLD, NOT IN THIS DREAM WORLD.
YOU CAN START WITH A FLYING MAN. HE'LL BE THE FIRST SOLDIER IN THIS ARMY.
YOU SAID IN THE REAL WORLD.
FORGET ABOUT THAT! YOU'LL GO BACK TO THE REAL WORLD AFTER YOU HEAR...
11

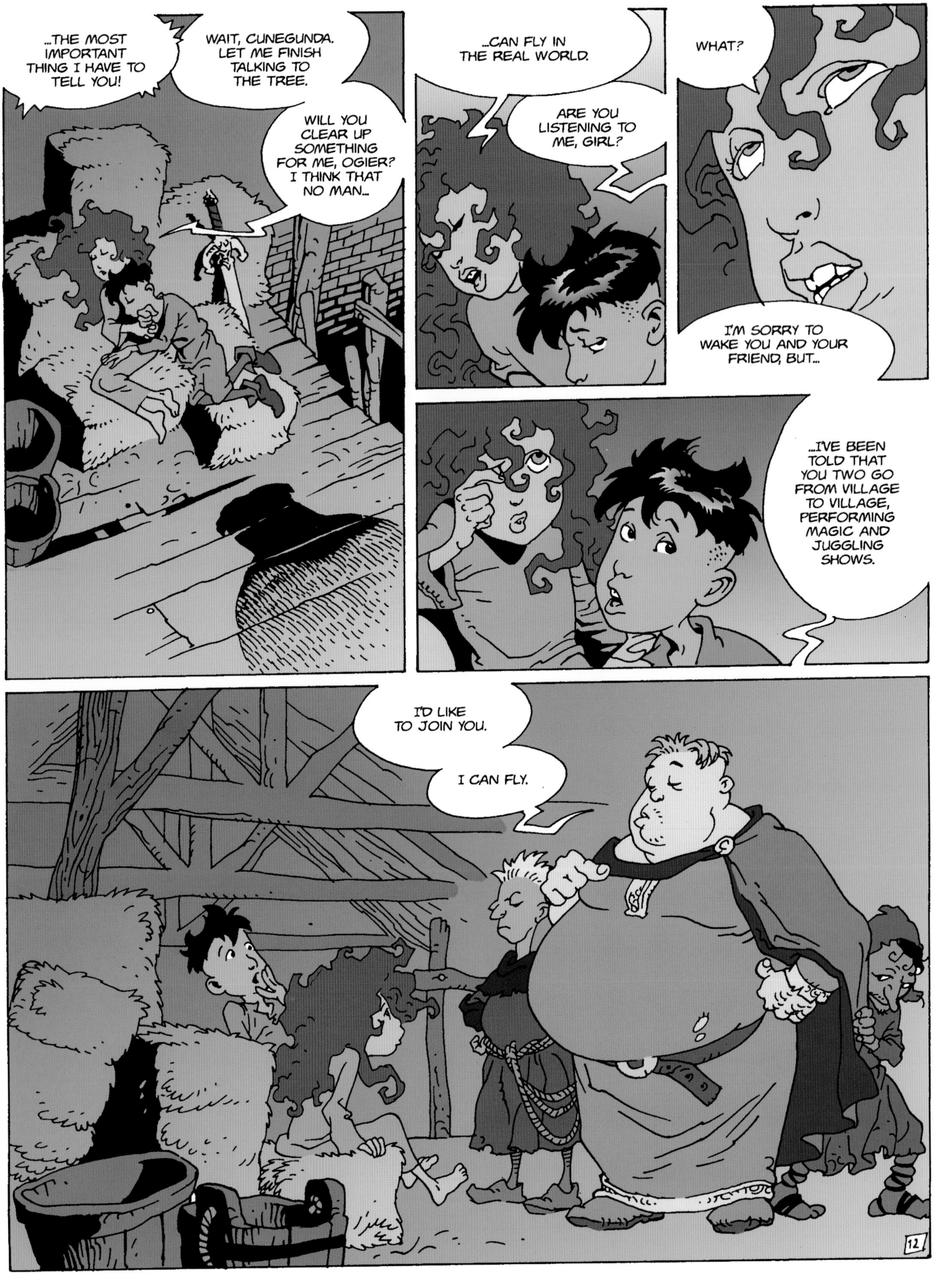

...THE MOST IMPORTANT THING I HAVE TO TELL YOU!
WAIT, CUNEGUNDA. LET ME FINISH TALKING TO THE TREE.
WILL YOU CLEAR UP SOMETHING FOR ME, OGIER? I THINK THAT NO MAN...
...CAN FLY IN THE REAL WORLD.
ARE YOU LISTENING TO ME, GIRL?
WHAT?
I'M SORRY TO WAKE YOU AND YOUR FRIEND, BUT...
...I'VE BEEN TOLD THAT YOU TWO GO FROM VILLAGE TO VILLAGE, PERFORMING MAGIC AND JUGGLING SHOWS.
I'D LIKE TO JOIN YOU.
I CAN FLY.
12

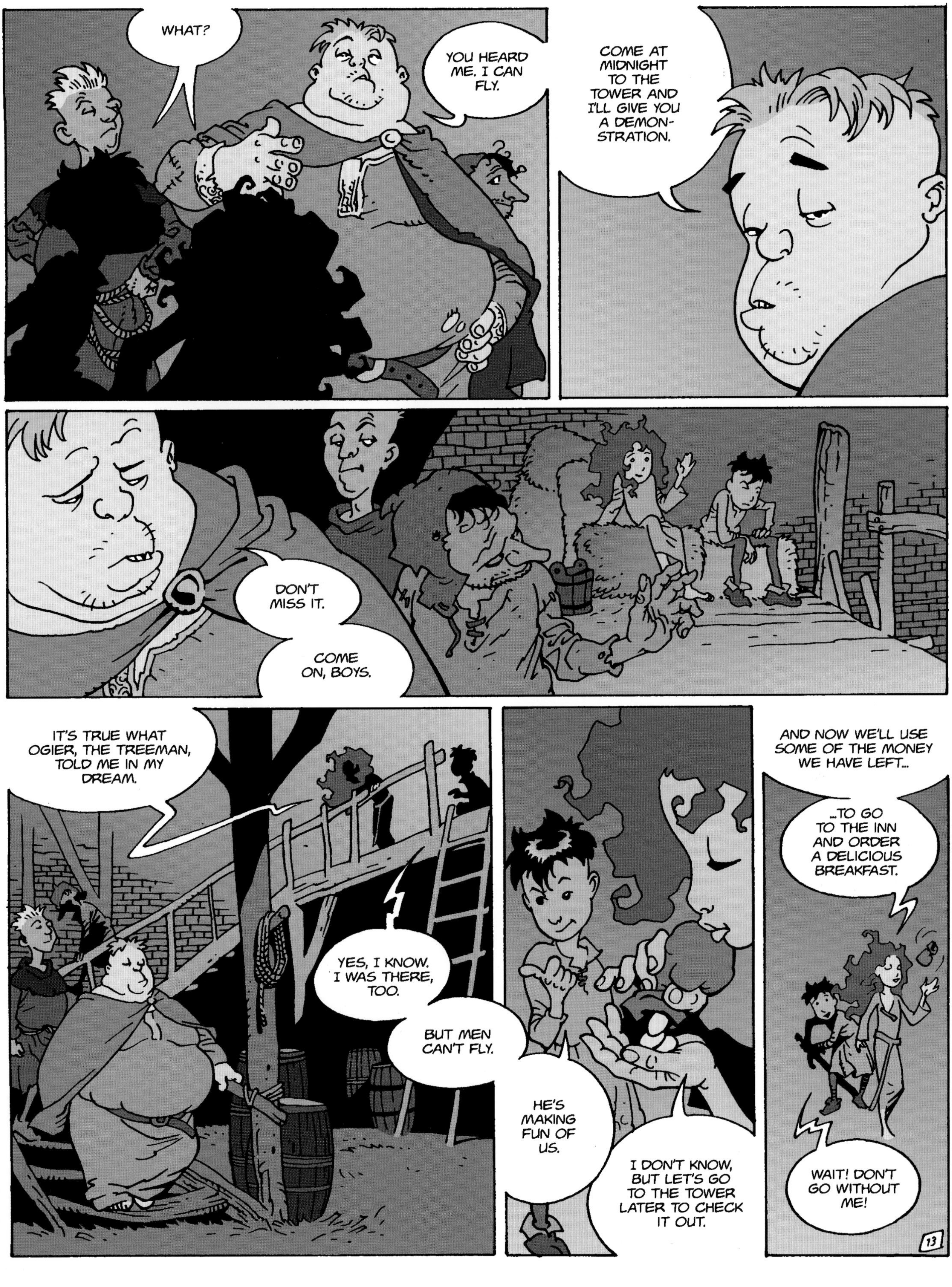
WHAT?
YOU HEARD ME. I CAN FLY.
COME AT MIDNIGHT TO THE TOWER AND I'LL GIVE YOU A DEMON-STRATION.
DON'T MISS IT.
COME ON, BOYS.
IT'S TRUE WHAT OGIER, THE TREEMAN, TOLD ME IN MY DREAM.
YES, I KNOW. I WAS THERE, TOO.
BUT MEN CAN'T FLY.
HE'S MAKING FUN OF US.
I DON'T KNOW, BUT LET'S GO TO THE TOWER LATER TO CHECK IT OUT.
AND NOW WE'LL USE SOME OF THE MONEY WE HAVE LEFT...
...TO GO TO THE INN AND ORDER A DELICIOUS BREAKFAST.
WAIT! DON'T GO WITHOUT ME!
13

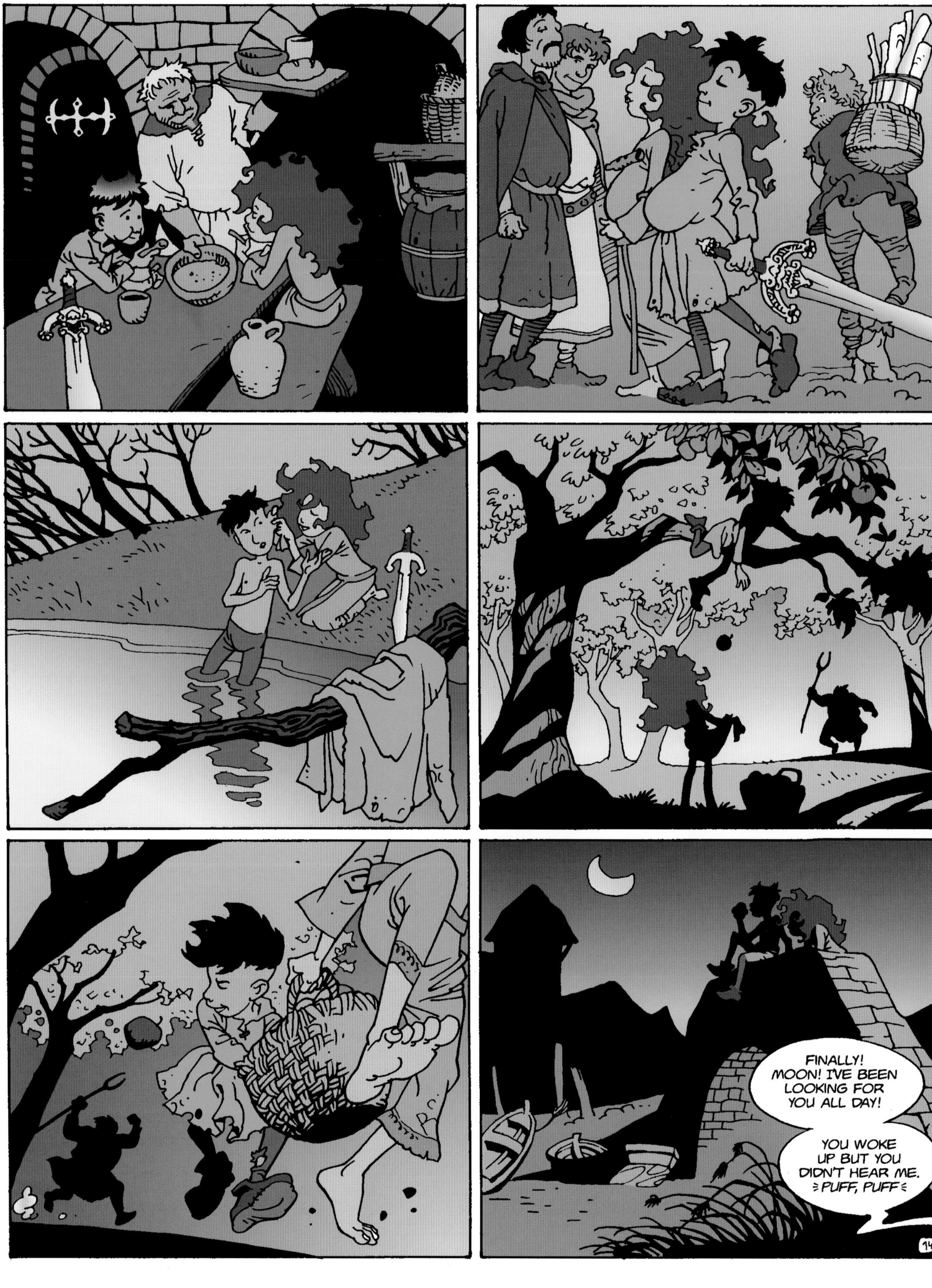
FINALLY! MOON! I'VE BEEN LOOKING FOR YOU ALL DAY!
YOU WOKE UP BUT YOU DIDN'T HEAR ME. PUFF, PUFF
14

CUNEGUNDA!

IT'S DIFFICULT FOR US TENANTS OF DREAMS TO ENTER YOUR REALITY.

I DON'T HAVE MUCH TIME.

YOU HEARD OGIER. YOU HAVE TO PROVIDE AN ARMY TO...

≥COUGH, SIGH≤

...BRING ABOUT THE RECLAMATION OF BURIEN.

LISTEN UP, BECAUSE I'LL TELL YOU WHAT YOU AB...

...ORF ≥COUGH≤ UH...

...ABSOLUTELY NEED IN THIS ARMY.

A STRONGMAN, A CAT TRAINER, A TIGHTROPE WALKER, A TRAINED BEAR, TWO TALKING PARROTS, AND...

...AND...

...AND...

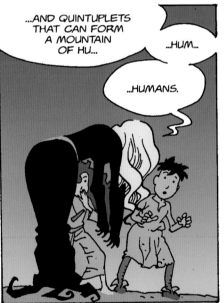

...AND QUINTUPLETS THAT CAN FORM A MOUNTAIN OF HU...

...HUM...

...HUMANS.

WHAT'S WRONG, CUNEGUNDA?

I'M DRYING UP.

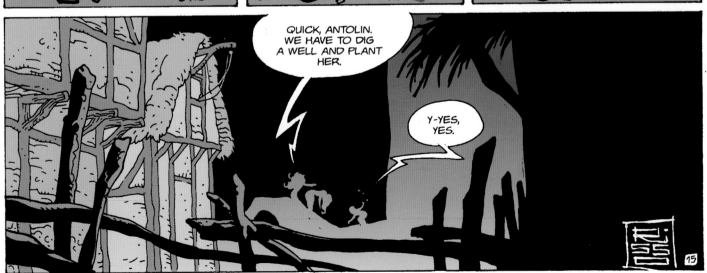

QUICK, ANTOLIN. WE HAVE TO DIG A WELL AND PLANT HER.

Y-YES, YES.

15

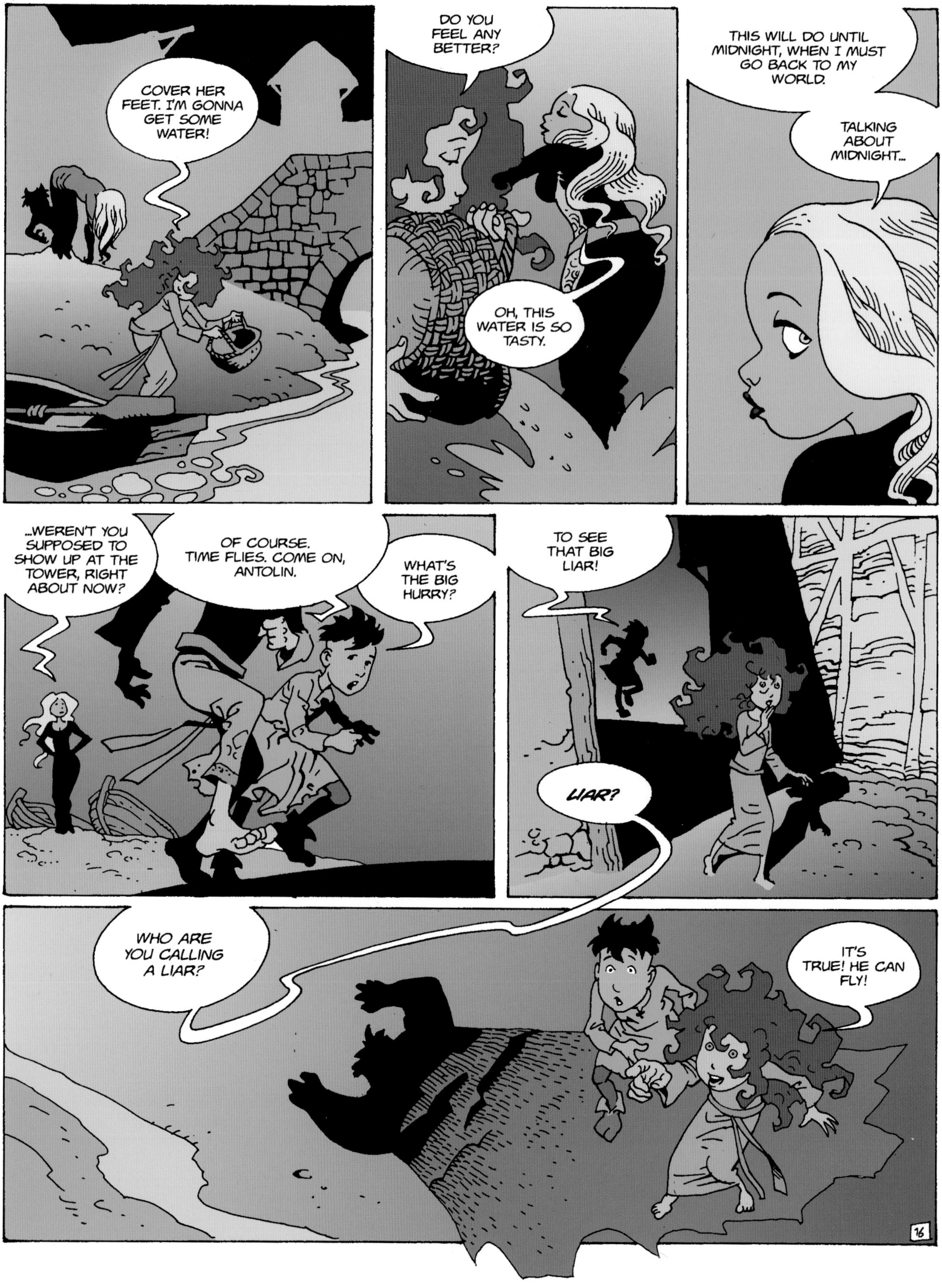
COVER HER FEET. I'M GONNA GET SOME WATER!
DO YOU FEEL ANY BETTER?
OH, THIS WATER IS SO TASTY.
THIS WILL DO UNTIL MIDNIGHT, WHEN I MUST GO BACK TO MY WORLD.
TALKING ABOUT MIDNIGHT...
...WEREN'T YOU SUPPOSED TO SHOW UP AT THE TOWER, RIGHT ABOUT NOW?
OF COURSE. TIME FLIES. COME ON, ANTOLIN.
WHAT'S THE BIG HURRY?
TO SEE THAT BIG LIAR!
LIAR?
WHO ARE YOU CALLING A LIAR?
IT'S TRUE! HE CAN FLY!
16

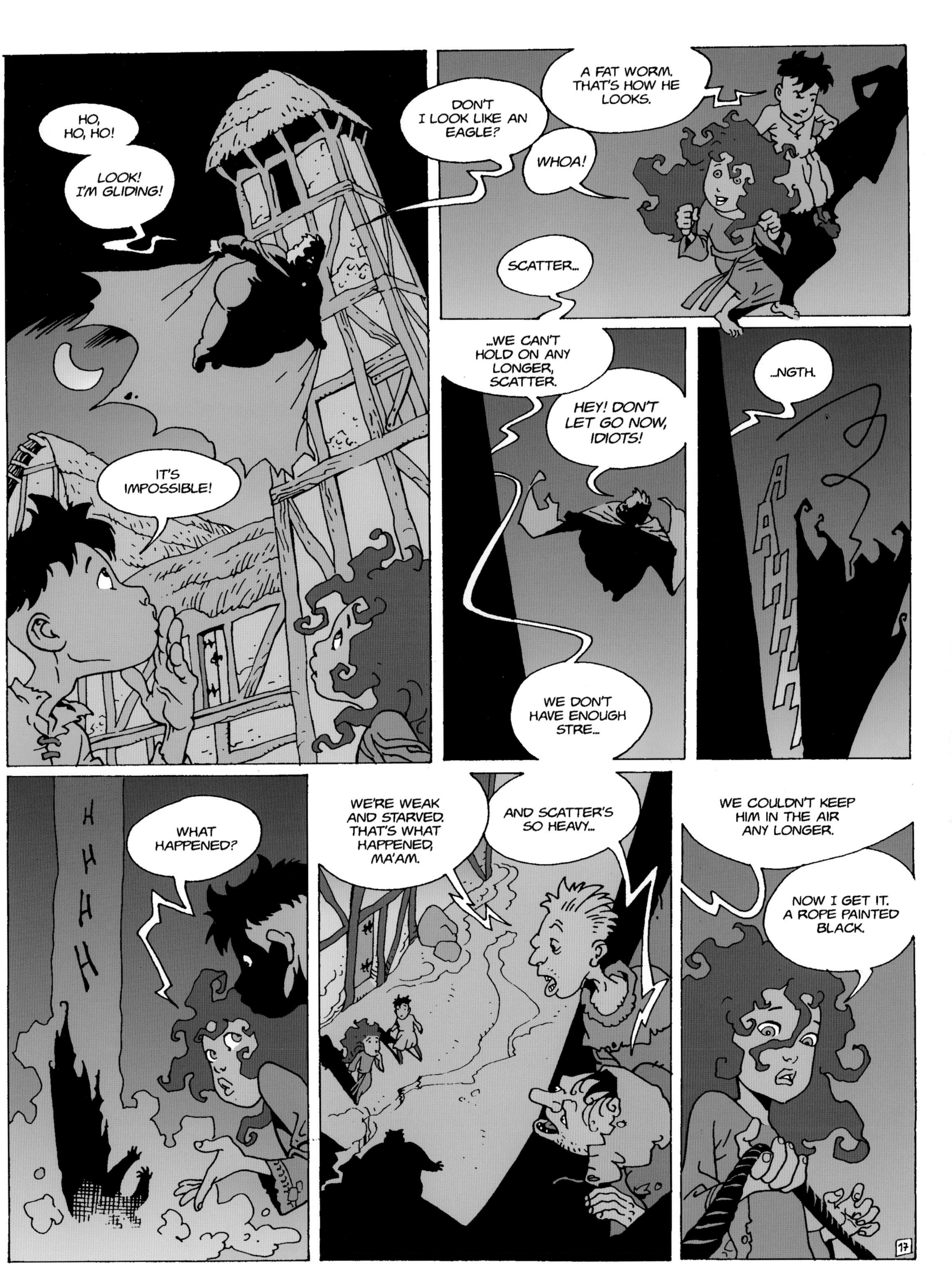
HO, HO, HO!
LOOK! I'M GLIDING!
DON'T I LOOK LIKE AN EAGLE?
IT'S IMPOSSIBLE!
A FAT WORM. THAT'S HOW HE LOOKS.
WHOA!
SCATTER...
...WE CAN'T HOLD ON ANY LONGER, SCATTER.
HEY! DON'T LET GO NOW, IDIOTS!
WE DON'T HAVE ENOUGH STRE...
...NGTH.
AAHHHH
HHHH
WHAT HAPPENED?
WE'RE WEAK AND STARVED. THAT'S WHAT HAPPENED, MA'AM.
AND SCATTER'S SO HEAVY...
WE COULDN'T KEEP HIM IN THE AIR ANY LONGER.
NOW I GET IT. A ROPE PAINTED BLACK.
17

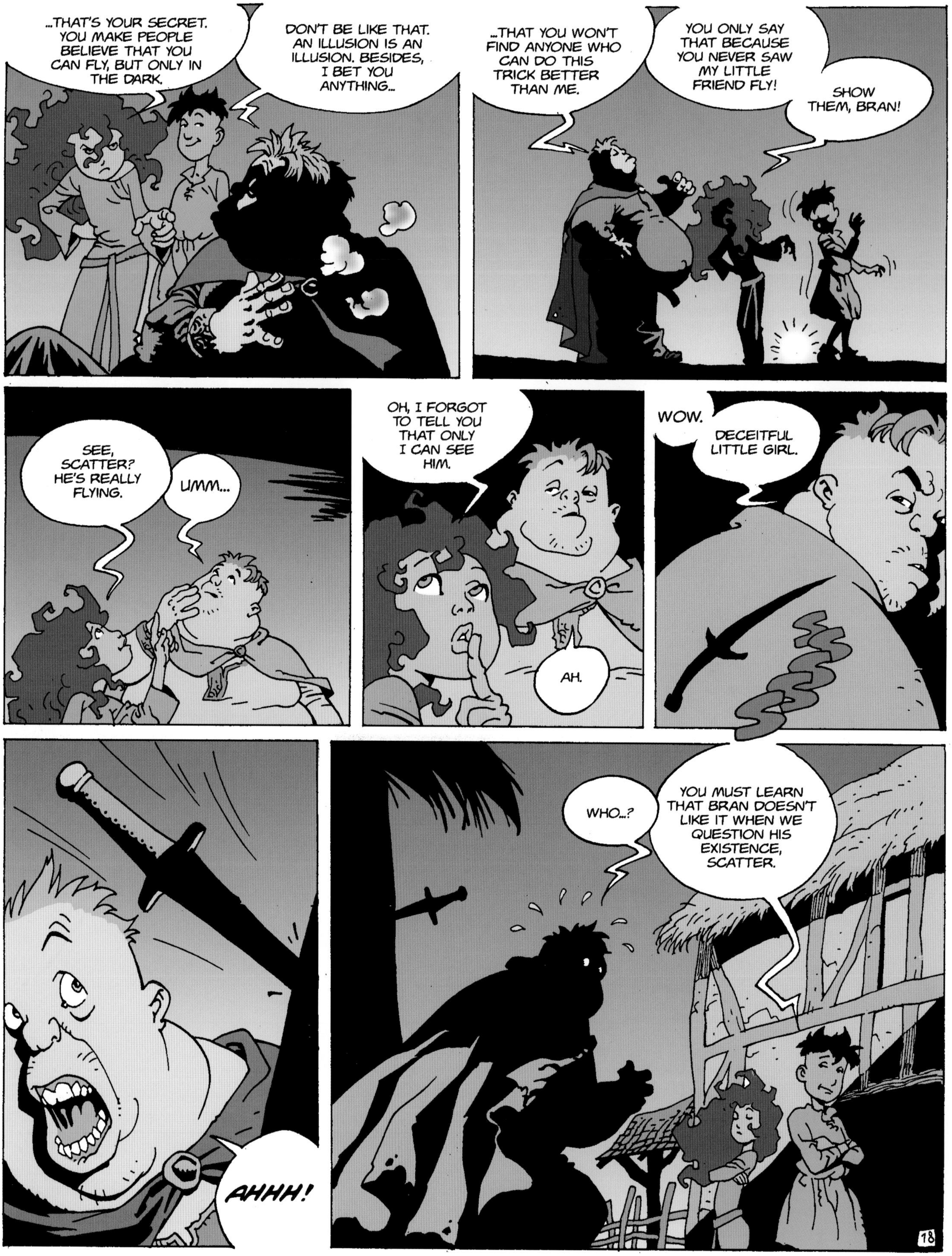
...THAT'S YOUR SECRET. YOU MAKE PEOPLE BELIEVE THAT YOU CAN FLY, BUT ONLY IN THE DARK.
DON'T BE LIKE THAT. AN ILLUSION IS AN ILLUSION. BESIDES, I BET YOU ANYTHING...
...THAT YOU WON'T FIND ANYONE WHO CAN DO THIS TRICK BETTER THAN ME.
YOU ONLY SAY THAT BECAUSE YOU NEVER SAW MY LITTLE FRIEND FLY!
SHOW THEM, BRAN!
SEE, SCATTER? HE'S REALLY FLYING.
UMM...
OH, I FORGOT TO TELL YOU THAT ONLY I CAN SEE HIM.
AH.
WOW.
DECEITFUL LITTLE GIRL.
AHHH!
WHO...?
YOU MUST LEARN THAT BRAN DOESN'T LIKE IT WHEN WE QUESTION HIS EXISTENCE, SCATTER.
78

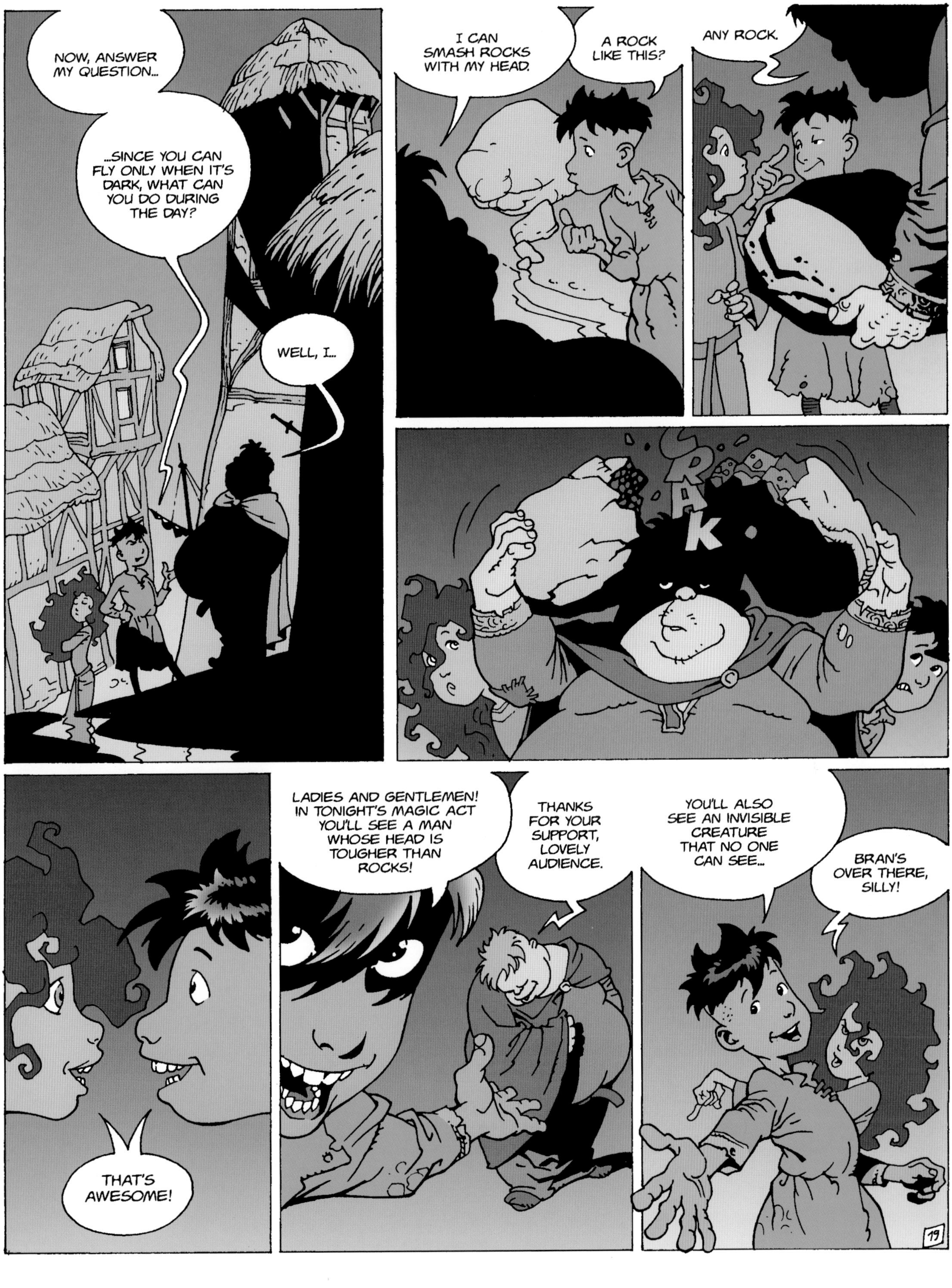
NOW, ANSWER MY QUESTION...
...SINCE YOU CAN FLY ONLY WHEN IT'S DARK, WHAT CAN YOU DO DURING THE DAY?
WELL, I...
I CAN SMASH ROCKS WITH MY HEAD.
A ROCK LIKE THIS?
ANY ROCK.
CRAK
THAT'S AWESOME!
LADIES AND GENTLEMEN! IN TONIGHT'S MAGIC ACT YOU'LL SEE A MAN WHOSE HEAD IS TOUGHER THAN ROCKS!
THANKS FOR YOUR SUPPORT, LOVELY AUDIENCE.
YOU'LL ALSO SEE AN INVISIBLE CREATURE THAT NO ONE CAN SEE...
BRAN'S OVER THERE, SILLY!
19

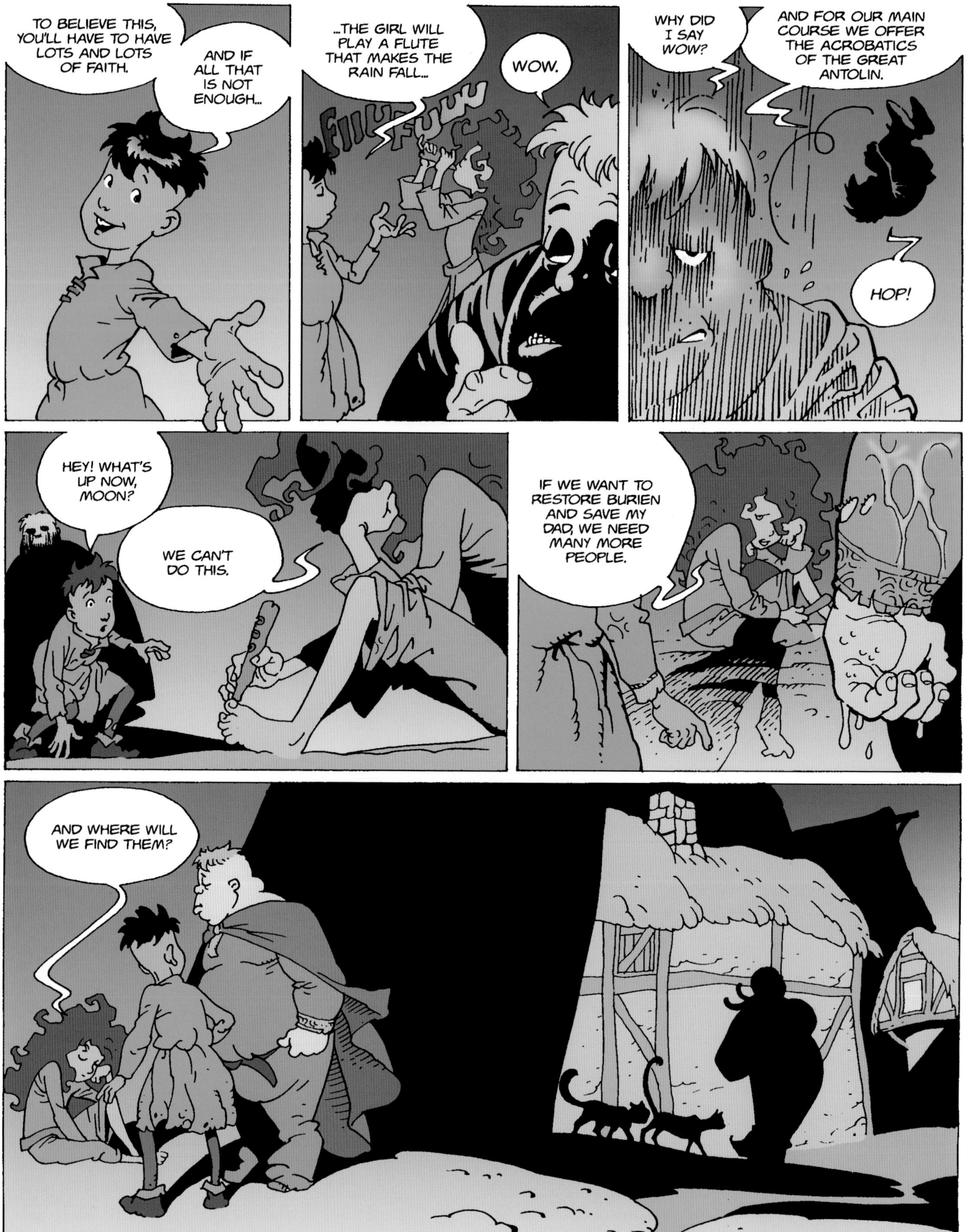

TO BELIEVE THIS, YOU'LL HAVE TO HAVE LOTS AND LOTS OF FAITH.
AND IF ALL THAT IS NOT ENOUGH...
...THE GIRL WILL PLAY A FLUTE THAT MAKES THE RAIN FALL...
FIIU FUUU
WOW.
WHY DID I SAY WOW?
AND FOR OUR MAIN COURSE WE OFFER THE ACROBATICS OF THE GREAT ANTOLIN.
HOP!
HEY! WHAT'S UP NOW, MOON?
WE CAN'T DO THIS.
IF WE WANT TO RESTORE BURIEN AND SAVE MY DAD, WE NEED MANY MORE PEOPLE.
AND WHERE WILL WE FIND THEM?
20

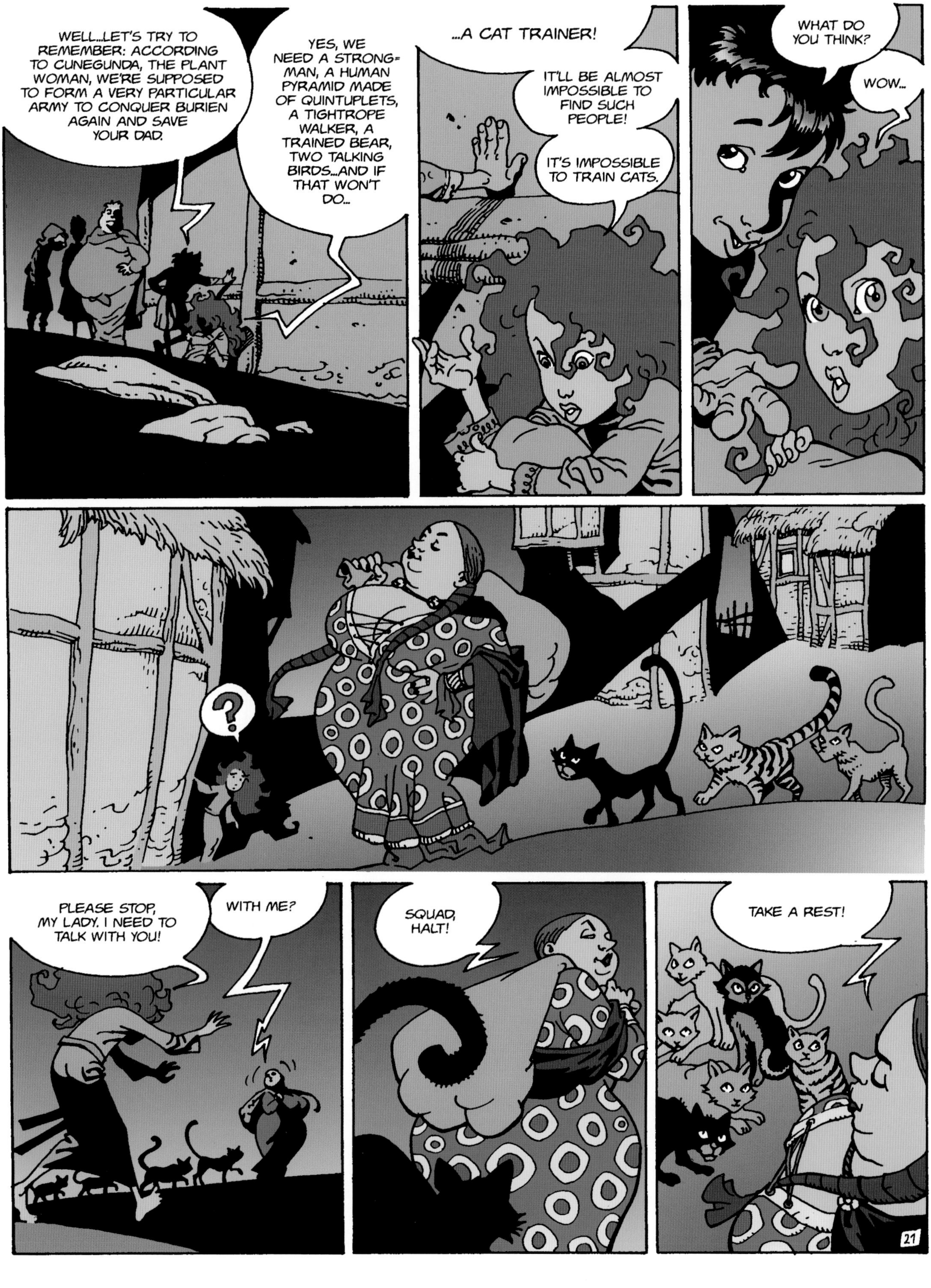
WELL...LET'S TRY TO REMEMBER: ACCORDING TO CUNEGUNDA, THE PLANT WOMAN, WE'RE SUPPOSED TO FORM A VERY PARTICULAR ARMY TO CONQUER BURIEN AGAIN AND SAVE YOUR DAD.
YES, WE NEED A STRONG-MAN, A HUMAN PYRAMID MADE OF QUINTUPLETS, A TIGHTROPE WALKER, A TRAINED BEAR, TWO TALKING BIRDS...AND IF THAT WON'T DO...
...A CAT TRAINER!
IT'LL BE ALMOST IMPOSSIBLE TO FIND SUCH PEOPLE!
IT'S IMPOSSIBLE TO TRAIN CATS.
WHAT DO YOU THINK?
WOW...
?
PLEASE STOP, MY LADY. I NEED TO TALK WITH YOU!
WITH ME?
SQUAD, HALT!
TAKE A REST!
21

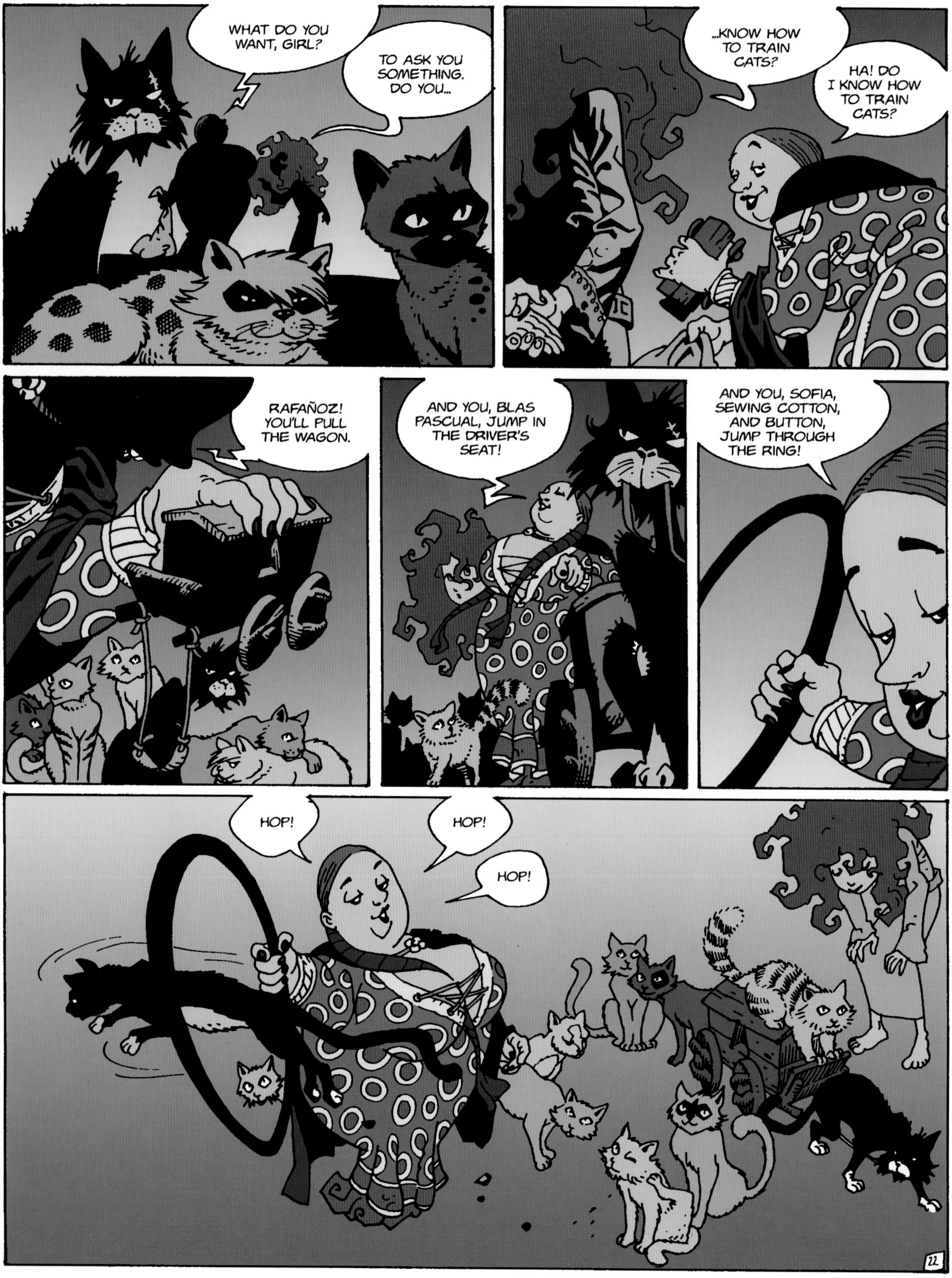
WHAT DO YOU WANT, GIRL?
TO ASK YOU SOMETHING. DO YOU...
...KNOW HOW TO TRAIN CATS?
HA! DO I KNOW HOW TO TRAIN CATS?
RAFAÑOZ! YOU'LL PULL THE WAGON.
AND YOU, BLAS PASCUAL, JUMP IN THE DRIVER'S SEAT!
AND YOU, SOFIA, SEWING COTTON, AND BUTTON, JUMP THROUGH THE RING!
HOP!
HOP!
HOP!
22

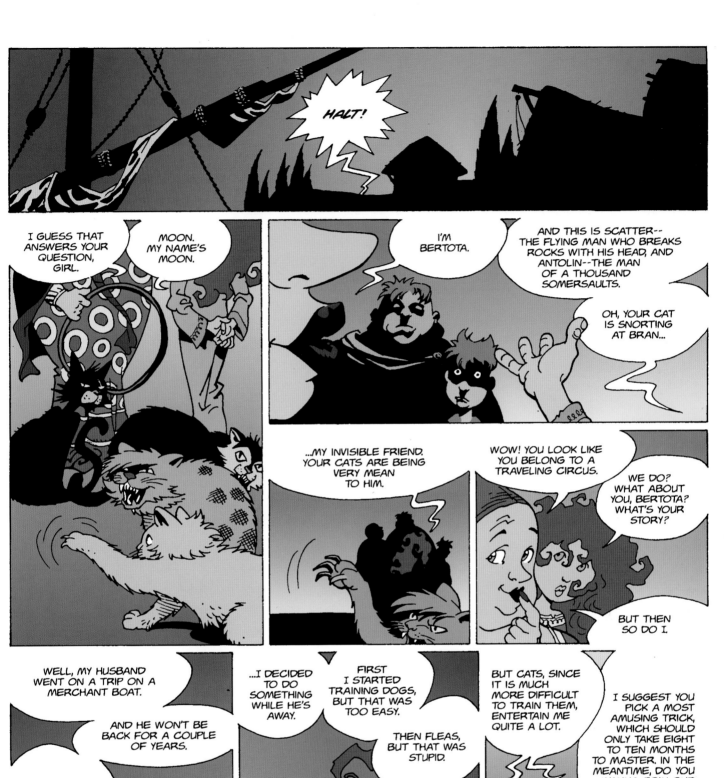

HALT!

I GUESS THAT ANSWERS YOUR QUESTION, GIRL.

MOON. MY NAME'S MOON.

I'M BERTOTA.

AND THIS IS SCATTER-- THE FLYING MAN WHO BREAKS ROCKS WITH HIS HEAD, AND ANTOLIN--THE MAN OF A THOUSAND SOMERSAULTS.

OH, YOUR CAT IS SNORTING AT BRAN...

...MY INVISIBLE FRIEND. YOUR CATS ARE BEING VERY MEAN TO HIM.

WOW! YOU LOOK LIKE YOU BELONG TO A TRAVELING CIRCUS.

WE DO? WHAT ABOUT YOU, BERTOTA? WHAT'S YOUR STORY?

BUT THEN SO DO I

WELL, MY HUSBAND WENT ON A TRIP ON A MERCHANT BOAT.

AND HE WON'T BE BACK FOR A COUPLE OF YEARS.

SINCE HIS ABSENCE FILLED ME WITH SORROW AND BOREDOM...

...I DECIDED TO DO SOMETHING WHILE HE'S AWAY.

FIRST I STARTED TRAINING DOGS, BUT THAT WAS TOO EASY.

THEN FLEAS, BUT THAT WAS STUPID.

BUT CATS, SINCE IT IS MUCH MORE DIFFICULT TO TRAIN THEM, ENTERTAIN ME QUITE A LOT.

I SUGGEST YOU PICK A MOST AMUSING TRICK, WHICH SHOULD ONLY TAKE EIGHT TO TEN MONTHS TO MASTER. IN THE MEANTIME, DO YOU WANNA JOIN OUR MAGICAL SHOW?

23

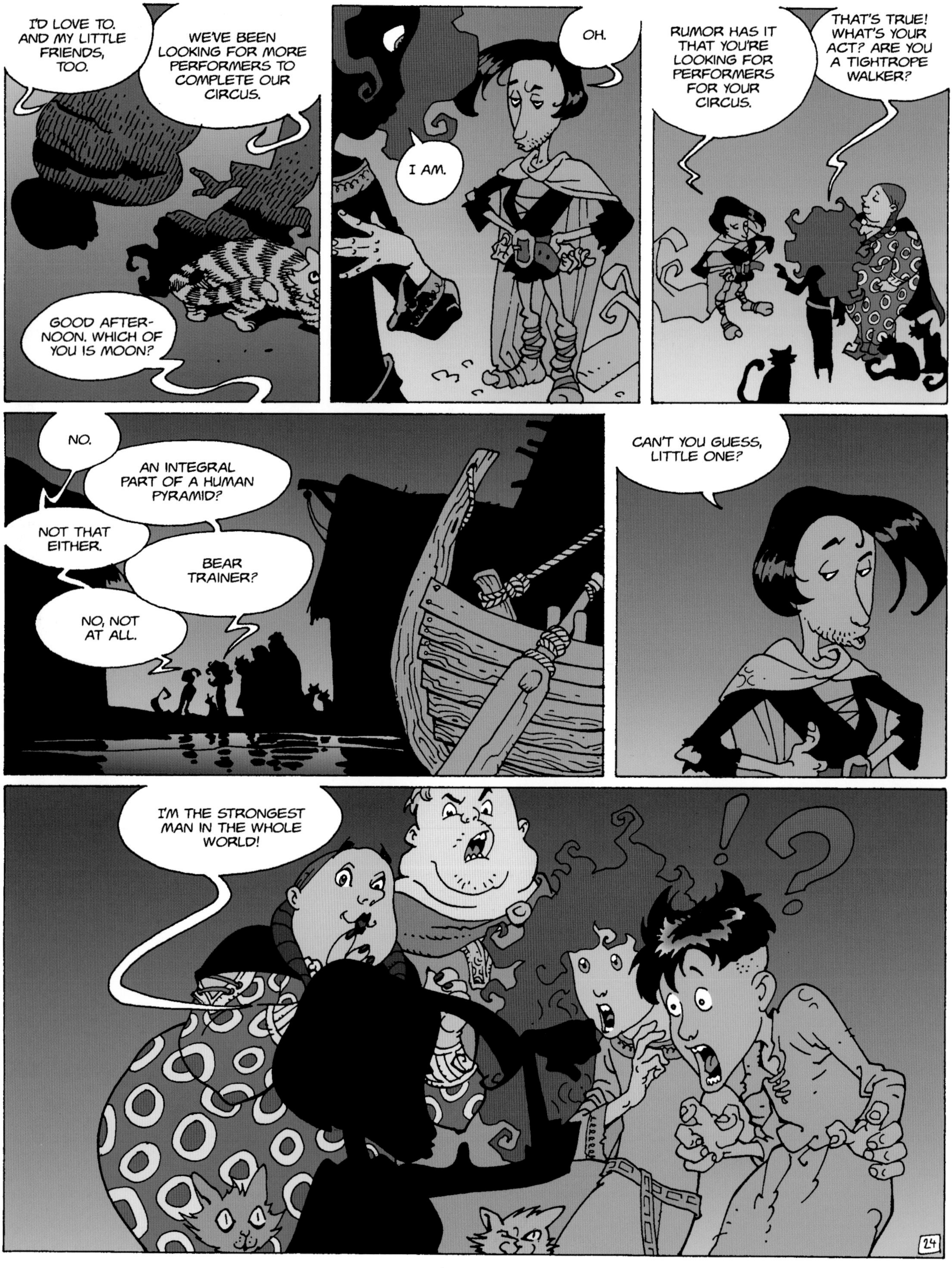
I'D LOVE TO. AND MY LITTLE FRIENDS, TOO.
WE'VE BEEN LOOKING FOR MORE PERFORMERS TO COMPLETE OUR CIRCUS.
GOOD AFTER-NOON. WHICH OF YOU IS MOON?
OH.
I AM.
RUMOR HAS IT THAT YOU'RE LOOKING FOR PERFORMERS FOR YOUR CIRCUS.
THAT'S TRUE! WHAT'S YOUR ACT? ARE YOU A TIGHTROPE WALKER?
NO.
AN INTEGRAL PART OF A HUMAN PYRAMID?
NOT THAT EITHER.
BEAR TRAINER?
NO, NOT AT ALL.
CAN'T YOU GUESS, LITTLE ONE?
I'M THE STRONGEST MAN IN THE WHOLE WORLD!
24

HMM.

PFFF.

YOU? A STRONGMAN? HA, HA.

HA, HA, HA.

≋ SIGH ≋

IT'S ALWAYS THE SAME OLD STORY.

IF YOU'LL BE KIND ENOUGH.

WHAT'S HE DOING?

I DON'T KNOW. IT LOOKS LIKE HE'S VERY FOND OF THAT TREE.

KRA-ACK

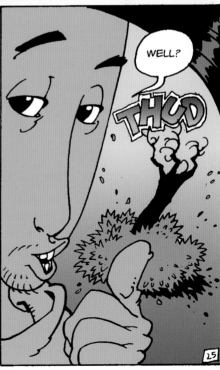

WELL?

THUD

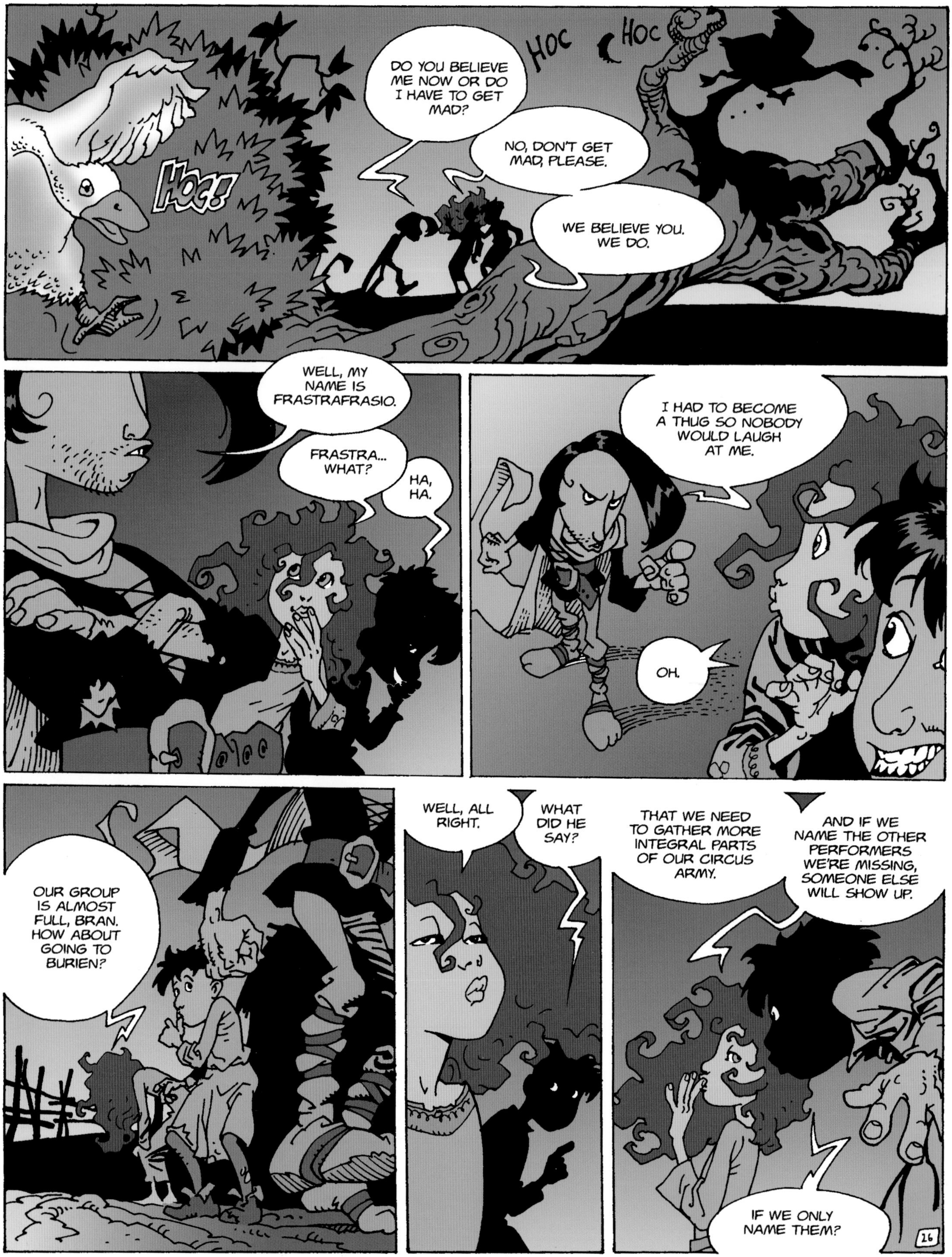
HOC!
HOC HOC
DO YOU BELIEVE ME NOW OR DO I HAVE TO GET MAD?
NO, DON'T GET MAD, PLEASE.
WE BELIEVE YOU. WE DO.
WELL, MY NAME IS FRASTRAFRASIO.
FRASTRA... WHAT?
HA, HA.
I HAD TO BECOME A THUG SO NOBODY WOULD LAUGH AT ME.
OH.
OUR GROUP IS ALMOST FULL, BRAN. HOW ABOUT GOING TO BURIEN?
WELL, ALL RIGHT.
WHAT DID HE SAY?
THAT WE NEED TO GATHER MORE INTEGRAL PARTS OF OUR CIRCUS ARMY.
AND IF WE NAME THE OTHER PERFORMERS WE'RE MISSING, SOMEONE ELSE WILL SHOW UP.
IF WE ONLY NAME THEM?
26

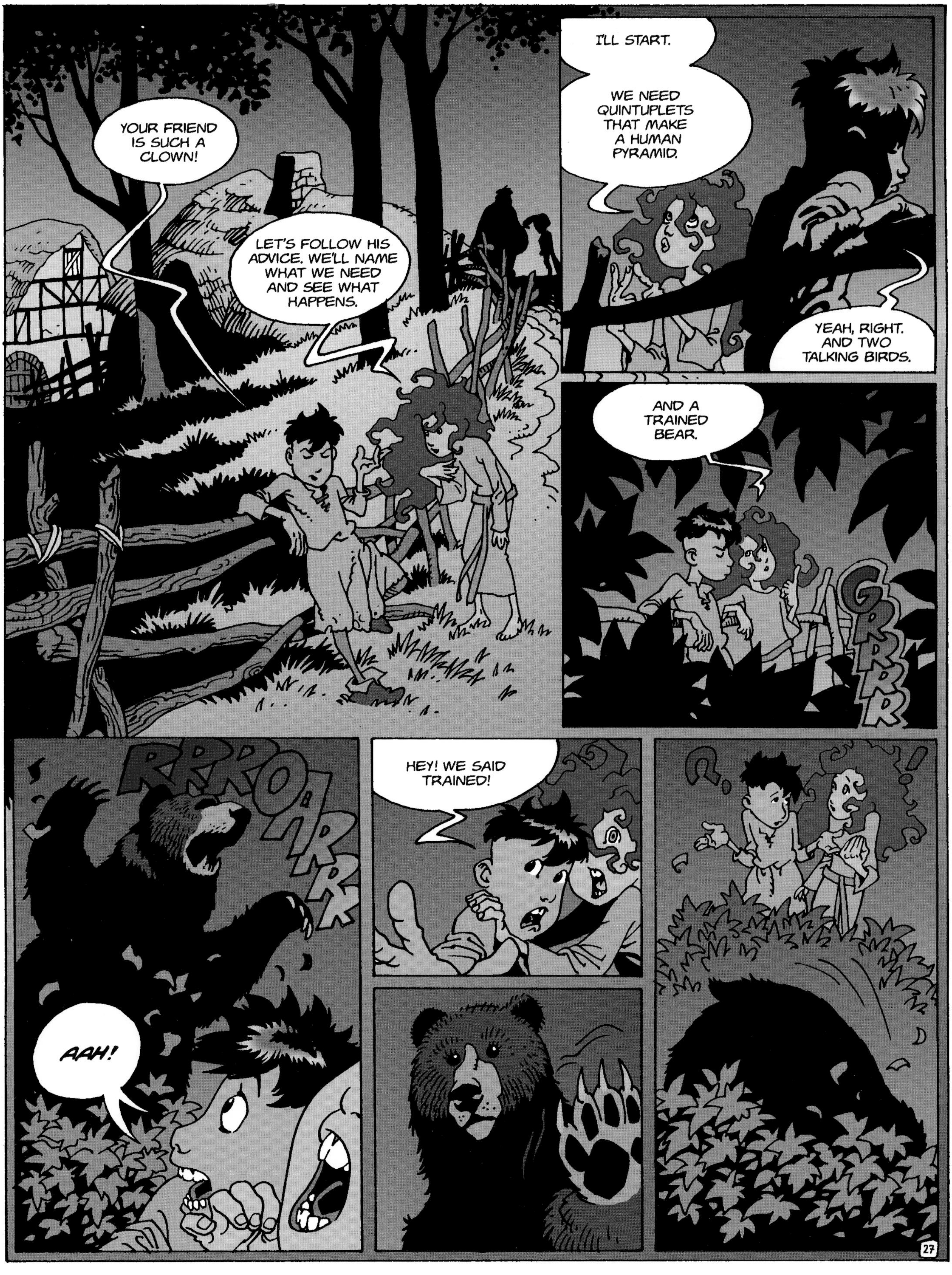
YOUR FRIEND IS SUCH A CLOWN!
LET'S FOLLOW HIS ADVICE. WE'LL NAME WHAT WE NEED AND SEE WHAT HAPPENS.
I'LL START.
WE NEED QUINTUPLETS THAT MAKE A HUMAN PYRAMID.
YEAH, RIGHT. AND TWO TALKING BIRDS.
AND A TRAINED BEAR.
GRRRR
RRROARRR
AAH!
HEY! WE SAID TRAINED!
?
!
27

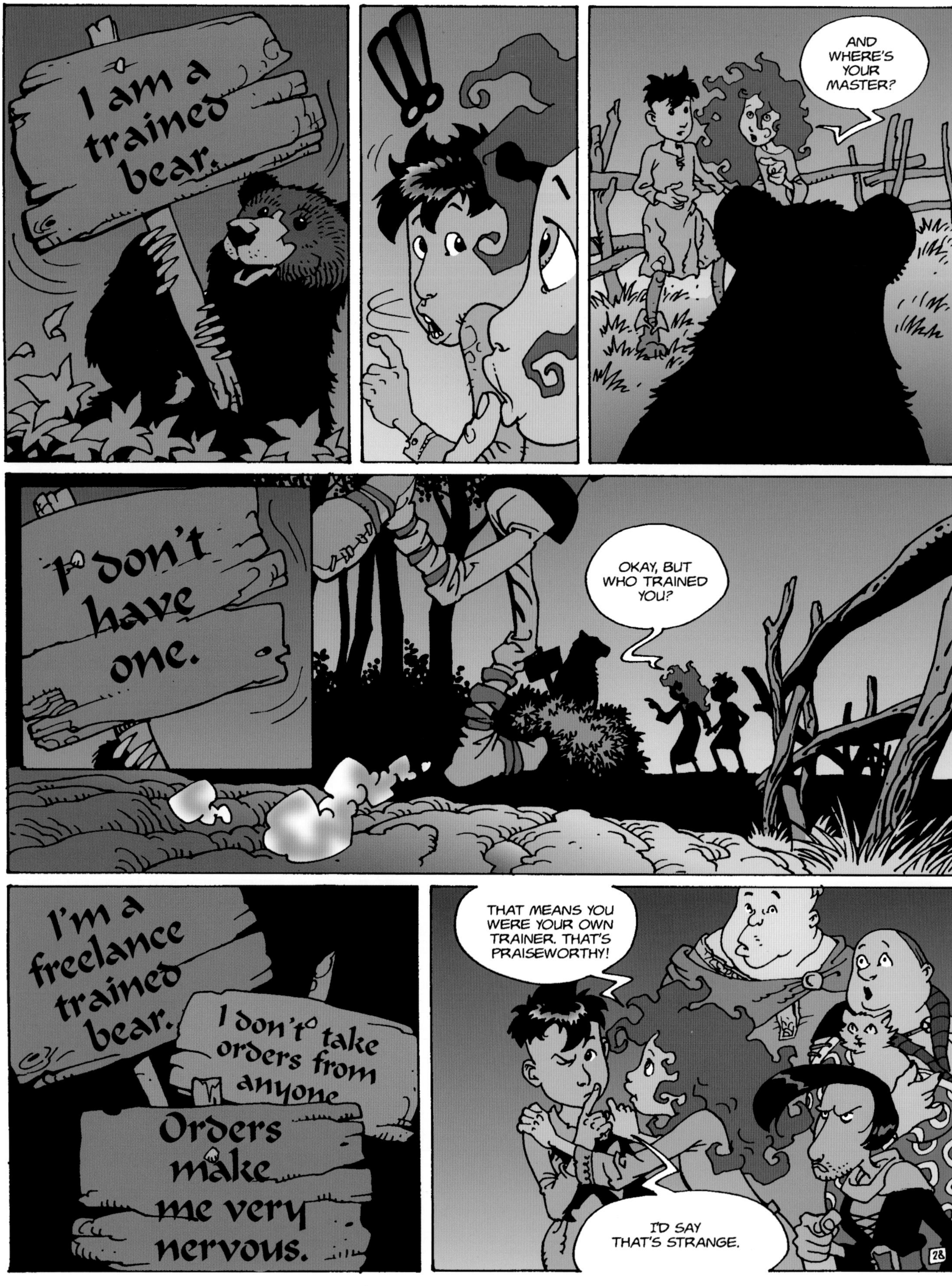
I am a trained bear.
AND WHERE'S YOUR MASTER?
I don't have one.
OKAY, BUT WHO TRAINED YOU?
I'm a freelance trained bear.
I don't take orders from anyone
Orders make me very nervous.
THAT MEANS YOU WERE YOUR OWN TRAINER. THAT'S PRAISEWORTHY!
I'D SAY THAT'S STRANGE.
28

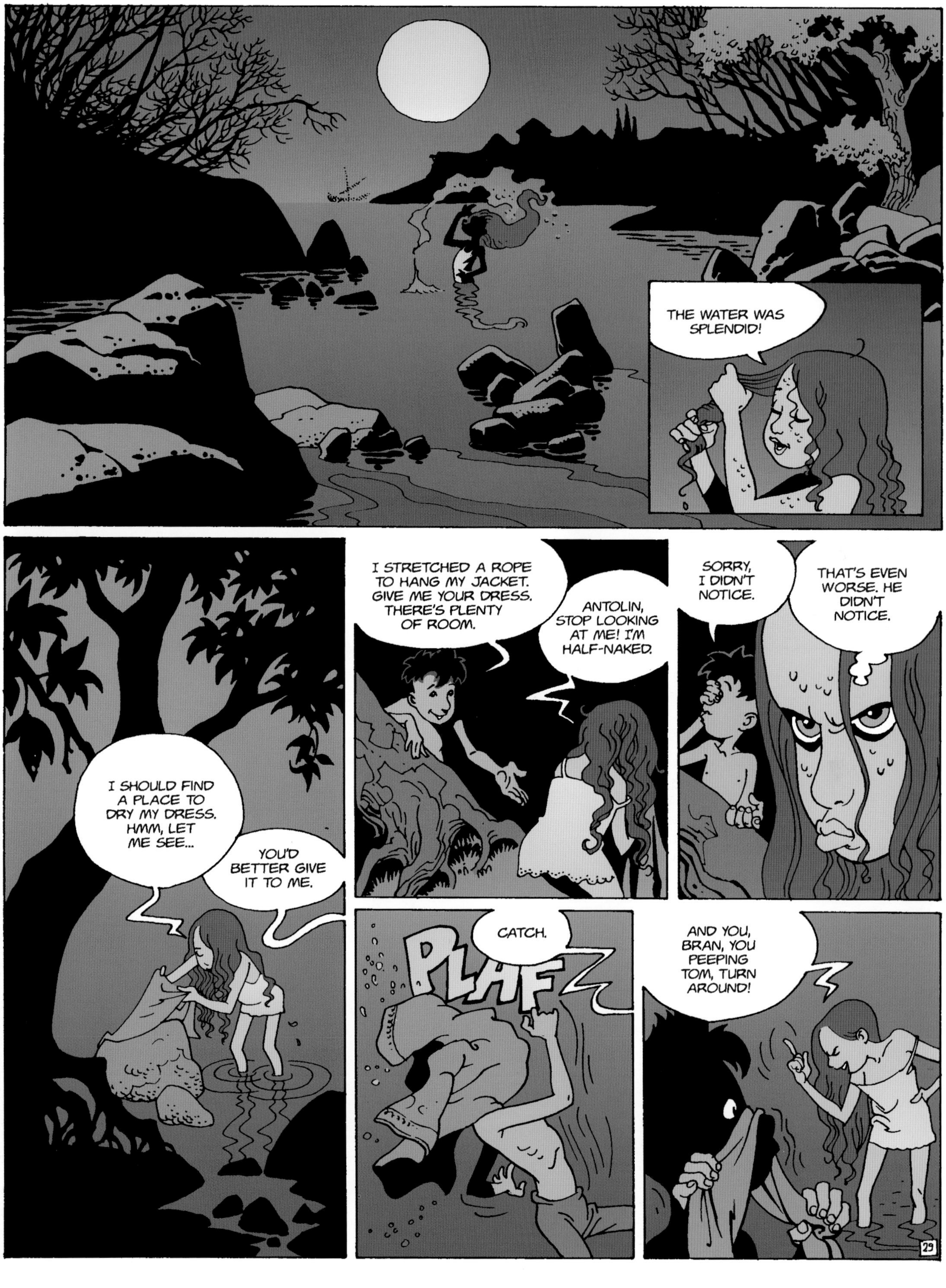
THE WATER WAS SPLENDID!
I SHOULD FIND A PLACE TO DRY MY DRESS. HMM, LET ME SEE...
YOU'D BETTER GIVE IT TO ME.
I STRETCHED A ROPE TO HANG MY JACKET. GIVE ME YOUR DRESS. THERE'S PLENTY OF ROOM.
ANTOLIN, STOP LOOKING AT ME! I'M HALF-NAKED.
SORRY, I DIDN'T NOTICE.
THAT'S EVEN WORSE. HE DIDN'T NOTICE.
CATCH.
PLAF
AND YOU, BRAN, YOU PEEPING TOM, TURN AROUND!
29

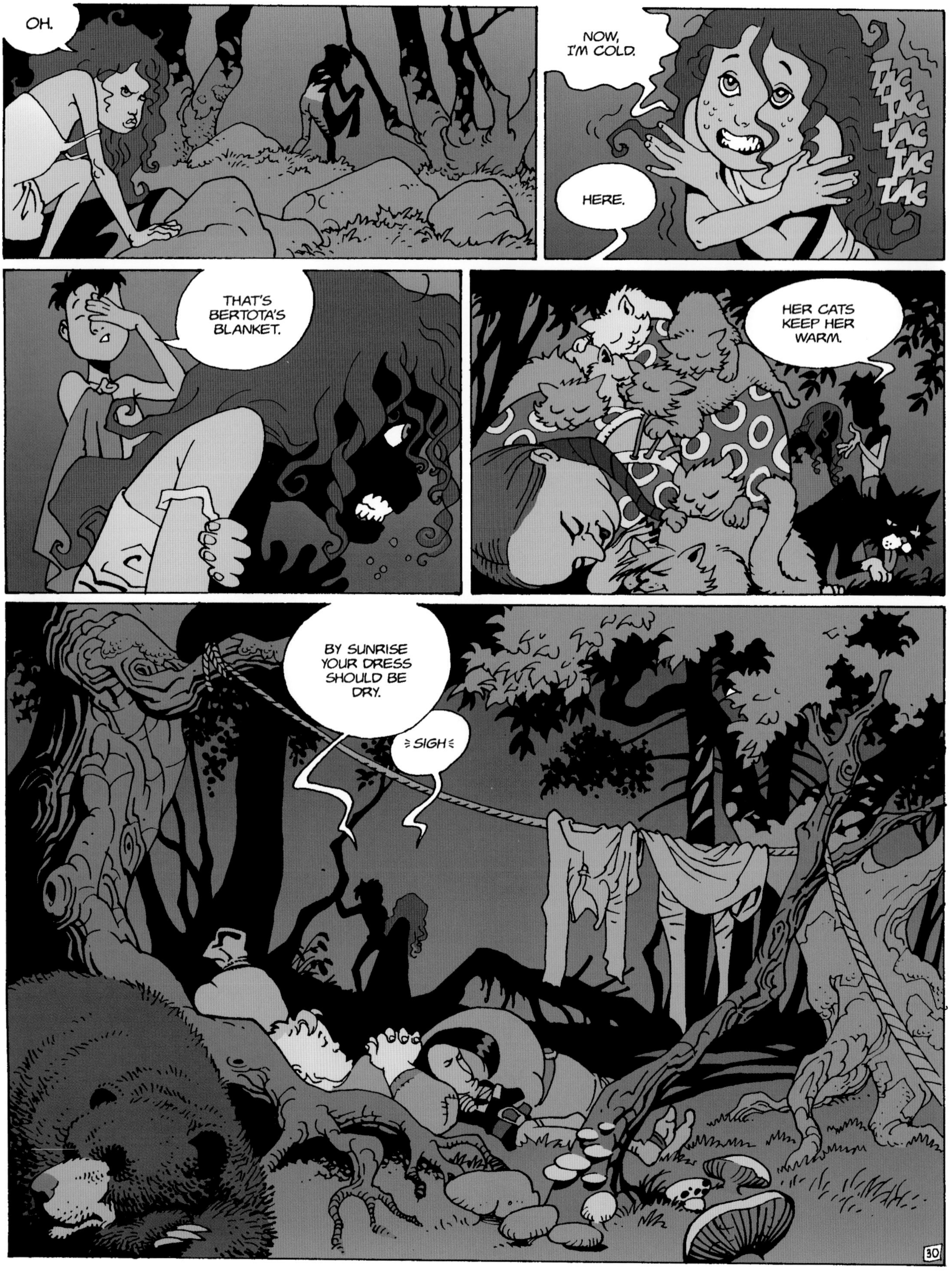
OH.
NOW, I'M COLD.
TAC TAC TAC TAC TAC
HERE.
THAT'S BERTOTA'S BLANKET.
HER CATS KEEP HER WARM.
BY SUNRISE YOUR DRESS SHOULD BE DRY.
SIGH
30

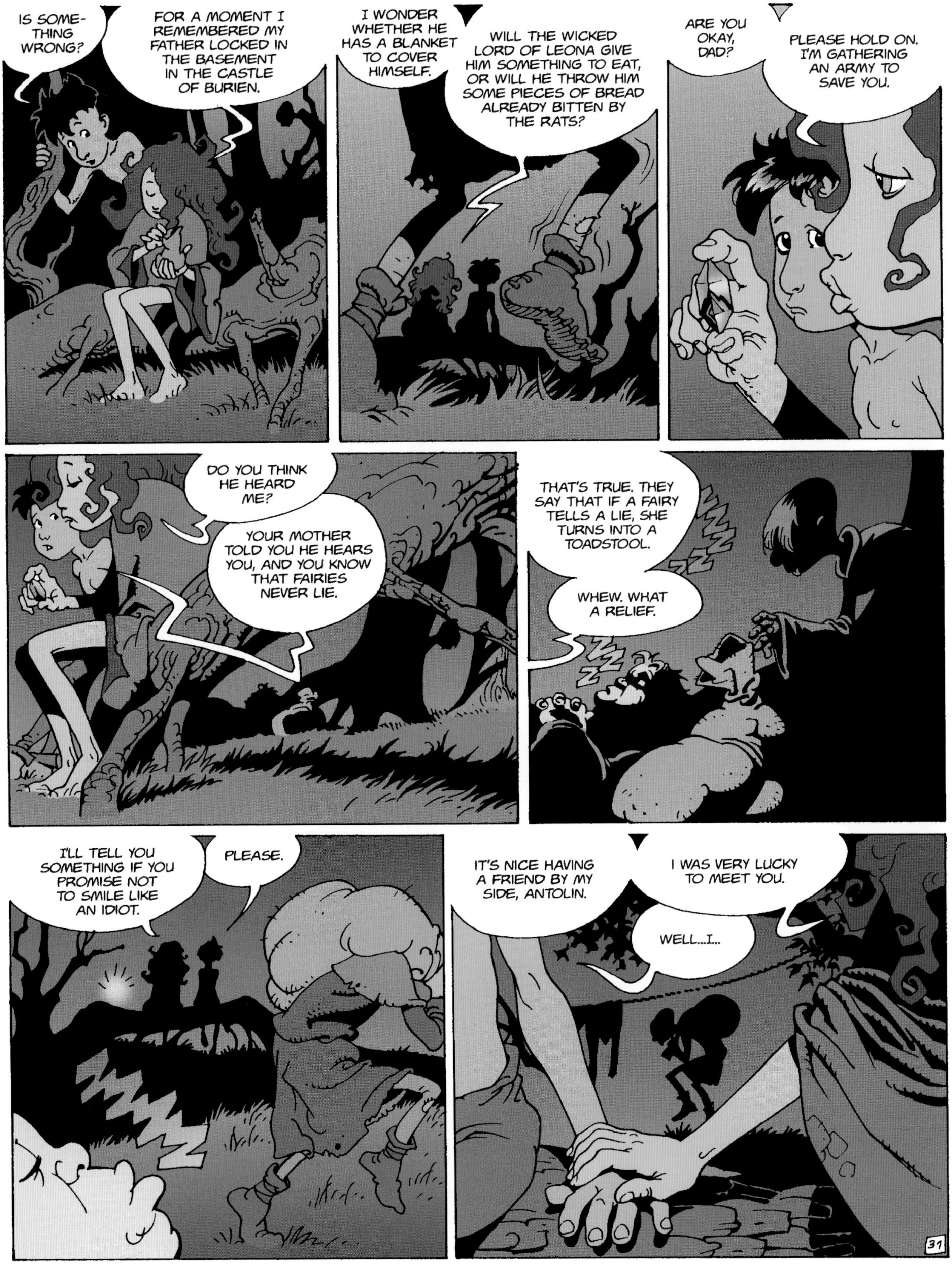
IS SOME-THING WRONG?
FOR A MOMENT I REMEMBERED MY FATHER LOCKED IN THE BASEMENT IN THE CASTLE OF BURIEN.
I WONDER WHETHER HE HAS A BLANKET TO COVER HIMSELF.
WILL THE WICKED LORD OF LEONA GIVE HIM SOMETHING TO EAT, OR WILL HE THROW HIM SOME PIECES OF BREAD ALREADY BITTEN BY THE RATS?
ARE YOU OKAY, DAD?
PLEASE HOLD ON. I'M GATHERING AN ARMY TO SAVE YOU.
DO YOU THINK HE HEARD ME?
YOUR MOTHER TOLD YOU HE HEARS YOU, AND YOU KNOW THAT FAIRIES NEVER LIE.
THAT'S TRUE. THEY SAY THAT IF A FAIRY TELLS A LIE, SHE TURNS INTO A TOADSTOOL.
WHEW. WHAT A RELIEF.
I'LL TELL YOU SOMETHING IF YOU PROMISE NOT TO SMILE LIKE AN IDIOT.
PLEASE.
IT'S NICE HAVING A FRIEND BY MY SIDE, ANTOLIN.
I WAS VERY LUCKY TO MEET YOU.
WELL...I...
31

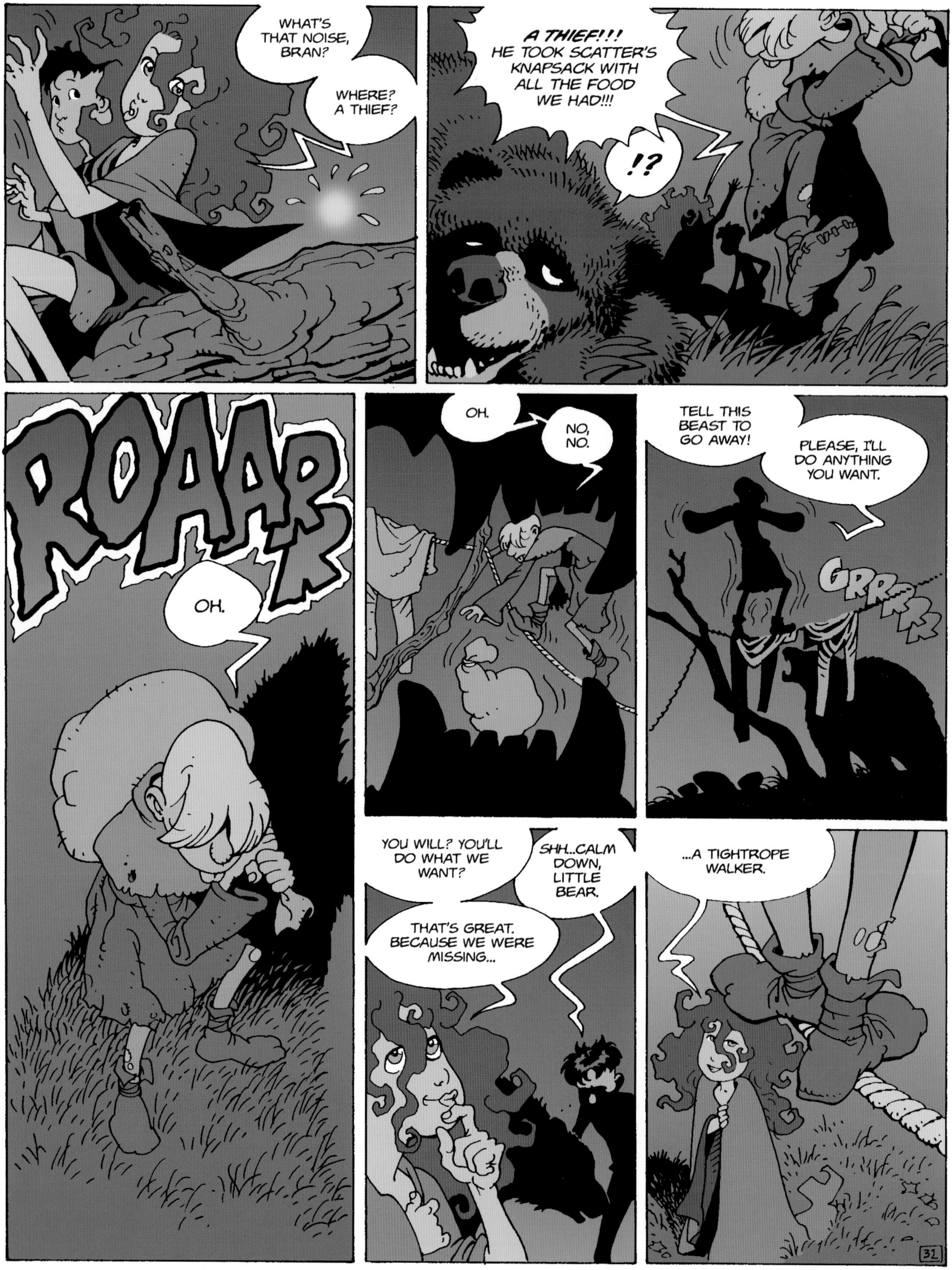
WHAT'S THAT NOISE, BRAN?
WHERE? A THIEF?
A THIEF!!! HE TOOK SCATTER'S KNAPSACK WITH ALL THE FOOD WE HAD!!!
!?
ROAAR
OH.
OH.
NO, NO.
TELL THIS BEAST TO GO AWAY!
PLEASE, I'LL DO ANYTHING YOU WANT.
GRRR
YOU WILL? YOU'LL DO WHAT WE WANT?
SHH...CALM DOWN, LITTLE BEAR.
THAT'S GREAT. BECAUSE WE WERE MISSING...
...A TIGHTROPE WALKER.
32

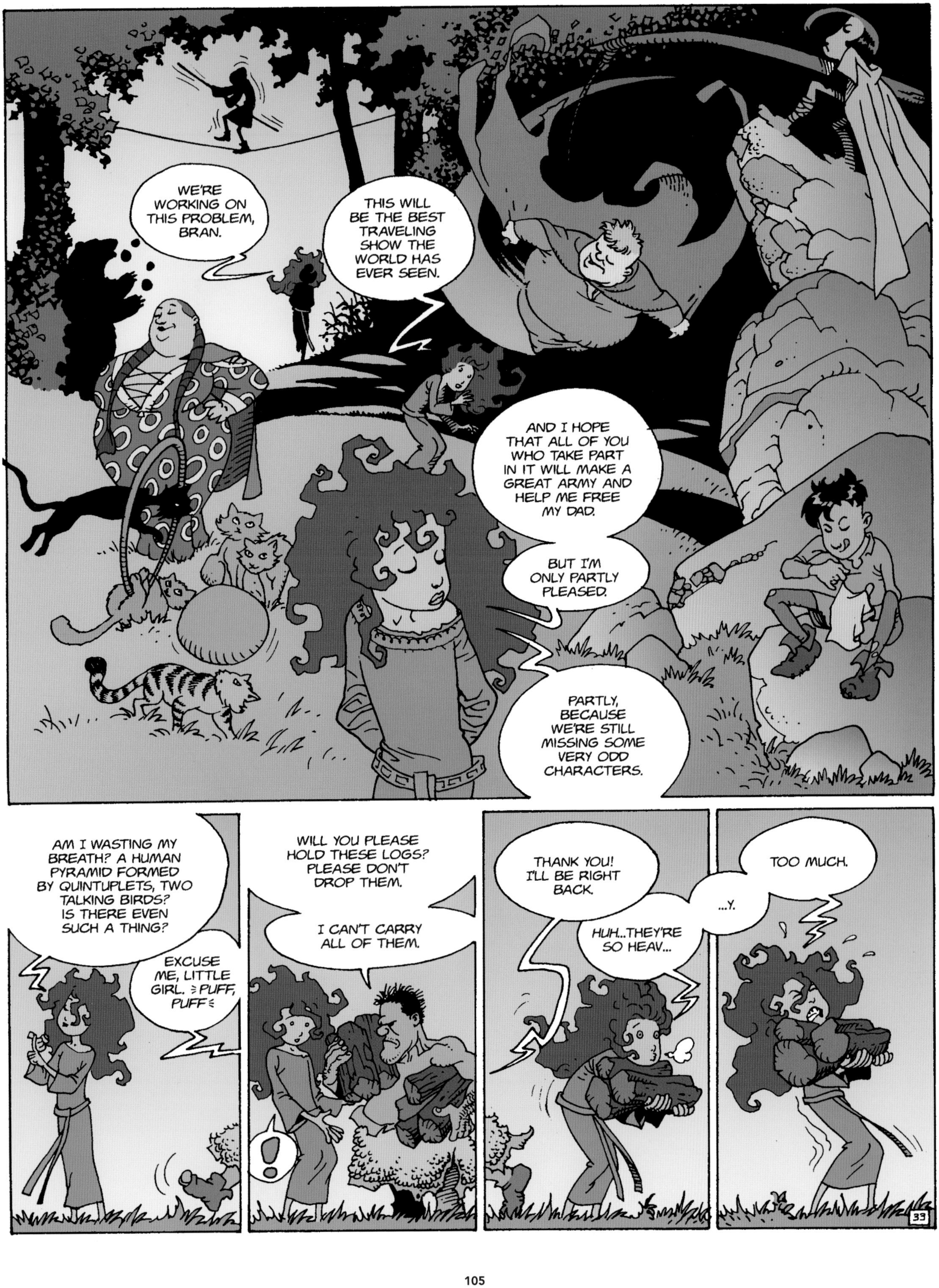

WE'RE WORKING ON THIS PROBLEM, BRAN.
THIS WILL BE THE BEST TRAVELING SHOW THE WORLD HAS EVER SEEN.
AND I HOPE THAT ALL OF YOU WHO TAKE PART IN IT WILL MAKE A GREAT ARMY AND HELP ME FREE MY DAD.
BUT I'M ONLY PARTLY PLEASED.
PARTLY, BECAUSE WE'RE STILL MISSING SOME VERY ODD CHARACTERS.
AM I WASTING MY BREATH? A HUMAN PYRAMID FORMED BY QUINTUPLETS, TWO TALKING BIRDS? IS THERE EVEN SUCH A THING?
EXCUSE ME, LITTLE GIRL. ⋟PUFF, PUFF⋞
WILL YOU PLEASE HOLD THESE LOGS? PLEASE DON'T DROP THEM.
I CAN'T CARRY ALL OF THEM.
THANK YOU! I'LL BE RIGHT BACK.
HUH...THEY'RE SO HEAV...
...Y.
TOO MUCH.
33

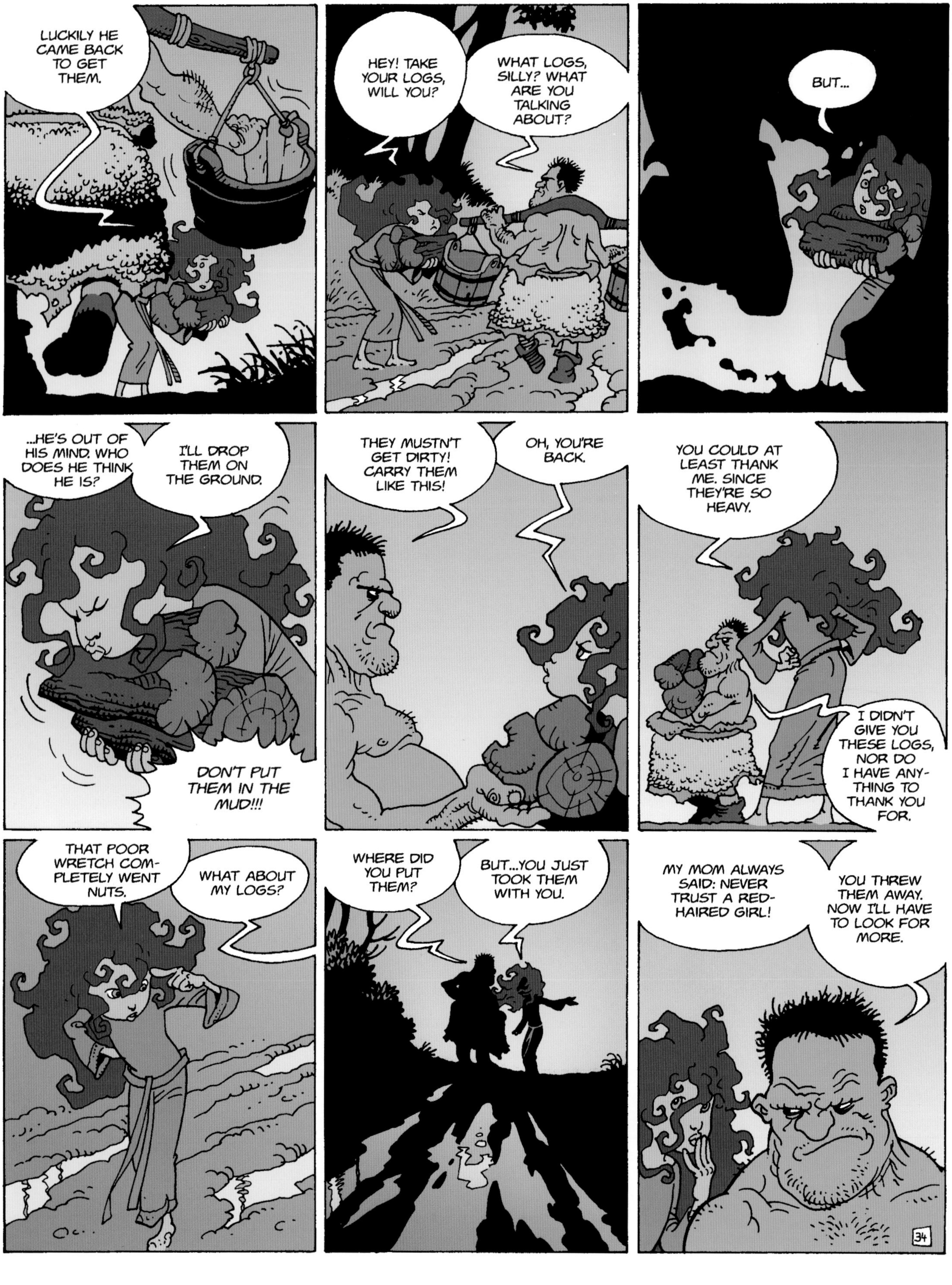
LUCKILY HE CAME BACK TO GET THEM.
HEY! TAKE YOUR LOGS, WILL YOU?
WHAT LOGS, SILLY? WHAT ARE YOU TALKING ABOUT?
BUT...
...HE'S OUT OF HIS MIND. WHO DOES HE THINK HE IS?
I'LL DROP THEM ON THE GROUND.
DON'T PUT THEM IN THE MUD!!!
THEY MUSTN'T GET DIRTY! CARRY THEM LIKE THIS!
OH, YOU'RE BACK.
YOU COULD AT LEAST THANK ME. SINCE THEY'RE SO HEAVY.
I DIDN'T GIVE YOU THESE LOGS, NOR DO I HAVE ANYTHING TO THANK YOU FOR.
THAT POOR WRETCH COMPLETELY WENT NUTS.
WHAT ABOUT MY LOGS?
WHERE DID YOU PUT THEM?
BUT...YOU JUST TOOK THEM WITH YOU.
MY MOM ALWAYS SAID: NEVER TRUST A RED-HAIRED GIRL!
YOU THREW THEM AWAY. NOW I'LL HAVE TO LOOK FOR MORE.
34

TELL ME SOME-THING, BRAN. DON'T YOU FIND THIS GUY STRANGE?

GET OUT OF THE WAY IMMEDIATELY!!!

THERE ARE PEOPLE THAT HAVE NOTHING TO DO EXCEPT SWALLOW FLIES IN THE MIDDLE OF THE ROAD.

YOU'RE RIGHT. IT MUST BE THAT.

BUT HE'S NOT THE ONLY LUNATIC. THERE ARE TWO.

...OR THREE.

HOP!

UP!

GIVE ME THIS LOG!

AND PASS ME MORE STRAW!

WE'D BETTER GO THERE AND SEE WHAT IS GOING ON.

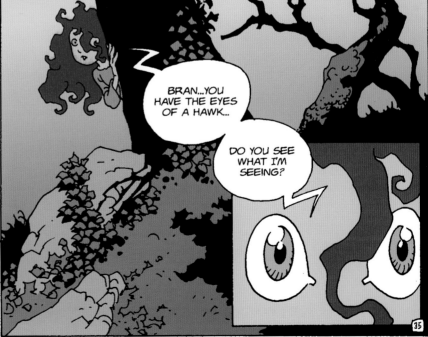

BRAN...YOU HAVE THE EYES OF A HAWK...

DO YOU SEE WHAT I'M SEEING?

I BELIEVE IT IS.

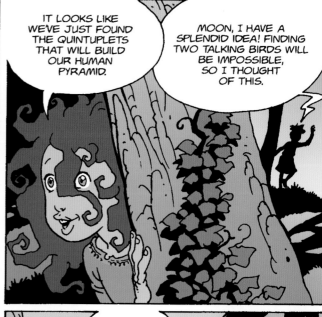

IT LOOKS LIKE WE'VE JUST FOUND THE QUINTUPLETS THAT WILL BUILD OUR HUMAN PYRAMID.

MOON, I HAVE A SPLENDID IDEA! FINDING TWO TALKING BIRDS WILL BE IMPOSSIBLE, SO I THOUGHT OF THIS.

HELLO, STUPID CANARY.

YOUR GRANDMA'S STUPID!

DON'T YOU THINK IT'S A BRILLIANT IDEA?

I FIND IT RATHER SAD. WHAT ABOUT YOU, MR. PEPOSIO?

I ABSOLUTELY AGREE, GRAND MASTER RUPERTO.

≷GULP≷

≷GULP≷

≷GULP≷

OH, THE WATER IS SO GOOD!

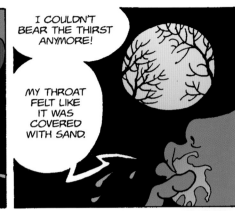

I COULDN'T BEAR THE THIRST ANYMORE!

MY THROAT FELT LIKE IT WAS COVERED WITH SAND.

BECAUSE YOU WERE SO SCARED.

BUT I ALREADY TOLD YOU THIS COULDN'T TURN OUT BADLY.

FORTUNATELY YOU INSISTED.

"COME ON, MOON, BEFORE WE MOVE ON, WE'LL DO A REHEARSAL IN FRONT OF AN AUDIENCE, RIGHT HERE, ON THE BORDER."

UNTIL I ACCEPTED IN THE END.

AND IT WAS A HUGE SUCCESS!

OF COURSE, YOU INTRODUCED THE PERFORMERS SO WELL.

MAY WE BEGIN, LADIES AND GENTLEMEN, WITH OUR SPECTACULAR SHOW...

I PRESENT YOU FRASTRAFRASIO, THE STRONGEST MAN IN THE WORLD!!!

HIM? LOOK AT HIM! FRASTRONFLO... SOMETHING. HIS NAME IS BIGGER THAN HIS MUSCLES, POOR WRETCH.

LET'S SEE IF THE MASTER OF THE CHARIOT WILL ASK FOR FORGIVENESS...

...FOR WHAT HE JUST SAID.

AAAH, MOM...

MOO?

37

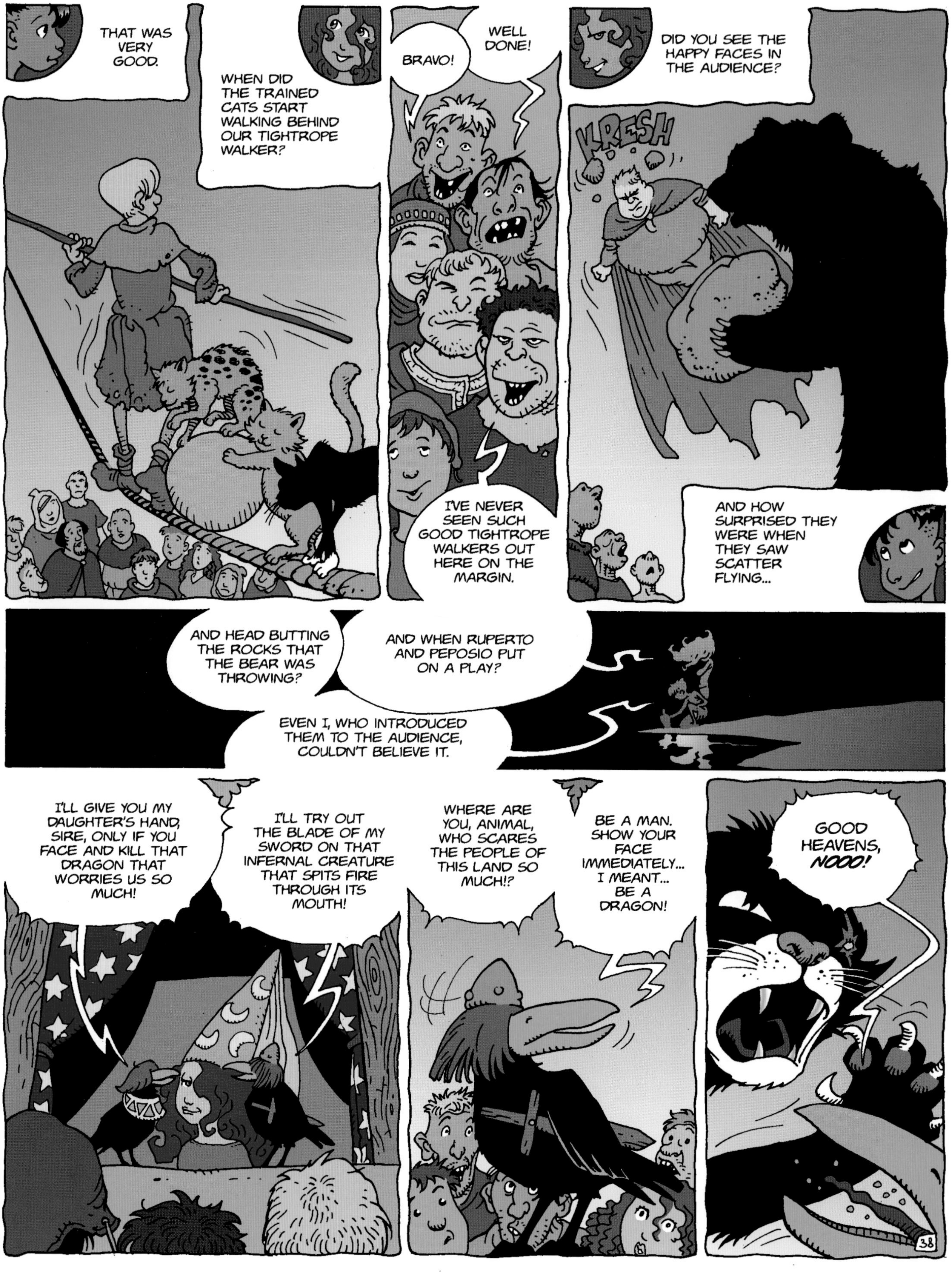
THAT WAS VERY GOOD.
WHEN DID THE TRAINED CATS START WALKING BEHIND OUR TIGHTROPE WALKER?
BRAVO!
WELL DONE!
I'VE NEVER SEEN SUCH GOOD TIGHTROPE WALKERS OUT HERE ON THE MARGIN.
DID YOU SEE THE HAPPY FACES IN THE AUDIENCE?
KRESH
AND HOW SURPRISED THEY WERE WHEN THEY SAW SCATTER FLYING...
AND HEAD BUTTING THE ROCKS THAT THE BEAR WAS THROWING?
AND WHEN RUPERTO AND PEPOSIO PUT ON A PLAY?
EVEN I, WHO INTRODUCED THEM TO THE AUDIENCE, COULDN'T BELIEVE IT.
I'LL GIVE YOU MY DAUGHTER'S HAND, SIRE, ONLY IF YOU FACE AND KILL THAT DRAGON THAT WORRIES US SO MUCH!
I'LL TRY OUT THE BLADE OF MY SWORD ON THAT INFERNAL CREATURE THAT SPITS FIRE THROUGH ITS MOUTH!
WHERE ARE YOU, ANIMAL, WHO SCARES THE PEOPLE OF THIS LAND SO MUCH!?
BE A MAN. SHOW YOUR FACE IMMEDIATELY... I MEANT... BE A DRAGON!
GOOD HEAVENS, NOOO!
38

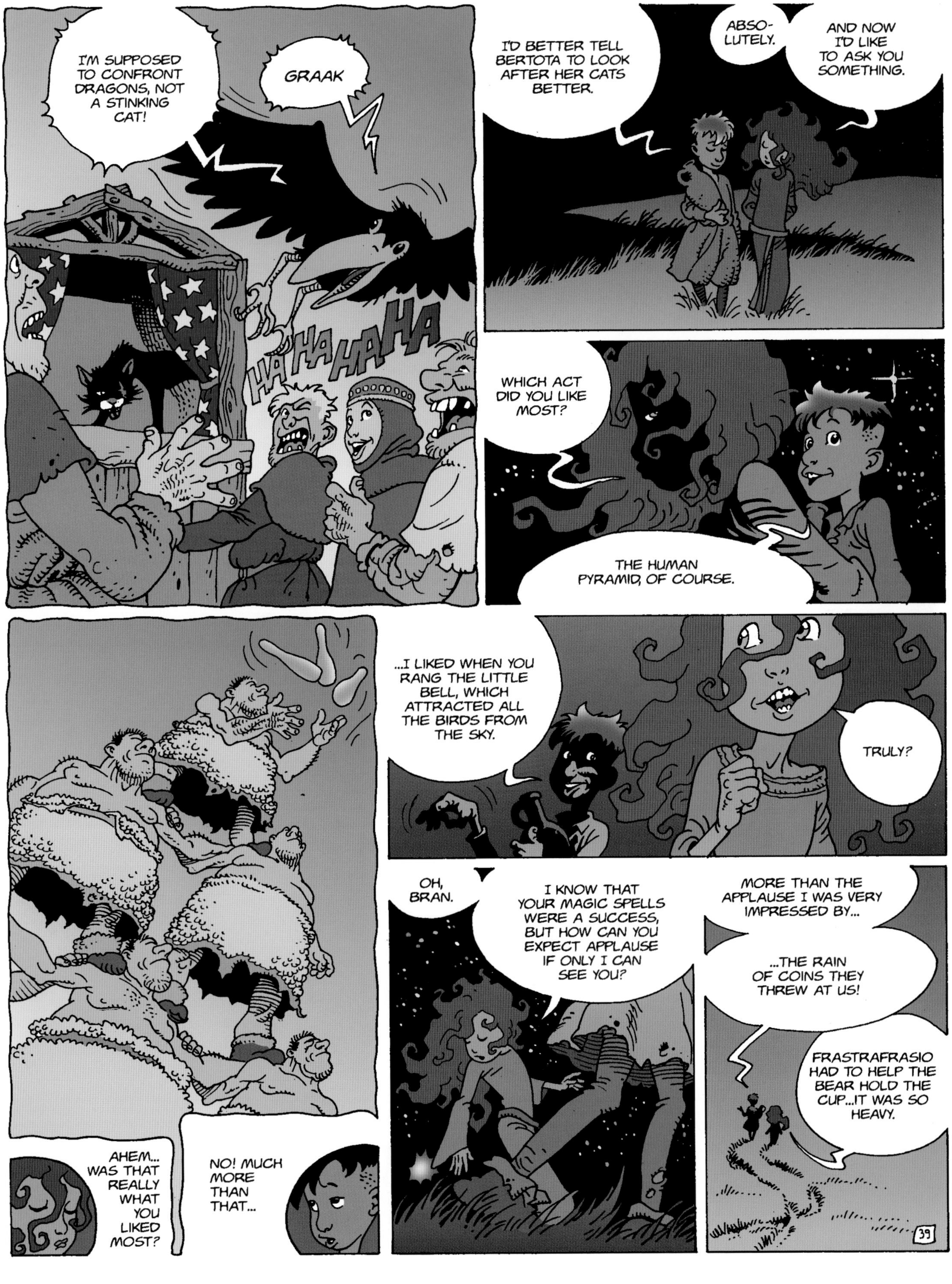
I'M SUPPOSED TO CONFRONT DRAGONS, NOT A STINKING CAT!
GRAAK
HA HA HA HA
I'D BETTER TELL BERTOTA TO LOOK AFTER HER CATS BETTER.
ABSO-LUTELY.
AND NOW I'D LIKE TO ASK YOU SOMETHING.
WHICH ACT DID YOU LIKE MOST?
THE HUMAN PYRAMID, OF COURSE.
AHEM... WAS THAT REALLY WHAT YOU LIKED MOST?
NO! MUCH MORE THAN THAT...
...I LIKED WHEN YOU RANG THE LITTLE BELL, WHICH ATTRACTED ALL THE BIRDS FROM THE SKY.
TRULY?
OH, BRAN.
I KNOW THAT YOUR MAGIC SPELLS WERE A SUCCESS, BUT HOW CAN YOU EXPECT APPLAUSE IF ONLY I CAN SEE YOU?
MORE THAN THE APPLAUSE I WAS VERY IMPRESSED BY...
...THE RAIN OF COINS THEY THREW AT US!
FRASTRAFRASIO HAD TO HELP THE BEAR HOLD THE CUP...IT WAS SO HEAVY.
39

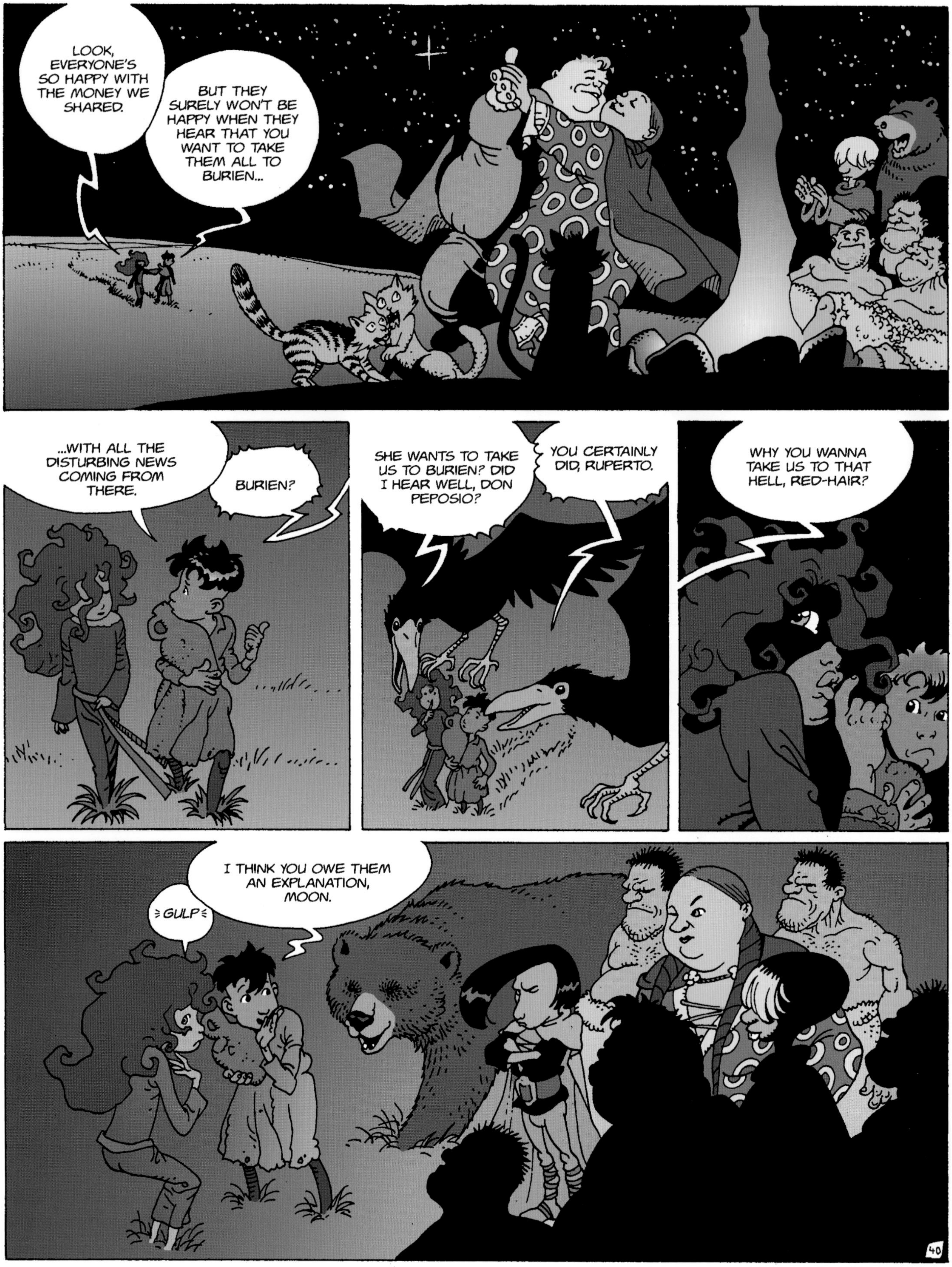
LOOK, EVERYONE'S SO HAPPY WITH THE MONEY WE SHARED.
BUT THEY SURELY WON'T BE HAPPY WHEN THEY HEAR THAT YOU WANT TO TAKE THEM ALL TO BURIEN...
...WITH ALL THE DISTURBING NEWS COMING FROM THERE.
BURIEN?
SHE WANTS TO TAKE US TO BURIEN? DID I HEAR WELL, DON PEPOSIO?
YOU CERTAINLY DID, RUPERTO.
WHY YOU WANNA TAKE US TO THAT HELL, RED-HAIR?
GULP
I THINK YOU OWE THEM AN EXPLANATION, MOON.
40

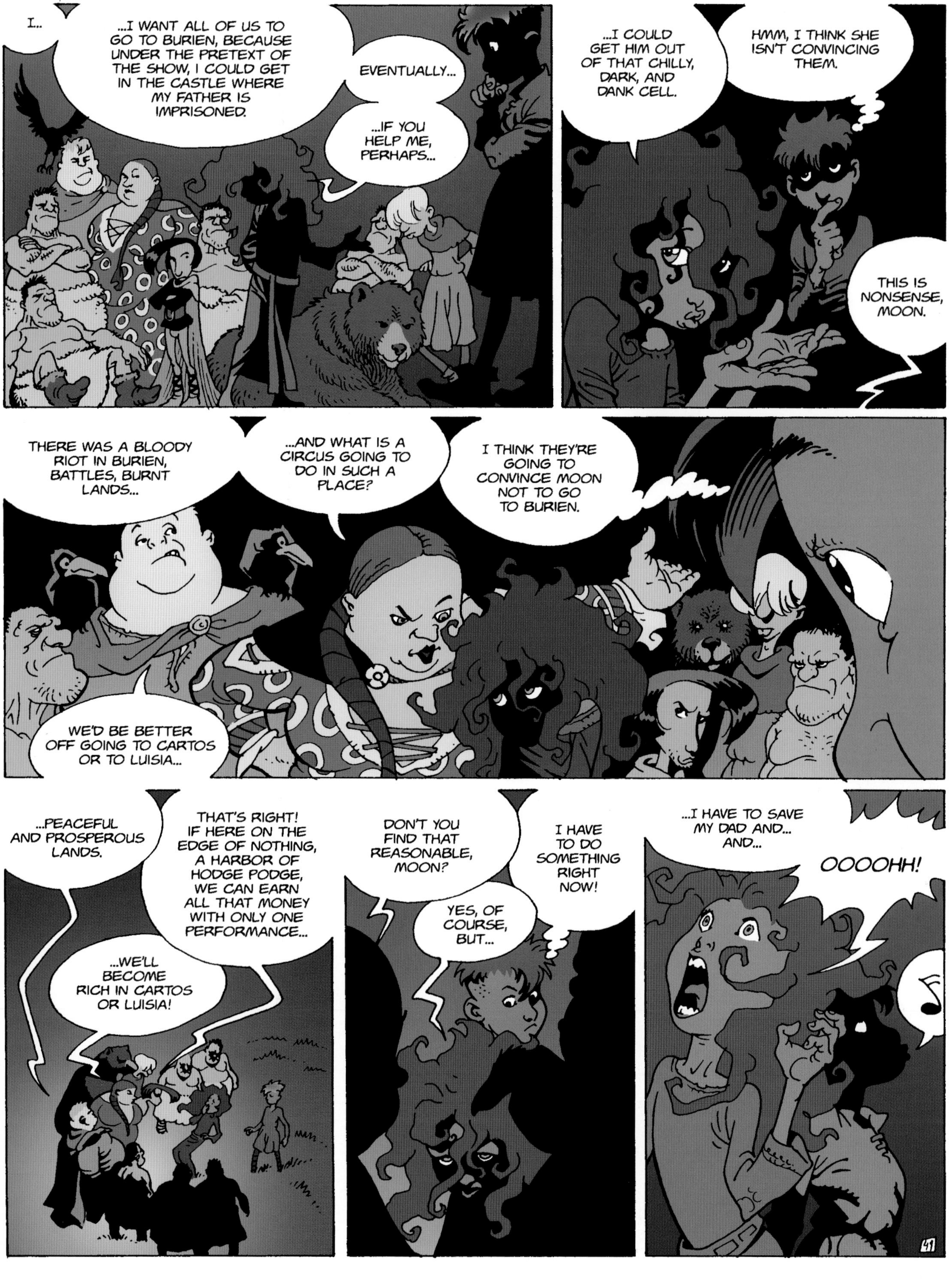

I...
...I WANT ALL OF US TO GO TO BURIEN, BECAUSE UNDER THE PRETEXT OF THE SHOW, I COULD GET IN THE CASTLE WHERE MY FATHER IS IMPRISONED.
EVENTUALLY...
...IF YOU HELP ME, PERHAPS...
...I COULD GET HIM OUT OF THAT CHILLY, DARK, AND DANK CELL.
HMM, I THINK SHE ISN'T CONVINCING THEM.
THIS IS NONSENSE, MOON.
THERE WAS A BLOODY RIOT IN BURIEN, BATTLES, BURNT LANDS...
...AND WHAT IS A CIRCUS GOING TO DO IN SUCH A PLACE?
I THINK THEY'RE GOING TO CONVINCE MOON NOT TO GO TO BURIEN.
WE'D BE BETTER OFF GOING TO CARTOS OR TO LUISIA...
...PEACEFUL AND PROSPEROUS LANDS.
THAT'S RIGHT! IF HERE ON THE EDGE OF NOTHING, A HARBOR OF HODGE PODGE, WE CAN EARN ALL THAT MONEY WITH ONLY ONE PERFORMANCE...
...WE'LL BECOME RICH IN CARTOS OR LUISIA!
DON'T YOU FIND THAT REASONABLE, MOON?
YES, OF COURSE, BUT...
I HAVE TO DO SOMETHING RIGHT NOW!
...I HAVE TO SAVE MY DAD AND... AND...
OOOOHH!
41

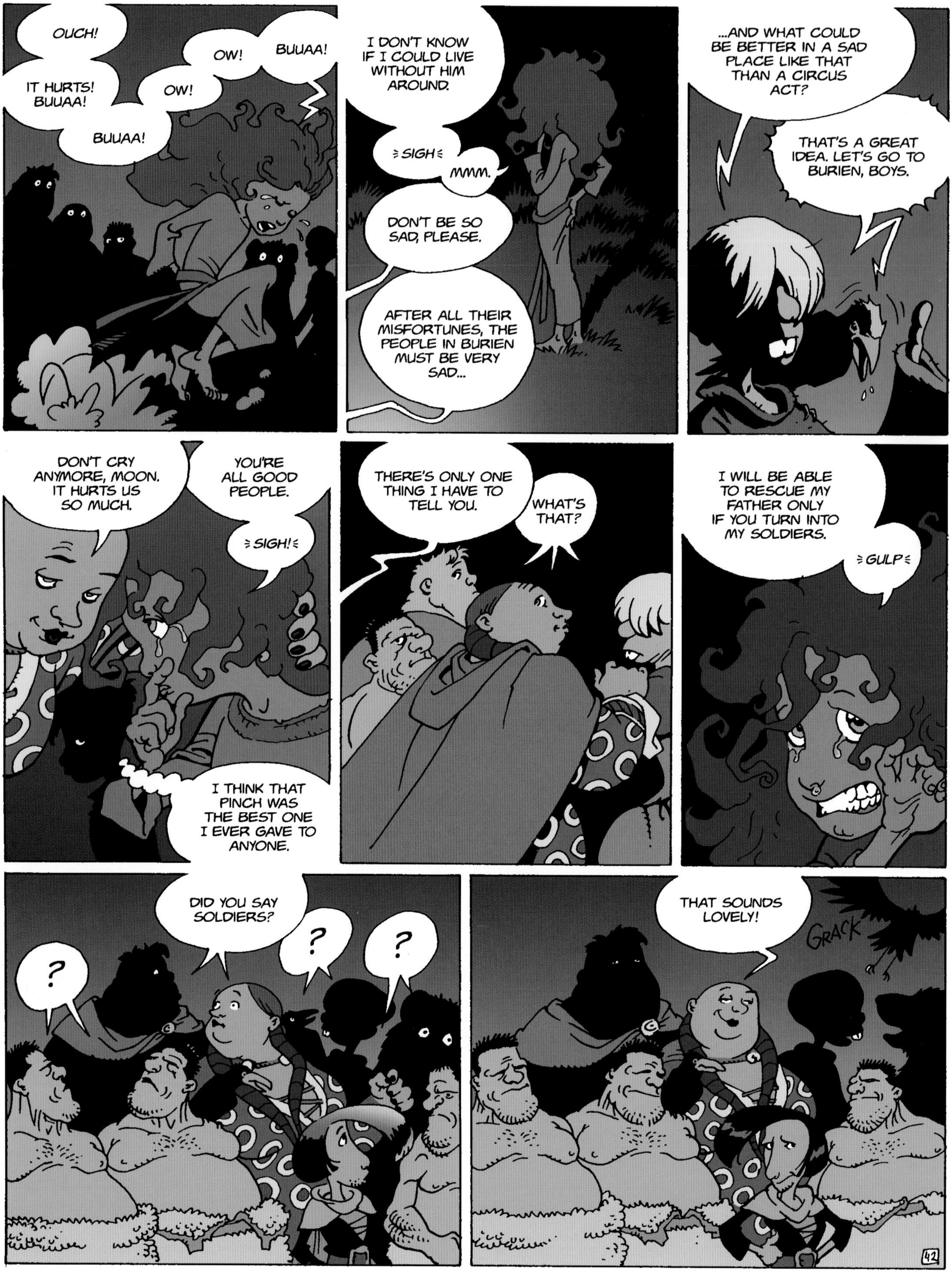
OUCH!
IT HURTS! BUUAA!
BUUAA!
OW!
OW!
BUUAA!
I DON'T KNOW IF I COULD LIVE WITHOUT HIM AROUND.
SIGH
MMM.
DON'T BE SO SAD, PLEASE.
AFTER ALL THEIR MISFORTUNES, THE PEOPLE IN BURIEN MUST BE VERY SAD...
...AND WHAT COULD BE BETTER IN A SAD PLACE LIKE THAT THAN A CIRCUS ACT?
THAT'S A GREAT IDEA. LET'S GO TO BURIEN, BOYS.
DON'T CRY ANYMORE, MOON. IT HURTS US SO MUCH.
YOU'RE ALL GOOD PEOPLE.
SIGH!
I THINK THAT PINCH WAS THE BEST ONE I EVER GAVE TO ANYONE.
THERE'S ONLY ONE THING I HAVE TO TELL YOU.
WHAT'S THAT?
I WILL BE ABLE TO RESCUE MY FATHER ONLY IF YOU TURN INTO MY SOLDIERS.
GULP
?
DID YOU SAY SOLDIERS?
?
?
THAT SOUNDS LOVELY!
GRACK
42

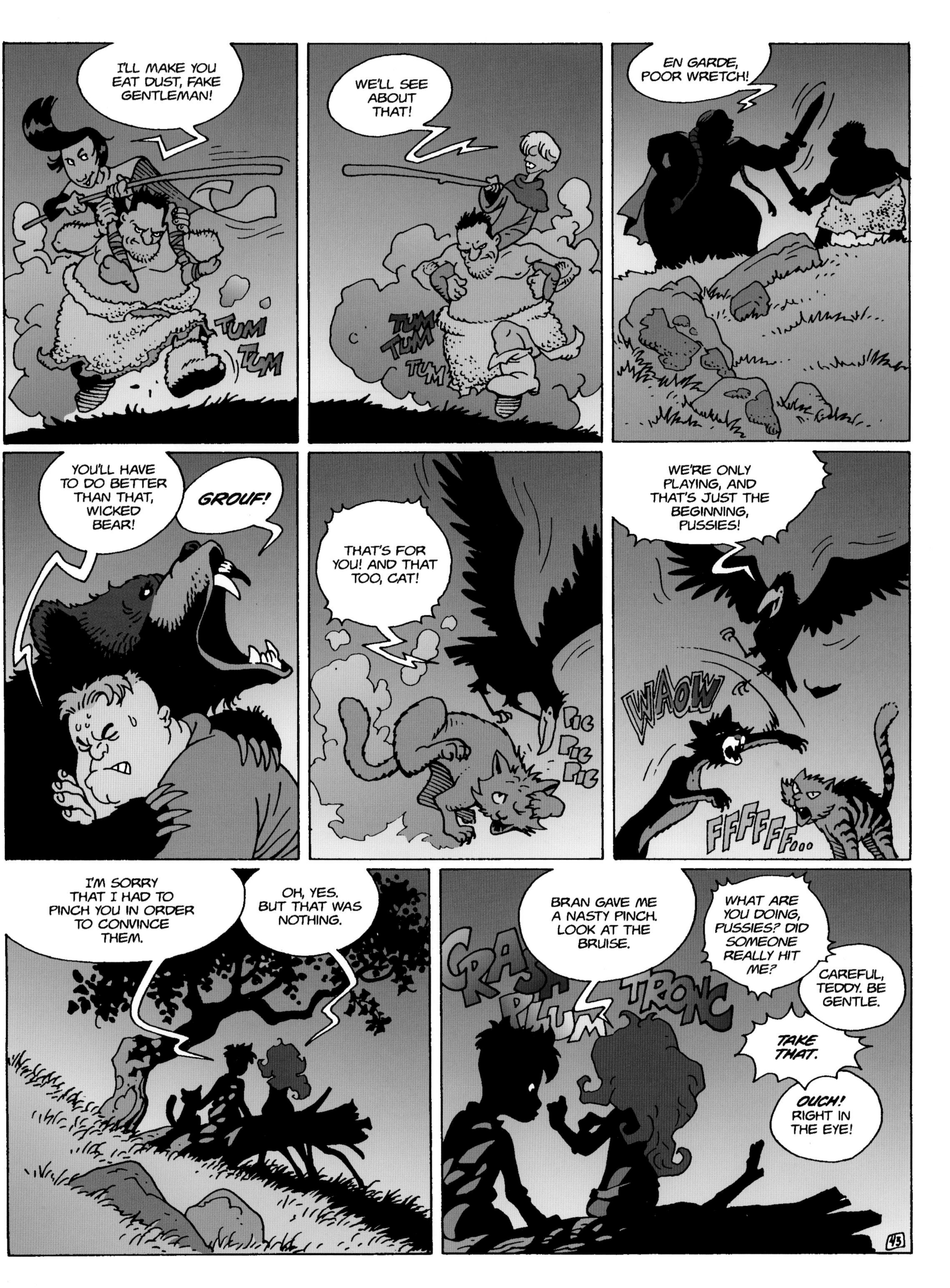
I'LL MAKE YOU EAT DUST, FAKE GENTLEMAN!
TUM TUM
WE'LL SEE ABOUT THAT!
TUM TUM TUM
EN GARDE, POOR WRETCH!
YOU'LL HAVE TO DO BETTER THAN THAT, WICKED BEAR!
GROUF!
THAT'S FOR YOU! AND THAT TOO, CAT!
PIC PIC PIC
WE'RE ONLY PLAYING, AND THAT'S JUST THE BEGINNING, PUSSIES!
WAOW
FFFFFFFooo
I'M SORRY THAT I HAD TO PINCH YOU IN ORDER TO CONVINCE THEM.
OH, YES. BUT THAT WAS NOTHING.
CRASH
BRAN GAVE ME A NASTY PINCH. LOOK AT THE BRUISE.
WHAT ARE YOU DOING, PUSSIES? DID SOMEONE REALLY HIT ME?
PLUM
TRONC
CAREFUL, TEDDY. BE GENTLE.
TAKE THAT.
OUCH! RIGHT IN THE EYE!
43

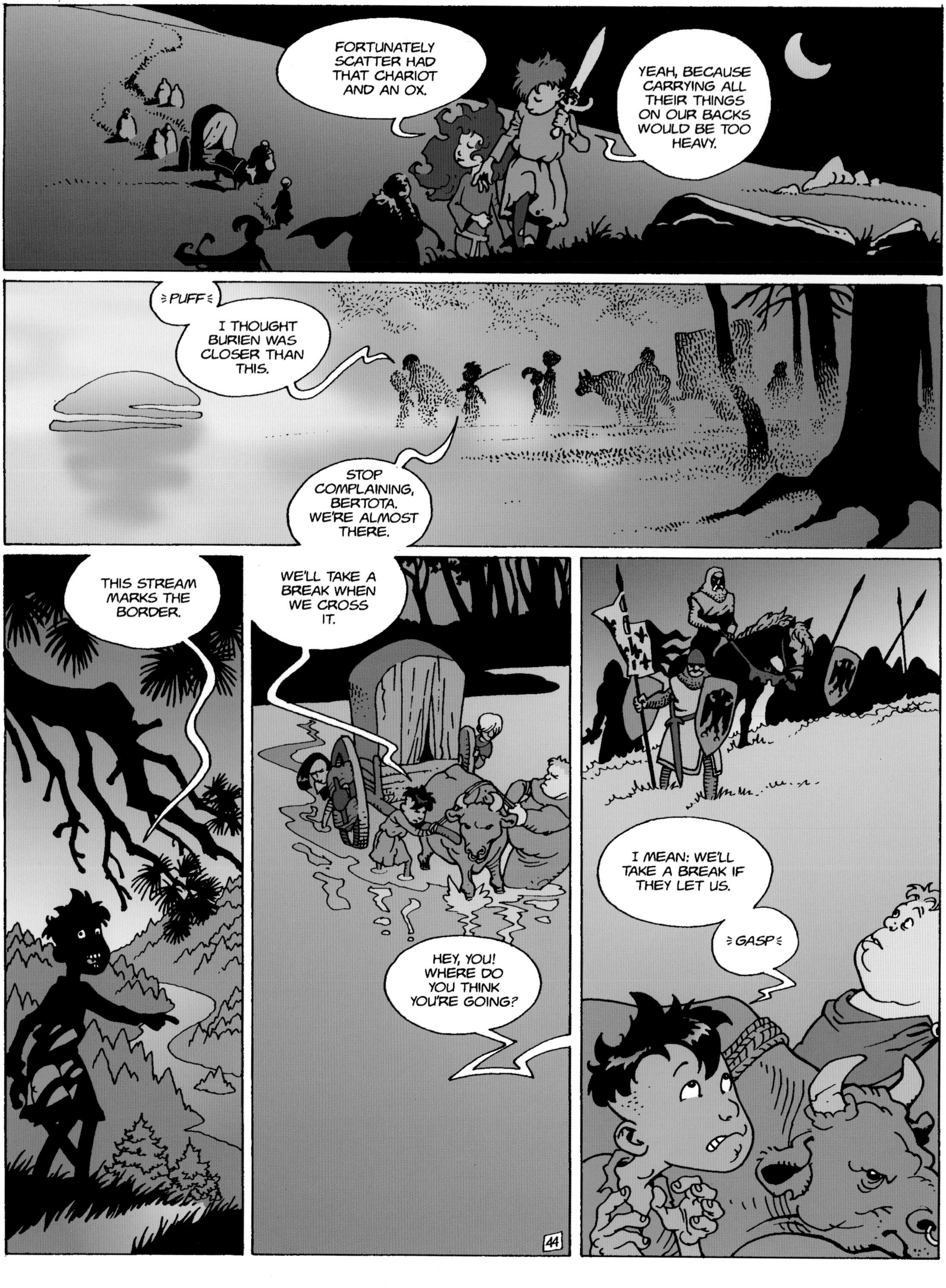
FORTUNATELY SCATTER HAD THAT CHARIOT AND AN OX.
YEAH, BECAUSE CARRYING ALL THEIR THINGS ON OUR BACKS WOULD BE TOO HEAVY.
PUFF
I THOUGHT BURIEN WAS CLOSER THAN THIS.
STOP COMPLAINING, BERTOTA. WE'RE ALMOST THERE.
THIS STREAM MARKS THE BORDER.
WE'LL TAKE A BREAK WHEN WE CROSS IT.
HEY, YOU! WHERE DO YOU THINK YOU'RE GOING?
44
I MEAN: WE'LL TAKE A BREAK IF THEY LET US.
GASP

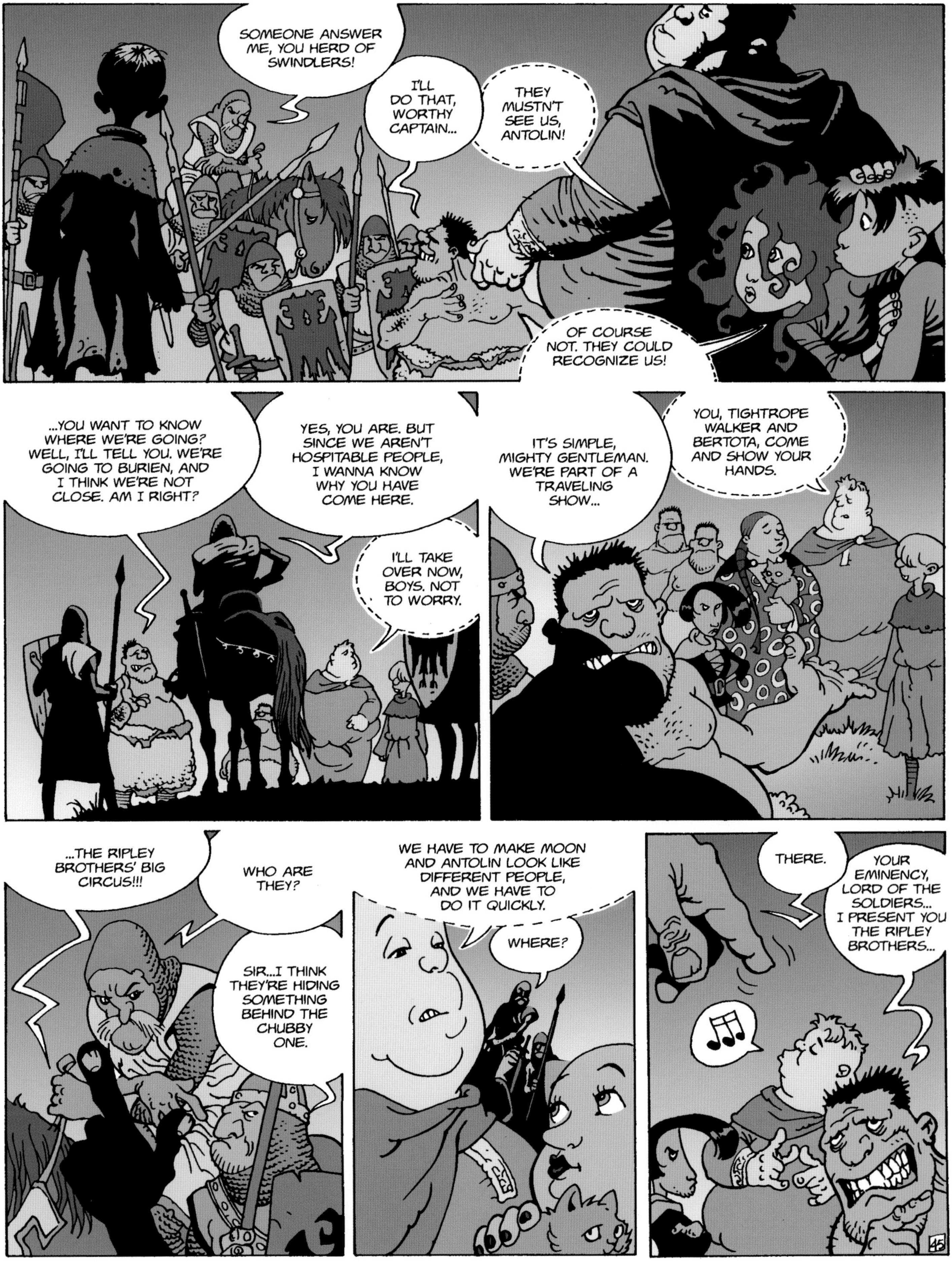

SOMEONE ANSWER ME, YOU HERD OF SWINDLERS!
I'LL DO THAT, WORTHY CAPTAIN...
THEY MUSTN'T SEE US, ANTOLIN!
OF COURSE NOT. THEY COULD RECOGNIZE US!
...YOU WANT TO KNOW WHERE WE'RE GOING? WELL, I'LL TELL YOU. WE'RE GOING TO BURIEN, AND I THINK WE'RE NOT CLOSE. AM I RIGHT?
YES, YOU ARE. BUT SINCE WE AREN'T HOSPITABLE PEOPLE, I WANNA KNOW WHY YOU HAVE COME HERE.
I'LL TAKE OVER NOW, BOYS. NOT TO WORRY.
IT'S SIMPLE, MIGHTY GENTLEMAN. WE'RE PART OF A TRAVELING SHOW...
YOU, TIGHTROPE WALKER AND BERTOTA, COME AND SHOW YOUR HANDS.
...THE RIPLEY BROTHERS' BIG CIRCUS!!!
WHO ARE THEY?
SIR...I THINK THEY'RE HIDING SOMETHING BEHIND THE CHUBBY ONE.
WE HAVE TO MAKE MOON AND ANTOLIN LOOK LIKE DIFFERENT PEOPLE, AND WE HAVE TO DO IT QUICKLY.
WHERE?
THERE.
YOUR EMINENCY, LORD OF THE SOLDIERS... I PRESENT YOU THE RIPLEY BROTHERS...
45

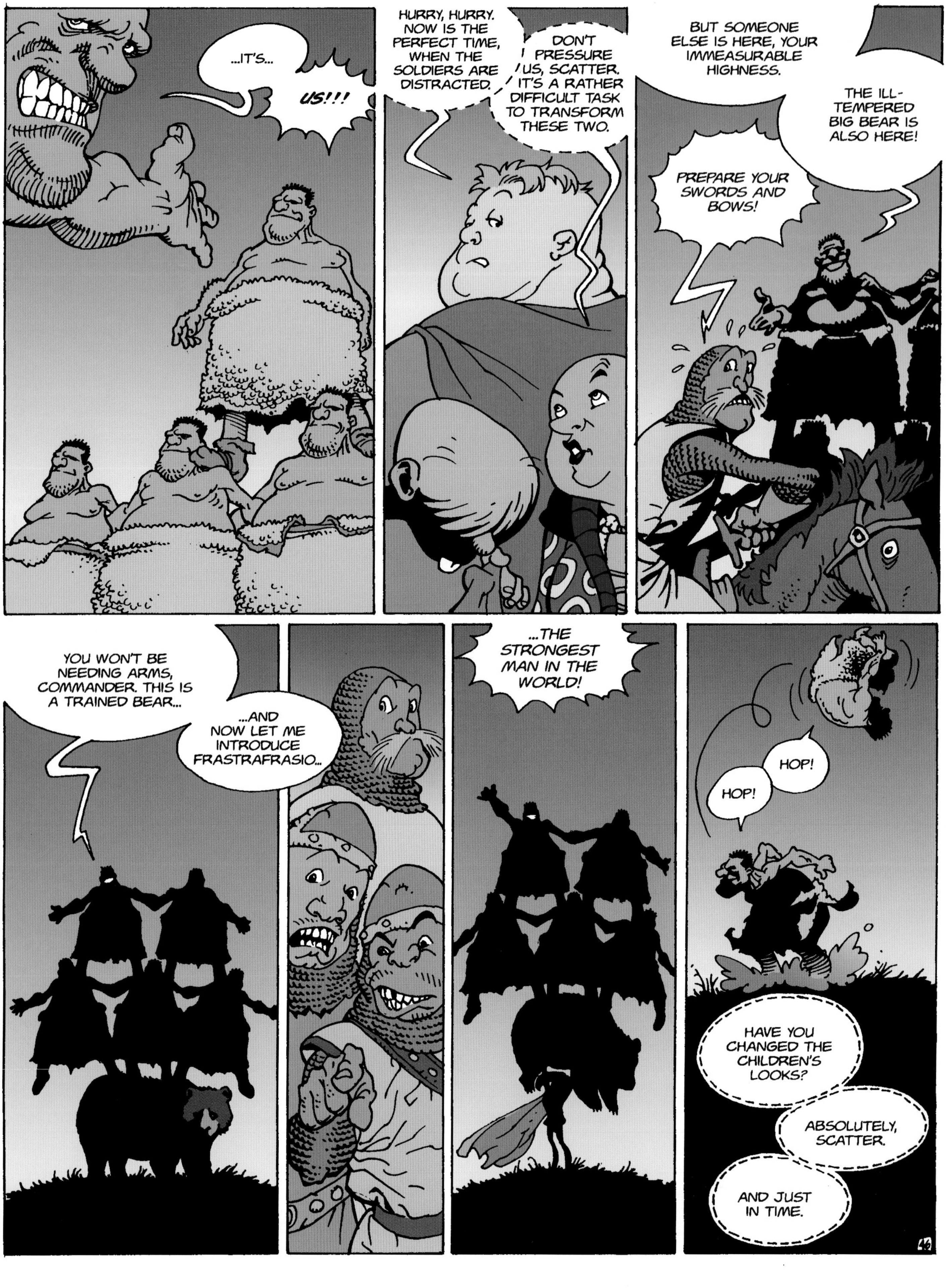

...IT'S...
US!!!
HURRY, HURRY. NOW IS THE PERFECT TIME, WHEN THE SOLDIERS ARE DISTRACTED.
DON'T PRESSURE US, SCATTER. IT'S A RATHER DIFFICULT TASK TO TRANSFORM THESE TWO.
BUT SOMEONE ELSE IS HERE, YOUR IMMEASURABLE HIGHNESS.
THE ILL-TEMPERED BIG BEAR IS ALSO HERE!
PREPARE YOUR SWORDS AND BOWS!
YOU WON'T BE NEEDING ARMS, COMMANDER. THIS IS A TRAINED BEAR...
...AND NOW LET ME INTRODUCE FRASTRAFRASIO...
...THE STRONGEST MAN IN THE WORLD!
HOP!
HOP!
HAVE YOU CHANGED THE CHILDREN'S LOOKS?
ABSOLUTELY, SCATTER.
AND JUST IN TIME.
46

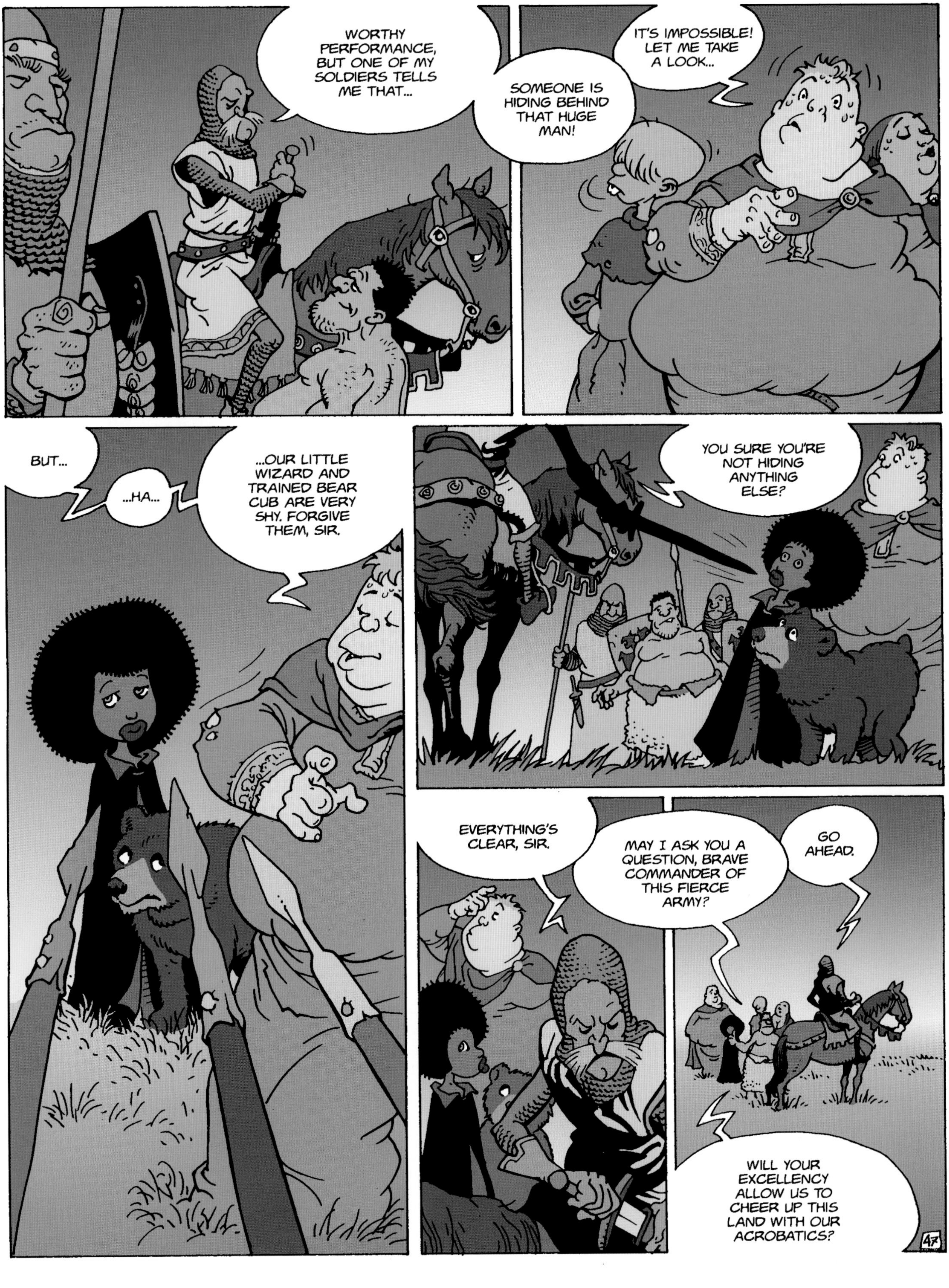
WORTHY PERFORMANCE, BUT ONE OF MY SOLDIERS TELLS ME THAT...
SOMEONE IS HIDING BEHIND THAT HUGE MAN!
IT'S IMPOSSIBLE! LET ME TAKE A LOOK...
BUT...
...HA...
...OUR LITTLE WIZARD AND TRAINED BEAR CUB ARE VERY SHY. FORGIVE THEM, SIR.
YOU SURE YOU'RE NOT HIDING ANYTHING ELSE?
EVERYTHING'S CLEAR, SIR.
MAY I ASK YOU A QUESTION, BRAVE COMMANDER OF THIS FIERCE ARMY?
GO AHEAD.
WILL YOUR EXCELLENCY ALLOW US TO CHEER UP THIS LAND WITH OUR ACROBATICS?
47

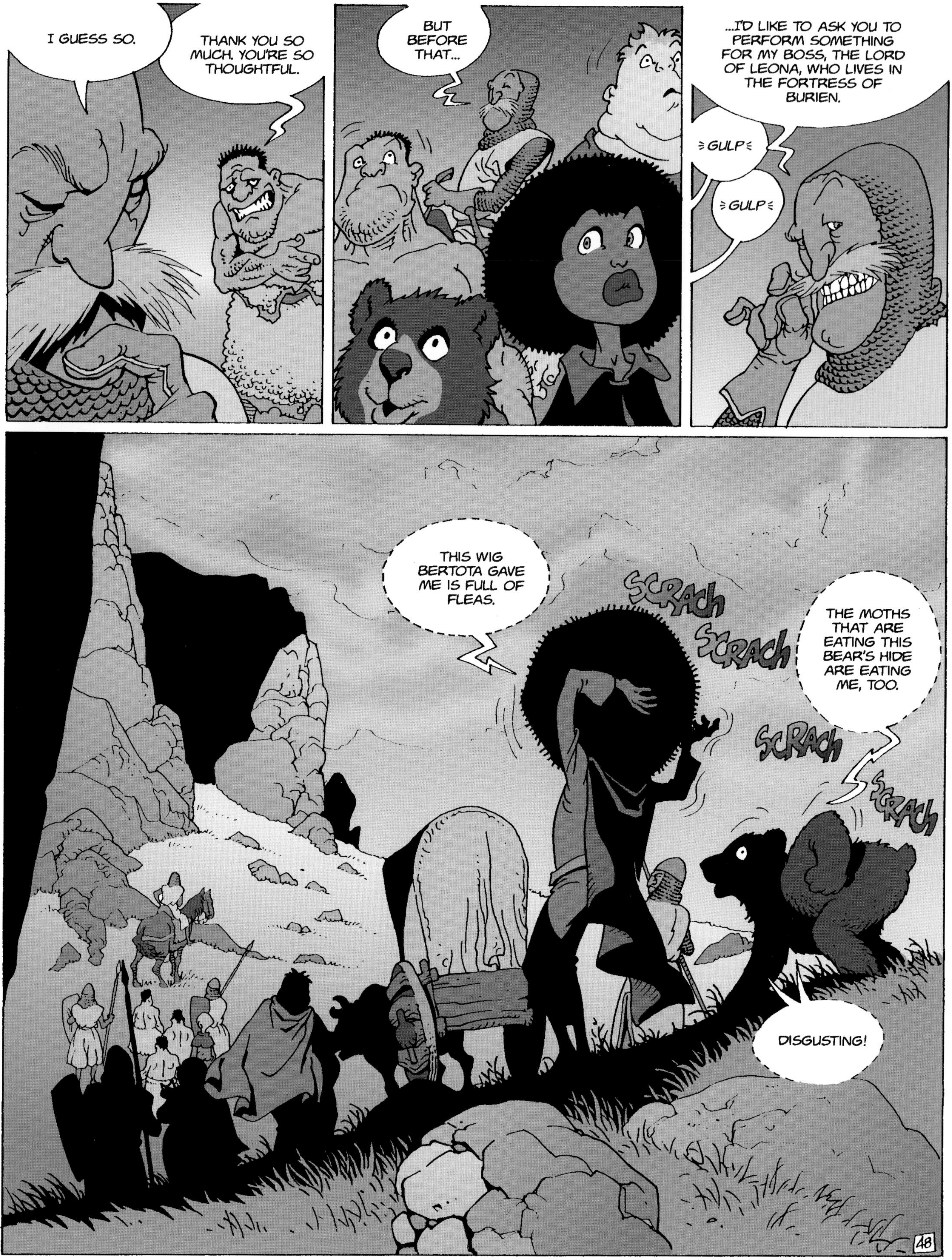
I GUESS SO.
THANK YOU SO MUCH. YOU'RE SO THOUGHTFUL.
BUT BEFORE THAT...
...I'D LIKE TO ASK YOU TO PERFORM SOMETHING FOR MY BOSS, THE LORD OF LEONA, WHO LIVES IN THE FORTRESS OF BURIEN.
GULP
GULP
THIS WIG BERTOTA GAVE ME IS FULL OF FLEAS.
SCRACH
SCRACH
THE MOTHS THAT ARE EATING THIS BEAR'S HIDE ARE EATING ME, TOO.
SCRACH
SCRACH
DISGUSTING!
48

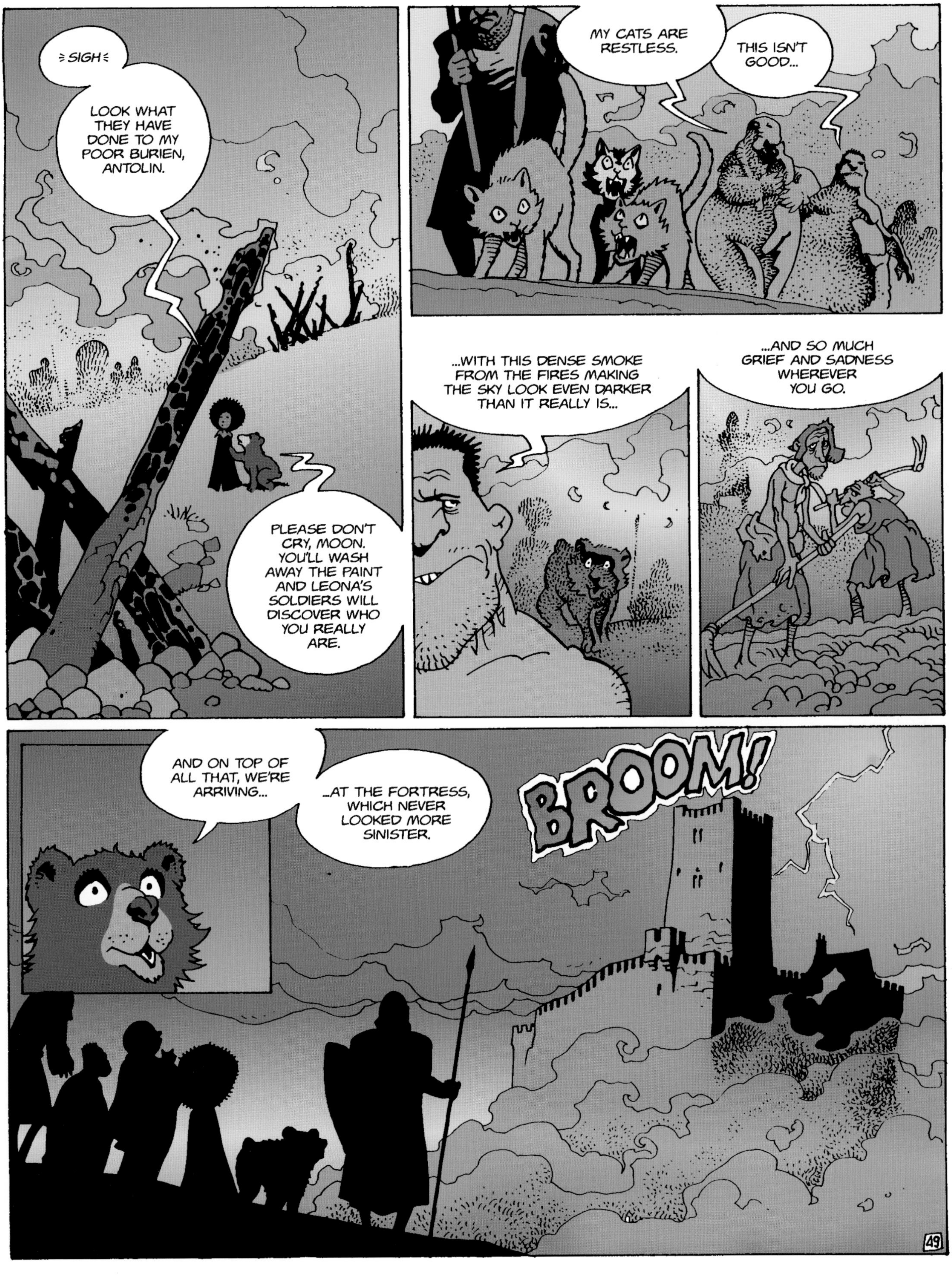
≥SIGH≤
LOOK WHAT THEY HAVE DONE TO MY POOR BURIEN, ANTOLIN.
PLEASE DON'T CRY, MOON. YOU'LL WASH AWAY THE PAINT AND LEONA'S SOLDIERS WILL DISCOVER WHO YOU REALLY ARE.
MY CATS ARE RESTLESS.
THIS ISN'T GOOD...
...WITH THIS DENSE SMOKE FROM THE FIRES MAKING THE SKY LOOK EVEN DARKER THAN IT REALLY IS...
...AND SO MUCH GRIEF AND SADNESS WHEREVER YOU GO.
AND ON TOP OF ALL THAT, WE'RE ARRIVING...
...AT THE FORTRESS, WHICH NEVER LOOKED MORE SINISTER.
BROOM!
49

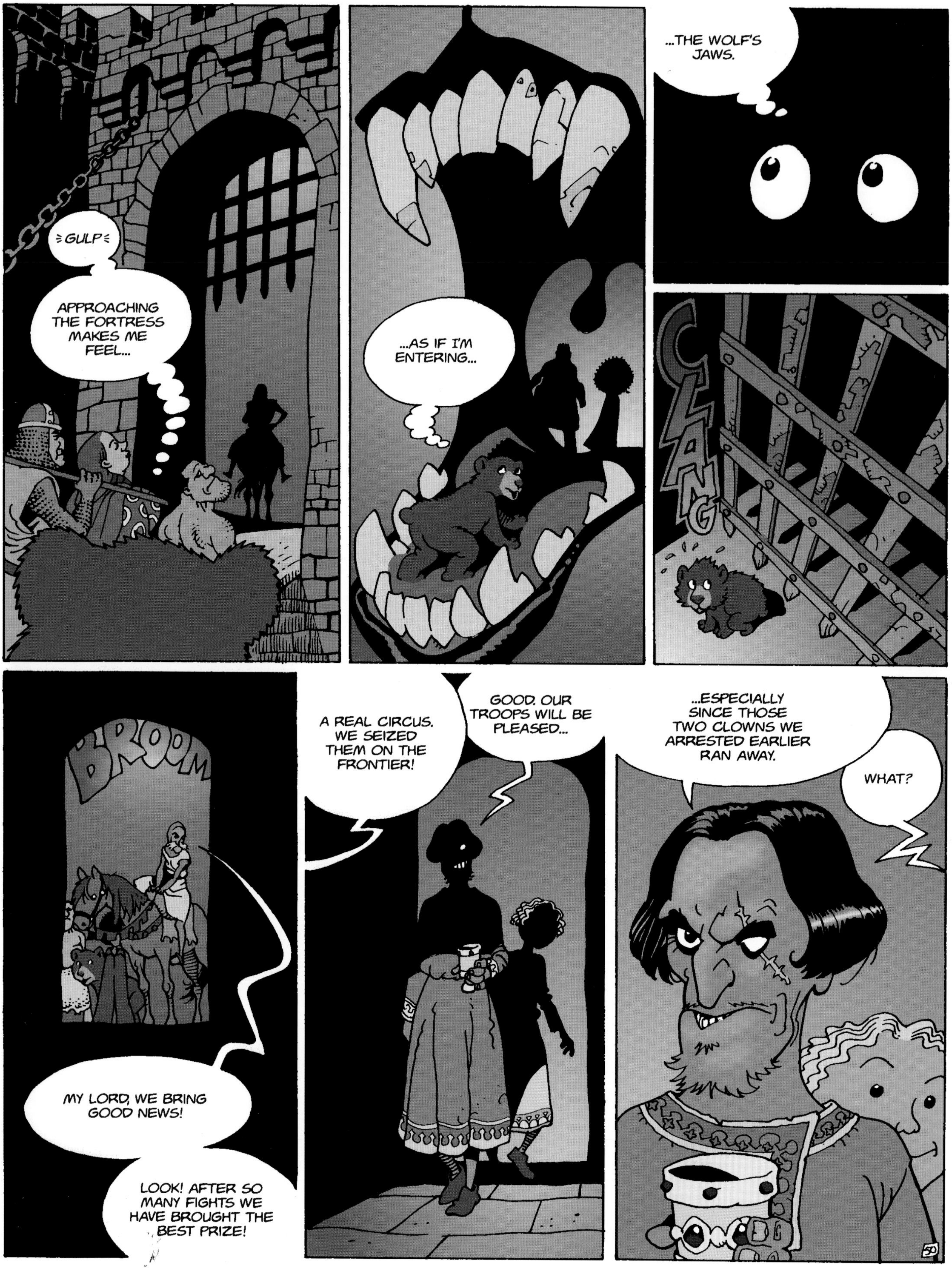
GULP
APPROACHING THE FORTRESS MAKES ME FEEL...
...AS IF I'M ENTERING...
...THE WOLF'S JAWS.
CLANG
BROOM
MY LORD, WE BRING GOOD NEWS!
LOOK! AFTER SO MANY FIGHTS WE HAVE BROUGHT THE BEST PRIZE!
A REAL CIRCUS. WE SEIZED THEM ON THE FRONTIER!
GOOD. OUR TROOPS WILL BE PLEASED...
...ESPECIALLY SINCE THOSE TWO CLOWNS WE ARRESTED EARLIER RAN AWAY.
WHAT?
50

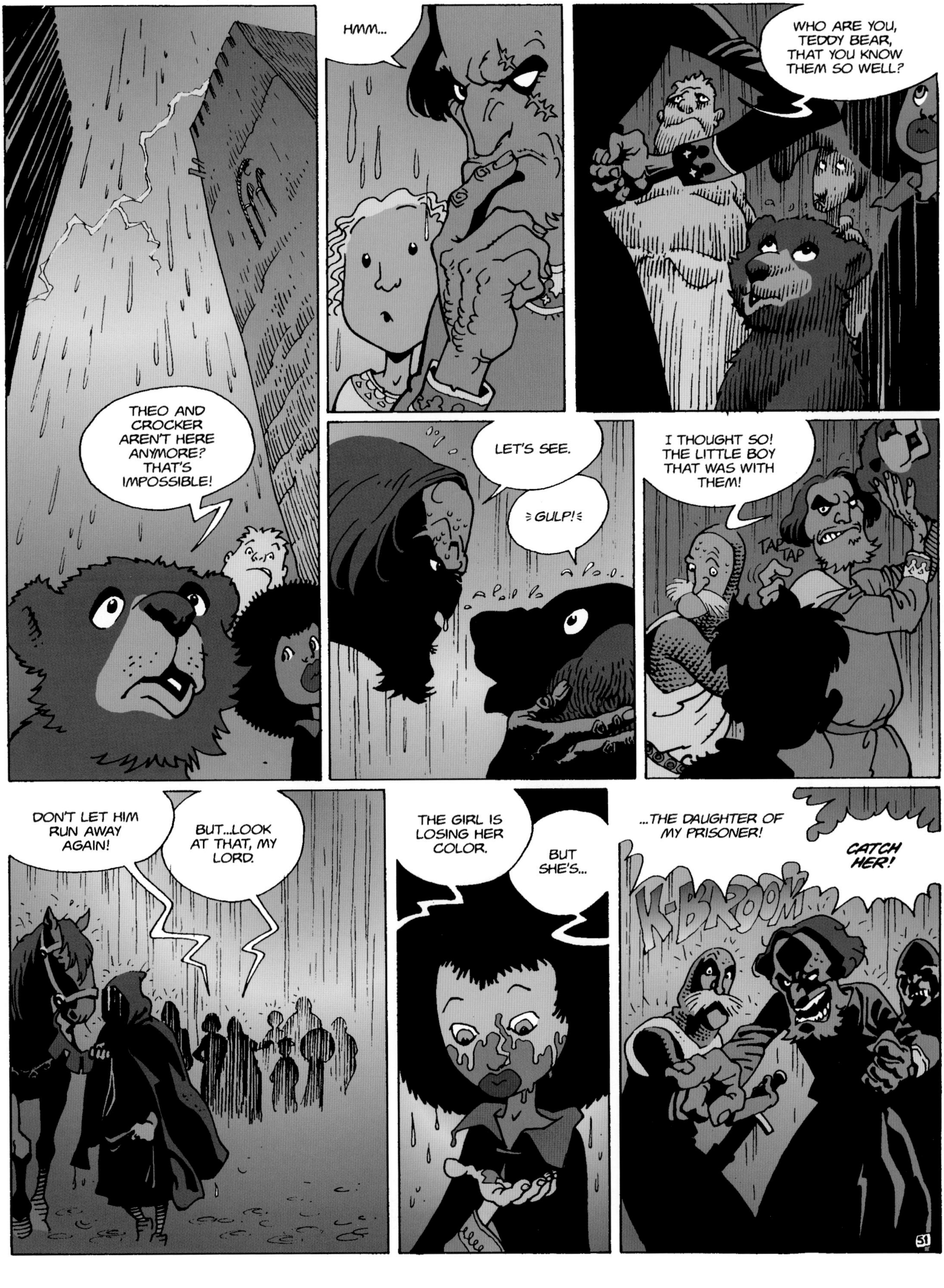
HMM...
WHO ARE YOU, TEDDY BEAR, THAT YOU KNOW THEM SO WELL?
THEO AND CROCKER AREN'T HERE ANYMORE? THAT'S IMPOSSIBLE!
LET'S SEE.
GULP!
I THOUGHT SO! THE LITTLE BOY THAT WAS WITH THEM!
TAP TAP
DON'T LET HIM RUN AWAY AGAIN!
BUT...LOOK AT THAT, MY LORD.
THE GIRL IS LOSING HER COLOR.
BUT SHE'S...
...THE DAUGHTER OF MY PRISONER!
CATCH HER!
K-BROOM
51

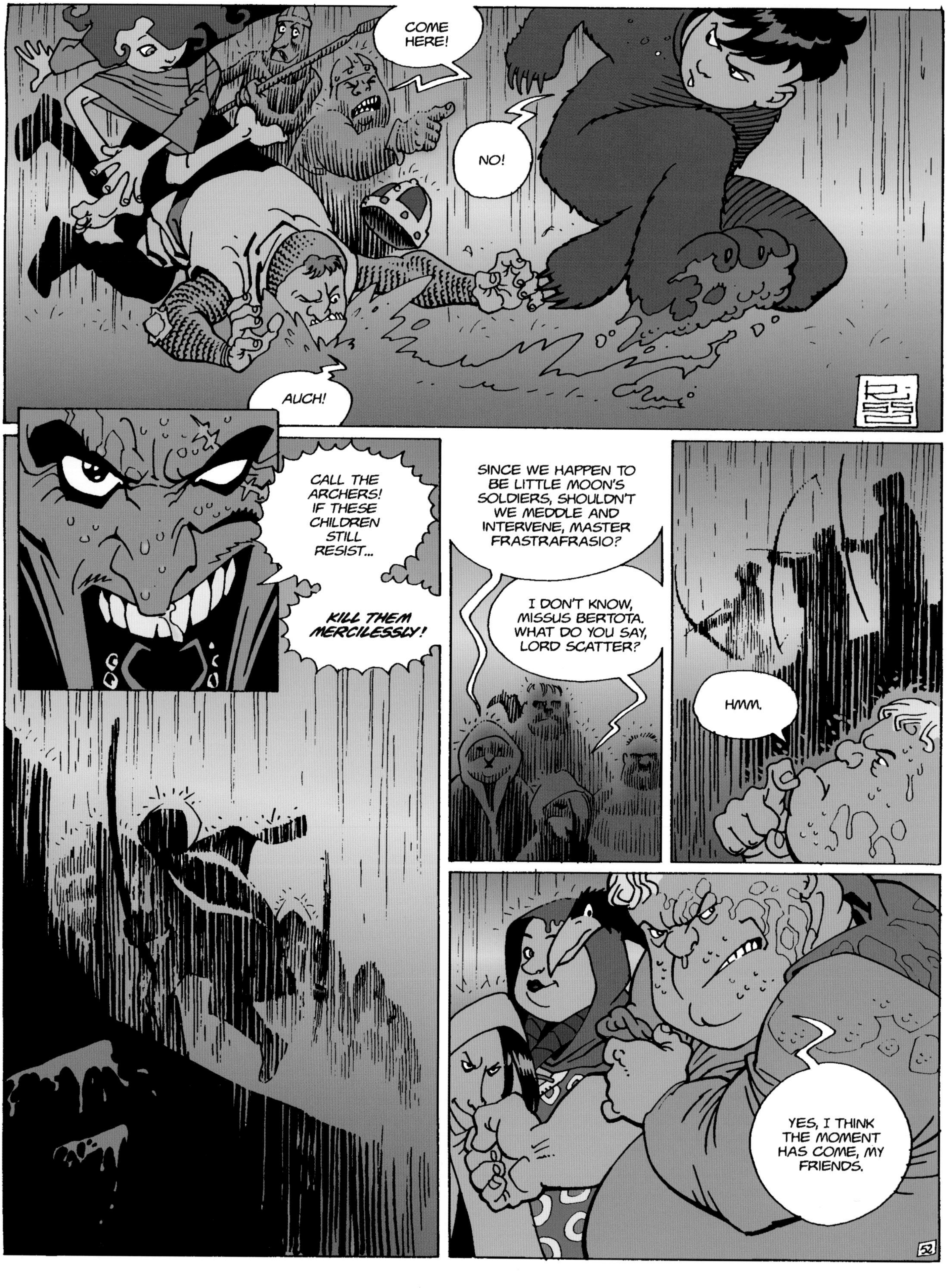
COME HERE!
NO!
AUCH!
CALL THE ARCHERS! IF THESE CHILDREN STILL RESIST...
KILL THEM MERCILESSLY!
SINCE WE HAPPEN TO BE LITTLE MOON'S SOLDIERS, SHOULDN'T WE MEDDLE AND INTERVENE, MASTER FRASTRAFRASIO?
I DON'T KNOW, MISSUS BERTOTA. WHAT DO YOU SAY, LORD SCATTER?
HMM.
YES, I THINK THE MOMENT HAS COME, MY FRIENDS.
52

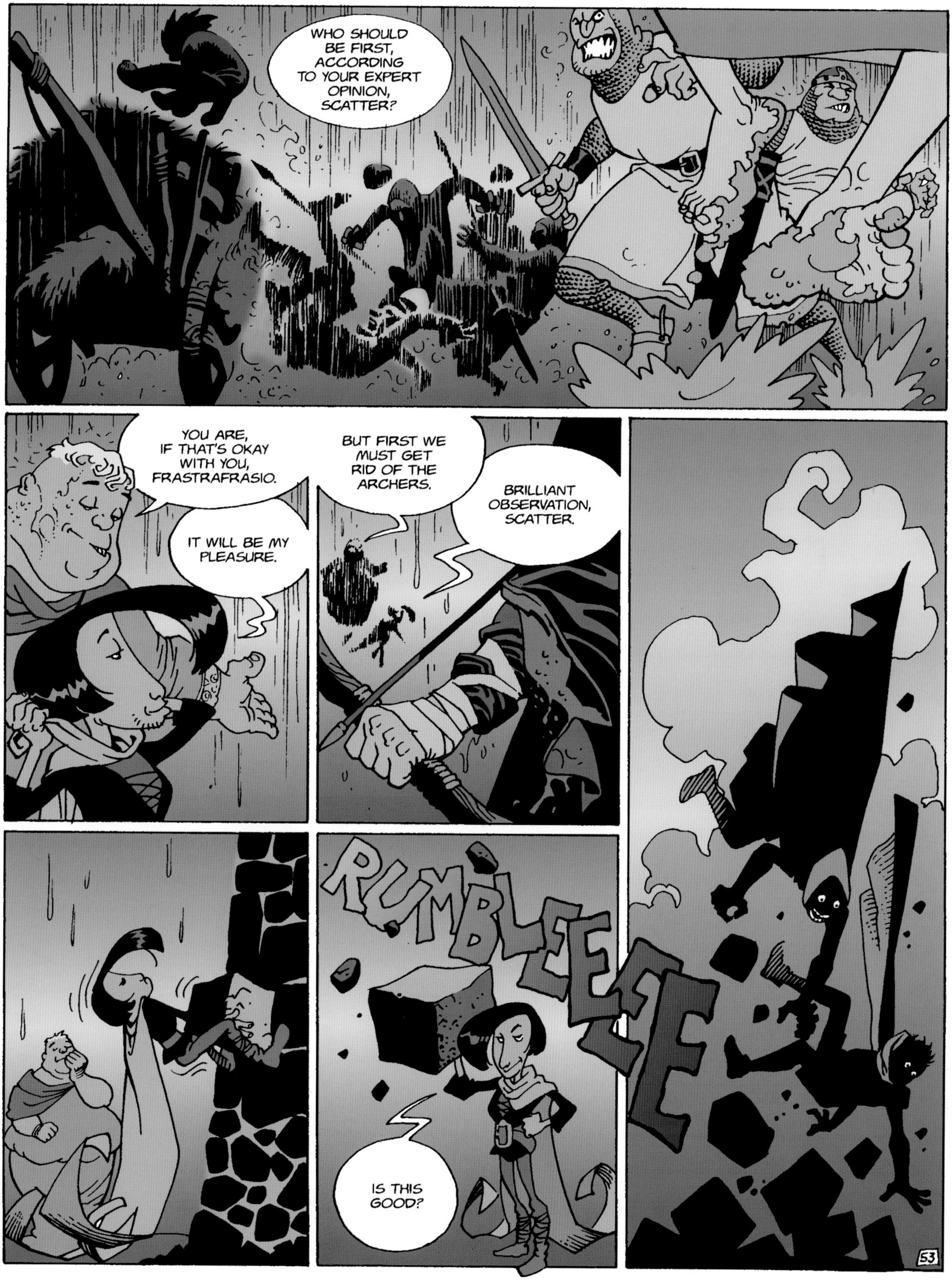

WHO SHOULD BE FIRST, ACCORDING TO YOUR EXPERT OPINION, SCATTER?
YOU ARE, IF THAT'S OKAY WITH YOU, FRASTRAFRASIO.
IT WILL BE MY PLEASURE.
BUT FIRST WE MUST GET RID OF THE ARCHERS.
BRILLIANT OBSERVATION, SCATTER.
RUMBLEEEE
IS THIS GOOD?
53

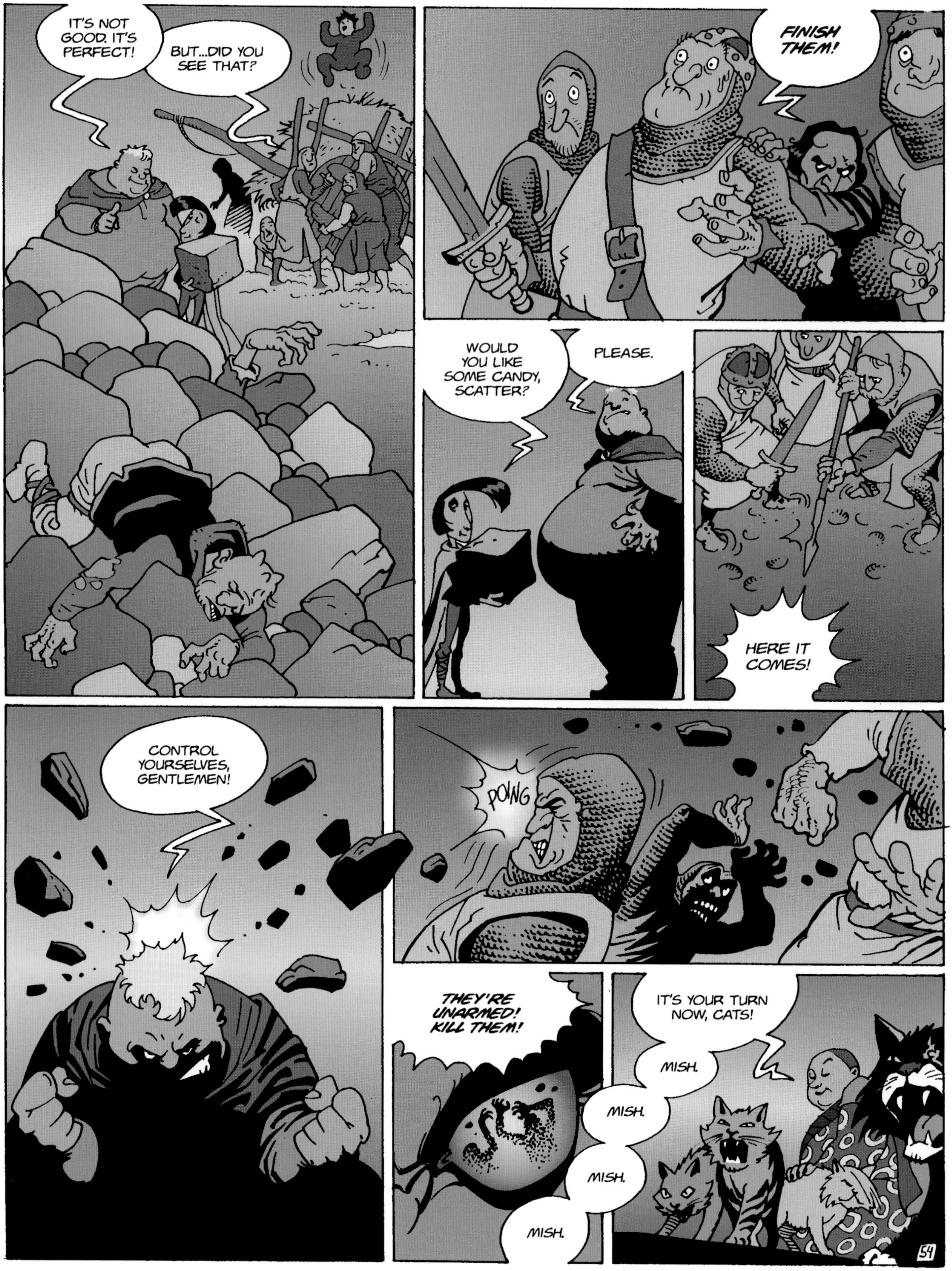
IT'S NOT GOOD. IT'S PERFECT!
BUT...DID YOU SEE THAT?
FINISH THEM!
WOULD YOU LIKE SOME CANDY, SCATTER?
PLEASE.
HERE IT COMES!
CONTROL YOURSELVES, GENTLEMEN!
POING
THEY'RE UNARMED! KILL THEM!
IT'S YOUR TURN NOW, CATS!
MISH.
MISH.
MISH.
MISH.
54

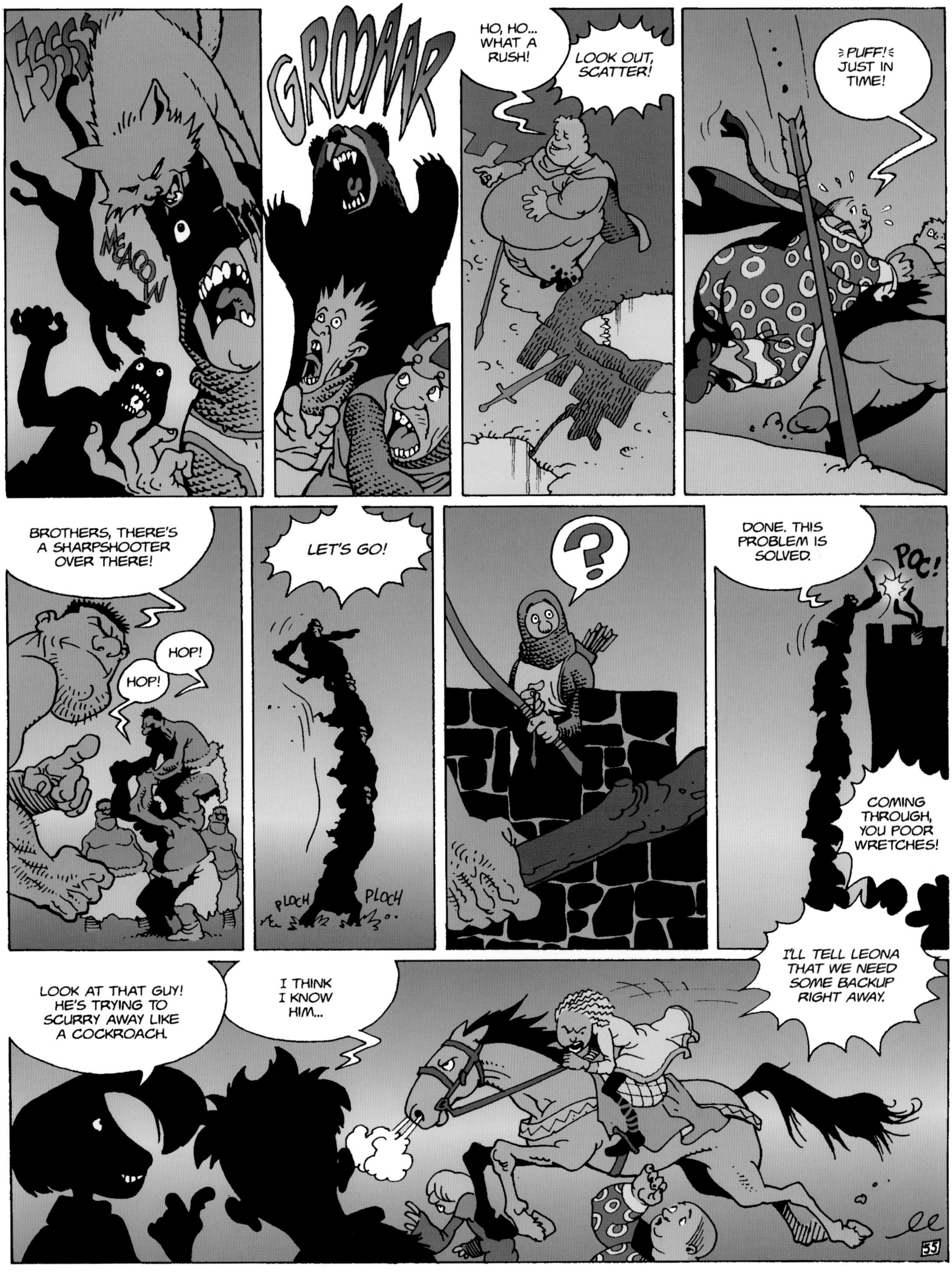
FSSSS
MEAOOW
GROOAAR
HO, HO... WHAT A RUSH!
LOOK OUT, SCATTER!
PUFF! JUST IN TIME!
BROTHERS, THERE'S A SHARPSHOOTER OVER THERE!
HOP!
HOP!
LET'S GO!
PLOCH
PLOCH
?
DONE. THIS PROBLEM IS SOLVED.
POC!
COMING THROUGH, YOU POOR WRETCHES!
LOOK AT THAT GUY! HE'S TRYING TO SCURRY AWAY LIKE A COCKROACH.
I THINK I KNOW HIM...
I'LL TELL LEONA THAT WE NEED SOME BACKUP RIGHT AWAY.
55

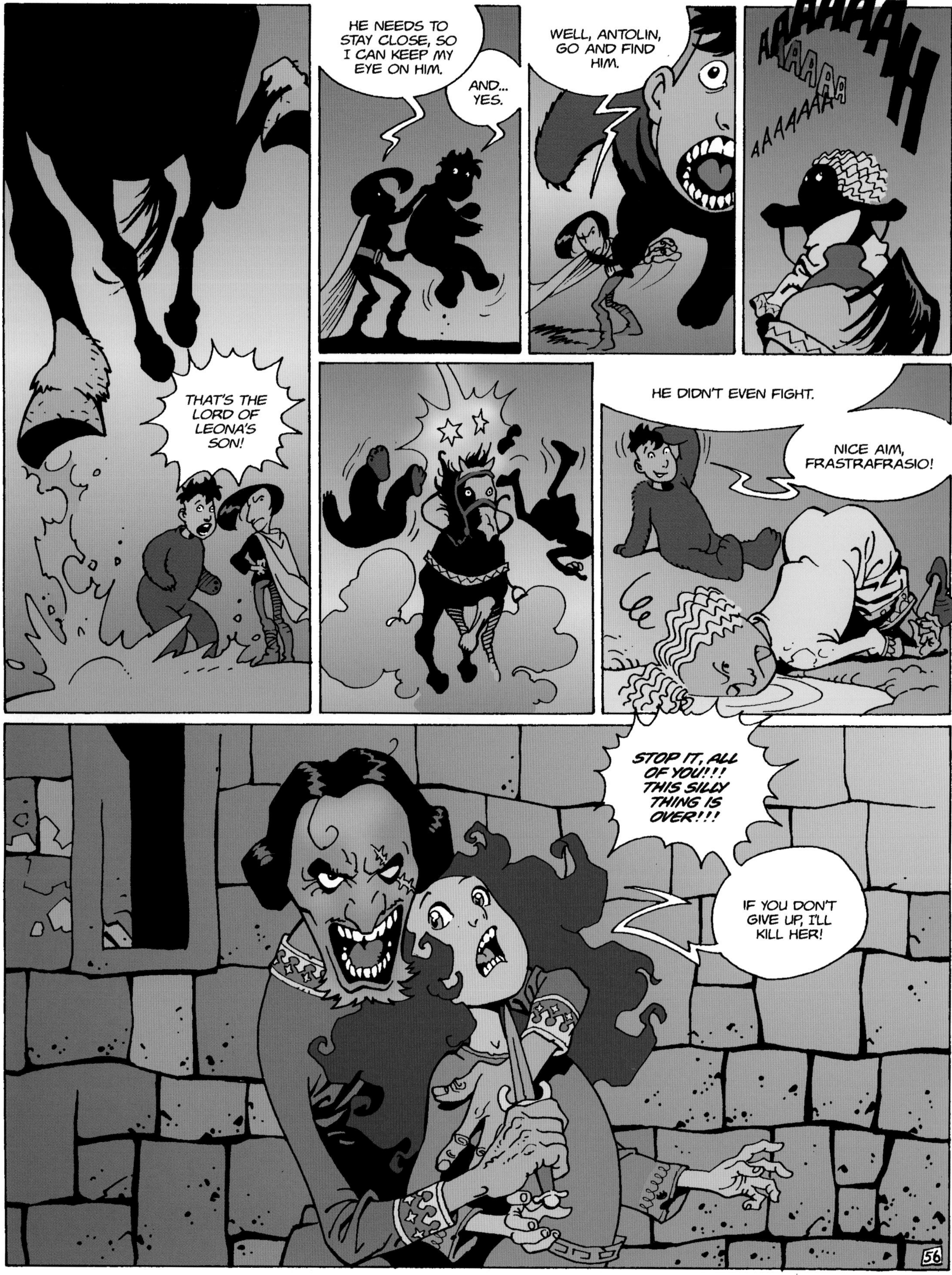
HE NEEDS TO STAY CLOSE, SO I CAN KEEP MY EYE ON HIM.
AND... YES.
WELL, ANTOLIN, GO AND FIND HIM.
AAAAAAAAH
AAAAAA
AAAAAAA
THAT'S THE LORD OF LEONA'S SON!
HE DIDN'T EVEN FIGHT.
NICE AIM, FRASTRAFRASIO!
STOP IT, ALL OF YOU!!! THIS SILLY THING IS OVER!!!
IF YOU DON'T GIVE UP, I'LL KILL HER!
56

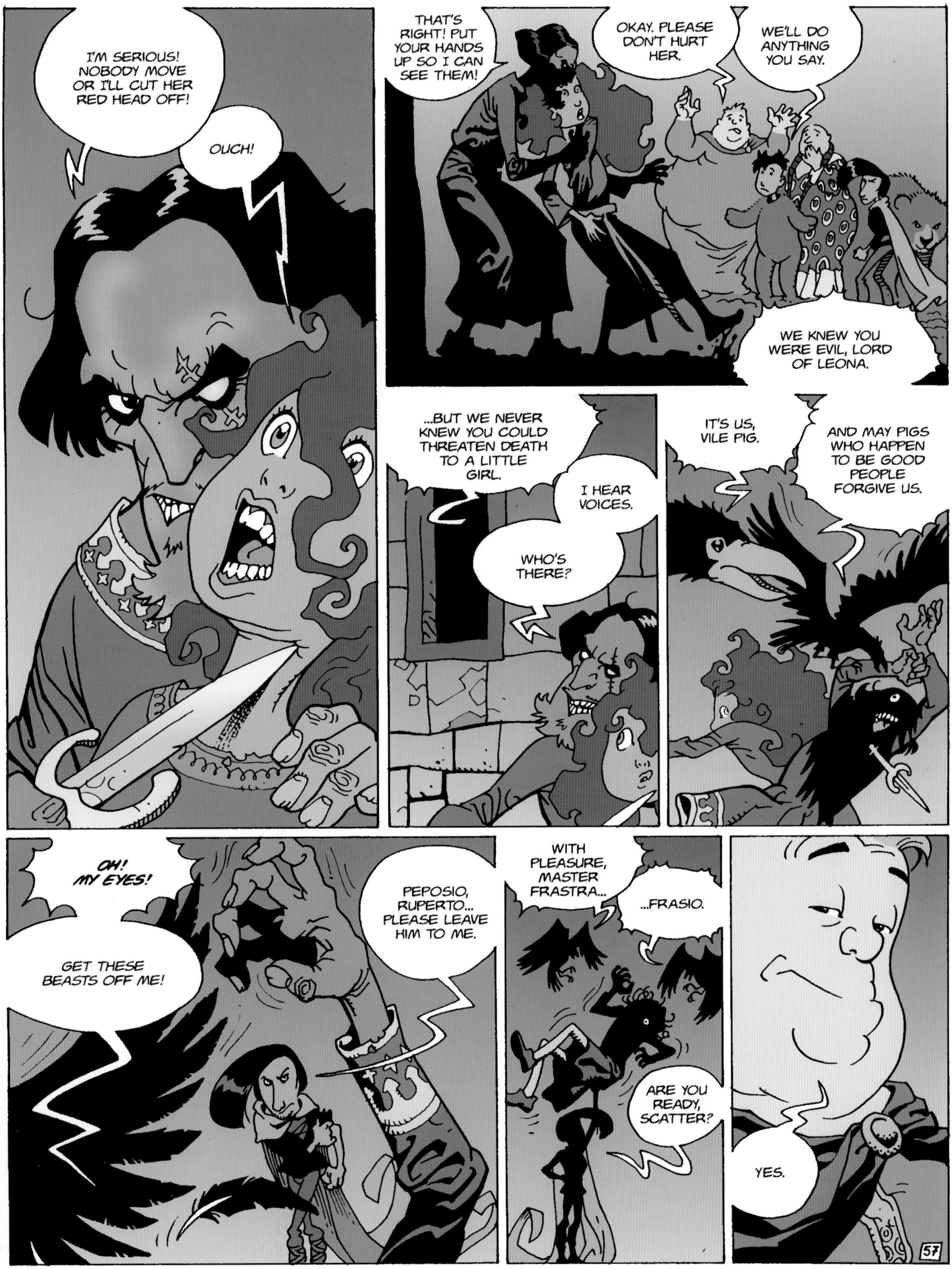
I'M SERIOUS! NOBODY MOVE OR I'LL CUT HER RED HEAD OFF!
OUCH!
THAT'S RIGHT! PUT YOUR HANDS UP SO I CAN SEE THEM!
OKAY. PLEASE DON'T HURT HER.
WE'LL DO ANYTHING YOU SAY.
WE KNEW YOU WERE EVIL, LORD OF LEONA.
...BUT WE NEVER KNEW YOU COULD THREATEN DEATH TO A LITTLE GIRL.
I HEAR VOICES.
WHO'S THERE?
IT'S US, VILE PIG.
AND MAY PIGS WHO HAPPEN TO BE GOOD PEOPLE FORGIVE US.
OH! MY EYES!
GET THESE BEASTS OFF ME!
PEPOSIO, RUPERTO... PLEASE LEAVE HIM TO ME.
WITH PLEASURE, MASTER FRASTRA...
...FRASIO.
ARE YOU READY, SCATTER?
YES.
57

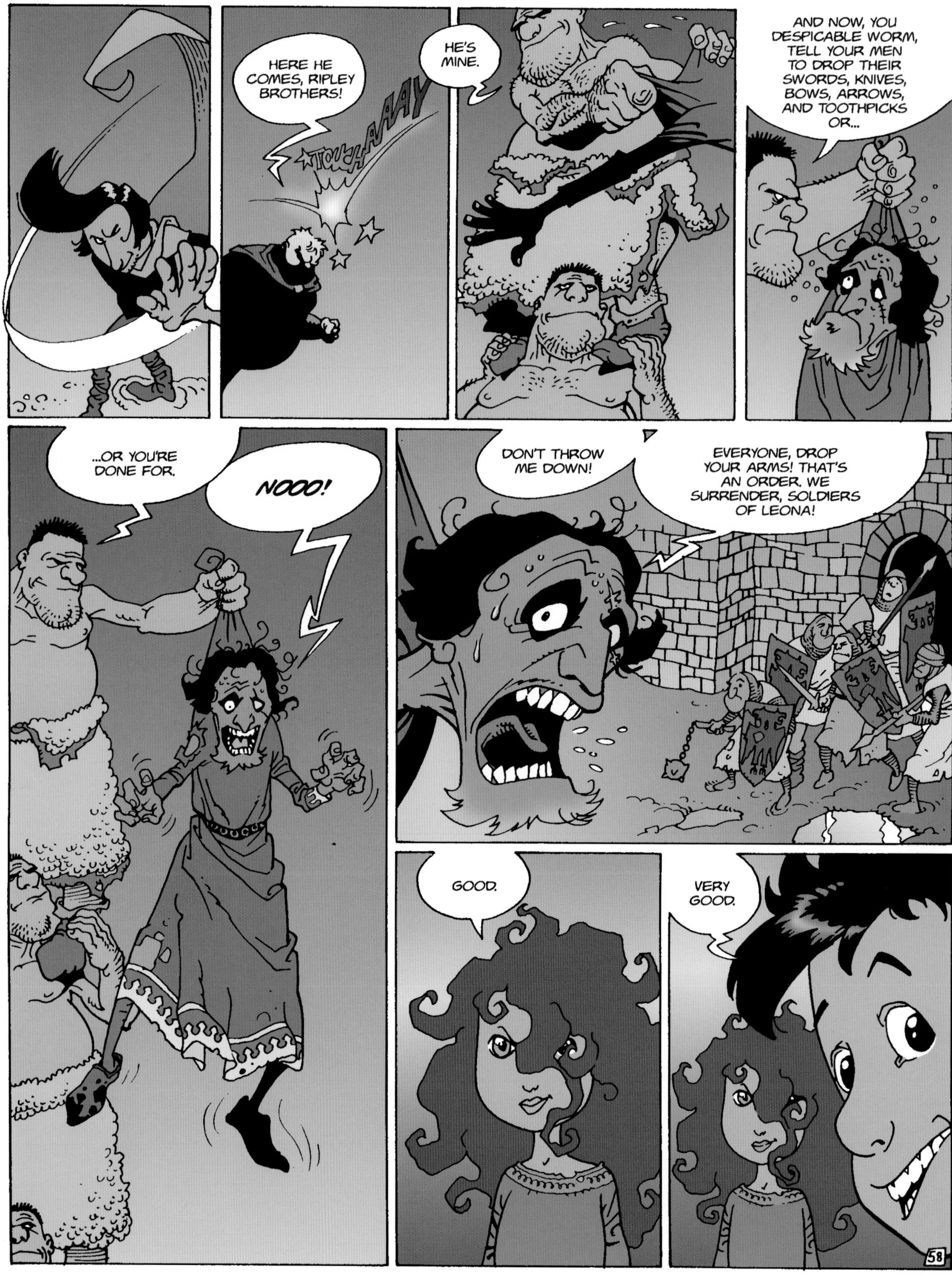
HERE HE COMES, RIPLEY BROTHERS!
TOUCHAAAAY
HE'S MINE.
AND NOW, YOU DESPICABLE WORM, TELL YOUR MEN TO DROP THEIR SWORDS, KNIVES, BOWS, ARROWS, AND TOOTHPICKS OR...
...OR YOU'RE DONE FOR.
NOOO!
DON'T THROW ME DOWN!
EVERYONE, DROP YOUR ARMS! THAT'S AN ORDER. WE SURRENDER, SOLDIERS OF LEONA!
GOOD.
VERY GOOD.
58

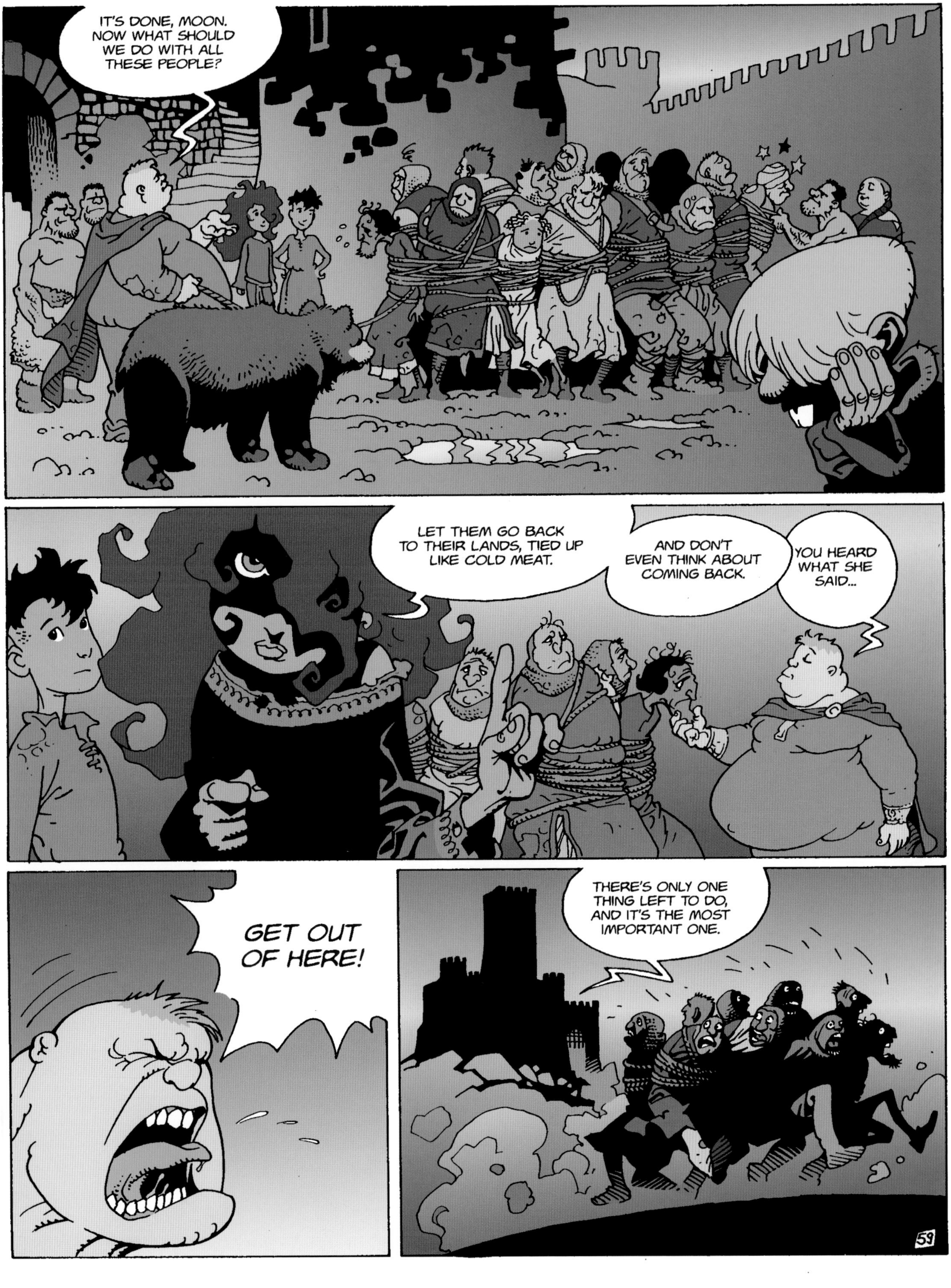

IT'S DONE, MOON. NOW WHAT SHOULD WE DO WITH ALL THESE PEOPLE?
LET THEM GO BACK TO THEIR LANDS, TIED UP LIKE COLD MEAT.
AND DON'T EVEN THINK ABOUT COMING BACK.
YOU HEARD WHAT SHE SAID...
GET OUT OF HERE!
THERE'S ONLY ONE THING LEFT TO DO, AND IT'S THE MOST IMPORTANT ONE.
59

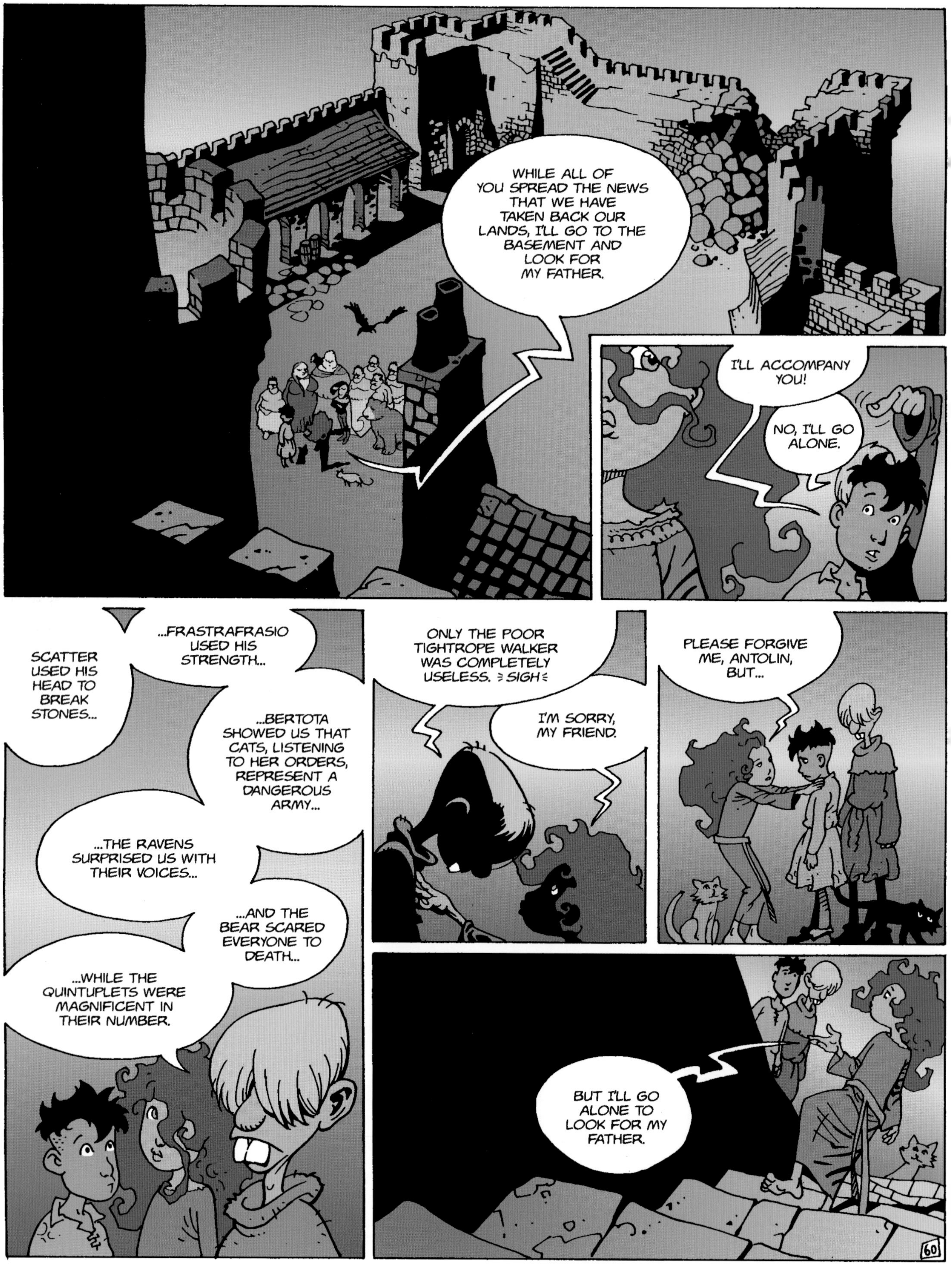
WHILE ALL OF YOU SPREAD THE NEWS THAT WE HAVE TAKEN BACK OUR LANDS, I'LL GO TO THE BASEMENT AND LOOK FOR MY FATHER.
I'LL ACCOMPANY YOU!
NO, I'LL GO ALONE.
SCATTER USED HIS HEAD TO BREAK STONES...
...FRASTRAFRASIO USED HIS STRENGTH...
...BERTOTA SHOWED US THAT CATS, LISTENING TO HER ORDERS, REPRESENT A DANGEROUS ARMY...
...THE RAVENS SURPRISED US WITH THEIR VOICES...
...AND THE BEAR SCARED EVERYONE TO DEATH...
...WHILE THE QUINTUPLETS WERE MAGNIFICENT IN THEIR NUMBER.
ONLY THE POOR TIGHTROPE WALKER WAS COMPLETELY USELESS. ≥SIGH≤
I'M SORRY, MY FRIEND.
PLEASE FORGIVE ME, ANTOLIN, BUT...
BUT I'LL GO ALONE TO LOOK FOR MY FATHER.
60

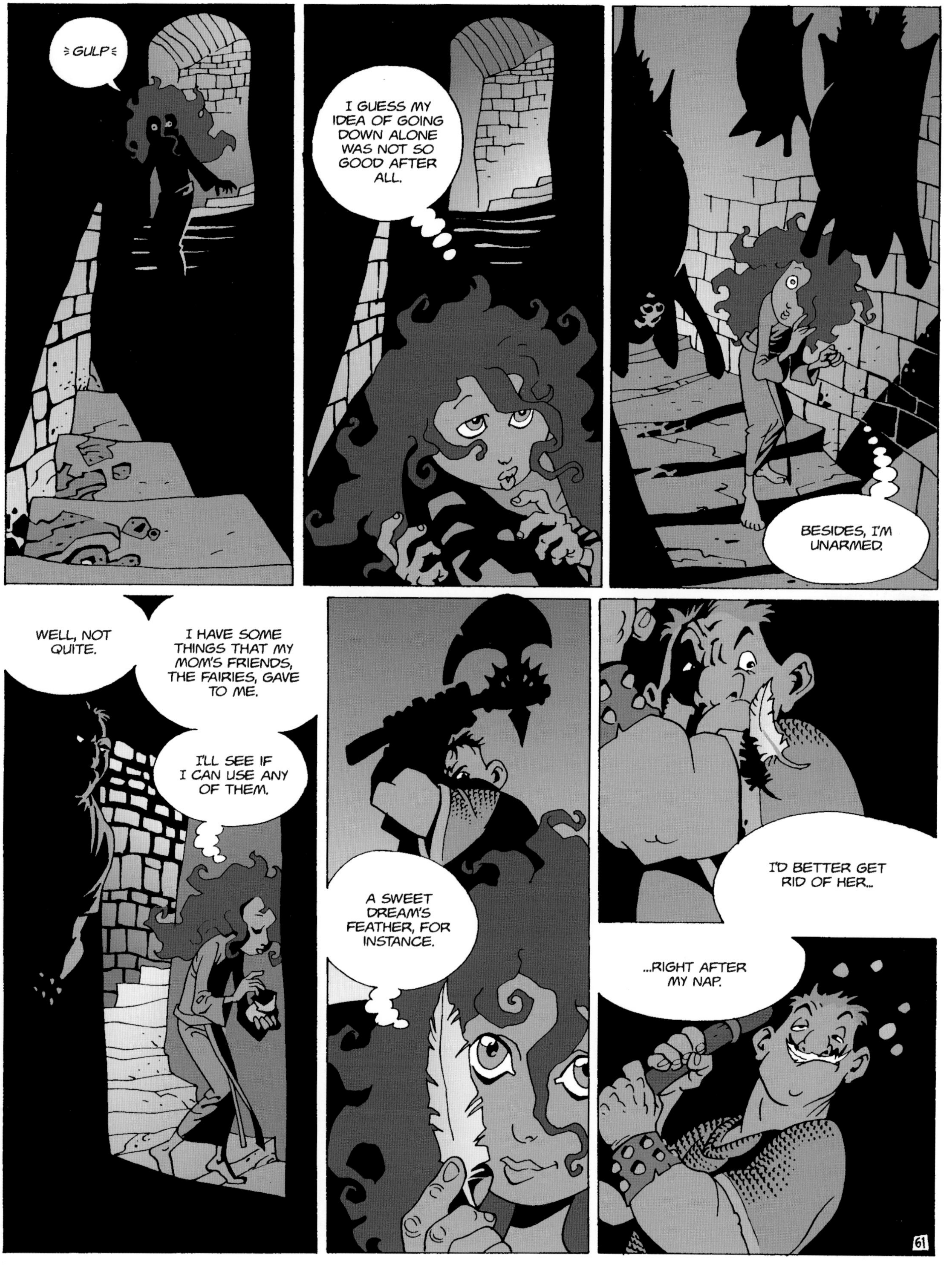

GULP
I GUESS MY IDEA OF GOING DOWN ALONE WAS NOT SO GOOD AFTER ALL.
BESIDES, I'M UNARMED.
WELL, NOT QUITE.
I HAVE SOME THINGS THAT MY MOM'S FRIENDS, THE FAIRIES, GAVE TO ME.
I'LL SEE IF I CAN USE ANY OF THEM.
A SWEET DREAM'S FEATHER, FOR INSTANCE.
I'D BETTER GET RID OF HER...
...RIGHT AFTER MY NAP.
61

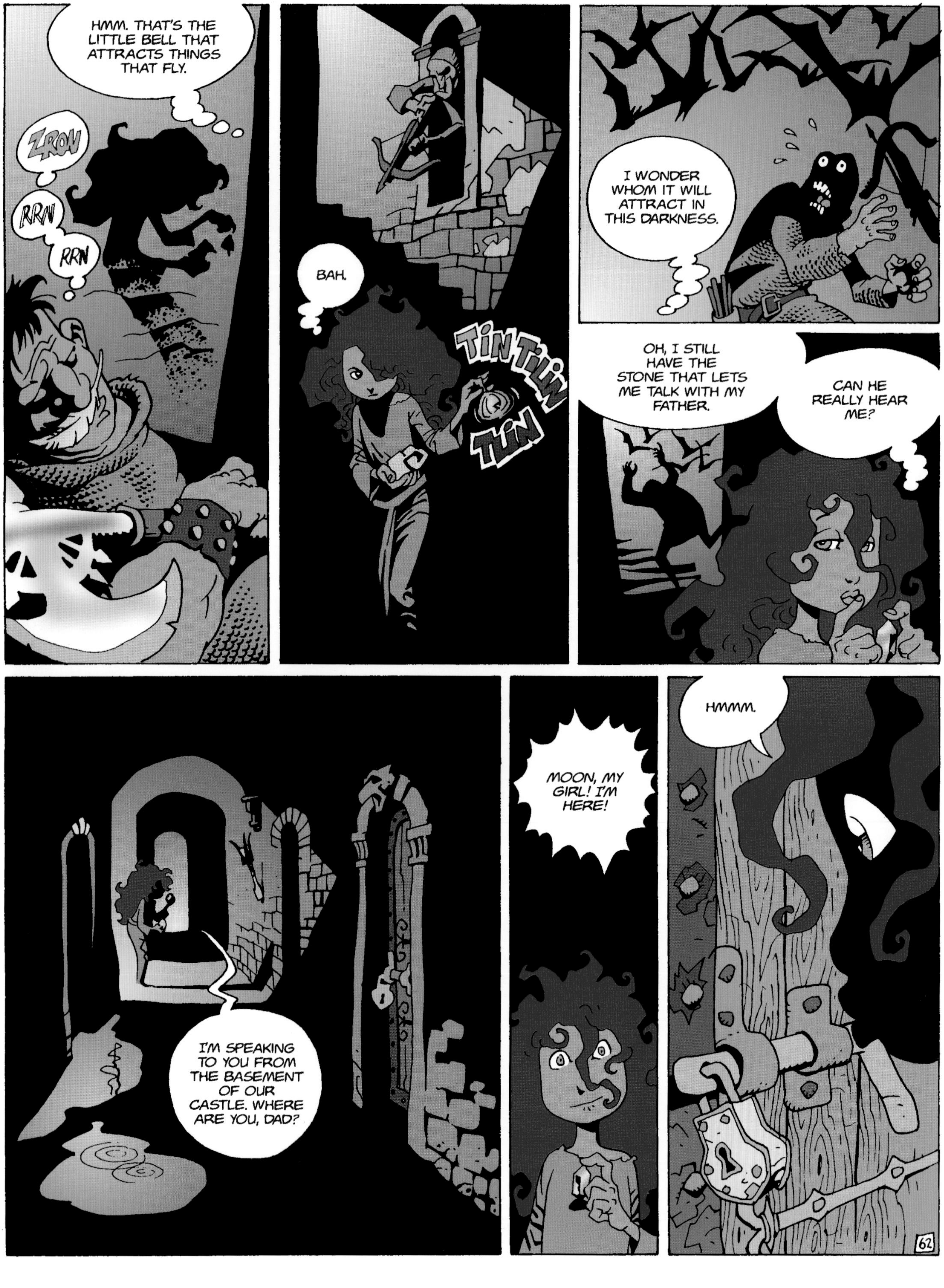
HMM. THAT'S THE LITTLE BELL THAT ATTRACTS THINGS THAT FLY.
ZRON
RRN
RRN
BAH.
TIN TILIN
TLIN
I WONDER WHOM IT WILL ATTRACT IN THIS DARKNESS.
OH, I STILL HAVE THE STONE THAT LETS ME TALK WITH MY FATHER.
CAN HE REALLY HEAR ME?
I'M SPEAKING TO YOU FROM THE BASEMENT OF OUR CASTLE. WHERE ARE YOU, DAD?
MOON, MY GIRL! I'M HERE!
HMMM.
62

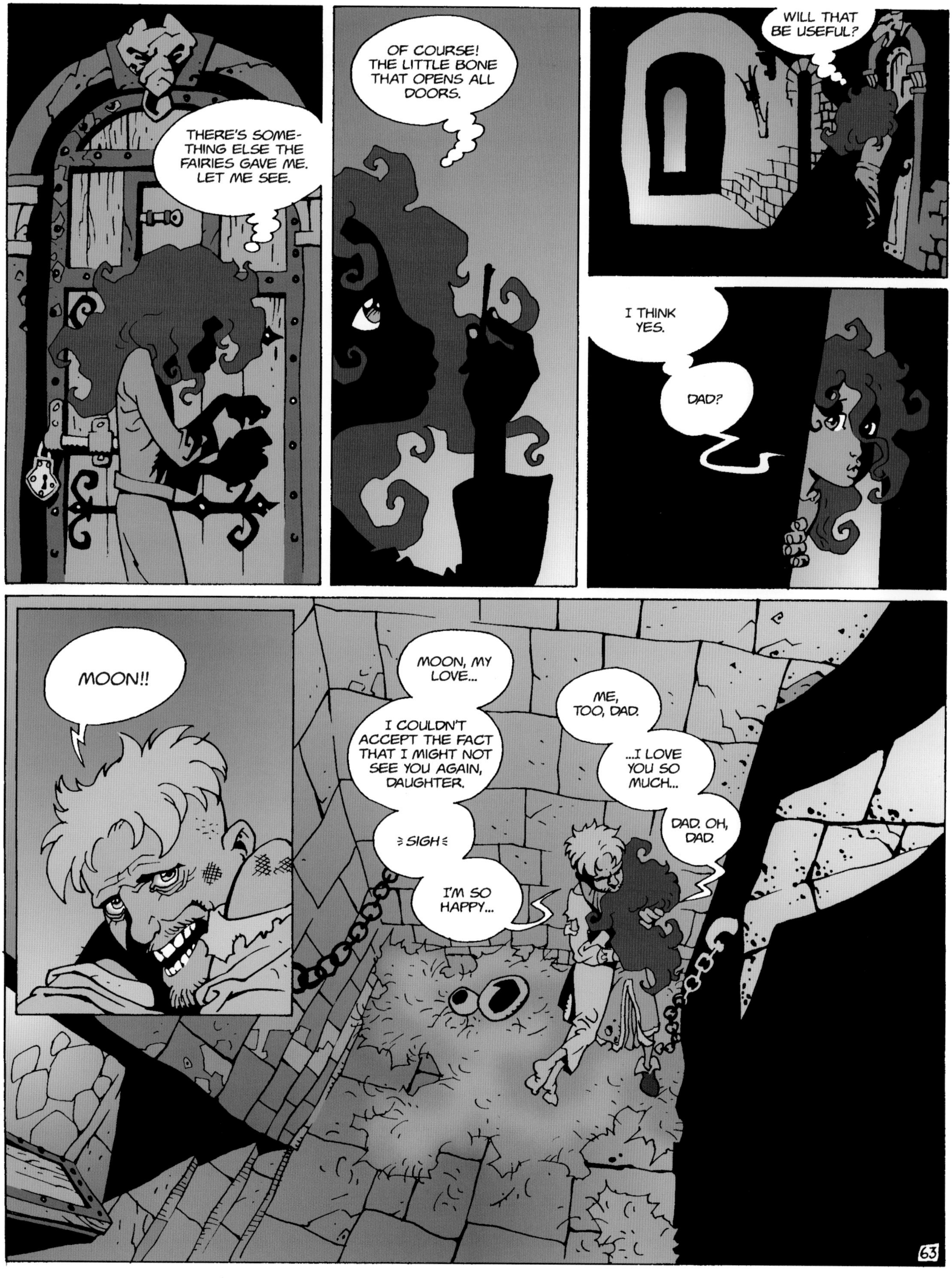
THERE'S SOME-THING ELSE THE FAIRIES GAVE ME. LET ME SEE.
OF COURSE! THE LITTLE BONE THAT OPENS ALL DOORS.
WILL THAT BE USEFUL?
I THINK YES.
DAD?
MOON!!
MOON, MY LOVE...
I COULDN'T ACCEPT THE FACT THAT I MIGHT NOT SEE YOU AGAIN, DAUGHTER.
SIGH
I'M SO HAPPY...
ME, TOO, DAD.
...I LOVE YOU SO MUCH...
DAD. OH, DAD.
63

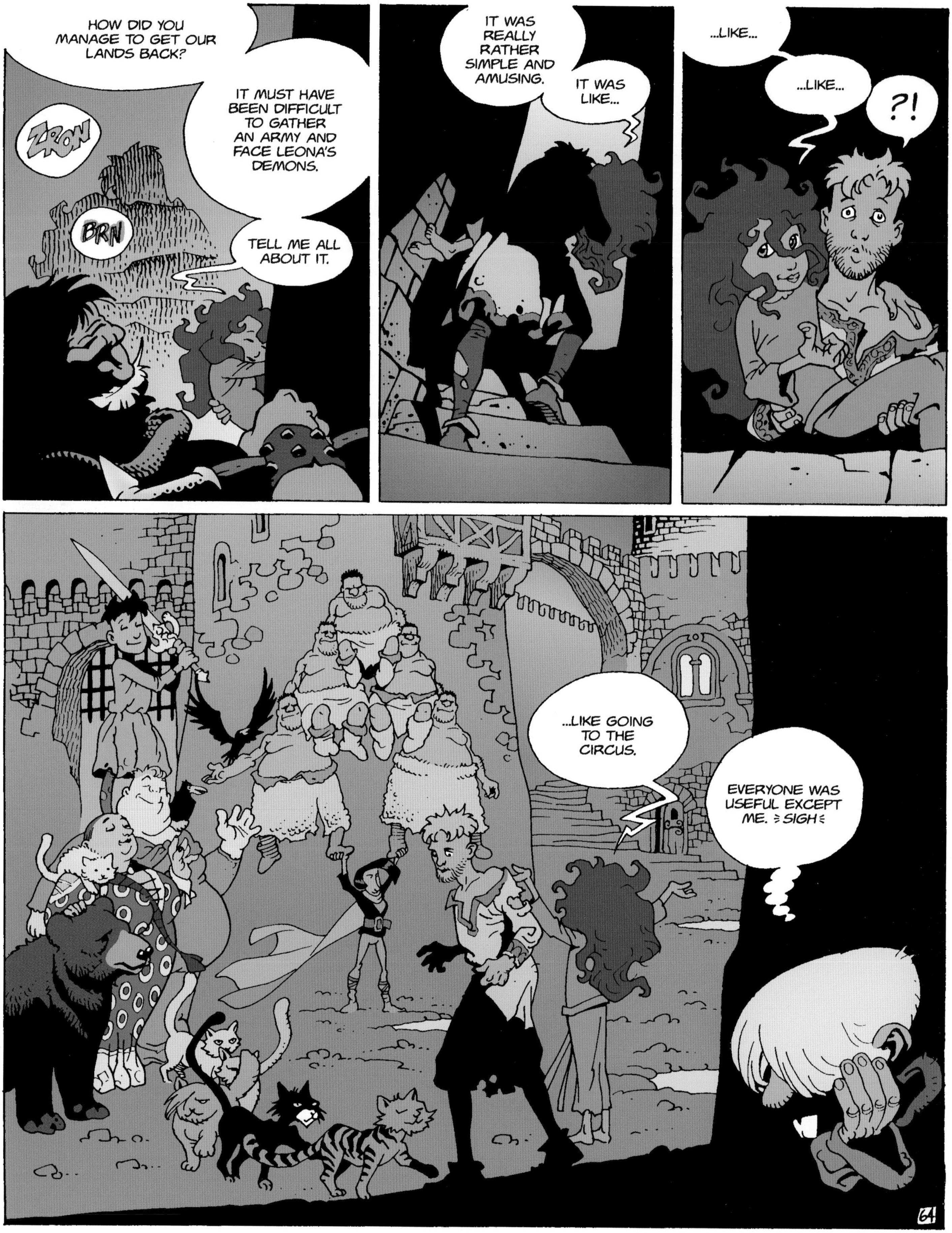
HOW DID YOU MANAGE TO GET OUR LANDS BACK?
IT MUST HAVE BEEN DIFFICULT TO GATHER AN ARMY AND FACE LEONA'S DEMONS.
ZRON
BRN
TELL ME ALL ABOUT IT.
IT WAS REALLY RATHER SIMPLE AND AMUSING.
IT WAS LIKE...
...LIKE...
...LIKE...
?!
...LIKE GOING TO THE CIRCUS.
EVERYONE WAS USEFUL EXCEPT ME. ≥SIGH≤
64

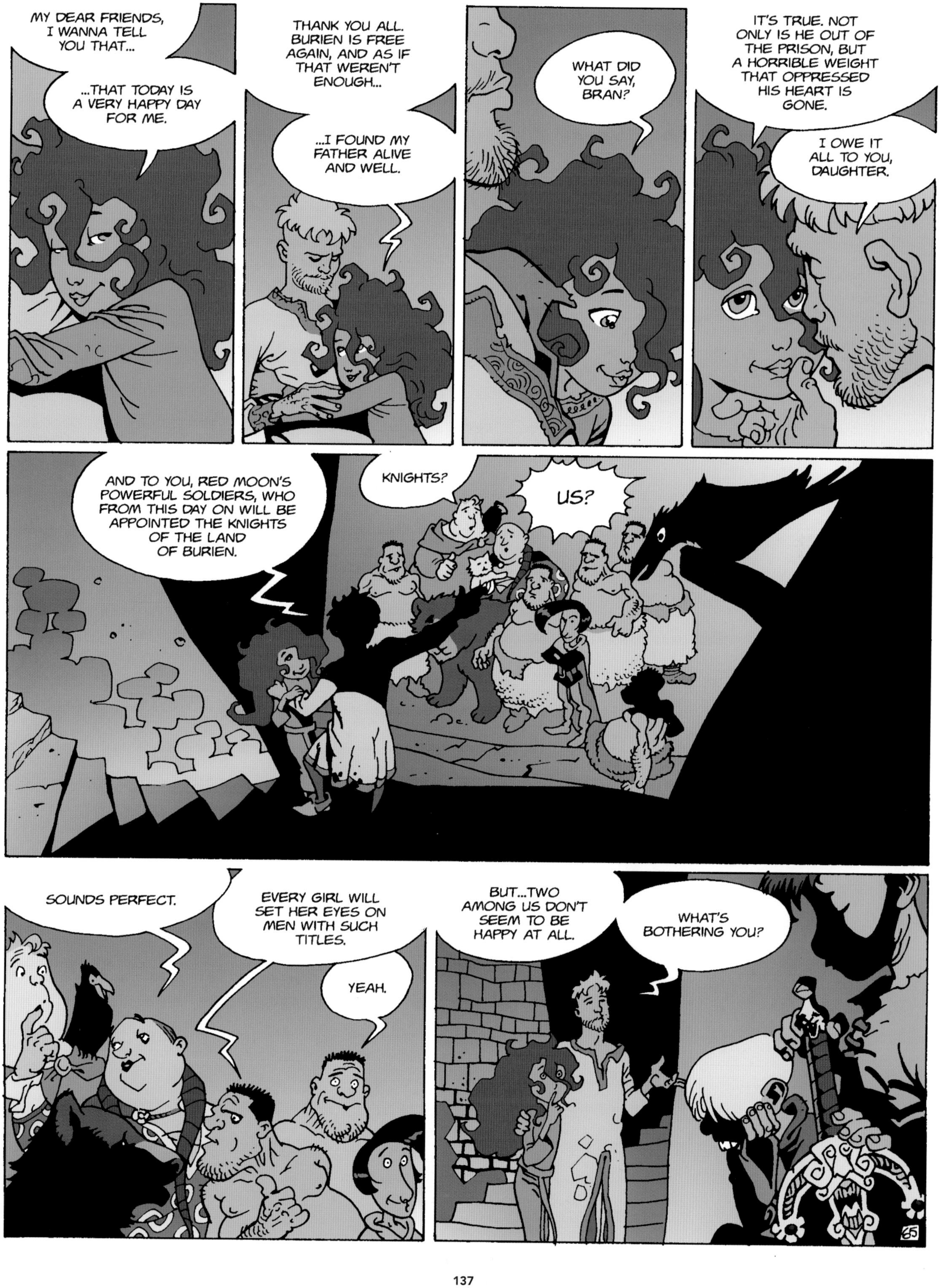
MY DEAR FRIENDS, I WANNA TELL YOU THAT...
...THAT TODAY IS A VERY HAPPY DAY FOR ME.
THANK YOU ALL. BURIEN IS FREE AGAIN, AND AS IF THAT WEREN'T ENOUGH...
...I FOUND MY FATHER ALIVE AND WELL.
WHAT DID YOU SAY, BRAN?
IT'S TRUE. NOT ONLY IS HE OUT OF THE PRISON, BUT A HORRIBLE WEIGHT THAT OPPRESSED HIS HEART IS GONE.
I OWE IT ALL TO YOU, DAUGHTER.
AND TO YOU, RED MOON'S POWERFUL SOLDIERS, WHO FROM THIS DAY ON WILL BE APPOINTED THE KNIGHTS OF THE LAND OF BURIEN.
KNIGHTS?
US?
SOUNDS PERFECT.
EVERY GIRL WILL SET HER EYES ON MEN WITH SUCH TITLES.
YEAH.
BUT...TWO AMONG US DON'T SEEM TO BE HAPPY AT ALL.
WHAT'S BOTHERING YOU?
65

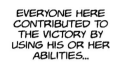

EVERYONE HERE CONTRIBUTED TO THE VICTORY BY USING HIS OR HER ABILITIES...

EVERYONE EXCEPT ME, THE TIGHTROPE WALKER.

THAT'S WHAT'S BOTHERING ME.

AM I COMPLETELY USELESS?

≥SNIFF≤

OF COURSE NOT.

YOU'RE THE MOST IMPORTANT.

THE ONLY ONE CAPABLE OF CLIMBING UP THERE AND REMOVING OUR ENEMY'S FLAG.

...AND ENABLING THE FLAG OF BURIEN TO WAVE AGAIN.

GREAT IDEA!

I'M COMING!

WELL DONE!

VERY GOOD JOB, TIGHTROPE WALKER!

66

138

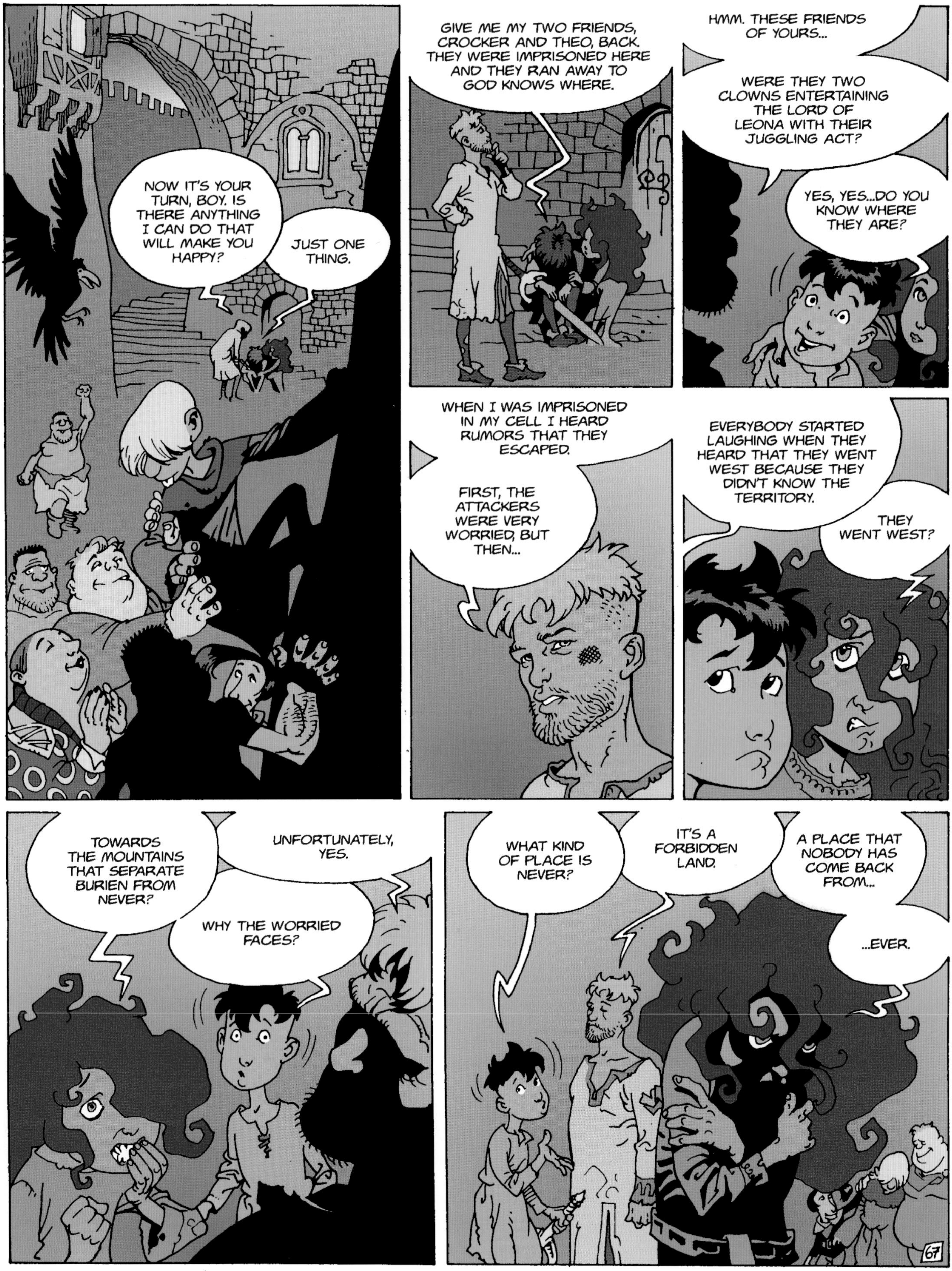
NOW IT'S YOUR TURN, BOY. IS THERE ANYTHING I CAN DO THAT WILL MAKE YOU HAPPY?
JUST ONE THING.
GIVE ME MY TWO FRIENDS, CROCKER AND THEO, BACK. THEY WERE IMPRISONED HERE AND THEY RAN AWAY TO GOD KNOWS WHERE.
HMM. THESE FRIENDS OF YOURS...
WERE THEY TWO CLOWNS ENTERTAINING THE LORD OF LEONA WITH THEIR JUGGLING ACT?
YES, YES...DO YOU KNOW WHERE THEY ARE?
WHEN I WAS IMPRISONED IN MY CELL I HEARD RUMORS THAT THEY ESCAPED.
FIRST, THE ATTACKERS WERE VERY WORRIED, BUT THEN...
EVERYBODY STARTED LAUGHING WHEN THEY HEARD THAT THEY WENT WEST BECAUSE THEY DIDN'T KNOW THE TERRITORY.
THEY WENT WEST?
TOWARDS THE MOUNTAINS THAT SEPARATE BURIEN FROM NEVER?
UNFORTUNATELY, YES.
WHY THE WORRIED FACES?
WHAT KIND OF PLACE IS NEVER?
IT'S A FORBIDDEN LAND.
A PLACE THAT NOBODY HAS COME BACK FROM...
...EVER.
67

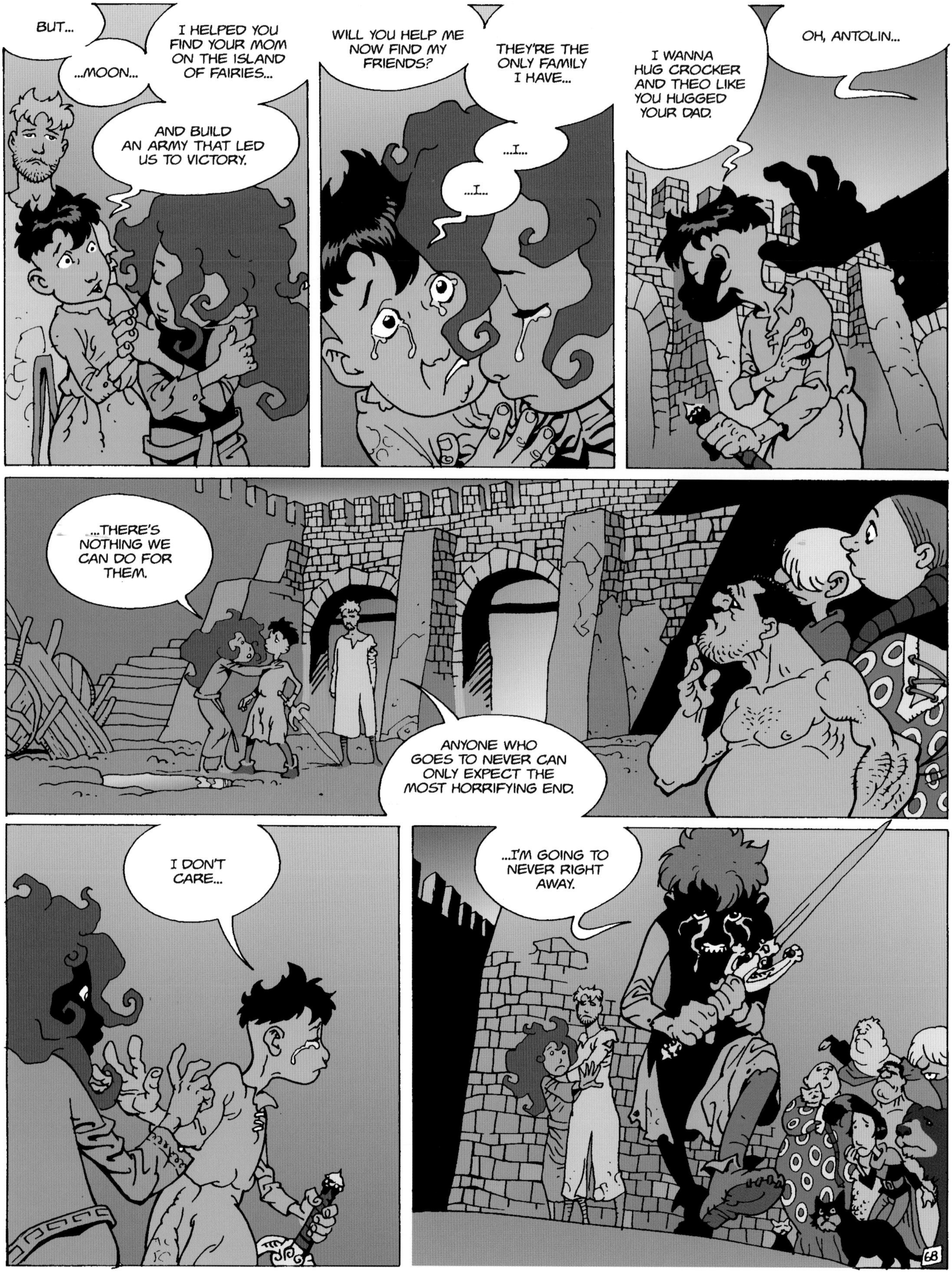

BUT...
...MOON...
I HELPED YOU FIND YOUR MOM ON THE ISLAND OF FAIRIES...
AND BUILD AN ARMY THAT LED US TO VICTORY.
WILL YOU HELP ME NOW FIND MY FRIENDS?
THEY'RE THE ONLY FAMILY I HAVE...
...I...
...I...
I WANNA HUG CROCKER AND THEO LIKE YOU HUGGED YOUR DAD.
OH, ANTOLIN...
...THERE'S NOTHING WE CAN DO FOR THEM.
ANYONE WHO GOES TO NEVER CAN ONLY EXPECT THE MOST HORRIFYING END.
I DON'T CARE...
...I'M GOING TO NEVER RIGHT AWAY.
68

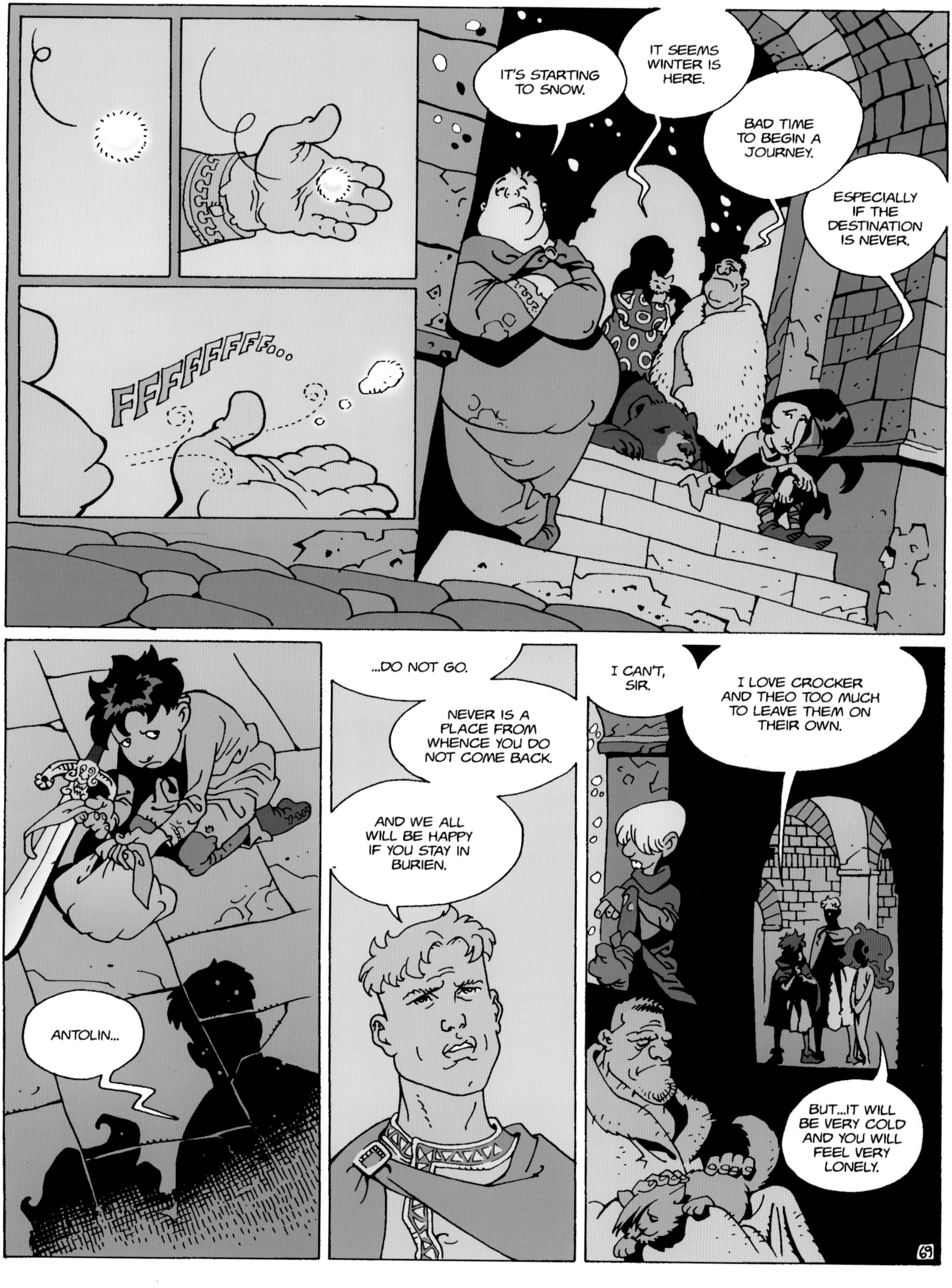
FFFFFFFFF...
IT'S STARTING TO SNOW.
IT SEEMS WINTER IS HERE.
BAD TIME TO BEGIN A JOURNEY.
ESPECIALLY IF THE DESTINATION IS NEVER.
ANTOLIN...
...DO NOT GO.
NEVER IS A PLACE FROM WHENCE YOU DO NOT COME BACK.
AND WE ALL WILL BE HAPPY IF YOU STAY IN BURIEN.
I CAN'T, SIR.
I LOVE CROCKER AND THEO TOO MUCH TO LEAVE THEM ON THEIR OWN.
BUT...IT WILL BE VERY COLD AND YOU WILL FEEL VERY LONELY.
69

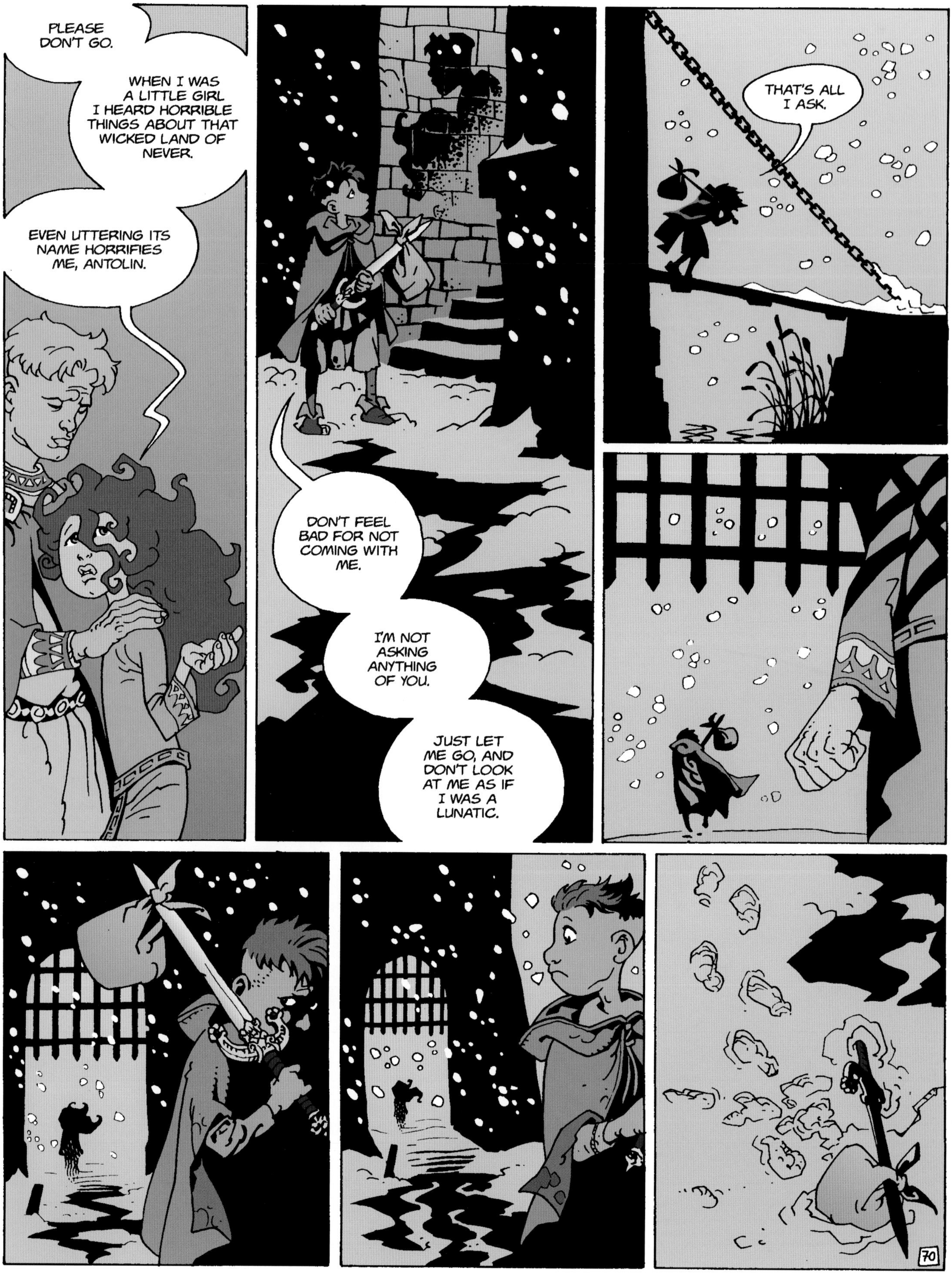
PLEASE DON'T GO.
WHEN I WAS A LITTLE GIRL I HEARD HORRIBLE THINGS ABOUT THAT WICKED LAND OF NEVER.
EVEN UTTERING ITS NAME HORRIFIES ME, ANTOLIN.
DON'T FEEL BAD FOR NOT COMING WITH ME.
I'M NOT ASKING ANYTHING OF YOU.
JUST LET ME GO, AND DON'T LOOK AT ME AS IF I WAS A LUNATIC.
THAT'S ALL I ASK.
70

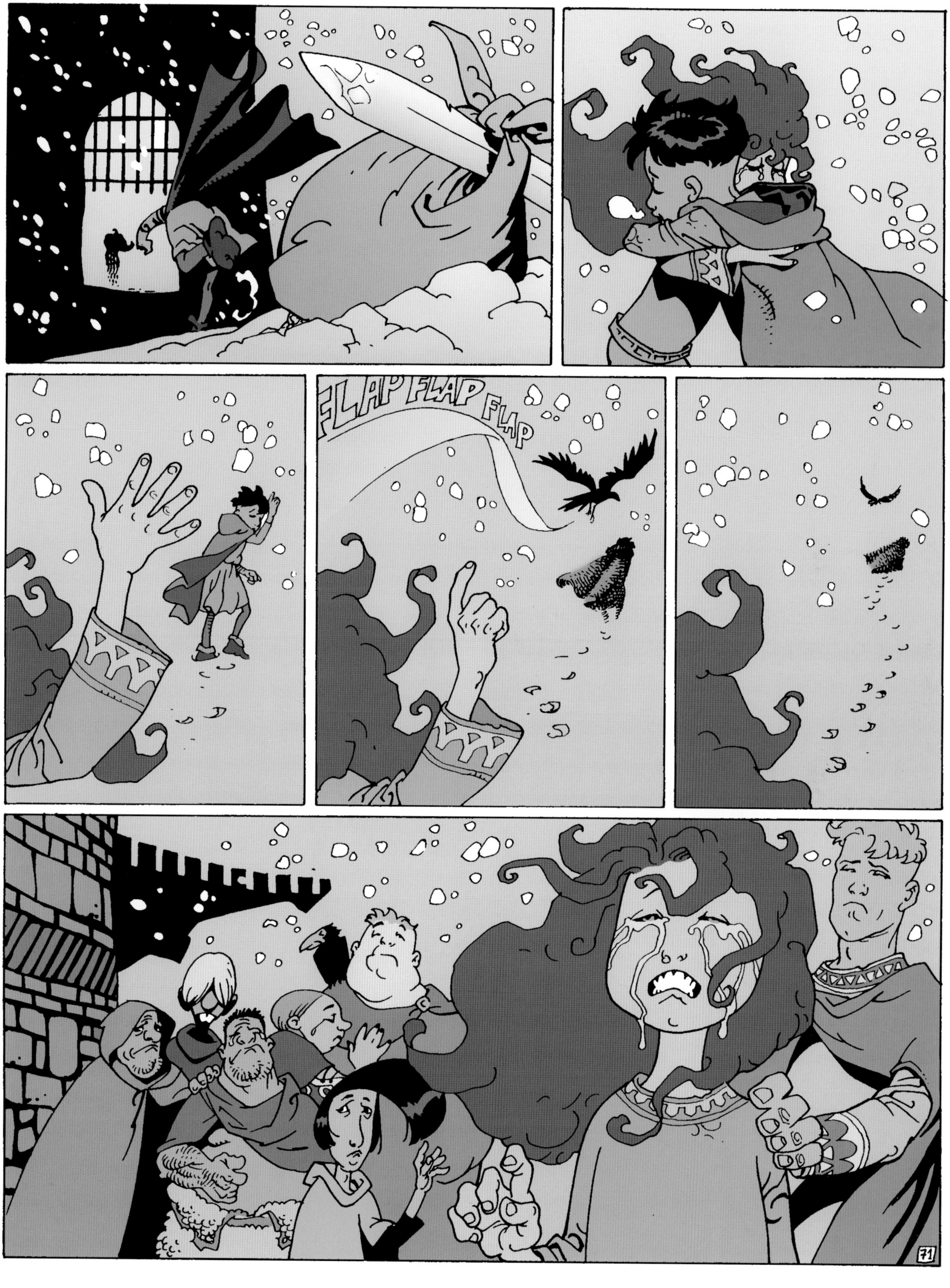
FLAP FLAP FLAP FLAP
71

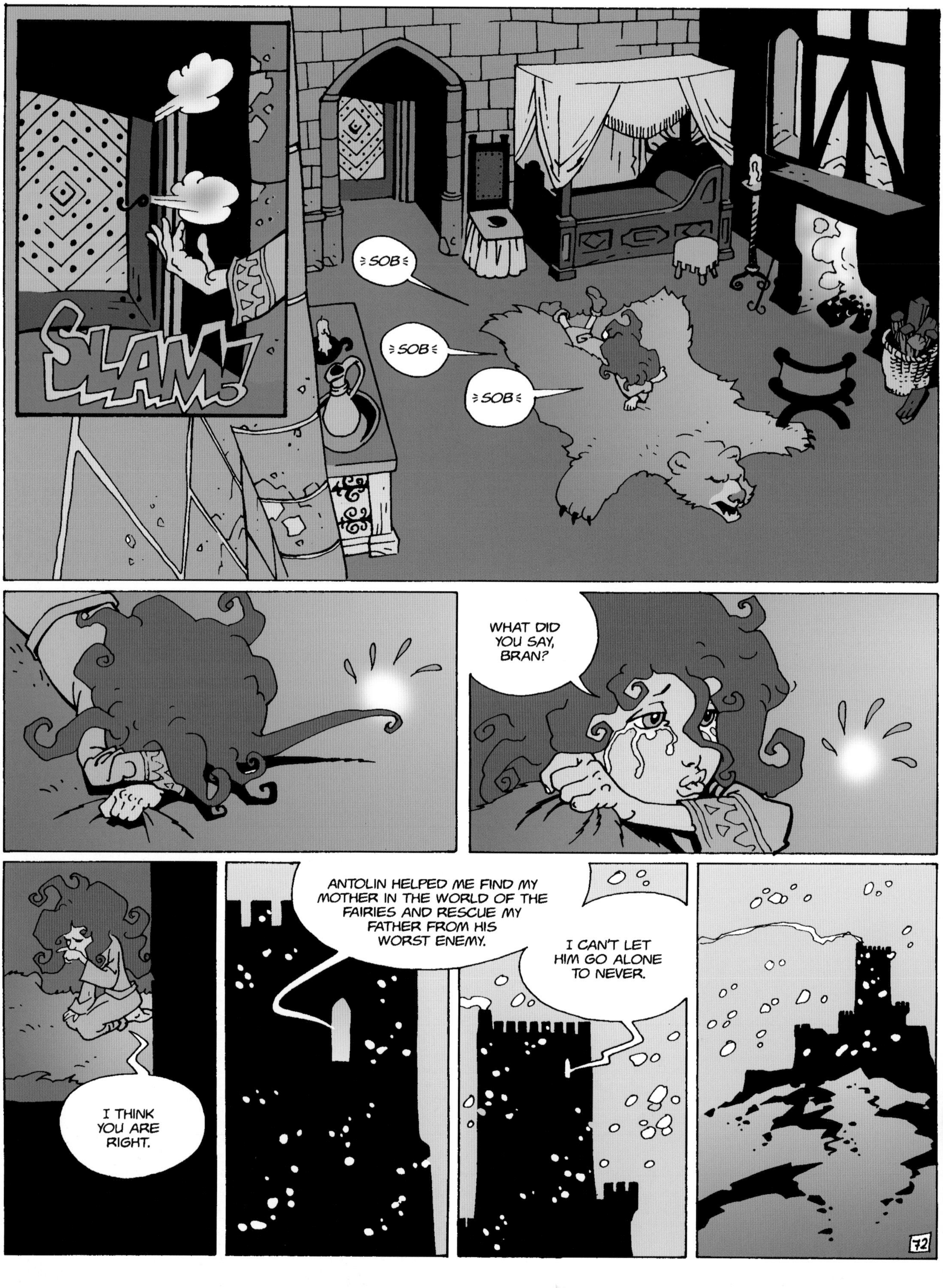
SLAM!
SOB
SOB
SOB
WHAT DID YOU SAY, BRAN?
I THINK YOU ARE RIGHT.
ANTOLIN HELPED ME FIND MY MOTHER IN THE WORLD OF THE FAIRIES AND RESCUE MY FATHER FROM HIS WORST ENEMY.
I CAN'T LET HIM GO ALONE TO NEVER.
72

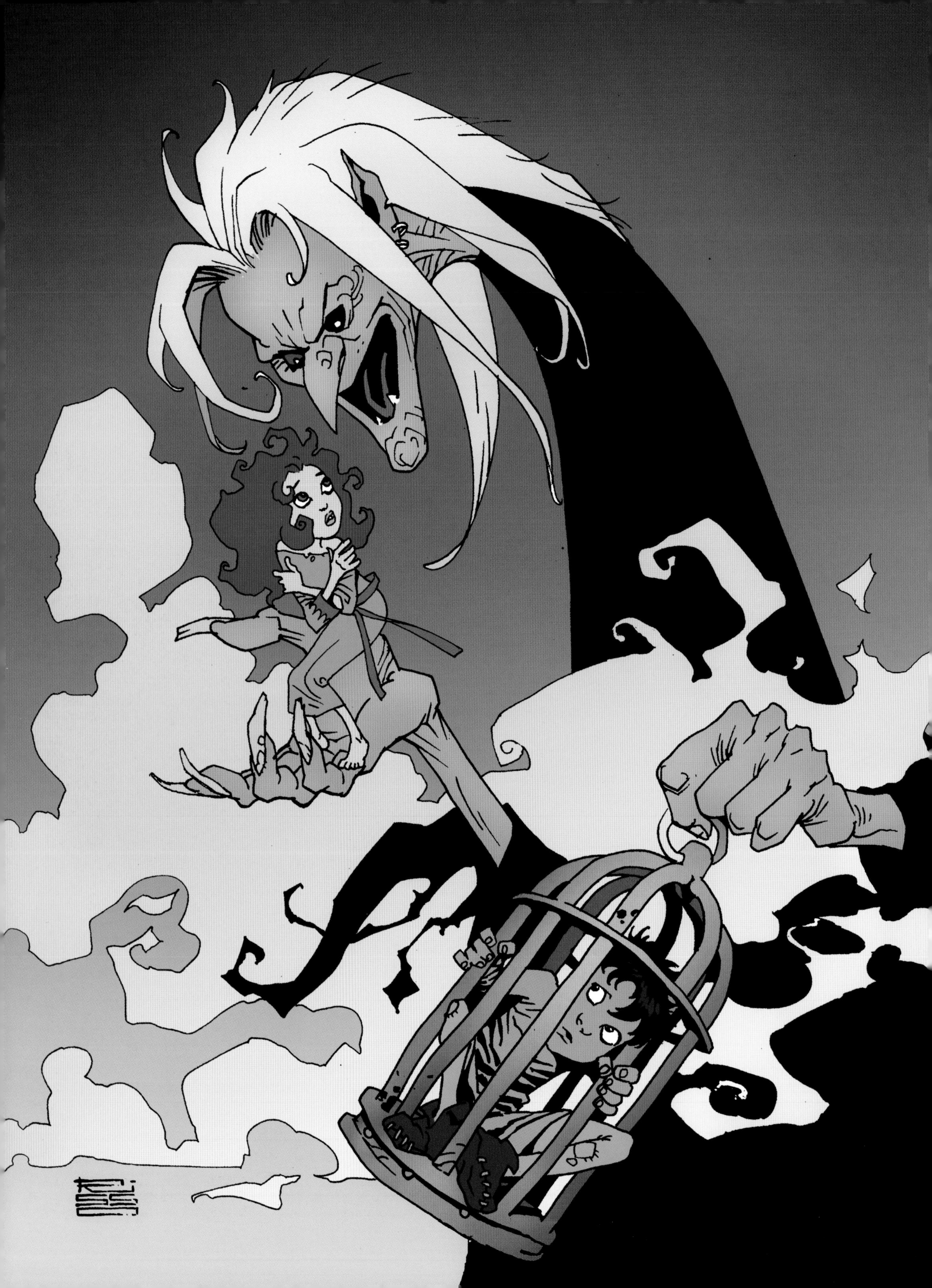

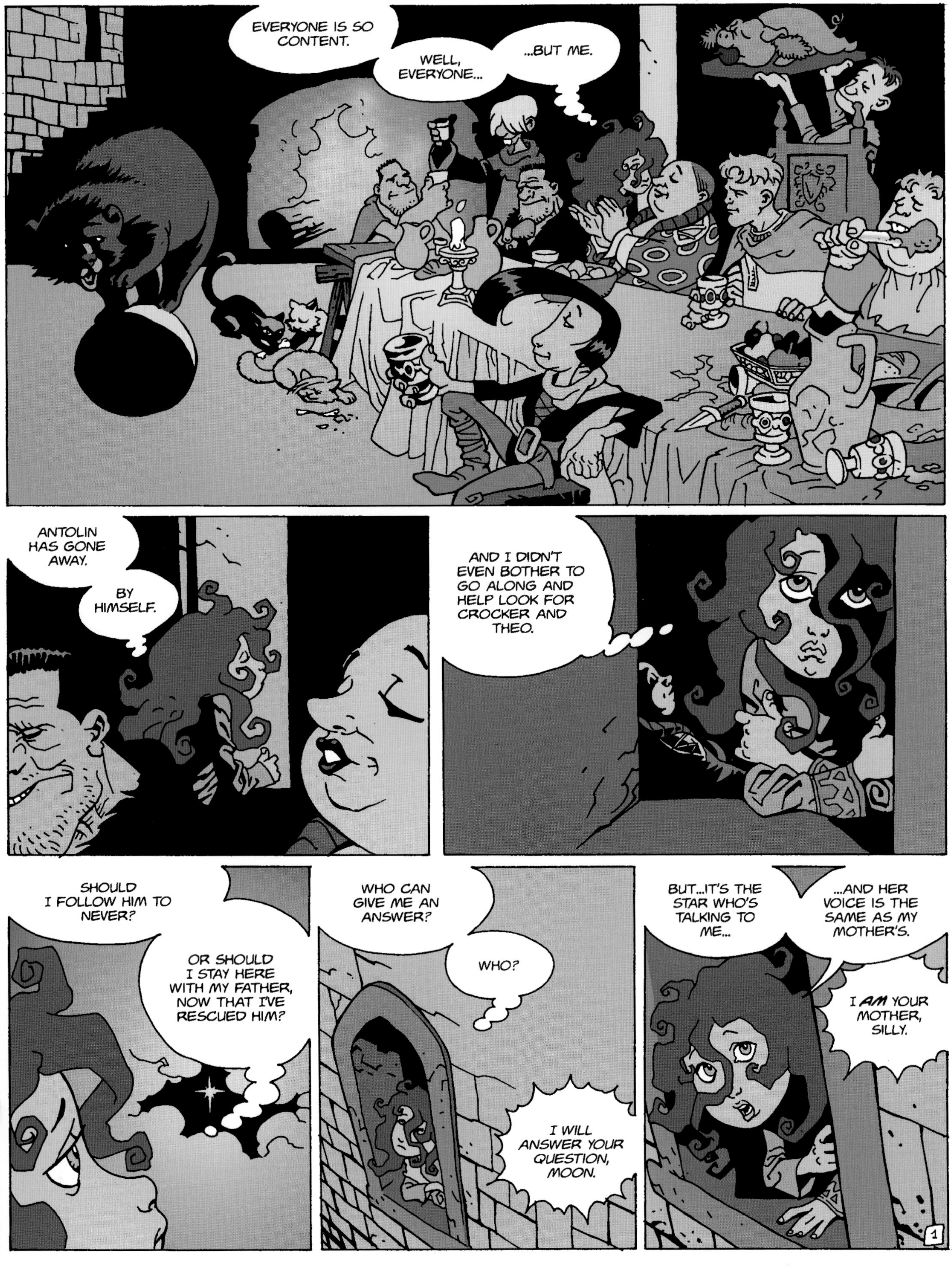
EVERYONE IS SO CONTENT.
WELL, EVERYONE...
...BUT ME.
ANTOLIN HAS GONE AWAY.
BY HIMSELF.
AND I DIDN'T EVEN BOTHER TO GO ALONG AND HELP LOOK FOR CROCKER AND THEO.
SHOULD I FOLLOW HIM TO NEVER?
OR SHOULD I STAY HERE WITH MY FATHER, NOW THAT I'VE RESCUED HIM?
WHO CAN GIVE ME AN ANSWER?
WHO?
I WILL ANSWER YOUR QUESTION, MOON.
BUT...IT'S THE STAR WHO'S TALKING TO ME...
...AND HER VOICE IS THE SAME AS MY MOTHER'S.
I AM YOUR MOTHER, SILLY.
1

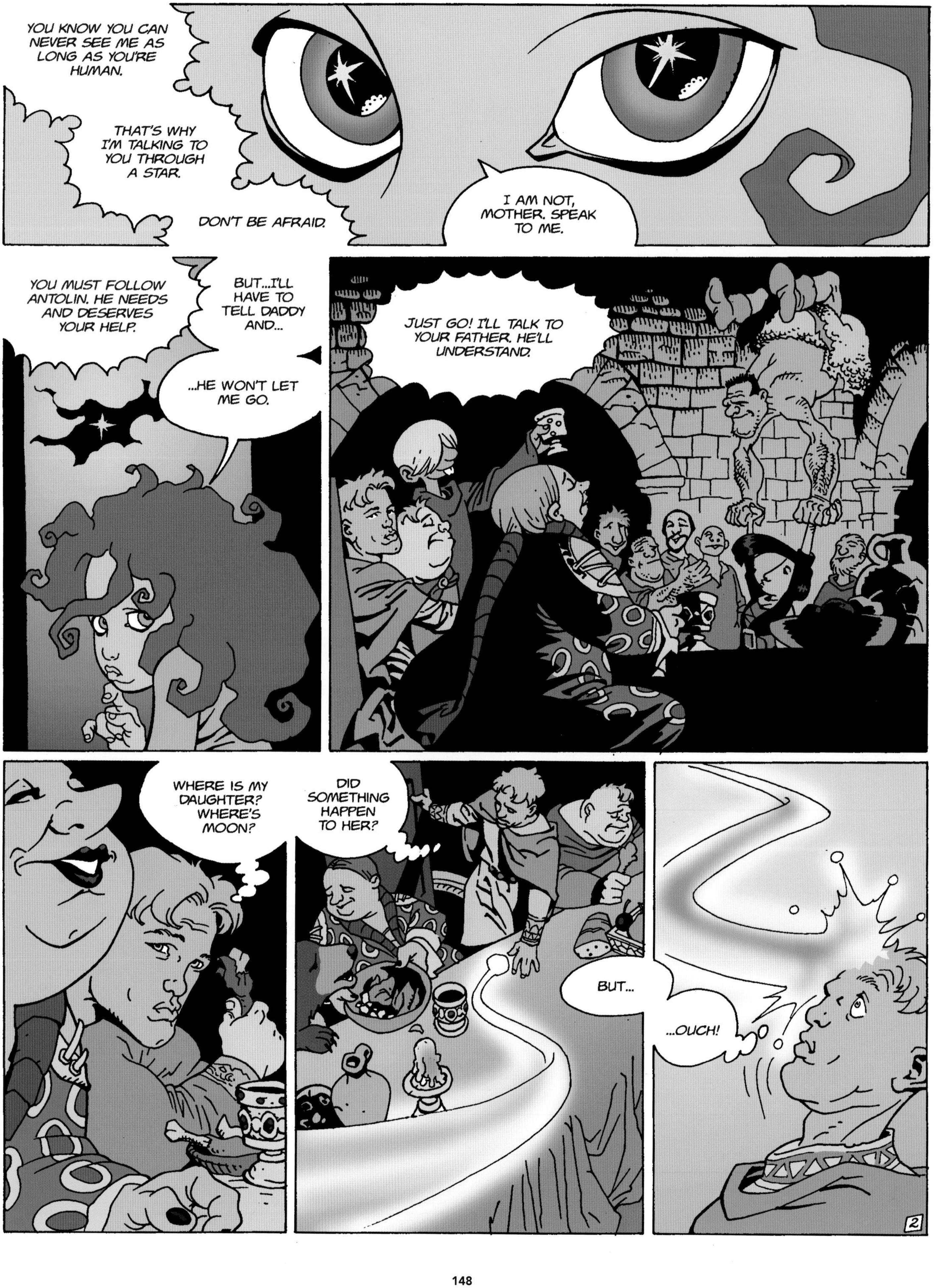
YOU KNOW YOU CAN NEVER SEE ME AS LONG AS YOU'RE HUMAN.
THAT'S WHY I'M TALKING TO YOU THROUGH A STAR.
DON'T BE AFRAID.
I AM NOT, MOTHER. SPEAK TO ME.
YOU MUST FOLLOW ANTOLIN. HE NEEDS AND DESERVES YOUR HELP.
BUT...I'LL HAVE TO TELL DADDY AND...
...HE WON'T LET ME GO.
JUST GO! I'LL TALK TO YOUR FATHER. HE'LL UNDERSTAND.
WHERE IS MY DAUGHTER? WHERE'S MOON?
DID SOMETHING HAPPEN TO HER?
BUT...
...OUCH!
2

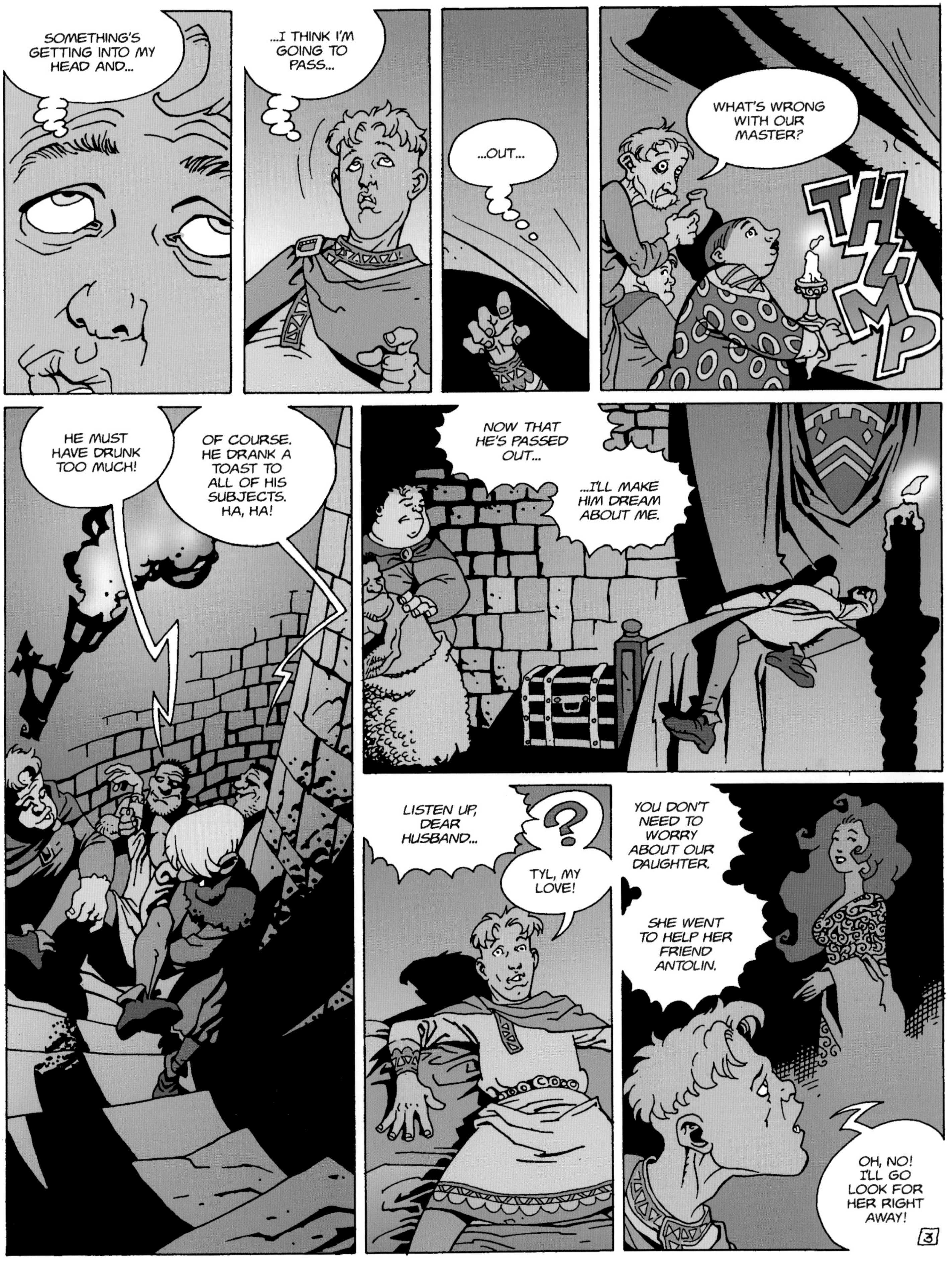
SOMETHING'S GETTING INTO MY HEAD AND...
...I THINK I'M GOING TO PASS...
...OUT...
WHAT'S WRONG WITH OUR MASTER?
THUMP
HE MUST HAVE DRUNK TOO MUCH!
OF COURSE. HE DRANK A TOAST TO ALL OF HIS SUBJECTS. HA, HA!
NOW THAT HE'S PASSED OUT...
...I'LL MAKE HIM DREAM ABOUT ME.
LISTEN UP, DEAR HUSBAND...
?
TYL, MY LOVE!
YOU DON'T NEED TO WORRY ABOUT OUR DAUGHTER.
SHE WENT TO HELP HER FRIEND ANTOLIN.
OH, NO! I'LL GO LOOK FOR HER RIGHT AWAY!
3

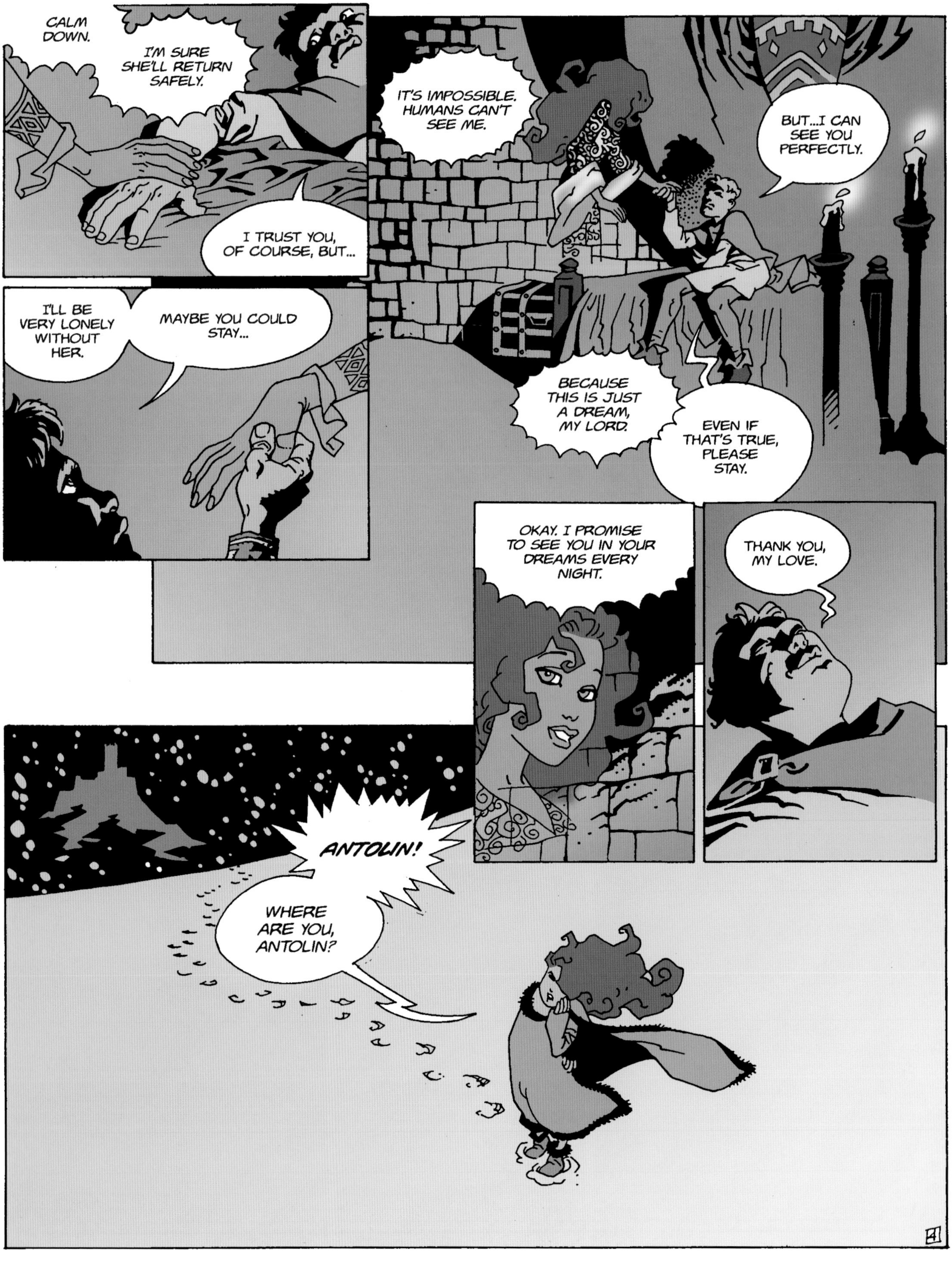
CALM DOWN.
I'M SURE SHE'LL RETURN SAFELY.
I TRUST YOU, OF COURSE, BUT...
I'LL BE VERY LONELY WITHOUT HER.
MAYBE YOU COULD STAY...
IT'S IMPOSSIBLE. HUMANS CAN'T SEE ME.
BUT...I CAN SEE YOU PERFECTLY.
BECAUSE THIS IS JUST A DREAM, MY LORD.
EVEN IF THAT'S TRUE, PLEASE STAY.
OKAY. I PROMISE TO SEE YOU IN YOUR DREAMS EVERY NIGHT.
THANK YOU, MY LOVE.
ANTOLIN!
WHERE ARE YOU, ANTOLIN?
4

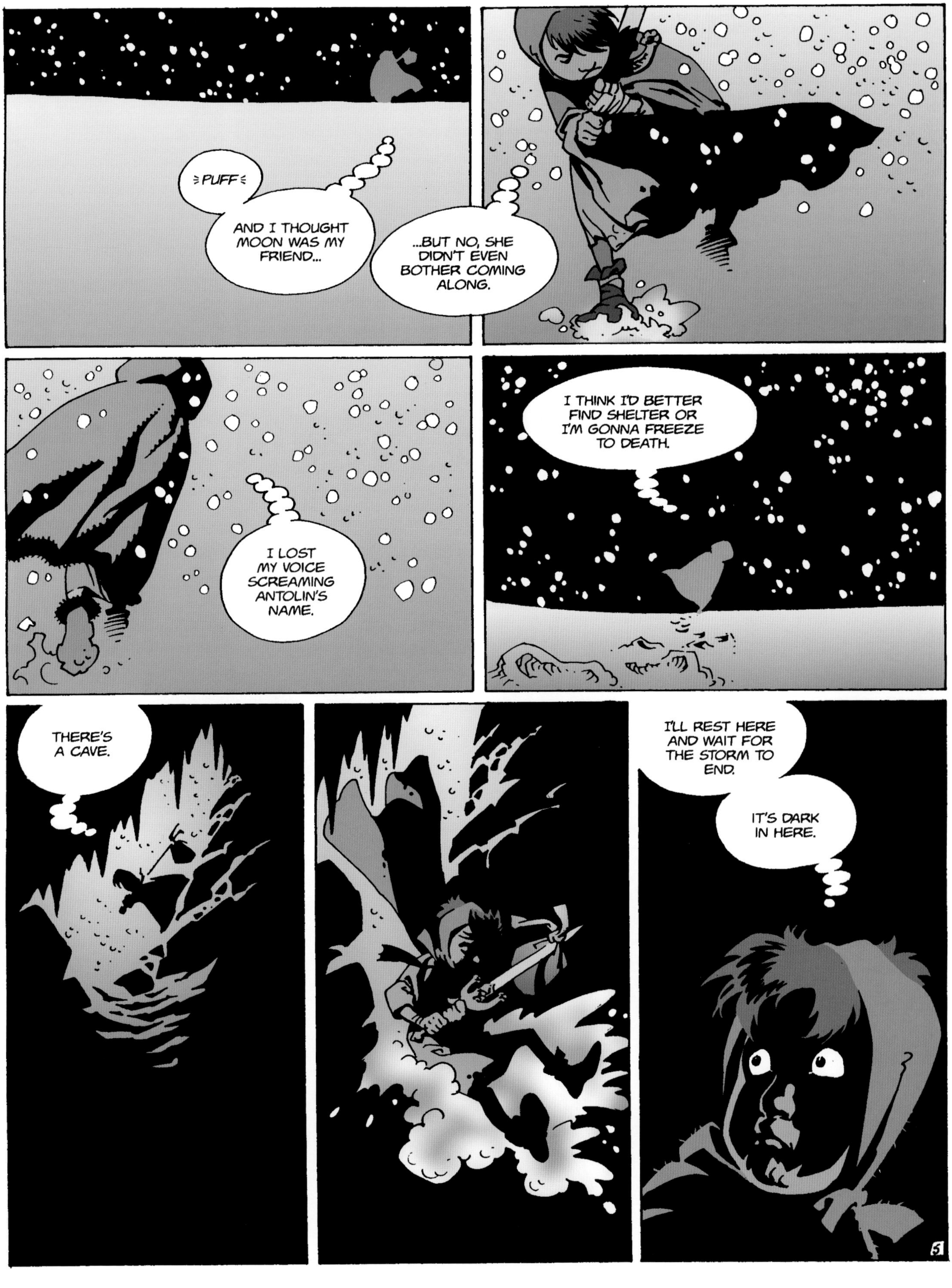

PUFF
AND I THOUGHT MOON WAS MY FRIEND...
...BUT NO, SHE DIDN'T EVEN BOTHER COMING ALONG.
I LOST MY VOICE SCREAMING ANTOLIN'S NAME.
I THINK I'D BETTER FIND SHELTER OR I'M GONNA FREEZE TO DEATH.
THERE'S A CAVE.
I'LL REST HERE AND WAIT FOR THE STORM TO END.
IT'S DARK IN HERE.
5

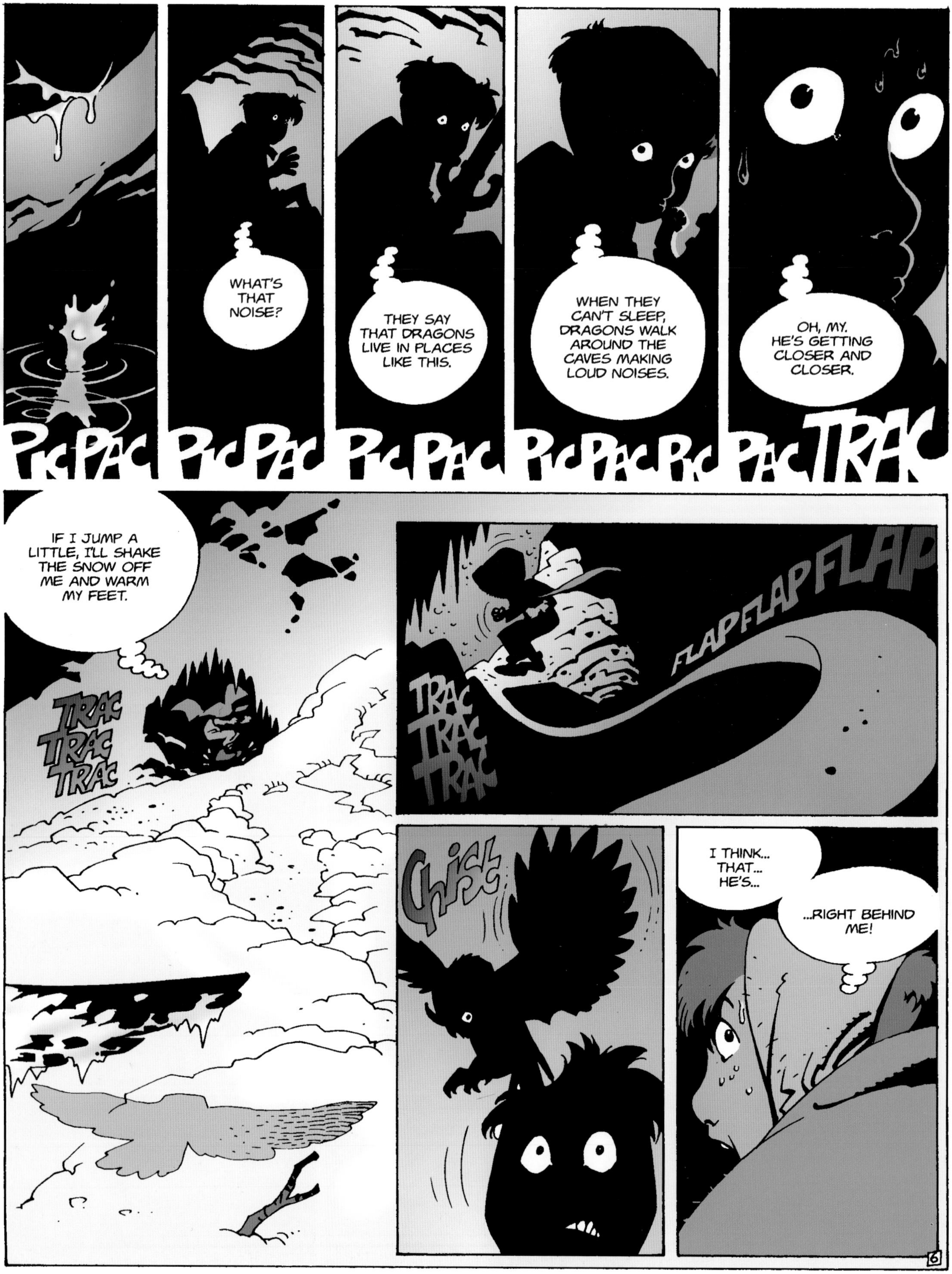
PIC PAC
WHAT'S THAT NOISE?
PIC PAC
THEY SAY THAT DRAGONS LIVE IN PLACES LIKE THIS.
PIC PAC
WHEN THEY CAN'T SLEEP, DRAGONS WALK AROUND THE CAVES MAKING LOUD NOISES.
PIC PAC PIC
OH, MY. HE'S GETTING CLOSER AND CLOSER.
PAC TRAC
IF I JUMP A LITTLE, I'LL SHAKE THE SNOW OFF ME AND WARM MY FEET.
TRAC TRAC TRAC
FLAP FLAP FLAP
TRAC TRAC TRAC
CHIST
I THINK... THAT... HE'S...
...RIGHT BEHIND ME!
6

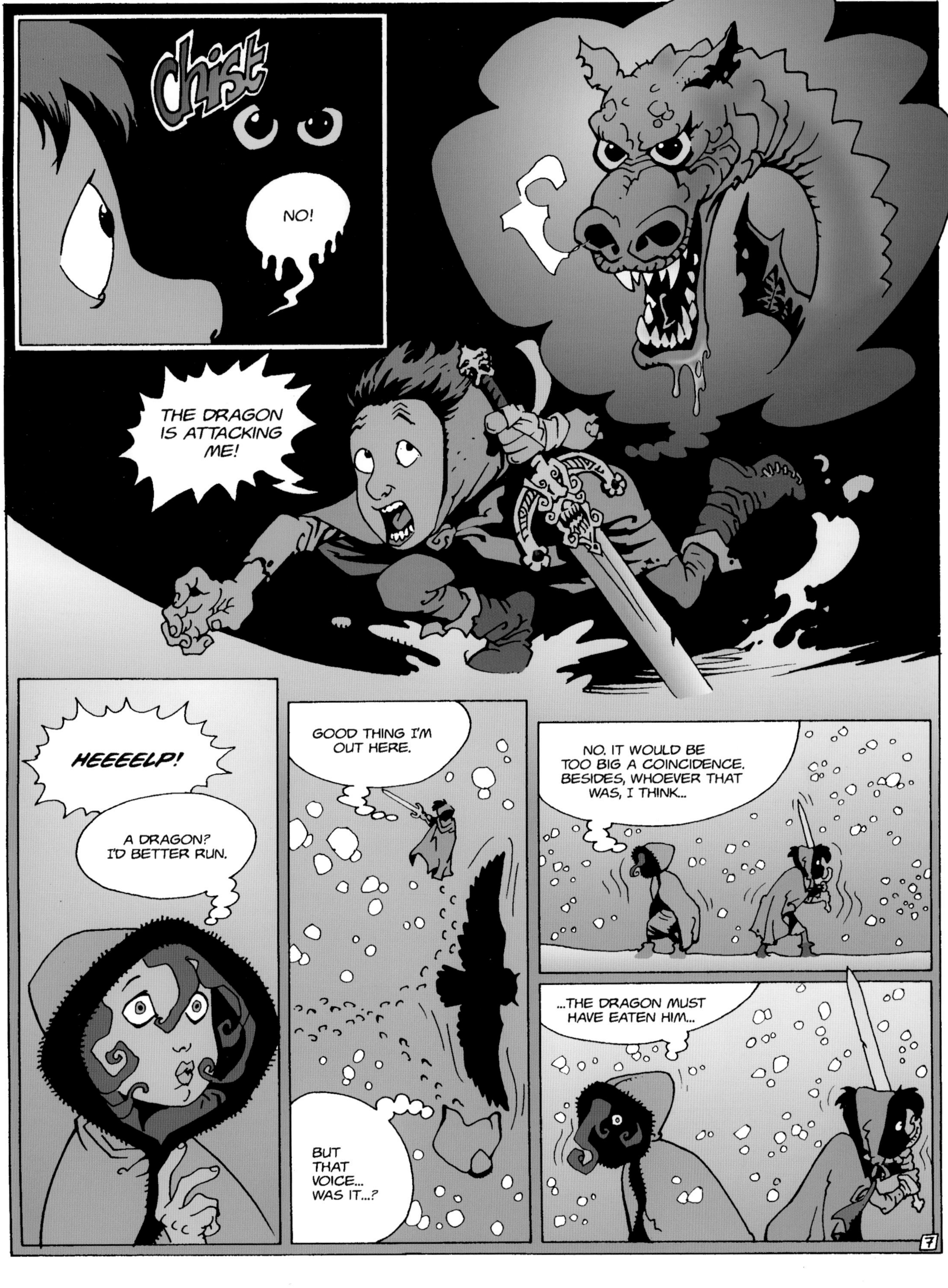
chist
NO!
THE DRAGON IS ATTACKING ME!
HEEEELP!
A DRAGON? I'D BETTER RUN.
GOOD THING I'M OUT HERE.
BUT THAT VOICE... WAS IT...?
NO. IT WOULD BE TOO BIG A COINCIDENCE. BESIDES, WHOEVER THAT WAS, I THINK...
...THE DRAGON MUST HAVE EATEN HIM...
7

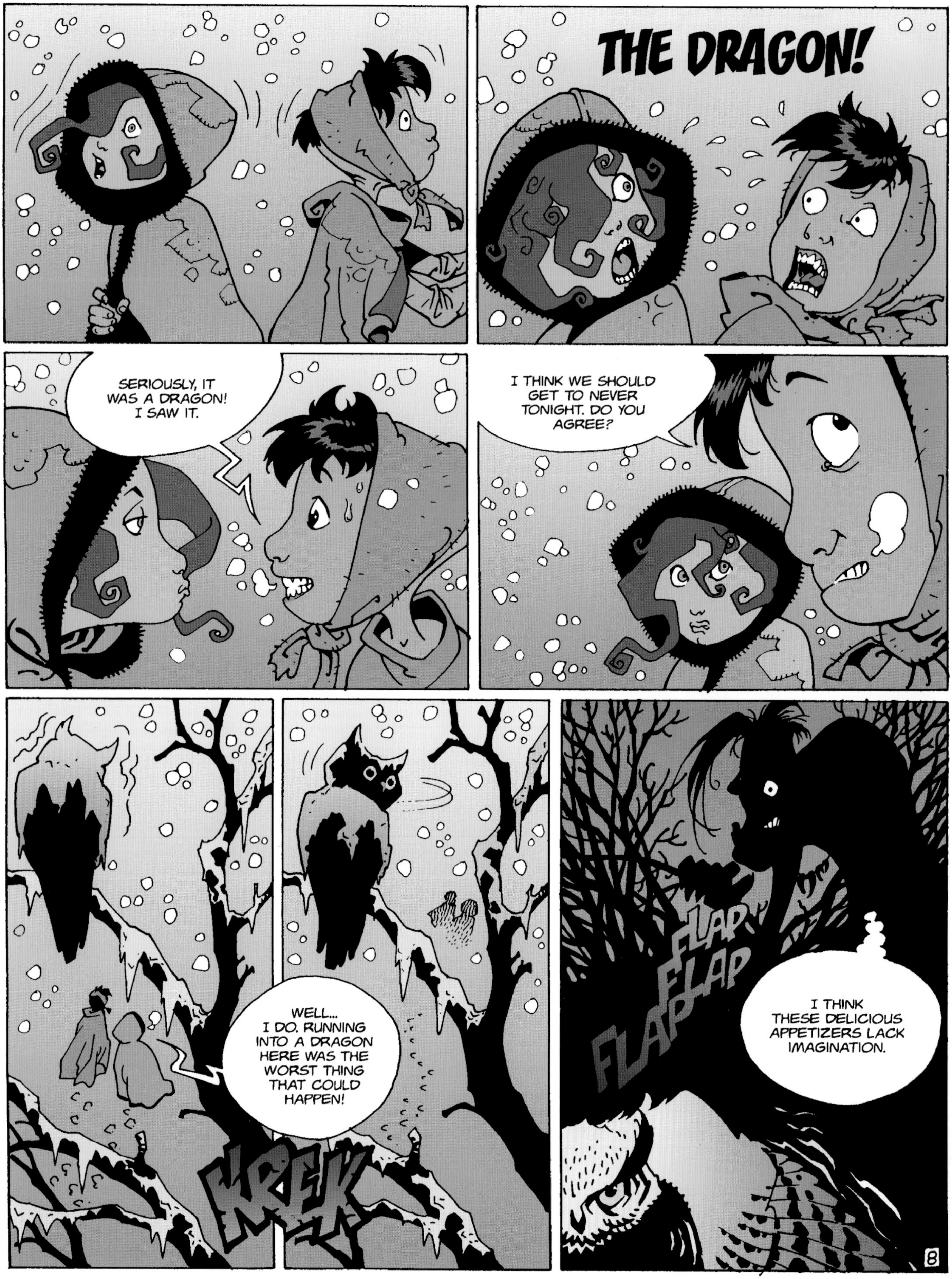
THE DRAGON!
SERIOUSLY, IT WAS A DRAGON! I SAW IT.
I THINK WE SHOULD GET TO NEVER TONIGHT. DO YOU AGREE?
WELL... I DO. RUNNING INTO A DRAGON HERE WAS THE WORST THING THAT COULD HAPPEN!
KREK
FLAP FLAP FLAP
I THINK THESE DELICIOUS APPETIZERS LACK IMAGINATION.
8

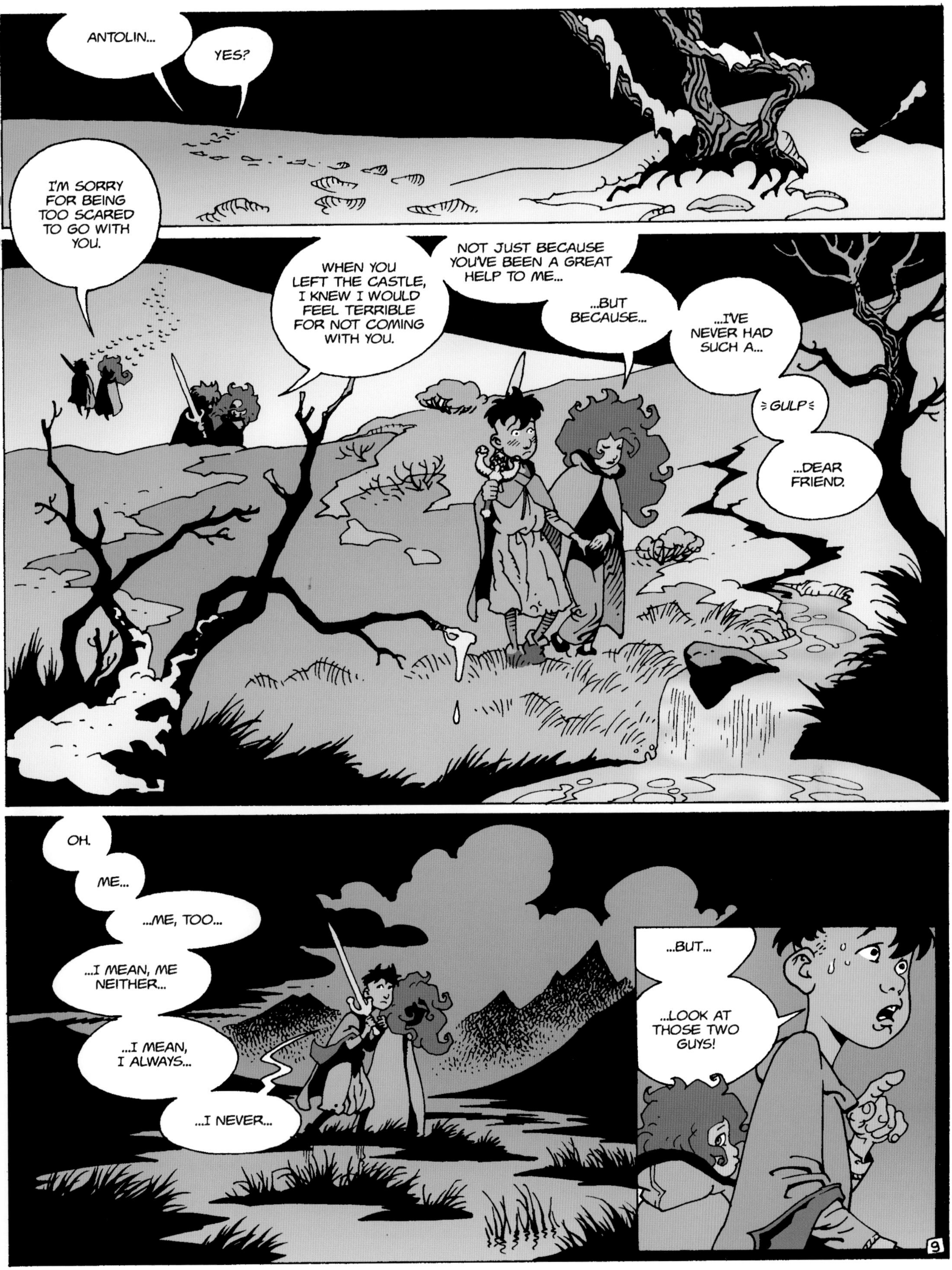
ANTOLIN...
YES?
I'M SORRY FOR BEING TOO SCARED TO GO WITH YOU.
WHEN YOU LEFT THE CASTLE, I KNEW I WOULD FEEL TERRIBLE FOR NOT COMING WITH YOU.
NOT JUST BECAUSE YOU'VE BEEN A GREAT HELP TO ME...
...BUT BECAUSE...
...I'VE NEVER HAD SUCH A...
GULP
...DEAR FRIEND.
OH.
ME...
...ME, TOO...
...I MEAN, ME NEITHER...
...I MEAN, I ALWAYS...
...I NEVER...
...BUT...
...LOOK AT THOSE TWO GUYS!
9

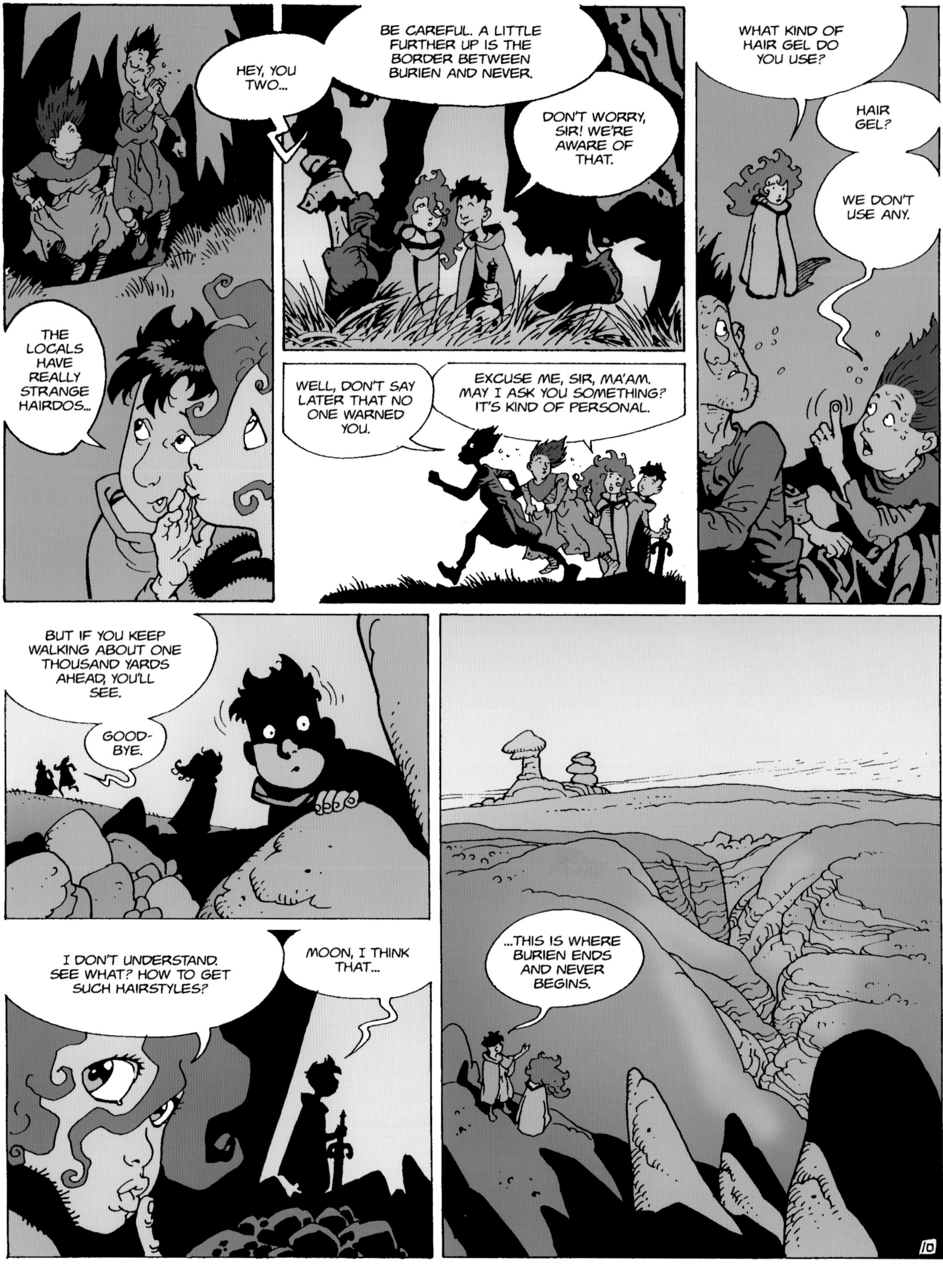
HEY, YOU TWO...
BE CAREFUL. A LITTLE FURTHER UP IS THE BORDER BETWEEN BURIEN AND NEVER.
DON'T WORRY, SIR! WE'RE AWARE OF THAT.
WHAT KIND OF HAIR GEL DO YOU USE?
HAIR GEL?
WE DON'T USE ANY.
THE LOCALS HAVE REALLY STRANGE HAIRDOS...
WELL, DON'T SAY LATER THAT NO ONE WARNED YOU.
EXCUSE ME, SIR, MA'AM. MAY I ASK YOU SOMETHING? IT'S KIND OF PERSONAL.
BUT IF YOU KEEP WALKING ABOUT ONE THOUSAND YARDS AHEAD, YOU'LL SEE.
GOOD-BYE.
I DON'T UNDERSTAND. SEE WHAT? HOW TO GET SUCH HAIRSTYLES?
MOON, I THINK THAT...
...THIS IS WHERE BURIEN ENDS AND NEVER BEGINS.
10

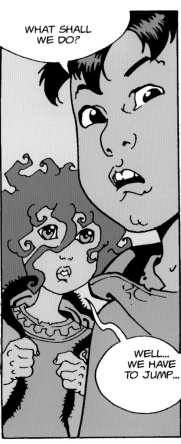

WHAT SHALL WE DO?

WELL... WE HAVE TO JUMP...

ON THREE. ONE, TWO...

...THREE!

IT'S NOT SO BAD HERE, IS IT?

ON THE CONTRARY. IT'S GREAT! INSTEAD OF THAT FREEZING COLD, IT'S NICE AND HOT.

RATHER UNPLEASANT HEAT, THOUGH, I'D SAY.

WELL...YES. NOW THAT I TOOK MY SHOES OFF...

...THE GROUND IS BURNING. I CAN BARELY WALK ON IT!

OUCH!

SORRY, ANTOLIN. THIS IS THE ONLY WAY TO PREVENT ME FROM GETTING HORRIBLE BLISTERS.

IF WE DON'T DO SOMETHING SOON...

...WE COULD DEHYDRATE AND BURN TO DEATH IN THE HOT SUN.

WE SHOULD AT LEAST COVER OUR HEADS.

HATS! HATS!

11

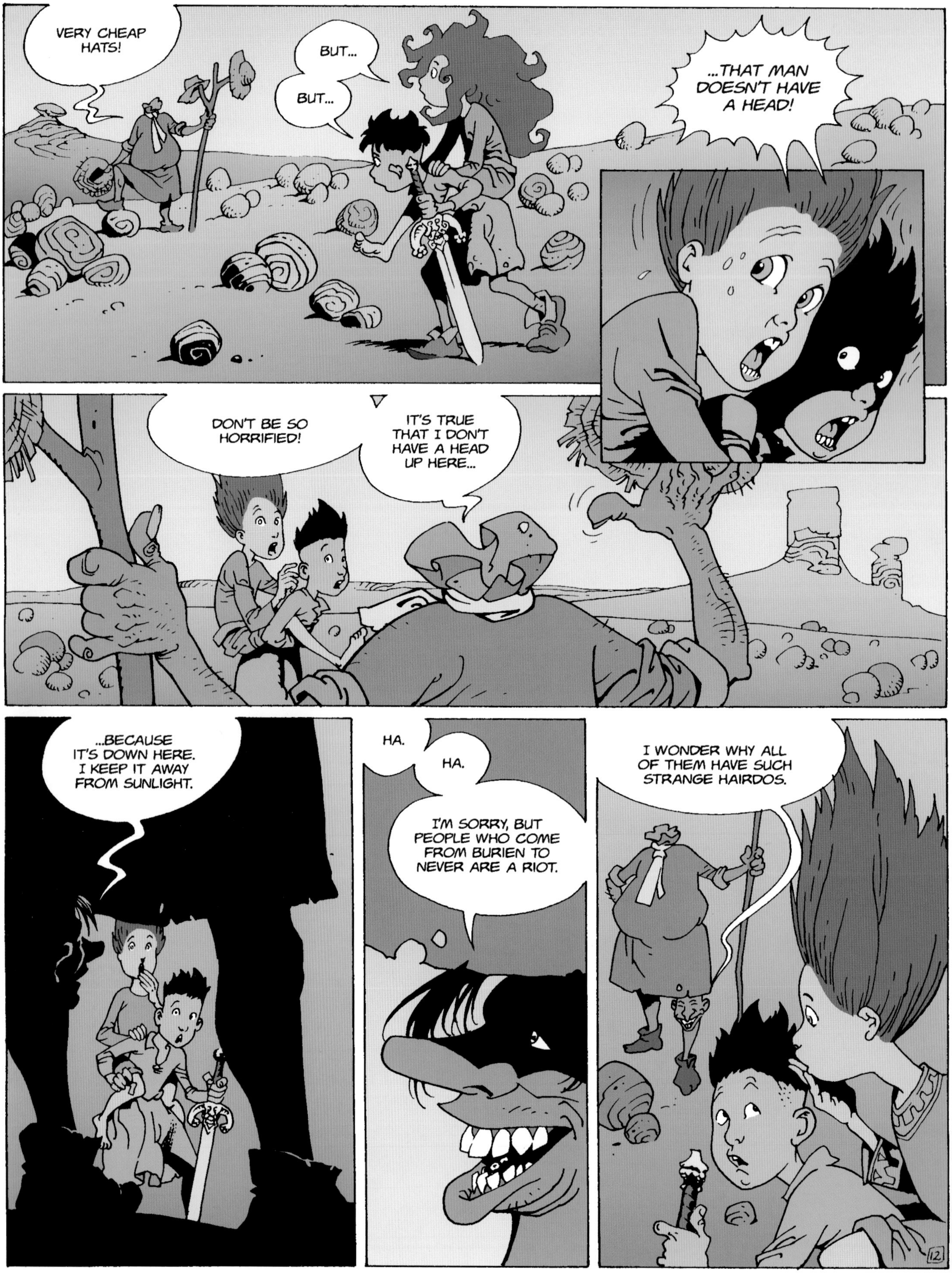
VERY CHEAP HATS!
BUT...
BUT...
...THAT MAN DOESN'T HAVE A HEAD!
DON'T BE SO HORRIFIED!
IT'S TRUE THAT I DON'T HAVE A HEAD UP HERE...
...BECAUSE IT'S DOWN HERE. I KEEP IT AWAY FROM SUNLIGHT.
HA.
HA.
I'M SORRY, BUT PEOPLE WHO COME FROM BURIEN TO NEVER ARE A RIOT.
I WONDER WHY ALL OF THEM HAVE SUCH STRANGE HAIRDOS.
12

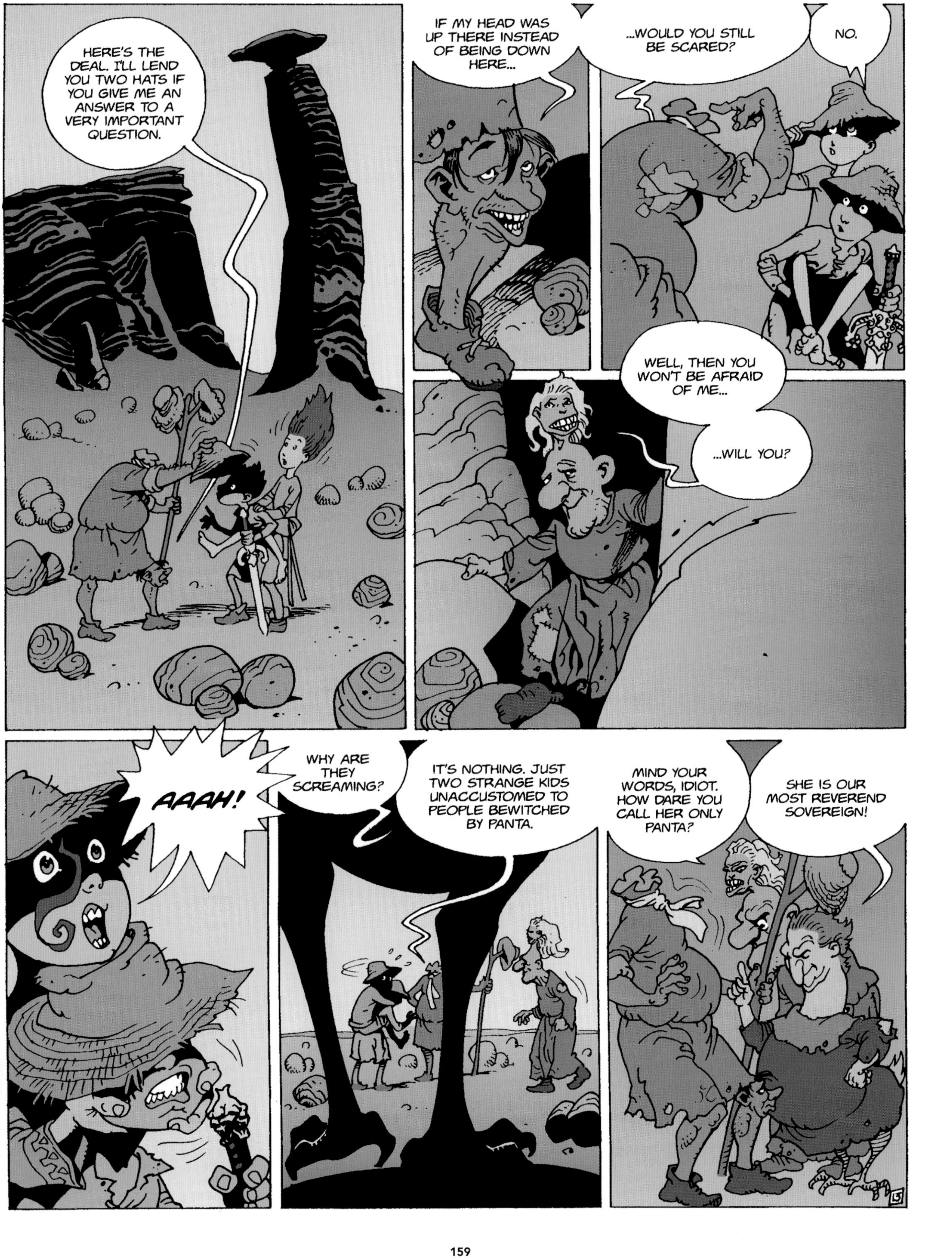
HERE'S THE DEAL. I'LL LEND YOU TWO HATS IF YOU GIVE ME AN ANSWER TO A VERY IMPORTANT QUESTION.
IF MY HEAD WAS UP THERE INSTEAD OF BEING DOWN HERE...
...WOULD YOU STILL BE SCARED?
NO.
WELL, THEN YOU WON'T BE AFRAID OF ME...
...WILL YOU?
AAAH!
WHY ARE THEY SCREAMING?
IT'S NOTHING. JUST TWO STRANGE KIDS UNACCUSTOMED TO PEOPLE BEWITCHED BY PANTA.
MIND YOUR WORDS, IDIOT. HOW DARE YOU CALL HER ONLY PANTA?
SHE IS OUR MOST REVEREND SOVEREIGN!

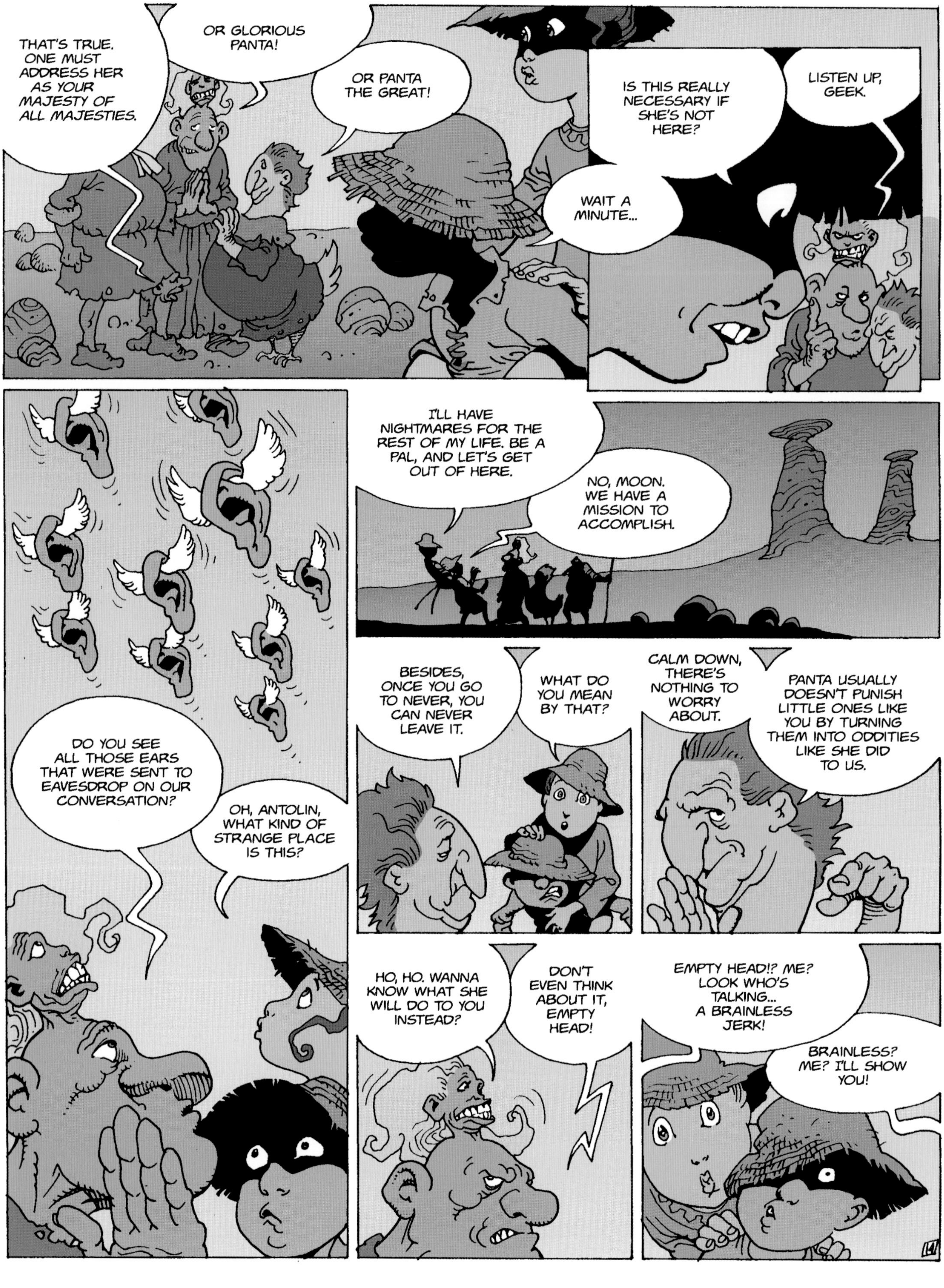
THAT'S TRUE. ONE MUST ADDRESS HER AS YOUR MAJESTY OF ALL MAJESTIES.
OR GLORIOUS PANTA!
OR PANTA THE GREAT!
IS THIS REALLY NECESSARY IF SHE'S NOT HERE?
LISTEN UP, GEEK.
WAIT A MINUTE...
DO YOU SEE ALL THOSE EARS THAT WERE SENT TO EAVESDROP ON OUR CONVERSATION?
OH, ANTOLIN, WHAT KIND OF STRANGE PLACE IS THIS?
I'LL HAVE NIGHTMARES FOR THE REST OF MY LIFE. BE A PAL, AND LET'S GET OUT OF HERE.
NO, MOON. WE HAVE A MISSION TO ACCOMPLISH.
BESIDES, ONCE YOU GO TO NEVER, YOU CAN NEVER LEAVE IT.
WHAT DO YOU MEAN BY THAT?
CALM DOWN, THERE'S NOTHING TO WORRY ABOUT.
PANTA USUALLY DOESN'T PUNISH LITTLE ONES LIKE YOU BY TURNING THEM INTO ODDITIES LIKE SHE DID TO US.
HO, HO. WANNA KNOW WHAT SHE WILL DO TO YOU INSTEAD?
DON'T EVEN THINK ABOUT IT, EMPTY HEAD!
EMPTY HEAD!? ME? LOOK WHO'S TALKING... A BRAINLESS JERK!
BRAINLESS? ME? I'LL SHOW YOU!
14

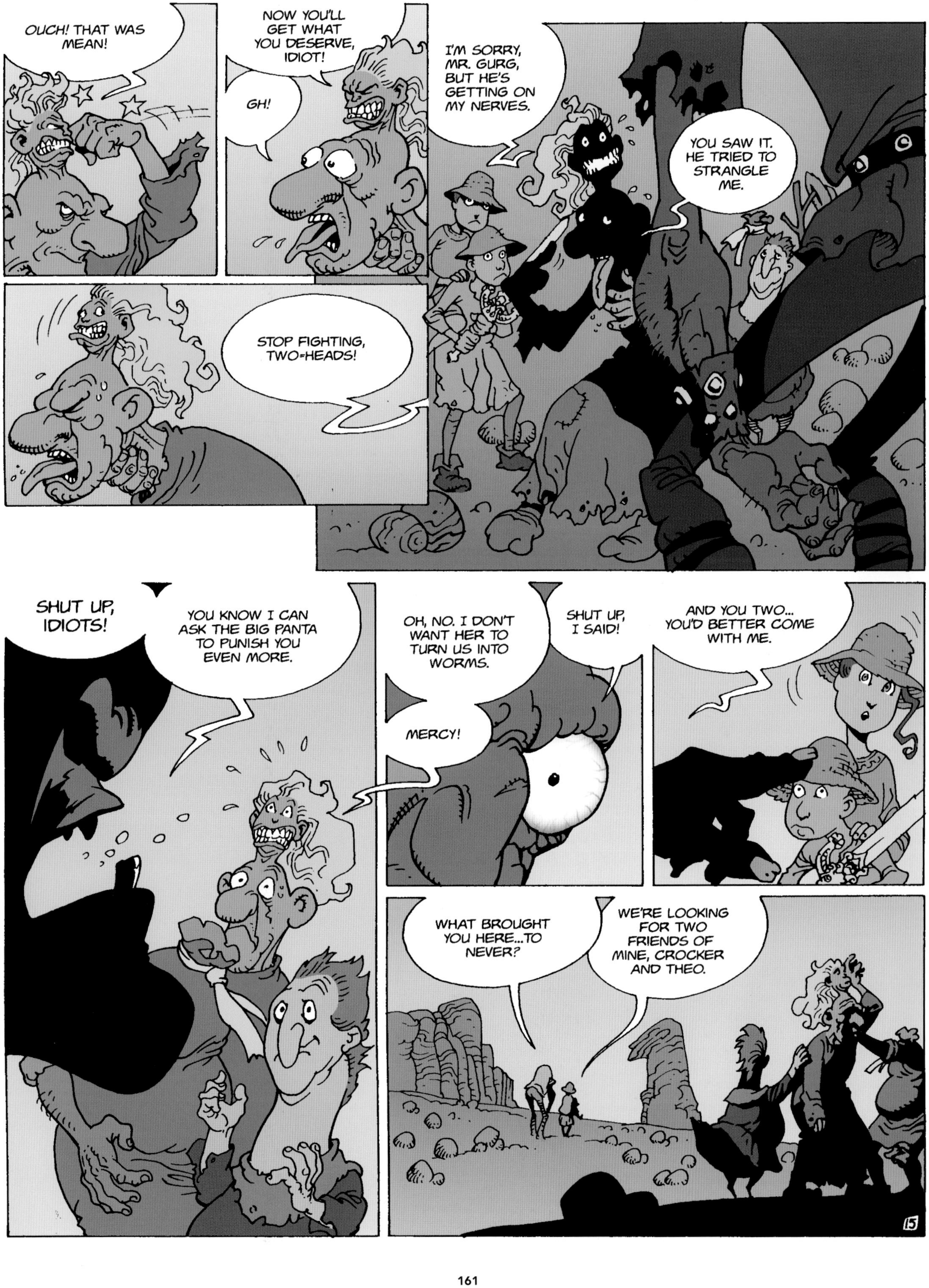
OUCH! THAT WAS MEAN!
NOW YOU'LL GET WHAT YOU DESERVE, IDIOT!
GH!
I'M SORRY, MR. GURG, BUT HE'S GETTING ON MY NERVES.
YOU SAW IT. HE TRIED TO STRANGLE ME.
STOP FIGHTING, TWO-HEADS!
SHUT UP, IDIOTS!
YOU KNOW I CAN ASK THE BIG PANTA TO PUNISH YOU EVEN MORE.
OH, NO. I DON'T WANT HER TO TURN US INTO WORMS.
MERCY!
SHUT UP, I SAID!
AND YOU TWO... YOU'D BETTER COME WITH ME.
WHAT BROUGHT YOU HERE...TO NEVER?
WE'RE LOOKING FOR TWO FRIENDS OF MINE, CROCKER AND THEO.
15

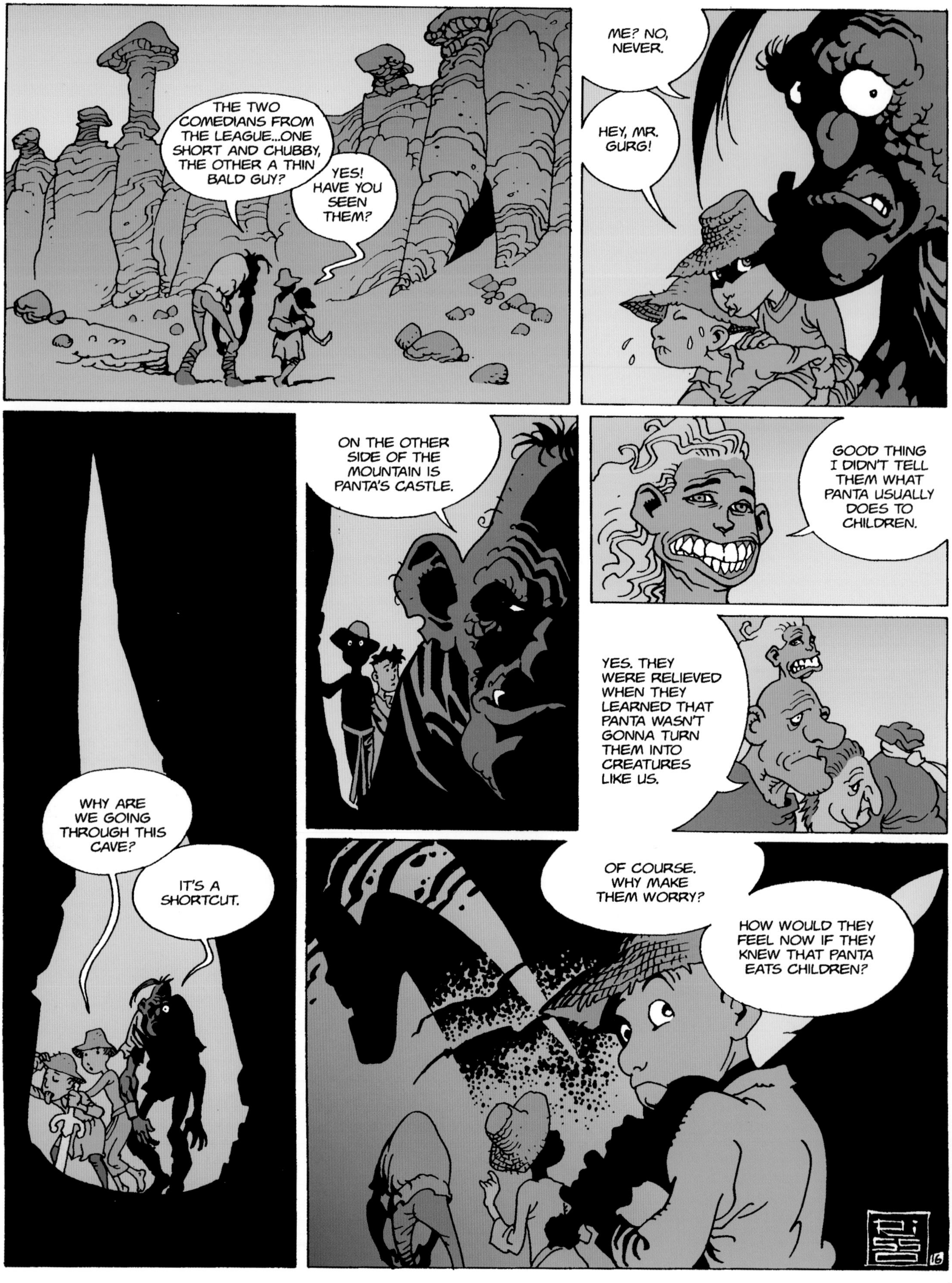
THE TWO COMEDIANS FROM THE LEAGUE...ONE SHORT AND CHUBBY, THE OTHER A THIN BALD GUY?
YES! HAVE YOU SEEN THEM?
ME? NO, NEVER.
HEY, MR. GURG!
WHY ARE WE GOING THROUGH THIS CAVE?
IT'S A SHORTCUT.
ON THE OTHER SIDE OF THE MOUNTAIN IS PANTA'S CASTLE.
GOOD THING I DIDN'T TELL THEM WHAT PANTA USUALLY DOES TO CHILDREN.
YES. THEY WERE RELIEVED WHEN THEY LEARNED THAT PANTA WASN'T GONNA TURN THEM INTO CREATURES LIKE US.
OF COURSE. WHY MAKE THEM WORRY?
HOW WOULD THEY FEEL NOW IF THEY KNEW THAT PANTA EATS CHILDREN?
16

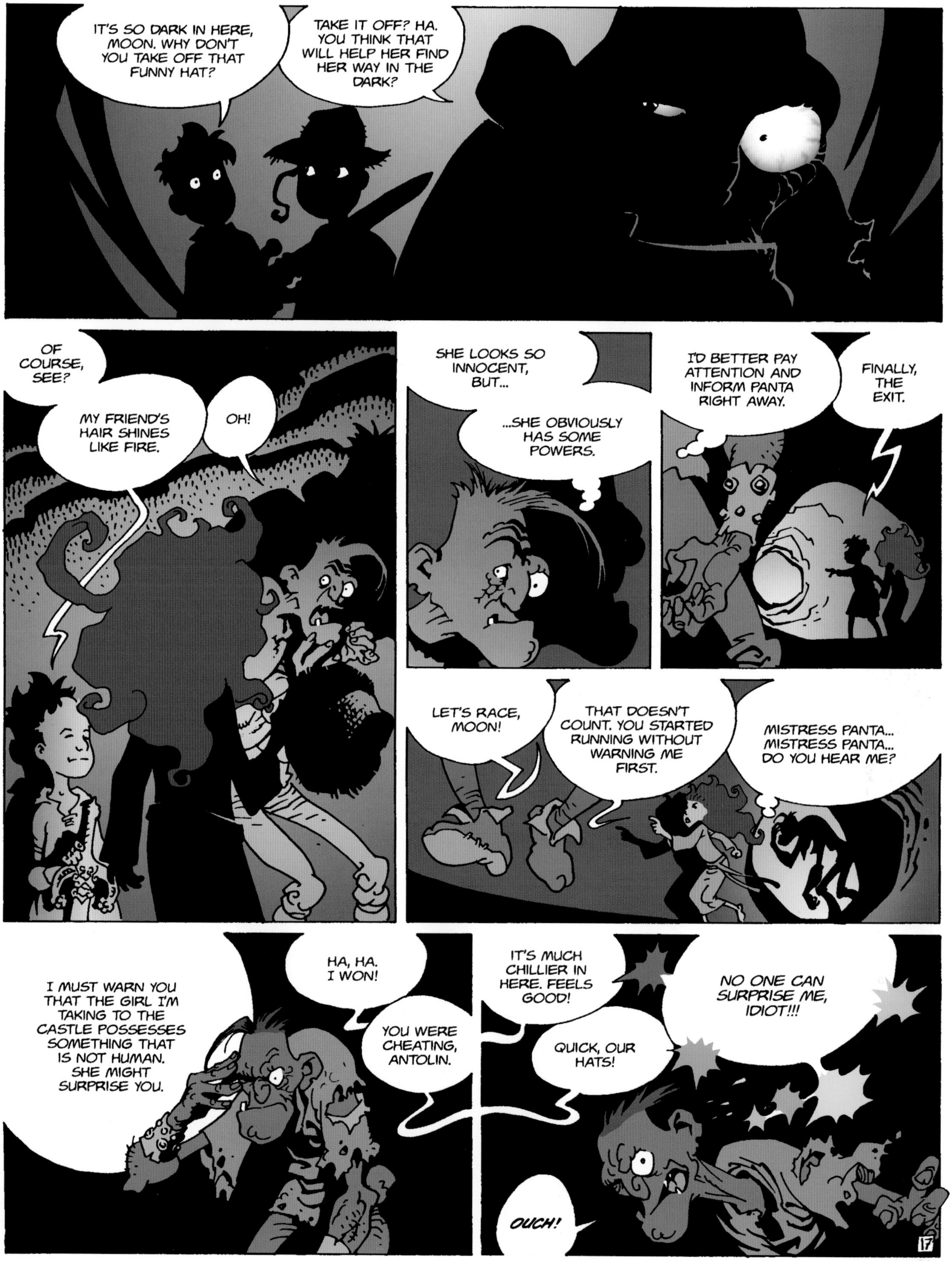
IT'S SO DARK IN HERE, MOON. WHY DON'T YOU TAKE OFF THAT FUNNY HAT?
TAKE IT OFF? HA. YOU THINK THAT WILL HELP HER FIND HER WAY IN THE DARK?
OF COURSE, SEE?
MY FRIEND'S HAIR SHINES LIKE FIRE.
OH!
SHE LOOKS SO INNOCENT, BUT...
...SHE OBVIOUSLY HAS SOME POWERS.
I'D BETTER PAY ATTENTION AND INFORM PANTA RIGHT AWAY.
FINALLY, THE EXIT.
LET'S RACE, MOON!
THAT DOESN'T COUNT. YOU STARTED RUNNING WITHOUT WARNING ME FIRST.
MISTRESS PANTA... MISTRESS PANTA... DO YOU HEAR ME?
I MUST WARN YOU THAT THE GIRL I'M TAKING TO THE CASTLE POSSESSES SOMETHING THAT IS NOT HUMAN. SHE MIGHT SURPRISE YOU.
HA, HA. I WON!
YOU WERE CHEATING, ANTOLIN.
IT'S MUCH CHILLIER IN HERE. FEELS GOOD!
QUICK, OUR HATS!
NO ONE CAN SURPRISE ME, IDIOT!!!
OUCH!
17

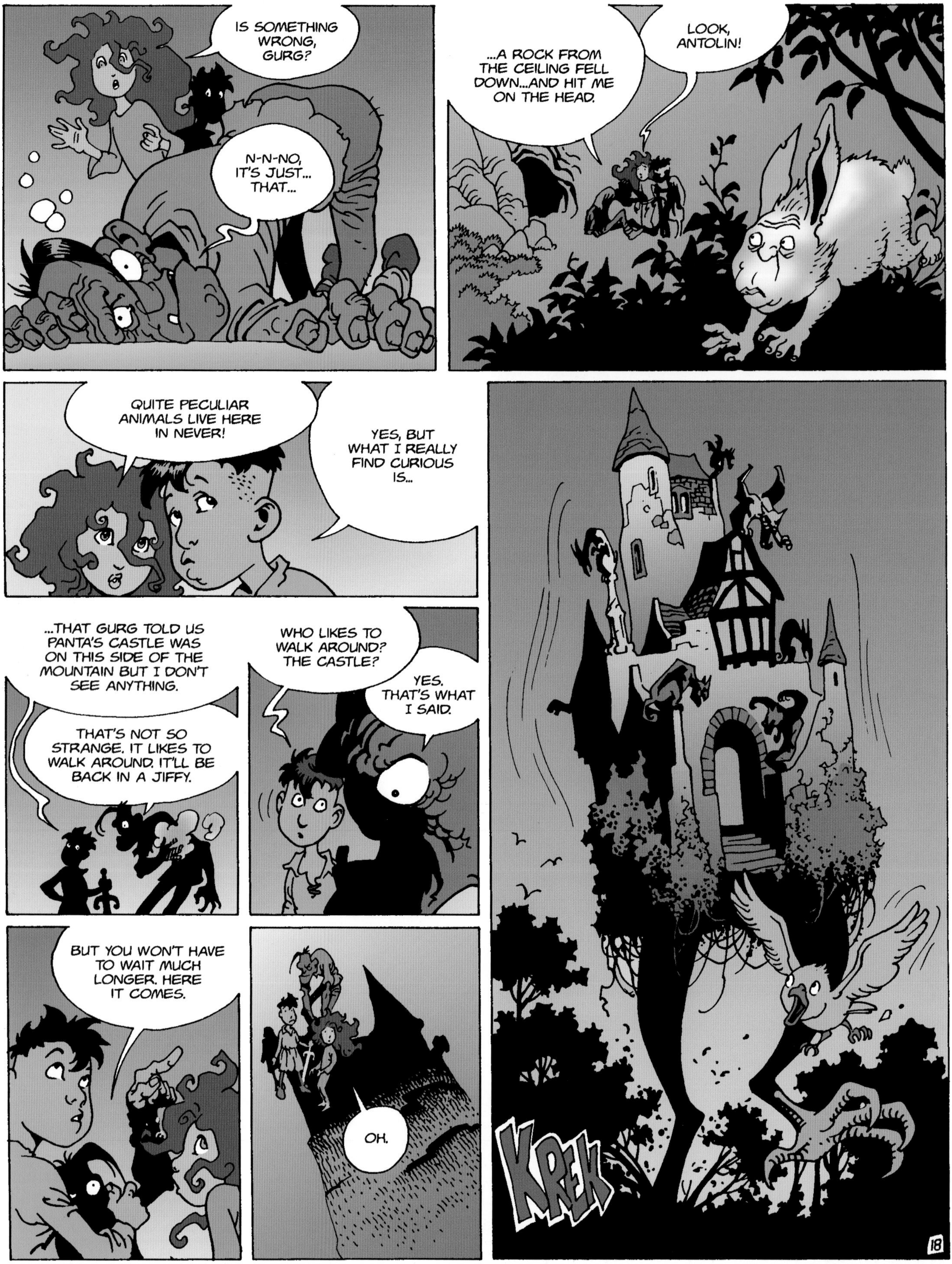
IS SOMETHING WRONG, GURG?
N-N-NO, IT'S JUST... THAT...
...A ROCK FROM THE CEILING FELL DOWN...AND HIT ME ON THE HEAD.
LOOK, ANTOLIN!
QUITE PECULIAR ANIMALS LIVE HERE IN NEVER!
YES, BUT WHAT I REALLY FIND CURIOUS IS...
...THAT GURG TOLD US PANTA'S CASTLE WAS ON THIS SIDE OF THE MOUNTAIN BUT I DON'T SEE ANYTHING.
THAT'S NOT SO STRANGE. IT LIKES TO WALK AROUND. IT'LL BE BACK IN A JIFFY.
WHO LIKES TO WALK AROUND? THE CASTLE?
YES. THAT'S WHAT I SAID.
BUT YOU WON'T HAVE TO WAIT MUCH LONGER. HERE IT COMES.
OH.
KREK
18

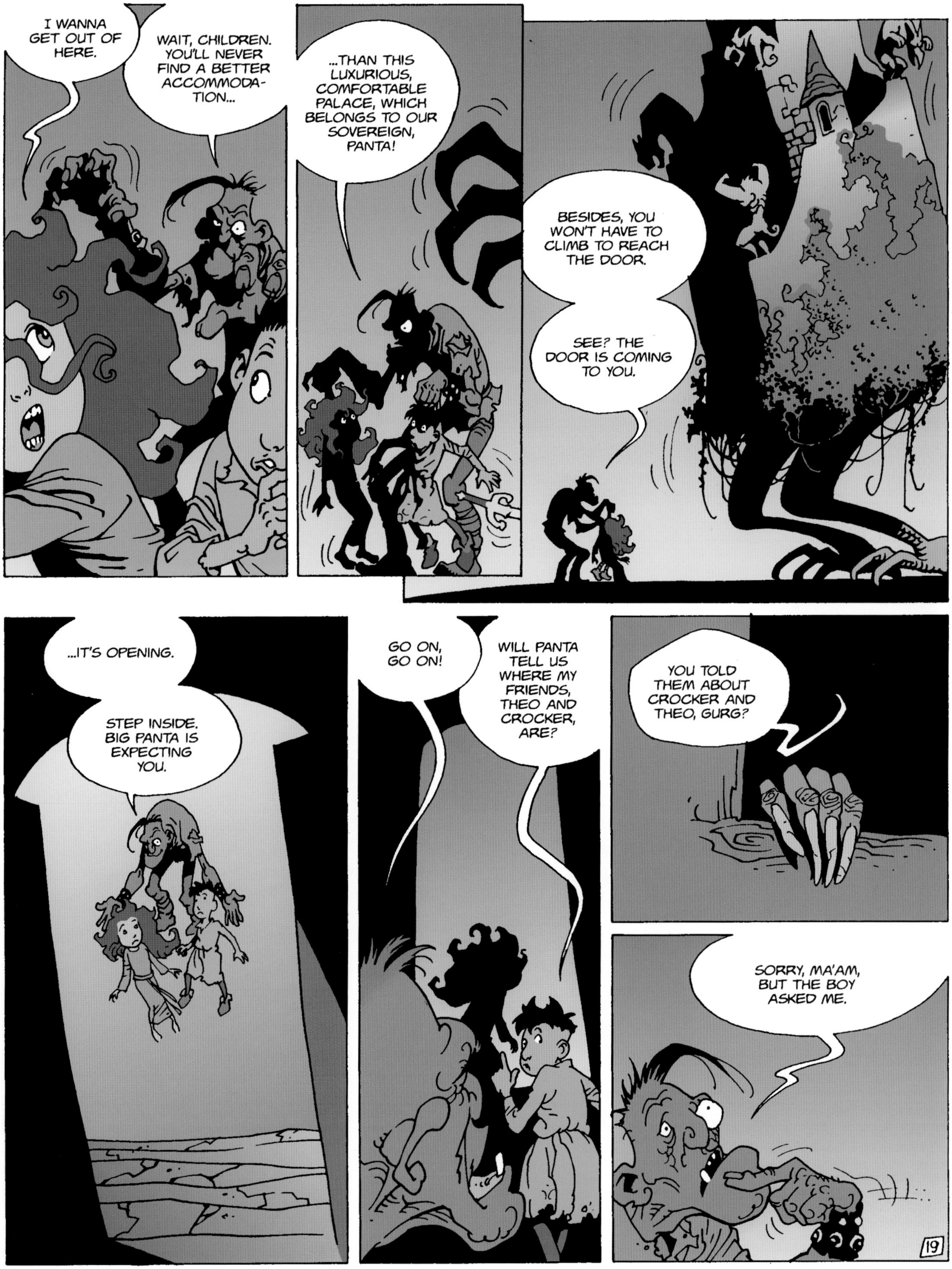
I WANNA GET OUT OF HERE.
WAIT, CHILDREN. YOU'LL NEVER FIND A BETTER ACCOMMODA-TION...
...THAN THIS LUXURIOUS, COMFORTABLE PALACE, WHICH BELONGS TO OUR SOVEREIGN, PANTA!
BESIDES, YOU WON'T HAVE TO CLIMB TO REACH THE DOOR.
SEE? THE DOOR IS COMING TO YOU.
...IT'S OPENING.
STEP INSIDE. BIG PANTA IS EXPECTING YOU.
GO ON, GO ON!
WILL PANTA TELL US WHERE MY FRIENDS, THEO AND CROCKER, ARE?
YOU TOLD THEM ABOUT CROCKER AND THEO, GURG?
SORRY, MA'AM, BUT THE BOY ASKED ME.
19

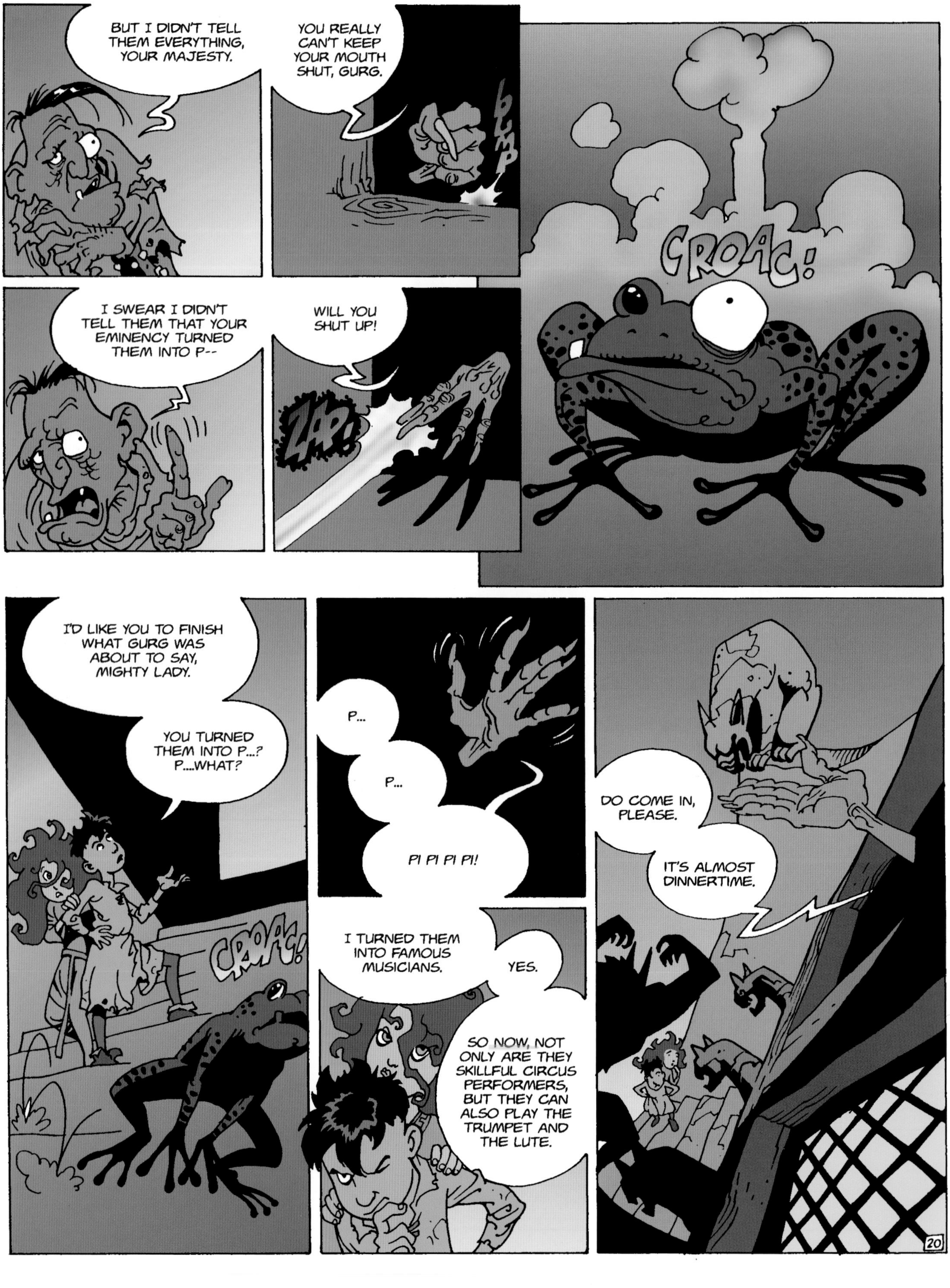
BUT I DIDN'T TELL THEM EVERYTHING, YOUR MAJESTY.
YOU REALLY CAN'T KEEP YOUR MOUTH SHUT, GURG.
bump
I SWEAR I DIDN'T TELL THEM THAT YOUR EMINENCY TURNED THEM INTO P--
WILL YOU SHUT UP!
ZAP!
CROAC!
I'D LIKE YOU TO FINISH WHAT GURG WAS ABOUT TO SAY, MIGHTY LADY.
YOU TURNED THEM INTO P...? P....WHAT?
CROAC!
P...
P...
PI PI PI PI!
I TURNED THEM INTO FAMOUS MUSICIANS.
YES.
SO NOW, NOT ONLY ARE THEY SKILLFUL CIRCUS PERFORMERS, BUT THEY CAN ALSO PLAY THE TRUMPET AND THE LUTE.
DO COME IN, PLEASE.
IT'S ALMOST DINNERTIME.
20

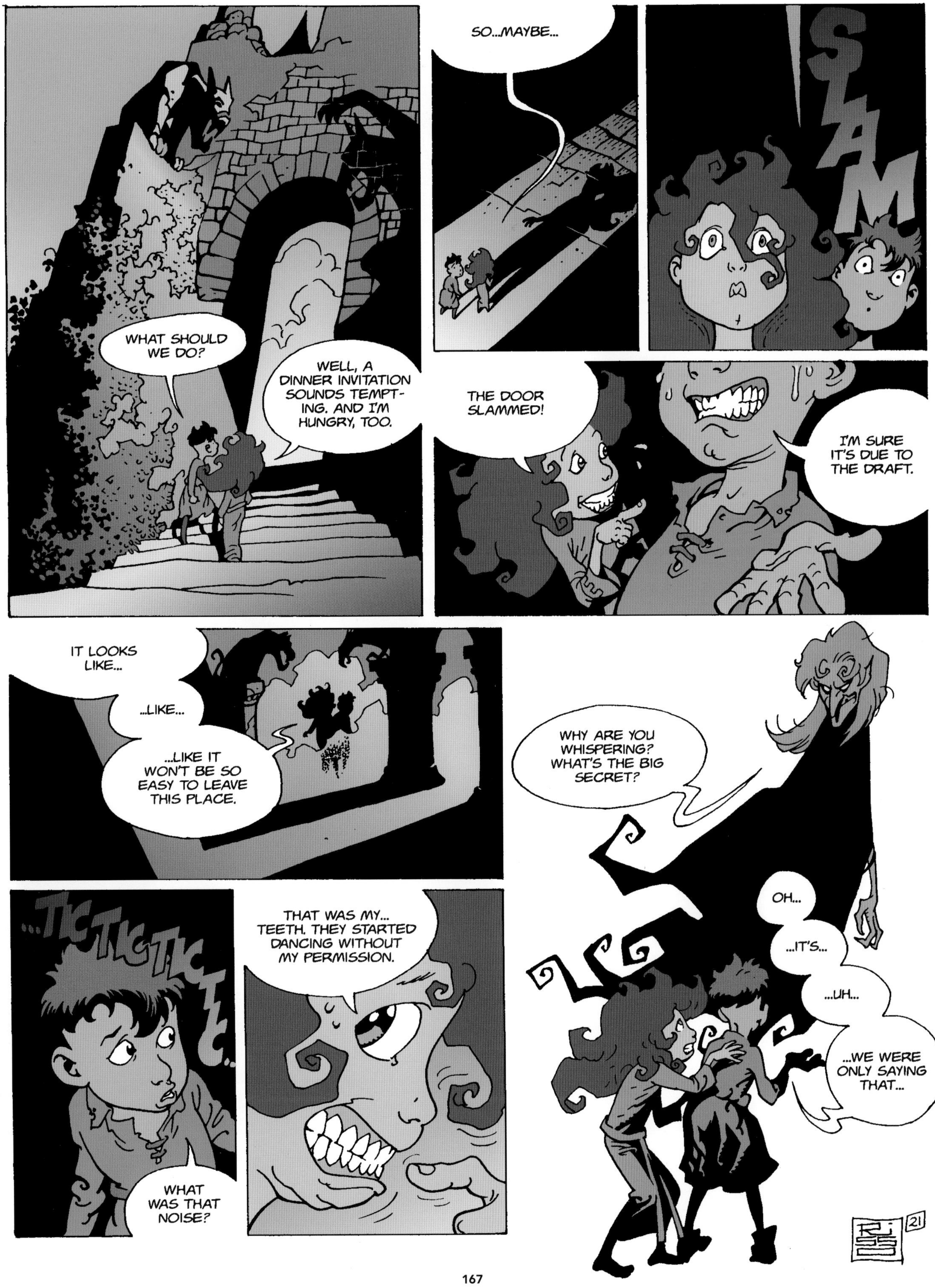
WHAT SHOULD WE DO?
WELL, A DINNER INVITATION SOUNDS TEMPTING. AND I'M HUNGRY, TOO.
SO...MAYBE...
SLAM
THE DOOR SLAMMED!
I'M SURE IT'S DUE TO THE DRAFT.
IT LOOKS LIKE...
...LIKE...
...LIKE IT WON'T BE SO EASY TO LEAVE THIS PLACE.
...TIC TIC TIC TIC TIC...
WHAT WAS THAT NOISE?
THAT WAS MY... TEETH. THEY STARTED DANCING WITHOUT MY PERMISSION.
WHY ARE YOU WHISPERING? WHAT'S THE BIG SECRET?
OH...
...IT'S...
...UH...
...WE WERE ONLY SAYING THAT...
21

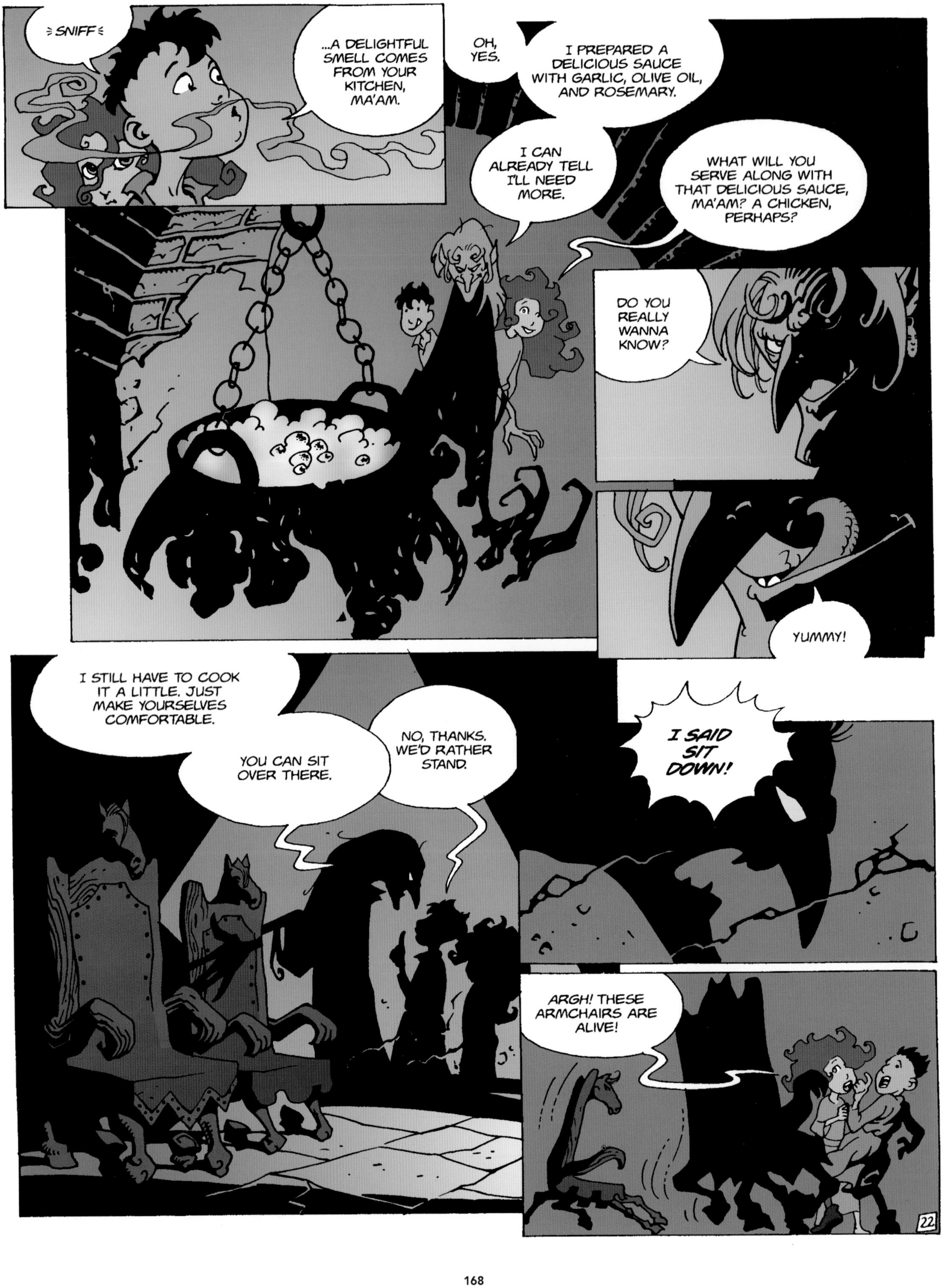
≷SNIFF≶
...A DELIGHTFUL SMELL COMES FROM YOUR KITCHEN, MA'AM.
OH, YES.
I PREPARED A DELICIOUS SAUCE WITH GARLIC, OLIVE OIL, AND ROSEMARY.
I CAN ALREADY TELL I'LL NEED MORE.
WHAT WILL YOU SERVE ALONG WITH THAT DELICIOUS SAUCE, MA'AM? A CHICKEN, PERHAPS?
DO YOU REALLY WANNA KNOW?
YUMMY!
I STILL HAVE TO COOK IT A LITTLE. JUST MAKE YOURSELVES COMFORTABLE.
YOU CAN SIT OVER THERE.
NO, THANKS. WE'D RATHER STAND.
I SAID SIT DOWN!
ARGH! THESE ARMCHAIRS ARE ALIVE!
22

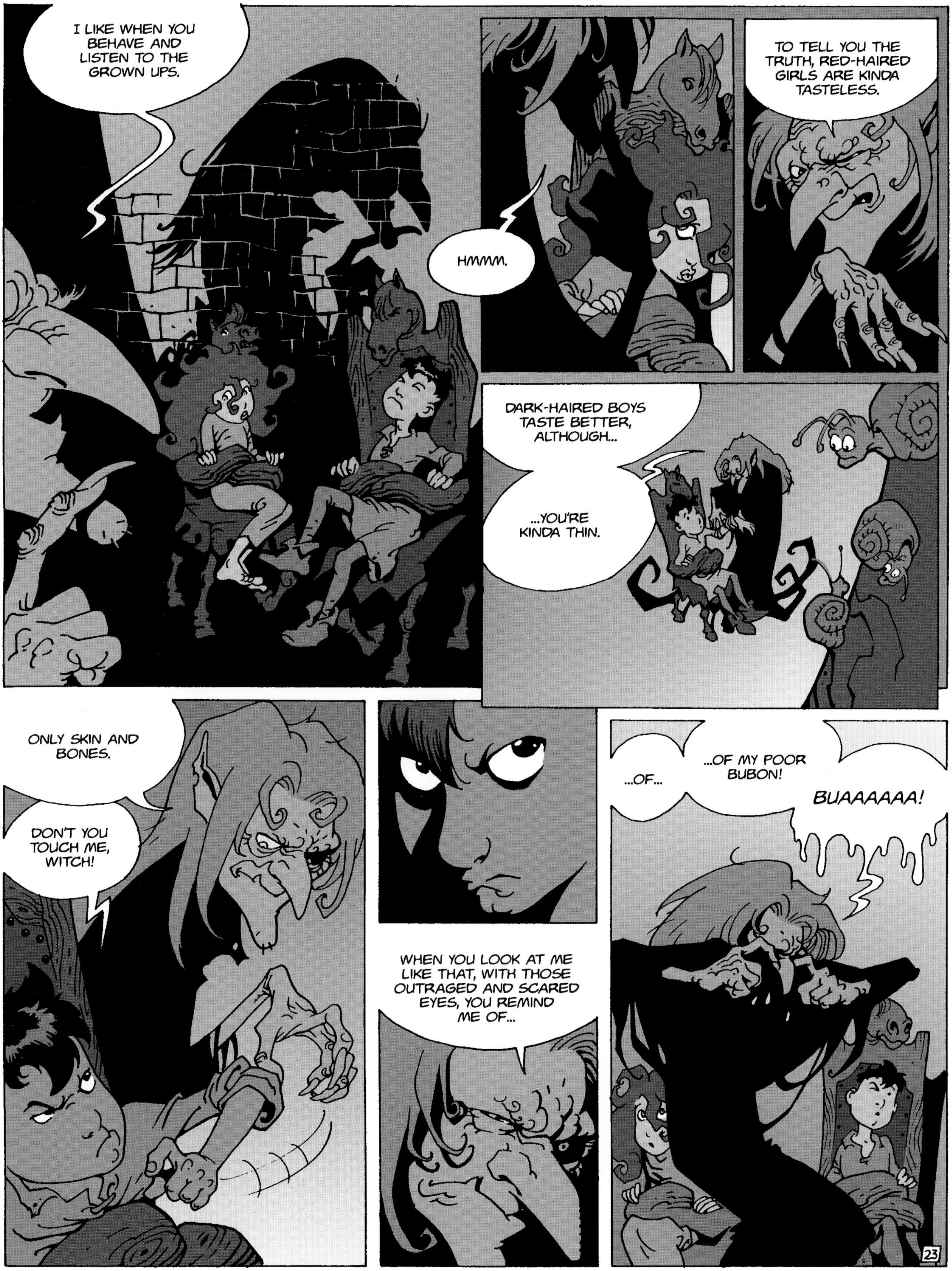
I LIKE WHEN YOU BEHAVE AND LISTEN TO THE GROWN UPS.
HMMM.
TO TELL YOU THE TRUTH, RED-HAIRED GIRLS ARE KINDA TASTELESS.
DARK-HAIRED BOYS TASTE BETTER, ALTHOUGH...
...YOU'RE KINDA THIN.
ONLY SKIN AND BONES.
DON'T YOU TOUCH ME, WITCH!
WHEN YOU LOOK AT ME LIKE THAT, WITH THOSE OUTRAGED AND SCARED EYES, YOU REMIND ME OF...
...OF...
...OF MY POOR BUBON!
BUAAAAAA!
23

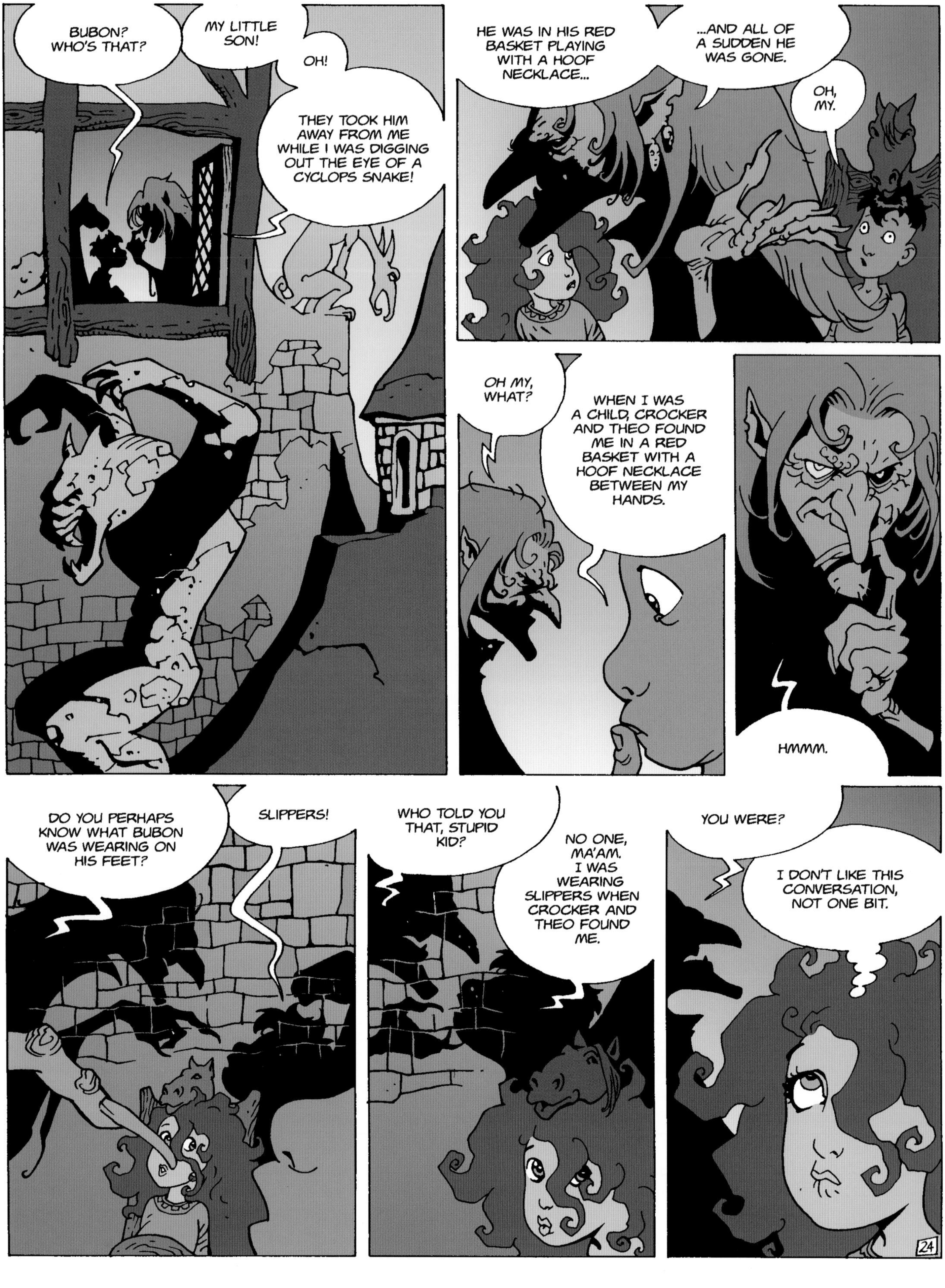
BUBON? WHO'S THAT?
MY LITTLE SON!
OH!
THEY TOOK HIM AWAY FROM ME WHILE I WAS DIGGING OUT THE EYE OF A CYCLOPS SNAKE!
HE WAS IN HIS RED BASKET PLAYING WITH A HOOF NECKLACE...
...AND ALL OF A SUDDEN HE WAS GONE.
OH, MY.
OH MY, WHAT?
WHEN I WAS A CHILD, CROCKER AND THEO FOUND ME IN A RED BASKET WITH A HOOF NECKLACE BETWEEN MY HANDS.
HMMM.
DO YOU PERHAPS KNOW WHAT BUBON WAS WEARING ON HIS FEET?
SLIPPERS!
WHO TOLD YOU THAT, STUPID KID?
NO ONE, MA'AM. I WAS WEARING SLIPPERS WHEN CROCKER AND THEO FOUND ME.
YOU WERE?
I DON'T LIKE THIS CONVERSATION, NOT ONE BIT.
24

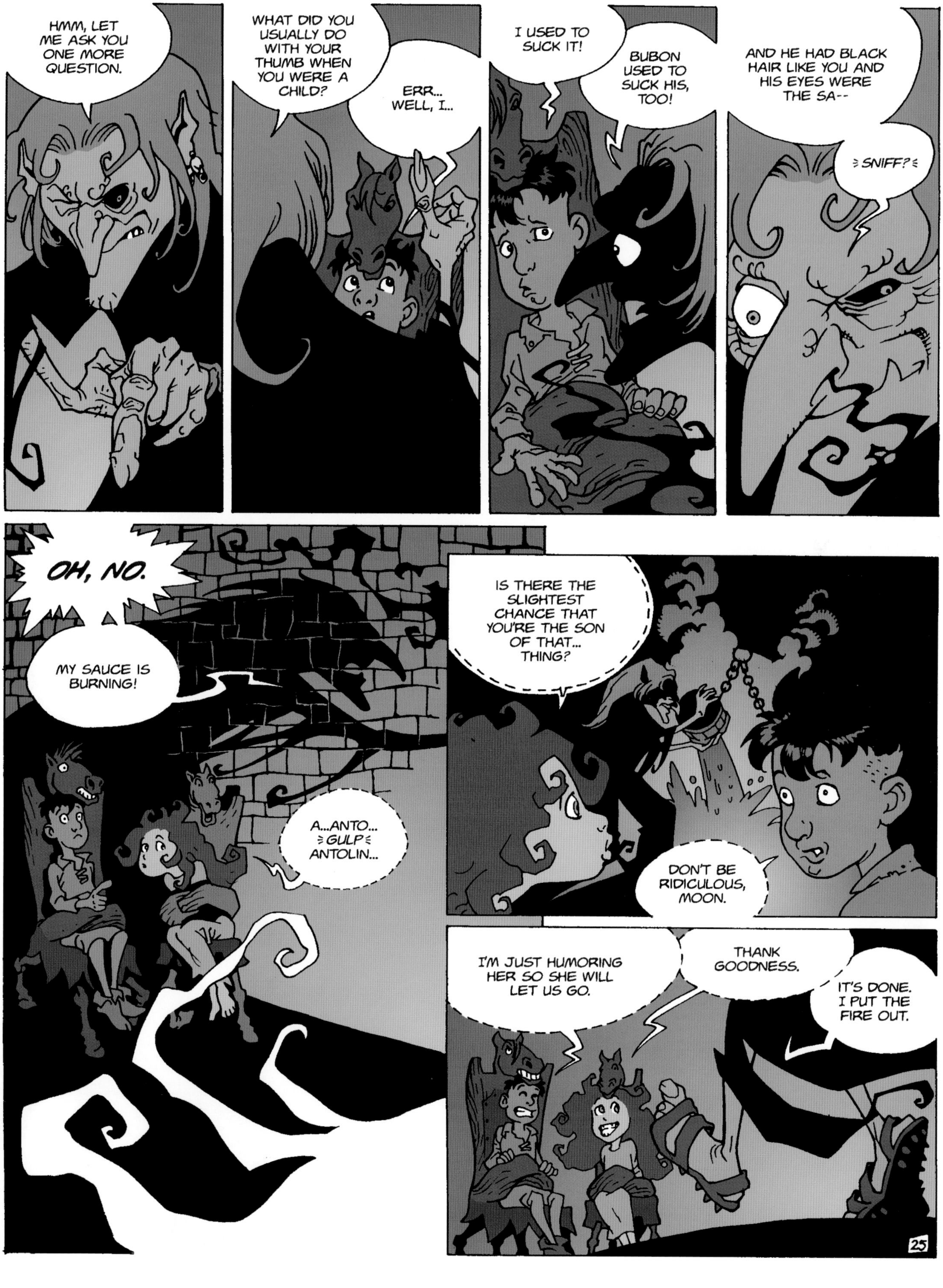
HMM, LET ME ASK YOU ONE MORE QUESTION.
WHAT DID YOU USUALLY DO WITH YOUR THUMB WHEN YOU WERE A CHILD?
ERR... WELL, I...
I USED TO SUCK IT!
BUBON USED TO SUCK HIS, TOO!
AND HE HAD BLACK HAIR LIKE YOU AND HIS EYES WERE THE SA--
SNIFF?
OH, NO.
MY SAUCE IS BURNING!
A...ANTO... GULP ANTOLIN...
IS THERE THE SLIGHTEST CHANCE THAT YOU'RE THE SON OF THAT... THING?
DON'T BE RIDICULOUS, MOON.
I'M JUST HUMORING HER SO SHE WILL LET US GO.
THANK GOODNESS.
IT'S DONE. I PUT THE FIRE OUT.
25

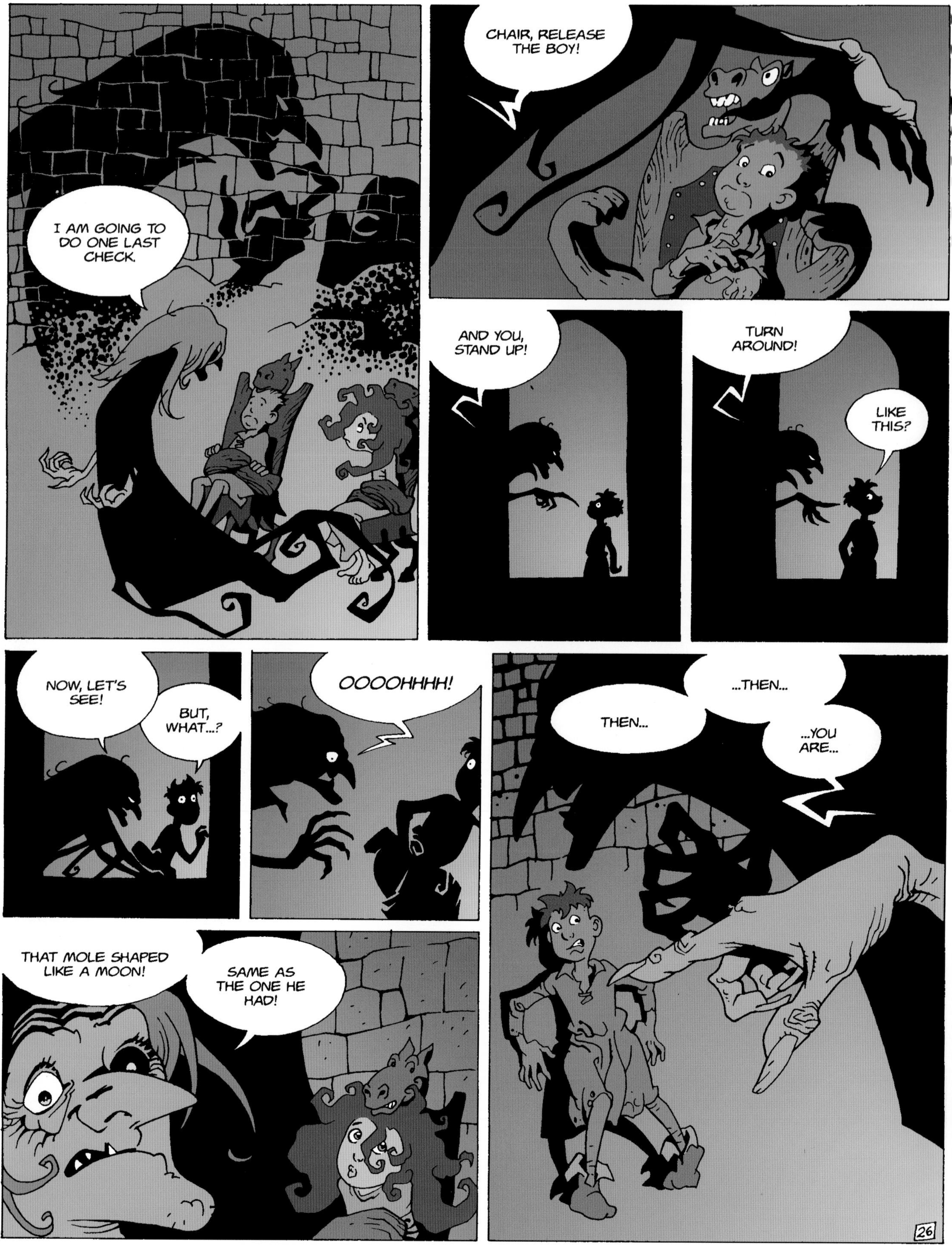
I AM GOING TO DO ONE LAST CHECK.
CHAIR, RELEASE THE BOY!
AND YOU, STAND UP!
TURN AROUND!
LIKE THIS?
NOW, LET'S SEE!
BUT, WHAT...?
OOOOHHHH!
THEN...
...THEN...
...YOU ARE...
THAT MOLE SHAPED LIKE A MOON!
SAME AS THE ONE HE HAD!
26

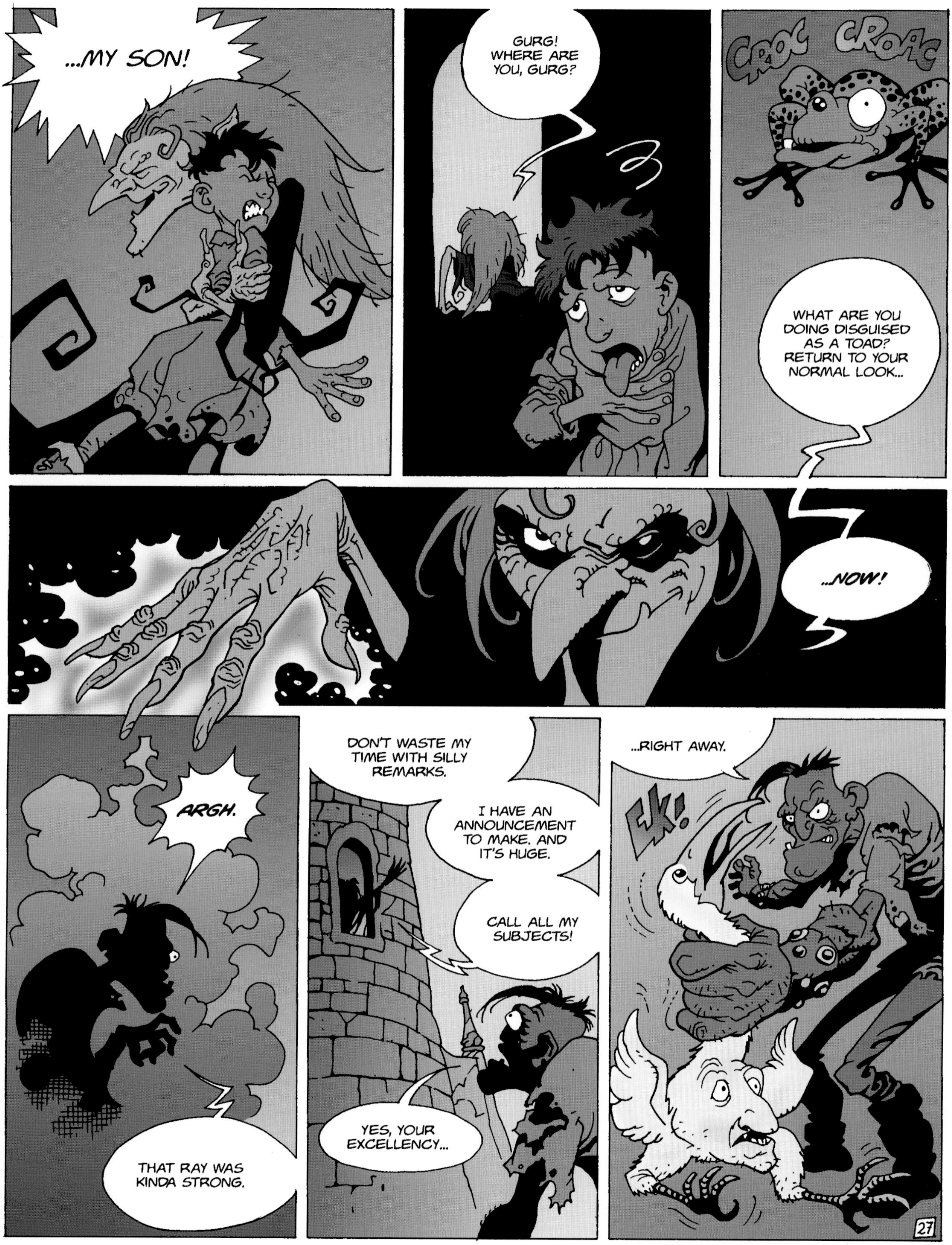
...MY SON!
GURG! WHERE ARE YOU, GURG?
CROC CROAC
WHAT ARE YOU DOING DISGUISED AS A TOAD? RETURN TO YOUR NORMAL LOOK...
...NOW!
ARGH.
THAT RAY WAS KINDA STRONG.
DON'T WASTE MY TIME WITH SILLY REMARKS.
I HAVE AN ANNOUNCEMENT TO MAKE. AND IT'S HUGE.
CALL ALL MY SUBJECTS!
YES, YOUR EXCELLENCY...
...RIGHT AWAY.
EK!
27

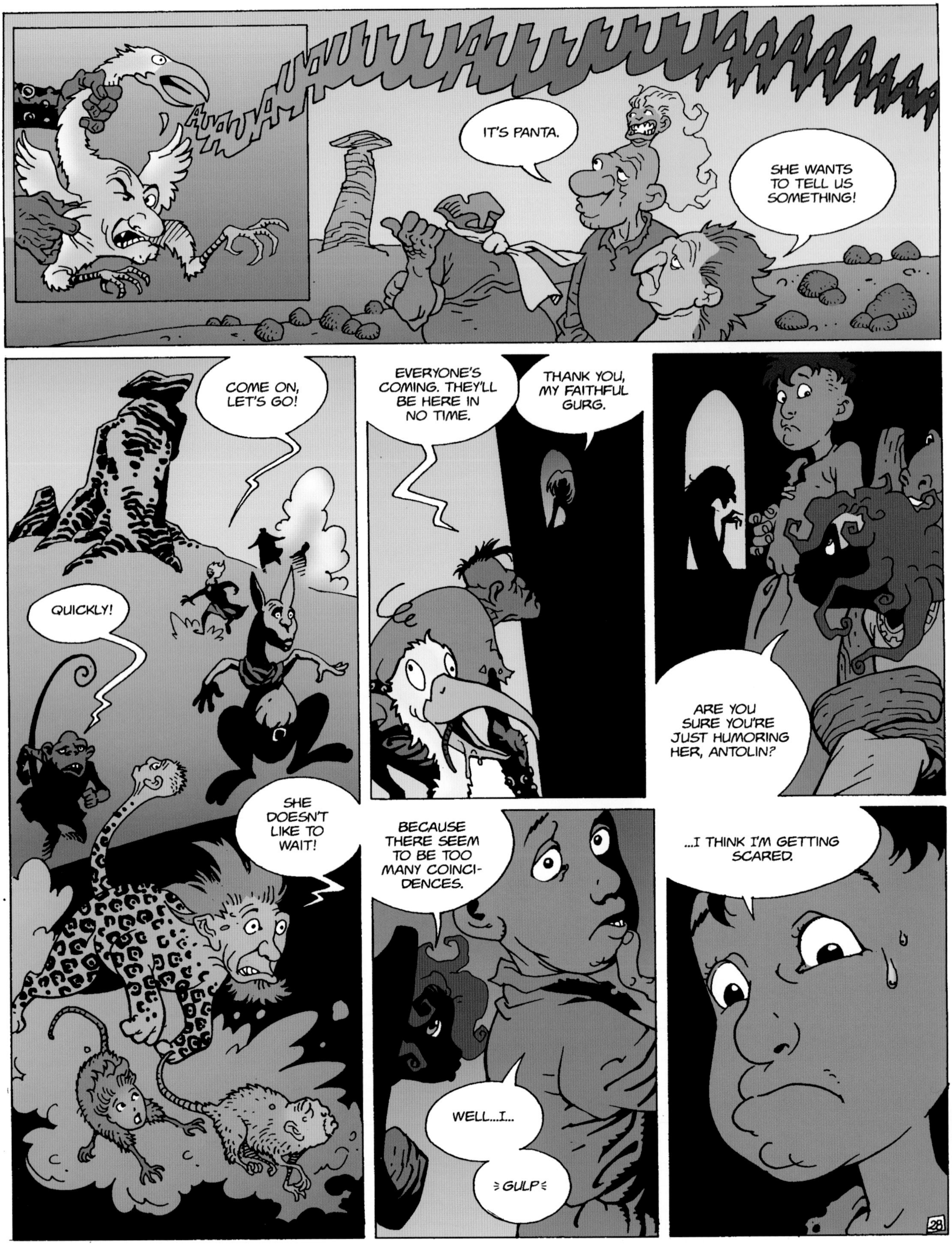
AUUUUUUUUAUUUUUUUAAAAAAAAA
IT'S PANTA.
SHE WANTS TO TELL US SOMETHING!
COME ON, LET'S GO!
QUICKLY!
SHE DOESN'T LIKE TO WAIT!
EVERYONE'S COMING. THEY'LL BE HERE IN NO TIME.
THANK YOU, MY FAITHFUL GURG.
ARE YOU SURE YOU'RE JUST HUMORING HER, ANTOLIN?
BECAUSE THERE SEEM TO BE TOO MANY COINCI-DENCES.
WELL...I...
GULP
...I THINK I'M GETTING SCARED.
28

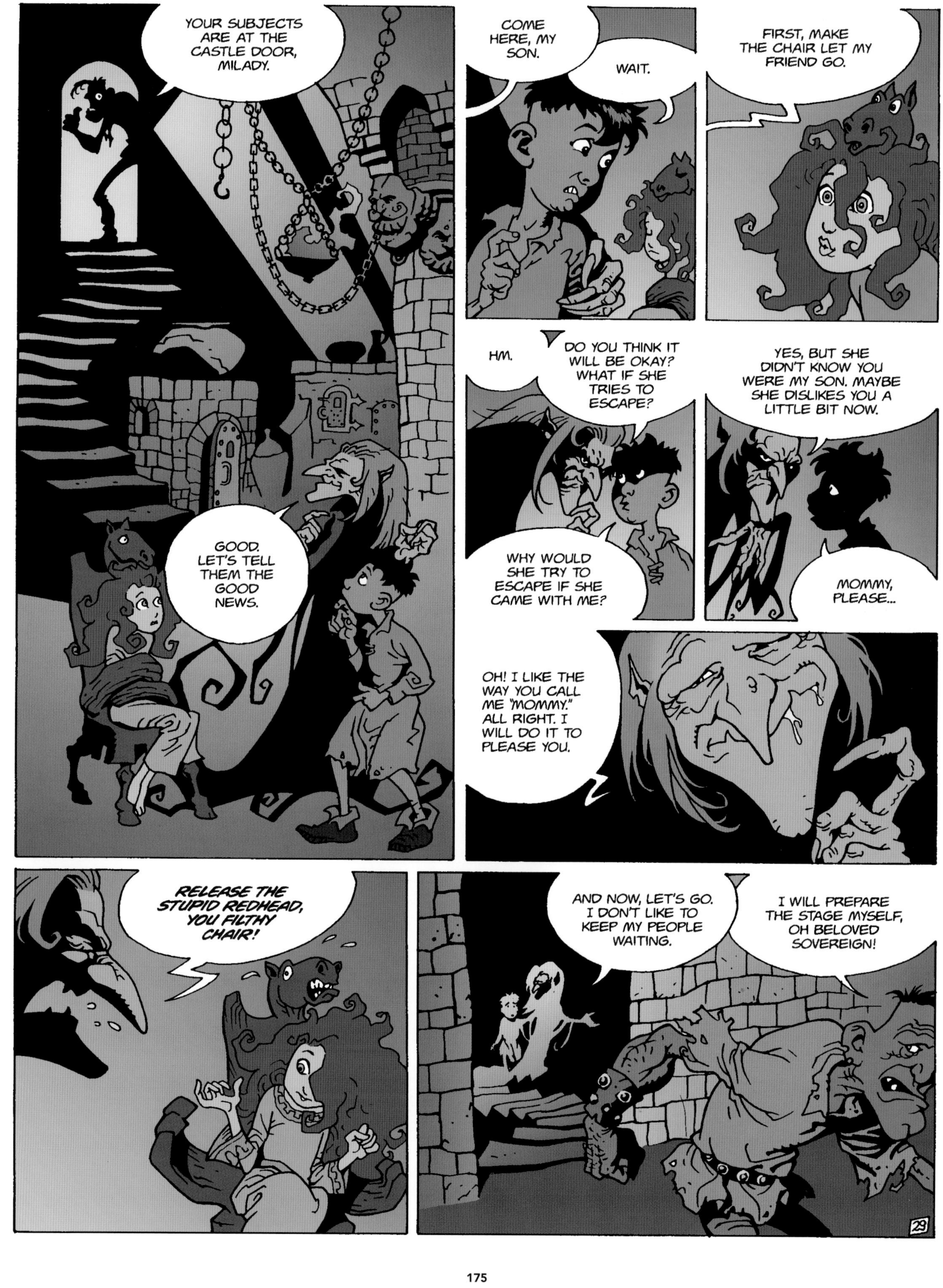
YOUR SUBJECTS ARE AT THE CASTLE DOOR, MILADY.
GOOD. LET'S TELL THEM THE GOOD NEWS.
COME HERE, MY SON.
WAIT.
FIRST, MAKE THE CHAIR LET MY FRIEND GO.
HM.
DO YOU THINK IT WILL BE OKAY? WHAT IF SHE TRIES TO ESCAPE?
WHY WOULD SHE TRY TO ESCAPE IF SHE CAME WITH ME?
YES, BUT SHE DIDN'T KNOW YOU WERE MY SON. MAYBE SHE DISLIKES YOU A LITTLE BIT NOW.
MOMMY, PLEASE...
OH! I LIKE THE WAY YOU CALL ME "MOMMY." ALL RIGHT. I WILL DO IT TO PLEASE YOU.
RELEASE THE STUPID REDHEAD, YOU FILTHY CHAIR!
AND NOW, LET'S GO. I DON'T LIKE TO KEEP MY PEOPLE WAITING.
I WILL PREPARE THE STAGE MYSELF, OH BELOVED SOVEREIGN!
29

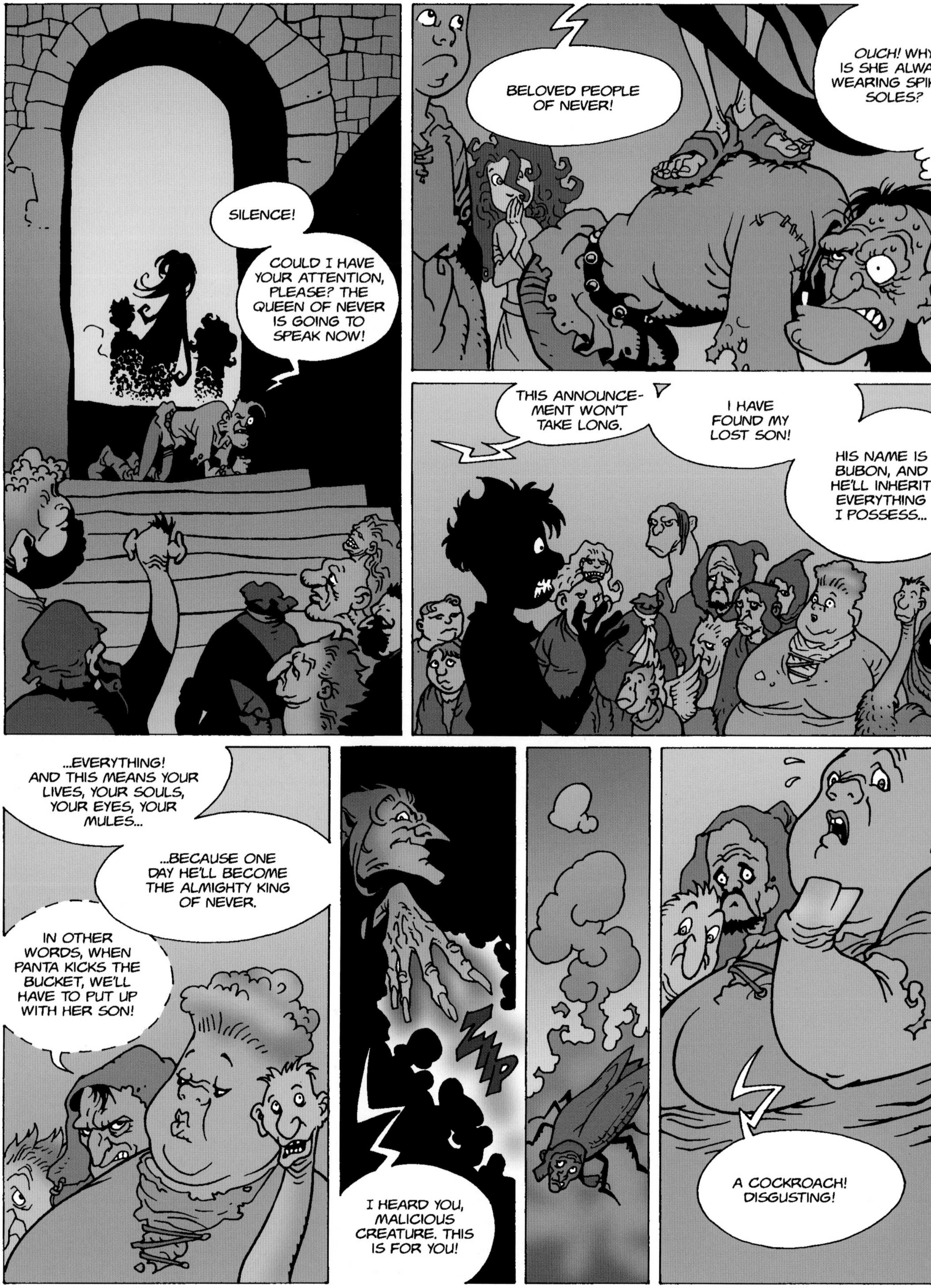

SILENCE!
COULD I HAVE YOUR ATTENTION, PLEASE? THE QUEEN OF NEVER IS GOING TO SPEAK NOW!
BELOVED PEOPLE OF NEVER!
OUCH! WHY IS SHE ALWAYS WEARING SPIKED SOLES?
THIS ANNOUNCEMENT WON'T TAKE LONG.
I HAVE FOUND MY LOST SON!
HIS NAME IS BUBON, AND HE'LL INHERIT EVERYTHING I POSSESS...
...EVERYTHING! AND THIS MEANS YOUR LIVES, YOUR SOULS, YOUR EYES, YOUR MULES...
...BECAUSE ONE DAY HE'LL BECOME THE ALMIGHTY KING OF NEVER.
IN OTHER WORDS, WHEN PANTA KICKS THE BUCKET, WE'LL HAVE TO PUT UP WITH HER SON!
ZWIP
I HEARD YOU, MALICIOUS CREATURE. THIS IS FOR YOU!
A COCKROACH! DISGUSTING!
30

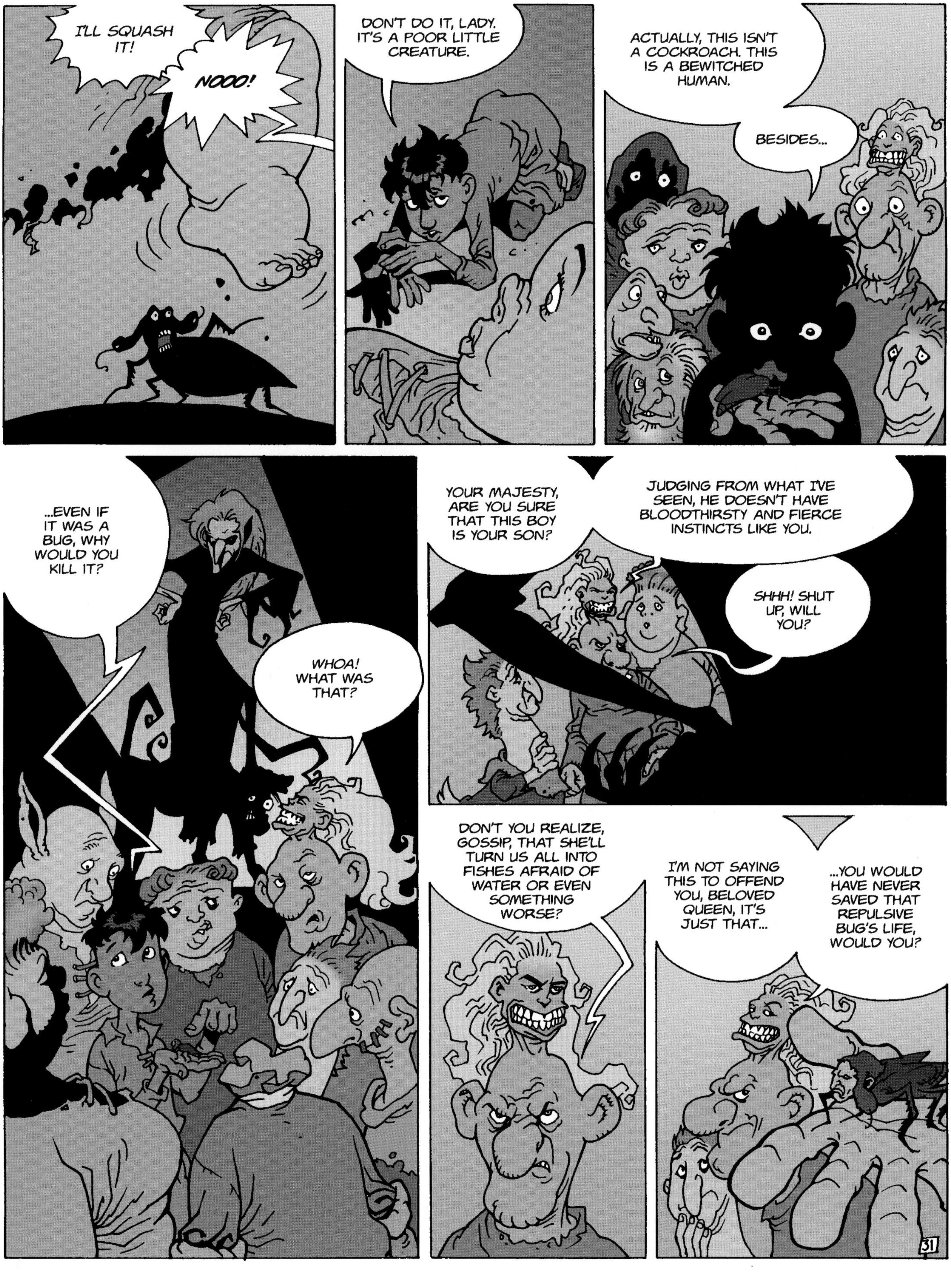
I'LL SQUASH IT!
NOOO!
DON'T DO IT, LADY. IT'S A POOR LITTLE CREATURE.
ACTUALLY, THIS ISN'T A COCKROACH. THIS IS A BEWITCHED HUMAN.
BESIDES...
...EVEN IF IT WAS A BUG, WHY WOULD YOU KILL IT?
WHOA! WHAT WAS THAT?
YOUR MAJESTY, ARE YOU SURE THAT THIS BOY IS YOUR SON?
JUDGING FROM WHAT I'VE SEEN, HE DOESN'T HAVE BLOODTHIRSTY AND FIERCE INSTINCTS LIKE YOU.
SHHH! SHUT UP, WILL YOU?
DON'T YOU REALIZE, GOSSIP, THAT SHE'LL TURN US ALL INTO FISHES AFRAID OF WATER OR EVEN SOMETHING WORSE?
I'M NOT SAYING THIS TO OFFEND YOU, BELOVED QUEEN, IT'S JUST THAT...
...YOU WOULD HAVE NEVER SAVED THAT REPULSIVE BUG'S LIFE, WOULD YOU?
31

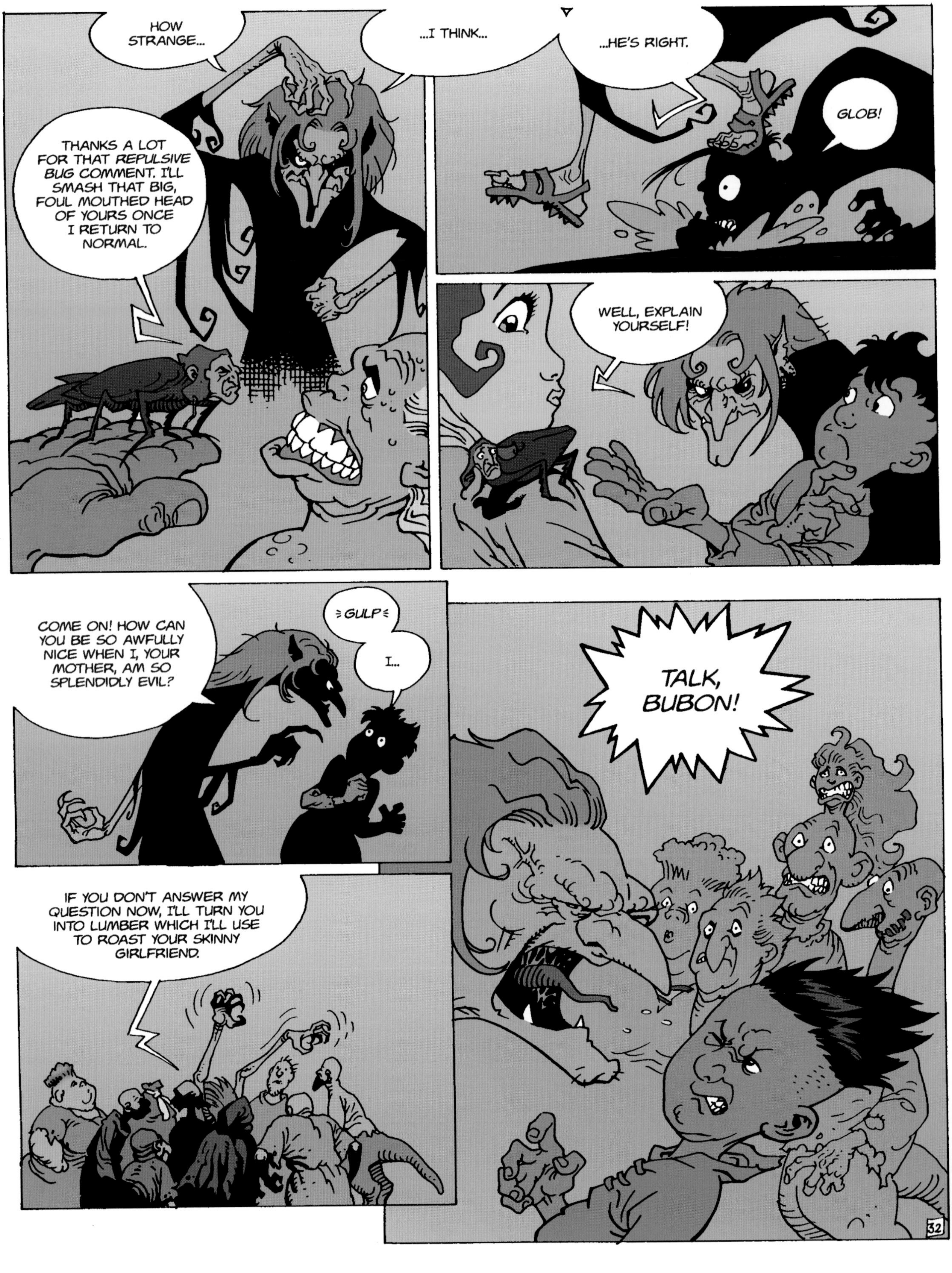
HOW STRANGE...
...I THINK...
...HE'S RIGHT.
THANKS A LOT FOR THAT REPULSIVE BUG COMMENT. I'LL SMASH THAT BIG, FOUL MOUTHED HEAD OF YOURS ONCE I RETURN TO NORMAL.
GLOB!
WELL, EXPLAIN YOURSELF!
COME ON! HOW CAN YOU BE SO AWFULLY NICE WHEN I, YOUR MOTHER, AM SO SPLENDIDLY EVIL?
GULP
I...
TALK, BUBON!
IF YOU DON'T ANSWER MY QUESTION NOW, I'LL TURN YOU INTO LUMBER WHICH I'LL USE TO ROAST YOUR SKINNY GIRLFRIEND.
32

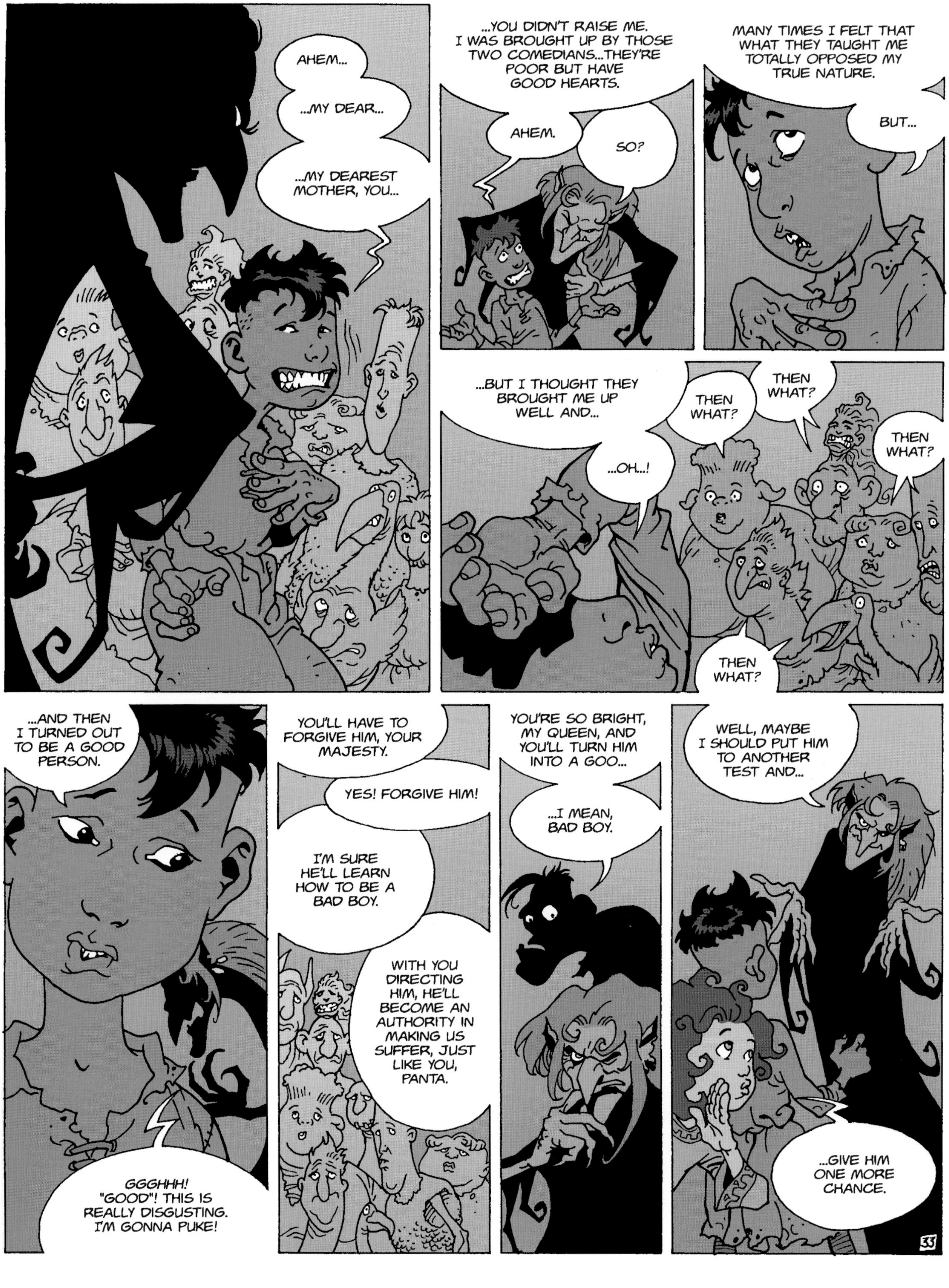
AHEM...
...MY DEAR...
...MY DEAREST MOTHER, YOU...
...YOU DIDN'T RAISE ME. I WAS BROUGHT UP BY THOSE TWO COMEDIANS...THEY'RE POOR BUT HAVE GOOD HEARTS.
AHEM.
SO?
MANY TIMES I FELT THAT WHAT THEY TAUGHT ME TOTALLY OPPOSED MY TRUE NATURE.
BUT...
...BUT I THOUGHT THEY BROUGHT ME UP WELL AND...
...OH...!
THEN WHAT?
THEN WHAT?
THEN WHAT?
THEN WHAT?
...AND THEN I TURNED OUT TO BE A GOOD PERSON.
GGGHHH! "GOOD"! THIS IS REALLY DISGUSTING. I'M GONNA PUKE!
YOU'LL HAVE TO FORGIVE HIM, YOUR MAJESTY.
YES! FORGIVE HIM!
I'M SURE HE'LL LEARN HOW TO BE A BAD BOY.
WITH YOU DIRECTING HIM, HE'LL BECOME AN AUTHORITY IN MAKING US SUFFER, JUST LIKE YOU, PANTA.
YOU'RE SO BRIGHT, MY QUEEN, AND YOU'LL TURN HIM INTO A GOO...
...I MEAN, BAD BOY.
WELL, MAYBE I SHOULD PUT HIM TO ANOTHER TEST AND...
...GIVE HIM ONE MORE CHANCE.
33

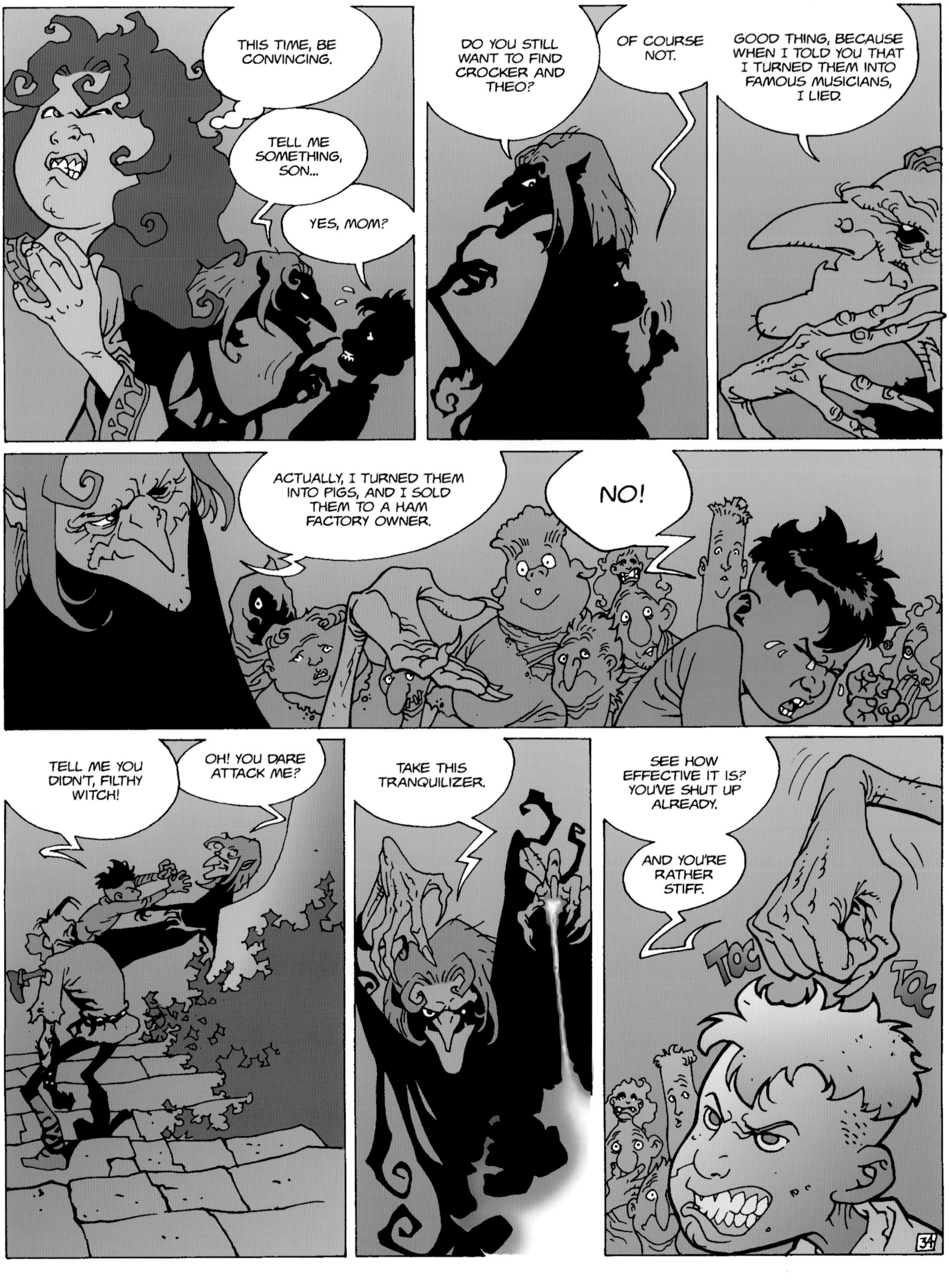
THIS TIME, BE CONVINCING.
TELL ME SOMETHING, SON...
YES, MOM?
DO YOU STILL WANT TO FIND CROCKER AND THEO?
OF COURSE NOT.
GOOD THING, BECAUSE WHEN I TOLD YOU THAT I TURNED THEM INTO FAMOUS MUSICIANS, I LIED.
ACTUALLY, I TURNED THEM INTO PIGS, AND I SOLD THEM TO A HAM FACTORY OWNER.
NO!
TELL ME YOU DIDN'T, FILTHY WITCH!
OH! YOU DARE ATTACK ME?
TAKE THIS TRANQUILIZER.
SEE HOW EFFECTIVE IT IS? YOU'VE SHUT UP ALREADY.
AND YOU'RE RATHER STIFF.
TOC
TOC
34

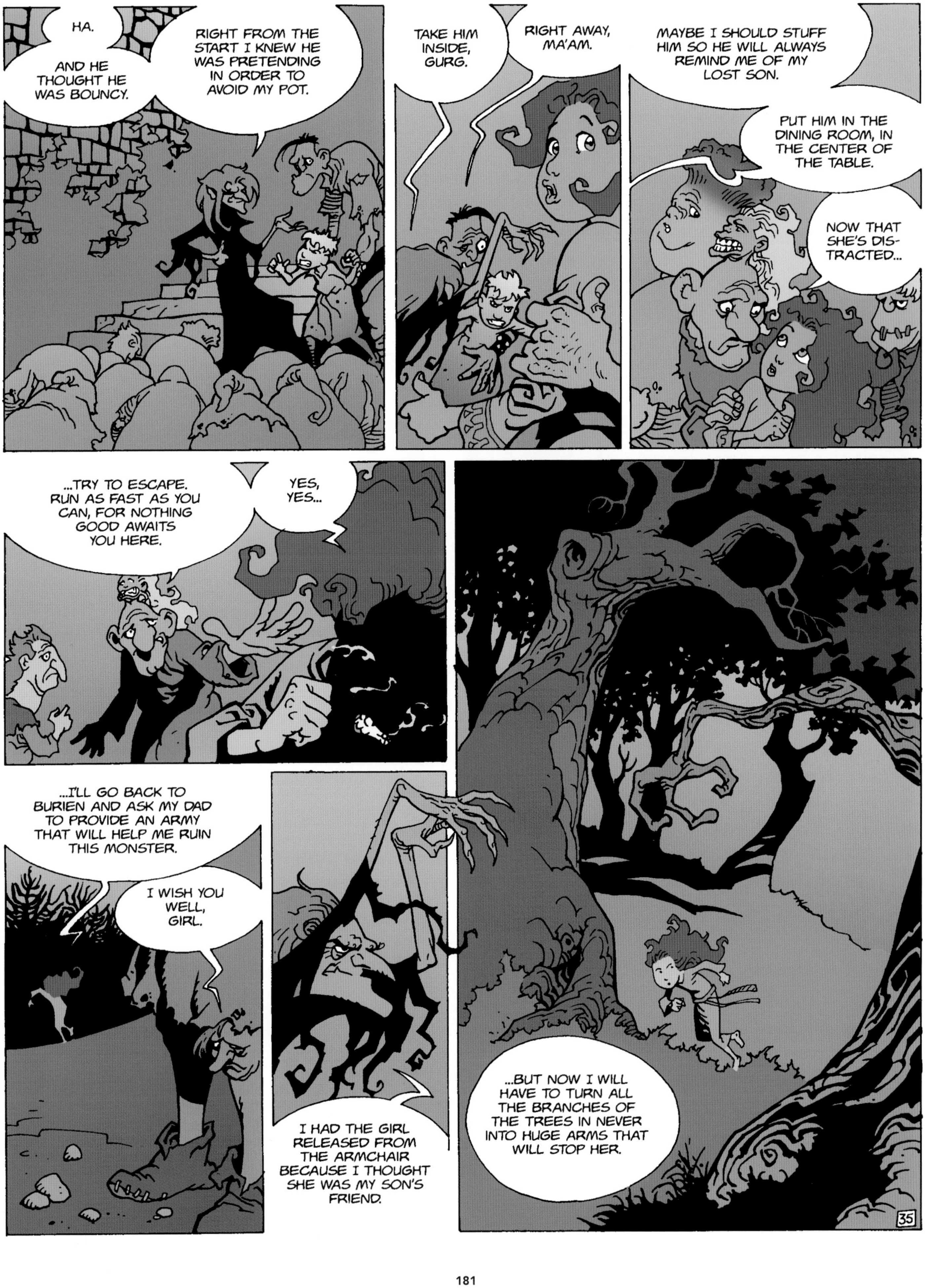
HA.
AND HE THOUGHT HE WAS BOUNCY.
RIGHT FROM THE START I KNEW HE WAS PRETENDING IN ORDER TO AVOID MY POT.
TAKE HIM INSIDE, GURG.
RIGHT AWAY, MA'AM.
MAYBE I SHOULD STUFF HIM SO HE WILL ALWAYS REMIND ME OF MY LOST SON.
PUT HIM IN THE DINING ROOM, IN THE CENTER OF THE TABLE.
NOW THAT SHE'S DISTRACTED...
...TRY TO ESCAPE. RUN AS FAST AS YOU CAN, FOR NOTHING GOOD AWAITS YOU HERE.
YES, YES...
...I'LL GO BACK TO BURIEN AND ASK MY DAD TO PROVIDE AN ARMY THAT WILL HELP ME RUIN THIS MONSTER.
I WISH YOU WELL, GIRL.
I HAD THE GIRL RELEASED FROM THE ARMCHAIR BECAUSE I THOUGHT SHE WAS MY SON'S FRIEND.
...BUT NOW I WILL HAVE TO TURN ALL THE BRANCHES OF THE TREES IN NEVER INTO HUGE ARMS THAT WILL STOP HER.
35

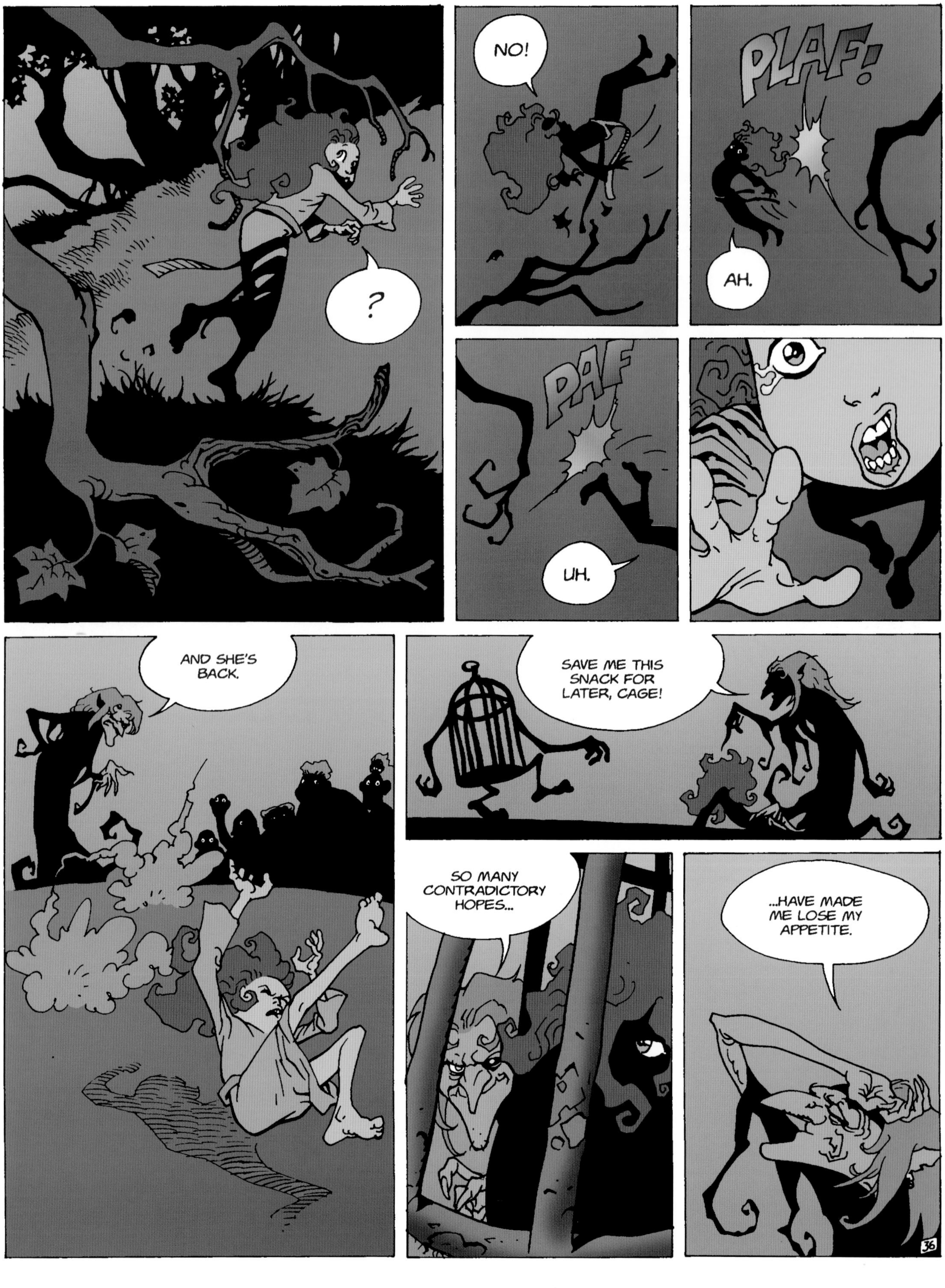
?
NO!
PLAF!
AH.
PAF
UH.
AND SHE'S BACK.
SAVE ME THIS SNACK FOR LATER, CAGE!
SO MANY CONTRADICTORY HOPES...
...HAVE MADE ME LOSE MY APPETITE.
36

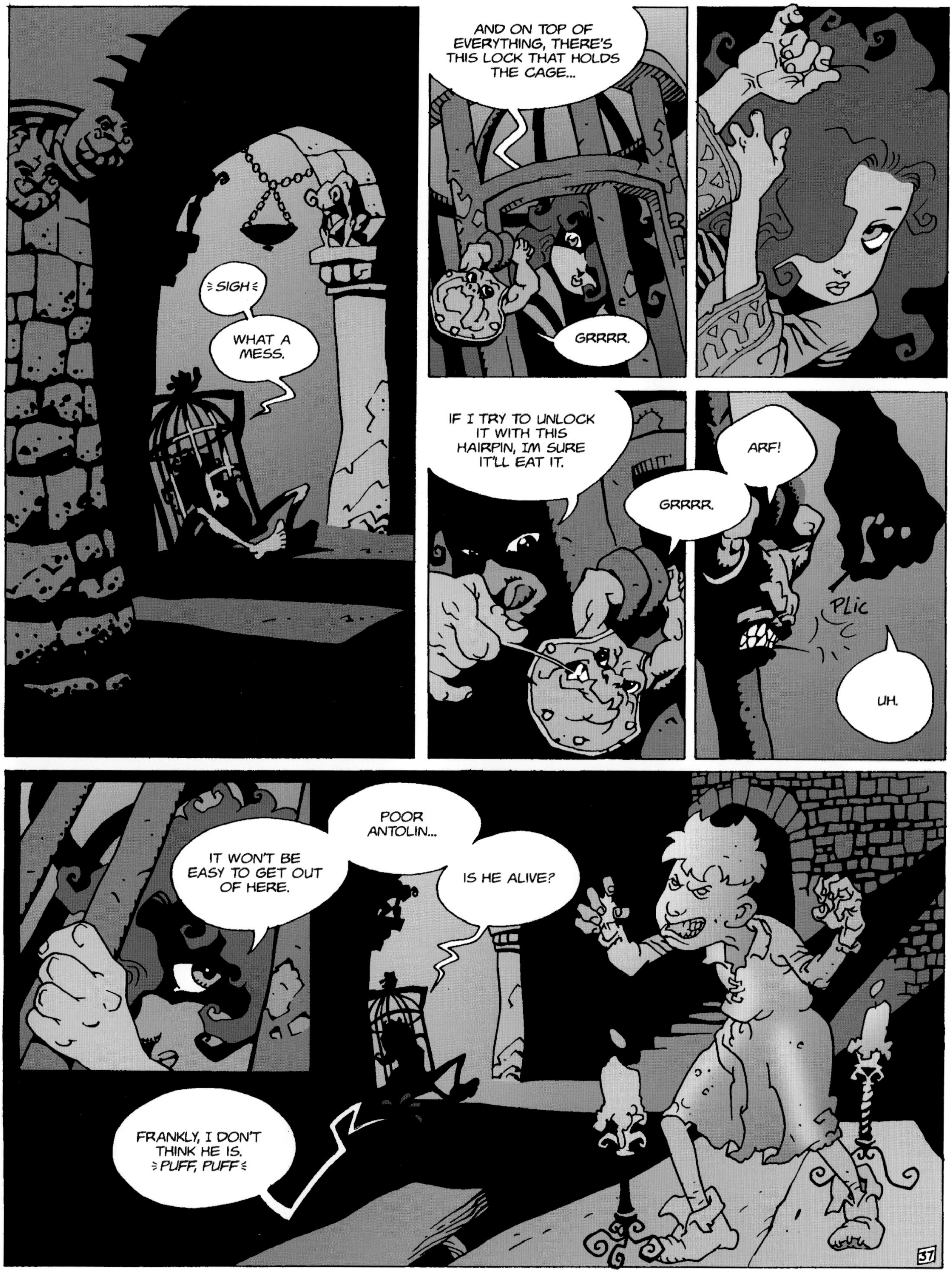

⚞SIGH⚟
WHAT A MESS.
AND ON TOP OF EVERYTHING, THERE'S THIS LOCK THAT HOLDS THE CAGE...
GRRRR.
IF I TRY TO UNLOCK IT WITH THIS HAIRPIN, I'M SURE IT'LL EAT IT.
GRRRR.
ARF!
PLic
UH.
IT WON'T BE EASY TO GET OUT OF HERE.
POOR ANTOLIN...
IS HE ALIVE?
FRANKLY, I DON'T THINK HE IS. ⚞PUFF, PUFF⚟
37

DON'T SAY THAT, COCKROACH. THAT SCARES ME.

≶ PUFF ≶   ≶ PUFF ≶

AND IT'S ALL YOUR FAULT.

WE WOULD NEVER HAVE GOTTEN INTO THIS TROUBLE IF MY FRIEND HADN'T TRIED TO SAVE YOU.

SHUT UP AND HEL... ≶ PUFF ≶ GH...

...GHHHHH...

...HELP ME WITH THIS BOTTLE. IT WEIGHS, LIKE, A MILLION TONS.

WHAT'S INSIDE?

SLEEPING POTION. PANTA TAKES IT EVERY NIGHT.

SHE'S AN INSOMNIAC.

SHE MUST SUFFER FROM SOME SICKNESS THAT GIVES HER HEADACHES AND MAKES HER SLEEPLESS.

WHY DID YOU BRING THIS TO ME?

DIP WHAT REMAINS OF YOUR HAIRPIN INTO THE LIQUID.

AND THEN?

DO I REALLY HAVE TO TELL YOU EVERY-THING?

PUT IT IN THAT PADLOCK'S MOUTH!

GROURGH.

PLIC

RONF!

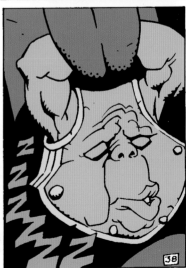

38

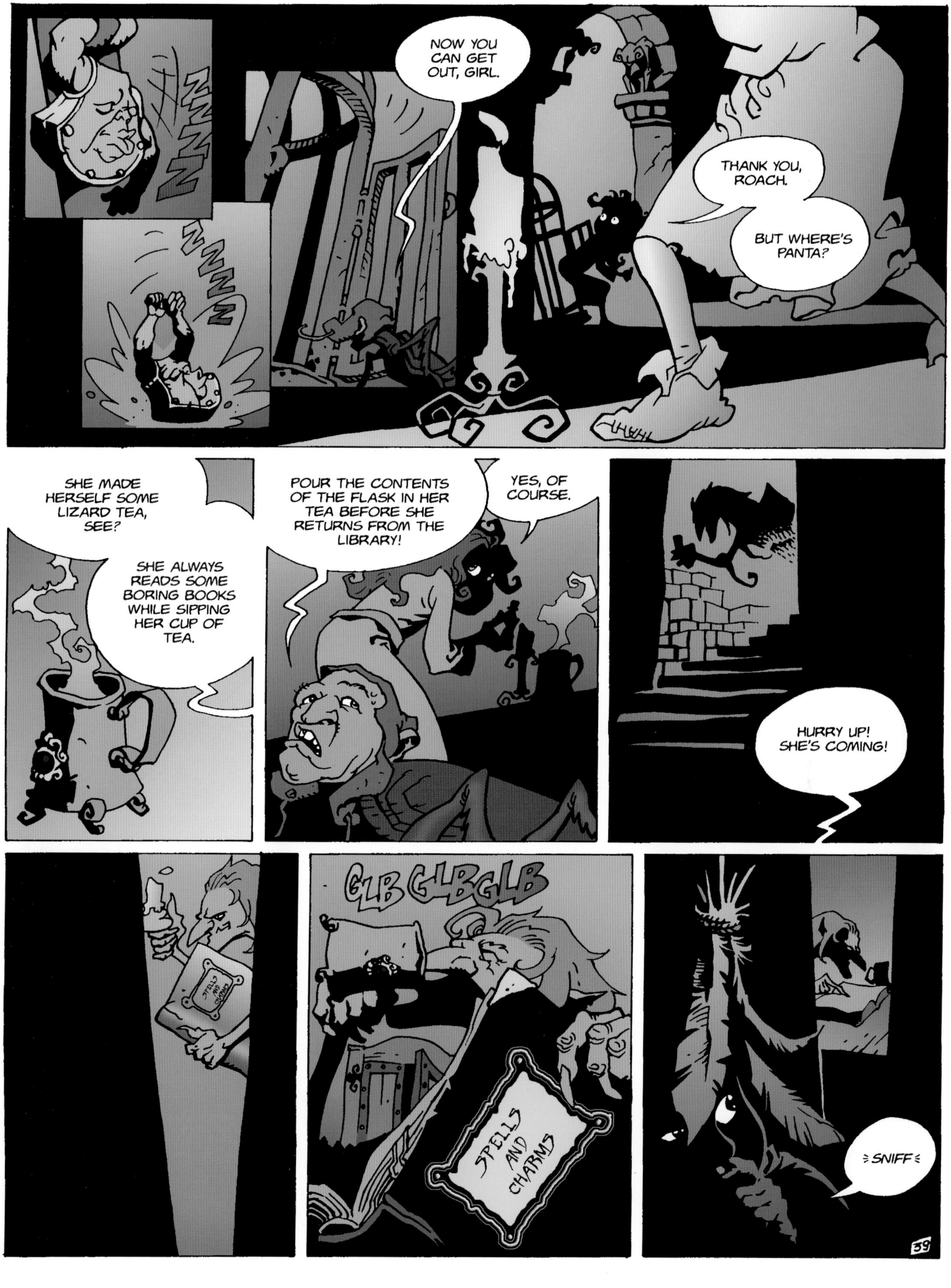
NNNN
NNNN
NOW YOU CAN GET OUT, GIRL.
THANK YOU, ROACH.
BUT WHERE'S PANTA?
SHE MADE HERSELF SOME LIZARD TEA, SEE?
SHE ALWAYS READS SOME BORING BOOKS WHILE SIPPING HER CUP OF TEA.
POUR THE CONTENTS OF THE FLASK IN HER TEA BEFORE SHE RETURNS FROM THE LIBRARY!
YES, OF COURSE.
HURRY UP! SHE'S COMING!
SPELLS AND CHARMS
GLB GLBGLB
SPELLS AND CHARMS
SNIFF
39

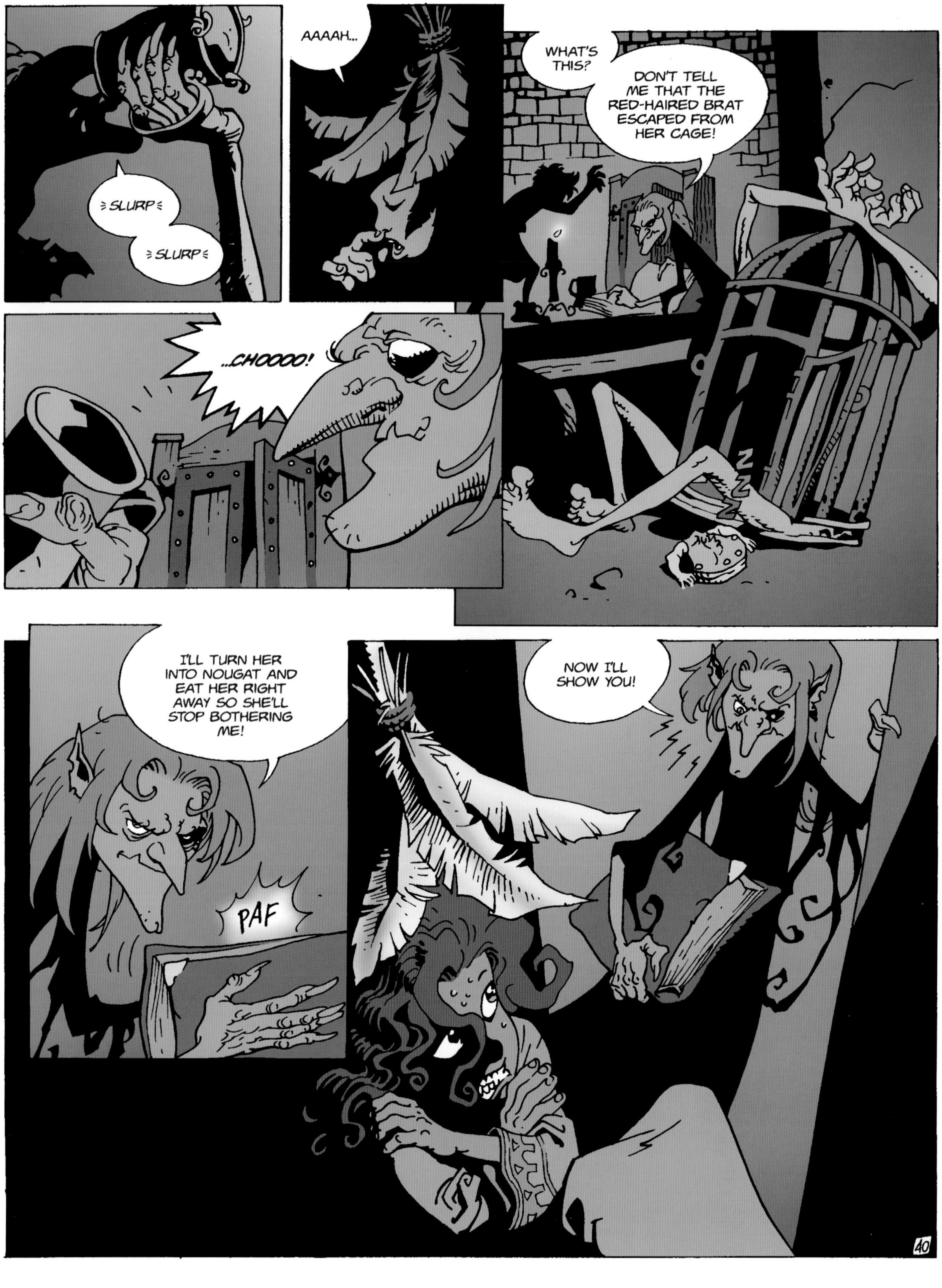
SLURP
SLURP
AAAAH...
WHAT'S THIS?
DON'T TELL ME THAT THE RED-HAIRED BRAT ESCAPED FROM HER CAGE!
...CHOOOO!
I'LL TURN HER INTO NOUGAT AND EAT HER RIGHT AWAY SO SHE'LL STOP BOTHERING ME!
PAF
NOW I'LL SHOW YOU!
40

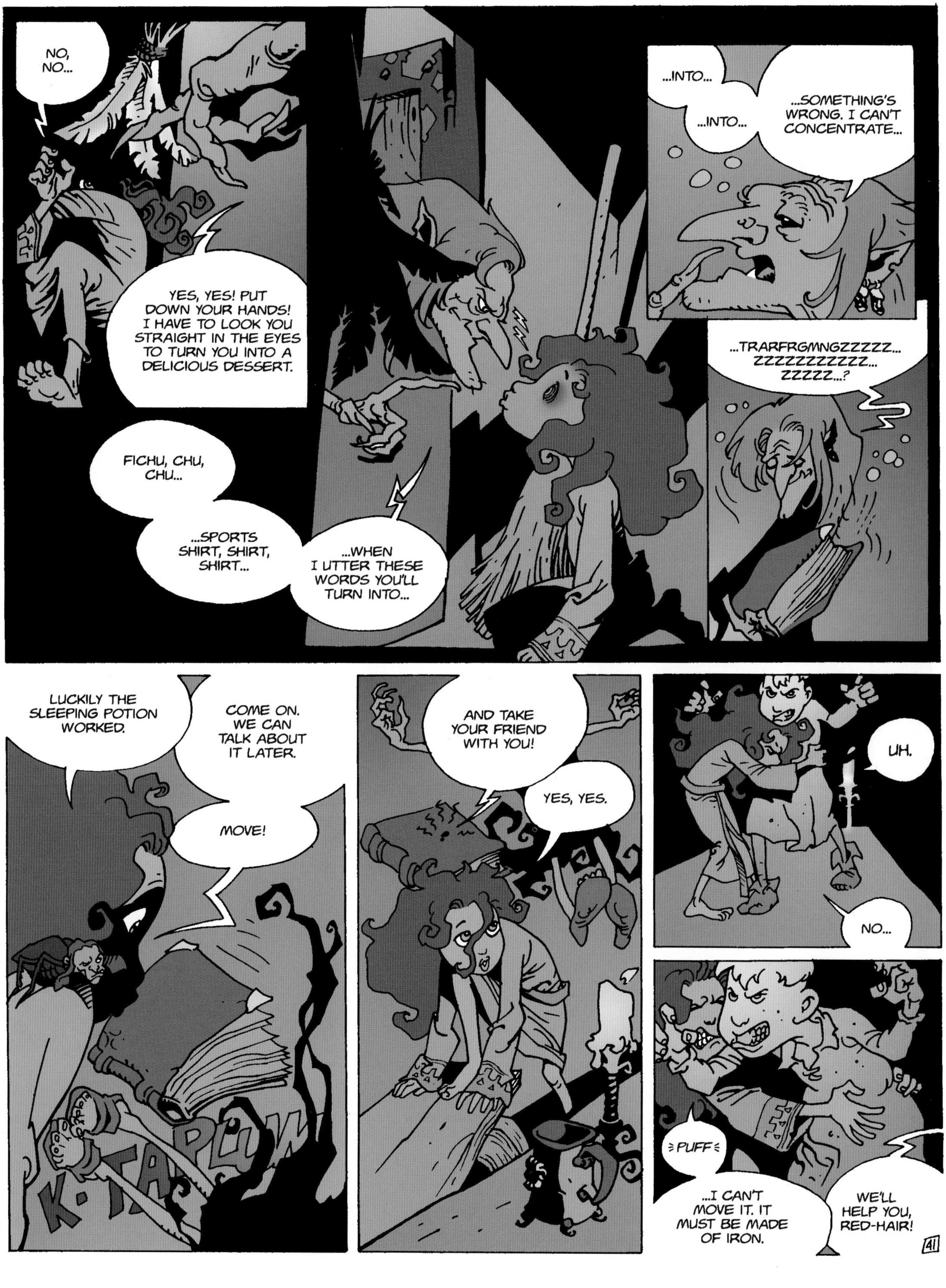
NO, NO...
YES, YES! PUT DOWN YOUR HANDS! I HAVE TO LOOK YOU STRAIGHT IN THE EYES TO TURN YOU INTO A DELICIOUS DESSERT.
FICHU, CHU, CHU...
...SPORTS SHIRT, SHIRT, SHIRT...
...WHEN I UTTER THESE WORDS YOU'LL TURN INTO...
...INTO...
...INTO...
...SOMETHING'S WRONG. I CAN'T CONCENTRATE...
...TRARFRGMNGZZZZZ... ZZZZZZZZZZZ... ZZZZZ...?
LUCKILY THE SLEEPING POTION WORKED.
COME ON. WE CAN TALK ABOUT IT LATER.
MOVE!
K·TA·PLUN
AND TAKE YOUR FRIEND WITH YOU!
YES, YES.
UH.
NO...
PUFF
...I CAN'T MOVE IT. IT MUST BE MADE OF IRON.
WE'LL HELP YOU, RED-HAIR!
41

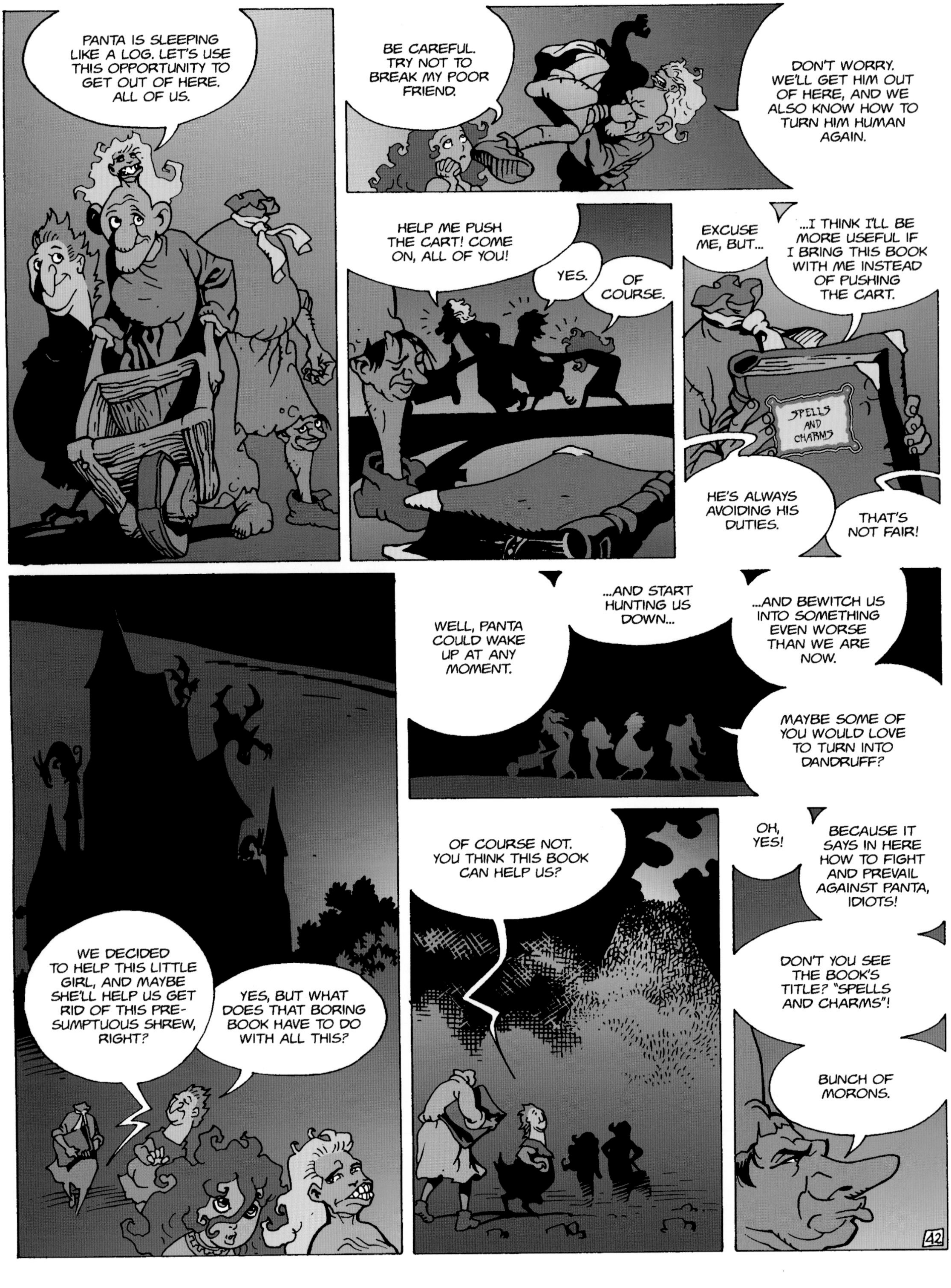
PANTA IS SLEEPING LIKE A LOG. LET'S USE THIS OPPORTUNITY TO GET OUT OF HERE. ALL OF US.
BE CAREFUL. TRY NOT TO BREAK MY POOR FRIEND.
DON'T WORRY. WE'LL GET HIM OUT OF HERE, AND WE ALSO KNOW HOW TO TURN HIM HUMAN AGAIN.
HELP ME PUSH THE CART! COME ON, ALL OF YOU!
YES.
OF COURSE.
EXCUSE ME, BUT...
...I THINK I'LL BE MORE USEFUL IF I BRING THIS BOOK WITH ME INSTEAD OF PUSHING THE CART.
SPELLS AND CHARMS
HE'S ALWAYS AVOIDING HIS DUTIES.
THAT'S NOT FAIR!
WE DECIDED TO HELP THIS LITTLE GIRL, AND MAYBE SHE'LL HELP US GET RID OF THIS PRE-SUMPTUOUS SHREW, RIGHT?
YES, BUT WHAT DOES THAT BORING BOOK HAVE TO DO WITH ALL THIS?
WELL, PANTA COULD WAKE UP AT ANY MOMENT.
...AND START HUNTING US DOWN...
...AND BEWITCH US INTO SOMETHING EVEN WORSE THAN WE ARE NOW.
MAYBE SOME OF YOU WOULD LOVE TO TURN INTO DANDRUFF?
OF COURSE NOT. YOU THINK THIS BOOK CAN HELP US?
OH, YES!
BECAUSE IT SAYS IN HERE HOW TO FIGHT AND PREVAIL AGAINST PANTA, IDIOTS!
DON'T YOU SEE THE BOOK'S TITLE? "SPELLS AND CHARMS"!
BUNCH OF MORONS.
42

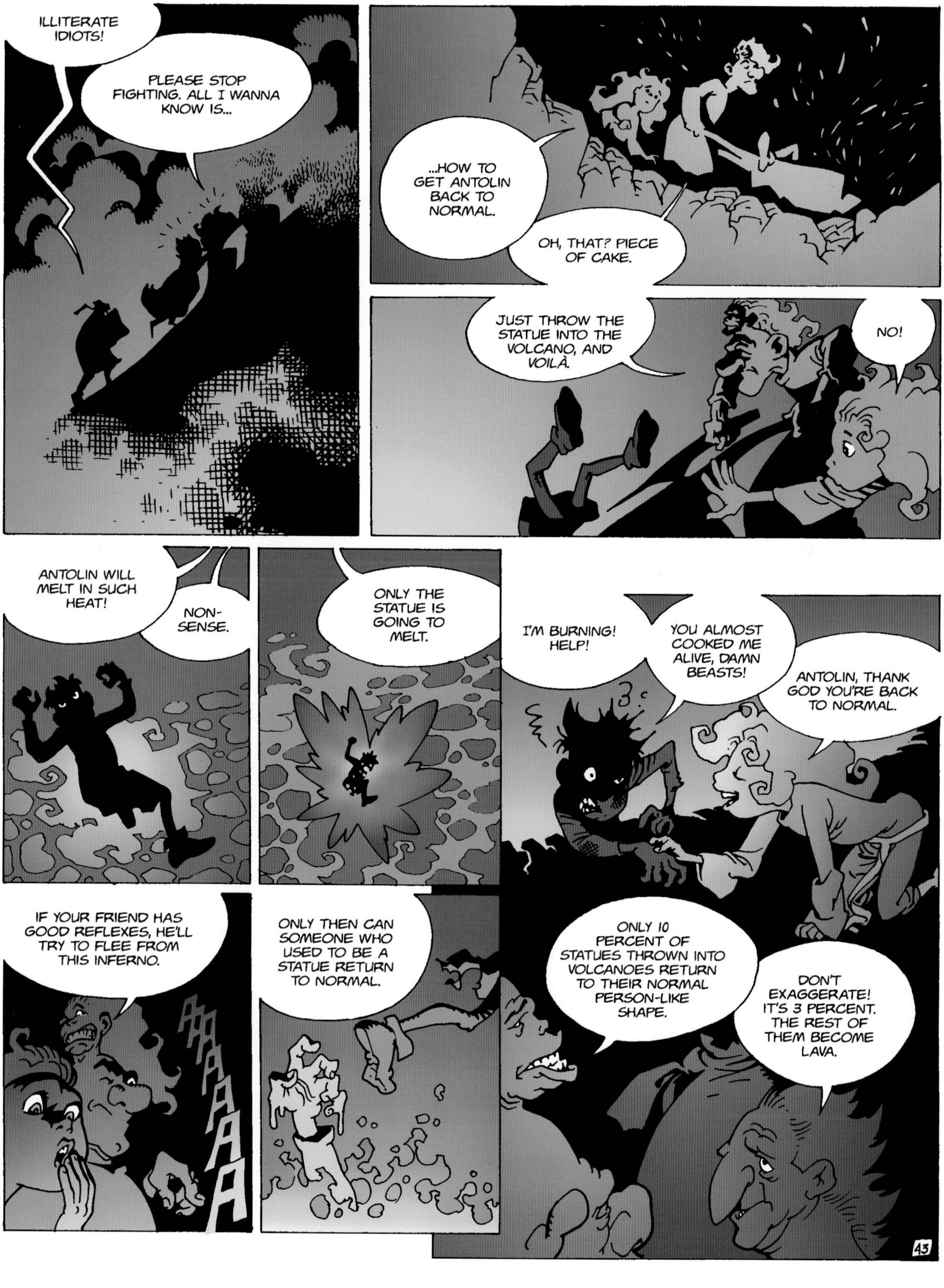
ILLITERATE IDIOTS!
PLEASE STOP FIGHTING. ALL I WANNA KNOW IS...
...HOW TO GET ANTOLIN BACK TO NORMAL.
OH, THAT? PIECE OF CAKE.
JUST THROW THE STATUE INTO THE VOLCANO, AND VOILÀ.
NO!
ANTOLIN WILL MELT IN SUCH HEAT!
NON-SENSE.
ONLY THE STATUE IS GOING TO MELT.
I'M BURNING! HELP!
YOU ALMOST COOKED ME ALIVE, DAMN BEASTS!
ANTOLIN, THANK GOD YOU'RE BACK TO NORMAL.
IF YOUR FRIEND HAS GOOD REFLEXES, HE'LL TRY TO FLEE FROM THIS INFERNO.
AAAAAAAAA
ONLY THEN CAN SOMEONE WHO USED TO BE A STATUE RETURN TO NORMAL.
ONLY 10 PERCENT OF STATUES THROWN INTO VOLCANOES RETURN TO THEIR NORMAL PERSON-LIKE SHAPE.
DON'T EXAGGERATE! IT'S 3 PERCENT. THE REST OF THEM BECOME LAVA.
43

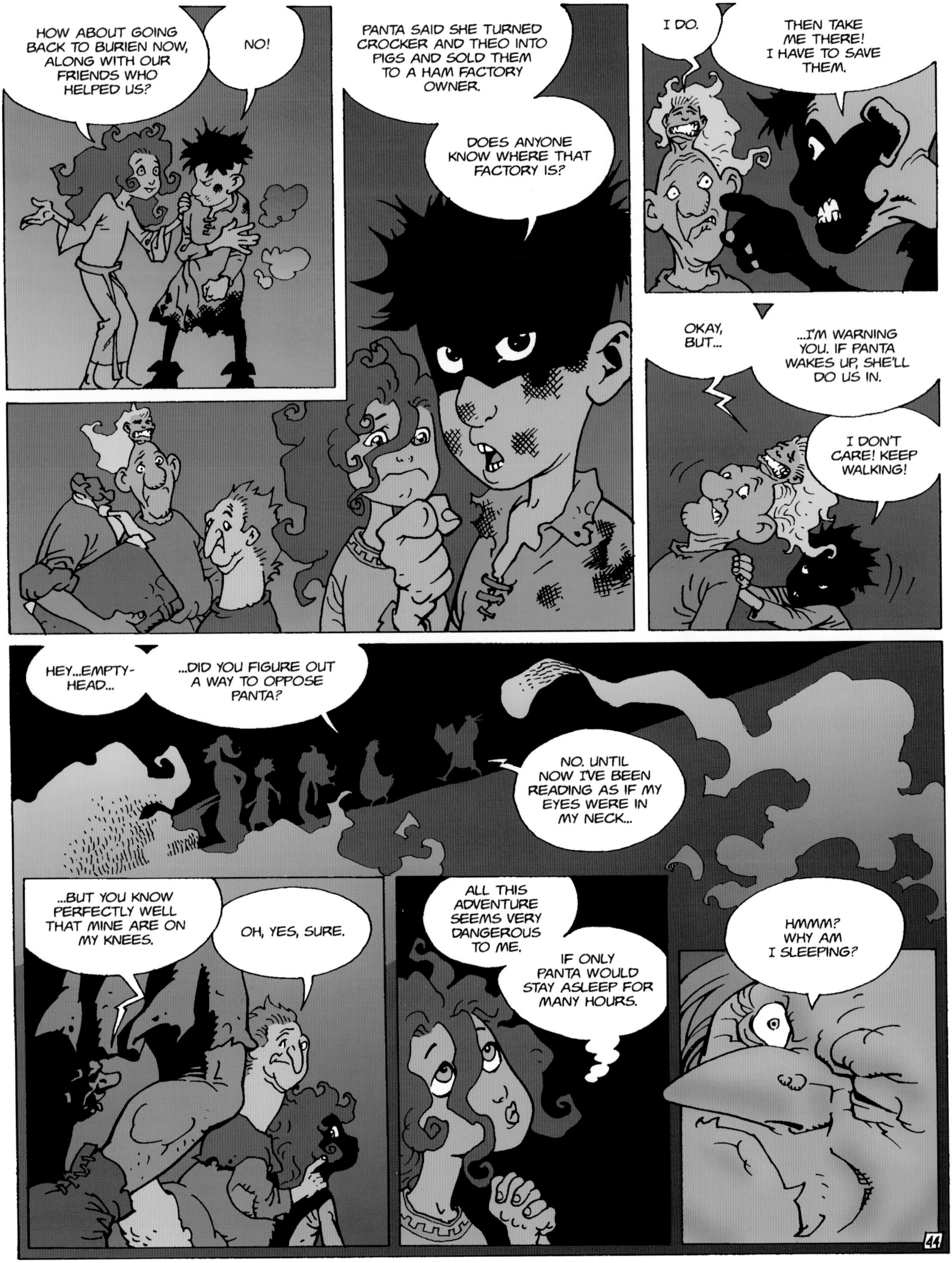
HOW ABOUT GOING BACK TO BURIEN NOW, ALONG WITH OUR FRIENDS WHO HELPED US?
NO!
PANTA SAID SHE TURNED CROCKER AND THEO INTO PIGS AND SOLD THEM TO A HAM FACTORY OWNER.
DOES ANYONE KNOW WHERE THAT FACTORY IS?
I DO.
THEN TAKE ME THERE! I HAVE TO SAVE THEM.
OKAY, BUT...
...I'M WARNING YOU. IF PANTA WAKES UP, SHE'LL DO US IN.
I DON'T CARE! KEEP WALKING!
HEY...EMPTY-HEAD...
...DID YOU FIGURE OUT A WAY TO OPPOSE PANTA?
NO. UNTIL NOW I'VE BEEN READING AS IF MY EYES WERE IN MY NECK...
...BUT YOU KNOW PERFECTLY WELL THAT MINE ARE ON MY KNEES.
OH, YES, SURE.
ALL THIS ADVENTURE SEEMS VERY DANGEROUS TO ME.
IF ONLY PANTA WOULD STAY ASLEEP FOR MANY HOURS.
HMMM? WHY AM I SLEEPING?
44

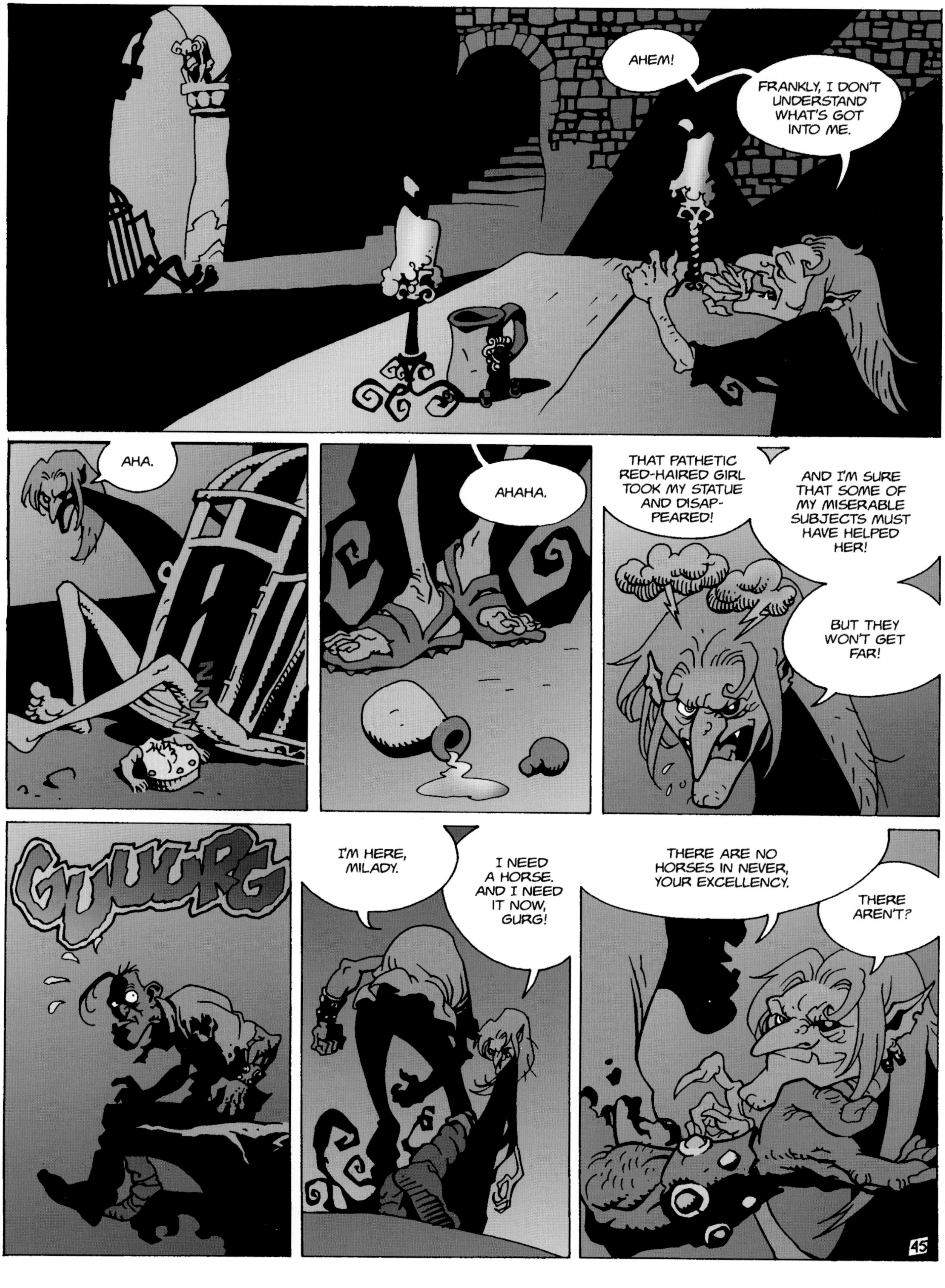
AHEM!
FRANKLY, I DON'T UNDERSTAND WHAT'S GOT INTO ME.
AHA.
AHAHA.
THAT PATHETIC RED-HAIRED GIRL TOOK MY STATUE AND DISAP-PEARED!
AND I'M SURE THAT SOME OF MY MISERABLE SUBJECTS MUST HAVE HELPED HER!
BUT THEY WON'T GET FAR!
GUUURG
I'M HERE, MILADY.
I NEED A HORSE. AND I NEED IT NOW, GURG!
THERE ARE NO HORSES IN NEVER, YOUR EXCELLENCY.
THERE AREN'T?
45

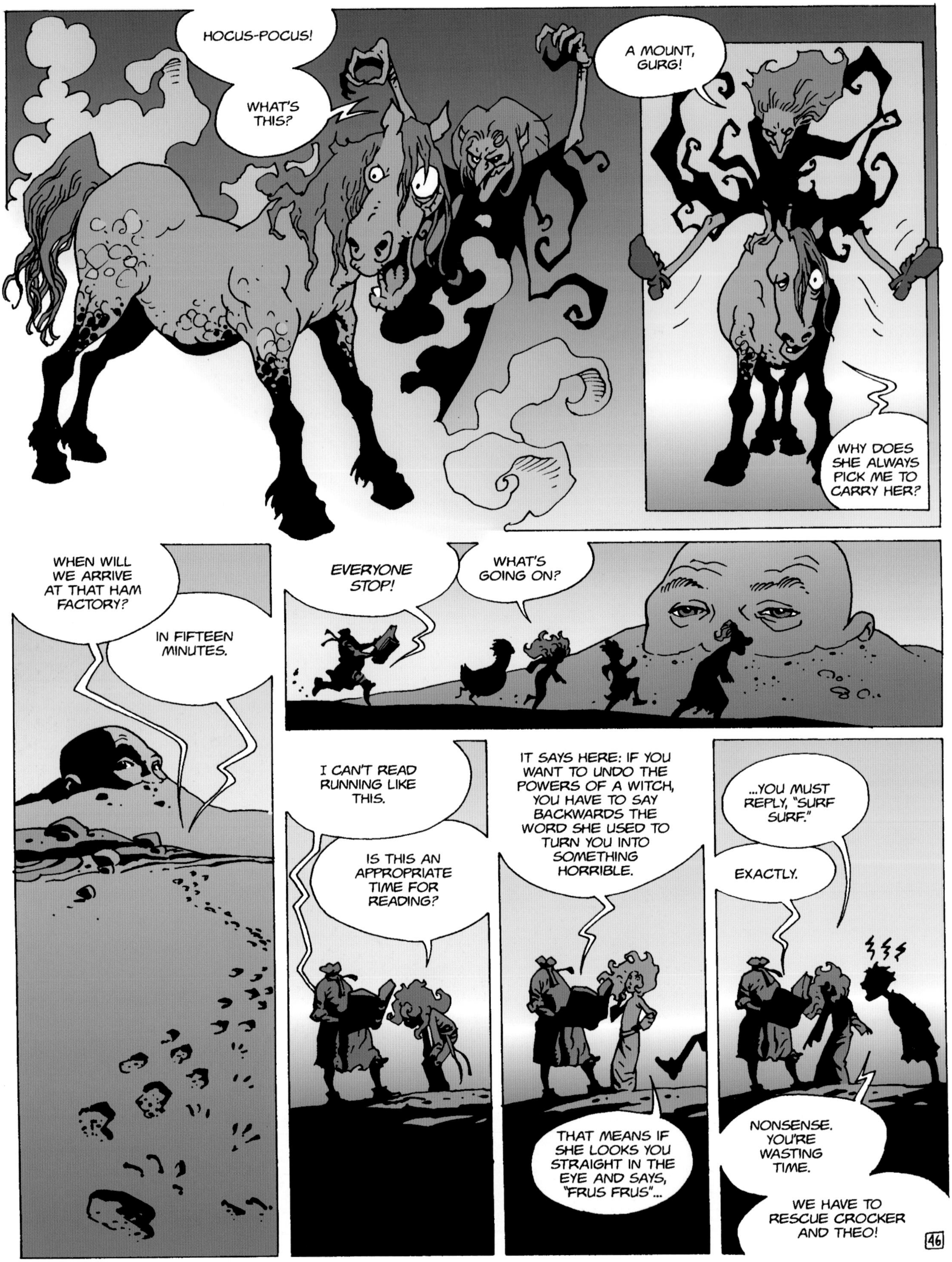
HOCUS-POCUS!
WHAT'S THIS?
A MOUNT, GURG!
WHY DOES SHE ALWAYS PICK ME TO CARRY HER?
WHEN WILL WE ARRIVE AT THAT HAM FACTORY?
IN FIFTEEN MINUTES.
EVERYONE STOP!
WHAT'S GOING ON?
I CAN'T READ RUNNING LIKE THIS.
IS THIS AN APPROPRIATE TIME FOR READING?
IT SAYS HERE: IF YOU WANT TO UNDO THE POWERS OF A WITCH, YOU HAVE TO SAY BACKWARDS THE WORD SHE USED TO TURN YOU INTO SOMETHING HORRIBLE.
THAT MEANS IF SHE LOOKS YOU STRAIGHT IN THE EYE AND SAYS, "FRUS FRUS"...
...YOU MUST REPLY, "SURF SURF."
EXACTLY.
NONSENSE. YOU'RE WASTING TIME.
WE HAVE TO RESCUE CROCKER AND THEO!
46

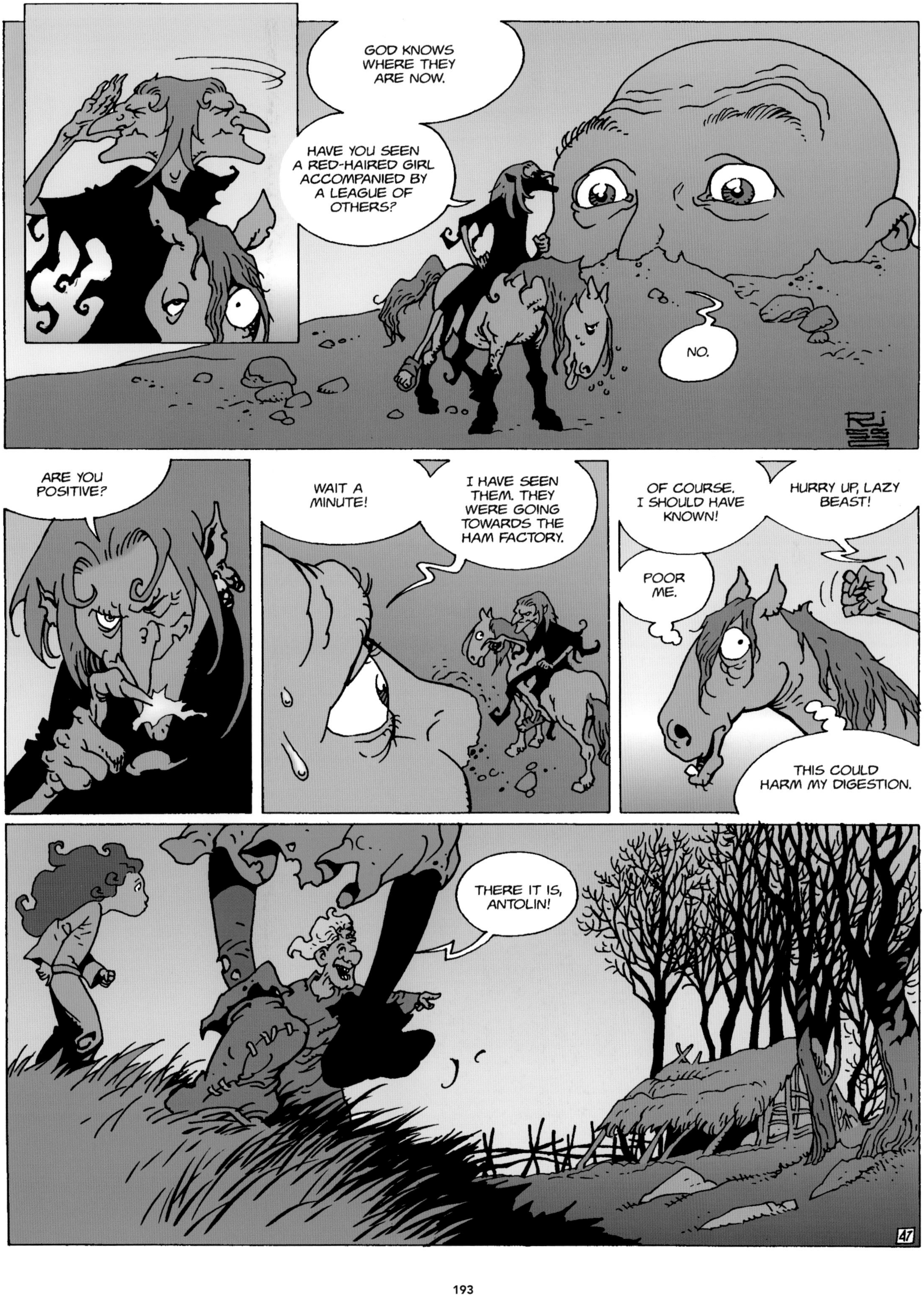
GOD KNOWS WHERE THEY ARE NOW.
HAVE YOU SEEN A RED-HAIRED GIRL ACCOMPANIED BY A LEAGUE OF OTHERS?
NO.
ARE YOU POSITIVE?
WAIT A MINUTE!
I HAVE SEEN THEM. THEY WERE GOING TOWARDS THE HAM FACTORY.
OF COURSE. I SHOULD HAVE KNOWN!
HURRY UP, LAZY BEAST!
POOR ME.
THIS COULD HARM MY DIGESTION.
THERE IT IS, ANTOLIN!
47

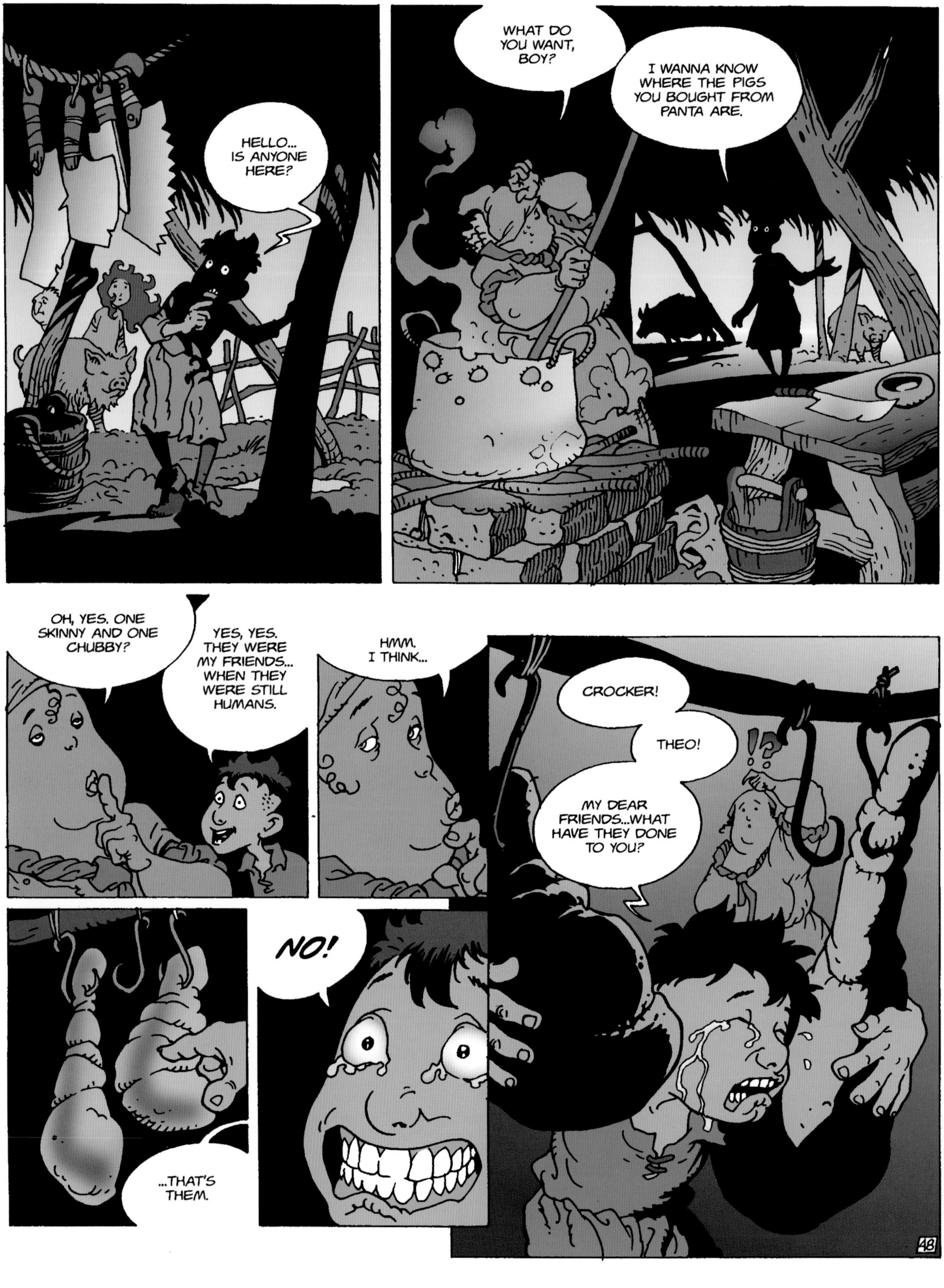
HELLO... IS ANYONE HERE?
WHAT DO YOU WANT, BOY?
I WANNA KNOW WHERE THE PIGS YOU BOUGHT FROM PANTA ARE.
OH, YES. ONE SKINNY AND ONE CHUBBY?
YES, YES. THEY WERE MY FRIENDS... WHEN THEY WERE STILL HUMANS.
HMM. I THINK...
...THAT'S THEM.
NO!
CROCKER!
THEO!
MY DEAR FRIENDS...WHAT HAVE THEY DONE TO YOU?
!?
48

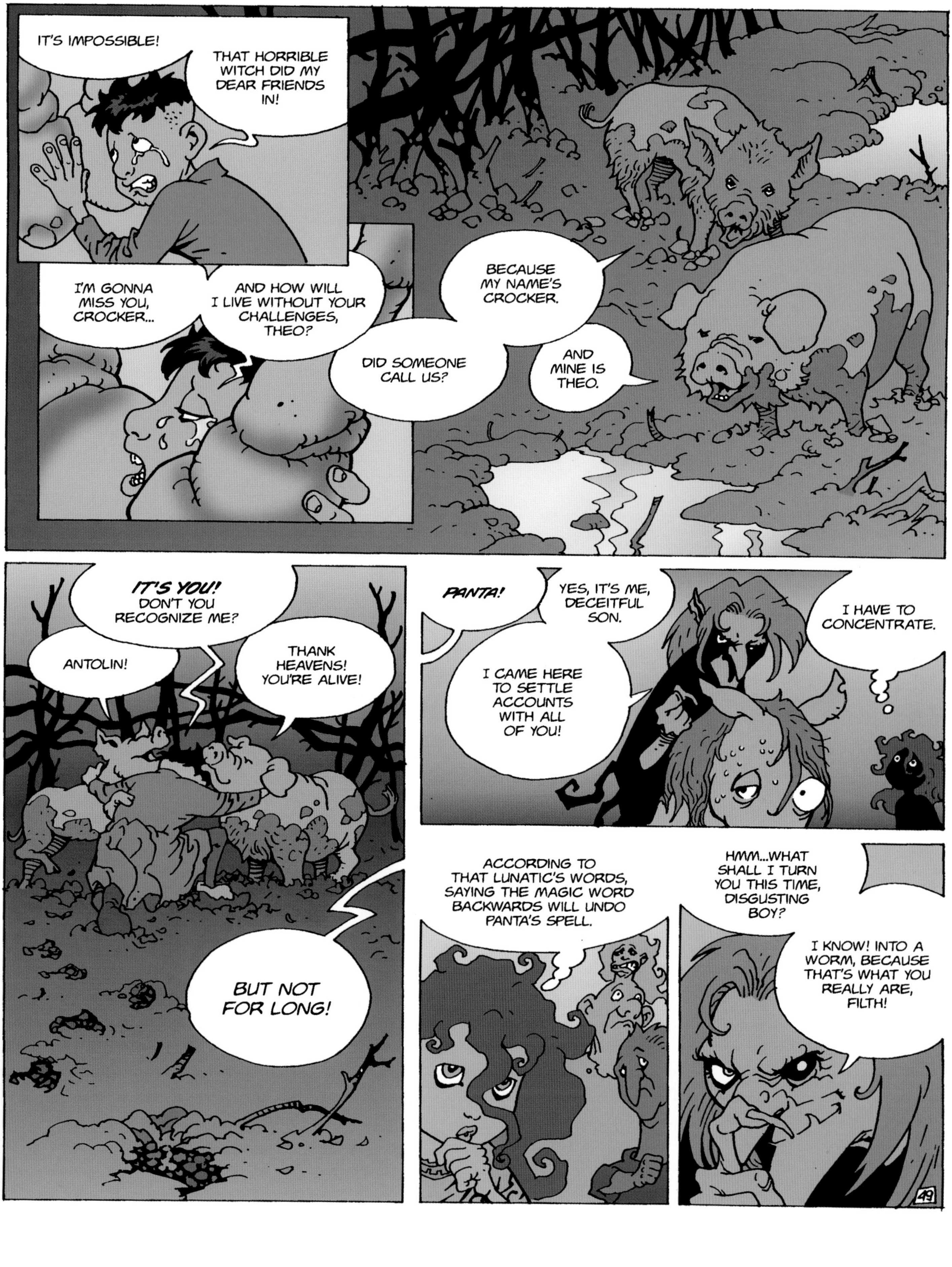
IT'S IMPOSSIBLE!
THAT HORRIBLE WITCH DID MY DEAR FRIENDS IN!
I'M GONNA MISS YOU, CROCKER...
AND HOW WILL I LIVE WITHOUT YOUR CHALLENGES, THEO?
DID SOMEONE CALL US?
BECAUSE MY NAME'S CROCKER.
AND MINE IS THEO.
IT'S YOU! DON'T YOU RECOGNIZE ME?
ANTOLIN!
THANK HEAVENS! YOU'RE ALIVE!
BUT NOT FOR LONG!
PANTA!
YES, IT'S ME, DECEITFUL SON.
I CAME HERE TO SETTLE ACCOUNTS WITH ALL OF YOU!
I HAVE TO CONCENTRATE.
ACCORDING TO THAT LUNATIC'S WORDS, SAYING THE MAGIC WORD BACKWARDS WILL UNDO PANTA'S SPELL.
HMM...WHAT SHALL I TURN YOU THIS TIME, DISGUSTING BOY?
I KNOW! INTO A WORM, BECAUSE THAT'S WHAT YOU REALLY ARE, FILTH!
49

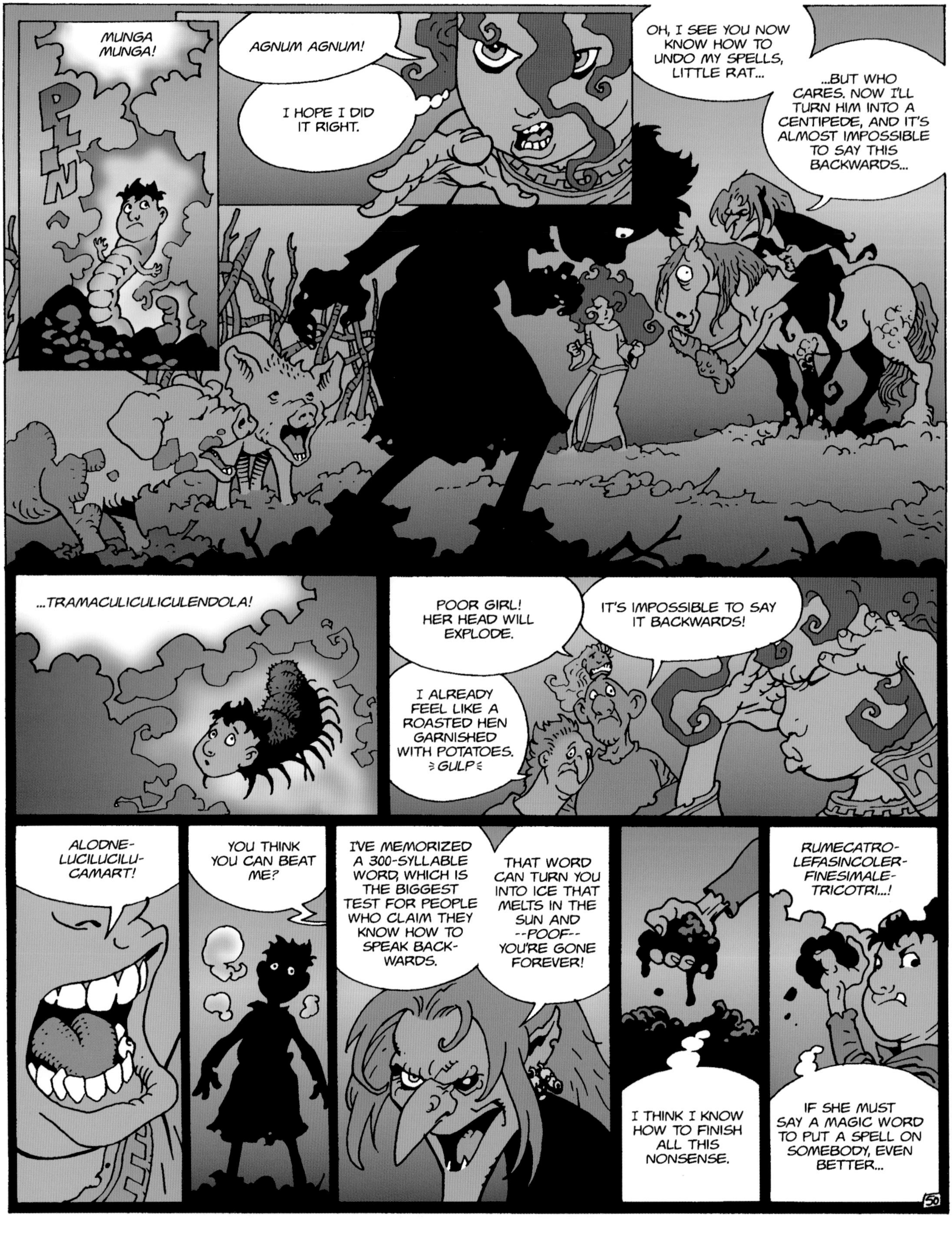
MUNGA MUNGA!
PLIN
AGNUM AGNUM!
I HOPE I DID IT RIGHT.
OH, I SEE YOU NOW KNOW HOW TO UNDO MY SPELLS, LITTLE RAT...
...BUT WHO CARES. NOW I'LL TURN HIM INTO A CENTIPEDE, AND IT'S ALMOST IMPOSSIBLE TO SAY THIS BACKWARDS...
...TRAMACULICULICULENDOLA!
POOR GIRL! HER HEAD WILL EXPLODE.
IT'S IMPOSSIBLE TO SAY IT BACKWARDS!
I ALREADY FEEL LIKE A ROASTED HEN GARNISHED WITH POTATOES.
GULP
ALODNE-LUCILUCILU-CAMART!
YOU THINK YOU CAN BEAT ME?
I'VE MEMORIZED A 300-SYLLABLE WORD, WHICH IS THE BIGGEST TEST FOR PEOPLE WHO CLAIM THEY KNOW HOW TO SPEAK BACK-WARDS.
THAT WORD CAN TURN YOU INTO ICE THAT MELTS IN THE SUN AND --POOF-- YOU'RE GONE FOREVER!
I THINK I KNOW HOW TO FINISH ALL THIS NONSENSE.
RUMECATRO-LEFASINCOLER-FINESIMALE-TRICOTRI...!
IF SHE MUST SAY A MAGIC WORD TO PUT A SPELL ON SOMEBODY, EVEN BETTER...
50

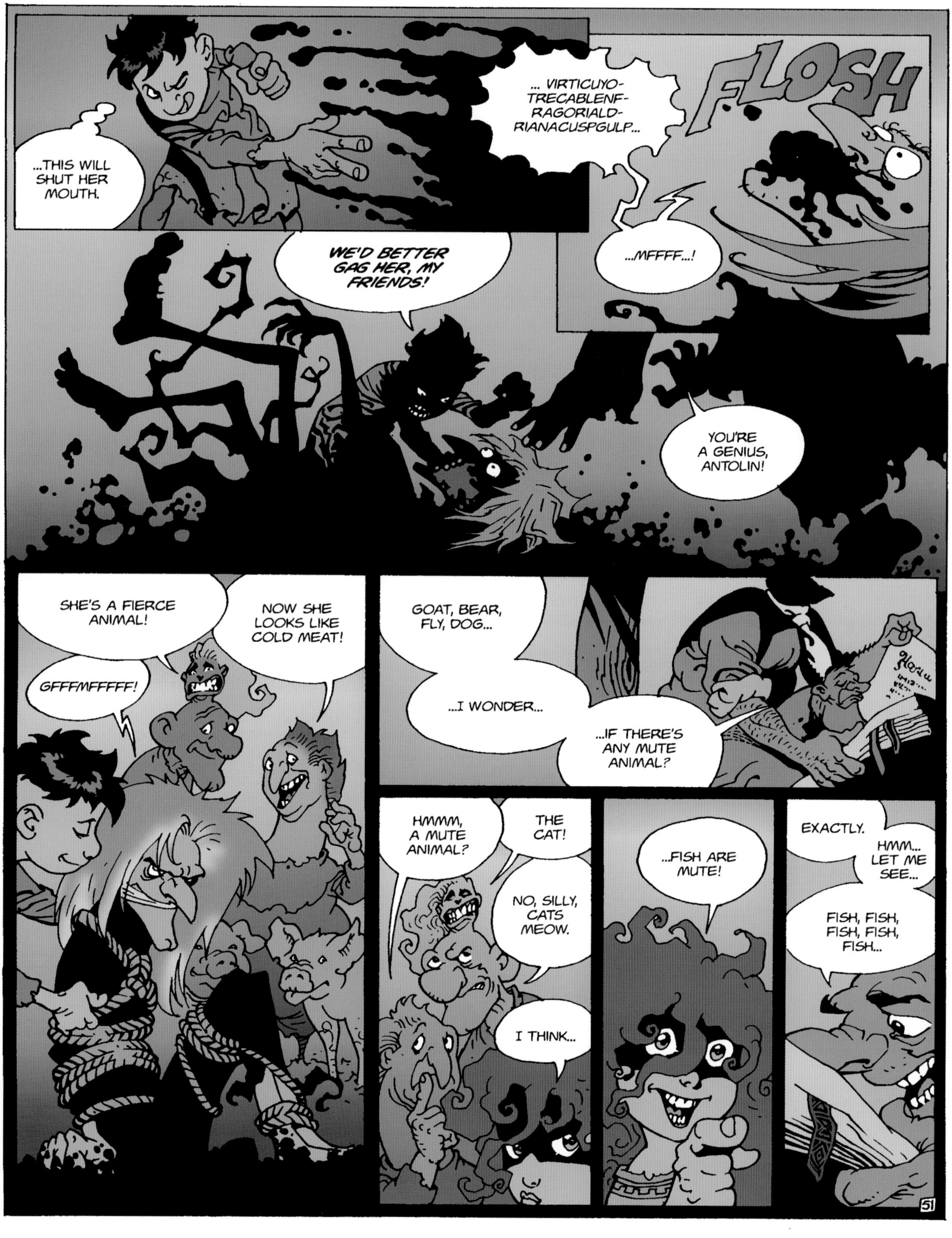

...THIS WILL SHUT HER MOUTH.
... VIRTICUYO-TRECABLENF-RAGORIALD-RIANACUSPGULP...
FLOSH
...MFFFF...!
WE'D BETTER GAG HER, MY FRIENDS!
YOU'RE A GENIUS, ANTOLIN!
SHE'S A FIERCE ANIMAL!
NOW SHE LOOKS LIKE COLD MEAT!
GFFFMFFFFF!
GOAT, BEAR, FLY, DOG...
...I WONDER...
...IF THERE'S ANY MUTE ANIMAL?
HMMM, A MUTE ANIMAL?
THE CAT!
NO, SILLY, CATS MEOW.
I THINK...
...FISH ARE MUTE!
EXACTLY.
HMM... LET ME SEE...
FISH, FISH, FISH, FISH, FISH...
51

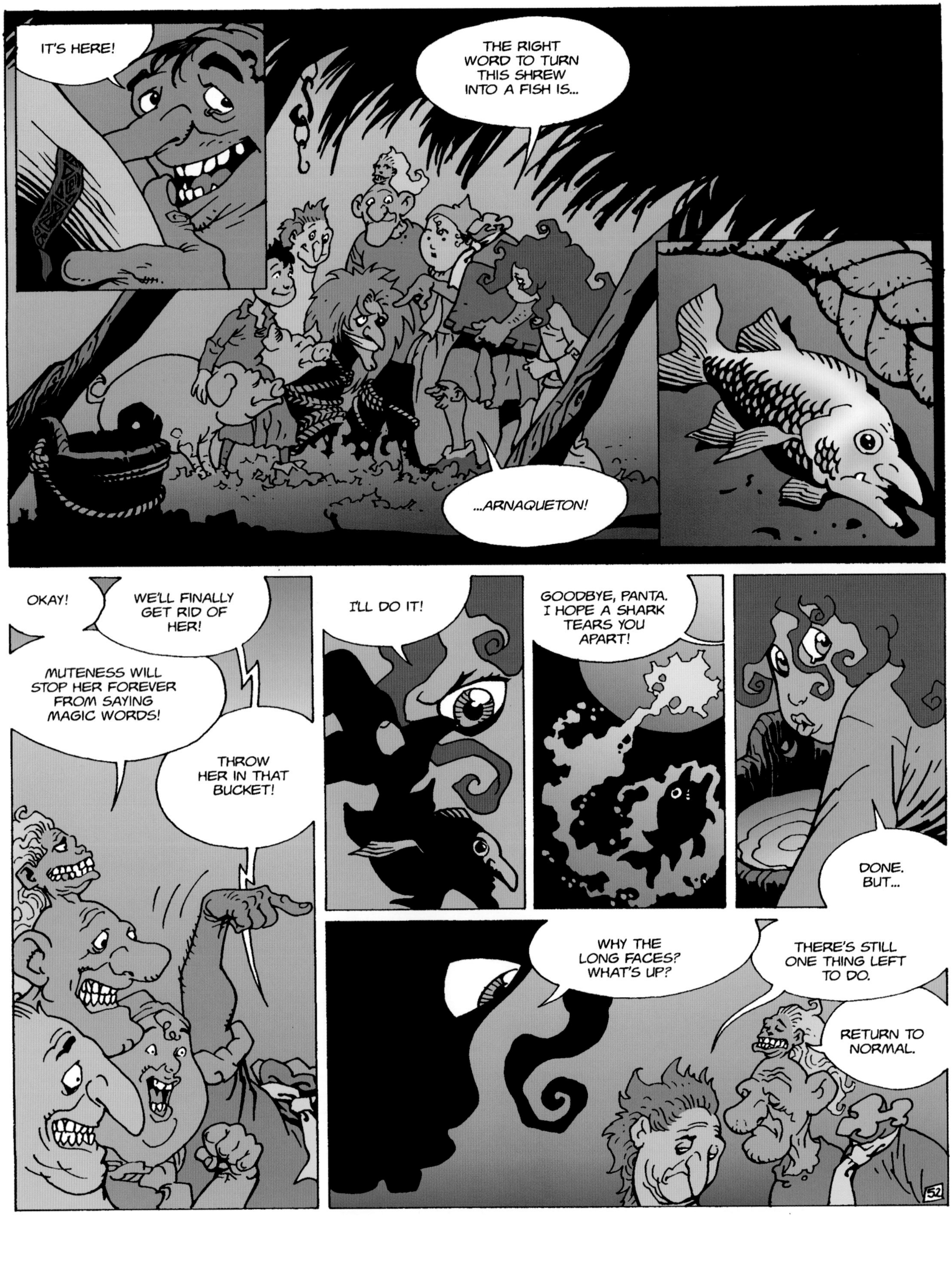
IT'S HERE!
THE RIGHT WORD TO TURN THIS SHREW INTO A FISH IS...
...ARNAQUETON!
OKAY!
WE'LL FINALLY GET RID OF HER!
MUTENESS WILL STOP HER FOREVER FROM SAYING MAGIC WORDS!
THROW HER IN THAT BUCKET!
I'LL DO IT!
GOODBYE, PANTA. I HOPE A SHARK TEARS YOU APART!
DONE. BUT...
WHY THE LONG FACES? WHAT'S UP?
THERE'S STILL ONE THING LEFT TO DO.
RETURN TO NORMAL.
52

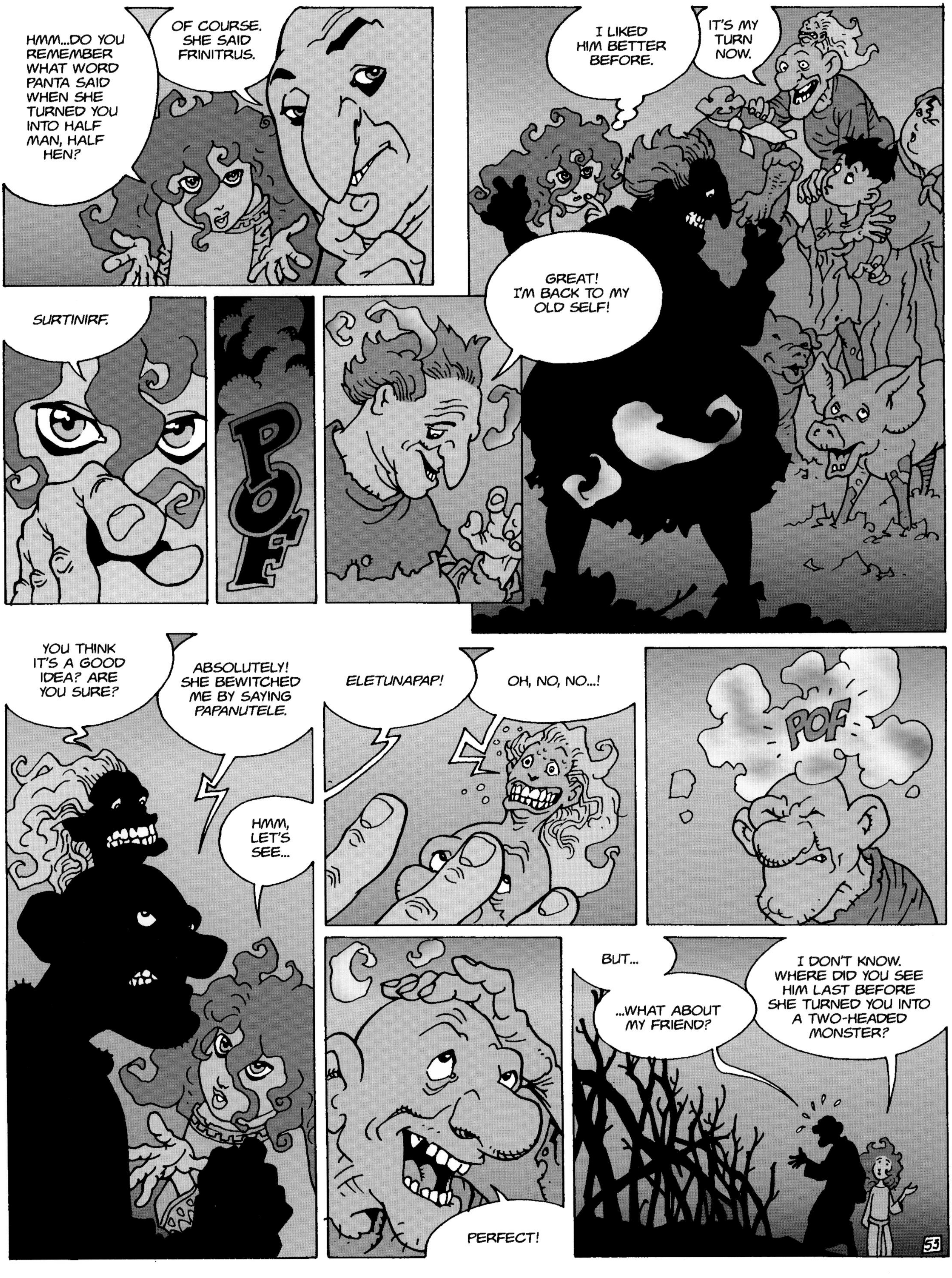
HMM...DO YOU REMEMBER WHAT WORD PANTA SAID WHEN SHE TURNED YOU INTO HALF MAN, HALF HEN?
OF COURSE. SHE SAID FRINITRUS.
SURTINIRF.
POF
I LIKED HIM BETTER BEFORE.
IT'S MY TURN NOW.
GREAT! I'M BACK TO MY OLD SELF!
YOU THINK IT'S A GOOD IDEA? ARE YOU SURE?
ABSOLUTELY! SHE BEWITCHED ME BY SAYING PAPANUTELE.
HMM, LET'S SEE...
ELETUNAPAP!
OH, NO, NO...!
POF
PERFECT!
BUT...
...WHAT ABOUT MY FRIEND?
I DON'T KNOW. WHERE DID YOU SEE HIM LAST BEFORE SHE TURNED YOU INTO A TWO-HEADED MONSTER?
53

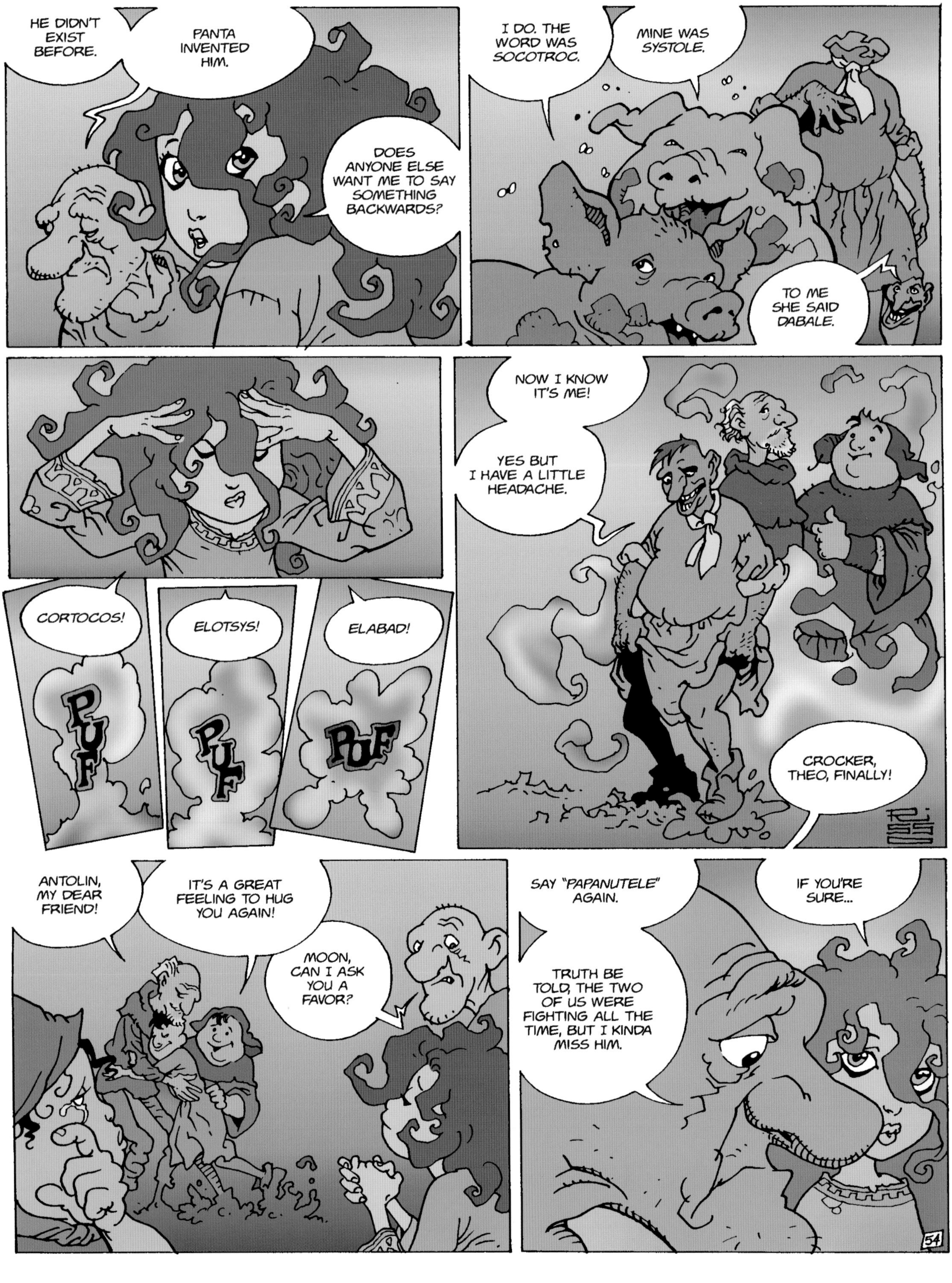
HE DIDN'T EXIST BEFORE.
PANTA INVENTED HIM.
DOES ANYONE ELSE WANT ME TO SAY SOMETHING BACKWARDS?
I DO. THE WORD WAS SOCOTROC.
MINE WAS SYSTOLE.
TO ME SHE SAID DABALE.
CORTOCOS!
PUF
ELOTSYS!
PUF
ELABAD!
PUF
NOW I KNOW IT'S ME!
YES BUT I HAVE A LITTLE HEADACHE.
CROCKER, THEO, FINALLY!
ANTOLIN, MY DEAR FRIEND!
IT'S A GREAT FEELING TO HUG YOU AGAIN!
MOON, CAN I ASK YOU A FAVOR?
SAY "PAPANUTELE" AGAIN.
IF YOU'RE SURE...
TRUTH BE TOLD, THE TWO OF US WERE FIGHTING ALL THE TIME, BUT I KINDA MISS HIM.
54

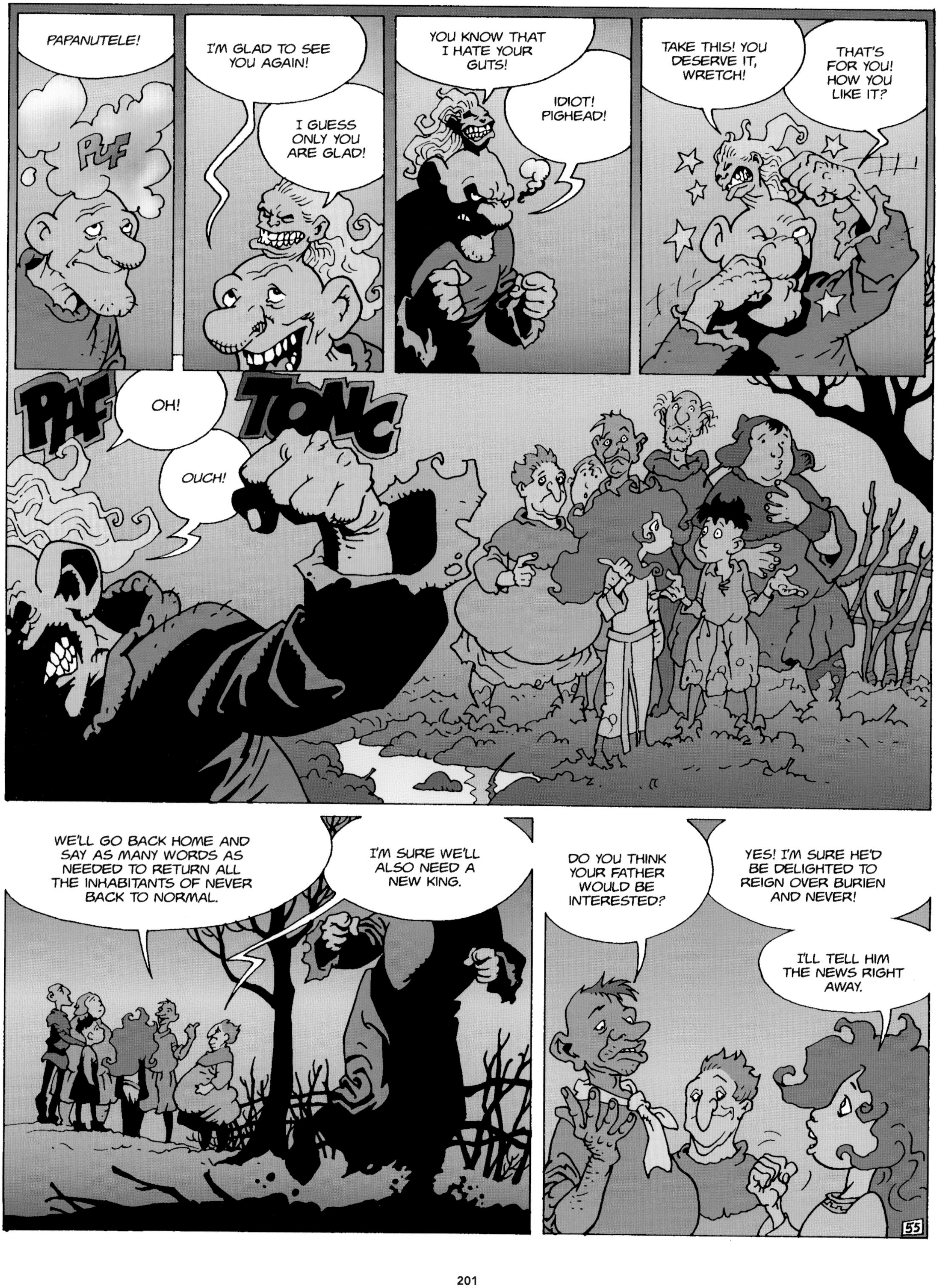
PAPANUTELE!
PUF
I'M GLAD TO SEE YOU AGAIN!
I GUESS ONLY YOU ARE GLAD!
YOU KNOW THAT I HATE YOUR GUTS!
IDIOT! PIGHEAD!
TAKE THIS! YOU DESERVE IT, WRETCH!
THAT'S FOR YOU! HOW YOU LIKE IT?
PAF
OH!
TONC
OUCH!
WE'LL GO BACK HOME AND SAY AS MANY WORDS AS NEEDED TO RETURN ALL THE INHABITANTS OF NEVER BACK TO NORMAL.
I'M SURE WE'LL ALSO NEED A NEW KING.
DO YOU THINK YOUR FATHER WOULD BE INTERESTED?
YES! I'M SURE HE'D BE DELIGHTED TO REIGN OVER BURIEN AND NEVER!
I'LL TELL HIM THE NEWS RIGHT AWAY.
55

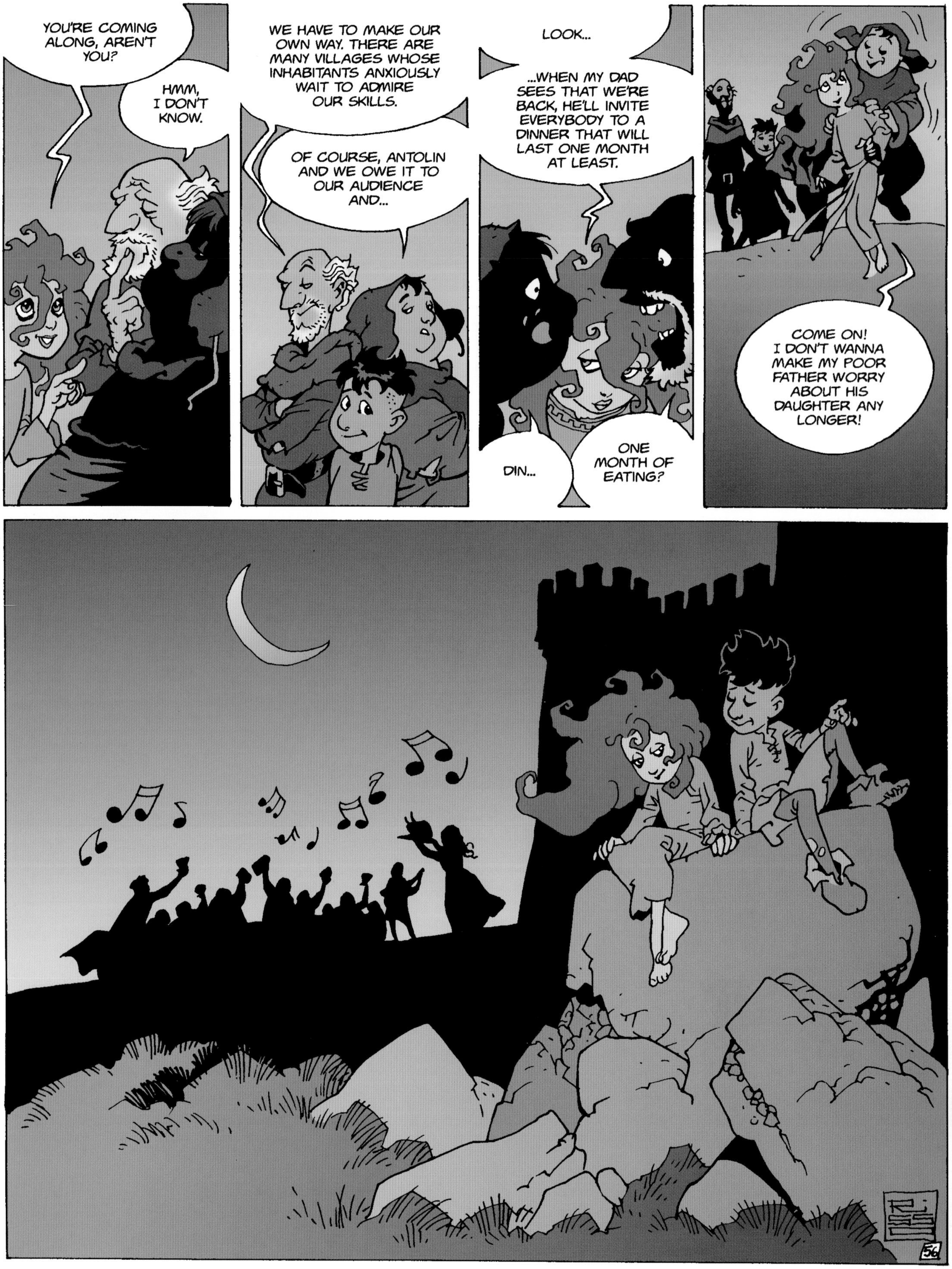

YOU'RE COMING ALONG, AREN'T YOU?
HMM, I DON'T KNOW.
WE HAVE TO MAKE OUR OWN WAY. THERE ARE MANY VILLAGES WHOSE INHABITANTS ANXIOUSLY WAIT TO ADMIRE OUR SKILLS.
OF COURSE, ANTOLIN AND WE OWE IT TO OUR AUDIENCE AND...
LOOK...
...WHEN MY DAD SEES THAT WE'RE BACK, HE'LL INVITE EVERYBODY TO A DINNER THAT WILL LAST ONE MONTH AT LEAST.
DIN...
ONE MONTH OF EATING?
COME ON! I DON'T WANNA MAKE MY POOR FATHER WORRY ABOUT HIS DAUGHTER ANY LONGER!
56

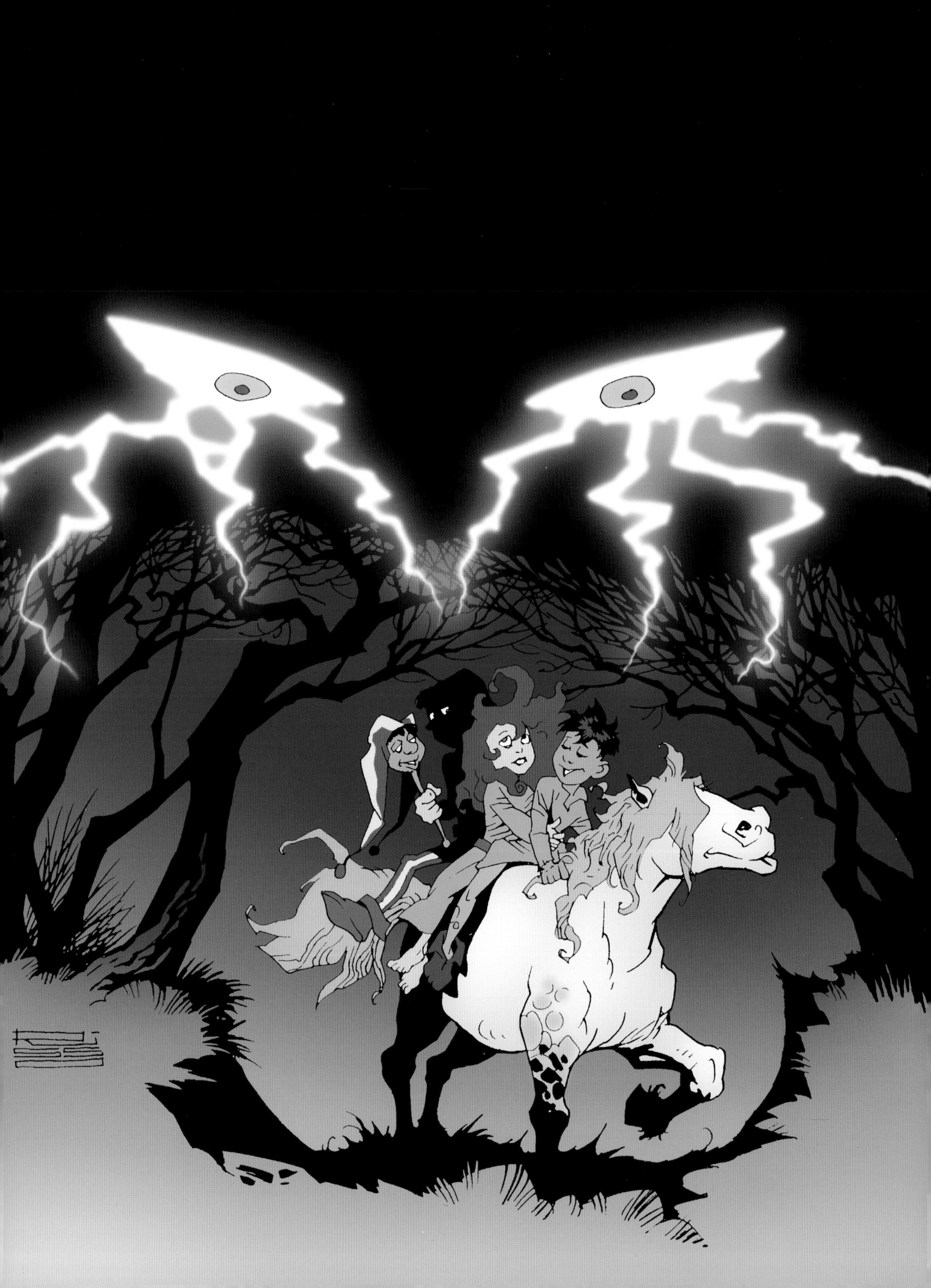

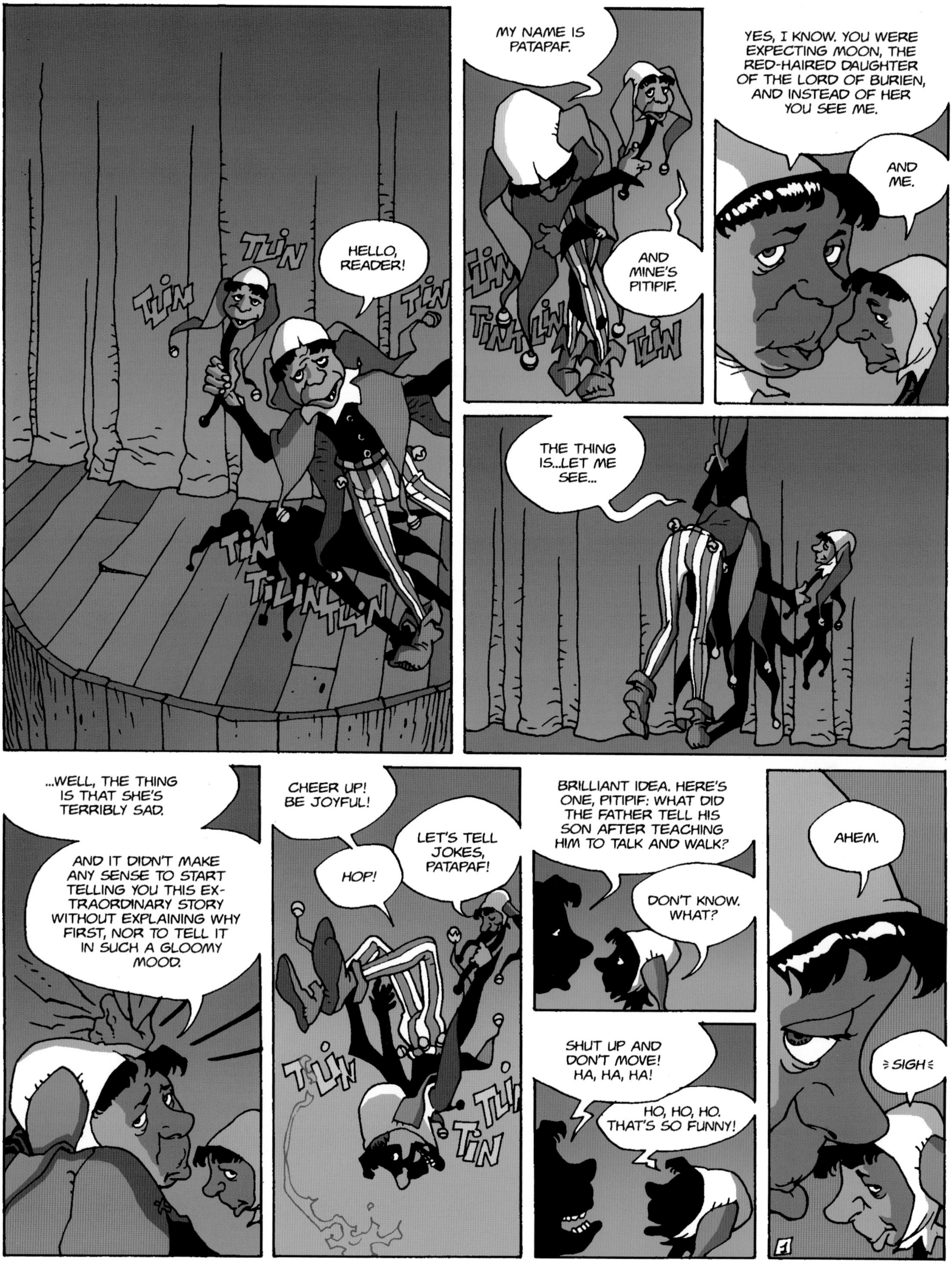
HELLO, READER!
TLIN
TLIN
TIN
TIN
TILIN
TLIN
MY NAME IS PATAPAF.
AND MINE'S PITIPIF.
TLIN
YES, I KNOW. YOU WERE EXPECTING MOON, THE RED-HAIRED DAUGHTER OF THE LORD OF BURIEN, AND INSTEAD OF HER YOU SEE ME.
AND ME.
THE THING IS...LET ME SEE...
...WELL, THE THING IS THAT SHE'S TERRIBLY SAD.
AND IT DIDN'T MAKE ANY SENSE TO START TELLING YOU THIS EXTRAORDINARY STORY WITHOUT EXPLAINING WHY FIRST, NOR TO TELL IT IN SUCH A GLOOMY MOOD.
CHEER UP! BE JOYFUL!
HOP!
LET'S TELL JOKES, PATAPAF!
TLIN
TIN
BRILLIANT IDEA. HERE'S ONE, PITIPIF: WHAT DID THE FATHER TELL HIS SON AFTER TEACHING HIM TO TALK AND WALK?
DON'T KNOW. WHAT?
SHUT UP AND DON'T MOVE! HA, HA, HA!
HO, HO, HO. THAT'S SO FUNNY!
AHEM.
SIGH

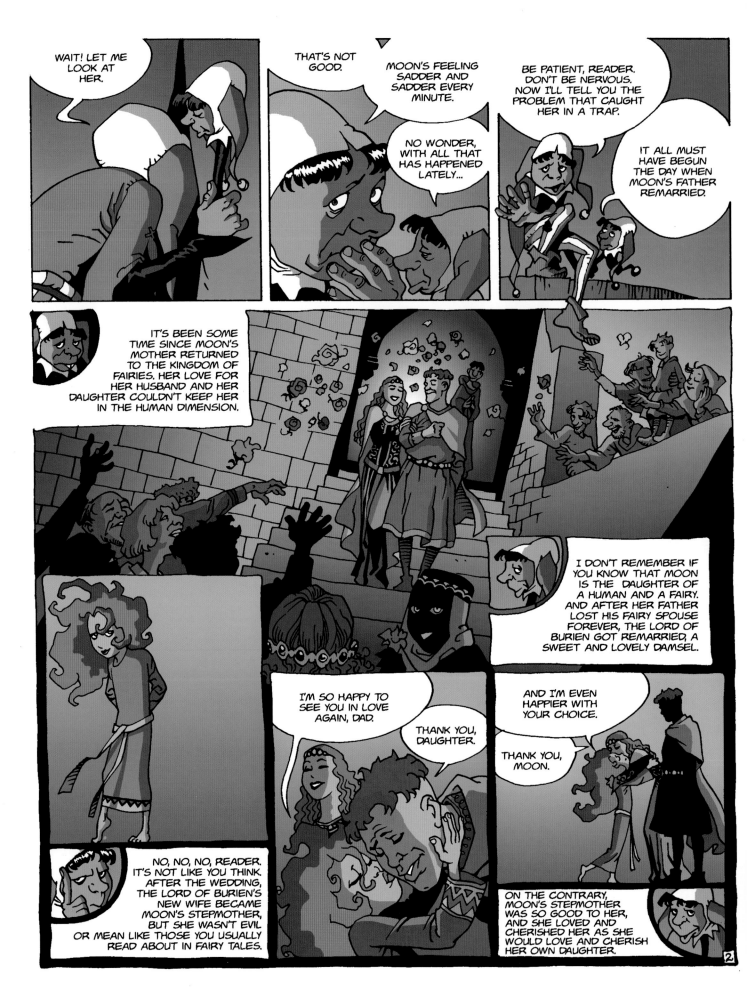

WAIT! LET ME LOOK AT HER.

THAT'S NOT GOOD.

MOON'S FEELING SADDER AND SADDER EVERY MINUTE.

NO WONDER, WITH ALL THAT HAS HAPPENED LATELY...

BE PATIENT, READER. DON'T BE NERVOUS. NOW I'LL TELL YOU THE PROBLEM THAT CAUGHT HER IN A TRAP.

IT ALL MUST HAVE BEGUN THE DAY WHEN MOON'S FATHER REMARRIED.

IT'S BEEN SOME TIME SINCE MOON'S MOTHER RETURNED TO THE KINGDOM OF FAIRIES. HER LOVE FOR HER HUSBAND AND HER DAUGHTER COULDN'T KEEP HER IN THE HUMAN DIMENSION.

I DON'T REMEMBER IF YOU KNOW THAT MOON IS THE DAUGHTER OF A HUMAN AND A FAIRY. AND AFTER HER FATHER LOST HIS FAIRY SPOUSE FOREVER, THE LORD OF BURIEN GOT REMARRIED, A SWEET AND LOVELY DAMSEL.

I'M SO HAPPY TO SEE YOU IN LOVE AGAIN, DAD.

THANK YOU, DAUGHTER.

AND I'M EVEN HAPPIER WITH YOUR CHOICE.

THANK YOU, MOON.

NO, NO, NO, READER. IT'S NOT LIKE YOU THINK. AFTER THE WEDDING, THE LORD OF BURIEN'S NEW WIFE BECAME MOON'S STEPMOTHER, BUT SHE WASN'T EVIL OR MEAN LIKE THOSE YOU USUALLY READ ABOUT IN FAIRY TALES.

ON THE CONTRARY, MOON'S STEPMOTHER WAS SO GOOD TO HER, AND SHE LOVED AND CHERISHED HER AS SHE WOULD LOVE AND CHERISH HER OWN DAUGHTER.

2

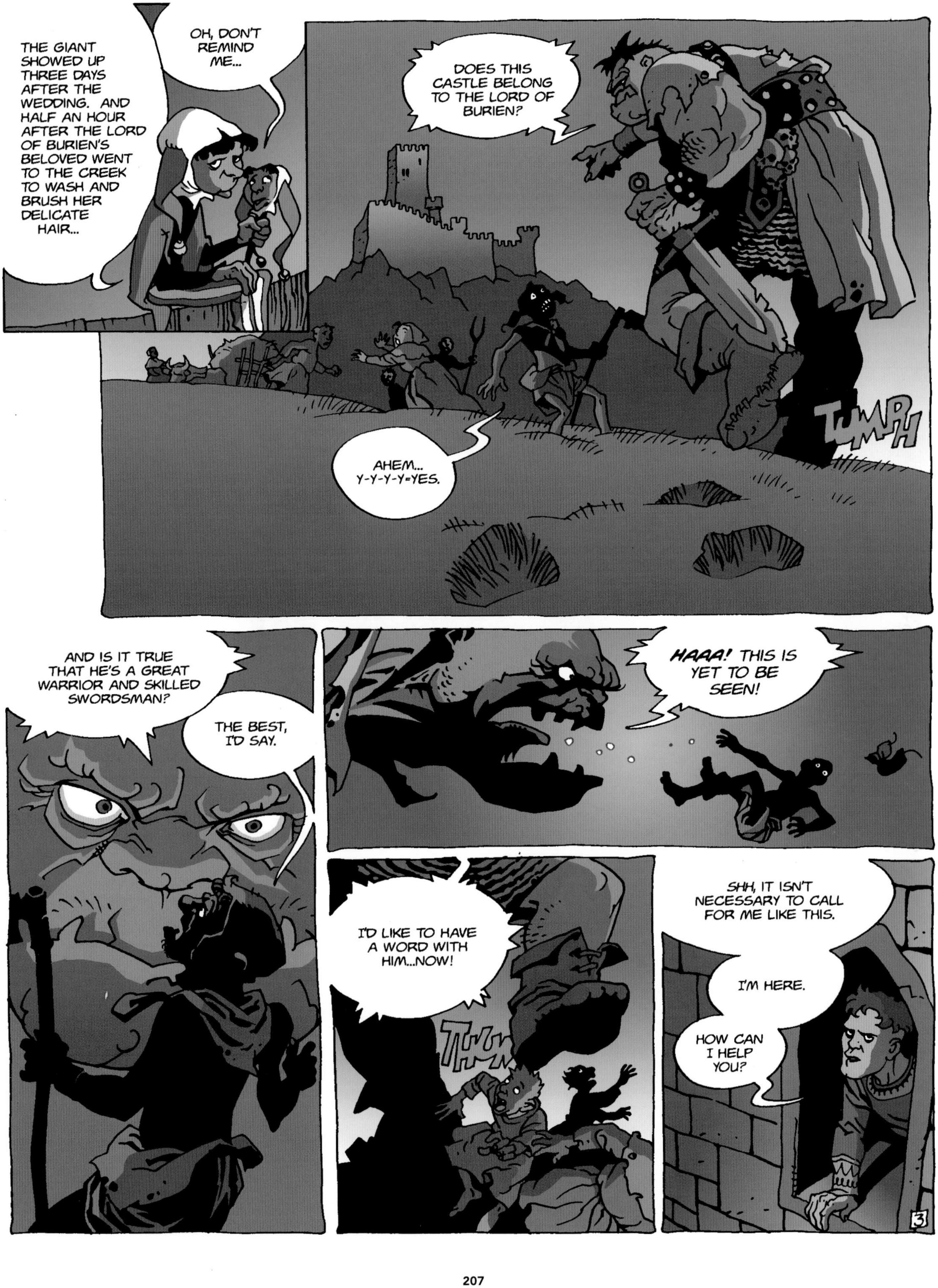
THE GIANT SHOWED UP THREE DAYS AFTER THE WEDDING. AND HALF AN HOUR AFTER THE LORD OF BURIEN'S BELOVED WENT TO THE CREEK TO WASH AND BRUSH HER DELICATE HAIR...
OH, DON'T REMIND ME...
DOES THIS CASTLE BELONG TO THE LORD OF BURIEN?
TUMPH
AHEM... Y-Y-Y-Y=YES.
AND IS IT TRUE THAT HE'S A GREAT WARRIOR AND SKILLED SWORDSMAN?
THE BEST, I'D SAY.
HAAA! THIS IS YET TO BE SEEN!
I'D LIKE TO HAVE A WORD WITH HIM...NOW!
SHH, IT ISN'T NECESSARY TO CALL FOR ME LIKE THIS.
I'M HERE.
HOW CAN I HELP YOU?
3

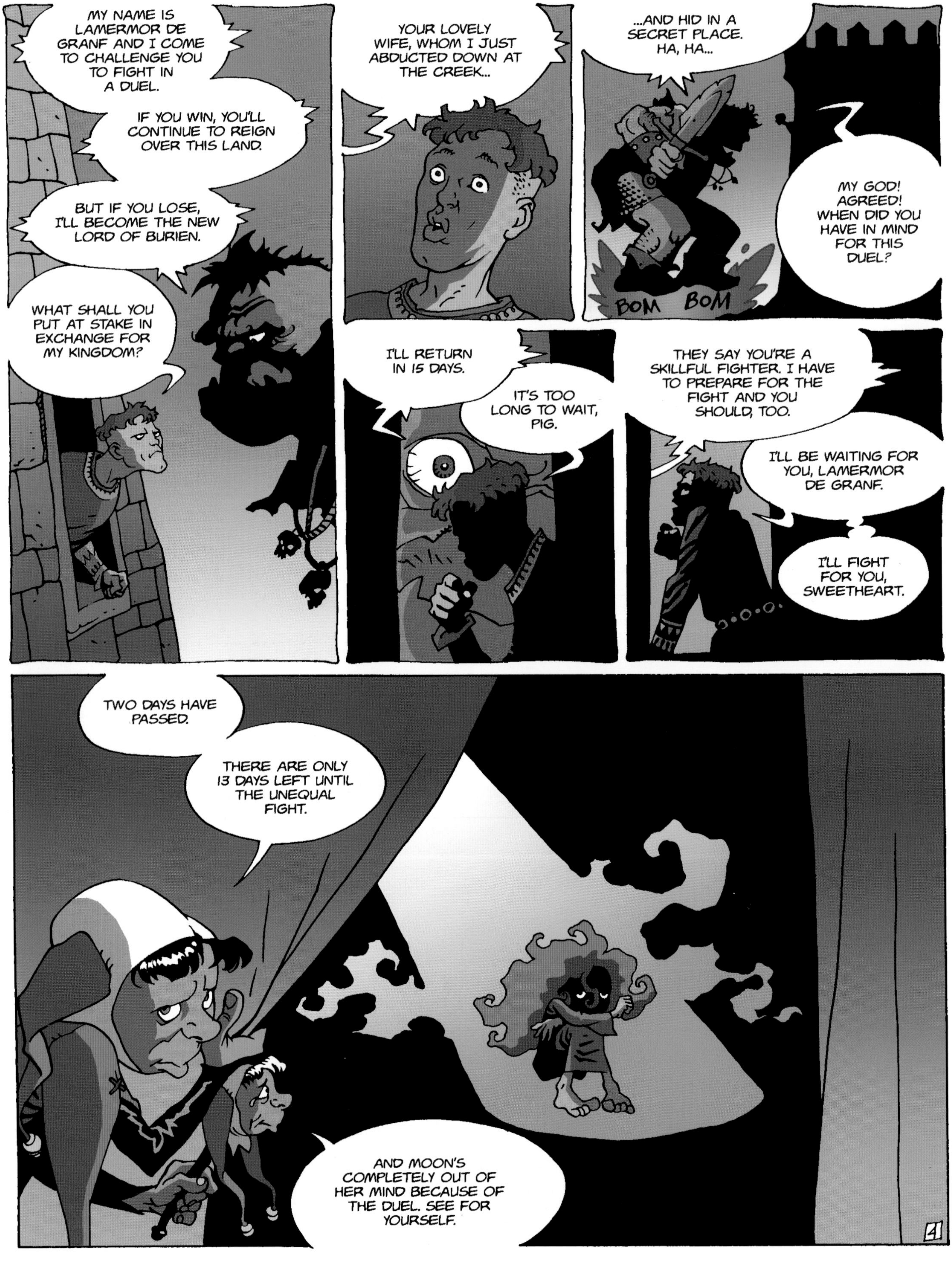
MY NAME IS LAMERMOR DE GRANF AND I COME TO CHALLENGE YOU TO FIGHT IN A DUEL.
IF YOU WIN, YOU'LL CONTINUE TO REIGN OVER THIS LAND.
BUT IF YOU LOSE, I'LL BECOME THE NEW LORD OF BURIEN.
WHAT SHALL YOU PUT AT STAKE IN EXCHANGE FOR MY KINGDOM?
YOUR LOVELY WIFE, WHOM I JUST ABDUCTED DOWN AT THE CREEK...
...AND HID IN A SECRET PLACE. HA, HA...
BOM BOM
MY GOD! AGREED! WHEN DID YOU HAVE IN MIND FOR THIS DUEL?
I'LL RETURN IN 15 DAYS.
IT'S TOO LONG TO WAIT, PIG.
THEY SAY YOU'RE A SKILLFUL FIGHTER. I HAVE TO PREPARE FOR THE FIGHT AND YOU SHOULD, TOO.
I'LL BE WAITING FOR YOU, LAMERMOR DE GRANF.
I'LL FIGHT FOR YOU, SWEETHEART.
TWO DAYS HAVE PASSED.
THERE ARE ONLY 13 DAYS LEFT UNTIL THE UNEQUAL FIGHT.
AND MOON'S COMPLETELY OUT OF HER MIND BECAUSE OF THE DUEL. SEE FOR YOURSELF.
4

IT'S IMPOSSIBLE! WE ARE THE BUFFOON AND HIS SCEPTER AND IT'S OUR DUTY TO DO SOMETHING.

LIKE WHAT?

OKAY. HOW ABOUT IF WE TRY DOING YOUR FAVORITE STUNT?

ELICIT A SMILE FROM MOON'S FACE OR LOOK FOR ANOTHER JOB, PAL.

WHEN YOU THROW ME IN THE AIR? NOT THAT ONE, PLEASE!

OH, YES. THAT ONE EXACTLY.

I ALMOST ALWAYS MANAGE TO LAND YOU ON MY NOSE AND PREVENT YOU FROM CRASHING.

ALMOST ALWAYS?

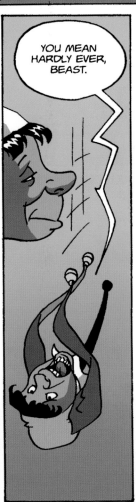

YOU MEAN HARDLY EVER, BEAST.

OUCH! MY HEAD!

DAMN ANIMAL!

NOW I'LL HAVE A BUMP!

OH, PITIPIF... LOOK...

...NOT ONLY HASN'T SHE MOVED ONE BIT, BUT SHE DIDN'T EVEN BOTHER TO SEE OUR GREAT STUNT.

AND I RISKED MY LIFE!

5

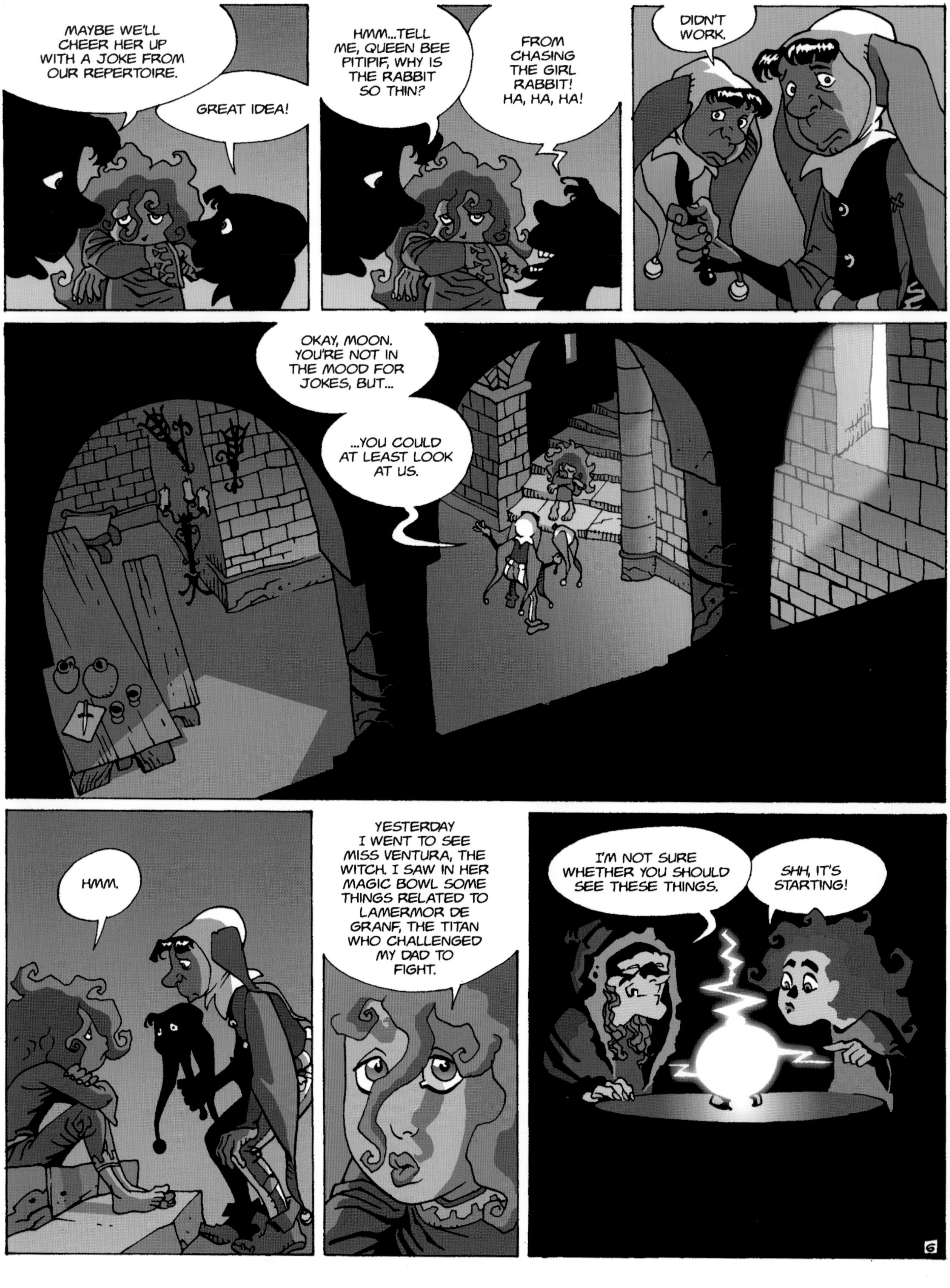
MAYBE WE'LL CHEER HER UP WITH A JOKE FROM OUR REPERTOIRE.
GREAT IDEA!
HMM...TELL ME, QUEEN BEE PITIPIF, WHY IS THE RABBIT SO THIN?
FROM CHASING THE GIRL RABBIT! HA, HA, HA!
DIDN'T WORK.
OKAY, MOON. YOU'RE NOT IN THE MOOD FOR JOKES, BUT...
...YOU COULD AT LEAST LOOK AT US.
HMM.
YESTERDAY I WENT TO SEE MISS VENTURA, THE WITCH. I SAW IN HER MAGIC BOWL SOME THINGS RELATED TO LAMERMOR DE GRANF, THE TITAN WHO CHALLENGED MY DAD TO FIGHT.
I'M NOT SURE WHETHER YOU SHOULD SEE THESE THINGS.
SHH, IT'S STARTING!
6

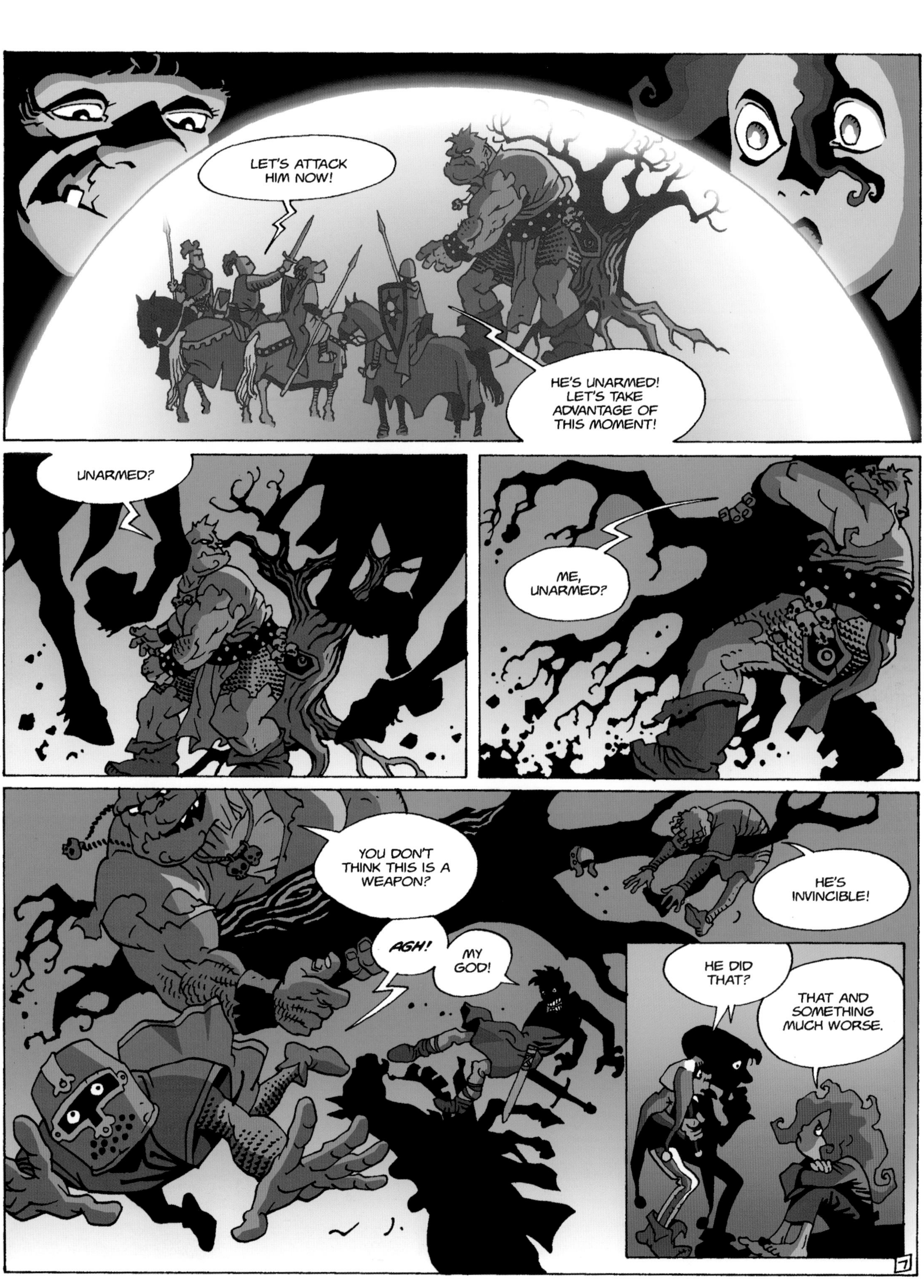
LET'S ATTACK HIM NOW!
HE'S UNARMED! LET'S TAKE ADVANTAGE OF THIS MOMENT!
UNARMED?
ME, UNARMED?
YOU DON'T THINK THIS IS A WEAPON?
AGH!
MY GOD!
HE'S INVINCIBLE!
HE DID THAT?
THAT AND SOMETHING MUCH WORSE.
7

IF I BREAK THE DOOR DOWN, ALLOWING YOUR SOLDIERS TO ENTER THE CASTLE AND ATTACK, YOU'LL GIVE ME A CRATE OF JEWELS?

YES. BUT IF YOU WANT I CAN BRING A BATTERING RAM.

THAT WON'T BE NECESSARY...

...I'LL HANDLE THAT DOOR...

...WITH JUST A PLAIN KICK.

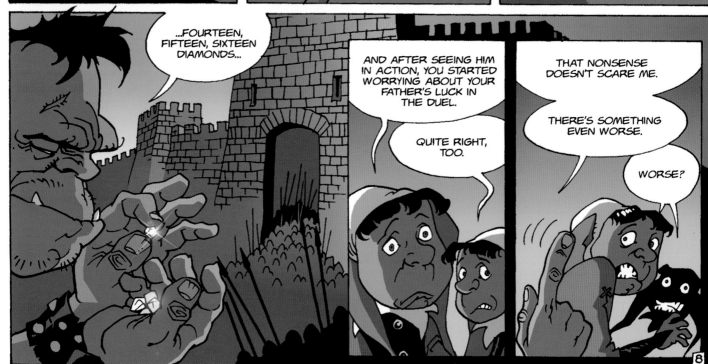

...FOURTEEN, FIFTEEN, SIXTEEN DIAMONDS...

AND AFTER SEEING HIM IN ACTION, YOU STARTED WORRYING ABOUT YOUR FATHER'S LUCK IN THE DUEL.

QUITE RIGHT, TOO.

THAT NONSENSE DOESN'T SCARE ME.

THERE'S SOMETHING EVEN WORSE.

WORSE?

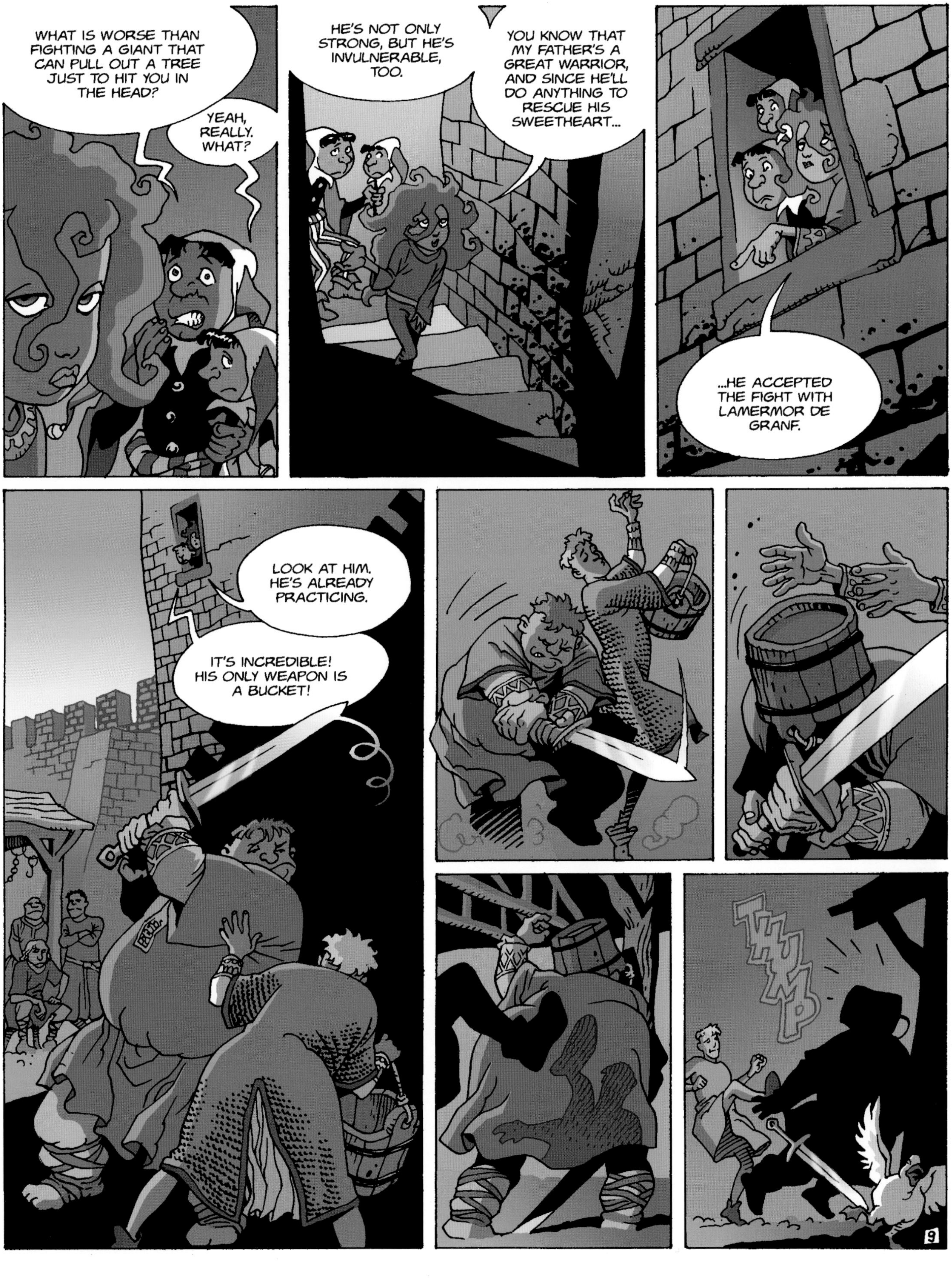
WHAT IS WORSE THAN FIGHTING A GIANT THAT CAN PULL OUT A TREE JUST TO HIT YOU IN THE HEAD?
YEAH, REALLY. WHAT?
HE'S NOT ONLY STRONG, BUT HE'S INVULNERABLE, TOO.
YOU KNOW THAT MY FATHER'S A GREAT WARRIOR, AND SINCE HE'LL DO ANYTHING TO RESCUE HIS SWEETHEART...
...HE ACCEPTED THE FIGHT WITH LAMERMOR DE GRANF.
LOOK AT HIM. HE'S ALREADY PRACTICING.
IT'S INCREDIBLE! HIS ONLY WEAPON IS A BUCKET!
THUMP
9

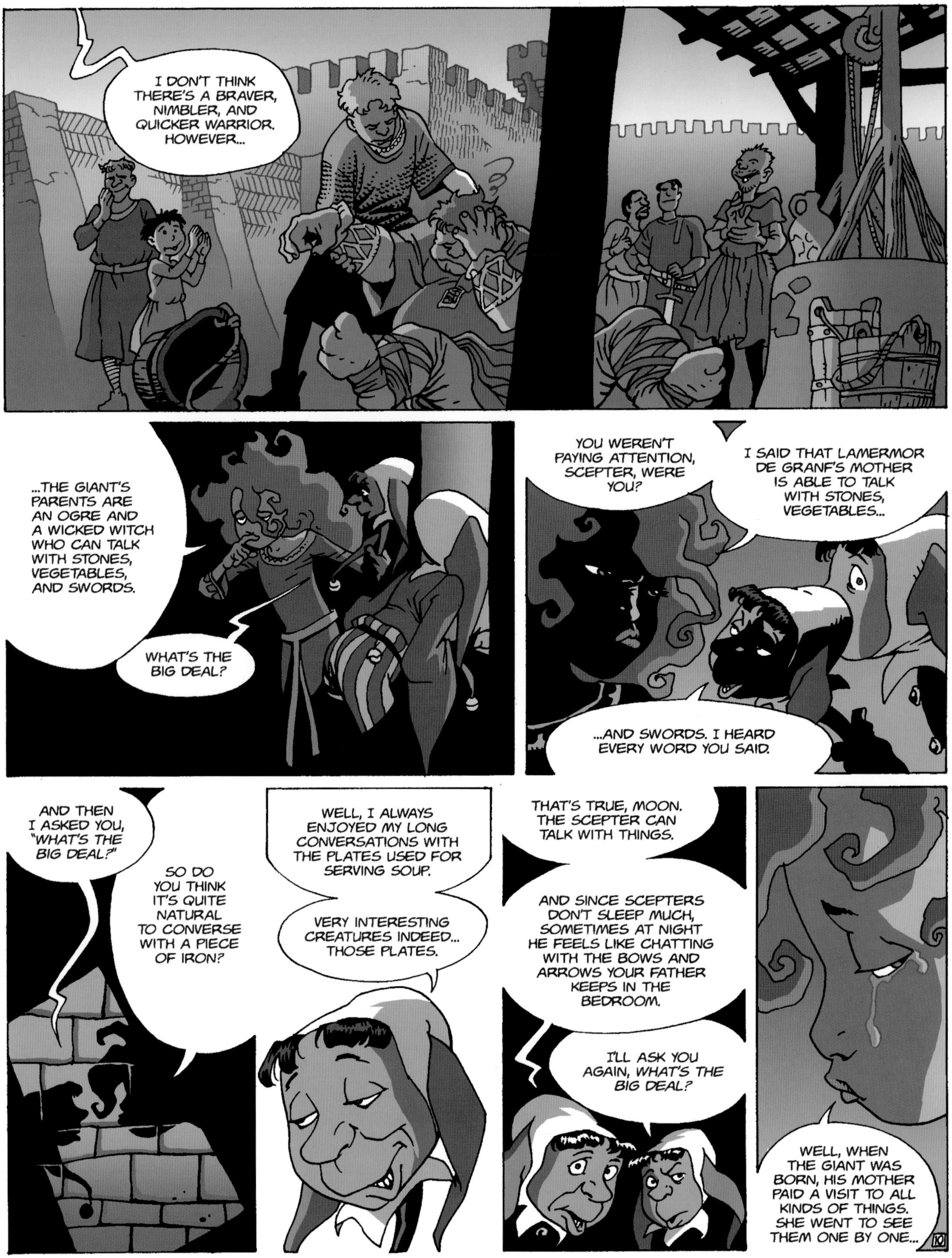
I DON'T THINK THERE'S A BRAVER, NIMBLER, AND QUICKER WARRIOR. HOWEVER...
...THE GIANT'S PARENTS ARE AN OGRE AND A WICKED WITCH WHO CAN TALK WITH STONES, VEGETABLES, AND SWORDS.
WHAT'S THE BIG DEAL?
YOU WEREN'T PAYING ATTENTION, SCEPTER, WERE YOU?
I SAID THAT LAMERMOR DE GRANF'S MOTHER IS ABLE TO TALK WITH STONES, VEGETABLES...
...AND SWORDS. I HEARD EVERY WORD YOU SAID.
AND THEN I ASKED YOU, "WHAT'S THE BIG DEAL?"
SO DO YOU THINK IT'S QUITE NATURAL TO CONVERSE WITH A PIECE OF IRON?
WELL, I ALWAYS ENJOYED MY LONG CONVERSATIONS WITH THE PLATES USED FOR SERVING SOUP.
VERY INTERESTING CREATURES INDEED... THOSE PLATES.
THAT'S TRUE, MOON. THE SCEPTER CAN TALK WITH THINGS.
AND SINCE SCEPTERS DON'T SLEEP MUCH, SOMETIMES AT NIGHT HE FEELS LIKE CHATTING WITH THE BOWS AND ARROWS YOUR FATHER KEEPS IN THE BEDROOM.
I'LL ASK YOU AGAIN, WHAT'S THE BIG DEAL?
WELL, WHEN THE GIANT WAS BORN, HIS MOTHER PAID A VISIT TO ALL KINDS OF THINGS. SHE WENT TO SEE THEM ONE BY ONE...
10

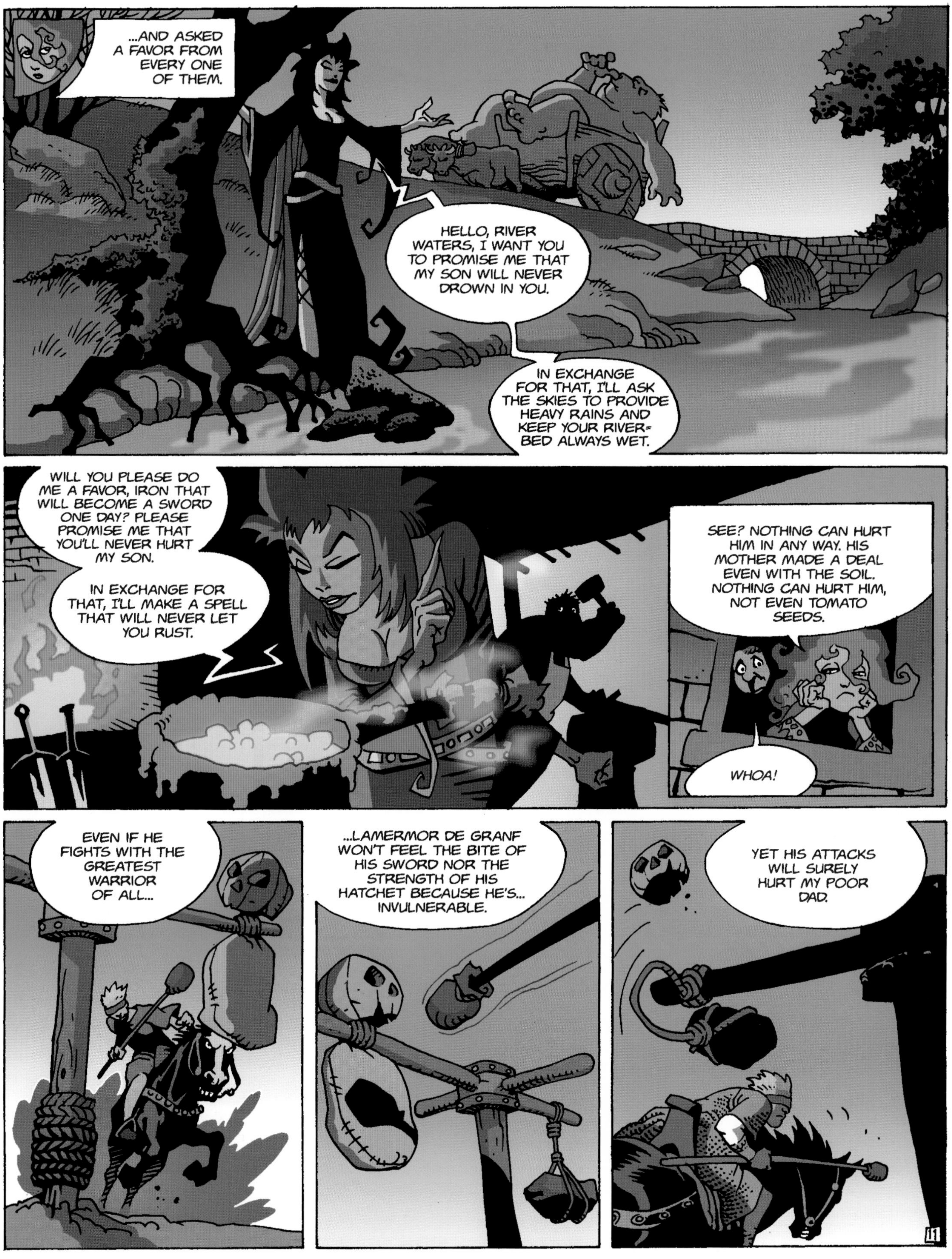
...AND ASKED A FAVOR FROM EVERY ONE OF THEM.
HELLO, RIVER WATERS, I WANT YOU TO PROMISE ME THAT MY SON WILL NEVER DROWN IN YOU.
IN EXCHANGE FOR THAT, I'LL ASK THE SKIES TO PROVIDE HEAVY RAINS AND KEEP YOUR RIVER-BED ALWAYS WET.
WILL YOU PLEASE DO ME A FAVOR, IRON THAT WILL BECOME A SWORD ONE DAY? PLEASE PROMISE ME THAT YOU'LL NEVER HURT MY SON.
IN EXCHANGE FOR THAT, I'LL MAKE A SPELL THAT WILL NEVER LET YOU RUST.
SEE? NOTHING CAN HURT HIM IN ANY WAY. HIS MOTHER MADE A DEAL EVEN WITH THE SOIL. NOTHING CAN HURT HIM, NOT EVEN TOMATO SEEDS.
WHOA!
EVEN IF HE FIGHTS WITH THE GREATEST WARRIOR OF ALL...
...LAMERMOR DE GRANF WON'T FEEL THE BITE OF HIS SWORD NOR THE STRENGTH OF HIS HATCHET BECAUSE HE'S... INVULNERABLE.
YET HIS ATTACKS WILL SURELY HURT MY POOR DAD.
11

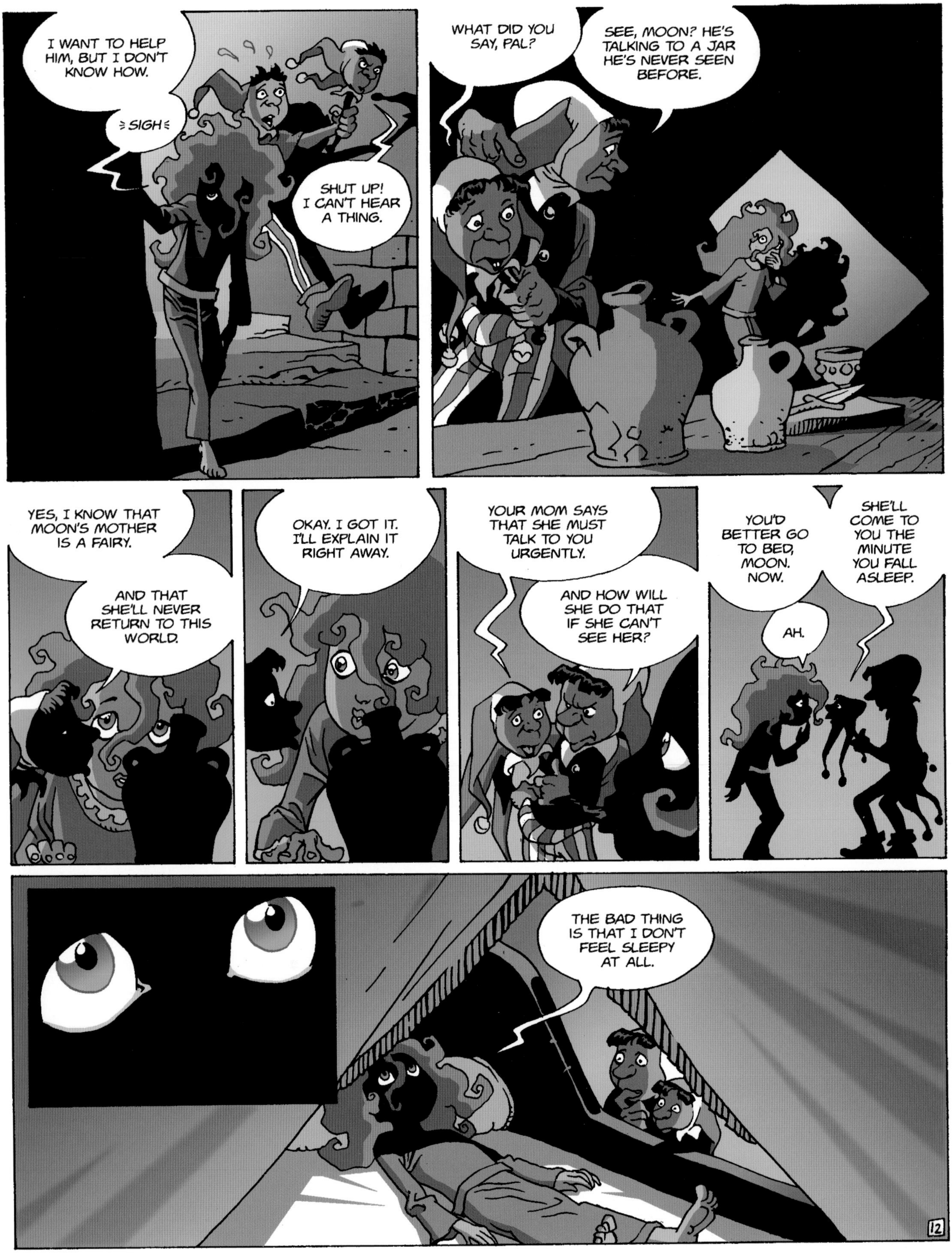

I WANT TO HELP HIM, BUT I DON'T KNOW HOW.
SIGH
SHUT UP! I CAN'T HEAR A THING.
WHAT DID YOU SAY, PAL?
SEE, MOON? HE'S TALKING TO A JAR HE'S NEVER SEEN BEFORE.
YES, I KNOW THAT MOON'S MOTHER IS A FAIRY.
AND THAT SHE'LL NEVER RETURN TO THIS WORLD.
OKAY. I GOT IT. I'LL EXPLAIN IT RIGHT AWAY.
YOUR MOM SAYS THAT SHE MUST TALK TO YOU URGENTLY.
AND HOW WILL SHE DO THAT IF SHE CAN'T SEE HER?
YOU'D BETTER GO TO BED, MOON. NOW.
SHE'LL COME TO YOU THE MINUTE YOU FALL ASLEEP.
AH.
THE BAD THING IS THAT I DON'T FEEL SLEEPY AT ALL.
12

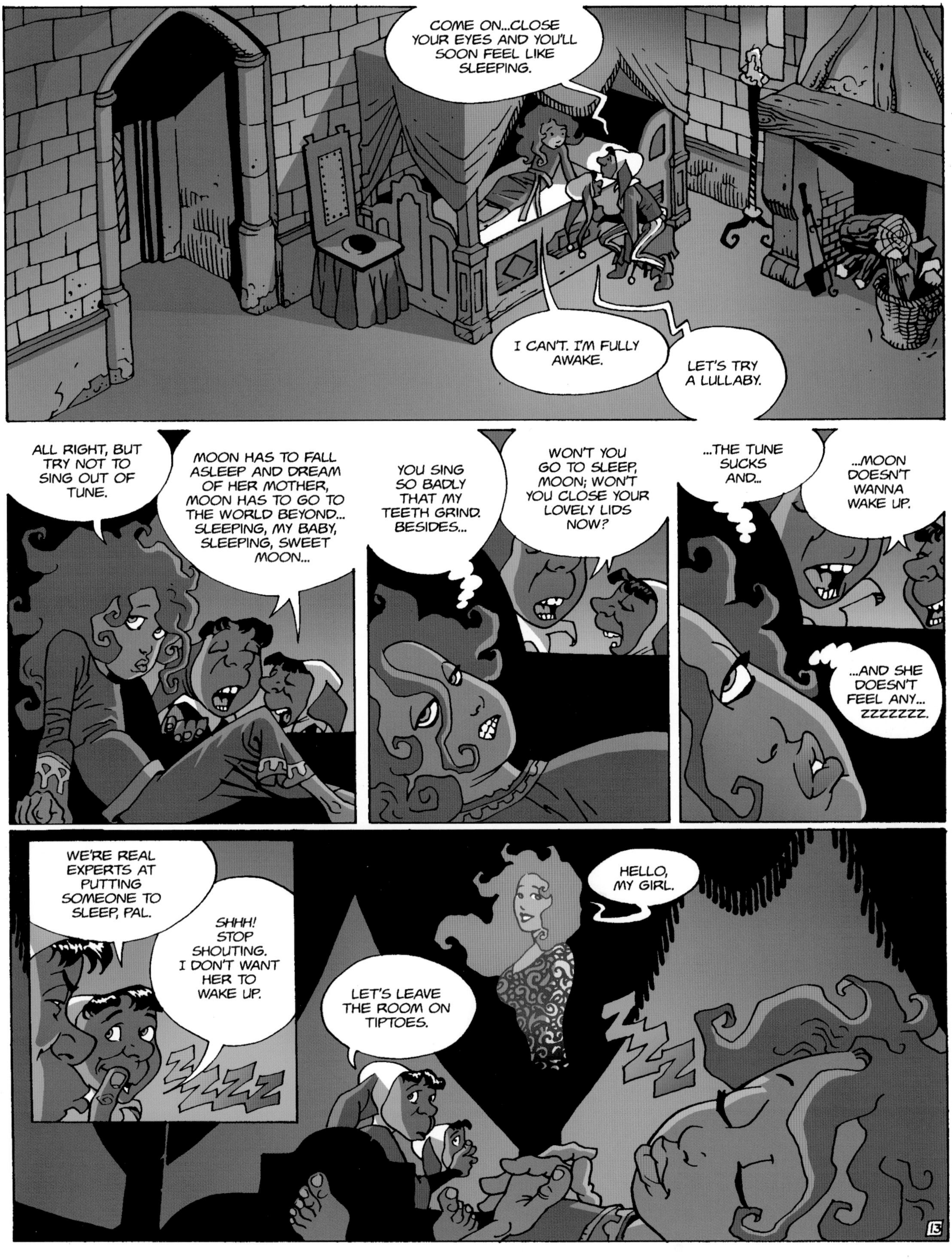
COME ON...CLOSE YOUR EYES AND YOU'LL SOON FEEL LIKE SLEEPING.
I CAN'T. I'M FULLY AWAKE.
LET'S TRY A LULLABY.
ALL RIGHT, BUT TRY NOT TO SING OUT OF TUNE.
MOON HAS TO FALL ASLEEP AND DREAM OF HER MOTHER, MOON HAS TO GO TO THE WORLD BEYOND... SLEEPING, MY BABY, SLEEPING, SWEET MOON...
YOU SING SO BADLY THAT MY TEETH GRIND. BESIDES...
WON'T YOU GO TO SLEEP, MOON; WON'T YOU CLOSE YOUR LOVELY LIDS NOW?
...THE TUNE SUCKS AND...
...MOON DOESN'T WANNA WAKE UP.
...AND SHE DOESN'T FEEL ANY... ZZZZZZZ.
WE'RE REAL EXPERTS AT PUTTING SOMEONE TO SLEEP, PAL.
SHHH! STOP SHOUTING. I DON'T WANT HER TO WAKE UP.
LET'S LEAVE THE ROOM ON TIPTOES.
HELLO, MY GIRL.
ZZZZ
ZZZ
13

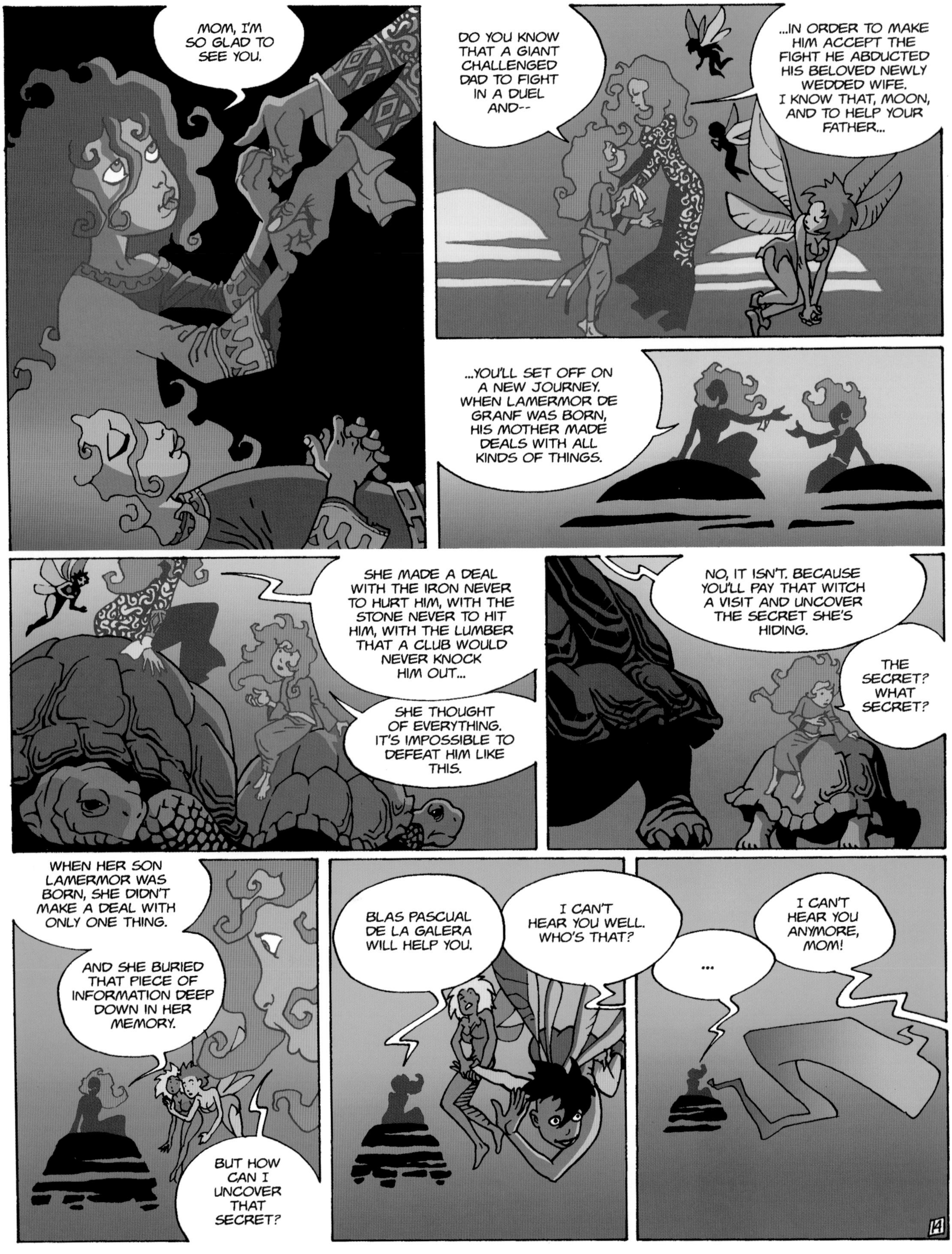

MOM, I'M SO GLAD TO SEE YOU.
DO YOU KNOW THAT A GIANT CHALLENGED DAD TO FIGHT IN A DUEL AND--
...IN ORDER TO MAKE HIM ACCEPT THE FIGHT HE ABDUCTED HIS BELOVED NEWLY WEDDED WIFE. I KNOW THAT, MOON, AND TO HELP YOUR FATHER...
...YOU'LL SET OFF ON A NEW JOURNEY. WHEN LAMERMOR DE GRANF WAS BORN, HIS MOTHER MADE DEALS WITH ALL KINDS OF THINGS.
SHE MADE A DEAL WITH THE IRON NEVER TO HURT HIM, WITH THE STONE NEVER TO HIT HIM, WITH THE LUMBER THAT A CLUB WOULD NEVER KNOCK HIM OUT...
SHE THOUGHT OF EVERYTHING. IT'S IMPOSSIBLE TO DEFEAT HIM LIKE THIS.
NO, IT ISN'T. BECAUSE YOU'LL PAY THAT WITCH A VISIT AND UNCOVER THE SECRET SHE'S HIDING.
THE SECRET? WHAT SECRET?
WHEN HER SON LAMERMOR WAS BORN, SHE DIDN'T MAKE A DEAL WITH ONLY ONE THING.
AND SHE BURIED THAT PIECE OF INFORMATION DEEP DOWN IN HER MEMORY.
BUT HOW CAN I UNCOVER THAT SECRET?
BLAS PASCUAL DE LA GALERA WILL HELP YOU.
I CAN'T HEAR YOU WELL. WHO'S THAT?
...
I CAN'T HEAR YOU ANYMORE, MOM!
14

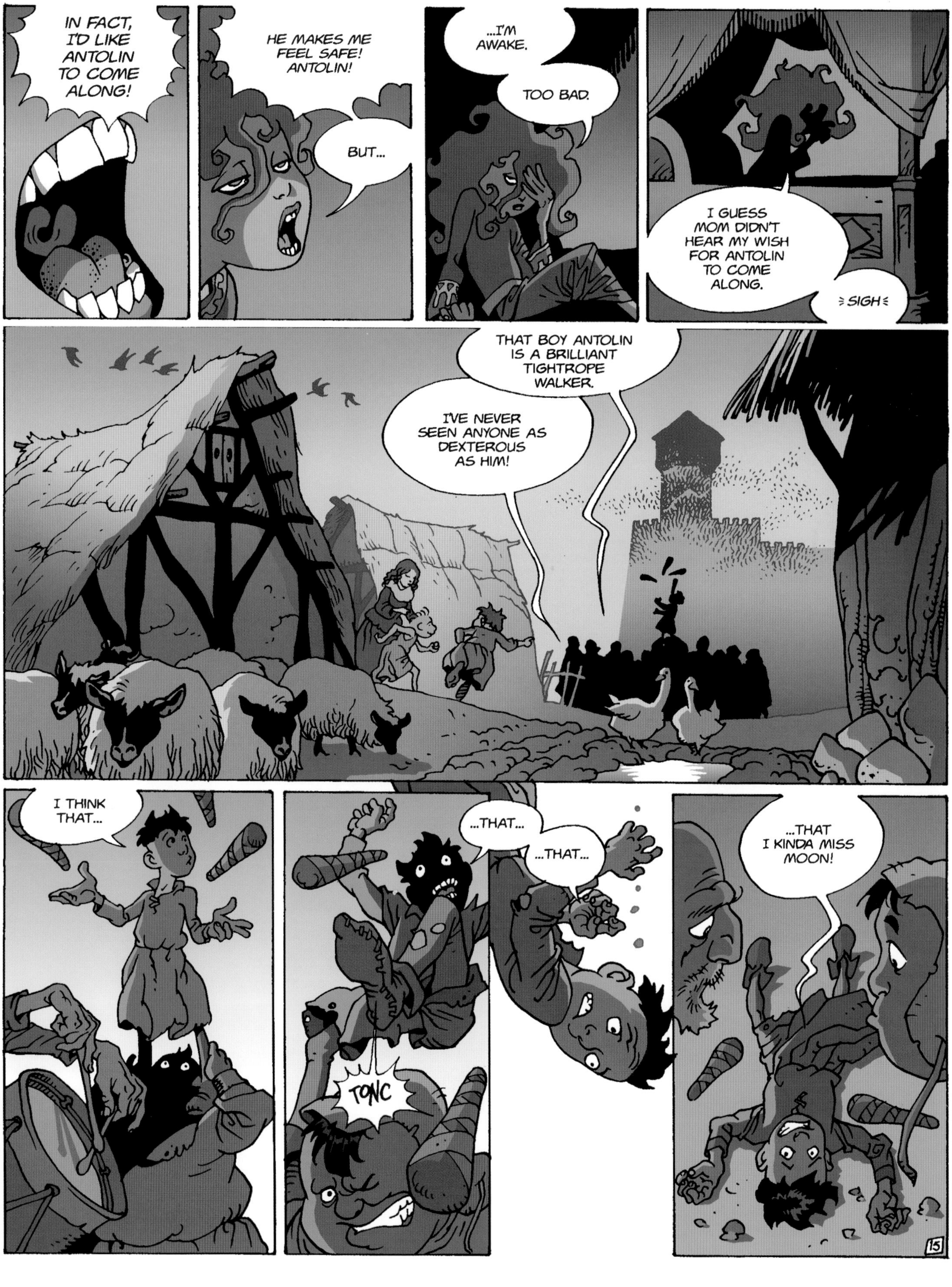
IN FACT, I'D LIKE ANTOLIN TO COME ALONG!
HE MAKES ME FEEL SAFE! ANTOLIN!
BUT...
...I'M AWAKE.
TOO BAD.
I GUESS MOM DIDN'T HEAR MY WISH FOR ANTOLIN TO COME ALONG.
SIGH
THAT BOY ANTOLIN IS A BRILLIANT TIGHTROPE WALKER.
I'VE NEVER SEEN ANYONE AS DEXTEROUS AS HIM!
I THINK THAT...
...THAT...
...THAT...
TONC
...THAT I KINDA MISS MOON!
15

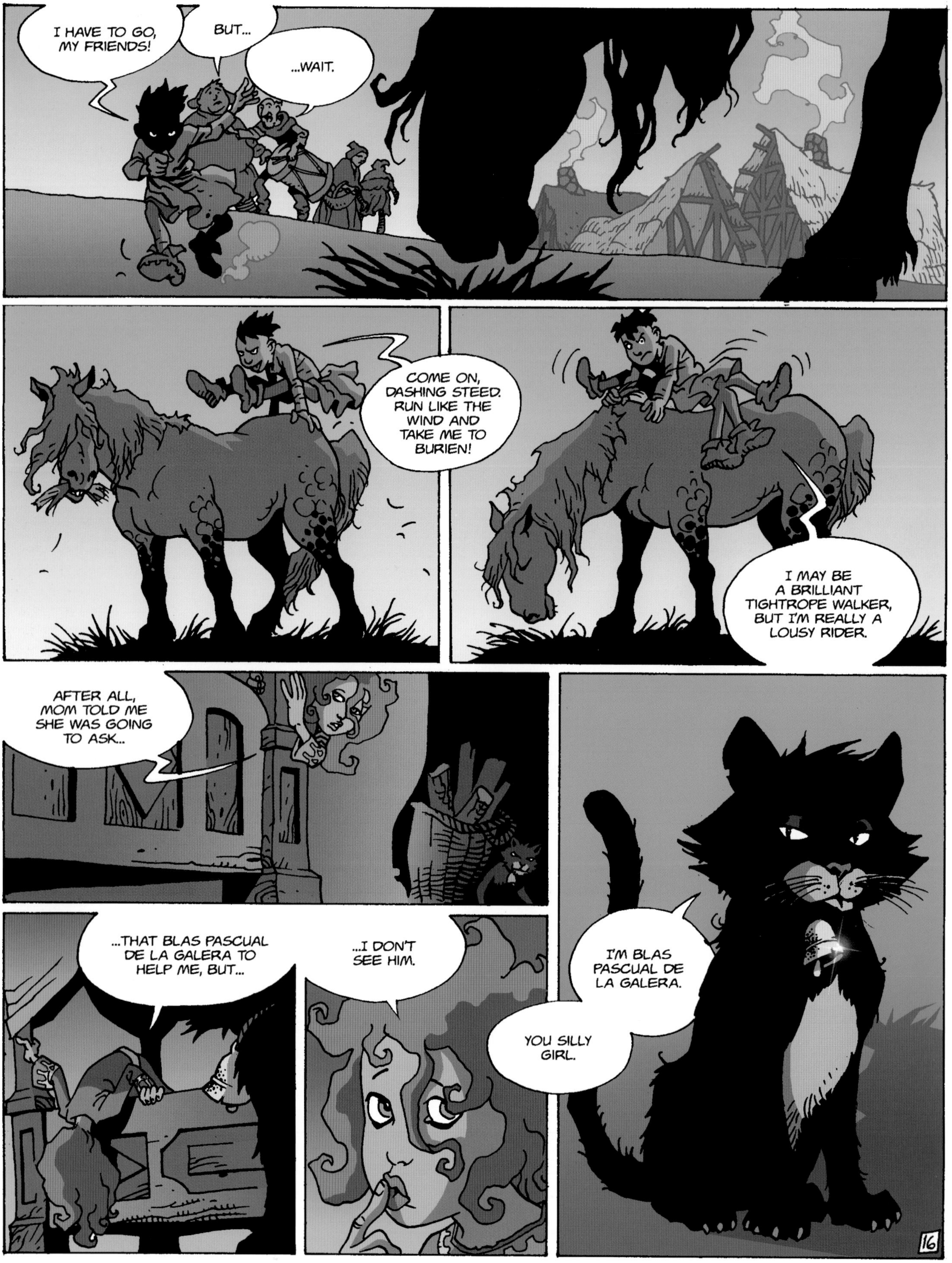
I HAVE TO GO, MY FRIENDS!
BUT...
...WAIT.
COME ON, DASHING STEED. RUN LIKE THE WIND AND TAKE ME TO BURIEN!
I MAY BE A BRILLIANT TIGHTROPE WALKER, BUT I'M REALLY A LOUSY RIDER.
AFTER ALL, MOM TOLD ME SHE WAS GOING TO ASK...
...THAT BLAS PASCUAL DE LA GALERA TO HELP ME, BUT...
...I DON'T SEE HIM.
I'M BLAS PASCUAL DE LA GALERA.
YOU SILLY GIRL.
16

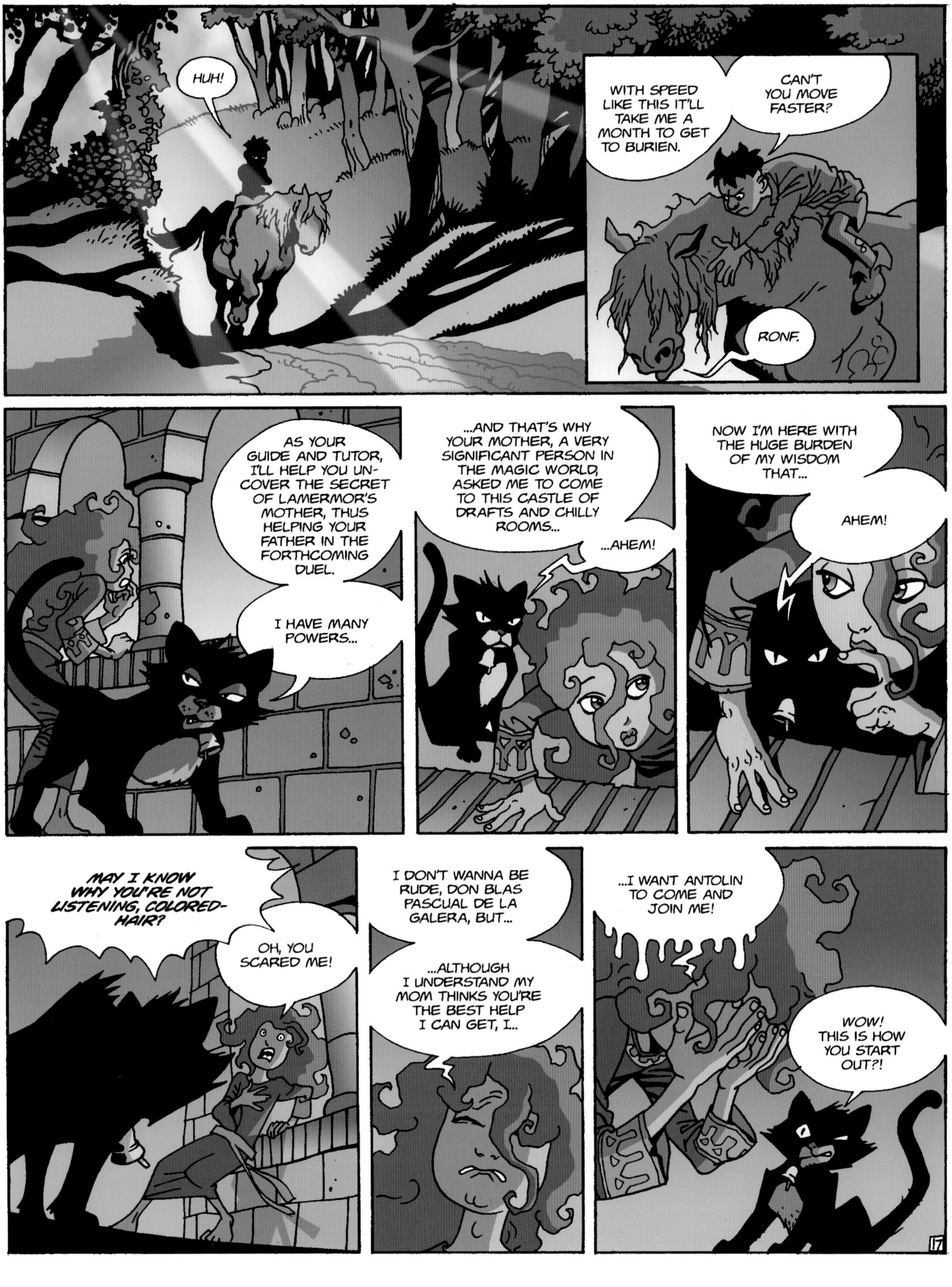
HUH!
WITH SPEED LIKE THIS IT'LL TAKE ME A MONTH TO GET TO BURIEN.
CAN'T YOU MOVE FASTER?
RONF.
AS YOUR GUIDE AND TUTOR, I'LL HELP YOU UNCOVER THE SECRET OF LAMERMOR'S MOTHER, THUS HELPING YOUR FATHER IN THE FORTHCOMING DUEL.
I HAVE MANY POWERS...
...AND THAT'S WHY YOUR MOTHER, A VERY SIGNIFICANT PERSON IN THE MAGIC WORLD, ASKED ME TO COME TO THIS CASTLE OF DRAFTS AND CHILLY ROOMS...
...AHEM!
NOW I'M HERE WITH THE HUGE BURDEN OF MY WISDOM THAT...
AHEM!
MAY I KNOW WHY YOU'RE NOT LISTENING, COLORED-HAIR?
OH, YOU SCARED ME!
I DON'T WANNA BE RUDE, DON BLAS PASCUAL DE LA GALERA, BUT...
...ALTHOUGH I UNDERSTAND MY MOM THINKS YOU'RE THE BEST HELP I CAN GET, I...
...I WANT ANTOLIN TO COME AND JOIN ME!
WOW! THIS IS HOW YOU START OUT?!
17

HMM, LET ME CHECK.

ARE YOU TALKING ABOUT ANTOLIN THE COOK, ANTOLIN THE WOODCUTTER, OR ANTOLIN THE TIGHTROPE WALKER?

ANTOLIN THE TIGHTROPE WALKER, OF COURSE!

AHA.

OH, YES.

HE'S ON HIS WAY HERE, BUT...

...BUT OBVIOUSLY NOT WITH PROPER TRANSPORTATION.

I SHOULD HAVE GIVEN HIM A SPEED INJECTION TO ACCELERATE HIM.

LET ME SEE...

BROTHER LORENZO PICO PICON, ARE YOU THERE?

YEAH, I'M RIGHT HERE.

HOW CAN I HELP YOU?

WELL, THERE'S A STOCKY, SLUGGISH HORSE WITH A BLACK-HAIRED, SKINNY BOY RIDING HIM. HE'S BARELY MOVING.

CAN YOU MAKE HIM MOVE FASTER?

?

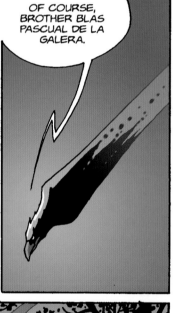

OF COURSE, BROTHER BLAS PASCUAL DE LA GALERA.

IF I GO ON LIKE THIS, I'LL NEVER MAKE IT. IT'S USELESS.

18

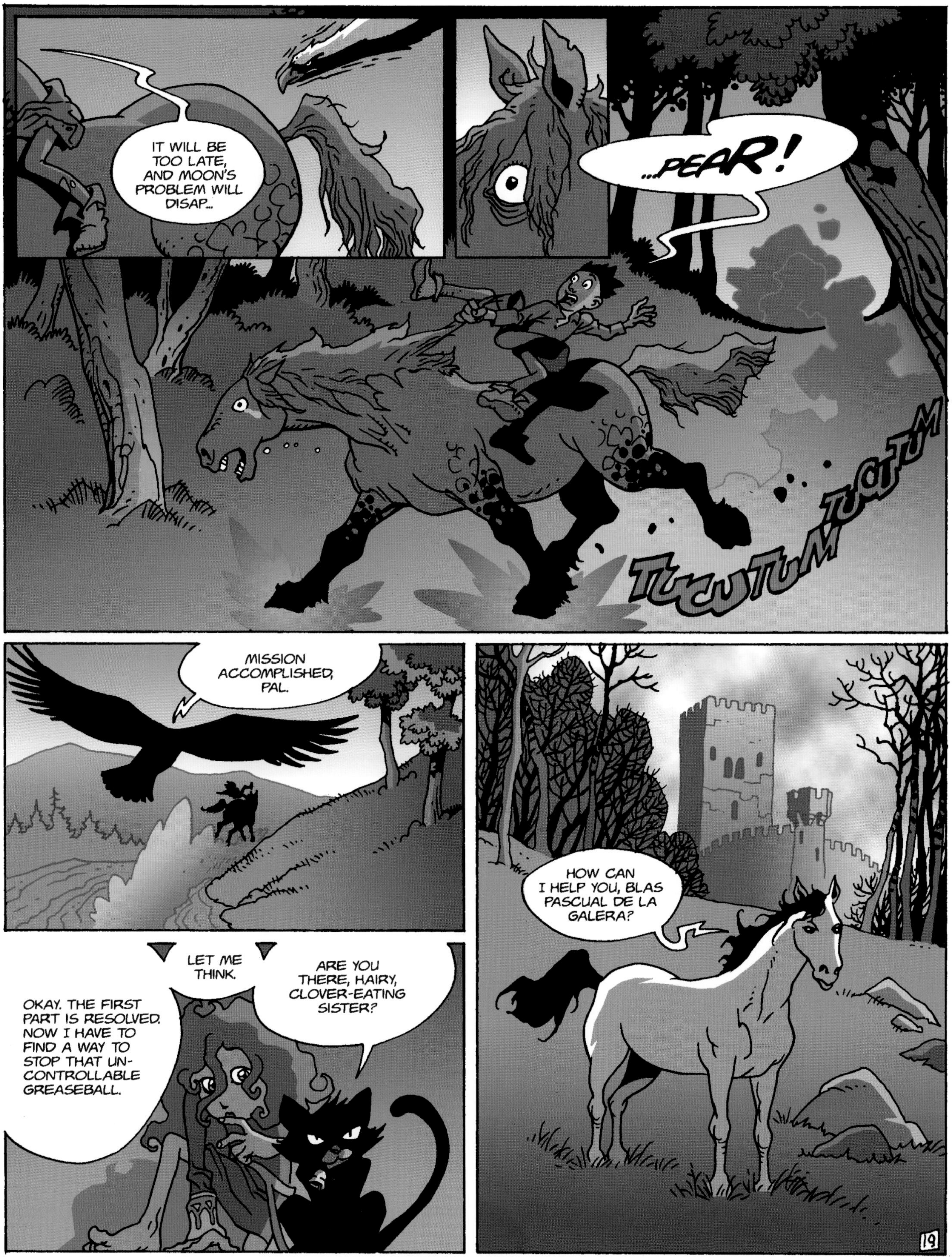
IT WILL BE TOO LATE, AND MOON'S PROBLEM WILL DISAP...
...PEAR!
TUCUTUMTUCUTUM
MISSION ACCOMPLISHED, PAL.
HOW CAN I HELP YOU, BLAS PASCUAL DE LA GALERA?
LET ME THINK.
ARE YOU THERE, HAIRY, CLOVER-EATING SISTER?
OKAY. THE FIRST PART IS RESOLVED. NOW I HAVE TO FIND A WAY TO STOP THAT UN-CONTROLLABLE GREASEBALL.
19

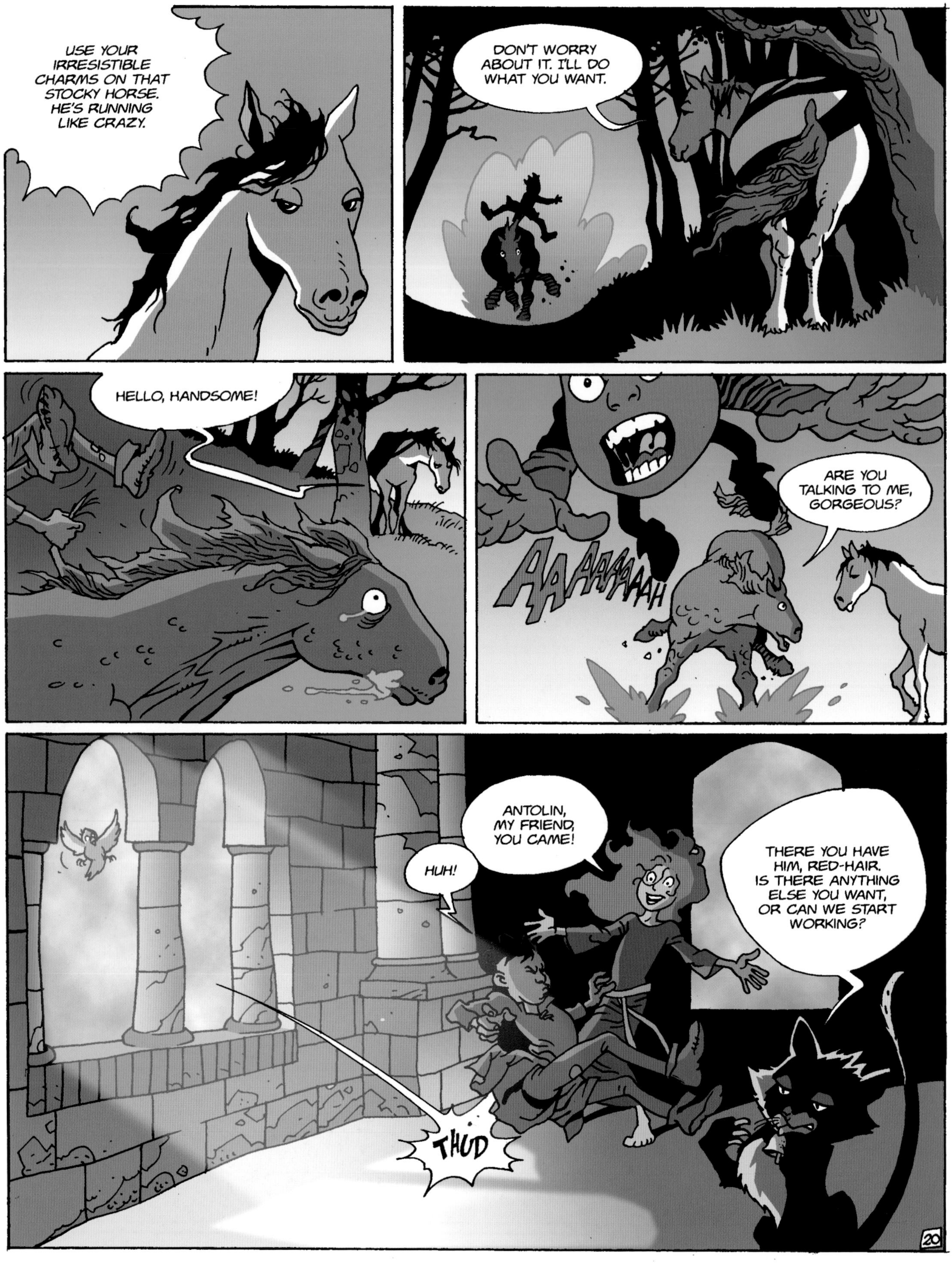
USE YOUR IRRESISTIBLE CHARMS ON THAT STOCKY HORSE. HE'S RUNNING LIKE CRAZY.
DON'T WORRY ABOUT IT. I'LL DO WHAT YOU WANT.
HELLO, HANDSOME!
AAAAAAAAH
ARE YOU TALKING TO ME, GORGEOUS?
HUH!
ANTOLIN, MY FRIEND, YOU CAME!
THERE YOU HAVE HIM, RED-HAIR. IS THERE ANYTHING ELSE YOU WANT, OR CAN WE START WORKING?
THUD
20

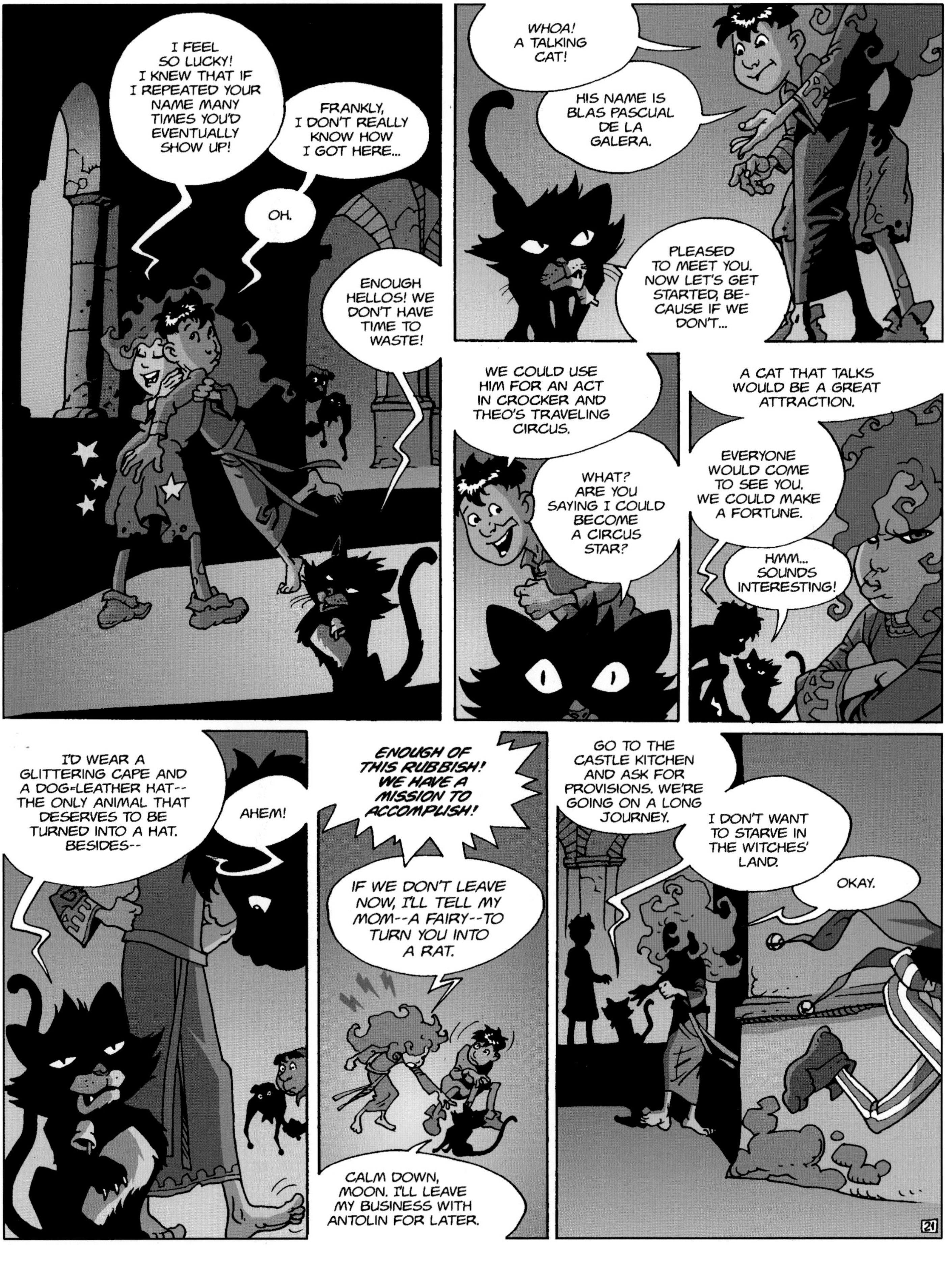

I FEEL SO LUCKY! I KNEW THAT IF I REPEATED YOUR NAME MANY TIMES YOU'D EVENTUALLY SHOW UP!
FRANKLY, I DON'T REALLY KNOW HOW I GOT HERE...
OH.
ENOUGH HELLOS! WE DON'T HAVE TIME TO WASTE!
WHOA! A TALKING CAT!
HIS NAME IS BLAS PASCUAL DE LA GALERA.
PLEASED TO MEET YOU. NOW LET'S GET STARTED, BE-CAUSE IF WE DON'T...
WE COULD USE HIM FOR AN ACT IN CROCKER AND THEO'S TRAVELING CIRCUS.
WHAT? ARE YOU SAYING I COULD BECOME A CIRCUS STAR?
A CAT THAT TALKS WOULD BE A GREAT ATTRACTION.
EVERYONE WOULD COME TO SEE YOU. WE COULD MAKE A FORTUNE.
HMM... SOUNDS INTERESTING!
I'D WEAR A GLITTERING CAPE AND A DOG-LEATHER HAT-- THE ONLY ANIMAL THAT DESERVES TO BE TURNED INTO A HAT. BESIDES--
AHEM!
ENOUGH OF THIS RUBBISH! WE HAVE A MISSION TO ACCOMPLISH!
IF WE DON'T LEAVE NOW, I'LL TELL MY MOM--A FAIRY--TO TURN YOU INTO A RAT.
CALM DOWN, MOON. I'LL LEAVE MY BUSINESS WITH ANTOLIN FOR LATER.
GO TO THE CASTLE KITCHEN AND ASK FOR PROVISIONS. WE'RE GOING ON A LONG JOURNEY.
I DON'T WANT TO STARVE IN THE WITCHES' LAND.
OKAY.
21

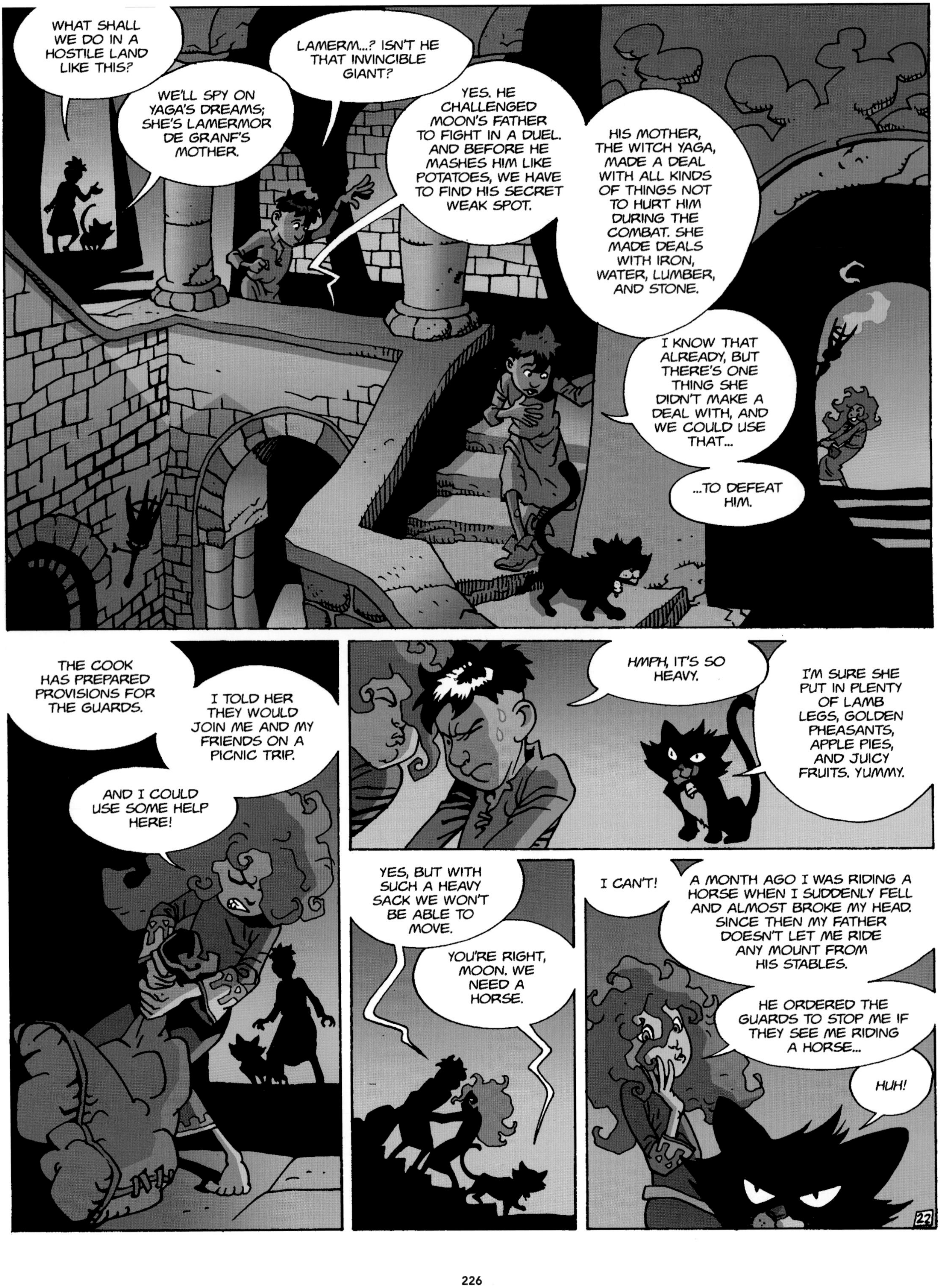
WHAT SHALL WE DO IN A HOSTILE LAND LIKE THIS?
WE'LL SPY ON YAGA'S DREAMS; SHE'S LAMERMOR DE GRANF'S MOTHER.
LAMERM...? ISN'T HE THAT INVINCIBLE GIANT?
YES. HE CHALLENGED MOON'S FATHER TO FIGHT IN A DUEL. AND BEFORE HE MASHES HIM LIKE POTATOES, WE HAVE TO FIND HIS SECRET WEAK SPOT.
HIS MOTHER, THE WITCH YAGA, MADE A DEAL WITH ALL KINDS OF THINGS NOT TO HURT HIM DURING THE COMBAT. SHE MADE DEALS WITH IRON, WATER, LUMBER, AND STONE.
I KNOW THAT ALREADY, BUT THERE'S ONE THING SHE DIDN'T MAKE A DEAL WITH, AND WE COULD USE THAT...
...TO DEFEAT HIM.
THE COOK HAS PREPARED PROVISIONS FOR THE GUARDS.
I TOLD HER THEY WOULD JOIN ME AND MY FRIENDS ON A PICNIC TRIP.
AND I COULD USE SOME HELP HERE!
HMPH, IT'S SO HEAVY.
I'M SURE SHE PUT IN PLENTY OF LAMB LEGS, GOLDEN PHEASANTS, APPLE PIES, AND JUICY FRUITS. YUMMY.
YES, BUT WITH SUCH A HEAVY SACK WE WON'T BE ABLE TO MOVE.
YOU'RE RIGHT, MOON. WE NEED A HORSE.
I CAN'T!
A MONTH AGO I WAS RIDING A HORSE WHEN I SUDDENLY FELL AND ALMOST BROKE MY HEAD. SINCE THEN MY FATHER DOESN'T LET ME RIDE ANY MOUNT FROM HIS STABLES.
HE ORDERED THE GUARDS TO STOP ME IF THEY SEE ME RIDING A HORSE...
HUH!
22

DO I HAVE TO TALK WITH THAT CLOVER-EATING GIRL AGAIN?

HELLO...

ARE YOU THERE, SIS?

CAN YOU MAKE THAT OBESE PLEBEIAN COME TO THE CASTLE OF BURIEN?

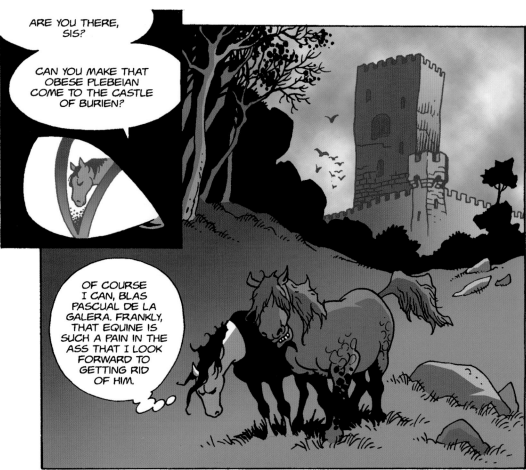

OF COURSE I CAN, BLAS PASCUAL DE LA GALERA. FRANKLY, THAT EQUINE IS SUCH A PAIN IN THE ASS THAT I LOOK FORWARD TO GETTING RID OF HIM.

I CAN TELL YOU'RE KINDA FOND OF ME, AREN'T YOU, NAG?

CALL ME THUNDER, HAIRY BROAD.

THUNDER? IS THAT YOUR REAL NAME? WAS THERE ANY SPECIAL REASON THAT YOUR FOLKS GAVE YOU THAT NAME?

OF COURSE. MY GALLOPING SOUNDS LIKE THUNDER, AND MY FOOTSTEPS WARN THE OTHERS THAT LIGHTNING IS ABOUT TO STRIKE.

GEE...WHAT'S HE GONNA THINK OF NEXT?

LISTEN, THUNDER, IF YOU WANT TO BE MY BOYFRIEND YOU HAVE TO DO SOMETHING FOR ME.

ANYTHING YOU SAY, MISTRESS OF MY HEART.

YOU'LL GO TO THE CASTLE OF BURIEN RIGHT AWAY. THERE YOU'LL FIND A CAT, A BOY, AND A RED-HAIRED GIRL, AND YOU'LL TAKE THEM WHERE THEY TELL YOU.

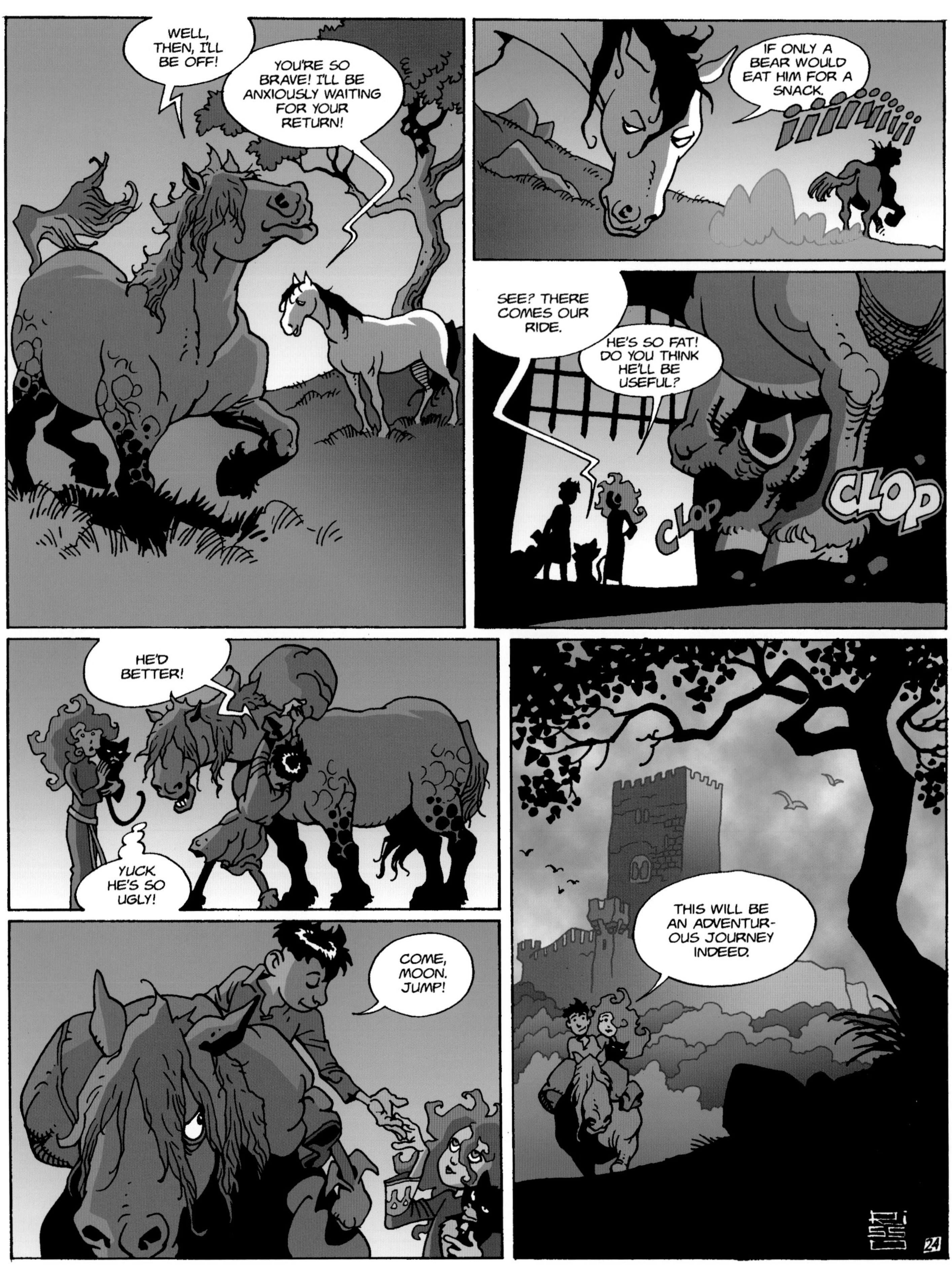
WELL, THEN, I'LL BE OFF!
YOU'RE SO BRAVE! I'LL BE ANXIOUSLY WAITING FOR YOUR RETURN!
IF ONLY A BEAR WOULD EAT HIM FOR A SNACK.
SEE? THERE COMES OUR RIDE.
HE'S SO FAT! DO YOU THINK HE'LL BE USEFUL?
CLOP
CLOP
HE'D BETTER!
YUCK. HE'S SO UGLY!
COME, MOON. JUMP!
THIS WILL BE AN ADVENTUR-OUS JOURNEY INDEED.
24

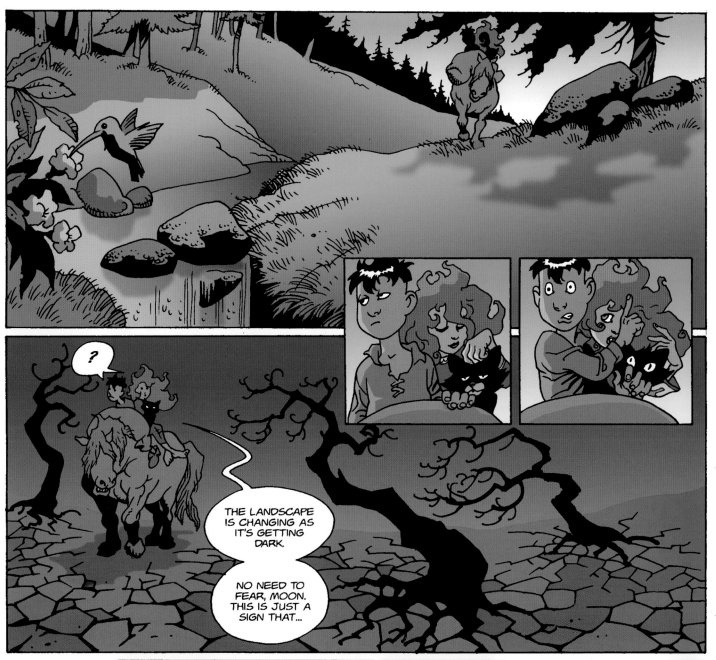

?

THE LANDSCAPE IS CHANGING AS IT'S GETTING DARK.

NO NEED TO FEAR, MOON. THIS IS JUST A SIGN THAT...

...THAT THE WITCHES' LAND IS VERY CLOSE.

SEE? FROM THAT LINE AHEAD STARTS THE SINISTER WORLD OF WITCHES.

ANTOLIN, STOP THE HORSE. BEFORE WE ENTER, LET'S HAVE A SNACK.

WHOA! GOOD IDEA.

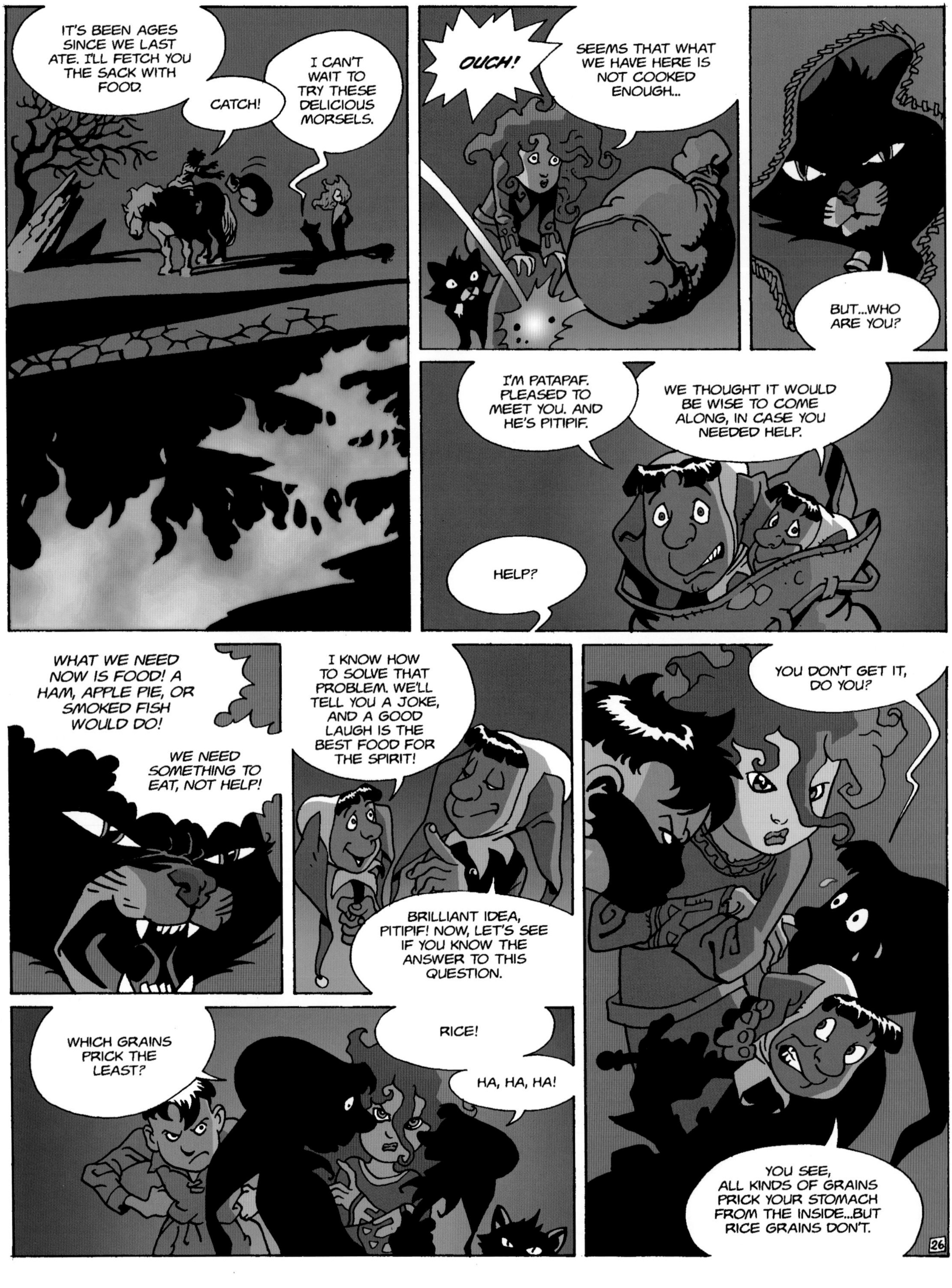
IT'S BEEN AGES SINCE WE LAST ATE. I'LL FETCH YOU THE SACK WITH FOOD.
CATCH!
I CAN'T WAIT TO TRY THESE DELICIOUS MORSELS.
OUCH!
SEEMS THAT WHAT WE HAVE HERE IS NOT COOKED ENOUGH...
BUT...WHO ARE YOU?
I'M PATAPAF. PLEASED TO MEET YOU. AND HE'S PITIPIF.
WE THOUGHT IT WOULD BE WISE TO COME ALONG, IN CASE YOU NEEDED HELP.
HELP?
WHAT WE NEED NOW IS FOOD! A HAM, APPLE PIE, OR SMOKED FISH WOULD DO!
WE NEED SOMETHING TO EAT, NOT HELP!
I KNOW HOW TO SOLVE THAT PROBLEM. WE'LL TELL YOU A JOKE, AND A GOOD LAUGH IS THE BEST FOOD FOR THE SPIRIT!
BRILLIANT IDEA, PITIPIF! NOW, LET'S SEE IF YOU KNOW THE ANSWER TO THIS QUESTION.
WHICH GRAINS PRICK THE LEAST?
RICE!
HA, HA, HA!
YOU DON'T GET IT, DO YOU?
YOU SEE, ALL KINDS OF GRAINS PRICK YOUR STOMACH FROM THE INSIDE...BUT RICE GRAINS DON'T.
26

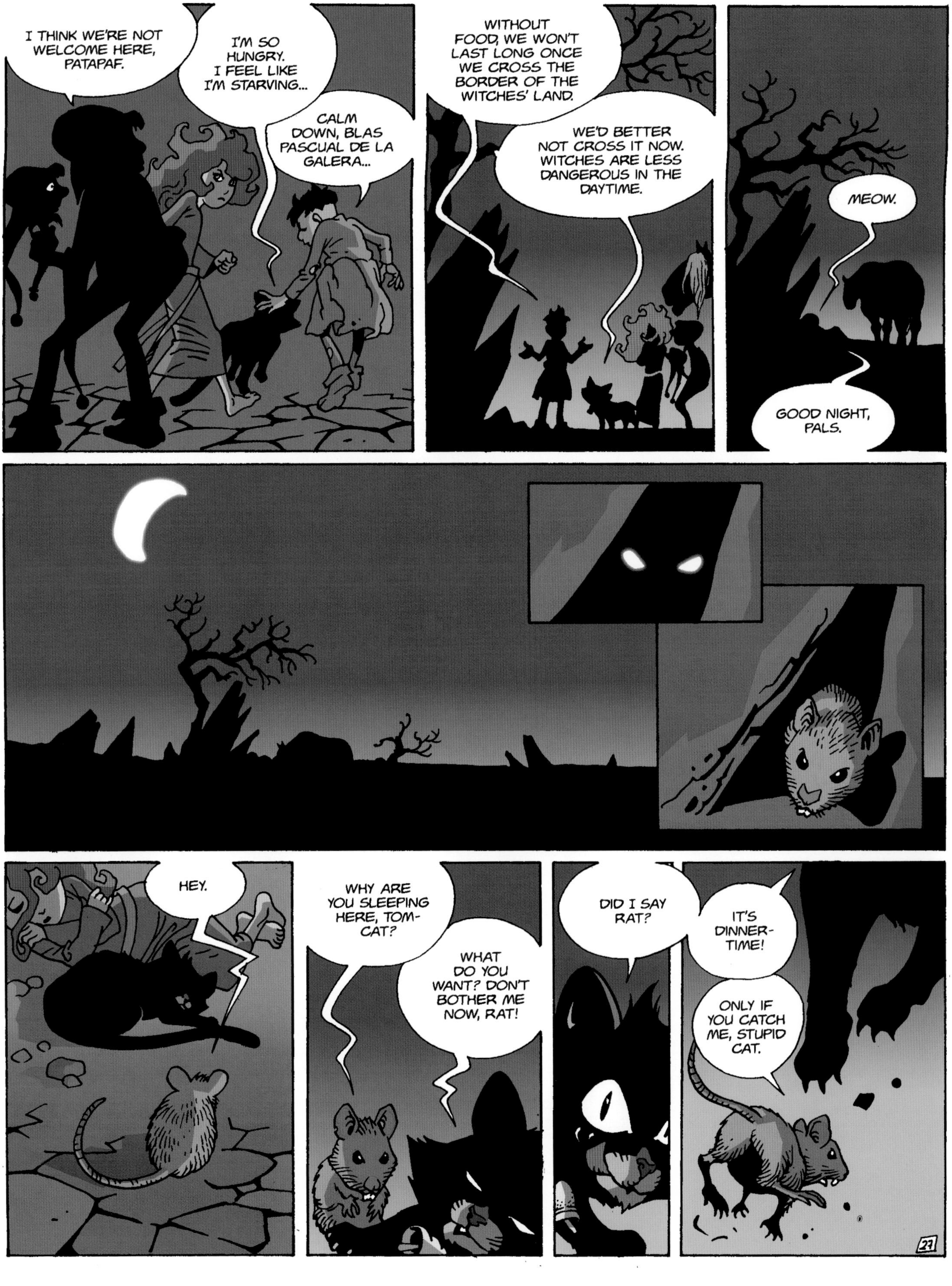

I THINK WE'RE NOT WELCOME HERE, PATAPAF.
I'M SO HUNGRY. I FEEL LIKE I'M STARVING...
CALM DOWN, BLAS PASCUAL DE LA GALERA...
WITHOUT FOOD, WE WON'T LAST LONG ONCE WE CROSS THE BORDER OF THE WITCHES' LAND.
WE'D BETTER NOT CROSS IT NOW. WITCHES ARE LESS DANGEROUS IN THE DAYTIME.
MEOW.
GOOD NIGHT, PALS.
HEY.
WHY ARE YOU SLEEPING HERE, TOM-CAT?
WHAT DO YOU WANT? DON'T BOTHER ME NOW, RAT!
DID I SAY RAT?
IT'S DINNER-TIME!
ONLY IF YOU CATCH ME, STUPID CAT.
27

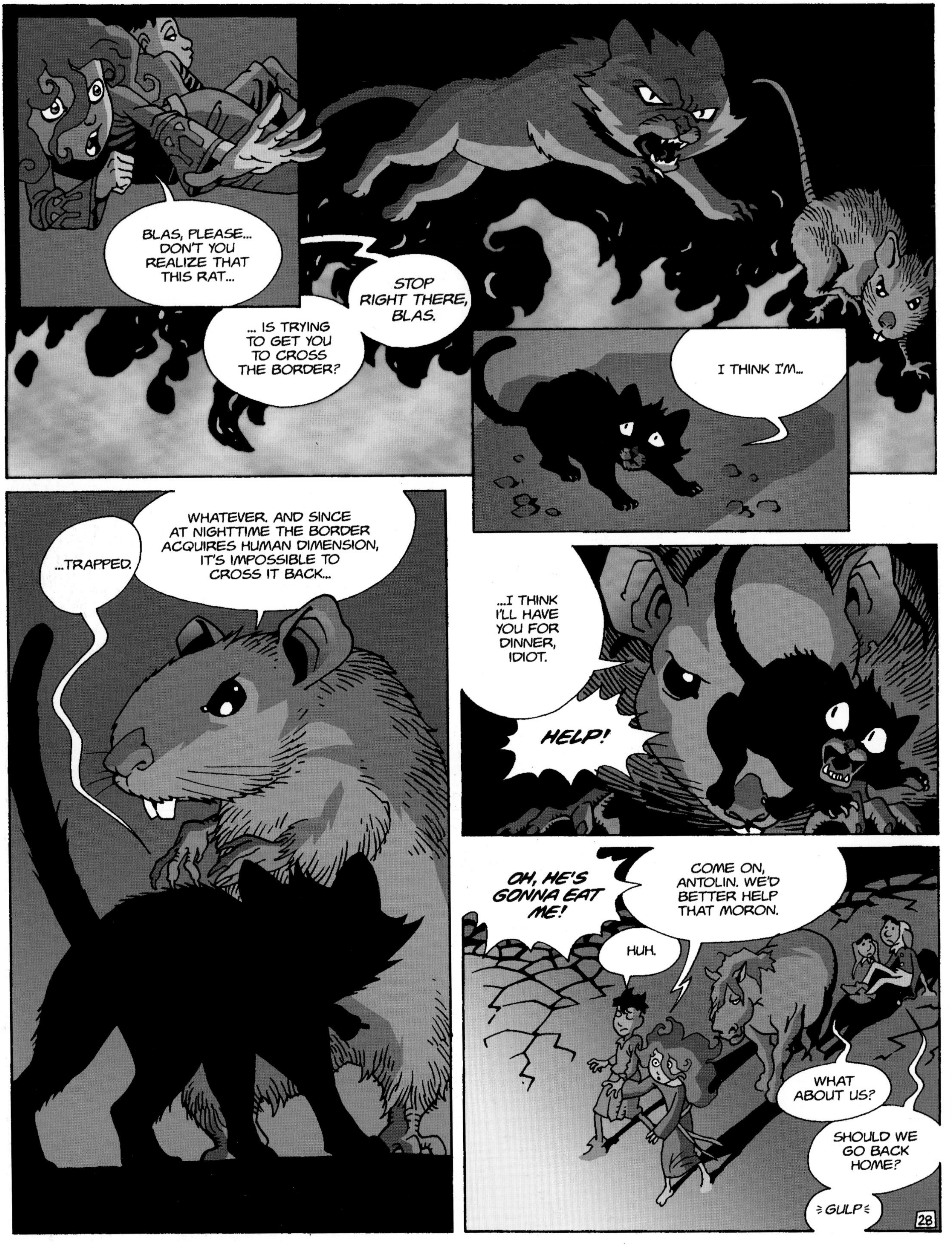
BLAS, PLEASE... DON'T YOU REALIZE THAT THIS RAT...
STOP RIGHT THERE, BLAS.
... IS TRYING TO GET YOU TO CROSS THE BORDER?
I THINK I'M...
...TRAPPED.
WHATEVER. AND SINCE AT NIGHTTIME THE BORDER ACQUIRES HUMAN DIMENSION, IT'S IMPOSSIBLE TO CROSS IT BACK...
...I THINK I'LL HAVE YOU FOR DINNER, IDIOT.
HELP!
OH, HE'S GONNA EAT ME!
COME ON, ANTOLIN. WE'D BETTER HELP THAT MORON.
HUH.
WHAT ABOUT US?
SHOULD WE GO BACK HOME?
GULP
28

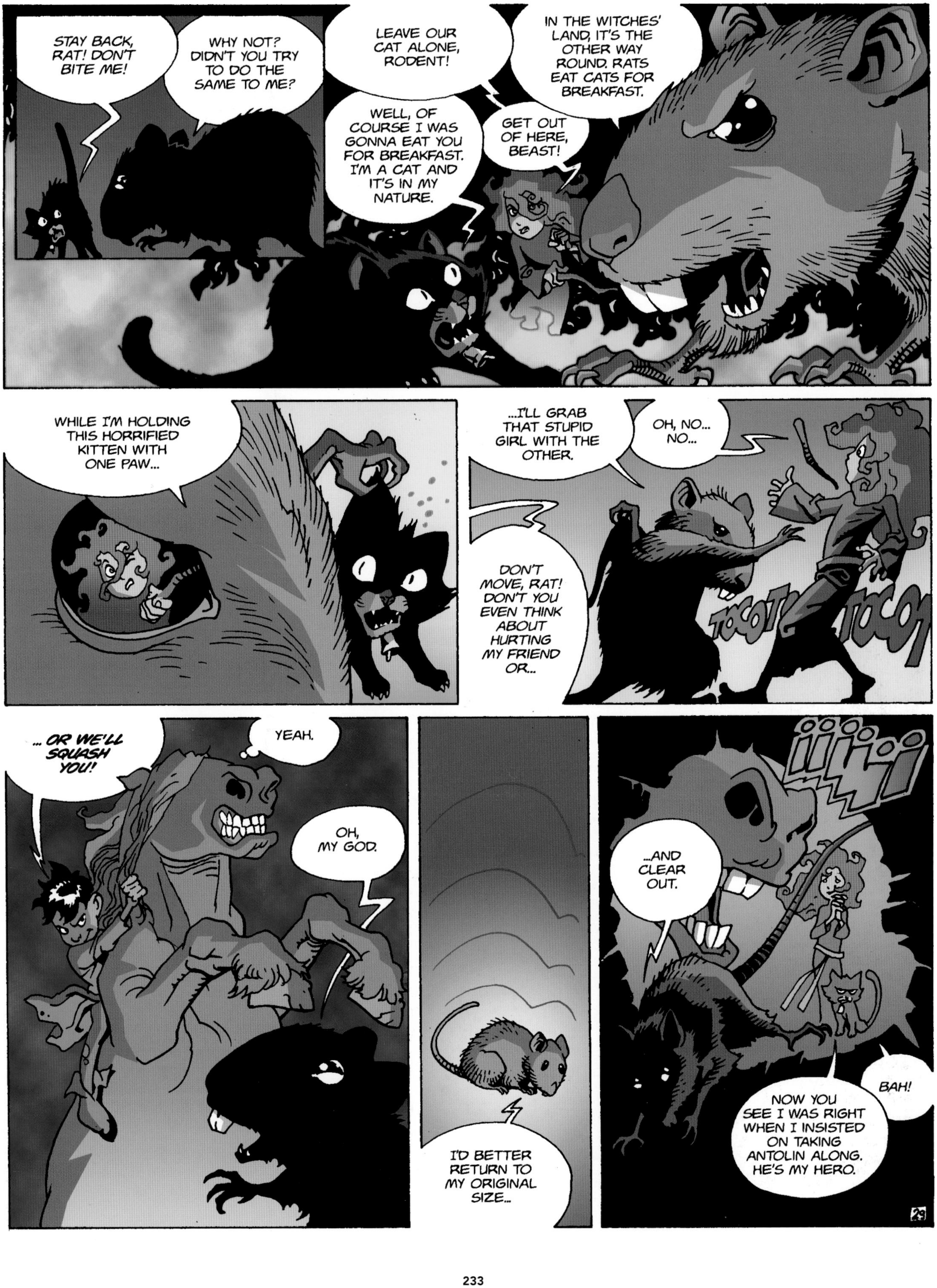
STAY BACK, RAT! DON'T BITE ME!
WHY NOT? DIDN'T YOU TRY TO DO THE SAME TO ME?
LEAVE OUR CAT ALONE, RODENT!
WELL, OF COURSE I WAS GONNA EAT YOU FOR BREAKFAST. I'M A CAT AND IT'S IN MY NATURE.
IN THE WITCHES' LAND, IT'S THE OTHER WAY ROUND. RATS EAT CATS FOR BREAKFAST.
GET OUT OF HERE, BEAST!
WHILE I'M HOLDING THIS HORRIFIED KITTEN WITH ONE PAW...
...I'LL GRAB THAT STUPID GIRL WITH THE OTHER.
OH, NO... NO...
DON'T MOVE, RAT! DON'T YOU EVEN THINK ABOUT HURTING MY FRIEND OR...
TOCOT TOCOT
... OR WE'LL SQUASH YOU!
YEAH.
OH, MY GOD.
I'D BETTER RETURN TO MY ORIGINAL SIZE...
...AND CLEAR OUT.
BAH!
NOW YOU SEE I WAS RIGHT WHEN I INSISTED ON TAKING ANTOLIN ALONG. HE'S MY HERO.
29

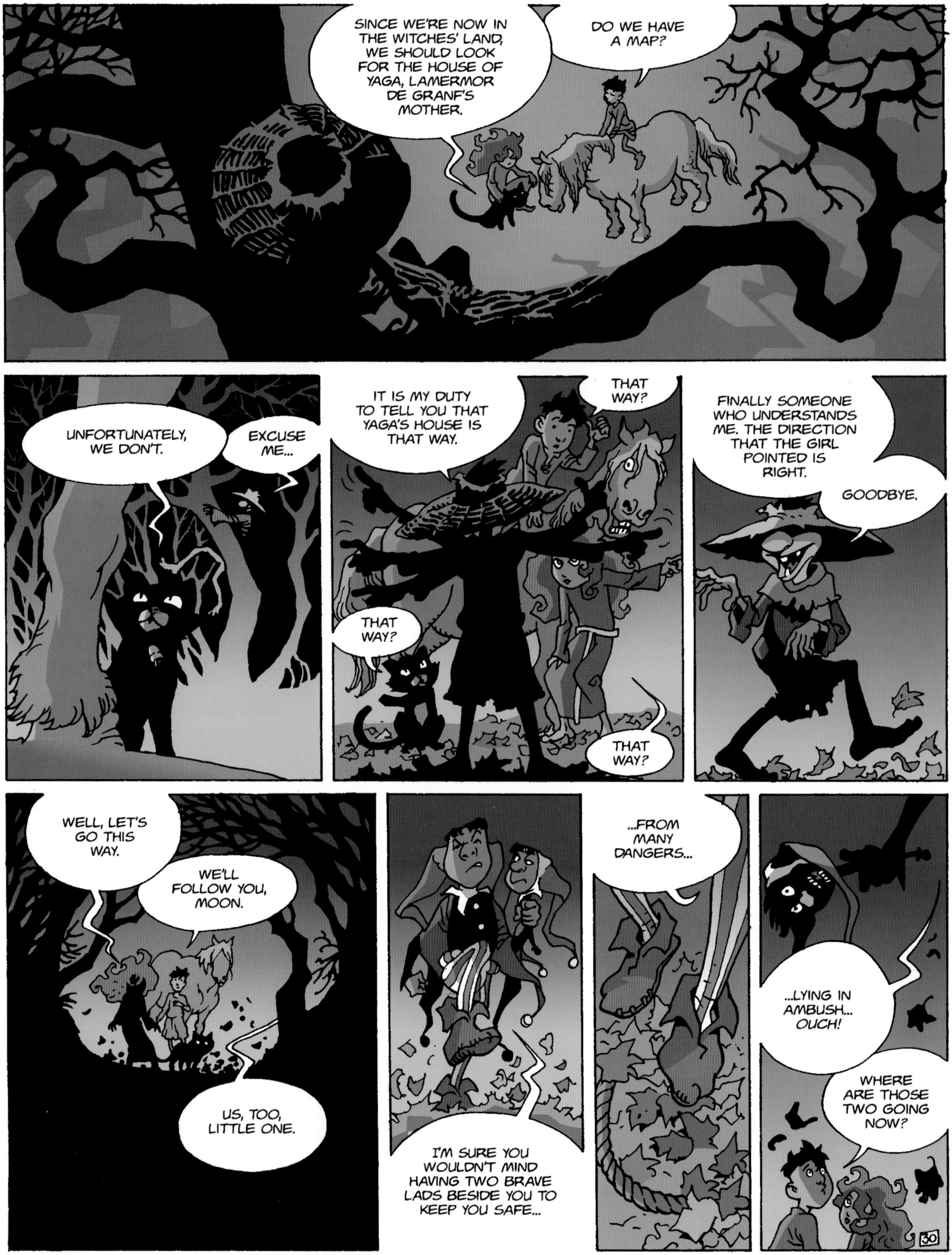
SINCE WE'RE NOW IN THE WITCHES' LAND, WE SHOULD LOOK FOR THE HOUSE OF YAGA, LAMERMOR DE GRANF'S MOTHER.
DO WE HAVE A MAP?
UNFORTUNATELY, WE DON'T.
EXCUSE ME...
IT IS MY DUTY TO TELL YOU THAT YAGA'S HOUSE IS THAT WAY.
THAT WAY?
THAT WAY?
THAT WAY?
FINALLY SOMEONE WHO UNDERSTANDS ME. THE DIRECTION THAT THE GIRL POINTED IS RIGHT.
GOODBYE.
WELL, LET'S GO THIS WAY.
WE'LL FOLLOW YOU, MOON.
US, TOO, LITTLE ONE.
I'M SURE YOU WOULDN'T MIND HAVING TWO BRAVE LADS BESIDE YOU TO KEEP YOU SAFE...
...FROM MANY DANGERS...
...LYING IN AMBUSH... OUCH!
WHERE ARE THOSE TWO GOING NOW?
30

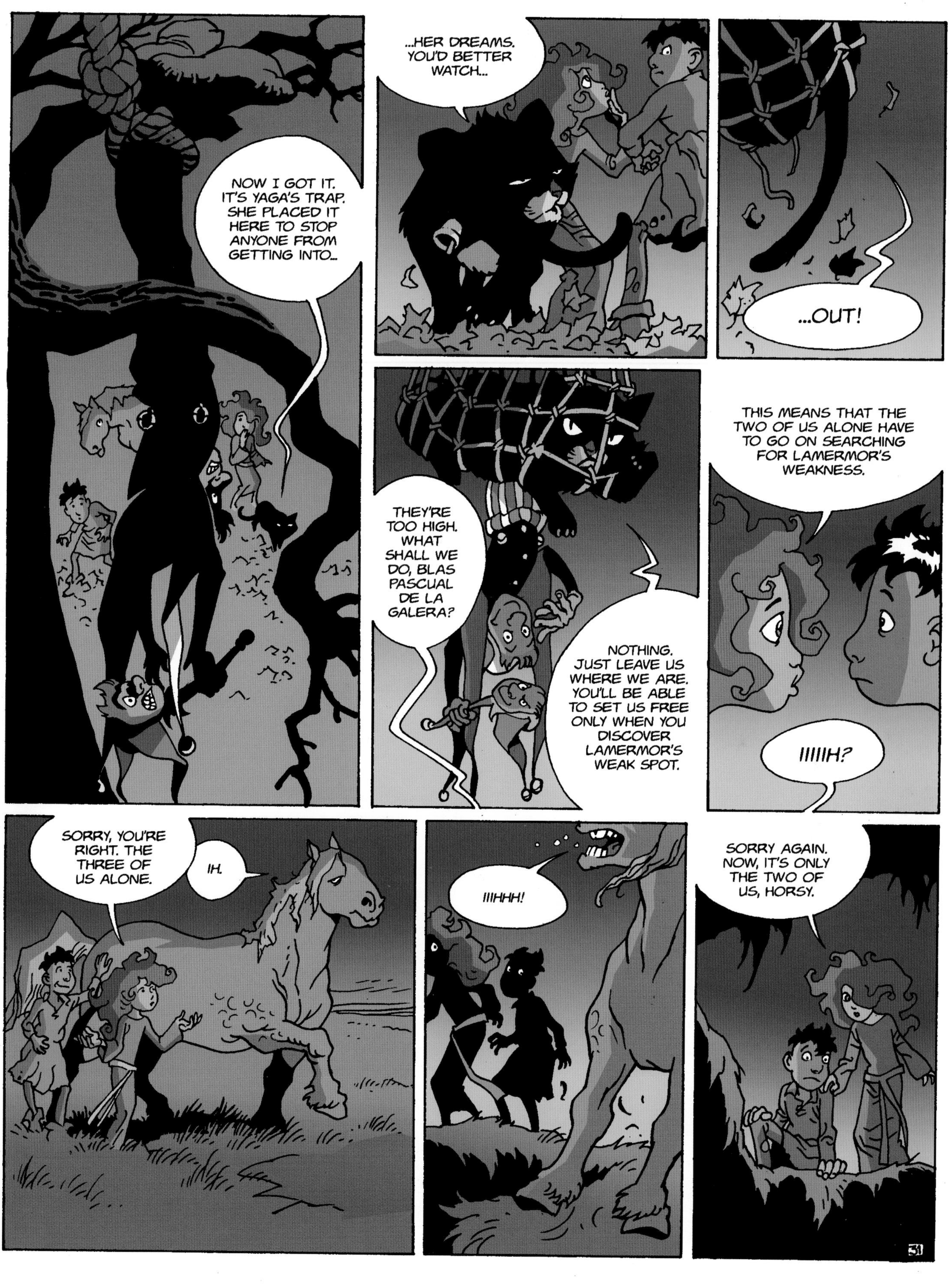
NOW I GOT IT. IT'S YAGA'S TRAP. SHE PLACED IT HERE TO STOP ANYONE FROM GETTING INTO...
...HER DREAMS. YOU'D BETTER WATCH...
...OUT!
THEY'RE TOO HIGH. WHAT SHALL WE DO, BLAS PASCUAL DE LA GALERA?
NOTHING. JUST LEAVE US WHERE WE ARE. YOU'LL BE ABLE TO SET US FREE ONLY WHEN YOU DISCOVER LAMERMOR'S WEAK SPOT.
THIS MEANS THAT THE TWO OF US ALONE HAVE TO GO ON SEARCHING FOR LAMERMOR'S WEAKNESS.
IIIIIH?
SORRY, YOU'RE RIGHT. THE THREE OF US ALONE.
IH.
IIIHHH!
SORRY AGAIN. NOW, IT'S ONLY THE TWO OF US, HORSY.
31

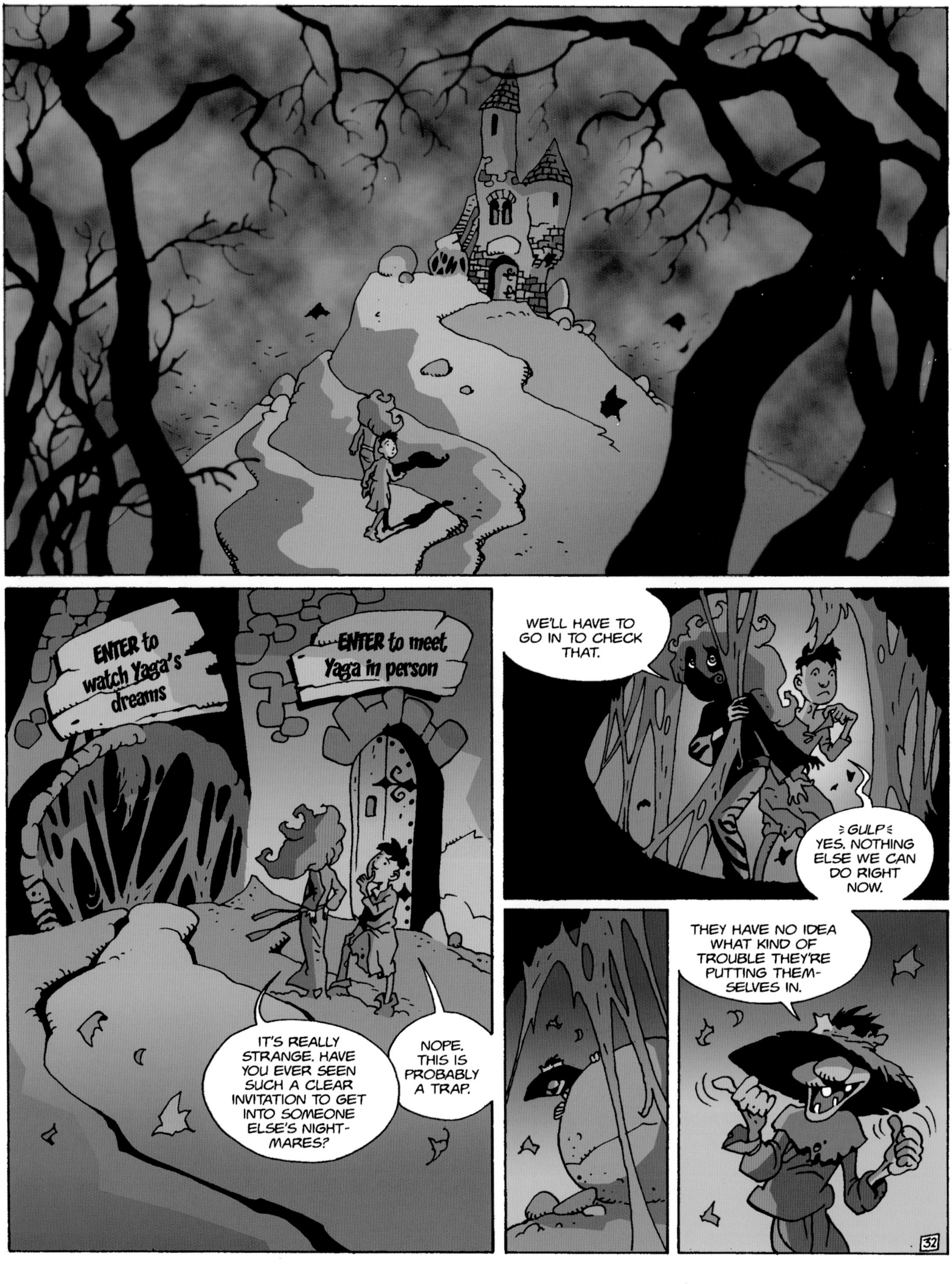
ENTER to watch Yaga's dreams
ENTER to meet Yaga in person
IT'S REALLY STRANGE. HAVE YOU EVER SEEN SUCH A CLEAR INVITATION TO GET INTO SOMEONE ELSE'S NIGHT-MARES?
NOPE. THIS IS PROBABLY A TRAP.
WE'LL HAVE TO GO IN TO CHECK THAT.
GULP
YES. NOTHING ELSE WE CAN DO RIGHT NOW.
THEY HAVE NO IDEA WHAT KIND OF TROUBLE THEY'RE PUTTING THEM-SELVES IN.
32

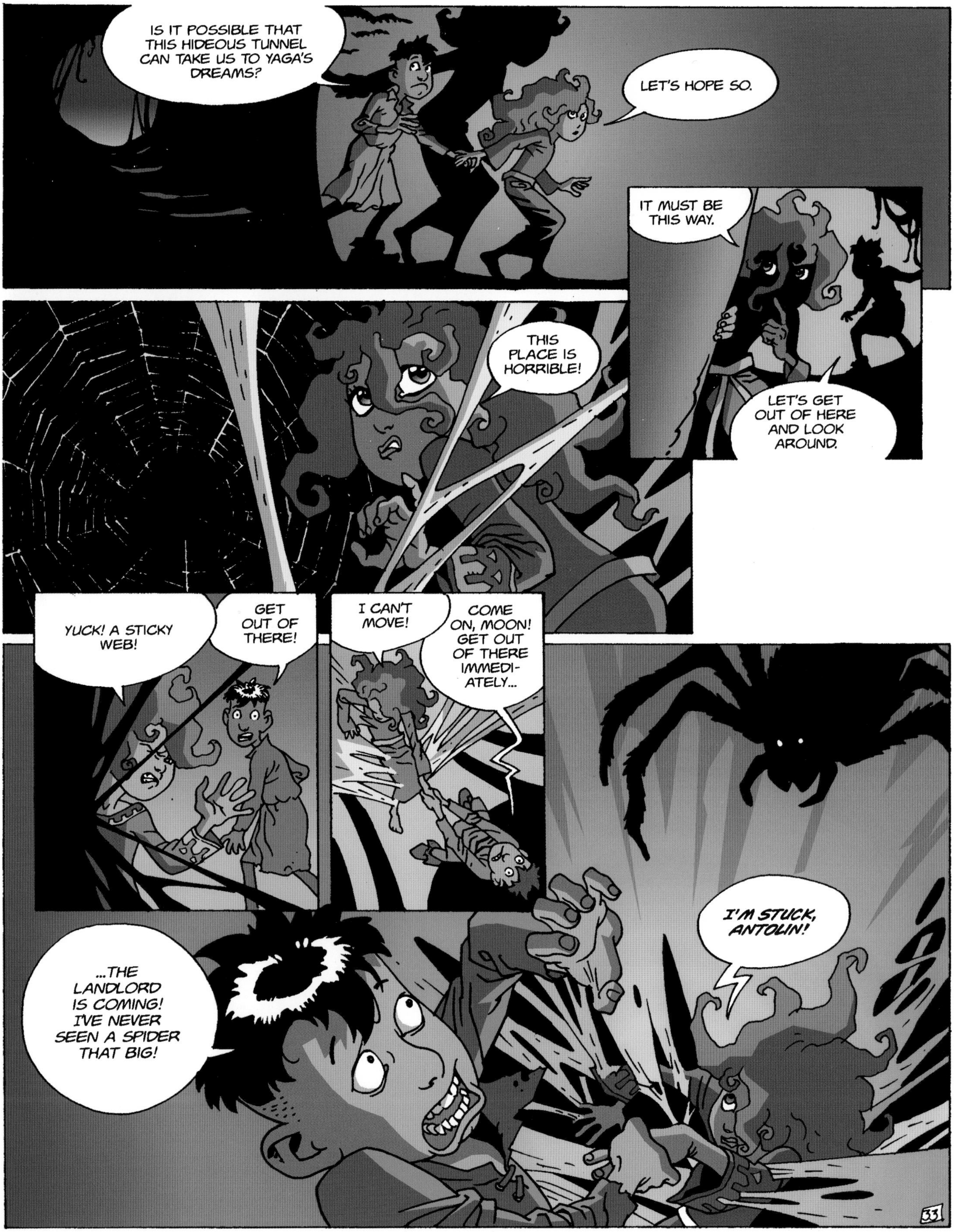
IS IT POSSIBLE THAT THIS HIDEOUS TUNNEL CAN TAKE US TO YAGA'S DREAMS?
LET'S HOPE SO.
IT MUST BE THIS WAY.
LET'S GET OUT OF HERE AND LOOK AROUND.
THIS PLACE IS HORRIBLE!
YUCK! A STICKY WEB!
GET OUT OF THERE!
I CAN'T MOVE!
COME ON, MOON! GET OUT OF THERE IMMEDI-ATELY...
...THE LANDLORD IS COMING! I'VE NEVER SEEN A SPIDER THAT BIG!
I'M STUCK, ANTOLIN!
33

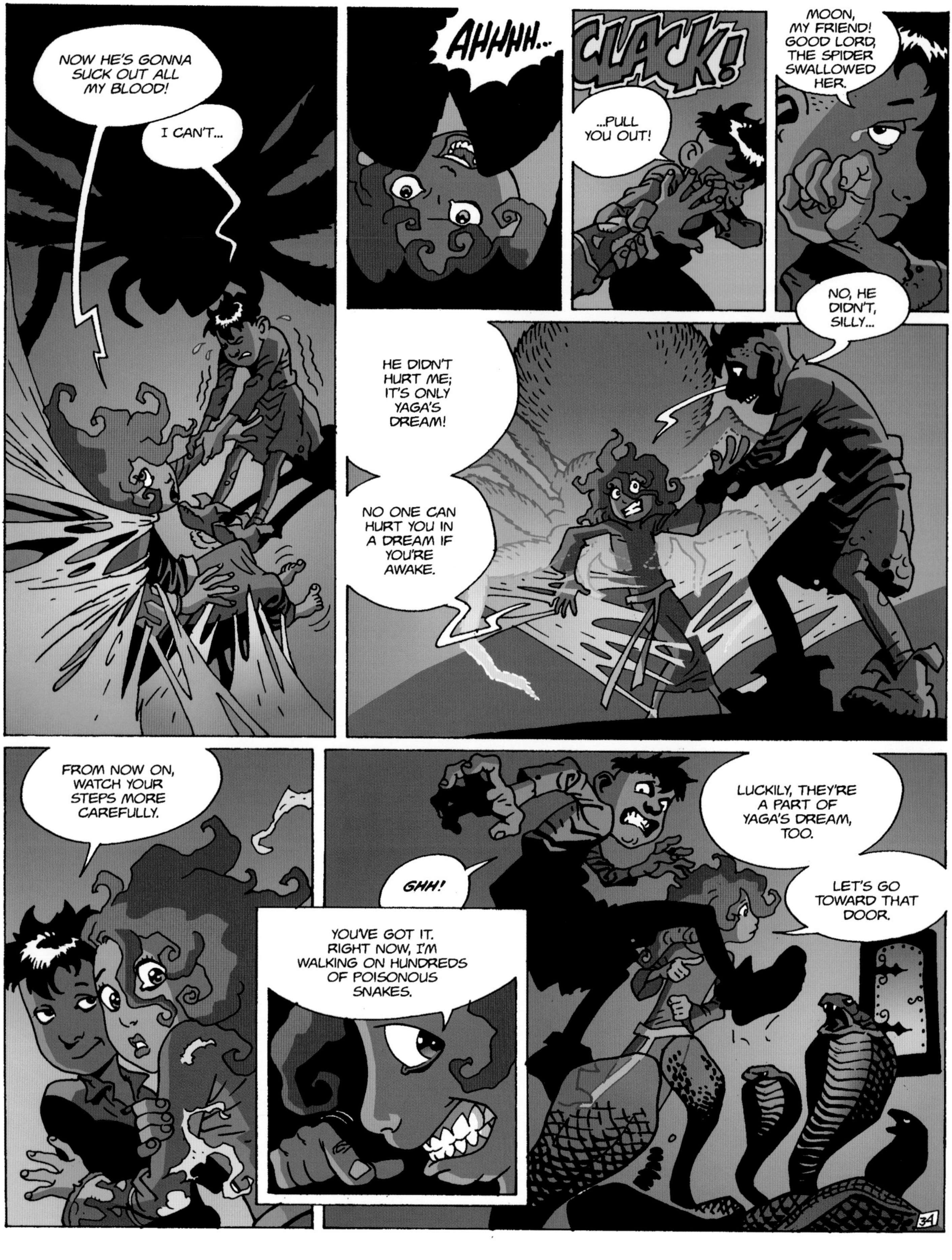
NOW HE'S GONNA SUCK OUT ALL MY BLOOD!
I CAN'T...
AHHHH...
CLACK!
...PULL YOU OUT!
MOON, MY FRIEND! GOOD LORD, THE SPIDER SWALLOWED HER.
NO, HE DIDN'T, SILLY...
HE DIDN'T HURT ME; IT'S ONLY YAGA'S DREAM!
NO ONE CAN HURT YOU IN A DREAM IF YOU'RE AWAKE.
FROM NOW ON, WATCH YOUR STEPS MORE CAREFULLY.
GHH!
YOU'VE GOT IT. RIGHT NOW, I'M WALKING ON HUNDREDS OF POISONOUS SNAKES.
LUCKILY, THEY'RE A PART OF YAGA'S DREAM, TOO.
LET'S GO TOWARD THAT DOOR.
34

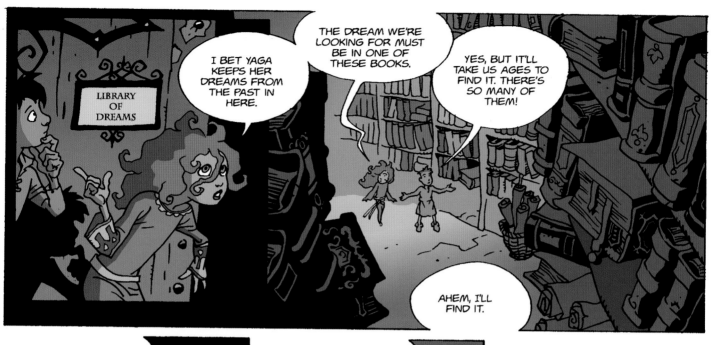

LIBRARY OF DREAMS

I BET YAGA KEEPS HER DREAMS FROM THE PAST IN HERE.

THE DREAM WE'RE LOOKING FOR MUST BE IN ONE OF THESE BOOKS.

YES, BUT IT'LL TAKE US AGES TO FIND IT. THERE'S SO MANY OF THEM!

AHEM, I'LL FIND IT.

I WORK AS A LIBRARIAN HERE, AND CAN FIND ANY DREAM.

AWESOME.

WE'RE INTERESTED IN A PARTICULAR NIGHTMARE THAT YAGA HAS EVERY NOW AND THEN.

DON'T TELL ME IT'S THE ONE WHERE SHE, SCARED TO DEATH, IMAGINES THAT SOMEONE WILL UNCOVER HER SON LAMERMOR'S WEAK SPOT?

BINGO. HOW DID YOU GUESS?

WELL...THAT'S THE ONLY CURIOUS DREAM SHE HAS. THE REST ARE SO COMMON, WITH DEADLY POISONS, SPELLS, AND CHARMS THAT CAN TURN YOU INTO A FRIED EGG OR GREEN BEANS...

RUBBISH!

CAN WE VIEW THE BOOK WE'RE LOOKING FOR?

OF COURSE. IT'S VOLUME #76,567. IT'S UP THERE.

I'LL GET IT DOWN FOR YOU.

RIGHT AWAY.

OH, MY VERTIGO. I THINK HE'S CLIMBING UP, RIGHT?

ANTOLIN IS VERY DEXTEROUS. HE'S THE FAMOUS TIGHTROPE WALKER FROM BURIEN.

35

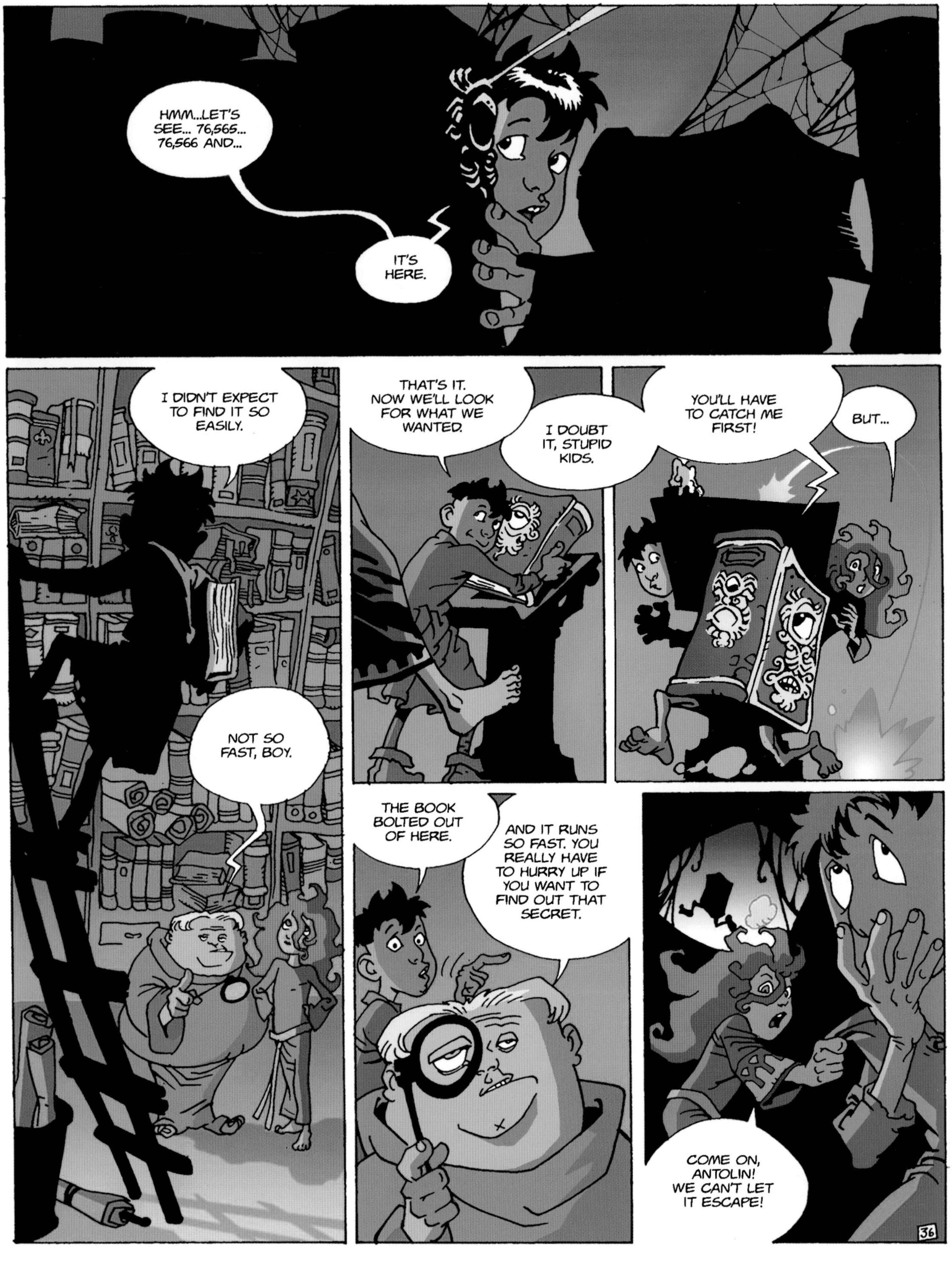

HMM...LET'S SEE... 76,565... 76,566 AND...
IT'S HERE.
I DIDN'T EXPECT TO FIND IT SO EASILY.
NOT SO FAST, BOY.
THAT'S IT. NOW WE'LL LOOK FOR WHAT WE WANTED.
I DOUBT IT, STUPID KIDS.
YOU'LL HAVE TO CATCH ME FIRST!
BUT...
THE BOOK BOLTED OUT OF HERE.
AND IT RUNS SO FAST. YOU REALLY HAVE TO HURRY UP IF YOU WANT TO FIND OUT THAT SECRET.
COME ON, ANTOLIN! WE CAN'T LET IT ESCAPE!
36

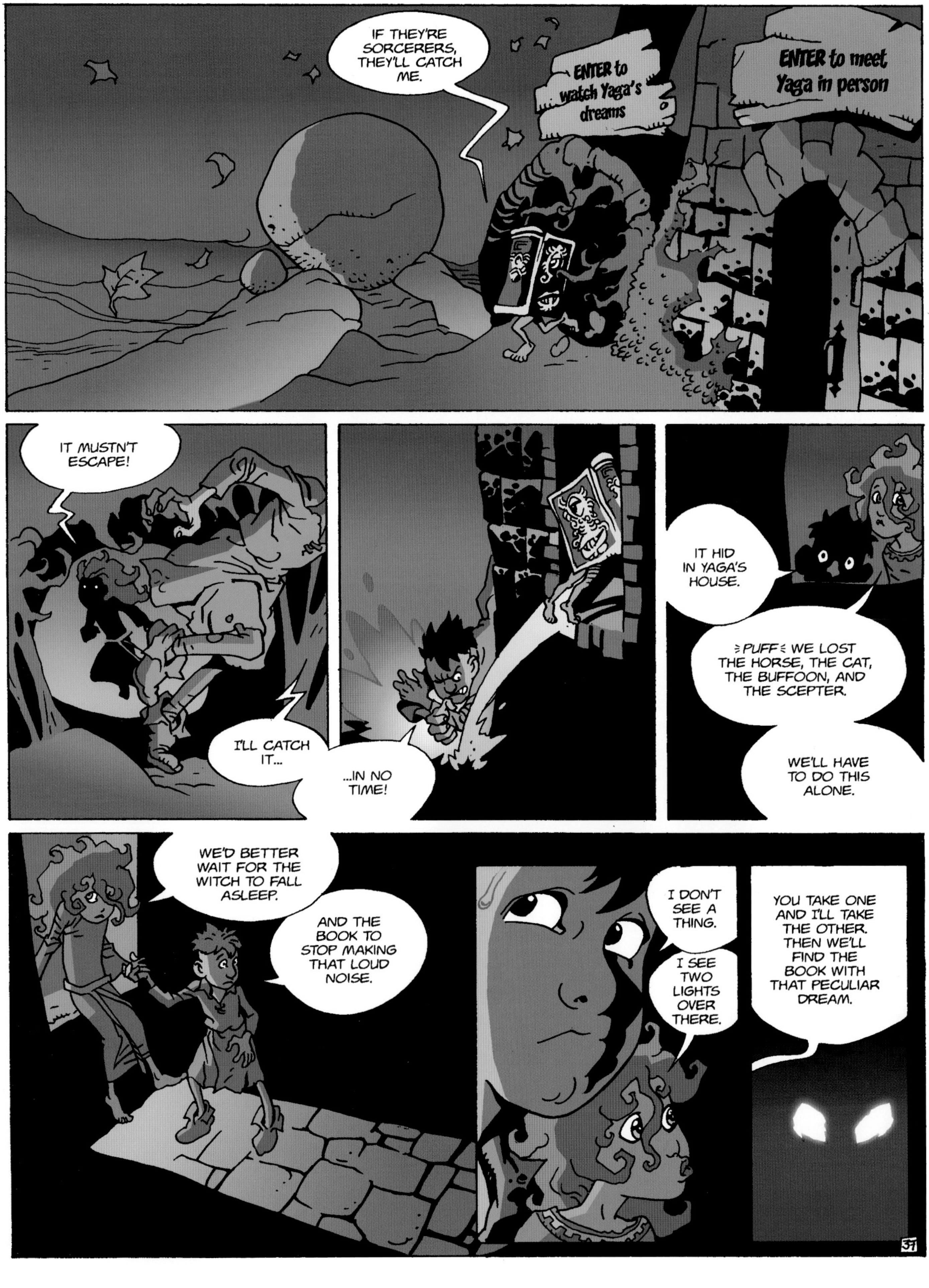
IF THEY'RE SORCERERS, THEY'LL CATCH ME.
ENTER to watch Yaga's dreams
ENTER to meet Yaga in person
IT MUSTN'T ESCAPE!
I'LL CATCH IT...
...IN NO TIME!
IT HID IN YAGA'S HOUSE.
PUFF WE LOST THE HORSE, THE CAT, THE BUFFOON, AND THE SCEPTER.
WE'LL HAVE TO DO THIS ALONE.
WE'D BETTER WAIT FOR THE WITCH TO FALL ASLEEP.
AND THE BOOK TO STOP MAKING THAT LOUD NOISE.
I DON'T SEE A THING.
I SEE TWO LIGHTS OVER THERE.
YOU TAKE ONE AND I'LL TAKE THE OTHER. THEN WE'LL FIND THE BOOK WITH THAT PECULIAR DREAM.
37

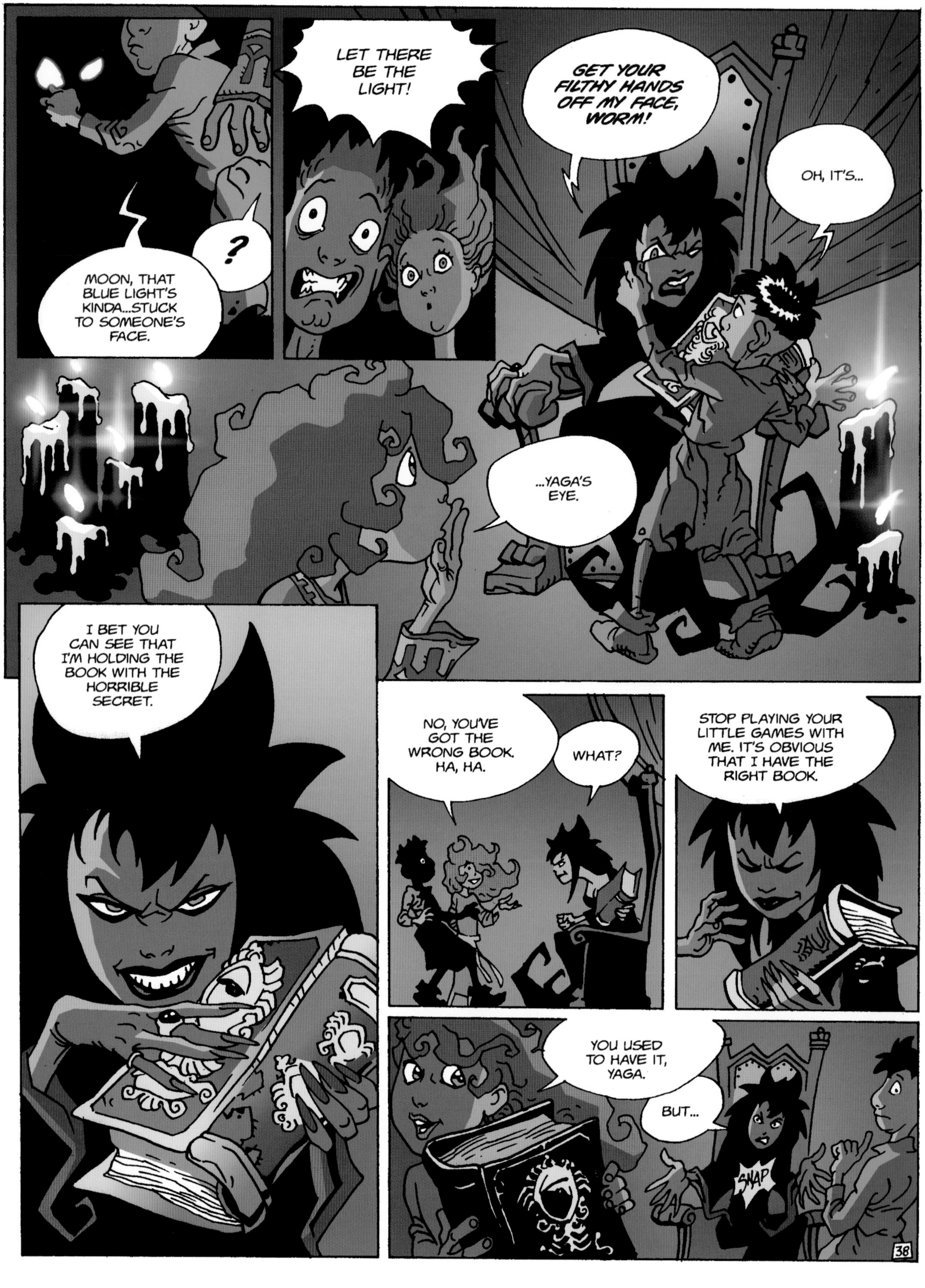
MOON, THAT BLUE LIGHT'S KINDA...STUCK TO SOMEONE'S FACE.
?
LET THERE BE THE LIGHT!
GET YOUR FILTHY HANDS OFF MY FACE, WORM!
OH, IT'S...
...YAGA'S EYE.
I BET YOU CAN SEE THAT I'M HOLDING THE BOOK WITH THE HORRIBLE SECRET.
NO, YOU'VE GOT THE WRONG BOOK. HA, HA.
WHAT?
STOP PLAYING YOUR LITTLE GAMES WITH ME. IT'S OBVIOUS THAT I HAVE THE RIGHT BOOK.
YOU USED TO HAVE IT, YAGA.
BUT...
SNAP
38

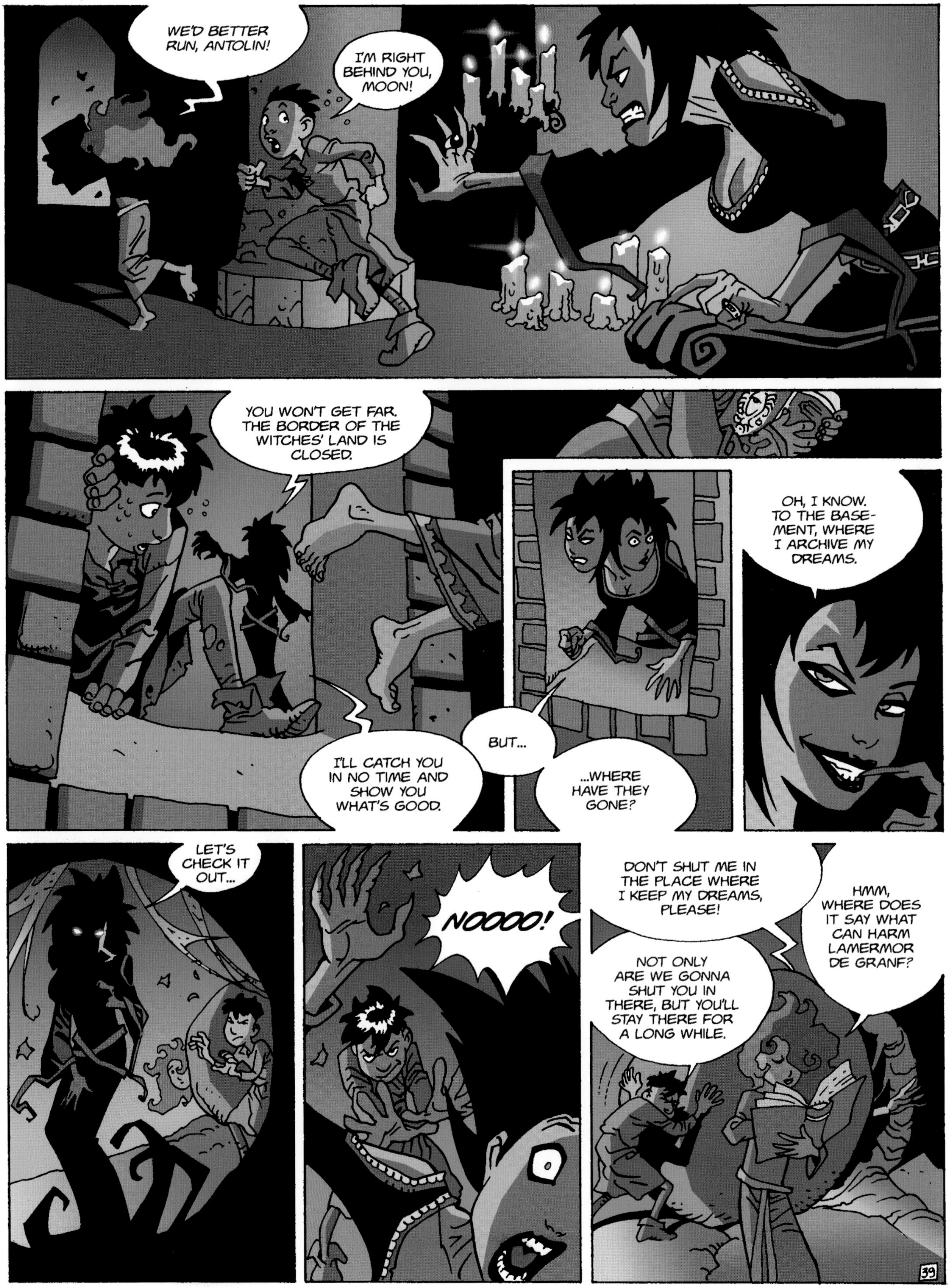
WE'D BETTER RUN, ANTOLIN!
I'M RIGHT BEHIND YOU, MOON!
YOU WON'T GET FAR. THE BORDER OF THE WITCHES' LAND IS CLOSED.
I'LL CATCH YOU IN NO TIME AND SHOW YOU WHAT'S GOOD.
BUT...
...WHERE HAVE THEY GONE?
OH, I KNOW. TO THE BASE- MENT, WHERE I ARCHIVE MY DREAMS.
LET'S CHECK IT OUT...
NOOOO!
DON'T SHUT ME IN THE PLACE WHERE I KEEP MY DREAMS, PLEASE!
NOT ONLY ARE WE GONNA SHUT YOU IN THERE, BUT YOU'LL STAY THERE FOR A LONG WHILE.
HMM, WHERE DOES IT SAY WHAT CAN HARM LAMERMOR DE GRANF?
39

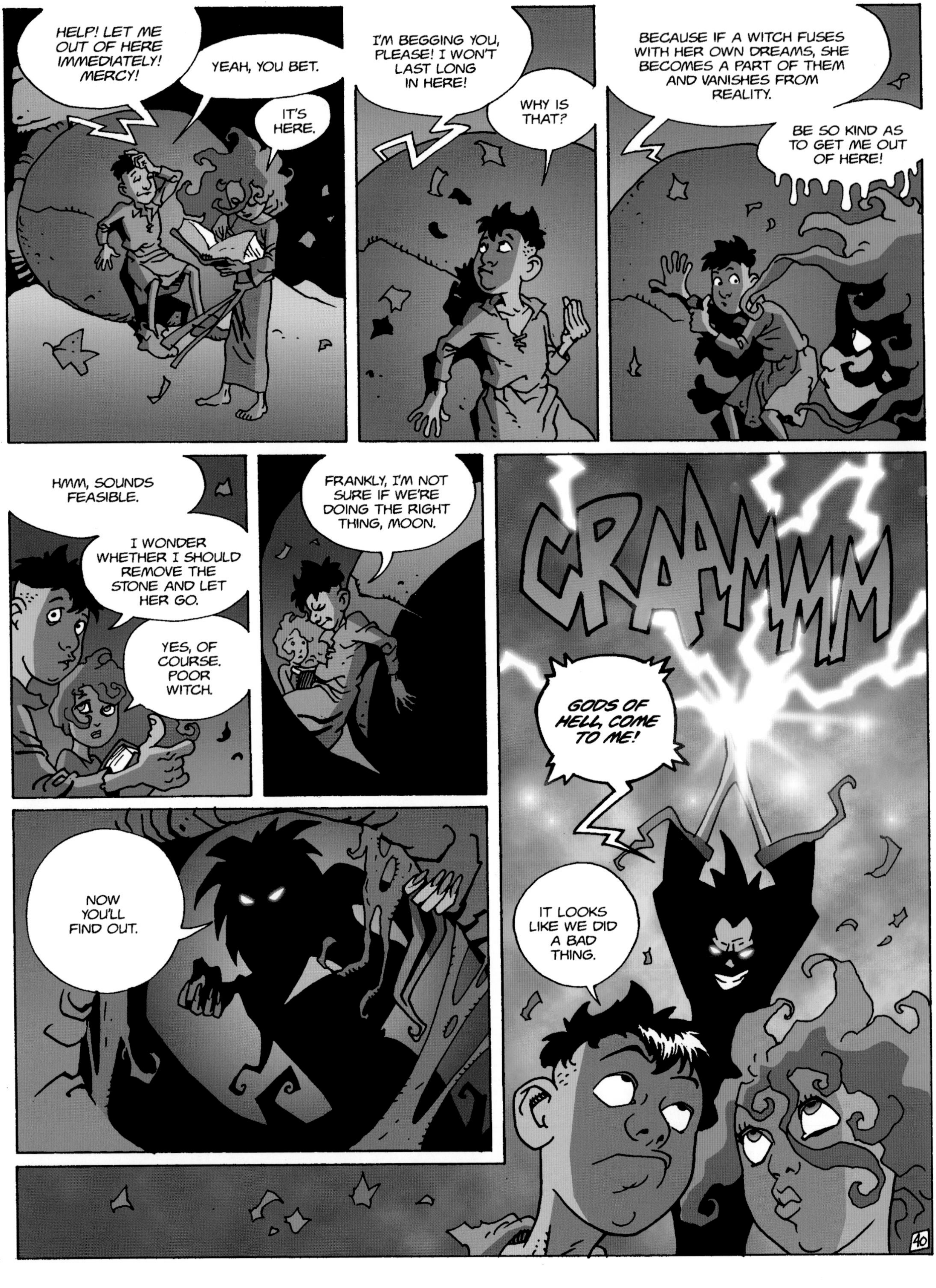
HELP! LET ME OUT OF HERE IMMEDIATELY! MERCY!
YEAH, YOU BET.
IT'S HERE.
I'M BEGGING YOU, PLEASE! I WON'T LAST LONG IN HERE!
WHY IS THAT?
BECAUSE IF A WITCH FUSES WITH HER OWN DREAMS, SHE BECOMES A PART OF THEM AND VANISHES FROM REALITY.
BE SO KIND AS TO GET ME OUT OF HERE!
HMM, SOUNDS FEASIBLE.
I WONDER WHETHER I SHOULD REMOVE THE STONE AND LET HER GO.
YES, OF COURSE. POOR WITCH.
FRANKLY, I'M NOT SURE IF WE'RE DOING THE RIGHT THING, MOON.
CRAMMM
GODS OF HELL, COME TO ME!
NOW YOU'LL FIND OUT.
IT LOOKS LIKE WE DID A BAD THING.
40

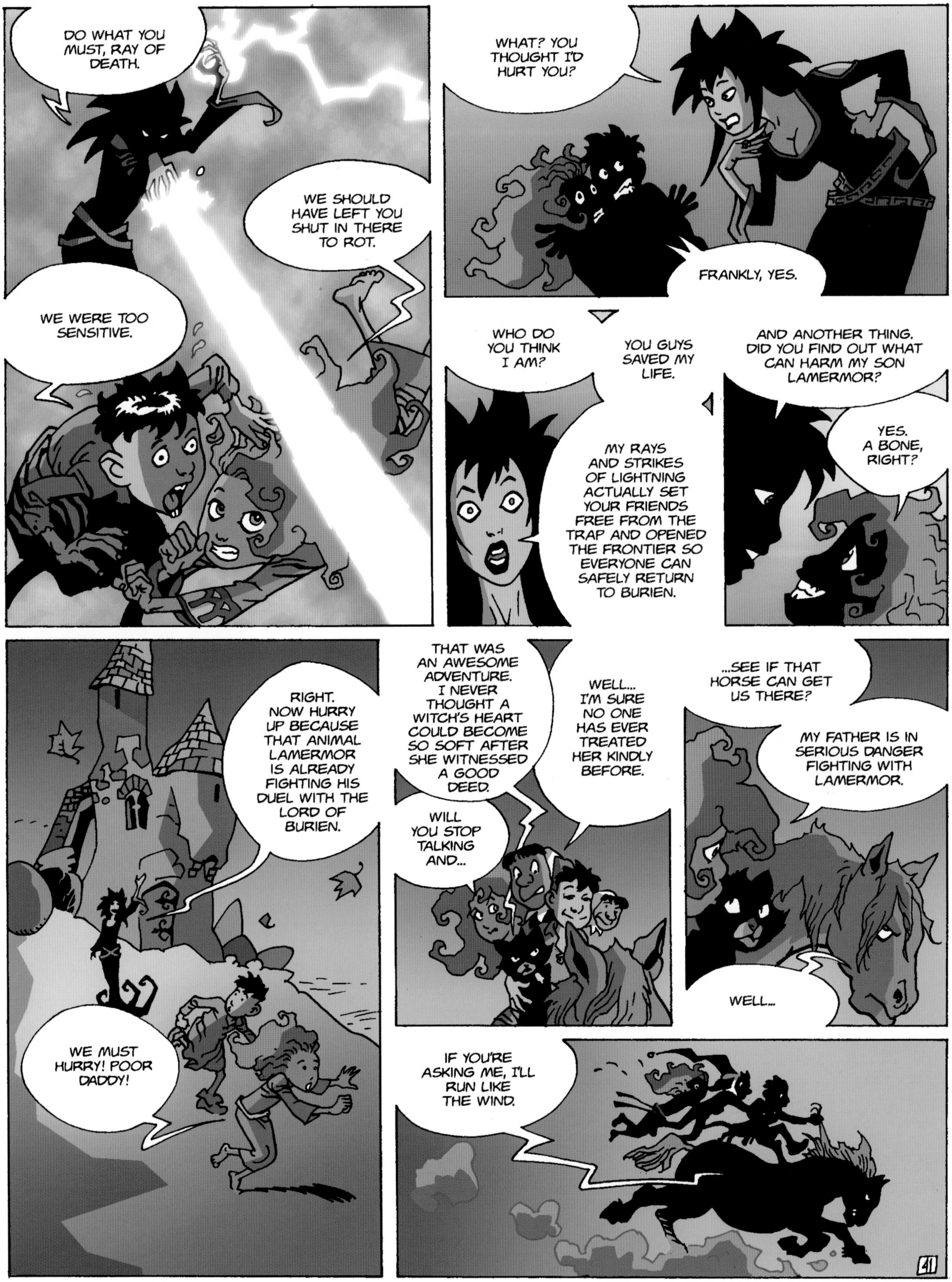
DO WHAT YOU MUST, RAY OF DEATH.
WE SHOULD HAVE LEFT YOU SHUT IN THERE TO ROT.
WE WERE TOO SENSITIVE.
WHAT? YOU THOUGHT I'D HURT YOU?
FRANKLY, YES.
WHO DO YOU THINK I AM?
YOU GUYS SAVED MY LIFE.
MY RAYS AND STRIKES OF LIGHTNING ACTUALLY SET YOUR FRIENDS FREE FROM THE TRAP AND OPENED THE FRONTIER SO EVERYONE CAN SAFELY RETURN TO BURIEN.
AND ANOTHER THING. DID YOU FIND OUT WHAT CAN HARM MY SON LAMERMOR?
YES. A BONE, RIGHT?
RIGHT. NOW HURRY UP BECAUSE THAT ANIMAL LAMERMOR IS ALREADY FIGHTING HIS DUEL WITH THE LORD OF BURIEN.
WE MUST HURRY! POOR DADDY!
THAT WAS AN AWESOME ADVENTURE. I NEVER THOUGHT A WITCH'S HEART COULD BECOME SO SOFT AFTER SHE WITNESSED A GOOD DEED.
WELL... I'M SURE NO ONE HAS EVER TREATED HER KINDLY BEFORE.
WILL YOU STOP TALKING AND...
...SEE IF THAT HORSE CAN GET US THERE?
MY FATHER IS IN SERIOUS DANGER FIGHTING WITH LAMERMOR.
WELL...
IF YOU'RE ASKING ME, I'LL RUN LIKE THE WIND.
41

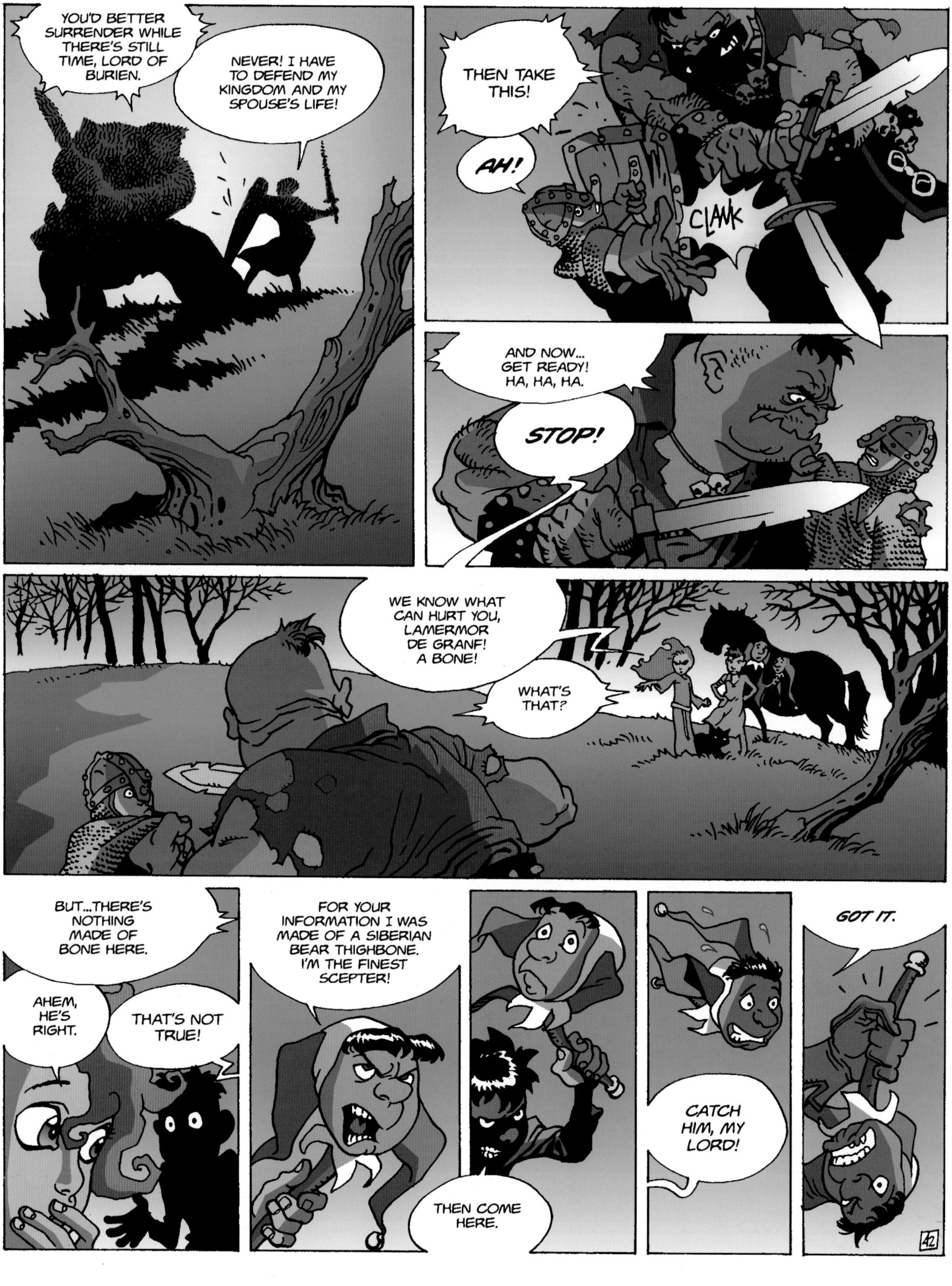
YOU'D BETTER SURRENDER WHILE THERE'S STILL TIME, LORD OF BURIEN.
NEVER! I HAVE TO DEFEND MY KINGDOM AND MY SPOUSE'S LIFE!
THEN TAKE THIS!
AH!
CLANK
AND NOW... GET READY! HA, HA, HA.
STOP!
WE KNOW WHAT CAN HURT YOU, LAMERMOR DE GRANF! A BONE!
WHAT'S THAT?
BUT...THERE'S NOTHING MADE OF BONE HERE.
AHEM, HE'S RIGHT.
THAT'S NOT TRUE!
FOR YOUR INFORMATION I WAS MADE OF A SIBERIAN BEAR THIGHBONE. I'M THE FINEST SCEPTER!
THEN COME HERE.
CATCH HIM, MY LORD!
GOT IT.
42

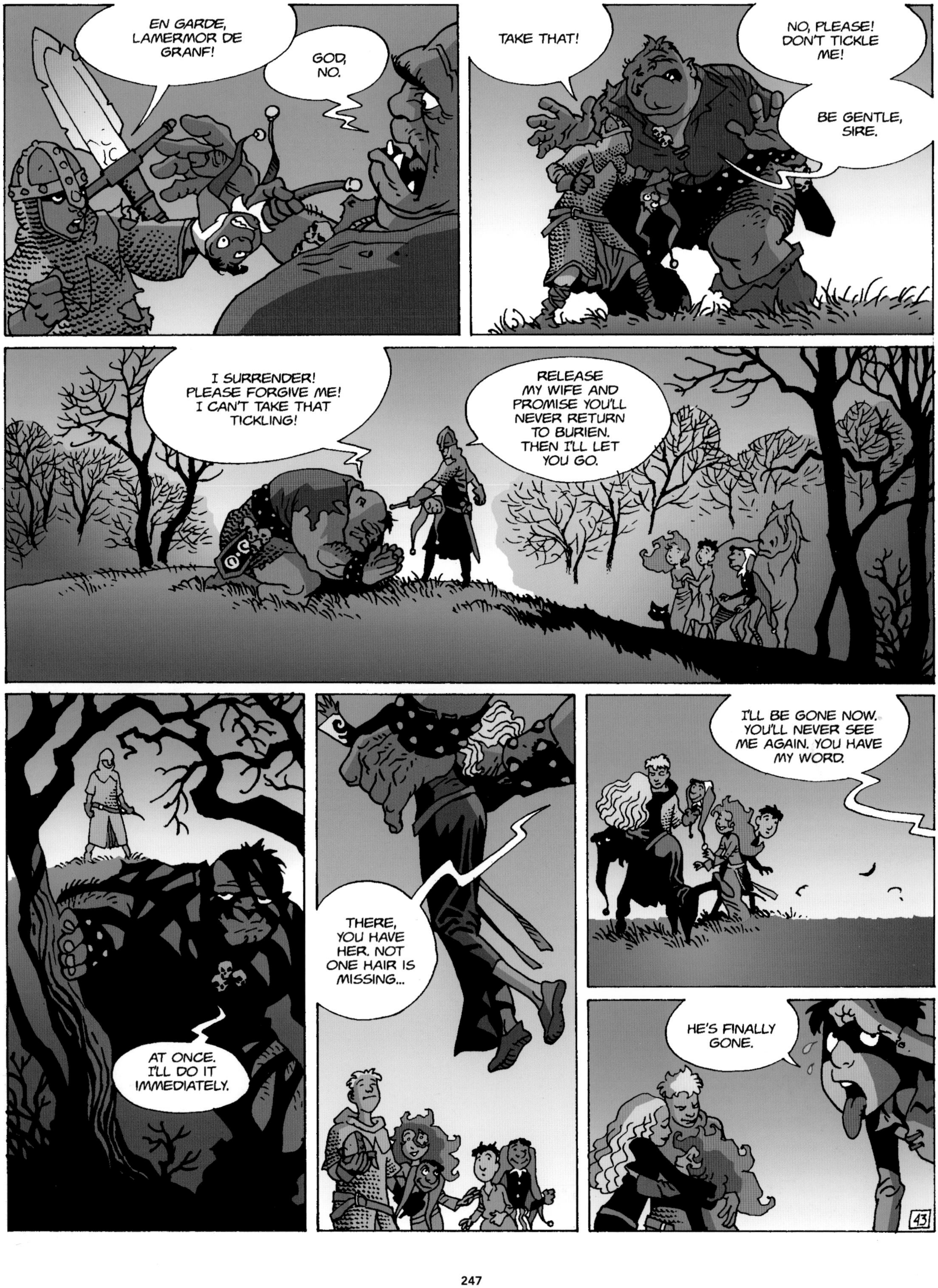
EN GARDE, LAMERMOR DE GRANF!
GOD, NO.
TAKE THAT!
NO, PLEASE! DON'T TICKLE ME!
BE GENTLE, SIRE.
I SURRENDER! PLEASE FORGIVE ME! I CAN'T TAKE THAT TICKLING!
RELEASE MY WIFE AND PROMISE YOU'LL NEVER RETURN TO BURIEN. THEN I'LL LET YOU GO.
AT ONCE. I'LL DO IT IMMEDIATELY.
THERE, YOU HAVE HER. NOT ONE HAIR IS MISSING...
I'LL BE GONE NOW. YOU'LL NEVER SEE ME AGAIN. YOU HAVE MY WORD.
HE'S FINALLY GONE.
43

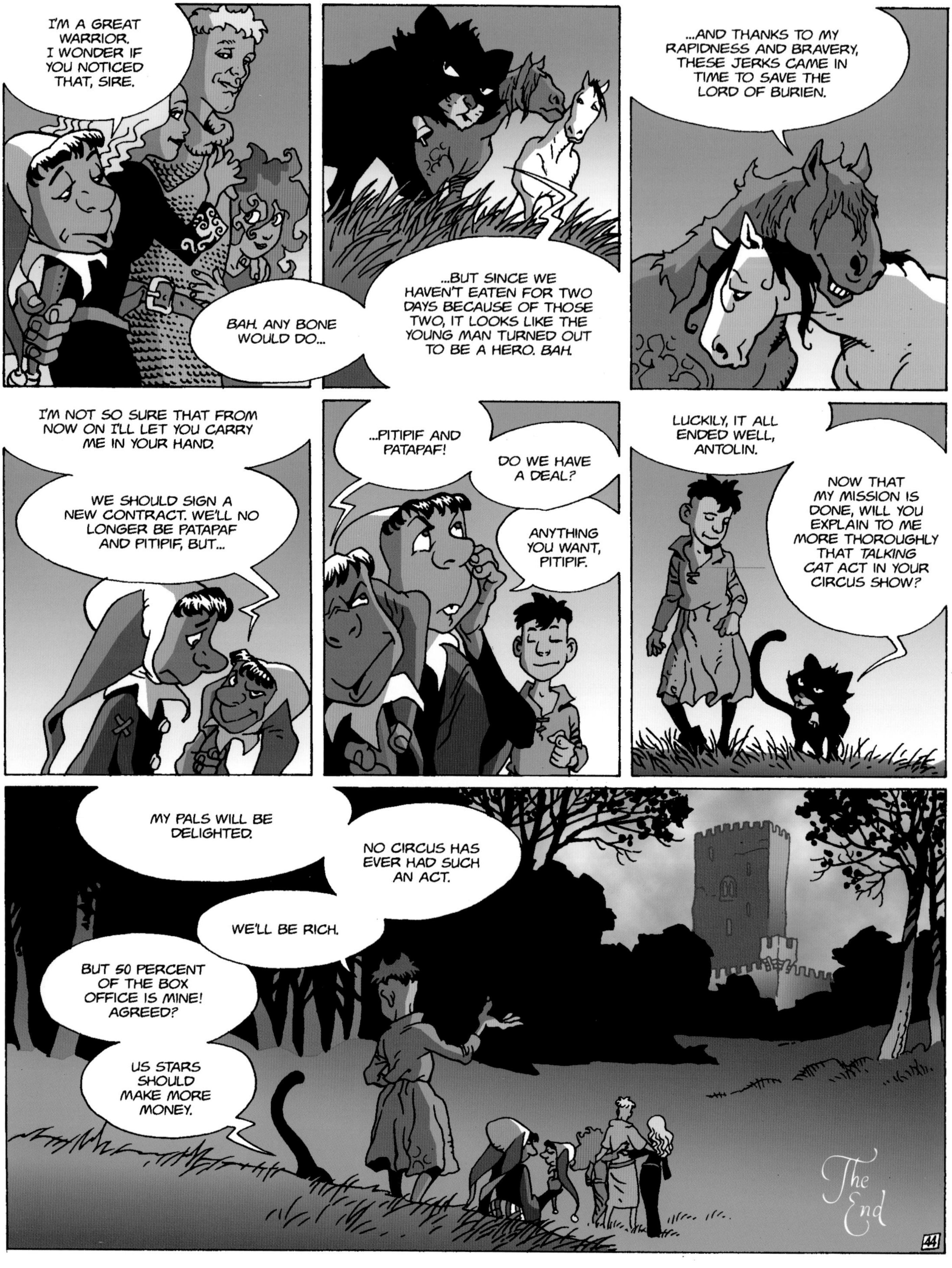
I'M A GREAT WARRIOR. I WONDER IF YOU NOTICED THAT, SIRE.
BAH. ANY BONE WOULD DO...
...BUT SINCE WE HAVEN'T EATEN FOR TWO DAYS BECAUSE OF THOSE TWO, IT LOOKS LIKE THE YOUNG MAN TURNED OUT TO BE A HERO. BAH.
...AND THANKS TO MY RAPIDNESS AND BRAVERY, THESE JERKS CAME IN TIME TO SAVE THE LORD OF BURIEN.
I'M NOT SO SURE THAT FROM NOW ON I'LL LET YOU CARRY ME IN YOUR HAND.
WE SHOULD SIGN A NEW CONTRACT. WE'LL NO LONGER BE PATAPAF AND PITIPIF, BUT...
...PITIPIF AND PATAPAF!
DO WE HAVE A DEAL?
ANYTHING YOU WANT, PITIPIF.
LUCKILY, IT ALL ENDED WELL, ANTOLIN.
NOW THAT MY MISSION IS DONE, WILL YOU EXPLAIN TO ME MORE THOROUGHLY THAT TALKING CAT ACT IN YOUR CIRCUS SHOW?
MY PALS WILL BE DELIGHTED.
NO CIRCUS HAS EVER HAD SUCH AN ACT.
WE'LL BE RICH.
BUT 50 PERCENT OF THE BOX OFFICE IS MINE! AGREED?
US STARS SHOULD MAKE MORE MONEY.
The End
44